Educational Research:

Competencies for Analysis & Application

Second Edition

L. R. Gay

Florida
International
University

Charles E. Merrill Publishing Company
A Bell & Howell Company
Columbus • Toronto • London • Sydney

Published by
Charles E. Merrill Publishing Co.

A Bell & Howell Company

Columbus, Ohio 43216

This book was set in Souvenir

Production Coordination: Linda Hillis Bayma

Cover Design Coordination: Will Chenoweth

Cover photo by Larry Hamill

Text Designer: Harry Voight

Library of Congress Catalog Card Number: 80–84219

International Standard Book Number: 0–675–08021–5

Printed in the United States of America

8 9 10—86

To R. J. Gay

Preface

Increasingly colleges and schools of education are acknowledging the need for professionals in all areas of education to possess research skills by including a course in educational research as a basic requirement for all graduate degrees. A number of factors, including rapid expansion of evaluation activities, make this assertion as valid today as it was when the first edition was written. This book is designed primarily for use in such an introductory course. Since the topic coverage is relatively comprehensive, however, this book may easily be adapted for use in either a senior-level undergraduate course or a more advanced graduate-level course.

The philosophy which guided the development of both the first and second editions of this text was the conviction that an introductory research course should be skill oriented, rather than knowledge oriented, and application oriented, rather than theory oriented. Thus the purpose of this book is *not* to have students become familiar with research, understand research, or acquire a body of knowledge, per se. The purpose of this book is *not* to mystify students with theoretical and statistical jargon. The purpose of this book is *not* to have students acquire in-depth understanding of theory. The purpose of this book *is* to aid students in the acquisition of the skills and knowledge required of a competent consumer and producer of education research, primarily the former; the emphasis is not on what the student knows, but rather on what the student can do with what he or she knows. It is recognized that being a "good" researcher involves more than the acquisition of skills and knowledge; in any field, significant research is usually produced by persons who through experience have acquired insights, intuitions, and strategies related to the research process. Research of any worth, however, is rarely conducted in the absence of basic research skills and knowledge. Further, a basic assumption of this text is that there is considerable overlap in the competencies required of a competent consumer of research and a competent producer of research, and that a person is in a much better position to evaluate the work of others after she or he has personally performed the major tasks involved in the research process.

The overall strategy of the text is to promote attainment of a degree of expertise in research through the acquisition of knowledge and by involvement in the research process. Part One discusses the scientific method and its application in education, and the major characteristics of the various types of research, in terms of purpose and method. In Part Two, each student selects and delineates a research problem of interest which has relevance to his or her professional area. In Part Two, and in succeeding Parts, the student then simulates the procedures which would be followed in conducting a study designed to investigate the problem; each Part develops a specific skill or set of skills required for the execution of a research study. Specifically, the student reviews and analyzes related literature and formulates hypotheses (Part Two), develops a research plan (Part Three), selects and defines samples (Part Four), evaluates and selects measuring instruments (Part Five), selects an experimental design and delineates experimental procedures (Part Six), statistically analyzes data (Part Seven), and prepares a research report (Part Eight). In Part Nine the student applies the skills and knowledge acquired in Parts One through Eight and evaluates a research report.

This book represents more than just a textbook to be incorporated into a course; it is actually a total instructional system which includes stated objectives, or competencies, instruction, and procedures for evaluation of each competency. The instructional strategy of the system emphasizes demonstration of skills and individualization within structure. The format for each Part is essentially the same. Following a brief introduction, each task to be performed is described. Tasks require students to demonstrate that they can perform particular research functions. Since each student works with a different problem, each student demonstrates the competency required by a task as it applies to her or his problem. With the exception of Part One, each Part is directed toward the attainment of one task, and the text discussion of chapters within each Part relates to that task. Each chapter begins with a list of Enablers, or chapter objectives. Enablers entail knowledge and skills which facilitate students' ability to perform a related task. In many instances enablers may be evaluated either as written exercises submitted by students or by tests, whichever the instructor prefers. For some enablers the first option is clearly preferable. Text discussion is intended to be as simple and straightforward as possible. Whenever feasible, procedures are presented as a series of steps and concepts are explained in terms of illustrative examples. In a number of cases, relatively complex topics or topics beyond the scope of the text are presented at a very elementary level and students are directed to other sources for additional, in-depth discussion. There is also a degree of intentional repetition; a number of concepts are discussed in different contexts and from different perspectives. Also, at the risk of eliciting more than a few groans, an *attempt* has been made to sprinkle the text with touches of humor. Each Part includes a rather lengthy summary and subheadings which directly parallel those in the chapters. The summaries are designed to facilitate both review and location of related text discussion. Finally, each Part concludes with suggested procedures for evaluation of the task.

The second edition reflects a combination of both unsolicited and solicited input. Positive feedback contained in unsolicited letters from instructors and students suggested aspects of the book which should *not* be changed, the writing style, for example. In order to systematically ascertain how well the text was meeting user needs, a questionnaire survey was conducted. The revisions made in the second edition reflect to a great extent the results of the survey. Every effort was made to incorporate all stated and implied suggestions, even if made by only a small percentage of responders. For example, several responders asked for the sample budget which appears in Chapter 3. In some instances it was not possible to be responsive because of conflicting requests. Most users, for example, were quite happy with the section on statistics. Those dissatisfied, however, were equally divided into two camps, those wanting more statistics and those wanting less. Thus, coverage of statistics remains basically the same. I am indebted to everyone who took the time to send a letter or return a questionnaire.

The major organizational change in the second edition is the division of the book into Parts, with each Part containing one or more chapters. Each Part in the second edition corresponds to a chapter in the first edition. A number of users felt that two of the original chapters were too long. These chapters have been divided into smaller, more manageable chapters. Corresponding enablers have been subdivided and assigned to the appropriate new chapters. Content changes were made for one of three reasons: (1) inclusion of new topics, (2) expansion of existing topics, or (3) clarification of existing topics. Use of certain techniques and strategies has increased dramatically since publication of the first edition; these include (among others) computer searches of the literature, ethnography, and single-subject experimental designs. Inclusion of these topics was deemed a necessity given the purpose of the text. Some topics which were treated briefly in the first edition were determined to be of sufficient importance to warrant more extensive coverage; these include (among others) standard error of measurement, observer reliability, and observation coding systems. Other topics, such as attitude scales, aptitude tests, and analysis of covariance were in need of clarification on one or more points. Content revision is reflected in both text discussion and in the addition of a number of new figures.

For each Part in the text there is a corresponding Part in the student guide and the professional supplement. The student guide primarily provides the student with model examples of tasks based on work submitted by previous students, additional examples, and self-test exercises. The professional supplement includes a number of test items, including some contributed by users of the first edition. In combination, the text, student guide, and professional supplement provide components which permit implementation of a variety of instructional approaches.

Sincere appreciation is expressed to Professor Paul Gallagher and to all the EDF 5481 students whose feedback stimulated constant revision and refinement of the content and methods of presentation reflected in this text. I am grateful to the Literary Executor of the late Sir Ronald A. Fisher, F.R.S., to Dr. Frank Yates, F.R.S., and to Longman Group Ltd., London, for permission to reprint Tables III, IV, V, and VII from their book *Statistical Tables for Biological, Agricultural and Medical Research* (6th edition, 1974). I also thank Professors John Follman, John Poggio, and especially Darrell Sabers for their conscientious and helpful reviews of the next-to-the-last draft of the original manuscript.

Appreciation beyond words is due my better half for continual and total understanding, encouragement, and reinforcement during the time this "magnum opus" was being written.

Photo Credits

Photograph page 2. Reprinted by permission of G. P. Putnam's Sons and Souvenir Press Ltd. from *Chariots of the Gods?* by Erich Von Däniken. Copyright© 1969 by Michael Heron and Souvenir Press.

Bookplate page 22. Courtesy of Antioch Bookplate Company, Yellow Springs, Ohio.

Photograph of *The Syndics* by Rembrandt, page 58. Reproduced by permission of Rijksmuseum, Amsterdam.

Photograph from *Gorgo*, p. 82. Reproduced by permission of King International Corporation.

Photograph page 104. From the MGM release *The Picture of Dorian Gray,*© 1945 by Loew's Inc. Reproduced by permission of Metro-Goldwyn-Mayer Inc.

Photograph of *Elizabeth Bathory* by István Csók, page 142. Copyright© 1972 by Raymond T. McNally and Radu Florescu. From *In Search of Dracula: A True History of Dracula and Vampire Legends* by Raymond T. McNally and Radu Florescu, by permission of the New York Graphic Society

Photograph page 203. Reproduced by permission of Strickler, Monkmeyer Press Photo Service.

Photograph page 272. From the motion picture *The Wolf Man*, 1941. Courtesy of Universal Pictures.

Photograph of *Study of Erasmus of Rotterdam* by Holbein, page 372. Courtesy of the Louvre Museum.

Acknowledgments

The author is indebted to the following individuals. The content and format of this edition reflect their input to a great extent.

Roland A. Alterman
Central Michigan University

E.C. Arch
Lewis & Clark College

Floyd W. Ayers
St. Cloud State University

F.B. Benson
Alabama A & M University

Gary A. Best
California State University,
Los Angeles

F. Lamar Blanton
West Georgia College

Rosemarie B. Bogal
Murray State University

Robert Branch
Gonzaga University

Taylor Byrd, Jr.
Alabama A & M University

Mary Reardon Castles
Wayne State University

Robert D. Clements
The University of Georgia

Clyde M. Combs, Jr.
Slippery Rock State College

Elizabeth Corld
Oklahoma State University

Jack L.R. Cudaback
Eastern Michigan University

Lloyd Davis
University of Tennessee,
Chattanooga

Ayres D'Costa
Ohio State University

Ann Beth Deily
College of St. Rose

Carl E. Edeburn
South Dakota State University

Charles Eiszler
Central Michigan University

Herbert Elover
Georgia College

George W. Fair
University of Texas, Dallas

Joseph Fearing
Texas Woman's University

Mel E. Finkenberg
California State University,
Los Angeles

Richard K. Fletcher, Jr.
Tennessee Technological University

Warren Fruechtel
Edinboro State College

Robert J. Garner
Towson State University

Harvey J. Goehring, Jr.
Slippery Rock State College

Robert T. Gray
San Diego State University

Mary Harris
University of New Mexico

Robert Hawkins
Southern Illinois University

David L. Henderson
Sam Houston State University

Max Jerman
Seattle Pacific University

Charles M. Johnson
Southwest Texas State University

Paul E. Jones
Towson State University

Sheldon Kleine
Good Samaritan Hospital
Puyallup, Washington

Thomas Kratochwill
University of Arizona

Norman L. Krong
Western Illinois University

James D. Lacey
State University College,
Potsdam

W. Iverson Lloyd
Alabama State University

Elizabeth McCorkle
Oklahoma State University

Pauline McCormick, C.S.J.
The College of Saint Rose

Richard K. McKay
Johns Hopkins University

S.M. Mattarazzo
Murray State University

Nolie Brown Mayo
University of Houston,
Clear Water City

Irene R. Mazer
Tacoma Public Schools–
Western Washington University

Larry Milbrandt
Wichita State University

Kathy Newell
University of Minnesota

Barbara Perry
James Madison University

John R. Ray
University of Tennessee,
Knoxville

A. Reid
Bowie State College

Joseph Riley
University of Georgia

Stephen A. Rollin
Florida State University

Carl Roseveare
Seattle Pacific University

William Ryan
Murray State University

Darrell Sabers
University of Arizona

Robert Schissel
University of Wisconsin,
Whitewater

Louis E. Shilling
Texas Woman's University

Jerry R. Shipman
Alabama A & M University

David L. Steinberg
James Madison University

Douglas E. Stone
University of South Florida

J. Nathan Swift
State University College,
Oswego

Beatrice Tignor
Bowie State College

Michael J. Williams
Central Connecticut State College

Leonard Zaichkowsky
Boston University

Gary H. Zarter
Seattle University

I. Zweibelson
Central Connecticut State College

Contents

Part One Introduction 2

Chapter 1 Introduction to Educational Research/5
The Scientific Method/5

Application of the Scientific Method in Education/6

Classification of Research by Purpose/8

Basic Versus Applied Research

Evaluation Research

Research and Development (R & D)

Action Research

Classification of Research by Method/11

Historical Research

Descriptive Research

Correlational Research

Causal-Comparative and Experimental Research

Guidelines for Classification

Summary/Chapter 1/17

Part Two Research Problems 22

Chapter 2 Selection and Definition of a Problem/25
Selection and Statement/25

Selection

Sources

Characteristics

Statement

Review of Related Literature/29

Definition, Purpose, and Scope

Preparation

Sources

Computer Searches

Abstracting

Analyzing, Organizing, and Reporting

Formulation and Statement of a Hypothesis/**45**
Definition and Purpose
Characteristics
Types of Hypotheses
Stating the Hypothesis
Testing the Hypothesis
Summary/Chapter 2/**50**

Part Three Research Plans 58

Chapter 3 Preparation and Evaluation of a Research Plan/61
Definition and Purpose/**61**
General Considerations/**62**
The Ethics of Research
Legal Restrictions
Cooperation
Training Research Assistants
Components/**66**
Introduction
Method
Data Analysis
Time Schedule
Budget
Evaluation of a Research Plan/**74**
Summary/Chapter 3/**75**

Part Four Subjects 82

Chapter 4 Selection of a Sample/85
Sampling: Definition and Purpose/**85**
Definition of a Population/**86**
Methods of Selecting a Sample/**87**
Random Sampling
Stratified Sampling
Cluster Sampling
Systematic Sampling
Conclusion
Determination of Sample Size/**97**
Avoidance of Sampling Bias/**98**
Summary/Chapter 4/**100**

Part Five Instruments 104

Chapter 5 Selection of Measuring Instruments/107
Purpose and Process/**108**

Characteristics of a Standardized Test/**109**
Validity
Reliability
Types of Tests/**124**
Achievement
Character and Personality
Aptitude
Selection of a Test/**132**
Sources of Test Information
Selecting from Alternatives
Test Administration/**136**
Summary/Chapter 5/**136**

Part Six Research Methods and Procedures 142

Chapter 6 The Historical Method/145
Definition and Purpose/**145**
The Historical Research Process/**146**
Definition of a Problem
Data Collection
Data Analysis: External and Internal Criticism
Data Synthesis
An Example of Historical Research/**151**

Chapter 7 The Descriptive Method/153
Definition, Purpose, and Process/**153**
Self-Report Research/**155**
Types of Self-report Research
Conducting Self-report Research
Observational Research/**168**
Types of Observational Research
Conducting Observational Research

Chapter 8 The Correlational Method/183
Definition and Purpose/**183**
The Basic Correlational Research Process/**184**
Problem Selection
Sample and Instrument Selection
Design and Procedure
Data Analysis and Interpretation
Relationship Studies/**189**
Data Collection
Data Analysis and Interpretation
Prediction Studies/**193**
Data Collection
Data Analysis and Interpretation

Chapter 9 The Causal-Comparative Method/197

Definition and Purpose/**197**

Conducting a Causal-Comparative Study/**200**
Design and Procedure
Control Procedures
Data Analysis and Interpretation

Chapter 10 The Experimental Method/207

Definition and Purpose/**207**
The Experimental Process
Manipulation and Control

Threats to Experimental Validity/**211**
Threats to Internal Validity
Threats to External Validity
Contamination and Experimenter Bias

Group Experimental Designs/**220**
Control of Extraneous Variables
Types of Group Designs

Single-Subject Experimental Designs/**237**
Single-Subject Versus Group Designs
External Validity
Internal Validity
Types of Single-Subject Designs

Summary/Part Six/**245**

Part Seven Data Analysis and Interpretation 272

Chapter 11 Preanalysis Procedures/275

Preparing Data for Analysis/**275**
Scoring Procedures
Tabulation Procedures

Types of Measurement Scales/**278**
Nominal Scales
Ordinal Scales
Interval Scales
Ratio Scales

Chapter 12 Descriptive Statistics/281

Types of Descriptive Statistics/**281**
Graphing Data
Measures of Central Tendency
Measures of Variability
The Normal Curve
Measures of Relationship
Measures of Relative Position

Calculation for Interval Data/**296**
Symbols
The Mean
The Standard Deviation
The Pearson **r**
Standard Scores

Chapter 13 Inferential Statistics/307

Concepts Underlying Application/**308**
Standard Error
The Null Hypothesis
Tests of Significance
Decision Making: Levels of Significance and Type I and Type II Errors
Two-Tailed and One-Tailed Tests
Degrees of Freedom
Tests of Significance: Types/**318**
The **t** *Test*
Simple Analysis of Variance
Multiple Comparisons
Factorial Analysis of Variance
Analysis of Covariance
Chi Square
Calculation and Interpretation of Selected Tests of Significance/**326**
The **t** *Test for Independent Samples*
The **t** *Test for Nonindependent Samples*
Simple Analysis of Variance (ANOVA)
The Scheffé Test
Chi Square

Chapter 14 Using the Computer for Data Analysis/343

When to Use the Computer/**343**
Costs Associated with Computer Use/**344**
Steps in Using the Computer/**345**

Chapter 15 Postanalysis Procedures/347

Verification and Storage of Data/**347**
Verification
Storage
Interpretation of Results/**349**
Hypothesized Results
Unhypothesized Results
Statistical Versus Practical Significance
Replication of Results
Summary/Part Seven/**351**

Part Eight Research Reports 372

Chapter 16 Preparation of a Research Report/375
General Guidelines/**375**
General Rules for Writing and Typing
Format and Style
Types of Research Reports/**378**
Theses and Dissertations
Journal Articles
Papers Read at Professional Meetings
Summary/Part Eight/**389**

Part Nine Research Critiques 396

Chapter 17 Evaluation of a Research Report/399
General Evaluation Criteria/**399**
Introduction
Method
Results
Conclusions and Recommendations
Summary (or Abstract)
Method-Specific Evaluation Criteria/**402**
Historical Research
Descriptive Research
Correlational Research
Causal-Comparative Research
Experimental Research
Summary/Part Nine/**404**

Appendix A Reference Tables/407
Table A.1. Ten Thousand Random Numbers/**408**
Table A.2. Values of the Correlation Coefficient for Different Levels of Significance (p)/**412**
Table A.3. Squares and Square Roots/**413**
Table A.4. Distribution of t/**423**
Table A.5. Distribution of F/**424**
Table A.6. Distribution of X^2/**428**

Appendix B Glossary/429

Author Index/439

Subject Index/441

List of Tables

8.1. Hypothetical Sets of Data Illustrating a High Positive Relationship Between Two Variables, No Relationship, and a High Negative Relationship/**186**

11.1. Hypothetical Summary Data Sheet for the Results of a Study Based on a 2 × 2 Factorial Design/**277**

12.1. Frequency Distribution Based on 85 Hypothetical Achievement Test Scores/**282**

List of Figures

3.1. Hypothetical, simplified example of a Gantt chart for a proposed research study/**74**

3.2. Hypothetical, simplified example of a budget for a proposed research study/**75**

4.1. Procedure for selecting a stratified sample based on IQ for a study designed to compare two methods (*A & B*) of mathematics instruction/**92**

5.1. Summary of methods for estimating reliability/**122**

7.1. Sample cover letter for a questionnaire/**163**

7.2. Flanders' interaction analysis categories (FIAC)/**177**

7.3. Sample line from a data sheet of a nursery school girl who changed activities with high frequency/**178**

7.4. Recording form for Flanders' interaction analysis categories/**178**

8.1. Data points for scores presented in Table 8.1 illustrating a high positive relationship (IQ and GPA), no relationship (IQ and weight), and a high negative relationship (IQ and errors)/**192**

8.2. The curvilinear relationship between age and agility/**193**

9.1. The basic causal-comparative design/**201**

10.1. Sources of invalidity for pre-experimental designs/**225**

10.2. Sources of invalidity for true experimental designs and quasi-experimental designs/**228**

10.3. Possible patterns for the results of a study based on a time-series design/**233**

10.4. An example of the basic 2 × 2 factorial design/**235**

10.5. Illustration of interaction and no interaction in a 2 × 2 factorial experiment/**236**

10.6. A record of talking-out behavior of an educable mentally retarded student/**243**

12.1. Frequency polygon based on 85 hypothetical achievement test scores/**283**

12.2. Characteristics of the normal curve/**289**

12.3. A positively skewed distribution and a negatively skewed distribution, each resulting from the administration of a 100-item test/**291**

13.1. The four possible outcomes of decision making concerning rejection of the null hypothesis/**313**

13.2. Summary of conditions for which selected statistics are appropriate/**326**

16.1. Common components of a research report submitted for a degree requirement/**379**

16.2. Example of a table and a figure illustrating appropriate use and format/**384**

Educational Research:

Competencies for Analysis & Application

Second Edition

Part One

Introduction

A cave drawing of a strange being, which is an ancient astronaut to Von Däniken, may be seen as simply an imaginary god to an archaeologist.

For most of you, educational research is probably a relatively unfamiliar discipline. Therefore, in order to meaningfully learn about and perform components of the research process, it is first necessary for you to develop a cognitive structure into which such experiences can be integrated.

The goal of Part One is for you to acquire an understanding of research process and methodology which will facilitate acquisition of specific research knowledge and skills. In succeeding parts, specific components of the research process will be systematically studied and executed. After you have read Part One, you should be able to perform the following tasks.

Task 1-A

Given a reprint of a research study, identify and briefly state:

(a) the problem (purpose of the study),
(b) the procedures,
(c) the method of analysis, and
(d) the major conclusions.

Task 1-B

Given reprints of three research studies, classify each as historical, descriptive, correlational, causal-comparative, or experimental research and list the characteristics of each study which support the classification chosen. (See Performance Criteria, p. 20.)

Introduction to Educational Research

Enablers

After reading chapter 1, you should be able to:

1. List and briefly describe the major steps involved in conducting a research study.

2. Select one article from a recent issue of the *Journal of Educational Research* and one from the *Journal of Educational Psychology*. For each article, identify and state:
   (a) the problem,
   (b) the procedures,
   (c) the method of analysis, and
   (d) the major conclusions.
   (Note: 1945 is not recent!)

3. Briefly define, and state the major characteristics of, each of the five methods of research.

4. For each of the five methods of research, briefly describe three possible research studies.
   Example:
   Experimental—A study to determine the effect of peer tutoring on the computational skill of third graders.

The Scientific Method

The goal of all scientific endeavors is to explain, predict, and/or control phenomena. This goal is based on the assumption that all behaviors and events are orderly and that they are effects which have discoverable causes. Progress toward this goal involves acquisition of knowledge and the development and testing of theories. The existence of a viable theory greatly facilitates scientific progress by simultaneously explaining many phenomena. Compared to other sources of knowledge, such as experience, authority, inductive reasoning, and deductive reasoning, application of the scientific method is undoubtedly the most efficient and reliable. Some of the problems associated with experience and authority as sources of knowledge are graphically illustrated by a story told about Aristotle. According to the story, one day Aristotle caught a fly and carefully counted and recounted its legs. He then announced that flies have five legs. No one questioned the word of Aristotle. For years his finding was uncritically

5

accepted. Of course the fly that Aristotle caught just happened to be missing a leg! Whether or not you believe the story, it does illustrate the limitations of relying on personal experience and authority as sources of knowledge.

Both inductive and deductive reasoning are also of limited value when used exclusively. Inductive reasoning involves formulation of generalizations based on observation of a limited number of specific events.

> **Example:** Every research textbook examined contains a chapter on sampling. Therefore, all research textbooks contain a chapter on sampling.

Deductive reasoning involves essentially the reverse process, arriving at specific conclusions based on generalizations.

> **Example:** All research textbooks contain a chapter on sampling. This book is a research text. Therefore, this book contains a chapter on sampling. (Does it?)

Although neither approach is entirely satisfactory, when used together as integral components of the scientific method, they are very effective. Basically, the scientific method involves induction of hypotheses based on observation, deduction of implications of the hypotheses, testing of the implications, and confirmation or disconfirmation of the hypotheses.

The scientific method is a very orderly process entailing a number of sequential steps: recognition and definition of the problem; formulation of hypotheses; collection of data; analysis of data; and statement of conclusions regarding confirmation or disconfirmation of the hypotheses. These steps can be applied informally in the solution of everyday problems such as the most efficient route to take from home to work or school, the best time to go to the drive-in window at the bank, or the best kind of electronic calculator to purchase. The more formal application of the scientific method to the solution of problems is what research is all about.

Application of the Scientific Method in Education

Research is the formal, systematic application of the scientific method to the study of problems; educational research is the formal, systematic application of the scientific method to the study of educational problems. The goal of educational research follows from the goal of all science, namely, to explain, predict, and/or control educational phenomena. The major difference between educational research and other scientific research is the nature of the phenomena studied. It is considerably more difficult to explain, predict, and control situations involving human beings, by far the most complex of all organisms. There are so many variables, known and unknown, operating in any educational environment that it is extremely difficult to generalize or replicate findings. The kinds of rigid controls that can be established and maintained in a biochemistry laboratory are virtually impossible in an educational setting. Observation is also more difficult in educational research. Observers may be subjective in recording behaviors, and persons observed may behave atypically just because they are being observed; chemical reactions tend to be oblivious to the fact that they are being observed! Precise measurement is also considerably more difficult in educational research. Most measurement must be indirect; there are no instruments comparable to a barometer for measuring intelligence, achievement, or attitude.

Perhaps it is precisely the difficulty and complexity of educational research that makes it such a challenging and exciting field. Despite a popular stereotype that depicts researchers as spectacled, stoop-shouldered, elderly gentlemen who endlessly add chemicals to test tubes, every day thousands of men and women of all ages, shapes, and sizes conduct educational research in a wide variety of settings. Every year many millions of dollars are spent in the quest for knowledge related to the teaching-learning process. Educational research has contributed many findings concerning principles of behavior, learning, and retention. In addition, significant contributions have been made related to curriculum, instruction, instructional materials, design, measurement, and analysis. Both the quantity and quality of research are increasing. This is partly because of better trained researchers. In fact, a great many graduate education programs, in such diverse areas as physical education, art education, and English education, now require a course in research for all students.

The steps involved in conducting research should look familiar since they directly parallel those of the scientific method:

1. Selection and definition of a problem. A problem is a hypothesis or question of interest to education which can be tested or answered through the collection and analysis of data.

2. Execution of research procedures. Procedures typically include selection of subjects and selection or development of measuring instruments. The design of the study will dictate to a great extent the specific procedures involved in the study.

3. Analysis of data. Data analysis usually involves application of one or more statistical techniques. Data are analyzed in a way that permits the researcher to test the research hypothesis or answer the research question.

4. Drawing and stating conclusions. The conclusions are based on the results of data analysis. They should be stated in terms of the original hypothesis or question. Conclusions should indicate, for example, whether the research hypothesis was supported or not supported.

In a research report, such as a published article in a journal, these steps should be readily evident if the report is well written. The problem will generally be presented in statements which begin with phrases like "the purpose of this study was to . . ." and "it was hypothesized that . . . ." The procedures section of a report may be quite lengthy and detailed, but there are certain major steps which can be identified, such as the number and characteristics of the subjects (the sample), a description of the measuring instruments including when they were administered (e.g., whether there was a pretest), and a description of treatment groups, if appropriate. Data analysis techniques are usually easy to identify; they will generally be presented in statements which include phrases like "data were analyzed using . . ." or "a . . . was used to analyze the data." Conclusions are usually labeled as such. While many conclusions may be presented, at least one of them should relate directly to the original hypothesis or question. Statements such as "it was concluded that more research is needed in this area" are fine but certainly do not represent *the* major conclusion of the study. More research is *always* needed!

Research studies can be classified in a number of ways. Two major approaches are to classify by purpose and to classify by method. When purpose is the classification criterion, all research studies fall into one of five categories: basic research, applied research, evaluation research, research and development (R & D), or action research. Research method refers to the overall strategy followed in collecting and analyzing data; this strategy is referred to as the research design. Even using research method as the criterion can lead to several different classification schemes. There are, however, five distinct types, kinds, or methods of research: historical, descriptive, correlational, causal-comparative, and experimental.

Classification of Research by Purpose

Classification of research by purpose is based primarily on the degree to which findings have direct educational application and the degree to which they are generalizable to other educational situations. Both of these criteria are a function of the research control exercised during the conduction of the study. Basic research involves the development of theory; applied research is concerned with the application of theory to the solution of problems; evaluation research involves decision making regarding the relative worth of two or more alternative actions; research and development is directed at the development of effective products that can be used in the schools; and action research is concerned with immediate solutions to local problems.

Basic Versus Applied Research

It is difficult to discuss basic and applied research separately as they are really on a continuum. There is disagreement, however, concerning toward which end of that continuum educational research should be directed. In its purest form, basic research is conducted solely for the purpose of theory development and refinement. It is not concerned with practical applicability and most closely resembles the laboratory conditions and controls usually associated with scientific research. Applied research, as the name implies, is conducted for the purpose of applying, or testing, theory and evaluating its usefulness in solving educational problems. Rightly or wrongly, most educational research studies would be classified at the applied end of the continuum; they are more concerned with "what" works best than with "why." Basic research is concerned with establishing general principles of learning; applied research is concerned with their utility in educational settings. For example, much basic research has been conducted with animals to determine principles of reinforcement and their effect on learning. Applied research has tested these principles to determine their effectivenss in improving learning (e.g., programmed instruction) and behavior (e.g., behavior modification). Some studies, those located in the middle of the continuum, try to integrate both approaches by conducting controlled research in special or simulated classrooms, using school children, and involving school-relevant topics and materials.

Both types of research are necessary. Basic research provides the theory that produces the implications for solving educational problems; applied research provides data to support theory, guide theory revision, or suggest development of new theory.

Evaluation Research

Evaluation is the systematic process of collecting and analyzing data in order to make decisions. Evaluation involves questions such as the following:

1. Is this special program worth what it costs?
2. Is the new, experimental reading curriculum better than the former curriculum?
3. Should Fenster be placed in a program for the gifted?

Answers to these questions require the collection and analysis of data and interpretation of that data with respect to one or more criteria. The more objective the criteria, the better, although some degree of subjectivity is unavoidable since people determine the criteria. For example, whether a new, experimental curriculum is "better" depends upon the criteria for success. One obvious criterion would be student achievement. Other criteria might include student attitudes and teacher attitudes. Examination of test scores might reveal that students averaged 2 points higher with the new curriculum. Objectively, and strictly speaking, the new curriculum was "better" with respect to student achievement. School administrators, however, may have decided that an achievement difference of at least 10 points would be necessary in order to justify the time, effort, and cost required to change over to the new curriculum. Similarly, determining whether Fenster meets the criteria for admittance to the program for the gifted (e.g., has a specific IQ score and grade point average) would be an objective process; setting the criteria themselves would be a more subjective process.

Deciding whether a special program is "worth" what it costs is even more complex and typically involves serious value judgments. If a special program cost a school system $100,000 per school year but reduced school vandalism by the amount of $150,000, there would not be much disagreement concerning whether the program was worth what it cost. But what if a program cost $100,000 per school year and reduced the ninth-grade dropout rate by 5%? How much is an education worth? How much is it worth to have a child increasing his or her knowledge instead of roaming the streets or attempting to enter an already crowded job market? Opinion on this issue varies greatly. The philosophy of the current school board would probably determine whether or not the program continued.

Notice that in none of the examples was the purpose of the evaluation to determine whether something was "good," or worthwhile, as opposed to "bad," or worthless, per se. That is not the function of evaluation. The purpose of evaluation is to select an alternative in order to make a decision. There may be only two alternatives (e.g., continue the program or not, adopt the new curriculum or keep the current one) or there may be several alternatives (e.g., many textbooks may be available for adoption).

A major point of disagreement among researchers is the issue of whether evaluation is a type of research or a separate discipline. A related issue is whether evaluations should be based on research designs, particularly when group comparisons are involved such as, Does curriculum A lead to higher achievement than curriculum B? Some argue that educational research and educational evaluation have distinctly different purposes, that research seeks control while evaluation assesses what is, and that the natural settings characteristic of evaluation essentially preclude that control. In reality, however, there is a fine line between research and evaluation, and an evaluation may very easily utilize a research design. Both research and evaluation involve decision making and both involve steps which parallel those of the scientific method. Further, many research studies are conducted in natural, real-world settings and are subject to the same control problems involved in many evaluations. Thus, while the issue has not yet been resolved, the case seems stronger for classifying evaluation as a type of research whose purpose is to facilitate decision making.

Research and Development (R & D)

The major purpose of R & D efforts is not to formulate or test theory but to develop effective products for use in schools. Products produced by R & D efforts include: teacher-training materials, learning materials, sets of behavioral objectives, media materials, and management systems. R & D efforts are generally quite extensive in terms of objectives, personnel, and time to completion. Products are developed to meet specific needs and according to detailed specifications. Once completed, products are field-tested and revised until a prespecified level of effectiveness is achieved. Although the R & D cycle is an expensive one, it does result in quality products designed to meet educational needs. School personnel who are the consumers of R & D endeavors may for the first time really see the value of educational research.

Action Research

The purpose of action research is to solve classroom problems through the application of the scientific method. It is concerned with a local problem and is conducted in a local setting. It is not concerned with whether the results are generalizable to any other setting and is not characterized by the same kind of control evident in other categories of research. The primary goal of action research is the solution of a given problem, not contribution to science. Whether the research is conducted in one classroom or in many classrooms, the teacher is very much a part of the process. The more research training the teachers involved have had, the more likely it is that the research will produce valid, if not generalizable, results.

The value of action research is confined to those conducting it. Despite its shortcomings, it does represent a scientific approach to problem solving that is considerably better than change based on the alleged effectiveness of untried procedures, and infinitely better than no change at all. It is a means by which concerned school personnel can attempt to improve the educational process, at least within their environment. Of course the value of action research to true scientific progress is limited. True progress requires the development of sound theories having implications for many classrooms, not just one or two. One sound theory that includes 10 principles of learning may eliminate the need for hundreds of would-be action research studies. Given the current status of educational theory, however, action research provides immediate answers to problems that cannot wait for theoretical solutions.

Classification of Research by Method

Although there is sometimes a degree of overlap, most research studies represent a readily identifiable method, or strategy. All studies have certain procedures in common—statement of a problem, collection of data, analysis of data, and drawing of conclusions. Beyond these, however, specific procedures are to a high degree determined by the research method. Each of the methods is designed to answer a different type of question. Knowledge of the various methods, and the procedures involved in each, is important both for conductors and consumers of research. Even using method as a criterion, there are several different ways in which research studies can be classified, for example, experimental versus nonexperimental, or historical versus descriptive versus experimental. However, these alternatives tend to lump together studies entailing distinctly different research strategies. A classification scheme that appears to be the most efficient, in that it minimizes categories and maximizes differentiation, places all research studies into one of five categories: historical, descriptive, correlational, causal-comparative, or experimental. The purpose of the following explanations is to provide you with an overview so that you will at least be able to read a research report and, based on its procedures, determine which of the five methods it represents. This competency is one which will aid you in reviewing the literature for the problem which you select in Part Two. The methods of research will be discussed further in Part Six.

Historical Research

Historical research involves studying, understanding, and explaining past events. The purpose of historical research is to arrive at conclusions concerning causes, effects, or trends of past occurrences that may help to explain present events and anticipate future events. While historical studies are less frequently conducted than other types, there are certain educational problems and issues (such as grading policies) that can be better understood in light of past experience. The steps involved in conducting a historical study are generally the same as for other types of research; a historical study should be guided by a hypothesis, just as an experimental study should, lest it degenerate into an aimless "treasure hunt."

Historical research studies do not gather data by administering instruments to individuals. They must seek out data that are already available. Sources of data are referred to as primary or secondary. Primary sources constitute firsthand knowledge, such as eyewitness reports and original documents; secondary sources constitute secondhand information, such as a description of an event by other than an eyewitness. If you interview someone who witnessed an accident, that someone is a primary source; if you interview that someone's husband or wife, who did not witness the accident but heard an account of what happened from his or her spouse, that person is a secondary source. Primary sources are admittedly harder to acquire (it would be quite a feat to find an eyewitness to the

Boston Tea Party!) but are generally more accurate and to be preferred. A major problem with much historical research is an excess of secondary sources.

Evaluation of historical data involves external criticism and internal criticism. External criticism assesses the authenticity of the data; internal criticism evaluates their worth. The worth of the data, the degree to which data are accurate and reliable and do indeed support the hypothesis, is judgmental and sometimes a matter of opinion. For example, a researcher investigating trends in classroom discipline might utilize a letter, allegedly written by George Washington, containing an expression of concern regarding the amount of physical punishment in the schools. The results of external criticism might verify that the letter was indeed written by George Washington. Internal criticism would be involved with whether he could be considered a reliable source concerning educational practices of the day. As another example, in his book *Chariots of the Gods?* Erich Von Däniken hypothesizes that thousands of years ago our ancestors were visited by intelligent beings from other worlds who, among other things, presented early humanity with advanced technology.[1] Von Däniken points to such remains as cave drawings, ancient maps, and relics of advanced, early civilizations as evidence in support of his theory. In general, authenticity of his evidence is without question; it is his interpretation of its meaning which is debatable. A cave drawing of a strange being, which is an ancient astronaut to Von Däniken, may be seen as simply an imaginary god to an archaeologist. In any event, his work represents a fascinating example of historical research.

The following are examples of typical historical research studies:

1. Factors leading to the development and growth of individualized instruction.

2. Effects of decisions of the United States Supreme Court on American education.

3. Trends in reading instruction, 1875–1975.

Descriptive Research

Descriptive research involves collecting data in order to test hypotheses or answer questions concerning the current status of the subject of the study. A descriptive study determines and reports the way things are. One common type of descriptive research involves assessing attitudes or opinions toward individuals, organizations, events, or procedures; pre-election political polls and market research surveys are examples of this type of descriptive research. Descriptive data are typically collected through a questionnaire survey, an interview, or observation.

Descriptive research sounds very simple; there is considerably more to it, however, than just asking questions and reporting answers. Since one is generally asking questions that have not been asked before, instruments usually have to be developed for specific studies; instrument development requires time and skill. A major problem further complicating descriptive research is lack of response— failure of subjects to return questionnaires or attend scheduled interviews. If the response rate is low, valid conclusions cannot be drawn. For example, suppose you are doing a study to determine attitudes of principals toward research. You

---

1. Von Däniken, E. *Chariots of the Gods?* New York: Bantam Books, 1972.

send a questionnaire to 100 principals and ask the question, "Do you usually cooperate if asked to participate in a research study?" Suppose 40 principals respond and they *all* answer "yes." Could you then conclude that principals cooperate? No! Even though all those who responded said "yes," those 60 who did not respond may never cooperate with research efforts. After all, they did not cooperate with you! Observational research also involves complexities that are not readily apparent. Observers must be trained and forms must be developed so that data will be collected objectively and reliably.

The following are examples of typical questions investigated by descriptive research studies:

1. How do second-grade teachers spend their time? Second-grade teachers would be observed for a period of time and results would probably be presented as percentages, e.g., 60% of their time is spent lecturing, 20% asking or answering questions, 10% administering discipline, and 10% performing administrative duties, such as collecting milk money.

2. How will citizens of Yortown vote in the next presidential election? A survey of citizens of Yortown would be taken (questionnaire or interview), and results would probably be presented as percentages; e.g., 70% indicate they will vote for Peter Pure, 20% for George Graft, and 10% are undecided.

3. How do parents feel about split-shift school days? Parents would be surveyed and results would probably be presented in terms of the percentages for, against, or undecided.

Correlational Research

Correlational research attempts to determine whether, and to what degree, a relationship exists between two or more quantifiable variables.[2] The purpose of a correlational study may be to establish relationship (or lack of it) or to use relationships in making predictions. Relationship studies typically study a number of variables believed to be related to a major, complex variable, such as achievement. Variables found not to be highly related are eliminated from further consideration; variables that are highly related may suggest causal-comparative or experimental studies to determine if the relationships are causal. For example, the fact that there is a relationship between self-concept and achievement does not imply that self-concept "causes" achievement or that achievement "causes" self-concept. Such a relationship only indicates that students with higher self-concepts have higher levels of achievement and students with lower self-concepts have lower levels of achievement. From the fact that two variables are highly related, one cannot conclude that one is the cause of the other; there may be a third factor which "causes" both of the related variables. For example, suppose it were determined that there is a high degree of relationship between number of years of schooling and income at age 40 (two quantifiable variables). The temptation might be to conclude that if you stay in school longer you will make more money; this conclusion would not necessarily be justified. There might be a third

---

2. A variable is a concept that can assume any one of a range of values. Examples of variables include height, weight, income, achievement, intelligence, and motivation. Got the idea?

variable, such as motivation, which "causes" people to stay in school *and* do well in their jobs. The important point to remember is that correlational research never establishes a cause-and-effect relationship, only a relationship.

Regardless of whether a relationship is a cause-effect relationship, the existence of a high relationship permits prediction. For example, high school grades and college grades are highly related; students who have high GPAs in high school tend to have high GPAs in college, and students who have low GPAs in high school tend to have low GPAs in college. Therefore, high school GPAs can be, and are, used to predict GPA in college. The degree of relationship between two variables is generally expressed as a correlation coefficient, which is a number between .00 and 1.00. Two variables that are not related will produce a coefficient near .00; two variables that are highly related will produce a coefficient near 1.00.[3] Since very few relationships are perfect, prediction is rarely perfect. However, for many decisions, predictions based on known relationships are very useful.

The following are examples of typical correlational studies:

1. The relationship between intelligence and creativity. Scores on an intelligence test and on a creativity test would be acquired from each member of a given group. The two sets of scores would be correlated and the resulting coefficient would indicate the degree of relationship.

2. The relationship between anxiety and achievement. Scores on an anxiety scale and on an achievement test would be acquired from each member of a group. The two sets of scores would be correlated and the resulting coefficient would indicate the degree of relationship.

3. Use of an aptitude test to predict success in an algebra course. Scores on an algebra aptitude test would be correlated with ultimate success in algebra as measured by final exam scores, for example. If the resulting coefficient was high, the aptitude test would be considered a good predictor.

Causal-Comparative and Experimental Research

While causal-comparative and experimental research represent distinctly different methods, they can best be understood through comparison and contrast. Both attempt to establish cause-effect relationships; both involve group comparisons. The major difference between them is that in experimental research the alleged "cause" is manipulated, and in causal-comparative research it is not. In experimental research, the alleged "cause," the activity or characteristic believed to make a difference, is referred to as a treatment; the more general term for "cause" is independent variable. The difference, or "effect," which is determined to occur or not occur, is referred to as the dependent variable. Dependent on what? Dependent on the independent variable. Thus, a study which investigates a cause-effect relationship investigates the effect of an independent variable on a dependent variable.

---

3. Two variables can be inversely related. When this occurs the coefficient is a negative number, and a high relationship is near −1.00. A negative relationship occurs when two variables are related in such a way that a high score on one is accompanied by a low score on the other, and vice versa. This will be discussed further in chapter 8.

In an experimental study the researcher manipulates at least one independent variable and observes the effect on one or more dependent variables. In other words, the researcher determines "who gets what," which group of subjects will get which treatment; the groups are generally referred to as experimental and control groups. Manipulation of the independent variable is the one single characteristic that differentiates experimental research from other methods. Ideally, in experimental research the groups to be studied are randomly formed before the experiment, a procedure not involved in the other methods of research. The essence of experimentation is control. The researcher strives to insure that the experiences of the groups are as equal as possible on all important variables except, of course, the independent variable. If, at the end of some period of time, groups differ in performance on the dependent variable, the difference can be attributed to the independent variable. Because of the direct manipulation and control of variables, experimental research is the only type of research that can truly establish cause-effect relationships.

The following are examples of typical experimental studies:

1. The comparative effectiveness of programmed instruction versus traditional instruction on computational skill. The independent variable, or cause, is type of instruction (programmed versus traditional); the dependent variable, or effect, is computational skill. Two groups (preferably randomly formed) would be exposed to essentially the same experiences, except for method of instruction. After some period of time, their computational skill would be compared.

2. The effect of self-paced instruction on self-concept. The independent variable, or cause, is pacing (self-pacing versus teacher pacing); the dependent variable, or effect, is self-concept. Two groups (preferably randomly formed) would be exposed to essentially the same experiences, except for the pacing of instruction. After some period of time, their self-concepts would be compared.

3. The effect of positive reinforcement on attitude toward school. The independent variable, or cause, is type of reinforcement (e.g., positive versus negative, or positive versus none); the dependent variable, or effect, is attitude toward school. Two groups (preferably randomly formed) would be exposed to essentially the same experiences, except for the type of reinforcement received. After some period of time, their attitudes toward school would be compared.

In a causal-comparative study the independent variable, or "cause," is not manipulated; it has already occurred. Independent variables in causal-comparative studies are variables which cannot be manipulated (e.g., sex, male-female), should not be manipulated (e.g., brain damage), or simply are not manipulated, but could be (e.g., method of instruction). In causal-comparative research, groups are also compared on some dependent variable; these groups, however, are different on some variable before the study begins. Perhaps one group possesses a characteristic and one does not, or perhaps each group is a member of a different socioeconomic level. In any event, the difference between the groups (the independent variable) is not, was not, or could not be determined by the researcher. Further, since the independent variable has already occurred, the same kinds of controls cannot be exercised as in an experimental study. Due to the lack of manipulation and control, cause-effect relationships established are at best tenuous and tentative. On the positive side, causal-comparative studies are less expensive and take much less time to conduct. Further, apparent cause-effect relationships may lead to experimental studies designed to confirm or disconfirm the findings. Also, there are a number of important variables which simply cannot be manipulated. Studies designed to investigate the effects of a broken home, intelligence, or sex on achievement must be causal-comparative, as none of these variables can be manipulated. The following are examples of typical causal-comparative studies:

1. The effect of kindergarten attendance on achievement at the end of the first grade. The independent variable, or cause, is kindergarten attendance (students attended kindergarten or they did not); the dependent variable, or effect, is achievement at the end of the first grade. Two groups of first graders would be identified—one group which had attended kindergarten, and one group which had not. The achievement of the two groups would be compared.

2. The effect of having a working mother on school absenteeism. The independent variable, or cause, is the employment status of the mother (the mother works or does not work); the dependent variable, or effect, is absenteeism, or number of days absent. Two groups of students would be identified—one group which had working mothers, and one group which did not. The absenteeism of the two groups would be compared.

3. The effect of sex on algebra achievement. The independent variable, or cause, is sex (male versus female); the dependent variable, or effect, is algebra achievement. The achievement of males would be compared to the achievement of females.

Guidelines for Classification

Which of the five methods is most appropriate for a given study depends upon the way in which the problem is defined. The same general problem can often be investigated using several of the methods. Research in a given area is often sequential; preliminary descriptive and/or correlational studies may be conducted followed by causal-comparative and/or experimental studies, if such seem warranted. As an example, let us look at anxiety and achievement. The following studies might be conducted:

1. Descriptive: A survey of teachers to determine how and to what degree they believe anxiety affects achievement.

2. Correlational: A study to determine the relationship between scores on an anxiety scale and scores on an achievement measure.

3. Causal-comparative: A study to compare the achievement of a group of students classified as high-anxious and a group classified as low-anxious.

4. Experimental: A study to compare the achievement of two groups—one group taught in an anxiety-producing environment and one group taught in an anxiety-reducing environment.[4]

---

4. There are generally considered to be two types of anxiety—trait anxiety and state anxiety. Trait anxiety is a personality characteristic that cannot be manipulated (Study 3). State anxiety is a temporary condition that can be manipulated, i.e., heightened or lessened (Study 4). In an anxiety-producing environment, for example, the teacher would constantly emphasize the importance of doing well on all tests.

When analyzing a study in order to determine the method represented, one approach is to ask yourself the following series of questions. First, Was the researcher attempting to establish a cause-effect relationship? If yes, the research is either causal-comparative or experimental. The next question is, Was the alleged cause, or independent variable, manipulated by the researcher? Did the researcher control who got what and what they got? If yes, the research is experimental; if no, the research is causal-comparative. If the answer to the very first question is no, the next question should be, Was the researcher attempting to establish a relationship or use a relationship for prediction? If yes, the research is correlational. If no, the research is either descriptive or historical, and you should have no difficulty discriminating between the two. The following examples should further clarify the differences among the methods:

1. Teacher attitudes toward unions. Probably descriptive. The study is determining the current attitudes of teachers. Data are probably collected through use of a questionnaire or an interview.

2. Effect of socioeconomic status (SES) on self-concept. Probably causal-comparative. The effect of SES on self-concept is being investigated. The independent variable, socioeconomic status, cannot be manipulated.

3. Comparison of large-group versus small-group instruction on achievement. Probably experimental. The effect of size of group on achievement is being investigated. The independent variable, group size, can be manipulated by the researcher.

4. Prediction of success in graduate school based on Graduate Record Examination (GRE) scores. Probably correlational. A cause-effect relationship is not involved, but a relationship is involved, namely the relationship between GRE scores and success in graduate school (e.g., GPA).

5. Participation of women in higher education, 1900–1980. Probably historical. The study is investigating a trend, probably increased participation by women.

Of course, one cannot usually identify method simply by reading the title of a research report. However, by reading the report, looking for identifying characteristics, and asking appropriate questions, you should have no trouble classifying most studies. Classifying a study by method is the first step in both conducting and reviewing a study, since each method entails different specific procedures and analyses.

Summary/Chapter 1

The Scientific Method

1. The goal of all scientific endeavors is to explain, predict, and/or control phenomena.
2. Compared to other sources of knowledge, such as experience, authority, inductive reasoning, and deductive reasoning, application of the scientific method is undoubtedly the most efficient and reliable.

3. Basically, the scientific method involves induction of hypotheses based on observations, deduction of implications of the hypotheses, testing of the implications, and confirmation or disconfirmation of the hypotheses.

Application of the Scientific Method in Education

4. Research is the formal, systematic application of the scientific method to the study of problems; educational research is the formal, systematic application of the scientific method to the study of educational problems

5. The major difference between educational research and other scientific research is the nature of the phenomena studied. It is considerably more difficult to explain, predict, and control situations involving human beings, by far the most complex of all organisms.

6. The steps involved in conducting research directly parallel those of the scientific method: selection and definition of a problem; execution of research procedures (collection of data); analysis of data; and drawing and stating conclusions.

Classification of Research by Purpose

7. Classification of research by purpose is based primarily on the degree to which findings have direct educational application and the degree to which they are generalizable. Both of these criteria are a function of the research control exercised during the conduction of the study.

Basic Versus Applied Research

8. In its purest form, basic research is conducted solely for the purpose of theory development and refinement.

9. Applied research, as the name implies, is conducted for the purpose of applying, or testing, theory and evaluating its usefulness in solving educational problems.

Evaluation Research

10. The purpose of evaluation research is to facilitate decision making regarding the relative worth of two or more alternative actions.

Research and Development (R & D)

11. The major purpose of R & D efforts is not to formulate or test theory but to develop effective products for use in schools.

Action Research

12. The purpose of action research is to solve classroom problems through the application of the scientific method.

Classification of Research by Method

13. While there is sometimes a degree of overlap, most research studies represent a readily identifiable method, or strategy.

14. All studies have certain procedures in common—statement of a problem, collection of data, analysis of data, and drawing of conclusions; beyond these, specific procedures are to a high degree determined by the research method.

Historical Research

15. Historical research involves studying, understanding, and explaining past events.

16. The purpose of historical research is to arrive at conclusions concerning causes, effects, or trends of past occurrences that may help to explain present events and anticipate future events.

17. Primary sources of data constitute firsthand knowledge; secondary sources constitute secondhand information.

18. External criticism assesses the authenticity of the data; internal criticism evaluates their worth.

Descriptive Research

19. Descriptive research involves collecting data in order to test hypotheses or answer questions concerning the current status of the subject of the study.

20. Descriptive data are typically collected through a questionnaire survey, an interview, or observation.

21. Since one is generally asking questions that have not been asked before, instruments usually have to be developed for specific studies.

22. A major problem further complicating descriptive research is lack of response—failure of subjects to return questionnaires or attend scheduled interviews.

Correlational Research

23. Correlational research attempts to determine whether, and to what degree, a relationship exists between two or more quantifiable variables.

24. The purpose of a correlational study may be to establish a relationship (or lack of it) or to use relationships in making predictions.

25. From the fact that two variables are highly related, one cannot conclude that one is the cause of the other; there may be a third factor which "causes" both of the related variables.

26. Regardless of whether a relationship is a cause-effect relationship, the existence of a high relationship permits prediction.

27. The degree of relationship between two variables is generally expressed as a correlation coefficient, which is number between .00 and 1.00.

Causal-Comparative and Experimental Research

28. The activity or characteristic believed to make a difference is referred to as the "cause" or treatment, and more generally as the independent variable.

29. The difference, or "effect," which is determined to occur or not occur is referred to as the dependent variable.

30. In an experimental study the researcher manipulates at least one independent variable and observes the effect on one or more dependent variables.

31. Ideally, in experimental research the groups to be studied are randomly formed before the experiment, a procedure not involved in the other methods of research.

32. The essence of experimentation is control.
33. Only experimental research can truly establish cause-effect relationships.
34. In a causal-comparative study the independent variable, or "cause," is not manipulated; it has already occurred.
35. In causal-comparative research, the difference between the groups (the independent variable) is not, was not, or could not be determined by the researcher.
36. Due to the lack of manipulation and control, cause-effect relationships established through causal-comparative research are at best tenuous and tentative.

Guidelines for Classification

37. Which of the five methods is most appropriate for a given study depends upon the way in which the problem is defined. The same general problem can often be investigated using several of the methods.
38. When analyzing a study in order to determine the method represented, one approach is to ask the following series of questions: Was the researcher attempting to establish a cause-effect relationship? Was the alleged cause, or independent variable, manipulated by the researcher? Was the researcher attempting to establish a relationship or use a relationship for prediction?

Task 1 Performance Criteria

Task 1-A

If the study that you are given was designed to investigate one major problem, one sentence should be sufficient to describe the problem. If several problems were investigated, one sentence per problem should be sufficient.

Six sentences or less will adequately describe the major procedures of most studies. Do not copy the procedures section of the study or describe each and every step. Briefly describe the subjects, instrument(s), and major steps.

As with the problem, one or two sentences will usually be sufficient to state the major analyses. You are not expected to understand the analyses, only identify them. By the time you get to chapter 13 you will be at least somewhat desensitized and will not be frightened by terms like *t* test and analysis of variance.

The major conclusions that you identify and state (one or two sentences should be sufficient) should directly relate to the original problem or problems. Remember, statements like "more research is needed in this area" do not represent major conclusions.

Task 1-B

The characteristics of the study which you describe should be characteristics which are unique to the research method represented by the study. The following are illustrative examples of responses you might give for studies representing each of the methods of research.

1. This study was historical *because* trends in instructional grouping practices during the past 50 years were investigated.
2. This study was descriptive *because* a questionnaire was used in order to determine how social studies teachers feel about the inquiry method of instruction.
3. This study was correlational *because* the predictive validity of a new scholastic aptitude test was investigated.

4. This study was causal-comparative *because* a cause-effect relationship was investigated but the independent variable was not manipulated; the researcher could not and did not determine "who got what," that is, which subjects were members of single-parent families and which were members of two-parent families.

5. This study was experimental *because* subjects were randomly assigned to treatments and the independent variable (cause) was manipulated; the researcher determined "who got what," that is, which subjects received peer counseling and which subjects received individual counseling.

See the *Student Guide* for practice examples for Task 1-A and Task 1-B.

Part Two
Research Problems

Since it will be a second home to you, at least for a while, you should become completely familiar with the library before beginning your review.

Selection and definition of a research problem is a refinement process that begins with the identification of a problem area and terminates with one or more testable hypotheses or answerable questions. The refinement process is based primarily upon a thorough review and critical analysis of related literature. Once a problem area is identified and a specific problem within it selected, a tentative hypothesis is formulated; this tentative hypothesis guides the literature review which in turn forms the basis for the final statement of the research hypothesis. Selection and definition of a problem is a very important component of the research process and entails much time and thought. The statement of the problem, the review of related literature, and the statement of the hypothesis comprise the introduction section of both research plans and research reports on completed research. The only difference may be the tense in which the introduction is written; research plans are usually written in the present tense ("it *is* hypothesized that . . ."), but research reports are always written in the past tense ("It *was* hypothesized that . . .").

The problem which you ultimately select in this part is the problem which you will work with in succeeding parts. Therefore, it is important that you select a problem which is (1) relevant to your area of study (e.g., English education) and (2) of particular interest to you. Also, since you will be responsible for a comprehensive literature search, it will be to your benefit to select a manageable, well-defined problem. For example, "the use of homework in mathematics instruction" is not manageable and well-defined; "the effect of daily homework assignments on the examination grades of ninth-grade algebra students" *is* manageable and well-defined.

The goal of Part Two is for you to acquire the ability to identify and define a meaningful problem, conduct an adequate review of related literature, and state the problem in terms of a testable hypothesis. After you have read Part Two, you should be able to perform the following task.

Task 2

Write an introduction for a research plan. This will include a statement of the specific problem to be investigated in the study, a statement concerning the significance of the problem, a review of related literature, and a testable hypothesis. Include definitions of terms where appropriate.

(See Performance Criteria, p. 56)

2

Selection and Definition of a Problem

Enablers

After reading chapter 2, you should be able to:

1. Make a list of at least three educational problems for which you would be interested in conducting a research study.

2. Select one of the problems; identify at least 15 complete references which directly relate to the selected problem. The sources of the references should include at least the following:

(a) *Education Index*—minimum three references.

(b) *Readers' Guide to Periodical Literature*—minimum one reference.

(c) *Dissertation Abstracts International*—minimum one reference.

(d) *Psychological Abstracts*—minimum one reference.

(e) *Resources in Education*—minimum one reference.

(f) *Current Index to Journals in Education*—minimum three references.

(g) *Review of Educational Research*—minimum one reference.

While (a) and (d) index references included in the other sources, you need to learn how to use all of the above sources.

3. Read and abstract·the references you have listed.

4. Formulate at least one testable hypothesis for your problem.

(Note: These enablers will form the basis for Task 2.)

Selection and Statement

After a problem area of interest is identified, a specific problem is selected for investigation. Theory and experience are two major sources of problems. A good problem has a number of identifiable characteristics. A good statement of a problem also conforms to a set of important criteria.

Selection

For beginning researchers, selection of a problem is the most difficult step in the research process. Some graduate students spend many anxiety-ridden days and sleepless nights worrying about where they are going to "find" the problem they need for their thesis or dissertation. To the poor student it seems as if *every* problem she or he identifies is dismissed by her or his advisor as being trivial or "already done." The problem is not a lack of problems; there is almost an unlimited supply of problems which need researching. The problem is a lack of familiarity with the literature on the student's part. Learning how and where to locate problems, and systematically attacking this phase of the research process, is much better for one's mental health than worrying one's self into a nervous collapse!

The first step in selecting a problem is to identify a general problem area that is related to your area of expertise and of particular interest to you. Examples of problem areas might be reading programs for preschoolers, programmed materials for elementary mathematics, counseling techniques for disruptive high school students, the use of paraprofessionals in the elementary school, the inquiry approach to social studies, and the use of reviews to increase retention. Since you will be doing a great deal of reading in the area you select, and devoting many hours to the planning and conduction of the ultimate study, choosing a topic of interest which will increase your knowledge and understanding of your particular professional area makes good sense.

The next step is to narrow down the general problem area to a specific, researchable problem. A problem that is too general can only cause you grief. In the first place, the scope of the review of related literature that you must inevitably conduct will be unnecessarily increased, possibly resulting in many more hours being spent in the library. This will in turn complicate organization of the results of the review and subsequent hypothesis development. Even more important than the practicalities, a problem that is too general tends to result in a study which is too general, includes too many variables, and produces results that are difficult to interpret. Conversely, a well-defined, manageable problem results in a well-defined, manageable study. One major way to narrow down your problem is to read sources giving overviews or summaries of the current status of research in your area; references such as the *Review of Educational Research* and the *Encyclopedia of Educational Research* may be very helpful.[1] In narrowing the problem area you should select an aspect of the general problem area that is related to your area of expertise. For example, the general problem area "the use of reviews to increase retention" could generate many specific problems such as "the comparative effectiveness of immediate versus delayed review on the retention of geometric concepts" and "the effect of review games on the retention of vocabulary words by second graders." In your efforts to sufficiently delineate a problem, however, be careful not to get carried away; a problem that is too narrow is just as bad as a problem that is too broad. A study such as "the effectiveness of preclass reminders in reducing instances of pencil sharpening during class time" would probably contribute little, if anything, to the science of education!

Selecting a good problem is well worth the time and effort. As mentioned previously, there is no shortage of significant problems that need to be researched; there is really no excuse for selecting a trite problem. Besides, it is generally to your advantage to select a worthwhile problem; you will certainly get

---

1. *Review of educational research.* Washington, D.C.: American Educational Research Association, 1931 to date, and Ebel, R. (ed.). *Encyclopedia of educational research.* New York: Macmillan, 1969.

a great deal more "out of it" professionally and academically. If the subsequent study is well conducted and reported, besides making a contribution to knowledge, publication in a professional journal is also a probable consequence. The potential personal benefits to be derived from publication include increased professional status and job opportunities, not to mention tremendous self-satisfaction.

Sources

You may be asking yourself, "So where do I find one of those numerous significant problems that need researching?" While there are several major sources of problems, the most meaningful ones are generally those derived from theory. There are many educationally relevant theories, such as theories of learning and behavior, from which problems can be drawn. The fact that a theory *is* a theory and *not* a body of facts means that it contains generalizations and hypothesized principles which must be subjected to rigorous scientific investigation. Problems derived from a theoretical problem area are not only preferable in terms of contribution to true scientific progress in education, they also facilitate the formulation of hypotheses based on a sound rationale; these hypotheses in turn facilitate ultimate interpretation of study results. The results of a study based on a theoretical problem contribute to their related theory by confirming or disconfirming some aspect of the theory and also by suggesting additional studies that need to be done.

To be perfectly honest, however, selection of a problem based on theory may be a bit "heavy" for many beginning researchers. There are a great number of problems that need researching that are not theoretical in nature. An obvious source of such problems is the researcher's personal experiences. Most educational researchers come from the teaching profession. It is hard to imagine a teacher who has never had a hunch concerning a better way to do something (a way to increase learning or improve behavior, for example) or been a consumer of a program or materials whose effectiveness was untested. This is not to say that a hunch based on experience will never lead to a theoretical problem, it is just more probable that the problem will result in a very applied research study.

As mentioned previously, the literature is also a good source of problems. In addition to overviews and summaries, which are more helpful in narrowing down a problem area, specific studies often indicate "next-step" studies which need to be conducted. The suggested "next-step" may involve a logical extension of the described study or simply replication of the study in a different setting in order to establish the generalizability of its findings. For example, a study investigating the effectiveness of programmed instruction in elementary arithmetic might suggest the need for similar studies in other curriculum areas. It is generally not a good idea, however, to simply replicate a study as it was originally conducted; there is much to be learned from developing and executing your own study. Replication of certain studies, however, is highly desirable, especially those whose results conflict with previous research or disconfirm some aspect of an established theory.

Characteristics

Since a research problem by definition involves an issue in need of investigation, it follows that a basic characteristic of a research problem is that it is "researchable." A "researchable" problem is one that can be investigated through the collection and analysis of data. Problems dealing with philosophical or ethical issues are not researchable. Research can assess how people "feel" about such issues but research cannot resolve them. Whether or not there is reward and punishment in the hereafter may be an important problem to many people but it is not researchable; there is no way to resolve it through the collection and analysis of data (at least at the present time!). Similarly, in education there are a number of issues that make great topics for debates (such as "should prayer be allowed in the schools?") but are not researchable problems.

A major characteristic of a good problem is that it has theoretical or practical significance. Of course the most significant problems are those derived from theory; even if the problem is nontheoretical, however, its solution should contribute in some way to improvement of the educational process. If the typical reaction to your problem is "who cares?" it probably is not of sufficient significance to warrant a study!

A third major characteristic of a good problem is that it is a good problem *for you*. The fact that you have chosen a problem of interest to you, in an area in which you have expertise, is not sufficient. It must be a problem that you can adequately investigate given (1) your current level of research skill, (2) available resources, and (3) time and other restrictions. The availability of appropriate subjects and measuring instruments, for example, is an important consideration. As a beginning researcher, you more than likely have access to one or more faculty advisors who can help you to assess the feasibility of your problem.

Statement

A well-written statement of a problem generally indicates the variables of interest to the researcher and the specific relationship between those variables which is to be investigated.[2] A well-written problem statement also defines all relevant variables, either directly or operationally; operational definitions define concepts in terms of operations, or processes. An excellent source of definitions is the *Dictionary of Education*.[3] An example of a problem statement might be: "The problem to be investigated in this study is (or "the purpose of this study is to investigate") the effect of positive reinforcement on the quality of English compositions." The variables to be defined are "positive reinforcement" and "quality of English compositions." Positive reinforcement might be defined in terms of positive written comments on compositions such as "good thought" and "much better." The quality of the compositions might be defined in terms of such factors as number of complete sentences and number of words spelled incorrectly. In this example, the relationship to be investigated between the variables is cause-effect; the purpose of the study is to see if positive reinforcement (the cause) influences the quality of compositions (the effect).

A statement of the problem is invariably the first component of the introduction section of both a research plan and a research report on a completed study. Since

2. Certain descriptive studies simply state their problems in the form of questions to be answered. However, most meaningful descriptive studies are also concerned with relationships between variables. For example, a descriptive study concerned with voting patterns of various types of voters on a school bond issue would be preferable to a mere polling of voters.

3. Good, C.V. (ed.). *Dictionary of education.* New York: McGraw-Hill, 1973.

the problem statement gives direction to the rest of the plan or report, it should be stated as soon as possible. The statement of the problem should be accompanied by a presentation of the background of the problem, including a justification for the study in terms of the significance of the problem. Background of the problem means information required for an understanding of the problem. The problem should be justified in terms of its contribution to educational theory or practice. For example, an introduction might begin with a problem statement such as "the purpose of this study is to compare the effectiveness of salaried paraprofessionals and parent volunteers with respect to the reading achievement of first-grade children." This statement might be followed by a discussion concerning (1) the role of paraprofessionals, (2) increased utilization of paraprofessionals by schools, (3) the expense involved, and (4) the search for alternatives, such as parent volunteers. The significance of the problem would be that if parent volunteers are equally effective, their use can be substituted for salaried paraprofessionals at great savings. Any educational practice that might increase achievement at no additional cost is certainly worthy of investigation!

After a problem has been carefully selected, delineated, and clearly stated, the researcher is ready to attack the review of related literature. The researcher typically has a tentative hypothesis that guides the review. In the above example, the tentative hypothesis would be that parent volunteers are equally effective as salaried paraprofessionals. It is not unlikely that the tentative hypothesis will be modified, even changed radically, as a result of the review. It does, however, give direction to the literature search, and narrows its scope to include only relevant topics.

Review of Related Literature

Having happily found a suitable problem, the beginning researcher is usually "raring to go." Too often the review of related literature is seen as a necessary evil to be completed as fast as possible so that one can get on with the study. This feeling is due to a lack of understanding concerning the purpose and importance of the review, and to a feeling of uneasiness on the part of students who are not too sure exactly how to go about it. The review of related literature, however, is as important as any other component of the research process, and it can be conducted quite painlessly if it is approached in an orderly manner. Some researchers even find the process quite enjoyable!

Definition, Purpose, and Scope

The review of related literature involves the systematic identification, location, and analysis of documents containing information related to the research problem. These documents include periodicals, abstracts, reviews, books, and other research reports. The review has several important functions which make it well worth the time and effort. The major purpose of reviewing the literature is to determine what has already been done that relates to your problem. This knowledge not only avoids unintentional duplication, but it also provides the understandings and insights necessary for the development of a logical framework into which your problem fits. In other words, the review tells the researcher what has been done and what needs to be done. Studies that have been done will provide the rationale for your research hypothesis; indications of what needs to be done will form the basis for the justification for your study.

Another important function of the literature review is that it points out research strategies and specific procedures and measuring instruments that have and have not been found to be productive in investigating your problem. This information will help you to avoid other researchers' mistakes and to profit from their experiences. It may suggest approaches and procedures previously not considered. For example, suppose your problem involved the comparative effectiveness of programmed versus traditional instruction on the achievement of ninth-grade algebra students. The review of literature might reveal 10 studies already conducted which have found no differences in achievement. Several of the studies, however, might suggest that programmed instruction may be more effective for certain kinds of students than others. Thus, you might reformulate your problem to involve the comparative effectiveness of programmed versus traditional instruction in algebra on the achievement of *low-aptitude* ninth-grade algebra students.

Being familiar with previous research also facilitates interpretation of the results of your study. The results can be discussed in terms of whether they agree with, and support, previous findings or not; if the results contradict previous findings, differences between your study and the others can be described, providing a rationale for the discrepancy. If your results are consistent with other findings, your report should include suggestions for the "next step"; if they are not consistent, your report should include suggestions for studies that will resolve the conflict.

Beginning researchers seem to have difficulty in determining how broad their literature review should be. They understand that all literature directly related to their problem should be reviewed, they just don't know when to quit! They have trouble determining which articles are "related enough" to their problem to be included. Unfortunately, there is no statistical formula that can be applied; the decisions must be based on judgment. These judgments become easier as one acquires experience; there are some general guidelines, however, which can assist the beginner. First, avoid the temptation to include everything you find; bigger does not mean better. A smaller, well-organized review is definitely to be preferred to a review containing many studies that are more or less related to the problem. Second, heavily researched areas usually provide enough references directly related to a specific problem to eliminate the need for relying on less related studies. For example, the role of feedback in learning has been extensively researched for both animals and human beings, for verbal learning and nonverbal learning, and for a variety of different learning tasks. If you were concerned with the relationship between frequency of feedback and chemistry achievement, you would probably not have to review, for example, feedback studies related to animal learning. Third, and conversely, new or little-researched problem areas usually require review of any study related in some meaningful way to the problem in order to develop a logical framework for the study and a sound rationale for the research hypothesis. For example, a study concerned with the effectiveness of formal preschool reading instruction would probably include in its literature search any study concerned with preschool reading instruction, formal or informal. Ten years from now there will probably be enough research on formal programs to eliminate the need for reviewing informal efforts.

A common misconception among beginning researchers is the idea that the worth of their problem is a function of the amount of literature available on the topic. This is not the case. There are many new important areas of research for which there is comparatively little available literature; formal preschool reading instruction is one such area. The very lack of such research increases the worth of the study. On the other hand, the fact that 1,000 studies have already been done in a given problem area does not mean there is no further need for research in that area. Such an area will generally be very well developed with additional needed research readily identifiable. Such an area is anxiety theory, which is concerned with the relationships between anxiety and learning.

Preparation

Since it will be a second home to you, at least for a while, you should become completely familiar with the library before beginning your review. Time spent initially will save time in the long run. You should find out what references are available and where they are located. You should also be familiar with services offered by the library as well as the rules and regulations regarding the use of library materials. Since most of the references you will be seeking will be located in educational journals, you should spend extra time getting well acquainted with the various periodicals.

Many libraries provide written guides detailing what the library has to offer and the procedures for utilizing references and services. While many references are standard and can be found in most libraries, some sources, such as the ERIC microfiche collection, are not necessarily available.[4] Services also vary from library to library; the stacks, for example, may or may not be available for direct use by graduate students. One important service that is offered by most libraries is the interlibrary loan. This service permits you to obtain references not available in your library but available in another library. The small fee usually charged is generally happily paid by the researcher who "needs" a locally unavailable reference. Many libraries offer guided tours of the facilities; such tours are generally scheduled for groups. While librarians are usually very willing to help individuals, you should learn to use the library all by yourself; the librarian may not be as cheerful the tenth time you approach as he or she was the first time!

Having formulated your problem, and acquainted yourself with the library, there is one more thing you need to do before you go marching merrily off into the library—make a list of key words to guide your literature search. Most of the sources you will consult will have alphabetical subject indexes to help you locate specific references. You will look in these indexes under the key words you have selected. For example, if your problem concerned the effectiveness of peer counseling in the drug education of high school students, the logical key words would be *peer counseling*. You will also need to think of alternative words under which your topic might be listed. For example, some indexes include *peer groups* as a heading. Usually, the key words will be obvious; sometimes you may have to play detective. A student of mine was interested in the effect of artificial turf on knee injuries in football. He looked under every key word he could think of, such

---

4. The ERIC system will be discussed in the next section.

as *surface, playing surface, turf,* and *artificial turf.* He could find nothing. Since we both knew that studies had been done, he kept trying. When he finally did find a reference it was listed under, of all things, *lawns!* Identifying key words is usually not such a big deal. In looking in initial sources you may identify additional key words that will help you in succeeding sources. However, giving some thought initially to possible key words should facilitate an efficient beginning to a task that requires organization. After you have identified your key words, you will finally be ready to begin to consult appropriate sources.

Sources

There are usually many sources of literature that might be related to a given problem. In general, however, there are a number of major sources commonly used by educational researchers. Some of these sources are primary sources and some are secondary; as with historical research, primary sources are definitely preferable. In historical research, a primary source is an eyewitness or an original document or relic; in the literature, a primary source is a description of a study written by the person who conducted it. A secondary source in the literature is generally a much briefer description of a study written by someone other than the original researcher. The *Review of Educational Research,* for example, summarizes many research studies conducted on a given topic.[5] Since secondary sources usually give complete bibliographic information on references cited, they direct the researcher to relevant primary sources. You should not be satisfied with only the information contained in secondary sources; the corresponding primary sources will be considerably more detailed and will give you information "straight from the horse's mouth," as they say.

The number of individual references that could be consulted for a given problem is staggering; fortunately there are indexes, abstracts, and other retrieval mechanisms that facilitate identification of relevant references. In this section we will discuss the ones most often used in educational research. You should check the library for sources in your area of specialization.

Education Index

The *Education Index* is a major source of educational periodicals.[6] Educational periodicals (as other periodicals) typically are published at regular intervals (monthly or bimonthly, for example) and include such things as reports of research efforts, reviews of related research, and opinion articles on contemporary educational issues. The term *periodical* includes professional journals as well as yearbooks, bulletins, and other educational reports. The *Education Index* lists bibliographical information on references appearing in literally hundreds of educational periodicals. The *Education Index* is used much the same way as any other index; entries are listed alphabetically under subject, author, and title headings. Since the procedure for using the *Index* is similar to the procedure followed for other indexes, it will be described in detail:

---

5. *Review of educational research.* Washington, D.C.: American Educational Research Association, 1931 to date.

6. *Education index.* New York: H.W. Wilson, 1929 to date.

1. Start with the most recent issue of the *Index* and look under the key words you have already identified, *peer counseling* for example.

2. Under the key words you will find a list of references presented alphabetically by title, or you will be directed to other key words. For example, if you looked under *peer counseling* in the July 1978–June 1979 cumulative index, you would be directed to see *personnel service—student participation*. Under *student partici-pation* you would find the following entries (among others):

> Effects of reciprocal peer counseling on college student personality development. S. A. McWilliams. bibl J AM Coll Health Assn 27:210–18 F '79
>
> Moving from drugs to sex: new directions for youth-oriented peer counseling. B. A. Baldwin. bibl J Am Coll Health Assn 27:75–8 O '78
>
> Service delivery and high school peer counseling systems. A. M. Fink and others. Personnel & Guid J 57:80–3 O '78

3. Decide whether each reference is related to your problem or not. For example, assume your problem was concerned with the effectiveness of peer counseling in drug education for high school students. The first entry above, dealing with college student personality development, would probably not be related. The second entry, concerned with drugs and sex, probably would be related. The third entry might or might not be related.

4. If the reference is probably related or might be related, copy the complete reference.

5. If you are not familiar with the abbreviations used by the *Index,* look in the front of the volume. Where you have written the reference, replace each abbreviation with the complete term. In the entry from the *Index* concerned with service delivery, for example, Personnel & Guid J is the abbreviation for Personnel and Guidance Journal, and O is the abbreviation for October.

6. Repeat steps 1–5 for previous issues of the *Index.*

7. Locate each of the references on the library shelves.

The *Education Index* is similar in purpose to *Current Index to Journals in Education* (CIJE), which will be discussed later.[7] It is less useful in that since the *Index* does not contain abstracts, time is often wasted locating "might be related" references which turn out not to be related. Since CIJE was not available prior to 1969, however, the *Education Index* is the best source of educational periodicals published from 1929 to 1969. There are also a number of indexes similar to the *Education Index* available for specific fields such as business education.

Readers' Guide to Periodical Literature

Readers' Guide to Periodical Literature is an index very similar in format to the *Education Index.*[8] Instead of professional publications, however, it indexes articles in well over 100 widely read magazines. Articles located through the *Guide* will generally be nontechnical, opinion-type references. These can be very useful, however, particularly in documenting the significance of your problem. For exam-

7. *Current index to journals in education.* Phoenix: Ornyx Press, 1969 to date.
8. *Readers' guide to periodical literature.* New York: H.W. Wilson, 1900 to date.

ple, many articles have been written in popular magazines expressing concern on the part of the American public over the inability of many children to read adequately. *Readers' Guide* lists entries alphabetically by subject and author, and the procedures for its use are essentially the same as for using the *Education Index*. In addition to *Readers' Guide,* there are several other sources of popular literature such as *International Index* and *The New York Times Index.*[9]

Dissertation Abstracts International

Dissertation Abstracts International contains abstracts of doctoral dissertations conducted at hundreds of academic institutions.[10] Abstracts are summaries, usually brief; *Dissertation Abstracts International* summarizes the main components of dissertation studies. The advantage of having an abstract is that it usually allows you to classify all references as related to your problem or not related, and greatly reduces time spent looking up unrelated references with fuzzy titles. *Dissertation Abstracts International* classifies entries by subject, author, and institution. The procedure for using the *Abstracts* is similar to the procedure for using the *Educational Index;* the major difference is that once a related dissertation title is located, the next step is not to locate the dissertation but to locate an abstract of the dissertation using the entry number given with the reference. For example, if the entry number were 27/03B/3720, the abstract would be located in volume 27, issue number 3B, page number 3720. If after reading an abstract you wish to obtain a copy of the complete dissertation, check and see if it is available on microfiche in your library. If not, it can be obtained from University Microfilms on microfilm for a small fee. University Microfilms also provides a computer retrieval service called DATRIX. By filling out a request form available at most libraries and indicating appropriate key words, you can receive a bibliography of related dissertations for a nominal fee.

Psychological Abstracts

Psychological Abstracts presents summaries of completed psychological research studies.[11] Each issue contains 12 sections corresponding to 12 areas of psychology. The sections on developmental psychology and educational psychology are generally the most useful to educational researchers. The December issue contains an annual cumulative author index and subject index. In addition, cumulative subject indexes and cumulative author indexes, which cover approximately 30 years, are available. The procedure for using *Psychological Abstracts* is similar to the procedure for the *Education Index*. The major difference is that the *Psychological Abstracts* index does not give bibliographic information; for a given topic, abstract numbers of related references are given. This number is located in *Psychological Abstracts,* which provides the complete reference as well as an abstract of the reference. If the abstract indicates that the study is related to the

---

9. *International index.* New York: H.W. Wilson, 1907 to date and *The New York Times index.* New York: The New York Times Co., 1913 to date.

10. *Dissertation abstracts international.* Ann Arbor, Mich.: University Microfilms, 1969 to date (From 1955 to 1969, the title was *Dissertation abstracts*).

11. *Psychological abstracts.* Washington, D.C.: American Psychological Association, 1927 to date.

problem of interest, the original reference can then be located. In addition to the key words identified for a given problem, the word *bibliographies* should also be checked. A bibliography related to your problem may exist which might lead you to important references that might otherwise be missed.

How fruitful *Psychological Abstracts* will be for you will depend upon the nature of your problem. If it is a nontheoretical problem, such as the previously mentioned study concerned with in-class pencil-sharpening behavior, you probably will not find anything in *Psychological Abstracts.* If the problem does relate to some theory, such as a study on the effects of positive reinforcement, you more than likely will find useful references. In such cases, both *Psychological Abstracts* and the *Education Index* should be checked to make sure you do not miss anything. Since *Psychological Abstracts* does provide abstracts which help to determine the relevancy of a given reference, it makes sense to check it before going to the *Education Index.*

Another source of similar information is the *Annual Review of Psychology;* it includes reviews of psychological research that are often of relevance to educational research.[12] There are also a number of journals of abstracts for specific areas such as *Child Development Abstracts and Bibliography.* [13]

Educational Resources Information Center (ERIC)

Established in the mid-sixties by the United States Office of Education, ERIC is a national information system currently supported and operated by the National Institute of Education (NIE). Its primary purpose is to collect and disseminate reports of current educational research, evaluation, and development activities. Many educators are not fully aware of the range of services offered by the ERIC network. Although there is some overlap in the references included in ERIC, the *Education Index,* and *Psychological Abstracts,* ERIC contains abstracts for many additional references. Research reports that would not typically be included in other sources (such as papers presented at professional meetings and studies conducted in school districts) are indexed and abstracted by ERIC. Another factor in favor of ERIC is the comparatively short time interval between collection of a document and its dissemination. Documents become part of ERIC much more quickly than if they are published by a professional journal. Thus for very current topics, ERIC is often a source of data not available through other sources. The usefulness of the ERIC system is supported by some statistics reported by NIE:[14]

> In one year alone, ERIC products and services were used over 10 million times.
> Students accounted for 62% of the users; teachers, 21%; school administrators, 11%; others, 6%.
> 90% of the users reported that they obtained information through ERIC that they probably would not have found using other sources.
> 70% of the users reported that the information they obtained through ERIC helped them professionally.
> 75% of the school-based users considered RIE (a major ERIC publication) very useful.

---

12. *Annual review of psychology.* Palo Alto, Calif.: Annual Reviews, 1950 to date.

13. *Child development abstracts and bibliography.* Washington, D.C.: National Research Council of the Society for Research in Child Development, 1927 to date.

14. National Institute of Education. *How to use ERIC.* Washington, D.C.: Author, 1979.

ERIC comprises a central office and a number of clearinghouses, each devoted to a different area (such as career education, early childhood education, handi-capped and gifted children, reading and communication skills, and teacher educa-tion). Each clearinghouse collects, abstracts, stores, and disseminates documents specific to its area of specialization. Disseminated documents include information analysis products (books, monographs, and other publications), fact sheets, com-puter search reprints, and information bulletins.

Two major ERIC publications are *Resources in Education* (RIE) and *Current Index to Journals in Education* (CIJE).[15] Since they both use a common format, if you learn how to use one of them you know how to use the other. The first step in using ERIC resources is to become familiar with the terms which ERIC uses to index references. The *Thesaurus of ERIC Descriptors,* available in most libraries, is a compilation of the key words used in indexing ERIC documents.[16] The *Thesaurus* indicates the various terms under which a given topic is indexed. If, for example, your research problem was "The Effectiveness of Peer Counseling as a Component in a Drug Education Program for High School Students," you would find that *peer counseling* is a descriptor used in the ERIC system. Each issue of RIE and CIJE includes new additions to the pool of descriptors. After you have identified appropriate descriptors, the next logical step is to consult RIE.

RIE RIE is published monthly, and semiannual indexes are available. RIE in-dexes over 1,000 documents per issue and for many entries provides an abstract prepared by one of the clearinghouses. If the title of an article sufficiently conveys its content, an abstract is not included; otherwise an abstract is included. Entries are indexed by subject, author, institution, and accession number. Using the accession numbers given in each index, abstracts are located in the Document Resume section. For example, in the January 1979 issue of RIE, in the subject index under *peer counseling,* the following entries are listed:

> Peer Counseling: Academic Credit for Helping
>   Others   ED 158 181
> Utilization of Students as Peer Counselors and
>   Peer Tutors   ED 158 210

The second entry appears to be related to our problem. Using the accession number, ED 158 210, more complete information is located in the Document Resume section. This information includes the author's name, the publication date, the cost of obtaining the complete document in microfiche and hard copy, descriptors under which this entry is listed, and an abstract of the contents. Since most libraries have the ERIC document collection in microfiche form, it is usually not necessary to order documents, although instructions are given for doing so.

The next step in using ERIC is to consult the monthly and semiannual indexes of CIJE.

CIJE CIJE, mentioned previously as an improvement on the *Education Index,* indexes articles in the periodical literature and covers close to 800 education and

---

15. National Institute of Education. *Resources in education.* Washington, D.C.: Author, 1966 to date.
16. CCM Information Corporation. *Thesaurus of ERIC descriptors.* New York: Author, 1975.

education-related publications. The procedure for using CIJE is very similar to the procedure for using RIE. Using the same descriptors, relevant entries are identified in one of the indexes. Using the accession numbers, additional information is located in the Main Entry section. As with RIE, if the title of an article sufficiently conveys its content, an abstract is not included; otherwise an abstract is included. The addition of abstracts when needed makes CIJE more useful than the *Education Index* for those years for which it is available. Although CIJE was first published in 1969, abstracts were not included until 1970. After reading the abstract, the entire article may be read by consulting the appropriate journal. As an example, in the subject index, under the descriptor *peer counseling* the following entry is listed (among others):

Student to Student Helping Program. *Humanist Educator;*
    v17 n2 P81–90 Dec 1978   EJ 193 692

This entry tells us that in volume 17, issue number 2, of the journal *Humanist Educator,* we will find an article entitled "Student to Student Helping Program." If we wish to know more about the contents of the article, we use the accession number, EJ 193 692, to locate the abstract and other information in the Main Entry section.

Obtaining ERIC Documents   In addition to those already mentioned, a number of other services are provided by ERIC. For example, the various clearinghouses prepare and disseminate annotated bibliographies in their particular area of specialization. Also, a variety of curriculum guides, teachers' guides, and instructional materials can be obtained from the clearinghouses. You should ask your librarian for an up-to-date listing of the clearinghouses and their addresses.

As mentioned, all ERIC documents are available in both hard copy and microfiche. Hard copy is more convenient but microfiche is considerably less expensive. Most libraries have the complete ERIC microfiche collection and microfiche readers. If they are not available, you can order any document directly from the ERIC Document Reproduction Service, P.O. Box 190, Arlington, Virginia 22210.

If you would like more information on the documents and services obtainable from ERIC, read *How to Use ERIC.* If your library does not have a copy, you can order one directly from the Superintendent of Documents, United States Government Printing Office, Washington, D.C. 20402. If you would like to submit a document (report, speech, or paper) for possible inclusion in the ERIC system, send two clear, legible copies to the ERIC Processing and Reference Facility, 4833 Rugby Avenue, Suite 303, Bethesda, Maryland 20014. Your contribution will be forwarded to, and screened by, the appropriate clearinghouse.

Smithsonian Science Information Exchange (SSIE)

The SSIE disseminates information concerning research in progress, most of which is federally funded. Research in many fields besides education is reported, such as the biological sciences. Entries are classified by subject, location, chief investigator, and source of funding; information provided includes the above information and additional information, such as a brief summary of the status of the research. To receive more information concerning the SSIE, or to use its service, write to the Smithsonian Science Information Exchange, Inc., Room 300, 1830 M Street, N.W., Washington, D.C. 20036.

Review of Educational Research (RER)

The RER, mentioned previously, reviews and briefly summarizes a number of related studies on given topics. For example, volume 49 contains reviews of research on training counselors and clinicians,[17] the physical environment of the school,[18] and nonverbal communication in teaching.[19] Although the RER is a secondary source, each article concludes with an extensive bibliography. By reading the review article, and using the bibliography, you can easily identify important primary sources. To use the RER, simply check the table of contents of each issue. If a listed review is relevant to your problem, read the review and note specific studies of interest. Finally, use the bibliography to obtain the complete reference on the selected studies. Up until 1970, the RER was concerned with a limited number of general problem areas; however, the RER now accepts unsolicited reviews on a wide variety of topics.

Books

It is hard to imagine a graduate student who has never used the library card catalog to find books related to a given problem. However, without the data it would not be very "researchy" to say that there is no such graduate student, thus the inclusion of this discussion. Briefly, the card catalog alphabetically indexes (by author, subject, and title) all publications contained in the library, with the exception of the periodicals. Not infrequently, a comprehensive description of research in a given field will be compiled and published in book form. If such a book exists for your problem, it can be an invaluable reference.

Encyclopedias may also be useful, especially those in specialized areas such as educational research. General encyclopedias contain articles on a wide range of topics written by experts. Encyclopedias in specialized areas contain more detailed discussions on a restricted number of topics. A good example is the *Encyclopedia of Educational Research* which contains critical reviews and summaries on a number of educational topics.[20] Like the RER, the *Encyclopedia* is a secondary source which also follows each article with an extensive bibliography helpful in identifying pertinent primary sources. The *Second Handbook of Research on Teaching* is also a valuable resource for certain topics.[21]

17. Ford, J.D. Research on training counselors and clinicians. *Review of Educational Research,* 1979, *49* (1), 87–130.

18. Weinstein, C.S. The physical environment of the school: A review of the research. *Review of Educational Research,* 1979, *49* (4), 577–610.

19. Smith, H.A. Nonverbal communication in teaching. *Review of Educational Research,* 1979, *49* (4), 631–672.

20. Ebel, R. (ed.). *Encyclopedia of educational research.* New York: Macmillan, 1969.

21. Travers, R.M.W. (ed.). *Second handbook of research on teaching.* Chicago: Rand McNally, 1973.

Computer Searches

With relatively little effort, and for a relatively low cost (maybe even free), you can use a computer to identify related references for you. Searching that would take you days and days to do, a computer can do in a matter of minutes. No, a computer won't do your review of related literature for you. It won't check all sources, and it won't give you copies of articles. It will, however, search data bases such as the ERIC system and provide you with a list of references and, if provided by the data base, abstracts.

To initiate a computer search, you provide the key words, or descriptors. The computer then searches data bases for references having those descriptors.[22] If you do not know the appropriate descriptors, typically a search analyst will translate your key words into appropriate descriptors. For example, the key words *drug instruction* might be changed to *drug education*. If you are willing to take less related references, not just those specifically on your topic, you have to use broader descriptors. Of course, whether this is necessary depends upon how many references there are that are directly related to your problem. If you conduct a search on-line, that is, actually at a computer terminal, you may or may not receive assistance in defining your search strategy. Either way, but especially if not, you should give your search strategy careful thought ahead of time. If your descriptors are too general, for example, you will spend unnecessary time on-line and this time may cost you money (not to mention the fact that you will have an unwieldy number of references to sort through).

As a result of the computer search you receive a computer printout listing the identified references and abstracts as they appear in CIJE or RIE (or *Psychological Abstracts,* or whatever). The printout is mailed to you within 7 to 10 days.

Data Sources

Computer searches are made possible by the fact that various data bases, such as ERIC, *Psychological Abstracts,* and *Exceptional Child Education Resources,* are available on computer tapes. Information retrieval systems, such as the Lockheed DIALOG system, provide institutions with access to the tapes in their system. Some institutions have some tapes themselves. It is safe to say, however, that virtually any institution that provides computer search services accesses the ERIC system.

ERIC searches can be obtained at hundreds of locations across the United States (and around the world). These locations are listed in the *Directory of ERIC Search Services* (to be discussed shortly).[23] Most state departments of education, for example, have the ERIC tapes and provide assistance and searches at no charge for members of the education community. Many universities provide computer searches of the ERIC system, and a number of them access a major information retrieval system such as the Lockheed DIALOG program. The ad-

---

22. Full-text searching is an option at some locations. Full-text searching does not involve descriptors alone. Instead, each entry is searched for a particular word, words, or phrase. For example, we could request a full-text search for the words *peers* and *drugs.* Any entry containing those words (not necessarily next to each other), in the abstract for example, would be listed.

23. Pugh, E., Howder, M.L., Brandhorst, W.T., & Weber, E. *Directory of ERIC search services.* Washington, D.C.: Educational Resources Information Center, National Institute of Education, 1978.

vantage to access to a major system is the availability of multiple data bases. The DIALOG program, for example, provides access to some 90 different data bases. The costs associated with a computer search depend on a number of factors, the major one being the length of the search. There is usually a charge for on-line computer time and a fee for each entry on the printout. While it is impossible to quote exact amounts since they change with regularity (inflation, you know), by the time you read this, on-line time will probably cost a minimum of $30 per hour and a printout with 100 references and abstracts will probably cost around $15. At these rates, a search taking 6 minutes of computer time and yielding 60 references would cost $12. Even though students may get a break on charges (there may be no charge at all), it is still to your advantage to plan your search strategy very carefully. Hundreds of more-or-less related abstracts take a *long* time to read and analyze.

The *Directory of ERIC Search Services,* referred to previously, lists and describes the organizations that provide computer searches of literature. The *Directory* is organized geographically. Organizations and institutions are presented by state and within state by city. A number of foreign institutions are listed following the alphabetized state listings. Information presented in the *Directory* includes:

1. The mailing address and phone number of each organization or institution and the person to contact for further information.

2. Populations to whom each organization provides services, e.g., "New York State residents." If there are no restrictions, this is indicated by the term "Open."

3. Data bases available, e.g., "RIE, Lockheed files."

4. Directions for submitting a search request and the format for such a request, e.g., "Walk-in, Keywords."

5. Search outputs, e.g., "Abstracts."

6. Cost per search, e.g., "$25 per hour, plus $.10 per abstract."

7. Turnaround time (time between the search request date and the delivery date), e.g., "1 week. On-line printout available immediately as an option."[24]

8. The search system used, e.g., "DIALOG, ORBIT."

9. Miscellaneous notes, e.g., "Microfiche duplication capability."

10. The latest date on which the information about the organization's or institution's services was reviewed and is known to be valid, e.g., "10/27/78."

How to Initiate a Computer Search

By now you may be thoroughly (or at least a little) confused by all the computer talk. The best thing to do is to march over to the library and ask the person at the information or reference desk, "How do I do a computer search?" Chances are very good that you'll find out everything you need to know. Until you feel secure, it is likely that there will be someone available to assist you in selecting your search words and planning your search strategy. At the very least, however, you

---

24. This option, although attractive, is typically expensive since it requires more connect time, i.e., on-line time.

have to have a specific statement of your problem. If multiple data bases are available to you, you will next have to select the ones you wish searched. Data bases are usually listed by area, for example, Social Sciences and Humanities, making it easy to select the ones of interest to you. Lastly, you need to specify your search strategy. Usually the best initial approach is to use search words that exactly match your problem. You can then test the adequacy of those search words by asking how many references there are for your selected combination of these words. If there are too few or too many references you can broaden or narrow your search accordingly. This adjusting is typically accomplished by use of the connectors *and* and *or.*

The *and* connector narrows the scope of the search while the *or* connector broadens the search. For example, if your problem was "The Effectiveness of Peer Counseling as a Component of a Drug Education Program for High School Students," your first-choice descriptors and connectors would be *peer counseling* and *drug education* and *high school students.* If this combination did not produce many references, you could expand your search by instructing the computer to search for related descriptors. Instead of requesting just *peer counseling,* you could give directions to search for entries under the descriptors *peer counseling* or *peer groups* or *peer teaching.* Or you could request that entries be searched under the descriptors *drug education* or *drug abuse* or *drug therapy.* Another approach to broadening the search would be to drop the descriptor *high school students.* This strategy would result in references being included which deal with the problem at a different level, junior high school for example.

When the number of references seems reasonable ("reasonable" will depend on the problem and the purpose of the search), you then make your request and wait for the printout. It must be emphasized that you will receive at most abstracts, not complete documents. Original sources will have to be located after the abstracts have been analyzed for relevance.

Abstracting

After you have identified the primary references related to your problem, using the appropriate indexes, abstracts, and reviews, you are ready to move on to the next phase of a review of related literature—abstracting the references. Basically, this involves locating, reviewing, summarizing, and classifying your references. Since the references you identified in each source are listed in reverse chronological order, starting with the most recent, the abstracting process will be conducted in the same order. The main advantage to beginning with the latest references on a given problem is that in terms of research strategy the most recent research is likely to have profited from previous research. Also, recent references may contain references to preceding studies you may not have identified. For each reference, a suggested procedure for abstracting is as follows:

1. If the article has an abstract or a summary, which most do, read it to determine the article's relevancy to your problem.

2. Skim the entire article, making mental note of the main points of the study.

3. On the top of an index card (4″ × 6″ is a convenient size) write the complete bibliographic reference, including the library call number if it is a book. If you know that your final report must follow a particular style, put your bibliographic reference in that form. If not, use the format of the American Psychological Association (APA).[25] The APA format is becoming increasingly popular, primarily because it eliminates the need for formal footnotes. For a journal article, the APA bibliographic reference would be:

> Snurd, B. J. The use of white versus yellow chalk in the teaching of advanced calculus. *Journal of Useless Findings,* 1984, *11*(7), 1–99.

In the above example, 1984 refers to the date of publication, *11* to the volume, (7) to the issue, and 1–99 to the page numbers. If this reference were cited in a paper, then its description would be followed by (Snurd, 1984), and no other footnote (beyond the bibliographic reference) would be required. Whatever format you use, be certain the reference you copy is accurate; you never know when you might have to go back and get additional information from an article. Besides, even if you do not have to find it again, it is very unscholarly to have an incorrect reference in a research report. Also, put only one reference on each index card. The purpose of using index cards is that they allow easy sorting and facilitate organization of the articles prior to writing the review of the literature.

4. Classify and code the article according to some system and place the code on the same index card in a conspicuous place, such as the upper right- or left-hand corner. For example, if your problem was concerned with salaried paraprofessionals versus parent volunteers (discussed earlier), you might use a three-part coding system to describe each article; the code might indicate whether the study was concerned with the use of paraprofessionals, parent volunteers, or both (PP versus PV versus B), whether it was an opinion article or a study (O versus S), and the degree of its relevance to your study (say 1, 2, or 3, with 3 meaning very relevant). Thus, PV/O/3 might be a code for an article describing the potential benefits to be derived from using parent volunteers. Any coding system that makes sense to you, given your problem, will facilitate your task later when you have to sort, organize, analyze, synthesize, and write your review of the literature.

5. On the same index card (under the bibliographic reference) abstract, or summarize, the reference. As neatly as you can (*you're* going to have to read them later!), write the essential points of the reference. If it is an opinion article write the main points of the author's position, for example, "Jones believes parent volunteers should be used because . . .," and list the "becauses." If it is a study, write the same kind of information you wrote for Task 1-A, chapter 1: the problem, the procedures (including the sample and instruments), the method of analysis, and the major conclusions. Make special note of any particularly interesting or unique aspect of the study, such as a new measuring instrument that was utilized. Double-check the reference to make sure you have not omitted any pertinent information.

6. Indicate on the index card any thoughts that come to your mind, such as points on which you disagree (make an *X,* for example) or components which you do not understand (put a ? next to them). For example, if an author stated that he had used a double-blind procedure, and you were unfamiliar with that

---

25. *Publication manual of the American Psychological Association* (2nd ed.). Washington, D.C.: American Psychological Association. 1974.

technique, you could indicate that with a ?. Later, you can seek out a knowledge-able person, such as your advisor, and quickly identify points on which you need clarification or explanation.

7. Indicate on the index card any statements that are direct quotations (plagiarism is a no-no) or personal reactions; if you do not put quotation marks around direct quotations on your index card, for example, you may not remember later which statements are, and which are not, direct quotations. Incidentally, direct quota-tions should be kept to a minimum in your research plan and report; both should be in your words, not other researchers'. Occasionally, however, a direct quota-tion may be quite appropriate.

An alternate strategy to making notes on index cards is to photocopy refer-ences whenever possible (you probably wouldn't want to copy a book!). If you copy the articles, you can take them with you and make your notes in the comfort of your home. The advantages of this approach are reduced time in the library and elimination of the possibility that you might have to go back and find a reference because you inadvertently left something out of your notes. The main disadvantage, of course, is the cost; photocopies cost a lot more than $4'' \times 6''$ index cards! Some researchers, however, feel that the approach is well worth the cost in terms of convenience. Whichever approach you use, guard your notes with your life. When you have completed your reviewing task, those notes will represent many hours of work. Students have been known to be literally in tears because they left their notes "on the bus" or "on a table in the cafeteria." Also, when the research report is completed, the index cards can be filed (photocopies can be placed in notebooks) and saved for future reference and future studies (nobody can do just one!).

Analyzing, Organizing, and Reporting

For beginning researchers, the hardest part about writing the review of related literature is thinking about how hard it is going to be to write the review of related literature. More time is spent worrying about doing it than acutally doing it. If you have efficiently abstracted the literature related to your problem, and if you approach the task in an equally systematic manner, then analyzing, organizing, and reporting it will be relatively painless. First, to get warmed up, read quickly through your notes. This will first of all refresh your memory and also you will more than likely identify some references which no longer seem sufficiently related. Do not force references into your review that do not really "fit"; the review forms the background and rationale for your hypothesis and should only contain references that serve this purpose. It may hurt a little to discard references representing work on your part, but your review will be better for it. The following guidelines and suggestions are based on experience acquired the hard way and should be helpful to you:

1. Make an outline. Don't groan; your eighth-grade teacher was right about the virtues of an outline. The time and thought you put into the outline will save you time in the long run and will increase your probability of having an organized review. The outline does not have to be excessively detailed. First, identify the main topics and the order in which they should be presented. For example, the outline I formulated for this chapter started out as three main headings—Selection and Statement, Review of Related Literature, and Formulation and Statement of a Hypothesis. As another example, the outline of the review for the problem concerned with the effectiveness of salaried paraprofessionals versus parent volunteers might begin with the headings Literature on Salaried Paraprofessionals, Literature on Parent Volunteers, and Literature Comparing the Two. The next step is to differentiate each major heading into logical subheadings. In my outline, for example, Review of Related Literature subdivided into the following:

Review of Related Literature
    Definition, Purpose, and Scope
    Preparation
    Sources
    Computer Searches
    Abstracting
    Analyzing, Organizing, and Reporting

The need for further differentiation will be determined by your problem; the more complex it is, the more subheadings will be required. When you have completed your outline you will invariably see topics that need rearranging. It is much easier, however, to reorganize an outline than it is to reorganize a document written in paragraph form.

2. Analyze each reference in terms of your outline; in other words, determine under which subheading each one fits. Then sort your references into appropriate piles. If you end up with one or more references without a home, there are three logical possibilities: (1) there is something wrong with your outline; (2) they do not belong in your review, and should be discarded; or (3) they do not belong in your review but do belong somewhere else in your introduction. For example, a reference concerned with the problem of school vandalism might state that school vandalism costs American taxpayers X thousands of dollars per year. Such a reference would belong in the significance section of the statement of the problem if the specific problem to be investigated was concerned with several alternative methods of reducing school vandalism. Opinion articles, or reports of descriptive research, will more often be useful in the problem statement portion of an introduction, whereas formal studies will almost always be included in the review of related literature portion.

3. Take all the references identified for a given subheading and analyze the relationships or differences between them. If three references say essentially the same thing, there is no need to describe each one; it is much better to make one summary statement followed by three references. For example:

Several studies have found white chalk to be more effective than yellow chalk in the teaching of advanced mathematics (Snurd, 1984; Trivia, 1925; Ziggy, 1976).

Do not present your references as a series of abstracts or annotations (Jones found X, Smith found Y, and Brown found Z). Your task is to organize and summarize the references in a meaningful way. Do not ignore studies which are contradictory to most other studies or to your personal bias. Analyze and evaluate contradictory studies and try to determine a possible explanation. For example:

Contrary to these studies is the work of Rautenstudee (1970), who found yellow chalk to be more effective than white chalk in the teaching of trigonometry. However, the size of the treatment groups (two students per group) and the duration of the study (one class period) may have seriously affected the results.

4. The review should flow in such a way that the references least related to the problem are discussed first, and the most related references discussed last, just prior to the statement of the hypothesis. Think in terms of a big **V**. At the bottom of the **V** is your hypothesis; directly above your hypothesis are the studies most directly related to it, and so forth. For example, if your hypothesis stated that white chalk would be more effective than yellow chalk in teaching biology to tenth graders, immediately preceding it would be the studies indicating the effectiveness of white chalk in the teaching of mathematics. Preceding those studies might be studies indicating that students prefer to read white chalk. At the top of the **V** (the beginning of the review), several references might be cited, written by well-known educators, expressing the belief that variables such as chalkboard color and color of chalk are important ones in the learning process, too often overlooked. These might be followed by similar references indicating that these variables might be even more critical in technical areas such as mathematics that entail a lot of chalkboard usage, and so forth. The idea is to organize and present your literature in such a way that it leads logically to a tentative, testable conclusion, namely your hypothesis. If your problem has more than one major aspect, you may have two **V**s or one **V** that logically leads to two tentative, testable conclusions.

5. The review should conclude with a brief summary of the literature and its implications. How lengthy this summary needs to be depends upon the length of the review. It should be detailed enough to clearly show the logic chain you have followed in arriving at your inplications and tentative conclusion.

Having systematically developed and presented your rationale, you will now be ready to state your hypothesis.

Formulation and Statement of a Hypothesis

Before you review the related literature, you have a tentative hypothesis which guides your search. Following the review, and preceding the actual conduction of the study, the hypothesis is refined and finalized.

Definition and Purpose

A hypothesis is a tentative explanation for certain behaviors, phenomena, or events that have occurred or will occur. A hypothesis states the researcher's expectations concerning the relationship between the variables in the research problem; a hypothesis is the most specific statement of a problem. It states what the researcher thinks the outcome of the study will be. The researcher does not then set out to "prove" his or her hypothesis, but rather collects data that either support the hypothesis or do not support it; research studies do not "prove" anything. Hypotheses are essential to all research studies with the possible exception of some descriptive studies whose purpose is to answer certain specific questions.

The hypothesis is formulated following the review of related literature and prior to the execution of the study. It logically follows the review since it is based on the implications of previous research. The related literature leads one to expect a certain relationship. For example, studies finding white chalk to be more effective than yellow chalk in teaching mathematics would lead a researcher to expect it to be more effective in teaching physics, if there were no other findings to the contrary. Hypotheses precede the study proper because the entire study is determined by the hypothesis. Every aspect of the research is affected by the hypothesis, including subjects (samples), measuring instruments, design, procedures, data analysis techniques, and conclusions. Although all hypotheses are based on previous knowledge and aimed at extending knowledge, they are not all of equal worth. There are a number of criteria that can be, and should be, applied to a given hypothesis to determine its value.

Characteristics

By now it should be clear that a hypothesis should be based on a sound rationale. It should follow from previous research and lead to future research; its confirmation or disconfirmation should contribute to educational theory or practice. Therefore, a major characteristic of a good hypothesis is that it is consistent with previous research. The chances of you being a Christopher Columbus of educational research who is going to show that something believed to be "square" is really "round" are slim! Of course, in areas of research where there are conflicting results, you will not be able to be consistent with all of them, but your hypothesis should follow from the rule, not the exception.

The previously stated definition of a hypothesis indicated that it is a tentative explanation for the occurrence of certain behaviors, phenomena, or events. A good hypothesis provides a reasonable explanation. If your telephone is out of order, you might hypothesize that it is because there are butterflies sitting on your telephone wires; such a hypothesis would not be a reasonable explanation. A reasonable hypothesis might be that you forgot to pay your bill, or that a repair crew is working outside. In a research study, a hypothesis suggesting that children with freckles pay attention longer than children without freckles would not be a reasonable explanation for attention behavior. On the other hand, a hypothesis suggesting that children who have a good breakfast pay attention longer would be.

A good hypothesis states as clearly and concisely as possible the expected relationship (or difference) between two variables and defines those variables in operational, measurable terms. A simply but clearly stated hypothesis makes it easier for consumers to understand, simplifies its testing, and facilitates formulation of conclusions following data analysis. The relationship expressed between two variables may or may not be a causal one. For example, the variables anxiety and math achievement might be hypothesized to be significantly related (there is a significant correlation between anxiety and math achievement), or it might be hypothesized that on low-difficulty math problems high-anxiety students perform better than low-anxiety students. The above example also illustrates the need for operational definitions. What is a low-difficulty math problem? What is a high-anxiety student? What does it mean to perform better? In this example, "high-anxiety student" might be defined as any student whose score of the A-State scale of the State-Trait Anxiety Inventory is in the upper 30% of the distribution of student scores.[26] The dependent variable in a hypothesis will often be operationally defined in terms of scores on a given test. For example, "better achievement" might be defined in terms of higher scores on the California Achievement Test Battery. If the appropriate terms can be operationally defined within the actual hypothesis statement without making it unwieldy, this should be done. If not, the hypothesis should be stated and the appropriate terms defined immediately following it.

A well-stated and defined hypothesis must be (and will be if well formulated and stated) testable. It should be possible to support or not support the hypothesis by collecting and analyzing data. It would not be possible to test a hypothesis that indicated that some students behave better than others because some have an invisible little angel on their right shoulder and some have an invisible little devil on their left shoulder. There would be no way to collect data to support or not support the hypothesis. In addition to being testable, a good hypothesis should normally be testable within some reasonable period of time. For example, the hypothesis that requiring first-grade students to brush their teeth after lunch every day will result in fewer people with false teeth at age 60 would obviously take a very long time to test. The researcher would very likely be long gone before the study was completed, not to mention the negligible educational significance of the hypothesis! A more manageable hypothesis with the same theme might be that requiring first-grade children to brush their teeth after lunch every day will result in fewer cavities at the end of the first grade.

Types of Hypotheses

Hypotheses can be classified in terms of how they are derived (inductive versus deductive hypotheses) or how they are stated (declarative versus null hypotheses). An inductive hypothesis is a generalization based on observation. Certain variables are noted to be related in a number of situations and a tentative explanation, or hypothesis formulated. Such inductively derived hypotheses can be very useful but are of limited scientific value in that they produce results that are not meaningfully related to any larger body of research. Deductive hypotheses derived from theory do contribute to the science of education by providing evidence that supports, expands, or contradicts a given theory and by suggesting future studies. For example, in a study conducted in 1966, Ausubel found no significant differences in retention between groups receiving a review one day after learning versus seven days after learning.[27] Ausubel suggested that the position of the review did not have a significant effect because early and late reviews each contribute to retention in a different way; an early review consoli-

---

26. Spielberger, C.D., Gorsuch, R.L. and Lushene, R.E. *Manual for the State-Trait Anxiety Inventory*. Palo Alto, Calif.: Consulting Psychologist Press, 1970.

27. Ausubel, D.P. Early versus delayed review in meaningful learning. *Psychology in the Schools*, 1966,3, 195–198.

dates material, while a delayed review promotes relearning of forgotten material. In a subsequent study, this author hypothesized that if Ausubel was correct, then two reviews, one early and one delayed, will be more effective than either two early reviews or two delayed reviews. The results generally supported this hypothesis.[28] In deriving a hypothesis from a theory, you should be sure that your V does not have any holes in it (you remember the big V!). In other words, your hypothesis should be a logical implication of previous efforts, not an inferential leap.

Hypotheses are classified as research hypotheses or statistical hypotheses; research hypotheses are stated in declarative form, and statistical hypotheses are stated in null form. A research hypothesis states an expected relationship or difference between two variables, in other words, what relationship the researcher expects to verify through the collection and analysis of data. Research, or declarative, hypotheses are nondirectional or directional. A nondirectional hypothesis simply indicates that a relationship or difference exists; a directional hypothesis indicates the nature of the relationship or difference. For example, a nondirectional hypothesis might state:

There is a significant difference in the behavior of ninth-grade students who participate in peer counseling and those who receive individual counseling.

The corresponding directional hypothesis might state:

Ninth-grade students who participate in peer counseling exhibit better behavior than ninth-grade students who receive individual counseling.

A directional hypothesis should not be stated if you have any reason to believe that the results may occur in the opposite direction. Nondirectional and directional hypotheses involve different types of statistical tests of significance; a nondirectional hypothesis usually requires a two-tailed test of significance and a directional hypothesis a one-tailed test.[29]

A statistical, or null, hypothesis states that there is no relationship (or difference) between variables, and that any relationship found will be a chance relationship, not a true one. For example, a null hypothesis might state:

There is no difference in the behavior of ninth-grade students who participate in peer counseling and those who receive individual counseling.

While a research hypothesis may be a null hypothesis, this is not very often the case. Statistical, or null, hypotheses are usually used because they suit statistical techniques which determine whether an observed relationship is probably a chance relationship or probably a true relationship. The disadvantage of null hypotheses is that they rarely express the researcher's true expectations regarding the results of a study, expectations based on insight and logic. One solution is to state two hypotheses, a declarative research hypothesis that communicates your

---

28. Gay, L.R. Temporal position of reviews and its effect on the retention of mathematical rules. *Journal of Educational Psychology,* 1973,*64*(2), 171–182.

29. These will be discussed further in chapter 13.

true expectation, and a statistical, null hypothesis that permits precise statistical testing. Another solution is to state a research hypothesis, analyze your data assuming a null hypothesis, and then make inferences concerning your research hypothesis based on your testing of a null hypothesis. Given that few studies are really designed to verify the nonexistence of a relationship, it seems logical that most studies should be based on a nonnull research hypothesis.

Stating the Hypothesis

As previously discussed, a good hypothesis is stated clearly and concisely, expresses the relationship between two variables, and defines those variables in operational measurable terms. A general paradigm, or model, for stating hypotheses for experimental studies which you may find useful is as follows:

X's who get Y do better on Z than
X's who do not get Y (or get some other Y)

If this model appears to be an oversimplification, it is because it is, and it may not always be appropriate. However, this model should help you to understand the nature of a hypothesis statement. Further, this model, or a variation of it, will be applicable in a surprising number of situations. In the model,

X = the subjects,
Y = the treatment, the independent variable (IV), and
Z = the observed outcome, the dependent variable (DV).

Study the following example and see if you can identify X, Y, and Z:

High school students who participate in peer counseling have less absenteeism than high school students who receive individual counseling.

In this example, X = high school students,
Y = type of counseling (peer versus individual), IV,
and Z = absenteeism (fewer days absent, or, stated positively, more days present), DV.

Got the idea? Try one more:

Sixth-grade students, whose measured reading comprehension is two or more levels below grade level, who receive token reinforcement in the form of free time contingent upon the completion of reading assignments, have higher reading comprehension at the end of sixth grade than sixth-grade students . . . who do not recieve token reinforcement for completed reading assignments.

In this example, X = Sixth-grade students whose measured reading achievement is two or more levels below grade level,
Y = token reinforcement contingent upon completion of reading assignments, IV,
and Z = reading comprehension, DV.

For a null hypothesis, the paradigm is:

> There is no difference on *Z* between *X*s who get *Y* and *X*s who do not get *Y* (or get some other *Y*).

See if you can think of an example that illustrates the model for null hypotheses.

Testing the Hypothesis

Hypothesis testing is really what scientific research is all about. In order to test a hypothesis, the researcher determines the sample, measuring instruments, design, and procedure that will enable her or him to collect the necessary data. Collected data are then analyzed in a manner that permits the researcher to determine the validity of the hypothesis. Analysis of collected data does not result in a hypothesis being proven or not proven, only supported or not supported. The results of a study only indicate whether a hypothesis was "true" for the particular subjects involved in the study. Many beginning researchers have the misconception that if their hypothesis is not supported by their data, then their study is a failure, and conversely, if it is supported then their study is a success. Neither of these beliefs is true. It is just as important, for example, to know what variables are *not* related as it is to know what variables *are* related. If a hypothesis is not supported, a valuable contribution may be made in the form of a revision of some aspect of a theory; such revision will generate new or revised hypotheses. Thus, hypothesis testing contributes to the science of education primarily by expanding, refining, or revising theory.

Summary/Chapter 2

Selection and Statement

Selection

1. The first step in selecting a problem is to identify a general problem area that is related to your area of expertise and of particular interest to you.
2. The next step is to narrow down the general problem area to a specific, researchable problem.

Sources

3. The most meaningful problems are generally derived from theory.
4. A major source of nontheoretical problems is the researcher's personal experiences.
5. The literature is also a good source of problems; in addition to overviews and summaries, specific studies often indicate "next-step" studies which need to be conducted.
6. It is generally not a good idea to simply replicate a study as it was originally conducted; there is much to be learned from developing and executing your own study.

Characteristics

7. A basic characteristic of a research problem is that it is "researchable," that is, can be investigated through the collection and analysis of data.

8. A good problem has theoretical or practical significance; its solution should contribute in some way to improvement of the educational process.

9. A good problem must be a good problem *for you.* It must be a problem that you can adequately investigate given (1) your current level of research skill, (2) available resources, and (3) time and other restrictions.

Statement

10. A well-written statement of a problem generally indicates the variables of interest to the researcher and the specific relationship between those variables which is to be investigated.

11. A well-written problem statement also defines all relevant variables, either directly or operationally; operational definitions define concepts in terms of operations, or processes.

12. Since the problem statement gives direction to the rest of the plan or report, it should be stated as soon as possible.

13. The statement of the problem should be accompanied by a presentation of the background of the problem, including a justification for the study in terms of the significance of the problem.

Review of Related Literature

Definition, Purpose, and Scope

14. The review of related literature involves the systematic identification, location, and analysis of documents containing information related to the research problem.

15. The major purpose of reviewing the literature is to determine what has already been done that relates to your problem.

16. Another important function of the literature review is that it points out research strategies and specific procedures and measuring instruments that have and have not been found to be productive in investigating your problem.

17. Being familiar with previous research also facilitates interpretation of the results of the study.

18. A smaller, well-organized review is definitely to be preferred to a review containing many studies that are more or less related to the problem.

19. Heavily researched areas usually provide enough references directly related to a specific problem to eliminate the need for relying on less related studies.

20. New or little-researched problem areas usually require review of any study related in some meaningful way to the problem in order to develop a logical framework for the study and a sound rationale for the research hypothesis.

21. A common misconception among beginning researchers is the idea that the worth of their problem is a function of the amount of literature available on the topic.

Preparation

22. Time spent initially will save time in the long run; you should find out what references are available and where they are located, especially the periodicals.

23. You should also be familiar with services offered by the library as well as the rules and regulations.

24. Many libraries provide written guides detailing what the library has to offer and the procedures for utilizing references and services.

25. One important service offered by most libraries is the interlibrary loan.

26. Before beginning the review, make a list of key words related to your problem to guide your literature search.

Sources

27. A primary source is a description of a study written by the person who conducted it; a secondary source is generally a much briefer description of a study written by someone other than the original researcher.

28. You should not be satisfied with only the information contained in secondary sources; the corresponding primary sources will be considerably more detailed and may be more accurate.

29. The number of individual references that could be consulted for a given problem is staggering; fortunately, there are indexes, abstracts, and other retrieval mechanisms that facilitate identification of relevant references.

Education Index

30. The *Education Index* lists bibliographic information on references appearing in literally hundreds of educational periodicals.

31. The *Education Index* is used much the same way as any other index; entries are listed alphabetically under subject, author, and title headings.

32. The procedure for using the *Education Index* is as follows: Start with the most recent issue and look under your key words; under the key words you will find a list of references presented alphabetically by title; decide whether each reference is related to your problem or not; if the reference is related, copy the complete reference; look up unfamiliar abbreviations in the front of the volume; repeat these steps for previous issues; locate each of the references.

33. The *Education Index* is the best source of educational periodicals published from 1929 to 1969.

Readers' Guide to Periodical Literature

34. *Readers' Guide* is an index very similar in format to the *Education Index* which indexes articles in widely read magazines.

35. *Reader's Guide* lists entries alphabetically by subject and author, and the procedures for its use are essentially the same as for using the *Education Index*.

Dissertation Abstracts International

36. *Dissertation Abstracts International* contains abstracts (usually brief summaries) of doctoral dissertations conducted at hundreds of academic institutions.

37. The procedure for using the *Abstracts* is similar to the procedure for using the *Education Index* with the exception that the reference also gives an entry number with which one locates an abstract.

Psychological Abstracts

38. *Psychological Abstracts* presents summaries of completed psychological research studies.

39. The procedure for using *Psychological Abstracts* is similar to the procedure for using the *Education Index;* the major difference is that the *Abstracts* index gives numbers that are used to locate both references and accompanying abstracts.

40. In addition to the key words identified for a given problem, the word *bibliographies* should also be checked.

41. *Psychological Abstracts* will be more useful for theoretical problems.

Educational Resources Information Center (ERIC)

42. The primary purpose of ERIC is to collect and disseminate reports of current educational research, evaluation, and development activities.

43. Research reports that would not typically be included in other sources are indexed and abstracted by ERIC.

44. The comparatively short time interval between collection of a document and its dissemination results in sources of data for very current issues being available that are not available through other sources.

45. ERIC comprises a central office and a number of clearinghouses, each devoted to a different area, which collect, store, and disseminate documents specific to their area of specialization.

46. The *Thesaurus of ERIC Descriptors* is a compilation of the key words used in indexing ERIC documents.

RIE

47. A major ERIC publication is *Resources in Education* (RIE) which indexes over 1,000 documents per issue and for many entries provides an abstract.

48. RIE entries are indexed by subject, author, institution, and accession number. Using accession numbers, abstracts are located in the Document Resume section.

CIJE

49. Another major ERIC publication, *Current Index to Journals in Education* (CIJE), indexes articles in the periodical literature and covers close to 800 education and education-related publications.

50. The procedure for using CIJE is very similar to the procedure for using RIE. Using the accession numbers, additional information is located in the Main Entry section.

51. The addition of abstracts when needed makes CIJE more useful than the *Education Index* for those years for which it is available.

Obtaining ERIC Documents

52. ERIC provides a number of additional services such as the preparation and dissemination of annotated bibliographies in various areas of specialization.

53. All ERIC documents are available in both hard copy and microfiche, which is less expensive.

Smithsonian Science Information Exchange (SSIE)

54. The SSIE disseminates information concerning research in progress, most of which is federally funded, in many fields besides education.

55. Entries are classified by subject, location, chief investigator, and source of funding; information provided also includes a brief summary of the status of the research.

Review of Educational Research (RER)

56. The RER reviews and briefly summarizes a number of related studies on given topics.

57. The RER is a secondary source; each article concludes with an extensive bibliography which facilitates location of important primary sources.

Books

58. The card catalog alphabetically indexes (by author, subject, and title) all publications contained in the library, with the exception of the periodicals.

59. Encyclopedias in special areas contain detailed discussions, written by experts, on a restricted number of topics. The *Encyclopedia of Educational Research,* for example, contains critical reviews and summaries on a number of educational topics.

Computer Searches

60. With relatively little effort, and for a relatively low cost, you can use a computer to identify related references for you.

61. A computer search checks data bases such as the ERIC system and provides you with a list of references and, if provided by the data base, abstracts.

62. To initiate a computer search, you provide the key words, or descriptors. The computer then searches data bases for references having those descriptors.

63. To save time and money, you should give your search strategy careful thought ahead of time.

Data Sources

64. ERIC searches can be obtained at hundreds of locations including state departments of education and universities.

65. The *Directory of ERIC Search Services* lists and describes the organizations which provide computer searches of literature.

How to Initiate a Computer Search

66. It is likely that there will be someone available to assist you in selecting your search words and planning your search strategy. At the very least, however, you have to have a specific statement of your problem.

67. If multiple data bases are available, you have to select the ones you wished searched.

68. If there are too few or too many references, you can broaden or narrow your search, usually by using the connectors *and* and *or.*

Abstracting

69. Abstracting references involves locating, reviewing, summarizing, and classifying your references.

70. The main advantage of beginning with the latest references on a given problem is that in terms of strategy, the most recent research is likely to have profited from previous research; also, recent references may contain references to preceding studies you may not have identified.

71. A suggested procedure for abstracting is as follows: if available, read the article abstract or summary first to determine the relevancy of the article to your problem; skim the entire article making mental note of main points; write the complete bibliographic reference, using either a required format or the APA format; classify and code the article according to some system; abstract or summarize the reference; write down any thoughts that come to your mind concerning the reference; and identify direct quotations.

72. An alternate strategy to taking notes on index cards is to photocopy references whenever possible.

73. Save your notes for future reference and future studies.

Analyzing, Organizing, and Reporting

74. All notes should be reread; this will first of all refresh your memory and also you will more than likely identify some references which no longer seem sufficiently related.

75. The following guidelines should be helpful: make an outline; analyze each reference in terms of your outline and sort your references into appropriate piles; take all the references identified for a given subheading and analyze the relationships and differences between them (do not present your references as a series of abstracts or annotations); the review should flow in such a way that the references least related to the problem are discussed first, and the most related references are discussed last, just prior to the statement of the hypothesis (think in terms of a big V); the review should conclude with a brief summary of the literature and its implications.

Formulation and Statement of a Hypothesis

Definition and Purpose

76. A hypothesis is a tentative explanation for certain behaviors, phenomena, or events that have occurred or will occur.

77. The researcher does not set out to "prove" his or her hypothesis but rather collects data that either support the hypothesis or do not support it.

78. The hypothesis is formulated following the review of related literature and prior to the execution of the study. The hypothesis logically follows the review and it is based on the implications of previous research; it precedes the study proper because the entire study is determined by the hypothesis (including subjects, instruments, design, procedures, analysis, and conclusions).

Characteristics

79. A major characteristic of a good hypothesis is that it is consistent with previous research.

80. A good hypothesis is a tentative, reasonable explanation for the occurrence of certain behaviors, phenomena, or events.

81. A good hypothesis states as clearly and concisely as possible the expected relationship (or difference) between two variables and defines those variables in operational, measurable terms.

82. A well-stated and defined hypothesis must be testable.

Types of Hypotheses

83. An inductive hypothesis is a generalization based on observation.

84. Deductive hypotheses derived from theory contribute to the science of education by providing evidence that supports, expands, or contradicts a given theory.

85. Research hypotheses are stated in declarative form, and statistical hypotheses are stated in null form.

86. A research hypothesis states the expected relationship (or difference) between two variables, in other words, what relationship the researcher expects to verify through the collection and analysis of data.

87. A nondirectional hypothesis simply indicates that a relationship or difference exists; a directional hypothesis indicates the nature of the relationship or difference.

88. A statistical, or null, hypothesis states that there will be no relationship (or difference) between variables, and that any relationship found will be a chance relationship, not a true one.

Stating the Hypothesis

89. A general paradigm, or model, for stating hypotheses for experimental studies is as follows:

Xs who get Y do better on Z than
Xs who do not get Y (or get some other Y).

90. In the model, Xs are the subjects, Y is the treatment (or independent variable), and Z is the observed outcome (or dependent variable).

Testing the Hypothesis

91. In order to test a hypothesis, the researcher determines the sample, measuring instruments, design, and procedure that will enable him or her to collect the necessary data; collected data are then analyzed in a manner that permits the researcher to determine the validity of the hypothesis.

92. It is just as important to know what variables are *not* related as it is to know what variables *are* related.

Task 2 Performance Criteria

The introduction which you develop for Task 2 will be the first part of the research report required for Task 8. Therefore, it may save you some revision time later if, when appropriate, statements are expressed in the past tense ("it *was* hypothesized," for example).

Your introduction should include the following subheadings and contain the following types of information:

INTRODUCTION
(Background and significance of the problem)
Statement of the Problem
(Problem statement and necessary definitions)
Review of Related Literature
(Don't forget the big **V**)
Statement of the Hypothesis(es)

As a guideline, three typed pages will generally be a sufficient length for Task 2. Of course for a *real* study you would review not just 15 references but all relevant references and the introduction would be correspondingly longer.

Because of feedback from your instructor on Enabler 4, and insight gained through developing your review of related literature, the hypothesis you state in Task 2 may very well be somewhat different from the one you stated for Enabler 4.

See the *Student Guide* for examples of Task 2.

Part Three
Research Plans

Having a research plan permits it to be carefully scrutinized . . . by others and allows others to not only identify problems, but also to make suggestions as to how the study might be improved.

Development of a research plan is a critical step in conducting research. Having formulated specific hypotheses, it is necessary to carefully delineate the method and procedure to be followed in testing them. Occasionally it will become apparent in formulating a plan that the proposed study is not feasible in its present form. That decision is best made *before* you have expended considerable time and energy on a study which cannot be adequately executed. While very few research plans are executed exactly as planned, the existence of a plan permits the researcher to assess the overall impact of any changes on the study as a whole.

You, of course, are not yet in a position to develop a complete plan. A research plan, for example, generally states the statistical technique which will be used to analyze the data; this ensures that data will be collected which are analyzable. By now, however, you have read enough research reports to be aware of some of the possibilities. It will be interesting for you to compare the plan you develop now with the research report you will develop in chapter 16 after you have acquired competencies related to the research process.

The goal of Part Three is for you to understand the importance of developing a research plan and become familiar with the components of such a plan. After you have read Part Three, you should be able to perform the following task.

Task 3

For the hypothesis you have formulated, develop the remaining components of a research plan for a study you would conduct in order to test your hypothesis. Include the following:

Method
    Subjects
    Instruments
    Design
    Procedure
Data Analysis
Time Schedule

Note: Assumptions, limitations, and definitions should be included where appropriate.

(See Performance Criteria, p. 79.)

3

Preparation and Evaluation of a Research Plan

Enablers

After reading chapter 3, you should be able to:

1. Briefly describe three ethical considerations involved in conducting and reporting educational research.
2. Briefly describe two major pieces of legislation affecting educational research.
3. Briefly describe each of the components of a research plan.
4. Briefly describe two major ways in which a research plan can be evaluated.

Definition and Purpose

A research plan is a detailed description of a proposed study designed to investigate a given problem. It includes justification for the hypothesis to be tested, a detailed presentation of the research steps that will be followed in collecting and analyzing required data, and a projected time schedule for each major step. A research plan may be relatively brief and informal, such as the one which you will develop for Task 3, or very lengthy and formal, such as the proposals which are submitted to governmental and private funding agencies. Graduate schools typically require that a proposal, or prospectus, be submitted for approval prior to the conduction of a thesis or dissertation study.

The research plan must be completed before a study is begun. Playing it by ear is all right for piano playing, but not for conducting research. After you have completed the review of related literature and formulated your hypothesis, you are ready to develop the rest of the plan. Since your study will be designed to test a hypothesis, it must be developed first. The nature of your hypothesis will determine to a high degree the sample group, measuring instruments, design, procedures, and statistical techniques used in your study. A research plan serves several important purposes. First, it makes you think; it forces you to think through every aspect of the study. The very process of getting it down on paper usually makes you think of something you might otherwise have overlooked. A second purpose of a written plan is that it facilitates evaluation of the proposed study, by you and by others. Sometimes great ideas do not look so great after all when they are written down. Also, certain problems may become apparent or some aspect may be seen to be infeasible. Having a written plan also allows others to not only identify flaws but also to make suggestions as to ways the study might be improved. This is as true for "old hands" as it is for beginning researchers. A third major purpose of a research plan is that it provides a guide for conducting the study. Detailed procedures need only be thought through once and then followed, not remembered. Also, if something unexpected occurs that alters some phase of the study, the overall impact on the rest of the study can be assessed. For example, suppose you ordered 60 copies of a test which was to be administered on May 1. If on April 15, you received a letter saying that due to a shortage of available tests your order could not be filled until May 15, your study might be seriously affected. At the very least it would be delayed several weeks. Reworking of the time schedule in your research plan might indicate that given your deadlines you could not afford to wait. Therefore, you might decide to use an alternate measuring instrument.

A well-thought-out plan saves time, reduces the probability of costly mistakes, and generally results in higher quality research. If your study is a disaster because of poor planning, *you* lose. The research plan is not really written for your advisor's or major professor's benefit, it is written for yours. If something goes wrong, which could have been avoided with a little foresight, you may have to redo the whole study at worst, or somehow salvage the remnants of a less-than-ideal study, at best.

Murphy's law states approximately that "if anything can go wrong, it will." Gay's law states that "if anything can go wrong, it will—unless you make sure that it doesn't!" Most of the minor tragedies that occur during studies could have been avoided with proper planning, good coordination, and careful monitoring. Part of good planning is anticipation. Do not wait until something happens before you figure out how to deal with it. Try to anticipate potential problems that might arise and then do what you can to prevent them. Plan your strategies for dealing with them if they do occur. For example, you might anticipate resistance on the part of some principals to giving you permission to use their students as subjects in your study. To deal with this contingency you should work up the best sales pitch possible. Do not ask, "Hey, can I use your kids for my study?" Instead, tell them how wonderful the study is and how it will benefit their students or their schools. If there is still opposition, you might tell them how enthusiastic central administration is about the study. Got the idea?

You may tend to get frustrated at times because you cannot do everything the way you would like to because of real or bureaucratic constraints. Don't let such obstacles exasperate you. Just relax and do your best. On the positive side, a sound plan critiqued by others is likely to result in a sound study conducted with a minimum of grief. You cannot guarantee that your study will be executed exactly as planned, but you can guarantee that things will go as smoothly as possible.

General Considerations

In planning the actual procedures of your study, there are a number of factors you should consider. Two of these factors, the ethics of conducting research and legal restrictions, are relevant to all research studies. Any potential subject in your study, for example, has the right to refuse to be involved *and* the right to stop being involved at any time. A third factor to consider is strategies for achieving and maintaining necessary cooperation, from school personnel, for example. A fourth factor is the need for training if others will be assisting you in conducting your study. Your research plan may not specifically addresss any of these factors, but the plan's chances of being properly executed will be increased if you are aware of them.

The Ethics of Research

There are ethical considerations involved in all research studies. Ethical concerns are, of course, more acute in experimental studies which, by definition, "manipulate" and "control" subjects. The ends do not justify the means, and perhaps the foremost rule of ethics is that subjects should not be harmed in any way (physically or mentally) in the name of science. If an experiment involves any risk to subjects, they should be completely informed concerning the nature of the risk, and permission for participation in the experiment should be acquired in writing from the subjects themselves, or from persons legally responsible for the subjects if they are not of age. The researcher should take every precaution and make every effort to minimize potential risk to subjects. Even if there is no risk to subjects, they should be completely informed concerning the nature of the study. Frequently, for control purposes, subjects are not aware of their participation in a study or, if aware, do not know the exact nature of the experiment. Such subjects should be debriefed, or informed, as soon as the study is completed. If school children are involved, it is also a good idea to inform parents, before the study is conducted if possible, concerning the purpose and procedures of the study. This may be done in writing or a presentation may be made to a parents' organization.

The subject's right to privacy is also an important consideration. Collecting information on subjects or observing them without their knowledge or without appropriate permission is not ethical. Furthermore, any information or data which are collected, either from or about a subject, should be strictly confidential, especially if it is at all personal. Individual scores should never be reported, or made public, even for an innocuous measure such as an arithmetic test. It is usually sufficient to present data in terms of group statistics; if individual scores, or raw data, need to be presented, they should be coded and should not be associated with subjects' names or other identifying information. Access to the data should be limited to persons directly involved in conducting the research.

Above all, the researcher must have personal integrity. The reader of a research report must be able to believe that what the researcher says happened, really happened; otherwise it is all for nothing. Falsifying data in order to make findings agree with a hypothesis is unprofessional, unethical, and unforgivable.

Legal Restrictions

The year 1974 marked the beginning of an era in which ethical standards are increasingly being given the force of law. The major provisions of legislation passed to date have been designed to protect subjects who participate in research and to ensure the confidentiality of students' records. Although provisions may seem to be overly restrictive at times, the intent of the legislation is clearly worthy.

Two major pieces of legislation affecting educational research are the National Research Act of 1974 and the Family Educational Rights and Privacy Act of 1974, more commonly referred to as the Buckley Amendment. The National Research Act requires that proposed research activities involving human subjects be reviewed and approved by an authorized group in an institution, prior to the execution of the research, to ensure protection of the subjects. Protection of subjects is broadly defined and requires that subjects not be harmed in any way and that they participate only if they freely agree to do so (informed consent). If subjects are not of age, informed consent must be given by parents or legal guardians.

Most colleges and universities have either formed such a review group or have assigned the review function to an already constituted group such as a university research committee. Typically, the researcher submits a proposal to the chair of the review group who in turn distributes copies to all the members. They in turn review the proposal in terms of proposed treatment of subjects. If there is any question as to whether subjects might be harmed in *any* way, the researcher is usually asked to meet with the review group to answer questions and to clarify proposed procedures. In rare cases the researcher is asked to rewrite the questionable or unclear areas in the research plan. When the review group is satisfied that the subjects will not be placed at risk (or that potential risk is minimal compared to the potential benefits of the study), the committee members sign the appropriate approval forms. Members' signatures on the approval forms signify that the proposal is acceptable with respect to subject protection and that the actual execution of the research will be periodically reviewed to insure that subjects are being properly treated. For complete information on the provisions of the National Research Act, write to the National Commission for the Protection of Human Subjects, 5333 Westbard Avenue, Bethesda, Maryland 20016.

The Buckley Amendment basically protects the privacy of the educational records of students. Among its provisions is the specification that data that actually identify the students may not usually be made available unless written permission is acquired from the students (if of age), parents, or legal guardians. The consent must indicate what data may be disclosed, for what purposes, and to whom. There are exceptions in terms of who is bound by the written consent provision. In most cases, however, the researcher does not need to identify individual data as the interest is in group results. Data can easily be coded in such a way that relevant information such as group membership is identifiable but the identity of individual students is not. For complete information on the provisions of the Buckley Amendment, write to the Family Educational Rights and Privacy Office, 200 Independence Avenue, S.W., Washington, D.C. 20201.[1]

---

1. For additional guidelines concerning the ethics and legal restrictions of research activities, see Ad Hoc Committee on Ethical Standards in Psychological Research. *Ethical principles in the conducting of research with human subjects.* Washington, D.C.: American Psychological Association, 1973; Michael, J.A., & Weinberger, J.A. Federal restrictions on educational research: Protection for research participants. *Educational Researcher,* 1977, *6*(1), 3–7; and Weinberger, J.A., & Michael, J.A. Federal restrictions on educational research. *Educational Researcher,* 1976, *5*(11), 3–8.

Cooperation

Very rarely is it possible to conduct educational research without the cooperation of a number of people, typically school personnel. The first step in acquiring the needed cooperation is to follow required procedures. Typically, approval for the proposed research must be granted by the superintendent or some other high-level administrator, the associate superintendent for instruction, for example. The approval process usually involves the completion of one or more forms on which the nature of the research and the specific request being made of the school system are described, and a meeting with the approval-granting administrator. Approval may also be required from the principal or principals whose schools will be involved. Even if such approval is not required it should be sought, both out of courtesy and for the sake of a smoothly executed study.

The key to gaining approval and cooperation is good planning. The key to good planning is a well-designed, carefully thought-out study. Administrators who are hesitant or hostile about people doing research in their schools have probably had a bad experience. They don't want anyone else running around their schools disrupting classes and administering useless, poorly constructed questionnaires. Unfortunately, there are instances in which improperly trained, though well-intended, persons go into a school and become a source of bad feelings regarding research. It is up to you to convince school personnel that what you are proposing is of value, that your study is carefully designed, and that you will work with teachers to minimize inconvenience.

Achieving full cooperation, and not just approval on paper, requires that you invest as much time as is necessary to discuss your study with the principal, the teachers, and perhaps even parents. These groups have varying levels of knowledge and understanding regarding the research process. Their concerns will focus mainly on the perceived value of the study, its potential affective impact, and the actual logistics of carrying it out. The principal, for example, will probably be more concerned with whether you are collecting any data that might be viewed as objectionable by the community than with the specific design you will be using. All groups will be interested in what you might be able to do *for them*. Potential benefits to be derived by the students, teachers, or principal as a result of your study should be explained fully. Your study, for example, might involve special instructional materials which are to be shared with the teachers and left with them after the study has ended. Even if all parties are favorably impressed, however, the spirit of cooperation will quickly dwindle if your study will involve considerable extra work on their part or will inconvenience them in any major way. Thus if changes can be made in the planned study to better accommodate their normal routine, they should be made *unless* the study will suffer as a consequence. No change should be made solely for the sake of compromise without considering its impact on the study as a whole.

Clearly, human relations is an important factor in conducting research in applied settings. That you should be your usual charming self goes without saying. But you should keep in mind that you are dealing with sincere, concerned educators who may not have your level of research expertise. Therefore, you must make a special effort to discuss your study in plain English (it is possible!)

and to never give the impression that you are talking down to them. Also, your task is not over once the study begins. The feelings of involved persons must be monitored and responded to throughout the duration of the study if the initial level of cooperation is to be maintained.

Training Research Assistants

In addition to determining *what* will be done, it must also be decided *who* will do it. Anyone who is going to assist you in any way in actually conducting your study, whether a colleague or a teacher, should be considered a research assistant. Regardless of who they are, or what role they will play, all assistants should participate in some type of orientation that explains the nature of the study and the part they will play in it. They should understand exactly *what* they are going to do and *how* they are to do it. Their responsibilities should be described in writing and, if necessary, they should receive training related to their assigned task and be given opportunities for supervised practice. Simulations, in which assistants go through the entire task (e.g., conducting an interview) with each other or with you, are an especially effective training strategy.

Before any data are actually collected, anyone involved in any way with data collection procedures should become thoroughly familiar with all relevant restrictions, legal or otherwise, related to the collection, storing, and sharing of obtained information. All necessary permissions from participants, school administrators, federal agencies, and the like should be obtained *in writing*. And finally, all data collection activities should be carefully and systematically monitored to ensure that correct procedures are being followed.

Components

Although they may go by other names, research plans typically include an introduction, a method section, a description of proposed data analyses, and a time schedule. Each component will be discussed in detail, but basically the format for a typical research plan is as follows:

Introduction
  Statement of the Problem
  Review of Related Literature
  Statement of the Hypothesis
Method
  Subjects
  Instruments
  Design
  Procedure
Data Analysis
Time Schedule
Budget (if appropriate)

Other headings may also be included, as needed. For example, if special materials are being developed for the study, or special equipment is being used (such as computer terminals), then headings such as Materials or Apparatus might be included under Method and before Design.

Introduction

If you have completed Task 2, you are very familiar with the content of the introduction: a statement of the problem, a review of related literature, and a statement of the hypothesis.

Statement of the Problem

Since the problem sets the stage for the rest of the plan, it should be stated as early as possible. The statement should be accompanied by a description of the background of the problem and a rationale for its significance.

Review of Related Literature

The review of related literature should present the least related references first and the most related references last, just prior to the statement of the hypothesis (do not forget the big **V**). The literature review should lead logically to a tentative, testable conclusion, your hypothesis. The review should conclude with a brief summary of the literature and its implications.

Statement of the Hypothesis

Each hypothesis should represent a reasonable explanation for some behavior, phenomenon, or event. It should clearly and concisely state the expected relationship (or difference) between the variables in your study, and should define those variables in operational, measurable terms. Finally, each hypothesis should be clearly testable within some reasonable period of time. Be certain that all terms in the introduction are either common-usage terms or are operationally defined. The persons reading your plan (and especially persons reading your final report of which this introduction will be a part) may not be as familiar with your terminology as you are.

Method

The specific method of research your study represents will affect the format and content of your method section. The method section for an experimental study, for example, typically includes a description of the experimental design, whereas a descriptive study may combine the design and procedure sections into one. In general, however, the method section includes a description of the subjects, measuring instruments, design, and procedure.

Subjects

The description of subjects should clearly define the population, the larger group, from which the sample will be selected. The description should indicate the size and major characteristics of the population. In other words, where are the subjects for your study going to come from? What are they like? How many do you have to choose from? For example, a description of subjects might include the following:

> Subjects will be selected from a population of 157 students enrolled in an algebra I course at a large urban high school in Miami, Florida. The population is tricultural, being composed primarily of Caucasian students, Black-American students, and Spanish-surnamed students. . . .

The procedural technique for selecting the sample or samples to be included in the study may be described here but usually is described in the procedure section of the plan.

Instruments

Since measurement in education is primarily indirect (there is no yardstick for achievement), the measuring instrument you select or develop really represents an operational definition of whatever construct you are trying to measure. For example, intelligence may be defined to be scores on the Wechsler Intelligence Scale for Children. Therefore, it is important to provide a rationale for the selection of the instrument to be used as well as a description of the instrument. Validity and reliability data should also be presented; the degree to which the instrument for collecting data is invalid is directly related to the degree to which the study is invalid. If you are going to develop your own instrument, you should describe how the instrument will be developed, what it will measure, and how you plan to evaluate its validity and reliability before its utilization in the actual study. For example, a description of the instrument might include the following:

> The Stanford Achievement Test: Arithmetic Test (level 7.0–9.9) will be utilized as the data-gathering instrument. Split-half reliability coefficients are reported to range from .86 to .93 and reviewers are in agreement concerning its high content validity. . . .

Of course, if more than one instrument is to be used, which is not uncommon, each should be described separately, and in detail. You are probably not yet able to identify and describe the instrument you would use in your study. Therefore, in Task 3, you should describe the *kind* of instrument which would be used.[2] This section may include a description of when each instrument will be administered and for what purpose (for example, as a pretest), but such a description is usually included in the procedure section. In writing this section of a research plan, a researcher may discover that an appropriate instrument for collecting data to test the hypothesis is not available. If this occurs, a decision needs to be made, probably to either alter the hypothesis and change the dependent variable (you remember Z!), or to develop an instrument. Again, it is better to be made aware

---

2. Task 5 will require you to select and describe a particular instrument of the kind which you describe here (unless, of course, you change your mind in the meantime!).

of the unavailability of an appropriate instrument *before* a study has begun than *during* its conduction.

Materials/Apparatus

As mentioned previously, if special materials (such as booklets, programmed units, or computer programs) are going to be developed, they should be described in some detail in the research plan. Also, if special apparatus (such as computer terminals) are going to be utilized, they also should be described. If computer terminals were going to be utilized, for example, the description might include the following:

> The learning materials will be presented by an IBM-1500 Computer-Assisted Instruction (CAI) system. Terminals for this system consist of a cathode-ray tube, a light pen, and a keyboard. . . .

Design

The description of the design indicates the basic structure of the study. The nature of the hypothesis, the variables involved, and the constraints of the "real world"—all contribute to the design to be used. For example, if the hypothesis involved comparing the effectiveness of isotonic versus isometric exercises with respect to increased arm strength, the study would involve comparing the final strength of two groups after some period of time, one group having engaged in isotonic exercises and one group in isometric exercises. Therefore, a design involving two groups would be needed. The "real world" might determine whether those groups could be randomly formed or whether existing groups would have to be used; these two alternatives dictate distinctly different designs. The nature of the variables also may affect the design. If the dependent variable involves measurement of attitudes, for example, use of a design involving a pretest may be precluded. Administration of a pretest of attitudes may alert students to what is coming, to what the study is all about—the "I know what you're up to" phenomenon. Subjects may then react differently to a treatment intended to change attitudes, for example, than they would have had they not been pretested. Thus, the design typically indicates the number of groups to be included in the study, whether the groups will be randomly formed, and whether there will be a pretest. Other factors may also be discussed such as particular arrangements of groups and time intervals between components of the design. For example, in the study by the author previously described (Gay, 1973), the design section indicated that "the design for both experiments followed that used by Peterson et al. (1935) and Sones and Stroud (1940) in that the interval between learning and retention testing was equated for all groups."[3] This entire discussion, it should be pointed out, is appropriate primarily for experimental

---

3. Peterson, H.A., Ellis, M., Toohill, N., & Kloess, P. Some measurements of the effects of reviews. *Journal of Educational Psychology*, 1935, *26*, 65–72, and Sones, A.M., & Stroud, J.B. Review, with special reference to temporal position. *Journal of Educational Psychology*, 1940, *31*, 665–676.

studies. The choice of designs is greatly reduced for a causal-comparative study, for example. Research plans and reports for studies involving the other methods of research typically do not include a separate design section.

There are a number of basic designs to select from as well as an almost endless number of variations on those designs which can be used. While the design can become very complex, especially if multiple independent and/or dependent variables are involved, such complex designs are really sophisticated variations of the basic designs. By the time you develop Task 6, you will be familiar with the basic designs and will be able to identify them by name and apply them to your study. In developing Task 3, you will not have this knowledge. You should be able, however, to describe the kinds of information which a given design conveys. In other words, you should be able to indicate the number and arrangement of groups, whether they will be randomly formed groups or existing groups, and whether there will be a pretest.

Procedure

The procedure section describes all the steps that will be followed in conducting the study, from beginning to end, in the order in which they will occur, in other words, how the design selected for testing the hypothesis will be operationalized. The procedure section typically begins with a description of the technique to be used in selecting the sample, or samples, for the study. A description might be as follows:

> In the summer of 1976, prior to the assignment of students to classes, a list of all students scheduled to take general math I in the fall (approximately 150 students) will be obtained. Using this list, 60 students will be randomly selected to participate in the study. These 60 students will then be randomly assigned to one of two general math I classes, one class to receive programmed instruction, and one class to receive lecture-discussion instruction.

Occasionally an entire population is used and simply randomly assigned to two or more groups. This situation might be described as follows:

> The entire eighth-grade population (approximately 200 students) will participate in the study. All students will be randomly assigned to one of six classes; three of those classes will randomly be designated as experimental classes, and three as control classes.

In both examples, the population would already have been described under Subjects at the beginning of the Method section.

If the design includes a pretest, the procedure for its administration—when it will be administered, and how—will usually be described next. Any other measure to be administered at the beginning of the study will also be discussed; for example, in addition to a pretest on current skill in reading music, a general musical achievement test might be administered in order to check for initial equivalence of groups. For a study designed in investigate a new method for improving reading comprehension, this portion of the procedure section might include a statement such as the following:

> In September, on the day following the first day of school, the Magoo Test of Reading Comprehension Form A will be administered to all experimental and control groups.

In research plans which do not include a separate section for a description of the instrument, relevant information concerning the measure will be presented here.

From this point on, the procedure section will describe exactly what is going to occur in the study. In an experimental study, this will basically involve a description of how the groups will be the same and how they will be different. How they will be different should be a function of the independent variable only; in other words, major differences between groups should be intentional treatment differences. How they will be the same will be a function of control procedures. Since the essence of experimentation is groups equivalent on all relevant variables except the experimental variable, all procedures designed to insure equivalence should be described; if two groups are equivalent to begin with, are treated the same for some period of time except for the independent variable, and are different at the end on some dependent variable, that difference can be attributed to the independent variable. Variables that typically need to be controlled include teacher skill and experience, materials, time on task, instructional environment, and testing conditions. For example, if an experimental group was taught by Carmel Kandee (teacher-of-the-year Mary Poppins type), and a control group was taught by Hester Hartless (wicked-witch-of-the-West type), then final differences between groups might be attributable to teacher differences, not treatment differences. In order to control for the teacher variable, you might have both groups taught by the same teacher, or you might have several experimental groups and several control groups and randomly assign teachers to groups. The following are examples of the kinds of statements which typically appear in the procedure section:

> The curriculum for both groups will be the same. . . .
> All experimental and control classes will utilize the Miss Muffet Reading
>   Series. . . .
> All eight teachers have more than five years' experience. . . .
> All students will meet for the same amount of time each day. . . .

The procedure section will generally conclude with a discussion concerning administration of the posttest similar to the discussion for the pretest. As an example:

> In June, on the next to the last day of school, the Magoo Test of Reading Comprehension, Form B will be administered to all experimental and control groups.

The procedure section should also include any identified assumptions and limitations. An assumption is any important "fact" presumed to be true but not actually verified. For example, in a study involving reading instruction for preschool children it might be assumed that, given the population, none of the children had received reading instruction at home. Such assumptions are probabilistic in nature; the reader of the research plan (and ultimately the research report) can determine whether he or she is willing to "buy" the researcher's assumption. For example, if the population were preschool children in an upper-middle-class suburban area, the assumption just discussed would be questionable. A limitation is some aspect of the study that the researcher knows may negatively affect the results or generalizability of the results but over which he or she probably has no control. In other words, something is not as "good" as it should be but the researcher cannot do anything about it. Two common limitations are sample size and length of the study. A research plan might state, for example:

Only one class of 30 students will be available for participation.

OR

While ideally subjects should be exposed to the experimental treatment for a longer period of time in order to more accurately assess its effectiveness, permission has been granted to the researcher to be in the school for a maximum of two weeks.

If such limitations are openly and honestly stated, the readers can judge for themselves how seriously the study may be affected.

Assumptions and limitations are generally stated within context; for example, a time limitation would be stated within the procedure section, probably at the same time administration of the posttest was discussed. Some colleges and universities require that assumptions and limitations be presented in a separate section. This forces the student to give some thought to where they occur in her or his study.

The procedure section should be as detailed as possible, and any new terms introduced should of course be defined. The key to writing this section is replicability. It should be precise to the point where someone else could read your plan and execute your study exactly as you intended it to be conducted. In fact, it should be detailed enough to permit *you* to execute it exactly as planned!

Data Analysis

The research plan must include a description of the statistical technique or techniques that will be used to analyze study data. For certain descriptive studies, data analysis may involve little more than simple tabulation and presentation of results. For most studies, however, one or more statistical methods will be required. Identification of appropriate analysis techniques is extremely important; very few situations cause as much "weeping and gnashing of teeth" as collecting data only to find that there is no appropriate analysis or that the analysis that is appropriate requires sophistication beyond the researcher's level of statistical competence. Once the data are collected, it is too late. Settling for a less appropriate technique in order to salvage the study is definitely a no-no, although this is done on occasion by poor planners. The hypothesis of the study determines the design which in turn determines the statistical analysis; an inappropriate analysis, therefore, does not permit a valid test of the research hypothesis. Which available analysis technique should be selected depends on a number of factors, such as how the groups will be formed (for example, by random assignment, by matching, or by using existing groups), how many different treatment groups will be involved, how many independent variables will be involved, and the kind of data to be collected (interval data, for example, will require different techniques than ordinal data). In a correlational study, similar factors will determine the appropriate correlational analysis.

If you do not understand any of the terms mentioned, do not worry about it; you are not supposed to, *yet!* They will be discussed in succeeding chapters. Although you probably are not familiar with any specific statistical analyses, you should be able to describe in your research plan the *kind* of analysis you would need. For example, you might say:

> An analysis will be used appropriate for comparing the achievement, on a test of reading comprehension, of two randomly formed groups of second-grade students.

By the time you get to Task 7, you *will* know exactly what you need (honest!).

Time Schedule

A realistic time schedule is equally important for both beginning researchers working on a thesis or dissertation and for experienced researchers working under the deadlines of a research grant or contract. It is an infrequent event when a researcher has as long as he or she pleases to conduct a study. The existence of deadlines typically necessitates careful budgeting of time. Basically, a time schedule includes a listing of major activities or phases of the proposed study and a corresponding expected completion time for each activity. Such a schedule in a research plan enables the researcher to assess the feasibility of conducting a study within existing time limitations. It also helps the researcher to stay on schedule during the conduction of the study. In developing a time frame, do not make the mistake of "cutting it too thin" by allowing a minimum amount of time for each activity. Allow yourself enough time so that if an unforeseen minor delay occurs, you can still meet your final deadline. You should also plan to have the completion date for your final activity a date sometime in advance of your actual deadline. Your schedule will not necessarily be a series of sequential steps such that one activity must be completed before another is begun. For example, while the study is being conducted, you may also be working on the first part of the research report.

A very useful approach for constructing a time schedule is to use what is called the Gantt chart method.[4] A Gantt chart lists the activities to be completed down the left-hand side of a page and the time to be covered by the entire project across the top of the page. A bar graph format is used to indicate the beginning and ending date for each activity. Such a chart permits the researcher to easily see the "big picture" and to identify concurrent activities (see Figure 3.1).

---

4. Archibald, R.D., and Villoria, R.L. *Network-based management systems (PERT/CPM)*, New York: John Wiley, 1967.

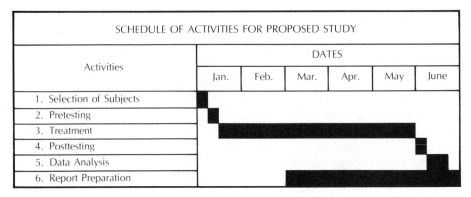

Figure 3.1.
Hypothetical, simplified example
of a Gantt chart for a proposed research study.

Budget

Formal research plans are referred to as proposals. Proposals are generally submitted to governmental or private funding agencies in the hope of receiving financial assistance for the conduction of a study. Proposals almost always require the inclusion of a tentative budget. Depending upon the amount requested and the agency to which the proposal is submitted, items included in the budget will vary. With the exception of some very small grants, however, budgets typically include such items as personnel, clerical assistance, expenses (such as travel and postage), equipment, and overhead (see Figure 3.2). Assistance in developing budgets is usually available at most colleges and universities, provided either formally by a research office or informally by colleagues who have had experience in developing proposals.

Evaluation of a Research Plan

Evaluation of a research plan can involve both informal and formal procedures. Informally, it should be reviewed and critiqued; formally, it may be field-tested in a preliminary pilot study. Having a research plan permits it to be carefully scrutinized by yourself and by others. Rereading a plan several days after having written it often results in flaws or weaknesses suddenly being very evident. Having a written plan also allows others not only to identify problems but also to make suggestions as to how the study might be improved. A research plan should be reviewed by at least one skilled researcher and at least one expert in the study's area of investigation, for example, reading. There is no researcher, no matter how long she or he has been "in the business," whose plan cannot benefit from the insight of others.

Formal evaluation of a research plan involves a pilot study, which is sort of a dress rehearsal. In a pilot study the entire study is conducted, each and every procedure is followed, and the resulting data are analyzed—all according to the research plan. Beginning researchers gain valuable experience from conducting a pilot study; the quality of one's dissertation, for example, may be considerably improved as a result. Even a small-scale pilot study, based on a small number of subjects, can help in refining procedures, such as instrument administration and scoring routines, and in trying out analysis techniques. The larger the scope of the

Budget

Direct costs	Amount
Personnel salaries	
Director (9 mos. at $20,000/yr.)	$15,000
Graduate assistant (9 mos. at $6,000/yr.)	4,500
Secretary (½ time for 9 mos. at $8,000/yr.)	3,000
Fringe benefits for director (12.2%)	1,830
	$24,330
Expenses	
Travel (60 on-site visits at $5/visit)	300
Instructional materials	500
Office supplies	200
Postage	200
Duplicating	150
Computer time	500
	1,850
Subtotal: Direct costs	26,180
Overhead (8% of direct costs)	2,094
Total costs	$28,274

Figure 3.2.
Hypothetical, simplified example
of a budget for a proposed research study.

pilot study, the more like the "real" study it is, the more likely it is that potential problems such as uncontrolled variables and inefficient data processing routines will be identified. The research plan will almost always be modified as a result of a pilot study, and in some cases it may be completely "overhauled." Besides time constraints, a major reason more large-scale pilot studies are not conducted is lack of available subjects. It is usually difficult enough to locate a sufficient number of subjects for the actual study, let alone a like number for a pilot study. Whenever feasible, however, a pilot study should be considered a very worthwhile use of your time.

Summary/Chapter 3

Definition and Purpose

1. A research plan is a detailed description of a proposed study designed to investigate a given problem; it includes justification for the hypothesis to be tested, a detailed presentation of the research steps that will be followed in collecting and analyzing required data, and a projected time schedule for each major step.

2. A research plan may be relatively brief and informal or very lengthy and formal, such as the proposals which are submitted to governmental and private funding agencies.

3. The research plan must be completed before a study is begun.

4. Since your study will be designed to test a hypothesis, it must be developed first; the nature of your hypothesis will determine to a high degree the sample group, measuring instruments, design, procedures, and statistical techniques used in your study.

5. The research plan makes you think; it forces you to think through every aspect of the study.

6. A written plan facilitates evaluation of the proposed study by you and by others.

7. A research plan provides a guide for conducting the study.

8. A well-thought-out plan saves time, reduces the probability of costly mistakes, and generally results in higher quality research.

9. Part of good planning is anticipation. Try to anticipate potential problems which might arise, do what you can to prevent them, and plan your strategies for dealing with them if they do occur.

General Considerations

The Ethics of Research

10. There are ethical considerations involved in all research studies. Ethical concerns are, of course, more acute in experimental studies which, by definition, "manipulate" and "control" subjects.

11. Perhaps the foremost rule of ethics is that subjects should not be harmed in any way (physically or mentally) in the name of science.

12. The subject's right to privacy is also an important consideration.

13. Above all, the researcher must have personal integrity.

Legal Restrictions

14. The major provisions of legislation passed to date have been designed to protect subjects who participate in research and to ensure the confidentiality of students' records.

15. The National Research Act of 1974 requires that proposed research activities involving human subjects be reviewed and approved by an authorized group in an institution, prior to the execution of the research, to ensure protection of the subjects.

16. The Family Educational Rights and Privacy Act of 1974, more commonly referred to as the Buckley Amendment, basically protects the privacy of the educational records of students.

17. Among the provisions of the Buckley Amendment is the specification that data that actually identify the students may not usually be made available unless written permission is acquired from the students (if of age), parents, or legal guardians.

Cooperation

18. The first step in acquiring needed cooperation is to follow required procedures.

19. The approval process usually involves the completion of one or more forms on which the nature of the research and the specific request being made of the school system are described, and a meeting with the approval-granting administrator.

20. The key to gaining approval and cooperation is good planning. The key to good planning is a well-designed, carefully thought-out study.

21. Achieving full cooperation, and not just approval on paper, requires that you invest as much time as is necessary to discuss your study with the principal, the teachers, and perhaps even parents. Potential benefits to be derived by the students, teachers, or principal as a result of your study should be explained fully.

22. If changes can be made in the planned study to better accommodate the normal routine of participating personnel, these changes should be made *unless* the study will suffer as a consequence.

23. The feelings of involved persons must be monitored and responded to throughout the duration of the study if the initial level of cooperation is to be maintained.

Training Research Assistants

24. Regardless of who they are, or what role they will play, all assistants should participate in some type of orientation that explains the nature of the study and the part they will play in it.

25. Responsibilities should be described in writing and, if necessary, assistants should receive training related to their assigned task and be given opportunities for supervised practice.

26. Before any data are actually collected, anyone involved in any way with data collection procedures should become thoroughly familiar with all relevant restrictions, legal or otherwise, related to the collection, storing, and sharing of obtained information.

Components

27. Although they may go by other names, research plans typically include an introduction, a method section, a description of proposed data analysis, a time schedule, and a budget, if appropriate.

Introduction

28. The introduction includes a statement of the problem, a review of related literature, and a statement of the hypothesis.

29. Be certain that all terms are either common-usage terms or are operationally defined.

Method

30. The specific method of research your study represents will affect the format and content of your method section.

Subjects

31. The description of subjects should clearly define the population, the larger group from which the sample will be selected.

32. The description should indicate the size and major characteristics of the population.

Instruments

33. Since measurement in education is primarily indirect, the measuring instrument you select or develop really represents an operational definition of whatever construct you are trying to measure.

34. It is important to provide a rationale for the selection of the instrument to be used as well as a description of the instrument.

35. If you are going to develop your own instrument, you should describe how the instrument will be developed, what it will measure, and how you plan to evaluate its validity and reliability.

Materials/Apparatus

36. If special materials (such as booklets, programmed units, or computer programs) are going to be developed, they should be described in some detail.

37. If special apparatus (such as computer terminals) are going to be utilized, they also should be described.

Design

38. The description of the design indicates the basic structure of the study.

39. The nature of the hypothesis, the variables involved, and the constraints of the "real world"—all contribute to the design to be used.

40. The design typically indicates the number of groups to be included in the study, whether the groups will be randomly formed, and whether there will be a pretest.

41. There are a number of basic designs to select from as well as an almost endless number of variations on those designs which can be used.

Procedure

42. The procedure section describes all the steps that will be followed in conducting the study, from beginning to end, in the order in which they will occur.

43. The procedure section typically begins with a description of the technique to be used in selecting the sample, or samples, for the study.

44. If the design includes a pretest, the procedure for its administration, when it will be administered, and how will usually be described next.

45. From this point on, the procedure section will describe exactly what is going to occur in the study. In an experimental study, this will basically involve a description of how the groups will be the same (control procedures) and how they will be different (the independent variable, or treatment).

46. The procedure section will generally conclude with a discussion concerning the administration of the posttest similar to the discussion for the pretest.

47. The procedure section should also include any identified assumptions and limitations. An assumption is any important "fact" presumed to be true but not actually verified; a limitation is some aspect of the study that the researcher knows may negatively affect the results or generalizability of the results, but over which he or she probably has no control.

48. The procedure section should be as detailed as possible and any new terms introduced should of course be defined; it should be precise to the point where someone else could read your plan and execute your study exactly as you intended it to be conducted.

Data Analysis

49. The research plan must include a description of the statistical technique or techniques that will be used to analyze study data.

50. The hypothesis of the study determines the design which in turn determines the statistical analysis; an inappropriate analysis, therefore, does not permit a valid test of the research hypothesis.

51. Which available analysis technique should be selected depends on a number of factors such as how the groups will be formed (for example, by random assignment, by matching, or by using existing groups), how many different treatment groups will be involved, how many independent variables will be involved, and the kind of data to be collected. (Interval data, for example, will require different techniques than ordinal data.) In a correlational study, similar factors will determine the appropriate correlational analysis.

Time Schedule

52. Basically, a time schedule includes a listing of major activities or phases of the proposed study and a corresponding expected completion time for each activity.

53. A very useful approach for constructing a time schedule is to use the Gantt chart method which uses a bar graph format.

Budget

54. Formal research plans are referred to as proposals; they almost always require the inclusion of a tentative budget.

55. Budgets typically include such items as personnel, clerical assistance, expenses, equipment, and overhead.

Evaluation of a Research Plan

56. Having a research plan permits it to be carefully scrutinized, by yourself and by others.

57. Having a plan also allows others not only to identify problems but also to make suggestions as to how the study might be improved.

58. A research plan should be reviewed by at least one skilled researcher and at least one expert in the study's area of investigation, for example, reading.

59. Formal evaluation of a research plan involves a pilot study; in a pilot study the entire study is conducted, each and every procedure is followed, and the resulting data are analyzed—all according to the research plan.

60. Even a small-scale pilot study based on a small number of subjects can help in refining procedures, such as instrument administration and scoring routines, and in trying out analysis techniques.

61. The research plan will almost always be modified as a result of a pilot study, and in some cases it may be completely "overhauled."

Task 3 Performance Criteria

As repeatedly pointed out, you are not yet in a position to develop a sound research plan. You are not expected to. The purpose of Task 3 is to have you demonstrate the ability to develop a complete research plan. What is required is that your plan contain all the components of a research plan, not that those components be technically correct. For example, you must describe how you will select your subjects, but it is not necessary that your selection method be a valid one. Beginning with chapter 4, you will learn the correct way to formulate each of the components. Feedback from your instructor concerning your research plan will alert you to specific sections of succeeding chapters.

See the *Student Guide* for examples of Task 3.

. . . every individual has the same
probability of being selected and selection of one individual in no way
affects selection of another individual

The purpose of selecting a sample is to gain information concerning a population. To use a former example, if you were interested in the effect of daily homework assignments on the examination grades of ninth-grade algebra students, it would not be possible for you to include *all* ninth-grade algebra students in the United States in your study. It would be necessary for you to select a sample. Since inferences concerning a population are made based on the behavior of a sample, it is imperative that the sample be representative and sufficiently large, and that care be taken to avoid possible sources of sampling error and bias.

The goal of Part Four is for you to understand the importance of selecting an adequate sample and be familiar with various sampling techniques. After you have read Part Four, you should be able to perform the following task.

Task 4

Having selected a problem, and having formulated one or more testable hypotheses or answerable questions, describe a sample appropriate for evaluating your hypotheses or answering your questions. This description will include:

(a) a definition of the population from which the sample would be drawn;

(b) the procedural technique for selecting the sample and forming the groups;

(c) sample sizes; and

(d) possible sources of sampling bias.

(See Performance Criteria, p. 102.)

4

Selection of a Sample

Sampling: Definition and Purpose

Sampling is the process of selecting a number of individuals for a study in such a way that the individuals represent the larger group from which they were selected. The individuals selected comprise a sample and the larger group is referred to as a population. The purpose of sampling is to gain information about a population; rarely is a study conducted that includes the total population of interest as subjects. In fact, not only is it generally not feasible to use the total group, it is also not necessary. If the group of interest is unmanageably large or geographically scattered, study of this group could result in considerable expenditure of time, money, and effort. Further, if a sample is well selected, research results based on it will be generalizable to the population. The degree to which the sample represents the population is the degree to which results for one are applicable to the other.

As an example, suppose the superintendent of a large school system wanted to find out how the 5,000 teachers in that system felt about teacher unions, whether they would join one, and for what reasons. If an interview were determined to be the best way to collect the desired data, it would take a very long time to interview each and every teacher; even if one interview only took 15 minutes, it would take a minimum of 1,250 hours, which is equivalent to 156 8-hour days, or approximately 30 school weeks to collect the desired information. On the other hand, if 10%, or 500, of the teachers were interviewed, it would take only 125 hours, or approximately 3 weeks. Assuming that the superintendent needed the information "now, not next year," as the saying goes, the latter approach would definitely be preferable *if* the same information could be acquired. As it happens, the conclusions based on the interviews of the sample of teachers would in all probability be the same as the conclusions based on interviews of all the teachers *if* the sample were correctly selected. Just any 500 teachers would not do. Interviewing 500 elementary teachers, for example, would not be satisfactory. In the first place, there is a highly disproportionate number of female teachers at that level and males might feel differently about unions. In the second place, opinions of elementary teachers might not be the same as those of junior high teachers or senior high teachers. How about 500 teachers who were members of the National Education Association (NEA)? While they would probably be more representative of all 5,000 teachers than the elementary teachers, they still would not do. Teachers who are already members of one professional organization would probably be more likely to join another organization. Of course it could also be argued that nonmembers of the NEA might be more likely to join a union since the approaches of the two organizations to certain problems would be distinctly different. In either case, however, it is reasonable to assume that the opinions toward unions of members and nonmembers of the NEA would be different. How then could it be done; how could a representative sample be selected?

Give up? Don't! As you will see shortly, there are several relatively simple procedures or sampling techniques which could be applied to select a very "nice" sample of teachers. These procedures would not guarantee a sample that was perfectly representative of the population, but they would definitely increase the odds. They would also correspondingly increase the degree of confidence that the superintendent could have regarding the generalizability of findings for the 500 teachers to all 5,000 teachers.

Definition of a Population

Regardless of the technique to be used in selecting a sample, the first step in sampling is definition of the population. The population is the group of interest to the researcher, the group to which she or he would like the results of the study to be generalizable. The defined population has at least one characteristic that differentiates it from other groups. Examples of research populations include all tenth-grade students in the United States, all primary-level gifted children in Utah, and all first-grade culturally deprived students in Utopia County who have participated in preschool training. These examples illustrate two important points about populations. First, populations may be virtually any size and may cover almost any geographical area. Second, the group the researcher would really like to generalize to is rarely available. Thus, the definition of a population is generally a realistic choice, not an idealistic one.

As an example, suppose you wanted to investigate a probelm discussed in chapter 2, that is, the effect of participation in a Head Start program on reading achievement at the end of the first grade. Ideally, your study would involve measurement of the reading achievement of all such students. Of course, this would not be very feasible. By the time the very last student was tested, he or she could well be in the fourth grade! By now it may have occurred to you that the "obvious" solution would be to select a representative sample and test all the members of the sample. A little more thought will reveal that this procedure would also probably be highly impractical. Since the population would be located from coast to coast, even if all appropriate students could be identified, you would still require a staff of qualified researchers and a healthy bank account (which very few researchers have!) to adequately conduct the study. Clearly, your idealistic research plan would have to be brought into line with cold, hard reality. In the end, you would probably settle for a more manageable population, such as all defined students in a given school system, and you would select your sample from this group. By selecting from a more narrowly defined population you would be saving time and money but you would also be losing generalizability. Assuming you selected an adequate sample, the results of your study would be directly generalizable to all appropriate students in the school system, but not to all appropriate students in the United States. The degree to which the students in your school system, or population, were similar to students in other systems would be the degree to which your results would have implications for other settings.

The key is to define your population in sufficient detail so that others may determine how applicable your findings might be to their situation.

Methods of Selecting a Sample

Selection of a sample is a very important step in conducting a research study. The "goodness" of the sample determines the generalizability of the results. Since conducting a study generally requires a great deal of time and energy, non-generalizable results are extremely wasteful; if all results were true only for the group on which they were based, educators could never benefit from anyone else's work and each and every study would have to be replicated an almost infinite number of times. Imagine how slow the progress of science would be if every scientist had to reconfirm Newton's laws!

As discussed previously, a "good" sample is one that is representative of the population from which it was selected. As we saw with our superintendent who needed to assess teachers' attitudes, selecting a representative sample is not a haphazard process. There are, however, several valid techniques for selecting a sample. While certain techniques are more appropriate for certain situations, each of the techniques does not give the same level of assurance concerning representativeness. However, as with populations, we sometimes have to compromise the ideal for the real, that is, what is feasible. This is true in many areas of scientific research, however, and is not a situation peculiar to educational research. Much medical research aimed at relieving human suffering, for example, must be conducted on lower forms of life such as rats; researchers in this field encounter similar problems to those faced by educational researchers with respect to the generalizability of their findings.

Regardless of the specific technique used, the steps in sampling are essentially the same: identification of the population, determination of required sample size, and selection of the sample. The degree to which the selected sample represents the population is the degree to which results are generalizable. There are four basic sampling techniques or procedures: random sampling, stratified sampling, cluster sampling, and systematic sampling.

Random Sampling

Random sampling is the process of selecting a sample in such a way that all individuals in the defined population have an equal and independent chance of being selected for the sample. In other words, every individual has the same probability of being selected and selection of one individual in no way affects selection of another individual. You may recall in physical education class the teacher occasionally formed teams by having the class line up and count off by twos, one-two-one-two and so on. With this method, you could never be on the same team as the person next to you. Selection was not independent; whether you were on one team or another was determined by where you were in line and the team for which the person next to you was selected. If selection of teams had been random, you would have had a 50-50 chance of being on either team regardless of which team the person next to you was on.

Random sampling is the best single way to obtain a representative sample. No technique, not even random sampling, *guarantees* a representative sample, but the probability is higher for this procedure than for any other. Differences between the sample and the population should be small and unsystematic. For example, you would not expect the exact same ratio of males and females in a sample as in a population; random sampling, however, assures that the ratio will be close and that the probability of having too many females is the same as the probability of having too many males. In any event, differences are a function of chance and are not the result of any conscious or unconscious bias on the part of the researcher.

Another point in favor of random sampling is that it is required by inferential statistics. This is very important since inferential statistics permit the researcher to make inferences about populations based on the behavior of samples. If samples are not randomly selected, then one of the major assumptions of inferential statistics is violated, and inferences are correspondingly tenuous.[1]

Steps in Random Sampling

In general, random sampling involves defining the population, identifying each member of the population, and selecting individuals for the sample on a completely chance basis. One way to do this is to write each individual's name on a separate slip of paper, place all the slips in a hat or other container, shake the container, and select slips from the container until the desired number of individuals is selected. This procedure is not exactly satisfactory, however; if a population had 1,000 members, for example, one would need a relatively large hat! A much more satisfactory approach is to use a table of random numbers. In essence, a table of random numbers selects the sample for you, each member being selected on a purely random, or chance, basis, Such tables are included in the appendix of most statistics books and some educational research books; they usually consist of columns of five-digit numbers which have been randomly generated by a computer. (See Table A.1 in the Appendix.) Using a table of random numbers to select a sample involves the following specific steps:

1. Identify and define the population.

---

1. In Part Seven, you will learn how to select and apply several commonly used inferential statistics. By the way, don't you dare groan and say you're no good at anything mathematical! You will be amazed at how easy statistics really is!

2. Determine the desired sample size.

3. List all members of the population.

4. Assign all individuals on the list a consecutive number from zero to the required number, for example, 000–249 or 00–89.

5. Select an arbitrary number in the table of random numbers. (Close your eyes and point!)

6. For the selected number, look at only the appropriate number of digits. For example, if a population has 800 members, you only need to use the last 3 digits of the number; if a population has 90 members, you only need to use the last 2 digits.

7. If the number corresponds to the number assigned to any of the individuals in the population, then that individual is in the sample. For example, if a population had 500 members and the number selected was 375, the individual assigned 375 would be in the sample; if a population had only 300 members then 375 would be ignored.

8. Go to the next number in the column and repeat step 7.

9. Repeat step 8 until the desired number of individuals has been selected for the sample.

Once the sample has been selected, members may then be randomly *assigned* to two or more treatment groups (by flipping a coin, for example) if an experimental study is being conducted.

Actually, the random selection process is not as complicated as the above explanation may have made it sound. The following example should make the procedure clear.

An Example of Random Sampling

It is now time to help our long-suffering superintendent who wants to select a sample of teachers so that their attitudes toward unions can be determined. We will apply each of the nine steps described above to the solution of this problem:

1. The population is all 5,000 teachers in the superintendent's school system.

2. The desired sample size is 10% of the 5,000 teachers, or 500 teachers.

3. The superintendent has supplied a directory which lists all teachers in the system.

4. Using the directory, the teachers are each assigned a number from 0000 to 4999.

5. A table of random numbers is entered at an arbitrarily selected number such as the one which is underlined.

59058
11859
53634
48708
71710
83942
33278
etc.

6. Since the population has 5,000 members, we only are concerned with the last four digits of the number, 3634.

7. There is a teacher assigned the number 3634; that teacher is therefore in the sample.

8. The next number in the column is 48708. The last four digits are 8708. Since there are only 5,000 teachers, there is no teacher assigned the number 8708. The number is therefore skipped.

9. Applying the above steps to the remaining numbers shown in the above column, teachers 1710, 3942, and 3278 are included. This procedure would be applied to numbers following 33278 in that column and succeeding columns until 500 teachers were selected.

At the completion of this process the superintendent would in all probability have a representative sample of all the teachers in the system. The 500 selected teachers could be expected to appropriately represent all relevant subgroups of teachers such as elementary teachers and male teachers. With random sampling, however, such representation of subgroups is probable but not guaranteed. The probable does not always occur. If you flip a quarter 100 times, the probable outcome is 50 heads and 50 tails. You may get 53 heads and 47 tails, or 45 heads and 55 tails, but most of the time you can expect to get close to a 50-50 split. Other outcomes are possible, however; they may be less probable but they are possible. In tossing a quarter 100 times, 85 heads and 15 tails is a possible, low-probability outcome. Similarly, it would be possible, although less probable, for the sample of teachers to be unrepresentative of the total group on one or more dimensions. For example, if 55% of the 5,000 teachers were female and 45% male, we would expect roughly the same percentages in the sample of 500. Just by chance, however, the sample might contain 30% females and 70% males.

If there were one or more variables which the superintendent believed might be highly related to attitudes toward unions, he might not be willing to leave accurate representation on those variables to chance. He might decide, for example, that teaching level (elementary, junior high, senior high) might be a significant variable and that elementary teachers might feel differently toward unions than junior high or senior high teachers. He would want to sample in such a way that appropriate representation on this variable would be guaranteed. In this case he would probably use stratified sampling rather than simple random sampling.

Stratified Sampling

Stratified sampling is the process of selecting a sample in such a way that identified subgroups in the population are represented in the sample in the same proportion that they exist in the population. It can also be used to select equal-sized samples from each of a number of subgroups if subgroup comparisons are desired. Proportional stratified sampling would be appropriate, for example, if you were going to take a survey prior to a national election in order to predict the probable winner. You would want your sample to represent the voting population. Therefore, you would want the same proportion of Democrats and Republicans, for example, in your sample as existed in the population. Other likely variables for proportional stratification might include race, sex, and socioeconomic status. On the other hand, equal-sized samples would be desired if you wanted to compare the performance of different subgroups.

Suppose, for example, that you were interested in comparing the performance of students of different IQ levels (say high, medium, and low) following two different methods of mathematics instruction. Simply randomly selecting a sample and assigning one-half of the sample of each of the methods would not (as you know!) guarantee equal representation of each of the IQ levels in each method. In fact, just by chance, one of the methods might not have any students from one of the levels. However, randomly selecting students from each level, and then assigning half of each selected group to each of the methods, would guarantee equal representation of each IQ level in each method. That is the purpose of stratified sampling, to *guarantee* desired representation of relevant subgroups.

Steps in Stratified Sampling

The steps in stratified sampling are very similar to those in random sampling *except* that selection is from subgroups in the population rather than the population as a whole. Stratified sampling involves the following steps:

1. Identify and define the population.
2. Determine desired sample size.
3. Identify the variable and subgroups (strata) for which you want to guarantee appropriate representation (either proportional or equal).
4. Classify all members of the population as members of one of the identified subgroups.
5. Randomly select (using a table of random numbers) an "appropriate" number of individuals from each of the subgroups, "appropriate" meaning either a proportional number of individuals or an equal number of individuals.

As with simple random sampling, once the samples from each of the subgroups have been randomly selected, each may be randomly assigned to two or more treatment groups. If we were interested in the comparative effectiveness of two methods of mathematics instruction for different levels of IQ, the steps in sampling might be as follows:

1. The population is all 300 eighth-grade students enrolled in general math at Central Junior High School.
2. The desired sample size is 45 students in each of the two methods.
3. The desired subgroups are three levels of IQ—high (over 115), average (85–115), and low (below 85).
4. Classification of the 300 students indicates that there are 45 high IQ students, 215 average IQ students, and 40 low IQ students.
5. Using a table of random numbers, 30 students are randomly selected from each of the IQ subgroups, that is, 30 high IQ, 30 average IQ, and 30 low IQ students.
6. The 30 students in each sample are randomly assigned to one of the two methods, that is 15 of each 30 are randomly assigned to one of the two methods. Therefore, each method contains 45 students—15 high IQ students, 15 average IQ students, and 15 low IQ students (see Figure 4.1).

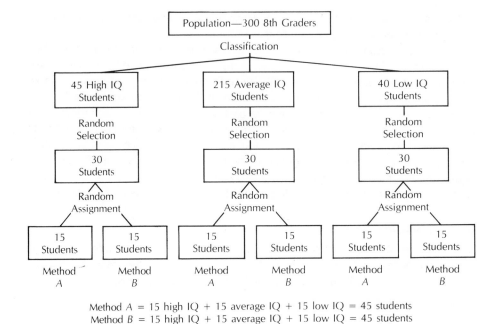

Method A = 15 high IQ + 15 average IQ + 15 low IQ = 45 students
Method B = 15 high IQ + 15 average IQ + 15 low IQ = 45 students

Figure 4.1
Procedure for selecting a stratified sample based on IQ for a study
designed to compare two methods (A and B) of mathematics instruction.

As you may have guessed, stratification can be done on more than one variable. In the above example, we could have stratified on IQ and math aptitude. The following example, based on a familiar situation, should help to further clarify the process of stratified sampling.

An Example of Stratified Sampling

Let us suppose that our old friend the superintendent wanted to guarantee appropriate representation of teaching level in the sample of teachers. We will apply each of the five steps previously described for selecting a stratified sample:

1. The population is all 5,000 teachers in the superintendent's school system.

2. Desired sample size is 10% of the 5,000 teachers, or 500 teachers.

3. The variable of interest is teaching level and there are three subgroups— elementary, junior high, and senior high.

4. Classify the teachers into the subgroups. Of the 5,000 teachers, 65% or 3,250 are elementary teachers, 20% or 1,000 are junior high teachers, and 15% or 750 are senior high teachers.

5. We want 500 teachers. Since we want proportional representation, 65% of the sample (325 teachers) should be elementary teachers, 20% (100 teachers) should be junior high teachers, and 15% (75 teachers) should be senior high teachers. Therefore, using a rable of random numbers, 325 of the 3,250 elementary teachers are randomly selected (makes sense since we want a total sample of

10%!), 100 of the 1,000 junior high teachers are selected, and 75 of the 750 senior high teachers are selected.

At the completion of this process, the superintendent would have a sample of 500 teachers (325 + 100 + 75), or 10% of the 5,000, and each teaching level would be proportionally represented.

So far we have discovered two ways in which the superintendent could get a sample of teachers, random sampling and stratified sampling. Both of these techniques, however, would result in a sample scattered over the entire district. The interviewer would have to visit many, many schools; any one school might contain only one teacher in the sample.[2] In the event that the superintendent wanted the information quickly, a more expedient method of sampling would be needed. For the sake of convenience, cluster sampling might be used.

Cluster Sampling

Cluster sampling is sampling in which groups, not individuals, are randomly selected. All the members of selected groups have similar characteristics. Instead of randomly selecting fifth graders, for example, you could randomly select fifth-grade classrooms and use all the students in each classroom. Cluster sampling is more convenient when the population is very large or spread out over a wide geographic area. Sometimes it is the only feasible method of selecting a sample. It is not always possible, for example, to obtain or compile a list of all members of the population; thus, in such cases, it is not possible to use simple random sampling. Also, often researchers do not have the control over subjects that they would like. For example, if your population were tenth-grade biology students, it is very unlikely that you would obtain administrative approval to randomly select tenth-grade students and remove a few students from each of many classrooms for your study. You would have a much better chance of securing permission to use several intact classrooms.

Any intact group of similar characteristics is a cluster. Examples of clusters include classrooms, schools, city blocks, hospitals, and department stores. Cluster sampling usually involves less time and less expense and is generally more convenient. Let us look at a few examples that illustrate this point. As the above example concerning tenth-grade biology students illustrated, it is easier to use all the students in several classrooms than several students in many classrooms. Similarly, in taking a survey, it is easier to use all the people in a limited number of city blocks, than a few people in many city blocks. You should be able to apply this logic to the examples of clusters mentioned above. In each case you should see that cluster sampling would be easier (though not necessarily as good, as we shall see later!) than either random sampling or stratified sampling.

Steps in Cluster Sampling

The steps in cluster sampling are not very different from those involved in random sampling. The major difference, of course, is that random selection of groups (clusters) is involved, not individuals. Cluster sampling involves the following steps:

---

2. It is highly unlikely that teachers would be asked to come to the interviewer.

1. Identify and define the population.
2. Determine the desired sample size.
3. Identify and define a logical cluster.
4. List all clusters (or obtain a list) that comprise the population.
5. Estimate the average number of population members per cluster.
6. Determine the number of clusters needed by dividing the sample size by the estimated size of a cluster.
7. Randomly select the needed number of clusters (using a table of random numbers).
8. Include in your study all population members in each selected cluster.

Cluster sampling can be done in stages, involving selection of clusters within clusters. This process is called multistage sampling. For example, schools can be randomly selected and then classrooms within each selected school can be randomly selected.

One common misconception that seems to exist among beginning researchers is the belief that it is all right to randomly select only one cluster. It is not uncommon, for example, for a beginning researcher to define a population as all fifth graders in X County, a cluster as a school, and to indicate random selection of a school. However, these same "researchers" would not dream of randomly selecting one student! The principle is the same. Keeping in mind that a good sample is representative of the population from which it is selected, it is highly unlikely that one randomly selected student could ever be representative of an entire population. Similarly, it is unlikely that one randomly selected school could be representative of all schools in a population. Thus, one would normally have to select a number of clusters in order for the results of a study to be generalizable to the population. The following example should make the procedures involved in cluster sampling clear.

An Example of Cluster Sampling

Let us see how our superintendent would get a sample of teachers if cluster sampling were used. We will follow the steps previously listed:

1. The population is all 5,000 teachers in the superintendent's school system.
2. The desired sample size is 500.
3. A logical cluster is a school.
4. The superintendent has a list of all the schools in the district; there are 100 schools.
5. Although the schools vary in the number of teachers per school, there are an average of 50 teachers per school.
6. The number of clusters (schools) needed equals the desired sample size, 500, divided by the average size of a cluster, 50. Thus, the number of schools needed is $500 \div 50 = 10$.
7. Therefore, 10 of the 100 schools are randomly selected.

8. All the teachers in each of the 10 schools are in the sample (10 schools, 50 teachers per school, equals the desired sample size).

Thus the interviewer could conduct interviews at 10 schools and interview many teachers at one time instead of traveling to a possible 100 schools.

The advantages of cluster sampling are evident. As with most things, however, nothing is all good. Cluster sampling has several drawbacks. For one thing, the chances are greater of selecting a sample that is not representative in some way of the population; the teachers in the above example are all from a limited number of schools, for example, not from a high percentage of the schools. Thus the possibility exists that the 10 schools selected are somehow different from the other 90 in the district (socioeconomic level of the students, racial composition, and so forth). One way to compensate for this problem is by selecting a larger sample, for example including more schools, thus increasing the likelihood that the schools selected adequately represent all the schools.

As another example, suppose our population were all fifth graders in 10 schools (each school having an average of 120 students in 4 classes of 30 students each), and we wanted a sample of 120 students. There are any number of ways we might select our sample. For example, we could: (a) randomly select one school and use all the fifth graders in that school, (b) randomly select 2 classes from each of 2 schools, or (c) randomly select 120 students from the 10 schools. In any of these ways we would wind up with 120 students, but our sample would probably not be equally "good" in each case. In case a we would have students from only one school. It is very likely that this school would be different from the other 9 in some significant way (e.g. socioeconomic level or racial composition). In case b we would be doing a little better, but we would still only have 2 of the 10 schools represented. Only in case c would we have a chance of selecting a sample containing students from all or most of the schools, and the classes within those schools. If random sampling was not feasible, selecting 2 classes from each of 2 schools would be preferable to selecting all the students in one school. Actually, if cluster sampling were used, it would be even better to select 1 class each from 4 of the schools. One way we could attempt to compensate for the loss of representativeness associated with cluster sampling would be to select more than 4 classes. As in most cases, however, the number of classes selected would be not just a matter of desirability but also of feasibility.

Another problem is that commonly used inferential statistics are not appropriate for analyzing data resulting from a study using cluster sampling. Such statistics generally require random sampling. Randomly assigning treatments to existing groups (clusters) is not enough; the groups must be randomly formed. The statistics that are available and appropriate for cluster samples are generally less sensitive to differences which may exist between groups. Thus, one should carefully weigh the advantages and disadvantages of cluster sampling before choosing this method of sampling.

There is one more type of sampling with which you should be familiar, systematic sampling. Although systematic sampling is not used very often, it is appropriate in certain situations and in some instances is the only feasible way to select a sample.

Systematic Sampling

Systematic sampling is sampling in which individuals are selected from a list by taking every Kth name. So what's a "Kth" name? That depends of what K is. If $K = 4$, selection involves taking every 4th name, if $K = 10$, every 10th name, and so forth. What K actually equals depends on the size of the list and the desired sample size. The major difference between systematic sampling and the other types of sampling so far discussed is the fact that all members of the population do not have an independent chance of being selected for the sample. Once the first name is selected, all the rest of the individuals to be included in the sample are automatically determined.

Even though choices are not independent, a systematic sample can be considered a random sample *if* the list of the population is randomly ordered. One or the other has to be random—either the selection process or the list. Since randomly ordered lists are rarely available, systematic sampling is rarely "as good" as random sampling. While some researchers argue this point, the major objection to systematic sampling of a nonrandom list is the possibility that certain subgroups of the population can be systematically excluded from the sample. The classic example usually given to support this contention is the statement that certain nationalities have distinctive last names that tend to group together under certain letters of the alphabet; when taking every Kth name, if K is at all large, it is possible that certain nationalities can be skipped over completely.

Steps in Systematic Sampling

Systematic sampling involves the following steps:

1. Identify and define the population.

2. Determine the desired sample size.

3. Obtain a list of the population.

4. Determine what K is equal to by dividing the size of the population by the desired sample size.

5. Start at some random place at the top of the population list.

6. Starting at that point, take every Kth name on the list until the desired sample size is reached.

7. If the end of the list is reached before the desired sample is reached, go back to the top of the list.

Now let us see how our superintendent would use systematic sampling.

An Example of Systematic Sampling

If our superintendent were to use systematic sampling, the process would be as follows:

1. The population is all 5,000 teachers in the superintendent's school system.

2. The desired sample size is 500.

3. The superintendent has supplied a directory which lists all teachers in the system in alphabetical order. The list is not randomly ordered, but it is the best available.

4. K is equal to the size of the population, 5000, divided by the desired sample size, 500. Thus $K = (5000 \div 500) = 10$.

5. Some random name at the top of the list of teachers is selected.

6. From that point, every following 10th name is automatically in the sample. For example, if the teacher selected in step 5 were the 3rd name on the list, then the sample would include the 13th name, the 23rd, the 33rd, the 43rd, and so forth.

In this case, due to the nonrandom nature of the list, the sample used would not be as likely to be representative as the samples resulting from application of the other techniques.

Conclusion

In most studies, simple, or stratified random, sampling will usually be the most appropriate sampling technique. Sometimes cluster sampling will be most expedient, and, in a few cases, systematic sampling will be appropriate. Depending upon the type of study, a sample may be used intact or may be randomly assigned to two or more treatements. A study will not necessarily use one of the four techniques discussed so far. It may not use any of them, if the entire population is used in the study, or it may use a combination of more than one. In addition to identification and definition of the population, determination of the desired sample size is a step common to all sampling techniques.

Determination of Sample Size

The question about sampling most frequently asked by beginning researchers is probably, "How do you know how large a sample should be?" And the answer is "large enough!" While the answer is not very comforting, the question is a difficult one. If the sample is too small, the results of the study may not be generalizable to the population. The results may hold only for the sample and may not be the same results that would have been obtained if the entire population had been used. Another way of looking at it is in terms of the hypothesis of the study. If the sample is not large enough, the wrong decision may be made concerning the validity of the hypothesis.

A sample which is too small can affect the generalizability of the study regardless of how well it is selected. Suppose, for example, the population were 300 first graders. If we randomly selected only one student, clearly that student could not represent all the students. Nor could 2, 3, or 4 students, even if randomly selected, adequately represent the population. On the other hand, we would all agree that a sample of 299, 298, or 297 students would represent the population. How about 10? Too small, you say. OK, how about 30? 75? 100? At what point does the sample size stop being "too small" and become "big enough?" That is a question without an easy answer. Knowing that the sample should be as large as possible helps some but still does not give any guidance as to what size sample is "big enough." In most cases, the researcher does not have access to many, many subjects. In fact, obtaining permission to involve students in a study, or finding adults willing to participate in a study, is generally not an easy task. Usually the problem is too few subjects rather than too many. In any event, there are some guidelines that can be applied in order to determine what size sample is "big enough."

In general, the minimum number of subjects believed to be acceptable for a study depends upon the type of research involved. For descriptive research, a sample of 10% of the population is considered minimum. For smaller populations, 20% may be required. For correlational studies at least 30 subjects are needed to establish the existence or nonexistence of a relationship. For causal-comparative studies and many experimental studies, a minimum of 30 subjects per group is generally recommended. Experimental studies with tight experimental controls may be valid with as few as 15 subjects per group.[3] Some authorities believe that 30 subjects per group should always be considered minimum. However, considering the difficulty involved in securing subjects, and the number of studies that are reported with less than 15 in a group, requiring 30 seems to be a little on the idealistic side. Further, while we would not be super-confident about the results of a single study based on small samples, if a number of such studies obtained similar results, our confidence in the findings would generally be as high, if not higher, than for a single study based on very large samples. There is a lot to be said for replication of findings.

The "minimums" discussed above are just that, minimums. If it is at all possible to use more subjects, you should do so. Using samples larger than the minimums is especially important in certain situations. For example, in an experimental study if the expected difference between groups is small, this difference might not "show up" if the samples are too small. Also, it should be noted that there are relatively precise statistical techniques which can be used to estimate required sample sizes for experimental studies; use of such techniques requires knowledge of certain facts about the population such as the difference expected between groups.[4] Although larger samples are in general better than smaller samples, even very large samples can lead to erroneous conclusions. There are many sources of sampling bias that can affect a study, regardless of sample size.

Avoidance of Sampling Bias

Selecting samples using the very best technique does not guarantee that they will be representative of the population. Sampling error, beyond the control of the researcher, can exist. Of course no sample will have a composition precisely identical to that of the population. The sample may have, for example, fewer males proportionally, or a higher average IQ. If well selected and sufficiently large, however, the chances are that the sample will be highly similar on such variables. Occasionally, however, just by chance, a sample will differ significantly from the

---

3 Roscoe, J.T. *Fundamental research statistics for the behavioral sciences* (2nd ed). New York: Holt, Rinehart and Winston, 1975.

4. For further discussion of these techniques see: Li, J.C.R. *Statistical inference I.* Ann Arbor: Edwards Brothers, 1969.

population on some major variable. Usually this will not make a significant difference. If there is a variable for which nonrepresentation might really affect the outcome of the study, the researcher should stratify on that variable rather than leaving all to chance.

Sampling bias is another story. Sampling bias does not result from random, chance differences between samples and populations. Sampling bias is systematic and is generally the fault of the researcher. If aware of sources of bias, a researcher can avoid bias if at all possible. The fact that size alone does not guarantee representativeness was graphically illustrated by the presidential election of 1936. The *Literary Digest* poll predicted that Roosevelt would be defeated by Landon. It based its prediction on a poll of several million people. Unfortunately for the *Literary Digest*, the prediction was wrong because it was based on a biased sample. The sample of people polled was selected primarily from automobile registration lists and telephone directories. In 1936, however, a sizable portion of the voting population did not own a car or have a telephone. Thus, the sample did not adequately represent the voting population. People without cars and telephones voted! The *Literary Digest*, of course, is no longer in business. Modern pollsters are more knowledgeable and take great care to insure that samples are representative of the voting population on relevant variables such as socioeconomic status.

A major source of bias is the use of volunteers. Volunteers are bound to be different from nonvolunteers. For example, they may be more motivated in general or more interested in the particular study. Since a population is composed of volunteers and nonvolunteers, the results of a study based on volunteers are not generalizable to the entire population, only to other volunteers. Two examples should help to make this point clear. Suppose you send a questionnaire to 100 randomly selected people and ask the question, "How do you feel about questionnaries?" Suppose that 40 people respond and all 40 indicate that they love questionnaires. Should you then conclude that the group from which the sample was selected loves questionnaires? Certainly not. The 60 who did not respond may not have done so simply because they hate questionnaires!

As a second example, suppose you want to do a study on the effectiveness of study-habit training on the achievement of college freshmen. You ask for volunteers from the freshman classes and 80 students volunteer. Of course right off the bat they are not representative of all freshmen! For example, they may be students who are not doing well academically but wish that they were. In any event, suppose you then randomly assign the volunteers to 2 groups of 40, one group to receive study-habit training, and one group to serve as a control. The experimental group is to receive study-habit training for one hour every day for two weeks, the control group is to do nothing special. Since they are all volunteers, the subjects feel free to drop out of the study. Members of the control group have no need to drop out since no demands are made on their time. Members of the experimental group, on the other hand, may drop out after one or more sessions, not wishing to "donate" any more of their time. Suppose at the end of the study, only 20 of the original 40 students in the training group remain while all 40 members of the control group remain. Suppose a comparison of their subsequent achievement indicates that the group which received training achieved significantly higher grades. Could you then conclude that the training was effective? Cer-tain-ly not! In essence, we would be comparing the achievement of those in the control group with those members of the experimental group who *chose to remain.* Thus, they might very well be more motivated to achieve, as a group, than the control group; the less motivated students dropped out of the study! It would be very difficult to determine how much of their achievement was due to the treatment (training) and how much was due to motivation.

Another common source of bias is the use of available groups just because "they are there." Suppose you want to do a study on the effectiveness of homework on the achievement of ninth-grade algebra students. You happen to have a friend who teaches two ninth-grade algebra classes. You ask your friend if you may conduct a study using those classes and your friend says yes. You then tell your friend to continue homework assignments in one class and to eliminate homework assignments in the other. At the end of the grading period the achievement of the two groups is compared and the homework group has achieved significantly more than the nonhomework group. Can you conclude that homework is effective? Not necessarily. In your study homework was effective for one class. Since the class was not selected from any larger group, you have no assurance that the class is representative of any other classes. Therefore, you have no assurance that your results are generalizable to any other ninth-grade algebra classes.

As mentioned before, securing administrative approval to involve students in a study is not generally easy. Researchers often use whatever subjects they can get, whatever is most convenient for the administration. This may amount to a researcher receiving permission to use several classes of the administration's choice. Cooperating with the administration is of course advisable, but not at the expense of good research. If the study cannot be conducted properly, the re-searcher should try hard to convince the administration to allow the study to be conducted the "researcher's way." If this fails, the researcher should look elsewhere for subjects. If suitable subjects cannot be found or selected properly, the study probably should be temporarily abandoned. Conducting a study re-quires considerable time and energy. To expend such time and energy on a study with little generalizability is a waste of both.

The researcher should be aware of sources of sampling bias and do his or her best to avoid it. If this is not possible, the researcher must decide whether the bias is so severe that the results will be seriously affected. If a decision is made to continue with the study, with full awareness of the existing bias, such bias should be completely reported in the final research report. The consumers of the research findings may then decide for themselves how serious they believe the bias to be.

Summary/Chapter 4

Sampling: Definition and Purpose

1. Sampling is the process of selecting a number of individuals for a study in such a way that the individuals represent the larger group from which they were selected.

2. The purpose of sampling is to use a sample to gain information about a population.

Definition of a Population

3. A population is the group to which a researcher would like the results of a study to be generalizable.
4. A defined population has at least one characteristic that differentiates it from other groups.

Methods of Selecting a Sample

5. Regardless of the specific technique used, the steps in sampling include identification of the population, determination of required sample size, and selection of the sample.
6. The degree to which the selected sample represents the population is the degree to which results are generalizable.

Random Sampling

7. Random sampling is the process of selecting a sample in such a way that all individuals in the defined population have an equal and independent chance of being selected for the sample.
8. Random sampling is the best single way to obtain a representative sample.
9. Random sampling involves defining the population, identifying each member of the population, and selecting individuals for the sample on a completely chance basis.
10. A random sample is generally selected using a table of random numbers.

Stratified Sampling

11. Stratified sampling is the process of selecting a sample in such a way that identified subgroups in the population are represented in the sample in the same proportion that they exist in the population.
12. Stratified sampling can also be used to select equal-sized samples from each of a number of subgroups if subgroup comparisons are desired.
13. The steps in stratified sampling are very similar to those in random sampling *except* that selection is from subgroups in the population rather than the population as a whole.

Cluster Sampling

14. Cluster sampling is sampling in which groups, not individuals, are randomly selected.
15. Any intact group of similar characteristics is a cluster.
16. The steps in cluster sampling are similar to those in random sampling except that the random selection of groups (clusters) is involved, not individuals.

Systematic Sampling

17. Systematic sampling is sampling in which individuals are selected from a list by taking every *K*th name, where *K* equals the number of individuals on the list divided by the number of subjects desired for the sample.

18. Even though choices are not independent, a systematic sample can be considered a random sample *if* the list of the population is randomly ordered (a relatively infrequent event).

Determination of Sample Size

19. Samples should be as large as possible; in general, the larger the sample, the more representative it is likely to be, and the more generalizable the results of the study are likely to be.
20. Minimum, acceptable sample sizes depend on the type of research: descriptive research—10% of the population; correlational research—30 subjects; causal-comparative research—30 subjects per group; and experimental research—15 subjects per group.
21. Even large samples can lead to erroneous conclusions if they are not well selected.

Avoidance of Sampling Bias

22 Sampling bias does not result from random, chance differences between samples and populations; sampling bias is systematic and is generally the fault of the researcher.
23. Two major sources of bias are the use of volunteers and the use of available groups.
24. You should not be talked into using a seriously biased sample for the sake of administrative convenience.
25. Any sampling bias present in a study should be fully described in the final research report.

Task 4 Performance Criteria

The definition of the population should describe its size and relevant characteristics (such as age, ability, and socioeconomic status).

The procedural technique for selecting subjects should be described in detail. For example, do not just say that stratified sampling will be used; indicate on what basis population members will be stratified and how (and how many) subjects will be selected from each subgroup. Also describe how selected subjects will be placed into treatment groups, by random assignment, for example. If the entire population will be used in the study, say so and simply describe how population members will be assigned to groups.

Include a summary statement that indicates resulting sample size for each group. For example:

Thus there will be 2 groups of 30 subjects each; each group will include 15 subjects with above-average intelligence and 15 subjects with below-average intelligence.

Any identifiable source of sampling bias should also be discussed, small sample sizes, for example.

See the *Student Guide* for practice problems and for examples of Task 4.

Part Five

Instruments

*The Thematic Apperception Test
presents the individual with a series of pictures; the respondent is then
asked to tell a story about each picture.*

Whether you are testing hypotheses or seeking answers to questions, you must have a valid, reliable instrument for collecting your data. In most cases it is a matter of selecting the best instrument for your purpose from those that are available. Sometimes, however, you may have to develop your own instrument. Whichever is the case, you must administer an instrument that will yield precisely the data you wish to collect in a quantifiable form.

When selecting a test, there are a number of factors which must be considered; some of these are more crucial than others. The major point to remember, however, is that one does not identify *an* instrument appropriate for a study, but rather selects *the best* instrument available.

The goal of Part Five is for you to be able to select the best instrument for a given study from those instruments that are available and appropriate. After you have read Part Five, you should be able to perform the following task.

Task 5

Having stated a problem, formulated one or more hypotheses or questions, and described a sample, describe three instruments appropriate for collection of data pertinent to the hypothesis or question. For each instrument selected, the description will include:

(a) the name, publisher, and cost;
(b) a description of the instrument;
(c) validity and reliability data;
(d) the type of subjects for whom the instrument is appropriate;
(e) instrument administration requirements;
(f) training requirements for scoring and interpretation of resulting data; and
(g) a synopsis of reviews.

Based on these descriptions, indicate which test is most acceptable for your "study," and why.

(See Performance Criteria, p. 141.)

Selection of Measuring Instruments

Enablers

After reading chapter 5, you should be able to:

Validity

1. Define or describe content validity.
2. Define or describe construct validity.
3. Define or describe concurrent validity.
4. List the procedures for determining concurrent validity by establishing relationship.
5. Define or describe predictive validity.
6. List the procedures for determining predictive validity.

Reliability

7. Define or describe reliability.
8. List the procedures for determining test-retest reliability.
9. List the procedures for determining equivalent-forms reliability.
10. List the procedures for determining split-half reliability.
11. Define or describe rationale equivalence reliability.
12. Explain the difference between interscorer and intrascorer reliability.
13. Define or describe standard error of measurement.

Types of Measuring Instruments

14. Describe the purpose of an achievement test; that is, describe what an achievement test measures.
15. Describe the purpose of each of the following types of nonprojective instruments:
    (a) personality inventories
    (b) attitude scales
    (c) tests of creativity
    (d) interest inventories
16. Describe the purpose of aptitude tests.

Selection of a Test

17. State the two most important guidelines, or rules, for test selection.
18. Identify and briefly describe three sources of test information.

19. List, in order of importance, the factors that should be considered in selecting one test from a number of alternatives.

Test Administration

20. List three guidelines for test administration.

Purpose and Process

All research studies involve data collection. Since all studies are designed to either test hypotheses or answer questions, they all require data with which to do so. Most studies use some sort of data collection instrument, often a published, standardized instrument. Actually, there are three major ways to collect data: (1) administer a standardized instrument, (2) administer a self-developed instrument, or (3) record naturally available data (such as grade point averages and absenteeism rates). For several good reasons, this chapter will be concerned only with the selection of published, standardized tests. Collection of available data, requiring a minimum of effort, sounds very attractive. There are not very many studies, however, for which this type of data is appropriate. Even when it is appropriate, that is, when it can be employed to test the intended hypothesis or answer the desired question, there are problems inherent in this type of data. For example, the same grade does not necessarily represent the same level of achievement, even in two different schools in the same system. Developing an instrument for a particular study also has several major drawbacks. The development of a "good" instrument requires considerable time, effort, *and* skill. Total time for execution of a study can be greatly increased if instrument development is involved. Also, training at least equivalent to a course in measurement is necessary in order to acquire the skills needed for good instrument development.[1]

On the positive side, the time it takes to select an appropriate standardized instrument is invariably less than the time it takes to develop an instrument that measures the same thing. Further, standardized instruments are developed by experts who possess the necessary skills. From a research point of view, an additional advantage of using a standardized instrument is that results from different studies using the same instrument can be compared. Suppose, for example, that two separate studies were conducted to determine which method of teaching algebra results in higher final achievement, method A or method B. Suppose further that study 1 utilized a self-developed test of algebra achievement and study 2 used a standardized test of algebra achievement. Now if study 1 found no difference between methods A and B, but study 2 found method B to be superior, interpretation of these conflicting results would be difficult. It might be that the two tests were measuring different abilities, for example, application of formulas versus word-problem solving. It might also be that the test used in study 1 was inadequately constructed. In any event, it would be difficult to distinguish differences due to the teaching method and differences due to the test used.

---

1. The nature of descriptive research often necessitates the development of instruments for particular studies. Guidelines for the development of certain types of instruments, such as questionnaires, will be presented in chapter 7.

Finally, use of a standardized instrument facilitates replication of a study by an independent researcher.

There are thousands of standardized instruments available which yield a wide variety of data for a wide variety of purposes. Major areas for which numerous measuring instruments have been developed include achievement, personality, intelligence, and aptitude. Each of these can in turn be further divided into many subcategories. Personality instruments, for example, can be classified as non-projective or projective; nonprojective instruments include measures of attitude and interest. Selection of an instrument for a particular research purpose involves identification and selection of the most appropriate one from among alternatives; a researcher does not find *an* instrument suited for his or her study but rather selects the *best* one of those that are available. The selection process involves determination of the most appropriate type of instrument, for example, reading comprehension, and then a comparative analysis of available tests of that type. Therefore, in order to intelligently select an instrument, a researcher must be familiar with the wide variety of types of instruments that exist and must also be knowledgeable concerning the criteria which should be applied in selecting one from among alternatives.

Characteristics of a Standardized Test

As you may have noticed, the word "test" has thus far been carefully avoided. This is because "test" has a very narrow connotation for many people. A test is not necessarily a written set of questions to which an individual responds in order to determine whether he or she "passes." A more inclusive definition of a test is . . . a means of measuring the knowledge, skill, feeling, intelligence, or aptitude of an individual or group. Tests produce numerical scores that can be used to identify, classify, or evaluate test takers. In addition, there are a number of characteristics shared by standardized tests. While these characteristics are desirable for all tests, they are much more likely to be in evidence for a standardized test. Regardless of the type of test being sought, there are certain kinds of information that should be available about any standardized test. This information, or lack of it, forms the basis for test selection.

Standardized tests are typically developed by experts and are therefore well constructed. Individual test items are analyzed and revised until they meet given standards of quality. Directions for administering, scoring, and interpreting a standardized test are carefully specified. One resulting characteristic of a standard-ized test is referred to as objectivity. In essence, test objectivity means that an individual's score is the same, or essentially the same, regardless of who is doing the scoring. Another major characteristic of standardized tests is the existence of validity and reliability data. Validity is the most important quality of any test. Validity is concerned with what a test measures and for whom it is appropriate; reliability refers to the consistency with which a test measures whatever it measures. Because of their importance, these two concepts will be discussed in considerable detail later in this section.

Specification of conditions of administration is a very important characteristic of a standardized test. This insures that if directions are carefully followed, the test will always be administered the same way and will always yield the same kind of data. If directions are carefully spelled out, even a beginning researcher should be able to properly administer most tests. The directions usually include instructions to be read to the test takers, restrictions on time, if any, and guidelines concerning the amount and nature of communication permitted between the test administrator and the test takers. Last, but not least, standardized tests generally include directions for scoring and guidelines for interpretation of scores. Directions for scoring include specifications such as the criteria for acceptable responses, when such are appropriate, the number of points to be assigned to various responses, and the procedure for computing total scores. Guidelines for test score interpretation generally include a table of norms. In fact, the availability of normative data is part of the essence of standardization. Typically, a test is administered to a large number of appropriately defined individuals, and resulting test scores are analyzed. A table of norms presents raw scores and one or more equivalent transformations, such as corresponding percentile ranks, which facilitate interpretation of an individual's score with respect to the performance of the group. Since researchers generally work with raw scores, this type of information is generally of more value to other consumer groups such as public school personnel.

As stated previously, the most important characteristic of a standardized test, or any test for that matter, is validity. Validity is totally indispensable; there is no quality or virtue of a test that can compensate for inadequate validity.

Validity

The most simplistic definition of validity is that it is the degree to which a test measures what it is supposed to measure. A common misconception is that a test is, or is not, valid. A test is not valid per se; it is valid for a particular purpose and for a particular group. The question is not "valid or invalid" but rather "valid for what and for whom?" A valid test of biology achievement is not very likely to be a valid personality test. It would be obvious to almost anyone looking at a test of biology achievement that the test did not measure any aspect of personality. It would probably not be quite as evident whether the test was a valid measure of biology facts or biology principles, if either. With respect to the "for whom" aspect of validity, a test which is a valid measure of vocabulary for high school students is certainly not a valid measure for second graders. Again, this would undoubtedly be self-evident to anyone examining a high school-level vocabulary test. It might not be as evident whether the test was valid for both ninth graders and seniors, if either. To further clarify the concept of valid "for what and for whom," let us apply the concept of validity to teaching. In general, a valid teacher is one who teaches whatever he or she is supposed to teach (or, if you prefer, whose students learn what they are supposed to learn!). But a teacher, no matter how outstanding, is not valid per se. A teacher is valid for a particular purpose, that is, a particular area of instruction, and a particular age or grade level. A valid kindergarten teacher is not very likely also to be a valid high school teacher, and a valid high school trigonometry teacher is not very likely also to be a valid high school physical education teacher. While the above analogy is admittedly loose, the concept it illustrates is important.

It is the "valid for whom" concern that makes the description of the norm group so important. Only to the degree that persons in the norm group are like the persons to whom we wish to administer the test can proper interpretation of results be made. Twenty-year-old achievement norms are not likely to be appropriate for students in the 1980s. The usefulness of norms based on a sample of 50,000 upper-middle-class high school students in the Midwest is certainly questionable if the test is to be administered to inner-city students in Boston. And so forth. Of course even an "ideal" norm group with a cast of thousands is not going to be *entirely* appropriate in any situation. There are just too many variables and student characteristics that might affect results. Thus care must always be taken in selecting a test and interpreting results. But if information concerning the norm group is insufficient or if the information given indicates any major way in which the norm group is inappropriate, then every effort must be made to locate a more suitable test. If none is available, then the shortcomings must be seriously considered when results are interpreted.

Since tests are designed for a variety of purposes, and since validity can be evaluated only in terms of purpose, it is not surprising that there are several different types of validity: content, construct, concurrent, and predictive. Because of the different ways in which they are determined, they are classified as either logical or empirical validity. Logical validity includes content validity and is so named because validity is determined primarily through judgment. Empirical validity includes concurrent and predictive validity and is so named because in each case validity is determined by relating performance on a test to performance on another criterion. Empirical validity is determined in a more objective manner. Assessment of construct validity involves both judgment and external criteria. For any given test it is important to seek evidence concerning the appropriate type of validity, given the intended purpose or purposes of the test.

Content Validity

Content validity is the degree to which a test measures an intended content area. Content validity requires both item validity and sampling validity. *Item validity* is concerned with whether the test items represent measurement in the intended content area, and *sampling validity* is concerned with how well the test samples the total content area. A test designed to measure knowledge of biology facts might have good item validity, because all the items do indeed deal with biology facts, but might have poor sampling validity, for example, if all the items deal only with vertebrates. A test with good content validity adequately samples the appropriate content area. This is important because we cannot possibly measure each and every aspect of a certain content area; the required test would be "humongously" long. And yet we do wish to make inferences about performance in the entire content area based on performance on the items included in the test. Such inferences are only possible if the test items adequately sample the domain of possible items. This sampling is of course easier for well-defined areas such as spelling than for fuzzier content areas such as social studies.

The term "face validity" is sometimes used in describing tests. While its meaning is somewhat ambiguous, basically *face validity* refers to the degree to which a test *appears* to measure what it purports to measure. While determining face validity is not a psychometrically sound way of estimating validity, the process is sometimes used as an initial screening procedure in test selection.

Content validity is of prime importance for achievement tests. A test score cannot accurately reflect a student's achievement if it does not measure what the student was supposed to learn. While this seems obvious, content validity has been a problem in a number of research studies. Many studies are designed to compare the effectiveness of two (or more) different ways of teaching the same thing. Effectiveness is often defined in terms of final achievement of the treatment groups as measured by a test. It is sometimes the case that the test used is more content valid for one of the groups than for the other. When this happens, final achievement differences may be at least partially attributable to the test used and not just to the teaching methods. This phenomenon frequently occurs when an "innovative" approach is compared to a traditional approach. The different approaches often emphasize different areas of content. A classic case is the early studies that compared the "new" math with the "old" math. These studies invariably found no achievement differences between students learning under the two approaches. The problem was that the "new" math was emphasizing concepts and principles while the achievement tests were emphasizing computational skill. When tests were developed which contained an adequate sampling of items measuring concepts and principles, studies began to find that the two approaches to teaching math resulted in essentially equal computational ability, but that the "new" math resulted in better conceptual understanding. The moral of the story is—in a study which compares treatments and measures achievement, take care that the test measures what the students learned in the treatments, that is, be sure that the test is valid *for your study* and *for your subjects*.

Content validity is determined by expert judgment. There is no formula by which it can be computed and there is no way to express it quantitatively. Usually experts in the area covered by the test are asked to assess its content validity. These experts carefully examine all items on the test and make a judgment concerning how well they represent the intended content area; this judgment is based on whether all subareas have been included, and in the correct proportions. In other words, a comparison is made between what ought to be included in the test, given its intended purpose, and what is actually included. When selecting a test for a research study, the researcher assumes the role of "expert" and determines whether the test is content valid for her or his study. The researcher compares what will be taught in the study with what is measured by the test.

Construct Validity

Construct validity is the degree to which a test measures an intended hypothetical construct. A construct is a nonobservable trait, such as intelligence, which explains behavior. You cannot see a construct, you can only observe its effect. In fact, constructs were "invented" to explain behavior. We cannot prove they exist; we cannot perform brain surgery on a person and "see" his intelligence. Constructs, however, do an amazingly good job of explaining certain differences between individuals. For example, it was always observed that some students learn faster than others, learn more, and retain longer. To explain these differences, a theory of intelligence was developed, and it was hypothesized that there is something called intelligence which is related to learning and which everyone possesses to a greater or lesser degree. Tests were developed designed to measure how much of it a person has. As it happens, students whose scores indicate that they have a "lot" of it, that is, they have high IQs, tend to do better in school and other learning environments. Other constructs which have been hypothesized to exist, and for which tests have been developed, include anxiety, creativity, and curiosity.

Research studies that involve a construct, either as an independent or a dependent variable, are only valid to the extent that the measure of the construct involved is valid. Anxiety, for example, can be an independent or a dependent variable. A study might be designed to determine whether high-anxiety students perform better on difficult tasks than low-anxiety students. A test of anxiety would need to be administered to the students in the study in order to classify them as "high-anxiety" or "low-anxiety." Another study might be designed to determine whether programmed instruction results in lower anxiety among slow learners than traditional instruction. A test of anxiety would need to be administered to both groups at the conclusion of the study. In both cases, the validity of the findings would be a direct function of the validity of the anxiety test used. If the test did not really measure anxiety, conclusions based on a study that utilized it would be meaningless. When selecting a test of a given construct, the researcher must look for and critically evaluate evidence presented related to the construct validity of the instrument.

The process of validating a test of a construct is by no means an easy task. Basically, it involves testing hypotheses deduced from a theory concerning the construct. If, for example, a theory of anxiety hypothesized that high-anxiety persons will work longer on a problem than low-anxiety persons, then if persons who scored high on the test under consideration did indeed work longer on a subsequent task this would be evidence to support the construct validity of the test. Of course if the high-anxiety persons did not, as hypothesized, work longer, then it would not necessarily mean that the test did not measure anxiety; the hypotheses related to the behavior of high-anxiety persons might be incorrect. Generally, a number of independent studies are required to establish the credibility of a test of a construct.

Concurrent Validity

Concurrent validity is the degree to which the scores on a test are related to the scores on another, already established, test administered at the same time, or to some other valid criterion available at the same time. Often, a test is developed that claims to do the same job as some other tests, easier or faster. If this is shown to be the case, that is, the concurrent validity of the new test is established, in most cases the new test will be utilized instead of the other tests. A paper-and-pencil test that does the same job as a performance test, or a short test that measures the same behaviors as a longer test, would certainly be preferred, especially in a research study.

Concurrent validity is determined by establishing relationship or discrimination. The relationship method involves determining the relationship between scores on the test and scores on some other established test or criterion (e.g., GPA). In this case, the steps involved in determining concurrent validity are as follows:

1. Administer the new test to a defined group of individuals.

2. Administer a previously established, valid test (or acquire such scores if already available).

3. Correlate the two sets of scores.

The resulting number, or validity coefficient, indicates the concurrent validity of the new test; if the coefficient is high, the test has good concurrent validity. Suppose, for example, that Professor Jeenyus developed a group test of intelligence for children which took only five minutes to administer. If scores on this test did indeed correlate highly with scores on the Wechsler Intelligence Scale for Children (which must be administered to one child at a time and takes at least an hour), then Professor Jeenyus' test would definitely be preferable in a great many situations. The discrimination method of establishing concurrent validity involves determining whether test scores can be used to discriminate between persons who possess a certain characteristic and those who do not, or those who possess it to a greater degree. For example, a test of mental adjustment would have concurrent validity if scores resulting from it could be used to correctly classify institutionalized and noninstitutionalized persons.

When selecting a test for a given research purpose, you will usually be seeking a test that measures what you wish in the most efficient manner. If you select a shorter or more convenient test that allegedly measures the desired behavior, be careful that concurrent validity has been established using a valid criterion.

Predictive Validity

Predictive validity is the degree to which a test can predict how well an individual will do in a future situation. An algebra aptitude test that has high predictive validity will fairly accurately predict which students will do well in algebra and which students will not. Predictive validity is extremely important for tests that are used to classify or select individuals. An example with which that you are all too familiar is the use of Graduate Record Examination (GRE) scores to select students for admission to graduate school. Many graduate schools require a certain minimum score for admission, often 1,000, in the belief that students who achieve that score have a higher probability of succeeding in graduate school. The predictive validity of the GRE has been the subject of many research studies. Results seem to indicate that the GRE has higher predictive validity for certain areas of graduate study than for others. For example, while it appears to have satisfactory predictive validity for predicting success in graduate studies in English, its validity in predicting success in an art education program appears to be questionable. Another example that illustrates the critical importance of predictive validity is the use of tests to determine which students should be assigned to special education classes. The decision to remove a child from the normal educational environment, and to place him or her in a special class, is a serious one. In this situation it is imperative that the decision be based on the results of valid measures.

As the GRE example illustrates, the predictive validity of a given instrument varies with a number of factors. The predictive validity of an instrument may vary depending upon such factors as the curriculum involved, textbooks used, and geographic location. The Mindboggling Algebra Aptitude Test, for example, may predict achievement better in courses using the Brainscrambling Algebra I text than in courses using other texts. Thus, if a test is to be used for prediction, it is important to compare the description of the manner in which it was validated with the situation in which it is to be used.

No test, of course, has perfect predictive validity. Therefore, predictions based on the scores of any test will be imperfect. However, predictions based on a combination of several test scores will invariably be more accurate than predictions based on the scores of any one test. Therefore, when important classification or selection decisions are to be made, they should be based on data from more than one indicator. For example, we can use high school grade point average (GPA) to predict college GPA at the end of the freshman year. We can also use scholastic aptitude score or rank in graduating class to predict college GPA. A prediction based on all three variables, however, will be more accurate than a prediction based on any one or two of them.

The predictive validity of a test is determined by establishing the relationship between scores on the test and some measure of success in the situation of interest. The test used to predict success is referred to as the predictor, and the behavior predicted is referred to as the criterion. In establishing the predictive validity of a test, the first step is to identify and carefully define the criterion. The criterion selected must be a valid measure of the behavior to be predicted. For example, if we wished to establish the predictive validity of an algebra aptitude test, final examination scores at the completion of a course in algebra might be considered a valid criterion, but number of days absent during the course probably would not. As another example, if we were interested in establishing the predictive validity of a given test for predicting success in college, grade point average at the end of the first year would probably be considered a valid criterion, but number of extracurricular activities in which the student participated probably would not. A word of caution is in order related to the concept of base rate. Base rate is the proportion of individuals who can be expected to meet a given criterion. You should avoid trying to predict a criterion for which the base rate is very high or very low. For example, suppose we wished to establish the predictive validity of a test designed to predict who will graduate summa cum laude. Since a very, very small percentage of students do so, all we would have to do is predict that no one would and we would be correct in almost every case! A test could hardly do better and would therefore be of very limited value.

Once the criterion has been identified and defined, the procedure for determining predictive validity is as follows:

1. Administer the test, the predictor variable.
2. Wait until the behavior to be predicted, the criterion variable, occurs.
3. Obtain measures of the criterion.
4. Correlate the two sets of scores.

The resulting number, or validity coefficient, indicates the predictive validity of the test; if the coefficient is high, the test has good predictive validity. For example, suppose we wished to determine the predictive validity of a physics aptitude test. First we would administer the test to a large group of potential physics students. Then we would wait until the students had completed a course in physics and would obtain a measure of their success, for example, final exam scores. The correlation between the two sets of scores would determine the predictive validity of the test; if the resulting correlation coefficient was high, the test would have high predictive validity.

As mentioned previously, often a combination of predictors is used to predict a criterion. In this case a prediction equation may be developed. A person's scores on each of a number of tests are inserted into the equation and her or his future performance is predicted. In this case the validity of the equation should be reestablished through cross-validation. Cross-validation involves administering the predictor tests to a different sample from the same population and developing a new equation. Of course, even if only one predictor test is involved, it is a good idea to determine predictive validity for more than just one sample of individuals. In other words, the predictive validity of a test should be reconfirmed.

You may have noticed (if you had a high score on the GRE!) that the procedures for determining concurrent validity and predictive validity are very similar. The major difference is in terms of when the criterion measure is administered. In establishing concurrent validity, it is administered at the same time as the predictor, or within a relatively short period of time; in establishing predictive validity, one usually has to wait for a much longer period of time to pass before criterion data can be collected. Occasionally, concurrent validity is substituted for predictive validity in order to save time and to eliminate the problems of keeping track of subjects. For example, we might administer a mechanical aptitude test to a group of mechanics and correlate scores on the test with some measure of their skill. The problem with this approach is that we would be dealing only with those who made it! Persons for whom the test would have predicted a low probability of success would not become mechanics. In other words, most of the persons in the sample would be persons for whom the test would have predicted success. Therefore, the resulting validity coefficient would probably be an underestimate of the predictive validity of the test.

In the discussion of both concurrent and predictive validity there was a statement to the effect that if the resulting coefficient is high, the test has good validity. You may have wondered, "How high is high?" The question of how high the coefficient must be in order to be considered "good" is not easy to answer. There is no magic number that a coefficient should reach. In general, it is a comparative matter. A coefficient of .50 might be acceptable if there is only one test available designed to predict a given criterion; on the other hand, a coefficient of .50 might be inadequate if there are other tests available with higher coefficients.

Closely related to the concept of validity is the concept of reliability, which deals with the question of score consistency.

Reliability

In everyday English, reliability means dependability, or trustworthiness. The term means essentially the same thing with respect to measurement. Basically, reliability is the degree to which a test consistently measures whatever it measures. The more reliable a test is, the more confidence we can have that the scores obtained from the administration of the test are essentially the same scores that would be obtained if the test were readministered. An unreliable test is essentially useless; if a test is unreliable then scores for a given sample would be expected to be different every time the test were administered. If an intelligence test was unreliable, for example, then a student scoring an IQ of 120 today might score an IQ of 140 tomorrow, and a 95 the day after tomorrow. If the test was reliable, and if the student's IQ was 110, then we would not expect his or her score to flucuate too greatly from testing to testing; a score of 105 would not be unusual, but a score of 145 would be very unlikely.

Reliability is expressed numerically, usually as a coefficient; a high coefficient indicates high reliability. If a test were perfectly reliable, the coefficient would be 1.00; this would mean that a student's score perfectly reflected her or his true status with respect to the variable being measured. However, alas and alack, no test is perfectly reliable. Scores are invariably affected by errors of measurement resulting from a variety of causes. High reliability indicates minimum error variance; if a test has high reliability then the effect of errors of measurement have been reduced. Errors of measurement affect scores in a random fashion; some scores may be increased while others are decreased. Errors of measurement can be caused by characteristics of the test itself (ambiguous test items, for example, that some students just happen to interpret correctly), by conditions of administration (directions not properly followed, for example), by the current status of the persons taking the test (some may be tired, others unmotivated), or by a combination of any of the above. High reliability indicates that these sources of error have been eliminated as much as possible.

Errors of measurement that affect reliability are random errors; systematic or constant errors affect validity. If an achievement test was too dificult for a given group of students, all scores would be systematically lowered; the test would have low validity for that group (remember "valid for whom"). The test might, however, yield consistent scores, i.e. might be reliable; in other words, the scores might be systematically lowered in the same way every time. A given student whose "true" achievement score was 80 and who scored 60 on the test (invalidity) might score 60 every time he took the test (reliability). This illustrates an interesting relationship between validity and reliability: a valid test is always reliable but a reliable test is not necessarily valid. In other words, if a test is measuring what it is supposed to be measuring, it will be reliable and do so every time, but a reliable test can consistently measure the wrong thing and be invalid! Suppose a test that purported to measure social studies concepts really measured facts. It would not be a valid measure of concepts but it could certainly measure the facts very consistently.

All this talk about error might lead you to believe that measurement in education is pretty sloppy and imprecise to say the least. Actually it's not as bad as it may sound. There are many tests that measure intended traits quite accurately. In fact, as Nunnally has pointed out, measurement in other areas of science often involves as much, if not more, random error.[2] To use his example, the measurement of blood pressure, a physiological trait, is far less reliable than most psychological measures. There are any number of "conditions of the moment" which may temporarily affect blood pressure—joy, anger, fear, and anxiety, to name a few. Thus, a person's blood pressure reading is also the result of a combination of "true" blood pressure and error.

Reliability is much easier to assess than validity. There are a number of different types of reliability; each is determined in a different manner and each deals with a different kind of consistency. Test-retest, equivalent-forms, and

---

2. Nunnally, JC. *Psychometric theory.* New York: McGraw-Hill, 1967.

split-half reliability are all determined through correlation; rationale equivalence reliability is established by determining how each item on a test relates to all other items on the test and to the total test.

Test-Retest Reliability

Test-retest reliability is the degree to which scores are consistent over time. It indicates score variation that occurs from testing session to testing session as a result of errors of measurement. In other words, we are interested in evidence that the score a person obtains on a test at some moment in time is the same score, or close to the same score, that the person would get if the test were administered some other time. We want to know how consistently the test measures whatever it measures. This type of reliability is especially important for tests used as predictors, aptitude tests, for example. Such a test would not really be too helpful if it indicated a different aptitude level each time it was given.

Determination of test-retest reliability is appropriate when alternate (equivalent) forms of a test are not available, and when it is unlikely that persons taking the test the second time will remember responses made on the test the first time. Test takers are more likely to remember items from a test with a lot of history facts, for example, than from a test with algebra problems. The procedure for determining test-retest reliability is basically quite simple:

1. Administer the test to an appropriate group.

2. After some time has passed, say a week, administer the *same test* to the *same group.*

3. Correlate the two sets of scores.

If the resulting coefficient, referred to as the *coefficient of stability,* is high, the test has good test-retest reliability. A major problem with this type of reliability is the difficulty of knowing how much time should elapse between the two testing sessions. If the interval is too short, the chances of students' remembering responses made on the test the first time are increased, and the estimate of reliability tends to be artificially high. If the interval is too long, students' ability to do well on the test may increase due to intervening learning or maturation, and the estimate of reliability tends to be artificially low.

Thus, when test-retest information is given concerning a test, the time interval between testings should be given as well as the actual coefficient. Although it is difficult to say precisely what, in general, the ideal time interval should be, one day will generally be too short and one month too long. The problems associated with test-retest reliability are taken care of by equivalent-forms reliability.

Equivalent-Forms Reliability

Equivalent forms of a test are two tests that are identical in every way except for the actual items included. The two forms measure the same variable, have the same number of items, the same structure, the same difficulty level, and the same directions for administration, scoring, and interpretation. In fact, if the same group takes both tests, the average score as well as the degree of score variability should be essentially the same on both tests. Only the specific items are not the same, although they do measure the same traits, or objectives. In essence, we are selecting, or sampling, different items from the same behavior domain. We are interested in whether scores depend upon the particular set of items selected or whether performance on one set of items is generalizable to other sets. If items are well selected, and if each set adequately represents the domain of interest, the latter should be true.

Equivalent-forms reliability, also referred to as alternate-forms reliability, indicates score variation that occurs from form to form, and is appropriate when it is likely that test takers will recall responses made during the first session and, of course, when two different forms of a test are available. When alternate forms are available, it is important to know the equivalent-forms reliability; it is reassuring to know that a person's score will not be greatly affected by which form is administered. Also, sometimes in research studies two forms of a test are administered to the same group, one as a pretest and the other as a posttest. It is crucial, if the effects of the intervening activities are to be validly assessed, that the two tests be measuring essentially the same things.

The procedure for determining equivalent-forms reliability is very similar to that for determining test-retest reliability:

1. Administer one form of the test to an appropriate group.

2. At the same session, or shortly thereafter, administer the *second form* of the test to the *same group*.

3. Correlate the two sets of scores.

If the resulting coefficient (referred to as the *coefficient of equivalence*) is high, the test has good equivalent-forms reliability. If the two forms of the test are administered at two different times (the best of all possible worlds!) the resulting coefficient is referred to as the *coefficient of stability and equivalence*. In essence, this approach represents a combination of test-retest and equivalent-forms reliability and thus assesses stability of scores over time as well as the generalizability of the sets of items. Since more sources of measurement error are possible than with either method alone, the resulting coefficient is likely to be somewhat lower. Thus the coefficient of stability and equivalence represents a conservative estimate of reliability.

Equivalent-forms reliability is the single most acceptable and most commonly used estimate of reliability for most tests used in research. The major problem involved with this method of estimating reliability is the difficulty of constructing two forms that are essentially equivalent. Lack of equivalence is a source of measurement error. Even though equivalent-forms reliability is considered to be the best estimate of reliability, it is not always feasible to administer two different forms of the same test, or even the same test twice. Imagine telling your students that they had to take two final examinations! Imagine someone telling *you* to take the GRE or SAT twice! Fortunately, there are other methods of estimating reliability that require administering a test only once.

Split-Half Reliability

Internal consistency reliability, as the name implies, is a type of reliability which is based on the internal consistency of the test. A common type of internal consistency reliability is referred to as split-half reliability. Since split-half reliability procedures require only one administration of a test, certain sources of errors of measurement are eliminated, such as differences in testing conditions, which can occur in establishing test-retest reliability. Split-half reliability is especially appropriate when a test is very long.

The procedure for determining split-half reliability is as follows:

1. Administer the *total* test to a group.

2. Divide the test into two comparable halves, or subtests—the most common approach is to include all odd items in one half and all even items in the other half.

3. Compute each subject's score on the two halves—each subject will consequently have two scores, a score for the odd items and a score for the even items.

4. Correlate the two sets of scores.

If the coefficient is high, the test has good split-half reliability. A number of logical and statistical methods can be used to divide a test in half, random selection of half of the items, for example. In reality, the odd-even strategy, however, is most often used. Actually, this approach works out rather well regardless of how a test is organized. Suppose, for example, a test is a 20-item power test and the items get progressively more difficult. Items 1, 3, 5, 7, 9, 11, 13, 15, 17, and 19 as a group should be approximately as difficult as items 2, 4, 6, 8, 10, 12, 14, 16, 18, and 20. Items 1 and 2 will be easy, 3 and 4 will be more difficult, and so forth. Or, suppose a test is organized by topic so that items 1–10 deal with circles, and items 11–20 deal with quadrilaterals. In this case the odd items will contain items on circles and quadrilaterals and so will the even items. Thus, regardless of how the test is organized, an odd-even split should produce essentially equivalent halves. In fact, what we are doing is artificially creating two equivalent forms of a test and computing equivalent-forms reliability; the two equivalent forms just happen to be in the same test. Thus the label "internal consistency reliability."

Since longer tests tend to be more reliable, and since split-half reliability represents the reliability of a test only half as long as the actual test, a correction formula must be applied to the coefficient. The correction formula which is used is the Spearman-Brown prophecy formula. For example, suppose the split-half reliability coefficient for a 50-item test were .80. The .80 would be based on the correlation between scores on 25 even items and 25 odd items and would therefore be an estimate of the reliability of a 25-item test, not a 50-item test. The Spearman-Brown formula would need to be applied to estimate the reliability (r) of the 50-item test. The formula is a very simple one, even for those of you who are not mathematically inclined:

$$r_{\text{total test}} = \frac{2r_{\text{split half}}}{1 + r_{\text{split half}}}$$

Applying the formula to our example:

$$r_{\text{total test}} = \frac{2\,(.80)}{1 + .80} = \frac{1.60}{1.80} = .89$$

Thus, the split-half estimate of .80 was corrected to an estimate of .89. One problem with the correction formula is that it tends to give a higher estimate of reliability than would be obtained using other procedures. Another approach to determining internal consistency is the method of rationale equivalence.

Rationale Equivalence Reliability

Rationale equivalence reliability is not established through correlation but rather estimates internal consistency by determining how all items on a test relate to all other items and to the total test. Rationale equivalence reliability is determined through application of one of the Kuder-Richardson formulas, usually formula 20 or 21 (KR-20 or KR-21). Application of a Kuder-Richardson formula results in an estimate of reliability that is essentially equivalent to the average of the split-half reliabilities computed for all possible halves. Use of formula 21 requires less time than any other method of estimating reliability. Its application also usually results in a more conservative estimate of reliability, especially if more than one trait is being measured.

The formula is as follows:

$$r_{total\ test} = \frac{(K)\ (SD^2) - \bar{X}\ (K - \bar{X})}{(SD^2)\ (K - 1)}$$

where

$$K = \text{the number of items in the test}$$
$$SD = \text{the standard deviation of the scores}$$
$$\bar{X} = \text{the mean of the scores}$$

In a later chapter you will learn how to compute the mean and standard deviation of a set of scores. For the moment, let it suffice to say that the mean ($\bar{X}$) is the average score on the test for the group that took it and the standard deviation (SD) is an indication of the amount of score variability, or how spread out the scores are. For example, assume that you have administered a 50-item test and have calculated the mean to be 40 ($\bar{X} = 40$) and the standard deviation to be 4 ($SD = 4$). The reliability of the test (which in this example turns out to be not too hot!) would be calculated as follows:

$$r_{total\ test} = \frac{(50)\ (4^2) - 40\ (50 - 40)}{(4^2)\ (50 - 1)}$$

$$= \frac{(50)\ (16) - 40\ (10)}{(16)\ (49)} = \frac{800 - 400}{784} = \frac{400}{784} = .51$$

This formula should be more comprehensible to you after you have completed the Task and Enablers for chapter 12 but even at this stage the ease of application of this formula should be evident.

Figure 5.1 summarizes the methods for estimating test reliability. One (1) test administration indicates either that only one test is administered (split-half and

		Number of Different Tests	
		1	2
Number of Administration Times	1	Split-half KR-21	Equivalent forms
	2	Test-retest	Stability and equivalence

Figure 5.1.
Summary of methods for estimating reliability.

KR-21 reliability) or that two tests are administered at essentially the same time (equivalent-forms reliability). Two (2) administration times indicates a time interval exists (say a week) between the two administrations (test-retest and stability and equivalence reliability). You should keep in mind when reviewing test information that while the size of the reliability coefficient is of prime importance, the method used to calculate it should also be considered.

Scorer/Rater Reliability

There are other situations for which reliability must be investigated. Such situations usually occur when the scoring of tests involves subjectivity, such as with essay tests, short-answer tests involving more than a one-word response, rating scales, and observation instruments. In such situations we are concerned with interjudge (interscorer, interrater, interobserver) reliability and/or intrajudge reliability. Interjudge reliability refers to the reliability of two (or more) independent scorers; intrajudge reliability refers to the reliability of the scoring of individual scorers. Scoring and rating are sources of errors of measurement, and it is important to estimate the consistency of scorers' assessments. Estimates of interjudge or intrajudge reliability are usually obtained using correlational techniques, as have already been discussed, but can also be expressed simply as percent agreement. While such reliabilities are unfortunately usually not very good, a number of standardized instruments have been developed to the point where interjudge and intrajudge reliability appear to be relatively quite good. Validation studies involving the Flanders system for the observation of classroom verbal behavior, for example, have reported interrater and intrarater reliabilities ranging from the mid eighties (e.g., .85) to the low nineties.

Reliability Coefficients

What constitutes an acceptable level of reliability is to some degree determined by the type of test although, of course, a coefficient over .90 would be acceptable for any test. The question really is concerned with what constitutes a minimum level of acceptability. For achievement and aptitude tests, there is generally no good reason for selecting a test whose reliability is not at least .90. There are a number of achievement and aptitude tests available that report such reliabilities and it is therefore not usually necessary to settle for less. Personality measures do not typically report such high reliabilities (although certainly some do) and one would therefore be very satisfied with a reliability in the eighties and might even accept a reliability in the seventies. When tests are developed in new areas, one usually has to settle for lower reliability, at least initially. For example, tests which measure curiosity are a relatively recent addition to the testing field. One would not expect high reliabilities for these new tests at this stage of their development.

If a test is composed of several subtests, then the reliability of each subtest must be evaluated, not just the reliability of the total test. Since reliability is a function of test length, the reliability of a given subtest is typically lower than the total test reliability. Examination of subtest reliability is especially important if one or more of the subtests is going to be used in the research rather than the total test. You, as a researcher, should be a good consumer of test information. If a test manual states that "the total test reliability is .90, and all subtest reliabilities are satisfactory," you should immediately become suspicious. If subtest reliabilities are "satisfactory," the publisher will certainly want to tell you just how satisfactory they are. Most of the major, well-established tests report subtest reliabilities. Remember, test publishers are in the business of selling tests. If they omit pertinent information, it is your responsibility to be aware of such omissions and to request additional data.

Standard Error of Measurement

Reliability can also be expressed in terms of the *standard error of measurement.* This is a concept that you should be familiar with since such data are often reported for a test. Basically, the standard error of measurement is an estimate of how often you can expect errors of a given size. Thus, a small standard error of measurement indicates high reliability, and a large standard error of measurement indicates low reliability. If a test were perfectly reliable (which no test is), a person's obtained score would be his or her true score. As it is, an obtained score is an estimate of a true score. If you administered the same test over and over to the same group, the score of each individual would vary. How much variability would be present in individual scores would be a function of the test's reliability. The variability would be small for a highly reliable test (zero if the test were perfectly reliable) and large for a test with low reliability. If we could administer the test many times we could see how much variation actually occurred. Of course, realistically we can't do this; administering the same test twice to the same group is tough enough. Fortunately, it is possible to estimate this degree of variation (the standard error of measurement) using the data from the administration of a test once to a group. In other words, the standard error of measurement allows us to estimate how much difference there probably is between a person's obtained score and true score, the size of this difference being a function of the reliability of the test. We can estimate the standard error of measurement using the following simple formula:

$$SE_m = SD\sqrt{1 - r}$$

where

SE_m = standard error of measurement
SD = the standard deviation of the test scores
r = the reliability coefficient

For example, for a 25-item test we might calculate the standard deviation of a set of scores to be 5 ($SD = 5$) and the split-half reliability to be .84 ($r = .84$). In this case the standard error of measurement would be calculated as follows:

$$\begin{aligned} SE_m = SD\sqrt{1 - r} &= 5\sqrt{1 - .84} \\ &= 5\sqrt{.16} \\ &= 5(.4) \\ &= 2.0 \end{aligned}$$

As the above example illustrates, the size of the SE_m is a function of both the SD and r. Higher reliability is associated with a smaller SE_m and a smaller SD is associated with a smaller SE_m. If in the above example $r = .64$, would you expect SE_m to be larger or smaller? Right, larger, and in fact it would be 3.0. Also, if in the above example $SD = 10$, what would you expect to happen to SE_m? Right, it would be larger, 4.0 to be exact. While we prefer the SE_m to be small, indicating less error, it is impossible to say how small is "good." This is because SE_m is expressed in the same units as the test and how small is "small" is relative to the size of the test. Thus $SE_m = 5$ would be large for a 20-item test but small for a 200-item test. In our example, $SE_m = 2.0$ would be considered small.

To facilitate better interpretation of scores, some test publishers do not just present the SE_m for the total group but also give a separate SE_m for each of a number of identified subgroups.

Types of Tests

There are many different kinds of tests available and many different ways to classify them. Buros' *Mental Measurement Yearbooks* are the major source of test information for educational researchers.[3] In addition to a number of curriculum areas such as English, Mathematics, and Reading, major headings in the *Yearbooks* include: Achievement Batteries, Character and Personality, Intelligence, and Multi-Aptitude Batteries.

Achievement

Achievement tests measure the current status of individuals with respect to proficiency in given areas of knowledge or skill. Standardized achievement tests are carefully developed to include measurement of objectives common to many school systems. They measure knowledge of facts, concepts, and principles. An individual's level of achivement is compared to the norm, or average score, for his or her grade or age level. Standardized achievement tests are available for individual curriculum areas such as reading and mathematics, and also in the form of comprehensive batteries that measure achievement in several different areas. The California Achievement Test Battery, for example, is a commonly used battery which measures achievement in reading, language, and arithmetic. Depending upon such factors as the number of achievement areas included, batteries take from one hour to several days to administer.

---

3. Buros, O.K. *The eighth mental measurement yearbook.* Highland Park, N.J.: Gryphon, 1979 (the latest publication in a series which began in 1933).

Many research studies are designed to compare the effectiveness of two or more curriculum approaches or methods of instruction. Effectiveness is usually defined in terms of pupil achievement at the end of the study. Sometimes, studies are designed to investigate various aspects of remedial instruction. In such studies diagnostic instruments are occasionally utilized. A diagnostic test is a type of achievement test yielding multiple scores for each area of achievement; these scores facilitate identification of specific areas of deficiency. The Stanford Diagnostic Reading Test is an example of a commonly used diagnostic instrument.

Character and Personality

Tests of character and personality are designed to measure characteristics of individuals along a number of dimensions and to assess feelings and attitudes toward self, others, and a variety of other activities, institutions, and situations. They may well be the most used tests in educational research. Such tests come in many different varieties (performance versus paper and pencil, individual versus group, power versus speed), and there are tests to measure almost any aspect of personality you can think of. Although they can be classified many ways, a logical initial differentiation, the one used by the *Yearbooks,* is to categorize such tests as nonprojective or projective.

Nonprojective Tests

Most tests of character and personality are nonprojective, or self-report, measures; such tests ask an individual to respond to a series of questions or statements. Nonprojective tests are frequently used in descriptive studies (to describe, for example, the personality structure of various groups such as high school dropouts), correlational studies (to determine, for example, relationships between various personality traits and other variables such as achievement), and experimental studies (to investigate, for example, the comparative effectiveness of different instructional methods for different personality types).

Personality Inventories Personality inventories present lists of questions or statements describing behaviors characteristic of certain personality traits, and the individual is asked to indicate (yes, no, undecided) whether the statement describes him or her. Some inventories are presented as checklists; the individual simply checks items that characterize him or her. An individual's score is based on the number of responses characteristic of the trait being measured. An introvert, for example, would be expected to respond "yes" to the statement "Reading is one of my favorite pastimes" and "no" to the statement "I love large parties." Inventories may be specific and measure only one trait, such as introversion-extroversion, or may be general and measure a number of traits. Since general inventories measure more than one trait at the same time, they are typically relatively long and take at least an hour to complete.

General inventories frequently used in educational research studies include the following: Adjective Check List, California Psychological Inventory, Edwards Personal Preference Schedule, Minnesota Multiphasic Personality Inventory, Mooney

Problem Check List, and the Sixteen Personality Factor Questionnaire. The Minnesota Multiphasic Personality Inventory alone has been utilized in hundreds of educational research studies.

One serious problem involved with the use of self-report inventories is the problem of accurate responses. Personality scores are only valid to the degree that the respondent is honest and selects responses that truly characterize him or her. A common phenomenon is the concept of a response set, or the tendency of an individual to continually respond in a given way. A common response set is the tendency of an individual to select the responses that he or she believes are the most socially acceptable. Whether response sets result from conscious or unconscious motivations, they can seriously distort an appraisal of the individual's personality structure. If a large proportion of a research sample is not responding honestly, results of the study may be essentially meaningless. Therefore, in studies utilizing such tests, every effort should be made to increase the likelihood that valid test results are obtained.

Attitude Scales　Attitude scales attempt to determine what an individual believes, perceives, or feels. Attitudes can be measured toward self, others, and a variety of other activities, institutions, and situations. There are four basic types of attitude scales: Likert scales, semantic differential scales, Thurstone scales, and Guttman scales. The first two are used more often but you should at least be aware of the existence of the other two.

A *Likert scale* asks an individual to respond to a series of statements by indicating whether she or he strongly agrees (SA), agrees (A), is undecided (U), disagrees (D), or strongly disagrees (SD) with each statement.[4] Each response is associated with a point value, and an individual's score is determined by summing the point values for each statement. For example, the following point values might be assigned to responses to positive statements: SA = 5, A = 4, U = 3, D = 2, SD = 1. For negative statements, the point values would be reversed, that is, SA = 1, A = 2, and so on. An example of a positive statement might be "Short people are entitled to the same job opportunities as tall people." A high point value on a positively stated item would indicate a positive attitude and a high total score on the test would be indicative of a positive attitude.

A *semantic differential scale* asks an individual to give a quantitative rating to the subject of the attitude scale on a number of bipolar adjectives such as good-bad, friendly-unfriendly, positive-negative. The respondent indicates the point on the continuum between the extremes that represents her or his attitude. Based on their research, the original developers of this approach reported that most adjective pairs represent one of three dimensions which they labeled evaluation (e.g., good-bad), potency (e.g., strong-weak), and activity (e.g., active-passive).[5] For example, on a scale concerning attitudes toward property taxes, the following items might be included:

---

4. Likert, R. A technique for the measurement of attitudes. *Archives of Psychology*, 1932, No. 140.

5. Osgood, C.E., Suci, G.J., & Tannenbaum, P.H. *The measurement of meaning.* Urbana: University of Illinois Press, 1957.

Necessary ___ ___ ___ ___ ___ ___ ___ Unnecessary

Fair ___ ___ ___ ___ ___ ___ ___ Unfair

In practice, however, these dimensions are frequently ignored and/or replaced by other dimensions thought to be more appropriate in a particular situation.

Each position on a continuum has an associated score value; by totalling score values for all items, it can be determined whether the respondent's attitude is positive or negative. Semantic differential scales usually have 5 to 7 intervals with a neutral attitude being assigned a score value of 0. For the above items, the score values would be as follows:

Necessary ___ ___ ___ ___ ___ ___ ___ Unnecessary
          3   2   1   0   −1   −2   −3

Fair ___ ___ ___ ___ ___ ___ ___ Unfair
     3   2   1   0   −1   −2   −3

A person who checked the first interval (i.e., 3) on both of these items would be indicating a very positive attitude toward property taxes (fat chance!).[6]

A *Thurstone scale* asks an individual to select from a list of statements that represent different points of view those with which he or she is in agreement. Each item has an associated point value between 1 and 11; point values for each item are determined by averaging the values of the items assigned by a number of "judges." An individual's attitude score is the average point value of all the statements checked by that individual.[7] A *Guttman scale* also asks respondents to agree or disagree with a number of statements. A Guttman scale, however, attempts to determine whether an attitude is unidimensional; it is unidimensional if it produces a cumulative scale. In a cumulative scale, an individual who agrees with a given statement also agrees with all related preceding statements; for example, if you agree with statement 3, you also agree with statements 2 and 1.[8]

Measures of "attitude toward self" are referred to as measures of self-concept. Measures of self-concept are used in many educational research studies, especially studies designed to investigate: (1) the relationship between self-concept and other variables such as achievement; (2) the effects of self-concept on variables such as motivation; and (3) the effects of various curricula and teaching methods on self-concept.

Rating scales are also used to measure attitudes toward others. Such scales ask an individual to rate another individual on a number of behavioral dimensions. There are two basic types of such rating scales. One type is composed of items that ask an individual to rate another on a continuum (good to bad, excellent to

---

6. For further discussion of this approach, see: Snider, J.G., & Osgood, C.E. *Semantic differential technique: A sourcebook.* Chicago: Aldine, 1969.

7. Thurstone, L.L., & Chave, E.J. *The measurement of attitude.* Chicago: The University of Chicago Press, 1929.

8. Guttman, L. The basis for scaleogram analysis. In S. Stouffer, et al. (Eds.), *Measurement and prediction.* Princeton: Princeton University Press, 1950.

poor). The second type asks the individual to rate another on a number of items by selecting the most appropriate response category (e.g., excellent, above average, average, below average, poor). Two problems associated with rating scales are referred to as the "halo effect" and the "generosity error." The halo effect is the tendency of a rater to let overall feelings toward a person affect responses to individual items. A principal might rate one of his or her better teachers high on variables not directly related to teaching, such as honesty, even if he or she had no real basis for judgment. The generosity error is the tendency of a rater to give the person being rated the benefit of the doubt whenever the rater does not have enough knowledge to make an objective rating. Both the halo effect and the generosity error can work in reverse, of course. When rating scales are involved in a study, every effort should be made to reduce these problems by giving appropriate instructions to the raters.

Attitude scales suffer from the same problems as personality inventories. The researcher can never be sure that the individual is expressing his or her true attitude rather than a "socially acceptable" attitude. Again, the validity of a study is directly related to the validity of the responses made by individuals in the sample. Every effort should be made, therefore, to increase honesty of response by giving appropriate directions to those completing the instruments.

Creativity Tests   Tests of creativity are really tests designed to measure those personality characteristics that are related to creative behavior. One such trait is referred to as divergent thinking. Unlike convergent thinkers, who tend to look for *the* right answer, divergent thinkers tend to seek alternatives. J. P. Guilford, probably the most well-known researcher in this area, has developed a number of widely used tests of divergent thinking.[9] One such test asks the individual to list as many uses as he or she can think of for an ordinary brick. Think about it and list a few. If you listed uses such as build a school, build a house, build a library, etc., then you are not very creative; all of those uses are really the same, namely, you can use a brick to build something. Now, if you are creative, you listed different uses such as break a window, drown a rat, and hit a robber on the head.

Another test asks individuals to compose plot titles for brief stories. The titles are then rated for their originality. One of the stories concerns a missionary in Africa who is captured by cannibals. He is given a choice of being boiled alive or marrying a princess of the tribe. He chooses death. Take a few minutes and think of some possible titles. Perhaps you came up with a title like Missionary in Africa, The Cannibal and the Missionary, or Boiled in Africa. If you are especially clever, you may have come up with a title like Better Boil than Goil (my favorite!), A Mate Worse Than Death, or He Left a Dish for a Pot. The more clever titles a person comes up with, the higher the score on originality, which is one aspect of divergent thinking.

Another well-known researcher in this area is E. P. Torrance. The Torrance Tests of Creativity include graphic, or pictorial, items as well as verbal items. Tests

---

9. Guilford, J.P. *The nature of human intelligence.* New York: McGraw-Hill, 1967, *and* Guilford, J.P. Three faces of intellect. *American Psychologist,* 1959, *14*(8), 469–479.

are scored in terms of four factors: fluency, flexibility, originality, and elaboration.[10] The Torrance tests involve tasks such as listing as many uses as possible for an object and coming up with titles for pictures.

Interest Inventories   An interest inventory asks an individual to indicate personal likes and dislikes, such as the kinds of activities he or she prefers to engage in. Responses are generally compared to known interest patterns. The most widely used type of interest measure is the vocational interest inventory. Such inventories typically ask the respondent to indicate preferences with respect to leisure time activities, such as hobbies. The respondent's pattern of interest is then compared to the patterns of interest typical of successful persons in various occupational fields. The individual can then be counseled as to the fields in which she or he is more likely to be happy and successful. Two frequently used inventories are the Strong Vocational Interest Blank, which measures interest in professional and business fields, and the Kuder Interest Inventory—Vocational, which measures interest in broad occupational areas such as mechanical, scientific, persuasive, and social service.

Projective Tests

Projective tests were developed in an attempt to eliminate some of the major problems inherent in the use of self-report measures, such as the tendency of some respondents to give "socially acceptable" responses. The purposes of such tests are usually not obvious to respondents; the individual is typically asked to respond to ambiguous items. Since the purpose of the test is not clear, conscious dishonesty of response is reduced, and the respondent "projects" his or her true feelings. Projective tests are utilized mainly by clinical psychologists and very infrequently by educational researchers. This is due partly to their questionable validity and partly to the fact that administration, scoring, and interpretation of projective tests require very specialized training. However, if it is necessary to use a projective device in your research study, be sure to have it administered by qualified personnel.

The most commonly used projective technique is the method of association. This technique asks the respondent to react to a stimulus such as a picture, inkblot, or word. Word-association tests are probably the most well known of the association techniques (tell me the first thing that comes to your mind!). Two of the most commonly used association tests are the Rorschach Ink Blot Test and the Thematic Apperception Test; thousands of studies utilizing the Rorshach test have been conducted. The Rorschach test presents the respondent with a series of inkblots, and the respondent is asked to tell what he or she sees. The Thematic Apperception Test presents the individual with a series of pictures; the respondent is then asked to tell a story about each picture.

Until recently, all projective tests were required to be administered individually. There have been some recent efforts, however, to develop group projective tests.

---

10. Torrance, E.P. *Torrance Tests of Creative Thinking*. Princeton, N.J.: Personnel Press, 1966.

Although these tests are still in early stages of development, they offer great promise of becoming more objective projective devices.

Aptitude

Aptitude tests are measures of potential. They are used to predict how well someone is likely to perform in a future situation. Tests of general aptitude are variously referred to as scholastic aptitude tests, intelligence tests, and tests of general mental ability. Since intelligence tests have developed a bad reputation in recent years, the term "scholastic aptitude" has become more popular. The intents of all such tests, however, are basically the same. Aptitude tests are also available to predict a person's likely level of performance following some specific future instruction or training. Aptitude tests are available in the form of individual tests in specific areas, such as algebra, and in the form of batteries that measure aptitude in several related areas. While virtually all aptitude tests are standardized and are administered as part of a school testing program, the results are useful to teachers, counselors, and administrators.

General Aptitude

There are a variety of tests that fall into this category representing a variety of different definitions of general aptitude (or scholastic aptitude, or intelligence, or what have you). While the basic purpose of all such tests is to predict future academic performance, there is disagreement as to the factors that are being measured and are serving as the predictors. The term is variously defined to include variables such as abstract reasoning, problem solving, and verbal fluency. General aptitude tests typically ask the individual to perform a variety of verbal and nonverbal tasks that measure the individual's ability to apply knowledge and solve problems. Such tests generally yield three scores—an overall score, a verbal score, and a quantitative score—representing, for example, a total IQ, a verbal IQ, and a quantitative IQ. While general aptitude tests are intended to be measures of innate ability or potential, they appear actually to measure current ability; there is also some evidence to suggest that scores are to some degree affected by an individual's past and present environment. However, since they seem to do a reasonable job of predicting future academic success, and are in that sense measures of "potential," they are very useful to educators.

General aptitude tests may be group tests or individually administered tests. Each type has its relative advantages and disadvantages. Group tests are more convenient to administer, save considerable time, and provide an estimate of academic potential that is adequate for most educational research studies. Batteries are also available which comprise a number of tests suitable for different grade and age levels. Since tests in a battery are similarly structured, they permit the study of intellectual growth over time and comparisons among different levels. A commonly used group-administered battery is the California Test of Mental Maturity (CTMM). The CTMM has six levels and can be administered to all school-age children, college students, and adults. It includes 12 subtests representing five factors: logical reasoning, spatial relations, numerical reasoning, verbal concepts, and memory. The results include a language IQ, a nonlanguage IQ, and a total IQ. Although some of the subtests are not as good as they might be, overall the test is considered to be a respectable measure of potential. Another frequently administered group test is the Otis-Lennon Mental Ability Test, which also has six levels and is designed for school-age children in grades K–12. The Otis-Lennon Mental Ability Test measures four factors—verbal comprehension, verbal reasoning, figurative reasoning, and quantitative reasoning—and is also considered to be a respectable measure of potential.

A serious disadvantage of group tests is that they require a great deal of reading. Thus, students with poor reading ability are at a disadvantage and may receive scores reflecting, for example, an IQ level lower than their true level. Individual tests, on the other hand, require much less reading. Another advantage of individual tests is that since they are administered one-on-one, the examiner is aware of factors such as illness or anxiety that might be adversely affecting the individual's ability to respond. From a research point of view, the main disadvantage of individual tests is that they are more difficult to administer and score; trained personnel are required to administer them and to score them. However, if there is any reason to question the validity of group tests for a particular sample, very young children for example, an individual test should be used, even if this requires a reduction of sample size. Probably the most well known of the individually administered tests is the Stanford-Binet Intelligence Scale; it has been used extensively in research projects, and there is considerable data concerning its validity. More and more, however, the Wechsler scales are being utilized. While the Stanford-Binet is appropriate only for older adolescents and adults, Wechsler scales are available to measure the intelligence of persons from the age of 4 to adulthood: the Wechsler Preschool and Primary Scale of Intelligence (WPPSI)—ages 4–6½; the Wechsler Intelligence Scale for Children (WISC)—ages 5–15; and the Wechsler Adult Intelligence Scale (WAIS)—older adolescents and adults. As an example, the WISC is a scholastic aptitude test which includes verbal tests (e.g., general information, vocabulary) and performance tests (e.g., picture completion, object assembly). While the Stanford-Binet yields one IQ score, the Wechsler scales also yield a number of subscores.

As mentioned previously, there is evidence to indicate that IQ scores are affected by the individual's past and present environment. The validity of IQ tests for certain minority groups has been questioned, and such tests have been accused of being culturally biased. This criticism has prompted the development of "culture-fair" IQ tests. Culture-fair tests attempt to exclude culturally related items, such as items which include words that might not be familiar to certain groups of individuals. In fact, most of these tests do not require the use of language. Interestingly, however, there is some recent evidence which suggests that such tests may not be as culture-fair as originally believed; nonverbal tests may in fact be less culture-fair than verbal tests. The Culture-Fair Intelligence Test (ages 4 to adult) is probably the most frequently used culture-fair test.

Specific Aptitude

As the term is generally used, specific aptitude tests attempt to predict the level of performance that can be expected of an individual following future instruction or training in a specific area or areas. Aptitude tests are available for a wide variety of academic and nonacademic areas such as mathematics and mechanical reasoning. As with tests of general aptitude, they are used by teachers, counselors, and administrators, and for the same reasons. They are also used as a basis for grouping, in math classes, for example. Specific aptitude tests are also frequently used in research studies. Their most common use in this regard is probably to equate groups that are going to be compared on achievement after receiving different treatments. If groups are different in aptitude to begin with, then final achievement differences might be attributable to this initial difference rather than to differences in treatment. Aptitude scores can be used to equate groups either by using stratified sampling or through a statistical procedure called analysis of covariance. While most aptitude tests are standardized, written tests, some are performance tests. The latter are appropriate when the students taking the tests have an English language difficulty, foreign students, for example.

Aptitude tests are available for a number of specific areas such as algebra, music, and mechanical ability. Multi-aptitude batteries, which measure aptitudes in several related areas, are available for the assessment of both academic and nonacademic aptitudes. Multi-aptitude batteries include a number of subtests that have been normed on the same group. The Sequential Tests of Educational Progress (STEP) battery, an academic aptitude battery, includes tests on reading, writing, mathematics, and science, among others. The Differential Aptitude Tests (DAT), on the other hand, include tests on space relations, mechanical reasoning, and clerical speed and accuracy, among others, and is designed to predict success in various job areas.

Readiness

Readiness, or prognostic, tests are sometimes classified as aptitude tests, sometimes as achievement tests. Aptitude does seem to be a more appropriate categorization, however, since a readiness test is administered prior to instruction or training in a specific area in order to determine whether and to what degree a student is ready for, or will profit from, instruction. Due to increased interest in the basic skills, reading readiness tests have been given more attention than other types. Reading readiness tests typically include measurement of variables such as auditory discrimination, visual discrimination, and motor ability. Readiness batteries have also been developed to assess readiness in a number of areas. The Metropolitan Readiness Test, for example, was designed to measure the degree to which students starting school have developed the skills and abilities that contribute to readiness for first-grade instruction in areas such as reading, arithmetic, and writing. Given the state of the art, that is, the relative newness of readiness tests, the Metropolitan Readiness Test is considered to be a good test of its type.[11]

Selection of a Test

The most important guidelines for test selection are the following related rules: *Do not,* repeat, do not stop with the first test you find that appears to measure what

---

11. For a detailed description of a number of achievement, character and personality, and aptitude tests, see Mehrens, W.A., & Lehmann, I.J. *Standardized tests in education.* New York: Holt, Rinehart and Winston, 1975.

you want, say "Eureka I have found it!" and blithely use it in your study! *Do* identify those tests that are appropriate for your study, compare them on relevant factors, and select the best one. If you are knowledgeable concerning the qualities a test should possess, and familiar with the various types of tests that are available (which you are of course by now!), then the selection of an instrument is a very orderly process. Assuming you have defined the specific purpose of your study and defined your population, the first step is to determine precisely what type of test you need. The next step is to identify and locate appropriate tests. Finally, you must do a comparative analysis of the tests and select *the best one.* In order to locate appropriate tests, you need to be familiar with sources of test information.

Sources of Test Information

Once you have determined the type of test you need, for example, a test of reading comprehension for second graders, a logical place to start looking for tests is in Buros' *Mental Measurement Yearbooks.* The *Yearbooks* have been published for several decades and represent the most comprehensive source of test information available to educational researchers. Each volume contains information on tests published since the last *Yearbook* as well as additional information on tests that have been substantially revised. To use a *Yearbook,* the following procedure may be utilized:

1. Scan the Table of Contents and identify the category which matches the type of test you are seeking, i.e., Achievement Batteries.

2. Go to the back of the volume to the Classified Index of Tests. The Classified Index is an expanded Table of Contents that alphabetically lists, by category, all the tests which appear in that volume.

3. Identify promising test titles and their corresponding entry numbers.

4. Using the entry numbers, locate the test descriptions in the Tests and Reviews section of the *Yearbook* (the main body of the volume).

If you are seeking information on a particular test, you can locate its entry number by referring to the Index of Titles, which is also located in the back of the volume.

Entries for new tests in the Tests and Reviews section typically include the following information: title, author, publisher, cost, a brief description, a description of groups for whom the test is intended, validity and reliability data, whether the test is a group or individual test, time requirements, test references, and critical reviews by qualified reviewers. Among other things, the reviews generally cite any special requirements or problems involved in test administration, scoring, or interpretation. A very useful supplement volume to the *Yearbooks* is Buros' *Tests in Print.* This volume is a comprehensive bibliography of all tests that have appeared in preceding *Yearbooks.* The format is basically that of the Classified Index of Tests that appears in each volume but with considerably more information. Both the *Yearbooks* and *Tests in Print* are indispensable reference works for educational researchers.

After reading the descriptions and reviews in the *Yearbooks,* you will quickly eliminate many of the tests whose titles looked promising; some will not be appropriate for your sample, some will have inadequate validity and reliability data, and some will have one or more serious problems identified by reviewers. After you have narrowed the list of candidates you will still usually require additional information. A good source of information on a test is the publisher's test manual. Manuals typically include detailed validity and reliability data, a description of the subjects for whom the test is appropriate, conditions of administration, detailed scoring instructions, and requirements for score interpretation. As mentioned previously, however, you must be a good consumer. Relevant data omitted from the manual is probably unfavorable to the test. Thus, if information on subscore reliabilities is missing, they probably are not very good. As the Romans used to say, CAVEAT EMPTOR!

Sometimes you may be aware of a new test which sounds exactly like what you need but for which you can find no information. In this case there are several additional avenues of inquiry. The *Journal of Educational Measurement* is one possibility that should be checked; the *Journal* contains reviews of recently published tests. *Psychological Abstracts* is also a potential source of information. Using the monthly or annual index, you can quickly determine if the *Abstracts* contain any information on the test. If nothing can be found, or if available information is inadequate, you should be able to obtain additional data by writing to the test developer. Test developers will usually comply with such requests, especially if you agree to supply the results of your study in return.

Final selection of a test usually requires examination of the actual tests. A test which appears, from all descriptions, to be exactly what you need may have some problems detectable only by inspection of the test itself. The test may not be content valid; for example, it may contain items measuring content not covered by your treatment. An initial inspection copy of a test, as well as additional required copies if you select that test for your study, should be acquired from the test publisher. For most tests, the publisher's name and address are given in the *Mental Measurement Yearbooks*.

Selecting from Alternatives

Eventually a decision must be reached. Once you have narrowed the number of candidates and acquired all relevant information, a comparative analysis of the tests must be made. While there are a number of factors to be considered, for example, validity data and cost, these factors are not of equal importance; the least expensive test is not necessarily the best test! As you should know by now, the most important factor to be considered is validity. Is one of the tests more appropriate for your sample? If you are interested in prediction, does one of the tests have a significantly higher validity coefficient? If content validity is of prime importance, are the items of one test based on the same textbook that will be used in your study? These are typical of the questions which might be raised. If after the validity comparison there are still several tests that seem appropriate, the next factor for consideration is reliability.

Assuming all coefficients were acceptable, you would presumably select the test with the highest reliability, but there are other considerations. A factor to be considered in relation to reliability, for example, is the length of the test and the time it takes to administer it. Shorter tests are, in general, to be preferred. A test that can be administered during one class period, for example, would be considerably more convenient than a 2-hour test; shorter tests are also preferable in terms of student fatigue and motivation. However, since reliability is related to length, a shorter test will tend to be less reliable. For example, for many tests a short form is also available; the reliability of the short form is invariably lower. Thus, if a long form and a short form of a test (or two different tests of different lengths) are both valid for your study, the questions to be considered are: How much shorter? How much less reliable? If one test takes half as long to administer and is only slightly less reliable, the shorter test is probably better. For example, suppose Test A (or Form A) has a KR-20 reliability of .94 and takes 90 minutes to administer, and Test B (or Form B) has a KR-20 reliability of .90 and takes 50 minutes to administer; which would you choose? Most probably Test B. If after comparing validity and reliability data, you still have more than one candidate, you should consider administration, scoring, and interpretation requirements.

By the time you get to this point, you have probably already made a decision concerning whether you need an individually administered test. If not, and if there is no essential reason for using an individually administered test, now is the time to eliminate them from contention. Most of the time individually administered tests will not even be a consideration since they are used primarily for certain IQ and personality testing situations. However, when they are, you should keep in mind the potential disadvantages associated with their use: additional cost, additional time, the need for trained administrators, complicated scoring procedures, and the need for trained interpreters. Of course, if the nature of your subjects or the research variable of interest requires it, by all means use an individually administered test. In either case, you should consider the administration, scoring, and interpretation requirements. In addition to the time consideration mentioned previously, you should consider factors such as unusual administration conditions, difficult scoring procedures, and sophisticated interpretation. Are you qualified to execute the requirements of the test as specified? If not, can you afford to acquire the necessary personnel? If after all this soul-searching, by some miracle you still have more than one test in the running, by all means pick the cheapest one!

There are two additional considerations in test selection which have nothing to do with the psychometric qualities of a test. Both are related to the use of tests in schools. If you are planning to use school children in your study, you should check to see what tests they have already been administered. You would not want to administer a test with which subjects had familiarity. Second, you should be sensitive to the fact that some parents or administrators might object to a test which contains "touchy" items. Certain personality inventories, for example, ask questions related to the sexual behavior of the respondents. If there is any possibility that the test contains potentially objectionable items, either choose another test or acquire appropriate permissions before administering the test. There have been instances where researchers have been ordered to destroy (even burn!) test results. As the old saying goes, an ounce of prevention. . . .

Occasionally, hopefully not very often, you will find yourself in the position of not being able to locate a suitable test. The solution is *not* to use an inadequate test with the rationale, "Oh well, I'll do the best I can!" One logical solution is to develop your own test. Good test construction requires a variety of skills. As mentioned previously, training at least equivalent to a course in measurement is needed. If you do develop your own test, you must collect validation data; a self-developed test should not be utilized in a research study unless it has been pretested first with a group very similar to the group to be used in the actual study. In addition to collecting validity and reliability data, you will need to try out the administration and scoring procedures. In some cases, the results of pretesting will indicate the need for revisions and further pretesting. This procedure may also sometimes be followed for an existing test. You may find a test that seems very appropriate but for which certain relevant types of validation data are not available. In this case you may decide to try to validate this test with your population rather than develop a test "from scratch."

Test Administration

There are several general guidelines for test administration of which you should be aware. First, if testing is to be conducted in a school setting, arrangements should be made beforehand with the appropriate person, usually the principal. Consultation with the principal should result in agreement as to when the testing will take place, under what conditions, and with what assistance from school personnel. The principal can be very helpful in supplying such information as dates for which testing is inadvisable (e.g., assembly days and days immediately preceding or following holidays). Second, whether you are testing in the schools or elsewhere, you should do everything you can to insure ideal testing conditions; a comfortable, quiet environment is more conducive to subject cooperation. Also, if testing is to take place in more than one session, the conditions of the sessions should be as identical as possible. Third, follow the Scout motto and be prepared. Be thoroughly familiar with the administration procedures presented in the test manual and follow the directions precisely. If they are at all complicated, practice beforehand. Administer the test to some friends; if this is not feasible, stand in front of a mirror and give it to yourself!

As with everything in life, good planning and preparation usually pay off. If you have made all necessary arrangements, secured all necessary cooperation, and are completely familiar and comfortable with the administration procedures, the actual testing situation should go well. If some unforeseen catastrophe occurs during testing, such as an earthquake or a power failure, make careful note of the incident. If it is serious enough to invalidate the testing, you may have to try again another day with another group. If in your judgment the effects of the incident are not serious, at least relate its occurrence in your final research report. Despite the possibility of unforeseen tragedies, it is certain that the probability of all going well will be greatly increased if you adequately plan and prepare for the big day.

Summary/Chapter 5

Purpose and Process

1. The time and skill it takes to select an appropriate standardized instrument are invariably less than the time and skill it takes to develop an instrument that measures the same thing.

2. There are thousands of standardized instruments available which yield a wide variety of data for a wide variety of purposes.

3. Selection of an instrument for a particular research purpose involves identification and selection of the most appropriate one from among alternatives.

Characteristics of a Standardized Test

4. A test is a means of measuring the knowledge, skill, feeling, intelligence, or aptitude of an individual or group.

5. Test objectivity means that an individual's score is not affected by the person scoring the test.

6. Validity is the most important quality of any test. Validity is concerned with what a test measures and for whom it is appropriate; reliability refers to the consistency with which a test measures whatever it measures.

7. Specification of conditions of administration, directions for scoring, and guidelines for interpretation are important characteristics of standardized tests.

8. A table of norms presents raw scores and one or more equivalent transformations, such as corresponding percentile ranks.

Validity

9. Validity is the degree to which a test measures what it is supposed to measure.

10. A test is not valid per se; it is valid for a particular purpose and for a particular group.

Content Validity

11. Content validity is the degree to which a test measures an intended content area.

12. Item validity is concerned with whether the test items represent measurement in the intended content area, and sampling validity is concerned with how well the test samples the total content area.

13. Content validity is of prime importance for achievement tests.

14. Content validity is determined by expert judgment.

15. When selecting a test for a research study the researcher assumes the role of "expert" and determines whether the test is content valid for her or his study.

Construct Validity

16. Construct validity is the degree to which a test measures an intended hypothetical construct.

17. A construct is a nonobservable trait, such as intelligence, which explains behavior.

18. Validating a test of a construct involves testing hypotheses deduced from a theory concerning the construct.

Concurrent Validity

19. Concurrent validity is the degree to which the scores on a test are related to the scores on another, already established test administered at the same time, or to some other valid criterion available at the same time.

20. The relationship method of determining concurrent validity involves determining the relationship between scores on the test and scores on some other established test or criterion.

21. The discrimination method of establishing concurrent validity involves determining

whether test scores can be used to discriminate between persons who possess a certain characteristic and those who do not, or those who possess it to a greater degree.

Predictive Validity

22. Predictive validity is the degree to which a test can predict how well an individual will do in a future situation.
23. The predictive validity of a test is determined by establishing the relationship between scores on the test and some measure of success in the situation of interest.
24. The test that is used to predict success is referred to as the predictor, and the behavior that is predicted is referred to as the criterion.

Reliability

25. Reliability is the degree to which a test consistently measures whatever it measures.
26. Reliability is expressed numerically, usually as a coefficient; a high coefficient indicates high reliability.

Test-Retest Reliability

27. Test-retest reliability is the degree to which scores are consistent over time.
28. Test-retest reliability is established by determining the relationship between scores resulting from administering the same test, to the same group, on different occasions.

Equivalent-Forms Reliability

29. Equivalent forms of a test are two tests that are identical in every way except for the actual items included.
30. Equivalent-forms reliability is determined by establishing the relationship between scores resulting from administering two different forms of the same test, to the same group, at the same time.
31. Equivalent-forms reliability is the most acceptable estimate of reliability for most tests used in research and is the most commonly used.

Split-Half Reliability

32. Split-half reliability is determined by establishing the relationship between the scores on two equivalent halves of a test administered to a total group at one time.
33. Since longer tests tend to be more reliable, and since split-half reliability represents the reliability of a test only half as long as the actual test, a correction known as the Spearman-Brown prophecy formula must be applied to the coefficient.

Rationale Equivalence Reliability

34. Rationale equivalence reliability is not established through correlation but rather estimates internal consistency by determining how all items on a test relate to all other items and to the total test.
35. Rationale equivalence reliability is determined through application of the Kuder-Richardson formulas, usually formula 20 or 21 in educational research studies.

Scorer/Rater Reliability

36. Interjudge reliability refers to the reliability of two (or more) independent scorers; intrajudge reliability refers to the reliability of the scoring of individual scorers.
37. Estimates of interjudge or intrajudge reliability are usually obtained using correlational techniques but can also be expressed simply as percent agreement.

Reliability Coefficients

38. What constitutes an acceptable level of reliability is to some degree determined by the type of test, although, of course, a coefficient over .90 would be acceptable for any test.

39. If a test is composed of several subtests, then the reliability of each subtest must be evaluated, not just the reliability of the total test.

Standard Error of Measurement

40. The standard error of measurement is an estimate of how often you can expect errors of a given size.

41. A small standard error of measurement indicates high reliability; a large standard error of measurement, low reliability.

42. The standard error of measurement allows us to estimate how much difference there probably is between a person's obtained score and true score, the size of this difference being a function of the reliability of the test.

Types of Tests

Achievement

43. Achievement tests measure the current status of individuals with respect to proficiency in given areas of knowledge or skill.

44. Standardized achievement tests are available for individual curriculum areas such as reading and mathematics, and also in the form of comprehensive batteries that measure achievement in several different areas.

Character and Personality

45. Tests of character and personality are designed to measure characteristics of individuals along a number of dimensions and to assess feelings and attitudes toward self, others, and a variety of other activities, institutions, and situations.

46. They may well be the most used tests in educational research.

Nonprojective Tests

Personality Inventories

47. Personality inventories present lists of questions or statements describing behaviors characteristic of certain personality traits, and the individual is asked to indicate (yes, no, undecided) whether the statement describes her or him.

48. Personality inventories may be specific and measure only one trait, such as introversion-extroversion, or may be general and measure a number of traits.

Attitude Scales

49. Attitude scales attempt to determine what an individual believes, perceives, or feels.

50. Attitudes can be measured toward self, others, and a variety of other activities, institutions, or situations.

51. There are four basic types of attitude scales: Likert scales, semantic differential scales, Thurstone scales, and Guttman scales.

52. Measures of "attitude toward self" are referred to as measures of self-concept.

53. Rating scales are also used to measure attitudes toward others.

Creativity Tests

54. Tests of creativity are really tests designed to measure those personality characteristics that are related to creative behavior.

55. One such trait is referred to as divergent thinking; unlike convergent thinkers, who tend to look for *the* right answer, divergent thinkers tend to seek alternatives.

Interest Inventories

56. An interest inventory asks an individual to indicate personal likes and dislikes, such as kinds of activities he or she likes to engage in.

57. Responses are generally compared to known interest patterns.

58. The most widely used type of interest measure is the vocational interest inventory.

Projective Tests

59. Projective tests were developed in an attempt to eliminate some of the major problems inherent in the use of self-report measures, such as the tendency of some respondents to give "socially acceptable" responses.

60. The purposes of such tests are usually not obvious to respondents; the individual is typically asked to respond to ambiguous items.

61. The most commonly used projective technique is the method of association; this technique asks the respondent to react to a stimulus such as a picture, inkblot, or word.

Aptitude

62. Aptitude tests are used to predict how well someone is likely to perform in a future situation.

63. Tests of general aptitude are variously referred to as scholastic aptitude tests, intelligence tests, and tests of general mental ability.

General Aptitude

64. General aptitude tests typically ask the individual to perform a variety of verbal and nonverbal tasks that measure the individual's ability to apply knowledge and solve problems.

65. While general aptitude tests are intended to be measures of innate ability or potential, they appear actually to measure current ability.

66. Since they seem to do a reasonable job of predicting future academic success, and are in that sense measures of "potential," they are very useful to educators.

67. Culture-fair tests attempt to exclude culturally related items, such as items which include words that might not be familiar to certain groups of individuals.

Specific Aptitude

68. Specific aptitude tests attempt to predict the level of performance that can be expected of an individual following future instruction or training in a specific area or areas.

69. Aptitude tests are available for a number of specific areas such as algebra, music, and mechanical ability.

70. Multi-aptitude batteries, which measure aptitudes in several related areas, are available for the assessment of both academic and nonacademic aptitudes.

Readiness

71. A readiness test is administered prior to instruction or training in a specific area in order to determine whether and to what degree a student is ready for, or will profit from, instruction.

72. Reading readiness tests typically include measurement of variables such as auditory discrimination, visual discrimination, and motor ability.

Selection of a Test

73. *Do not* use the first test you find that appears to measure what you want.

74. *Do* identify those tests that are appropriate for your study, compare them on relevant factors, and select the best one.

Sources of Test Information

75. Buros' *Mental Measurement Yearbooks* represent the most comprehensive source of test information available to educational researchers.

76. Buros' *Tests in Print* is a comprehensive bibliography of all tests that have appeared in preceding *Mental Measurement Yearbooks*.

77. A good source of information on a test is the publisher's test manual.

78. Final selection of a test usually requires examination of the actual tests.

Selecting from Alternatives

79. Final selection of a test requires a comparative analysis of the alternatives.

80. The most important factor to be considered is validity.

81. The next factor for consideration is reliability.

82. Other important factors include administration, scoring, and interpretation requirements.

83. A self-developed test should not be utilized in a research study unless it has been pretested first with a group very similar to the group to be used in the actual study.

Test Administration

84. If testing is to be conducted in a school setting, arrangements should be made beforehand with the appropriate person, usually the principal.

85. Every effort should be made to insure ideal testing conditions.

86. Be thoroughly familiar with the administration procedures presented in the test manual and follow the directions precisely.

Task 5 Performance Criteria

All the information required for each test will be found in Buros' *Mental Measurement Yearbooks*. Following the description of the three tests, you should present a comparative analysis of the tests which forms a rationale for your selection of the "most acceptable" test for your study. As an example, you might indicate that all three tests have similar reliability coefficients reported but that one of the tests is more appropriate for your subjects.

See the *Student Guide* for practice problems and for examples of Task 5.

Part Six
Research Methods and Procedures

Meder hypothesizes quite simply that Dracula was (is?!) a woman—"beautiful, seductive, evil noblewoman of highest society. . . ."

While research studies have a number of similar components, such as a defined problem and a set of conclusions, specific procedures in a study are to a great extent determined by the particular method of research involved. As each of the five methods of research (historical, descriptive, correlational, causal-comparative, experimental) has a unique purpose, application of each method entails a unique set of procedures and concerns. As suggested above, however, there are procedural steps common to all research studies; all studies, for example, involve some type of data collection and analysis.

The purpose of Parts One through Five was to give you an overview of the basic steps involved in conducting research and the major characteristics differentiating each of the methods of research. The purpose of Part Six is to facilitate acquisition of specific competencies related to each of the methods.

The goal of Part Six is for you to be able to describe the procedures involved in each of the methods of research and apply them in designing specific studies. After you have read Part Six, you should be able to perform the following task.

Task 6

Having stated a problem, formulated one or more hypotheses, described a sample, and selected one or more measuring instruments, develop the method section of a research report. This should include a description of subjects, instrument(s), research design, and specific procedures.

(See Performance Criteria, p. 271.)

6

The Historical Method

Enablers

After reading chapter 6, you should be able to:

1 Briefly state the purpose of historical research.

2. List and briefly describe the major steps involved in designing and conducting a historical research study.

3. Explain why primary sources of data are preferable to secondary sources.

4. Briefly describe external and internal criticism of data.

5. Briefly describe four factors which should be considered in determining the accuracy of documents.

Definition and Purpose

Historical research is the systematic collection and objective evaluation of data related to past occurrences in order to test hypotheses concerning causes, effects, or trends of those events that may help to explain present events and anticipate future events. Many beginning researchers tend to think of historical research as a rather unscientific method of investigation. This is only true, however, of poorly designed and conducted historical research. Admittedly, the nature of historical research precludes exercise of many of the control procedures characteristic of other methods; if well done, however, historical research also involves systematic, objective data collection and analysis, and the confirmation or disconfirmation of hypotheses.

Many current educational practices, theories, and issues can be better understood in light of past experiences. The grading issue, for example, is not a new one in education, nor is individualized instruction an innovation of the sixties. A knowledge of the history of education can yield insight into the circumstances involved in the evolution of the current educational system as well as practices and approaches that have been found to be ineffective or infeasible. In fact, studying the history of education might lead one to believe that not only is nothing new under the educational sun but also that educators never learn; some practices seem to appear and disappear with regularity. For over 150 years, for example, individualized instruction and group instruction have seemingly taken turns being the favored approach of the day. Miehl, however, does not view this constant shifting as the proverbial pendulum that swings from one approach to another and back, with no progress being made along the way. Instead, she sees educational change as a spiral phenomenon, with each ascending loop profiting from the former:

> In common with the pendulum swing, this view allows for renewed attention to a problem and line of solution which have been neglected for a time. The difference in the spiral view is that it accounts for the fact that proposals made at a later point in educational history usually are much more refined, with wisdom distilled from experience at both sides of the spiral built into them. At each new point on the upward and outward spiral the concepts are clearer and the language of education is more precise.[1]

Miehl has tested the spiral pattern on a number of educational issues, including the individualized versus group instruction question:

> During the depression years, when interest developed in helping children become more skillful, involved members of groups, new information on the dynamics of groups was available. The profession also could carry into the new movement better understanding of the individual within the group. At each new turn of the spiral the practices advocated could be more sophisticated, for educators could look back on the experiences had at previous positions on the lower levels of the spiral and could build into a new whole the useful residue from each previous stage.

As Miehl's position indicates, a knowledge of the history of education can not only increase understanding of the present but also facilitate anticipation of future trends.

The Historical Research Process

The steps involved in conducting a historical research study are essentially the same as for other types of research: definition of a problem, formulation of hypotheses (or questions to be answered), systematic collection of data, objective evaluation of data, and confirmation or disconfirmation of hypotheses. In conducting a historical study, the researcher can neither manipulate nor control any of the variables. On the other hand, there is no way the researcher can affect events of the past; what has happened has happened. The researcher can, however, apply scientific objectivity in attempting to determine exactly what did happen in the past.

Definition of a Problem

The purpose of a historical research study should *not* be to find out what is already known about a topic and to retell it. Recall that the goal of all scientific research in general, and educational research in particular, is to explain, predict, and/or control phenomena. The nature of historical research, of course, eliminates control of phenomena; therefore, the purpose of a historical research study should be to explain or predict, not to rehash. The purpose of a historical research study

---

1. Miel, A. Reassessment of the curriculum—why? In D. Huebner (Ed.), *A reassessment of the curriculum.* New York: Teachers College Press, 1964.

should also *not* be to prove a point or to support a pet position of the researcher. One can easily verify almost any point of view by consciously or unconsciously "overlooking" evidence to the contrary. There are probably data available to support almost any position; the historical researcher's task is to objectively evaluate and weigh all evidence in arriving at the most tenable conclusion. For example, one could cite data which would seemingly support the position that having more highly educated and trained teachers has led to increased school vandalism. One could do a historical study describing how requirements for teacher certification and recertification have increased over the years and how school vandalism has correspondingly increased. Of course such a study would indicate very poor critical analysis since two separate, independent sets of factors are probably responsible for each of these trends rather than one being the cause or effect of the other. To avoid this sort of biased data collection and analysis, one should probably avoid topics about which one has strong feelings; it is a lot easier to be objective when you are not emotionally involved.

As with the other methods of research, the purpose of a historical research study should be to discover new knowledge or to clarify, correct, or expand existing knowledge. Worthwhile historical research problems are identified much the same way as problems for other types of research. One especially valuable resource for acquainting beginning researchers with the kinds of historical research studies that have been conducted, and for suggesting possible future studies, is the *History of Education Quarterly.*[2] The *Quarterly,* for example, contains articles such as "The Origins of Public Education: A Reassessment" and "Pilgrim's Progress: Toward a Social History of the School Superintendency."[3] It is just as important in historical research as in any other method to formulate a manageable, well-defined problem; otherwise it is likely that an overwhelming amount of data will be collected, considerably complicating analysis and synthesis of the data and the drawing of adequately documented conclusions. On the other hand, a concern unique to historical research is the possibility that a problem will be selected for which insufficient data are available. Unlike researchers utilizing the other methods of research, the historical researcher cannot "create" data by administering instruments such as achievement tests, psychological inventories, or questionnaires to subjects.[4] The historical researcher is basically limited to whatever data are already available. Thus, if insufficient data are available, the problem will be inadequately investigated, and the hypothesis will be inadequately tested; conclusions concerning the confirmation or disconfirmation of such hypotheses will be at best extremely tentative.

It is better to study in depth a well-defined problem with one or more specific, well-stated hypotheses, than to investigate either a too-broadly stated problem with a fuzzy hypothesis, or a problem for which insufficient data are available with

---

2. *History of Education Quarterly.* New York: History of Education Society in cooperation with the School of Education, New York University, 1961 to date.

3. Katz, M.B. The origins of public education: A Reassessment. *History of Education Quarterly,* 1976, *16*(4), 381–407, *and* Tyack, D.B. Pilgrim's progress: Toward a social history of the school superintendency, 1860–1960. *History of Education Quarterly,* 1976, *16*(3), 257–300.

4. A historical study may involve interviews with participants in, or observers of, an event. Even in these cases, however, the number of persons who can be interviewed, and the kinds of questions that can be asked, are usually limited.

a virtually untestable hypothesis. As with other methods of research, the hypothesis guides the data collection. If the hypothesis is well stated, and if sufficient data are available, the collection and logical analysis of that data will confirm or disconfirm the hypothesis.

Data Collection

In a historical research study, the review of related literature and the study procedures are part of the same process (remember, there are no measuring instruments). The review of the literature does not take place before data collection; this does not mean, of course, that the literature may not be consulted to initially identify a problem. The term "literature" takes on a much broader meaning in a historical study and refers to all sorts of written communication; in addition, identification, acquisition, and review of such "literature" is considerably more complex. The written communication may be in the form of legal documents, records, minutes of meetings, letters, and other documents which will not normally be indexed alphabetically by subject, author, and title in a library. Thus, identification of such data requires considerably more "detective work" on the part of the researcher. Further, unless the problem deals with a very local event or issue, it is not uncommon for identified relevant documents to be available only at distant locations, in a special library collection, for example. In such cases, proper examination of the data requires either considerable travel or, when feasible, extensive reproduction. Both of these alternatives present the researcher with problems. Travel requires that the researcher have a healthy bank account (which very few do, as pointed out in chapter 4!) unless, of course, the effort is supported by a funding agency. Reproduction (for example, acquiring photocopies of documents in a private collection) can also become costly and often wasteful; a 50-page document may turn out to contain only one paragraph directly related to the problem under investigation.

A historical research study in education may also involve interviews with persons who participated in the event or process under investigation, if it occurred in the recent past (remember, it would be pretty tough to interview an observer of the Boston tea party!), or an examination of relics and remains, such as textbooks. Similar problems apply in these situations as when only written documents are involved; they are more difficult to identify, they may be located some distance from the researcher, and they may be unproductive sources after all. An interview with a person believed to have been involved in an incident, for example, may reveal that he or she was only peripherally involved or that he or she recollects only partially the details of the event.

Sources of data in a historical research study are classified as primary sources or secondary sources. Primary sources constitute firsthand information, such as original documents and reports by actual participants or direct observers; secondary sources constitute secondhand information, such as reference books (encyclopedias, for example) or reports by relatives of actual participants or observers. A student who participated in the takeover of the president's office at Rowdy U. would be a primary source of data concerning the event; her or his mother would be a secondary source. Primary sources are definitely to be preferred; the further removed the evidence is, the less comprehensive and accurate the resulting data are likely to be. You may have played a party game usually called "telephone" which illustrates how the facts get twisted as a story is passed from person to person. The first person hears the "true" story and whispers it to the second person, who whispers it to the third person, and so on until finally the last person tells out loud the story he or she was told. There is generally a considerable discrepancy between the first version and the last version; "John and Mary were seen holding hands at Burger Bugger" may well end up as "John and Mary were kicked out of El Ripoff Steakhouse because of their x-rated behavior on the dance floor!"

Because primary sources are admittedly more difficult to acquire, a common criticism of historical research is excessive reliance on secondary sources. It is better to select a "less grand" problem for which primary sources are available and accessible than to inadequately investigate the "problem of the year." Of course the further back in time the event under study occurred, the more likely it is that secondary sources may also have to be used. As a general rule, however, the more primary sources the better.

The process of reviewing and abstracting pertinent data from primary and secondary sources is essentially the one described in chapter 2: assessment of the source's relevancy to your problem; recording of complete bibliographic information; coding of the data from each source with respect to the hypothesis (or aspect of a hypothesis) to which it relates; summarization of the pertinent information; and notation of questions, comments, and quotations. One slight difference is that due to the nature of historical sources, several different note cards may be required for any one source. Minutes of a school board meeting, for example, might include information relating to two hypotheses; to facilitate later analysis and organization of data, they are best recorded separately. One major difference is that historical sources must also be subjected to a careful analysis to determine both their authenticity and their accuracy.

Data Analysis: External and Internal Criticism

When you read a report of a completed study in a professional journal, written by the person who conducted the research, you can generally assume that the report is accurate; the reported procedures and results can be assumed to be the procedure and results that actually occurred. This is not the case with historical sources. Historical sources exist independently of your study; they were not written or developed for use in a research project. Thus, while they may very well serve the purpose for which they were created, they may not serve your purpose. Recall the previously discussed letter, allegedly written by George Washington, containing an expression of concern regarding the amount of physical punishment in schools. Even if the letter were determined to be authentic, unless George Washington could be shown to be a reliable source concerning educational practices of his day, his letter could not be used as evidence to support a hypothesis concerning widespread corporal punishment during his era.

All sources of historical data must be subjected to rigorous scientific analysis to determine both their authenticity (external criticism) and their accuracy (internal criticism). As with Aristotle and his fly with five legs, too often statements are uncritically accepted as factual statements if they are made by well-known persons. An authority in one area may have *opinions* concerning other areas but they are not necessarily based on facts. Similarly, the fact that records are "official" does not necessarily mean that all information contained in those records is accurate. A school board member, for example, might state that teachers are losing control of their classrooms. This would be his opinion, however, and would not be objective evidence. Thus, for each source, first it must be determined whether it is authentic (was this letter really written by George Washington?), and second, a judgment must be made concerning the accuracy of its contents.

External criticism, establishment of authenticity, is generally not the problem in educational research. The researcher does not usually have to worry about possible hoaxes or forgeries; there is not a big market for forged school board minutes! If the researcher is dealing with a problem for which sources are relatively old, and for which authenticity is not necessarily a given, there are a number of scientific techniques available to her or him. Age of document or relic, for example, can be fairly accurately estimated by applying various physical and chemical tests. Internal criticism, establishment of accuracy, is considerably more difficult. In determining the accuracy of documents, for example, there are at least four factors that must be considered:

1. Knowledge and competence of the author. It must be determined whether the person who wrote the document is, or was, a competent person and a person in a position to be knowledgeable concerning what actually occurred.

2. Time delay. An important consideration is how much time is likely to have elapsed between the event's occurrence and the recording of the facts. Reports written while an event is occurring (such as minutes of meetings), or shortly after (such as entries in a diary), are more likely to be accurate than reports written some time after, such as an anecdote in an autobiography.

3. Bias and motives of the author. People often report or record incorrect information. Such distortion of the truth may be intentional or unintentional. People, for example, tend to remember what they want to remember. People also tend to amplify, add little details, in order to make a story more interesting. A more serious problem occurs when the recorder has motives for consciously or unconsciously misinterpreting the facts. Accounts of the Kent State shootings given by a National Guardsman and also by a student who were both present would probably differ considerably.

4. Consistency of data. Each piece of evidence must be compared with all other pieces to determine the degree of agreement. If one observer's account disagrees with those of other observers, his or her testimony may be suspect. Thus, in a sense, by the very fact that they agree, sources may validate their accuracy. Having reviewed, abstracted, and evaluated the data, the researcher then organizes and synthesizes the findings and prepares a research report.

Data Synthesis

As with a review of related literature, historical data should be organized and synthesized, and conclusions and generalizations formulated. Just as a review of literature should not be a series of annotations, the results of a historical study should not be a chronological listing of events. Critics of historical research question the validity of generalizations based on events that can never be exactly duplicated. This concern does have some merit and supports the need for extreme caution in forming generalizations. However, the generalization problem is not unique to historical research. It is virtually impossible to exactly duplicate any educational research study involving human beings, even highly controlled experimental studies. With historical research, as with other research methods, the more similar a new situation is to a former situation, the more applicable generalizations based on the past situation will be.

Since summarization of historical research data involves logical analysis rather than statistical analysis, the researcher must take care to be as objective as possible. It is very easy to "overlook" or to discard evidence that does not support, or contradicts, the research hypothesis. One may, for example, subconsciously apply stricter criteria when engaged in internal criticism of unwanted data.

You probably realize by now that there is a lot more to historical research than you originally thought. A historical research study is definitely not for rookies! The complex demands of data collection and analysis generally require skill, experience, and resources beyond those of the beginning researcher.[5]

An Example of Historical Research

Many beginning researchers tend to have a preconceived notion that historical research (and history in general) is really quite dull. As the example to be discussed will illustrate, nothing could be further from the truth. Conducting a historical study can be a very challenging, exciting pursuit. Many of the characteristics that would make one a good detective—such as a desire to collect objective evidence and pursue clues—also make a good historical researcher. The following example is not presented as a model of historical research; by the researcher's own admission, it is based primarily on secondary sources, and it is of very little educational significance. It is presented because it does represent a fascinating area of research in which primary sources are hard to come by, or, as the researcher himself puts it, "it is fun to be in sort of scholarly disagreement in such a 'fun' area as this Dracula business. . . ."[6]

Based on his experiences as a youth in Transylvania, his knowledge of the Romanian language, translations of court records, and other documentary evidence, Meder hypothesizes quite simply that Dracula was (is?!) a woman—"a beautiful, seductive, evil noblewoman of highest society. . . ."[7] As one piece of evidence, Meder cites the fact that "Dracula" translates into English literally as "the female devil." Further, there is a known historic figure, Countess Elizabeth Bathory of Transylvania, who in the seventheeth century was proven guilty in the highest court of the direct blood-ritual murders of more than 600 young girls. Convinced that the blood of beautiful young virgins was the key to eternal beauty and youth, the Countess would bathe in the warm blood drained from their main blood vessel. According to Meder, "scores of legal documents still exist in the

---

5. For more complete information on historical research see Berlinger, R.E. *Historical analysis: Contemporary approaches to Clio's craft.* New York: John Wiley & Sons, 1978, and Block, J. *Understanding historical research: A search for truth.* Glen Rock, N.J.: Research Publications, 1971.

6. Meder, Z., personal communication, November 17, 1974.

7. Meder, Z. *Dracula is a woman.* Manuscript in preparation.

Hungarian archives to attest to the truth of these blood orgies." Because of her high rank, she was only locked up in her bed-chamber where she was later found dead, lying face down on the floor, the characteristic position of the undead in the Dracula legend. Since nobody actually saw her die, and since the guard who found her only saw her lying face down, it is easy to see how stories could be originated suggesting that she did not really die, but rather escaped to continue her ghastly pursuits.

As further evidence, Meder describes a painting titled *Elizabeth Bathory*, by István Csók, that seems to depict preparations for a blood bath. The female image of Dracula is also supported by another painting by Csók, titled *The Vampires*, showing a woman sucking blood from the neck artery of a young victim.

In his work, Meder also refutes the evidence presented by McNally and Florescu in *In Search of Dracula* identifying Dracula with a male Wallachian ruler who was known as Vlad the Impaler.[8] Meder questions not their evidence or its veracity, but rather its consistency with the Dracula legend. Regardless of who is correct, the question of Dracula's sex is, as Meder puts it, definitely a "fun area" of historical research.

---

8. McNally, R.T., & Florescu, R. *In search of Dracula.* Greenwich, Conn.: New York Graphic Society, 1972.

7

The Descriptive Method

Enablers

After reading chapter 7, you should be able to:

1. Briefly state the purpose of descriptive research.
2. List the major steps involved in designing and conducting a descriptive research study.
3. State the major difference between self-report and observational research.
4. Briefly describe four types of self-report research.
5. List and briefly describe the steps involved in conducting a questionnaire study.
6. Identify and briefly describe four major differences between an interview study and a questionnaire study.
7. Briefly describe three types of observational research.
8. Briefly describe the steps involved in conducting an observational study.

Definition, Purpose, and Process

Descriptive research involves collecting data in order to test hypotheses or to answer questions concerning the current status of the subject of the study. A descriptive study determines and reports the way things are. The descriptive method in general, and specific types of descriptive research in particular, will be discussed in some detail for two major reasons. First, a high percentage of reported research studies are descriptive in nature. Second, the descriptive method is useful for investigating a variety of educational problems. Typical descriptive studies are concerned with the assessment of attitudes, opinions, demographic information, conditions, and procedures. Descriptive data are usually collected through a questionnaire survey, interviews, or observation. Just as the historical researcher has no control over what *was,* the descriptive researcher has no control over what *is,* and can only measure what already exists.

Descriptive research sounds very simple; there is considerably more to it, however, than just asking questions and reporting answers. The same basic process is involved as for the other methods of research, and each component must be just as conscientiously executed; for example, samples must be carefully selected, and appropriate relationships and conclusions must be derived from the data. In addition, descriptive studies involve a number of unique problems. For

153

example, self-report studies, such as those utilizing questionnaires or interviews, often suffer from lack of response; many subjects do not return mailed questionnaires or attend scheduled interviews. In these situations it is very difficult to interpret findings since people who do not respond may feel very differently from those who do. Twenty percent of a sample, for example, might feel very negatively about the quinmester system and might avail themselves of every opportunity to express their unhappiness, such as on your questionniare. The other 80 percent, who feel neutrally or positively, might not be as motivated to respond. Thus, if conclusions were based only on those who responded, very wrong conclusions might be drawn concerning feelings toward the quinmester system. Descriptive studies utilizing observational techniques to collect data also involve complexities that are not readily apparent. Observers must be trained and recording forms must be developed so that data will be collected objectively and reliably.

Once a descriptive problem has been defined, related literature has been reviewed, and hypotheses or questions stated, the researcher must give careful thought to sample selection and data collection. Which population has the desired information, for example, is not always readily apparent; this point is often not sufficiently thought through ahead of time. Also, there are frequently alternative methods available for collecting desired data, one of which is generally more appropriate. Suppose, for example, your problem was concerned with how elementary level teachers spend their time during the school day. You might hypothesize that they spend one-third of their time on noninstructional activities such as collecting milk money and maintaining order. Your first thought might be to mail a questionnaire to a sample of principals. This procedure, however, would be based on the assumption that principals *know* how teachers spend their time. While principals would of course be familiar with the duties and responsibilities of their teachers, it is not unlikely that teacher reports concerning time devoted to each activity would differ, perhaps significantly, from principal reports. Thus, directly asking the teachers themselves would probably result in more accurate information. On the other hand, it is possible that teachers might tend to subconsciously exaggerate the amount of time they spend on activities they consider to be distasteful, such as clerical operations (for example, grading papers). Thus, further thought might indicate that direct observation would probably yield the most objective, accurate data.

Having decided on a target population and a data collection strategy, the next steps are to identify your accessible population, determine needed sample size, select an appropriate sampling technique, and select or develop a data collection instrument. Frequently, since one is generally asking questions that have not been asked before, or seeking information that is not already available, a descriptive study requires the development of an instrument appropriate for obtaining the desired information. Of course if there is a valid, reliable instrument available, it can be used, but using an instrument just "because it is there" is not a good idea. If you want the correct answers, you have to ask the correct questions. If instrument development is necessary, the instrument should be tried out and revised where necessary before it is used in the actual study. Having identified an appropriate sample, and selected or developed a valid data collection instrument, the next step is to carefully plan and execute the specific procedures of the study (when the instrument will be administered, to whom, and how) and the data analysis procedures. Of course the basic steps in conducting a descriptive study will vary, depending upon the nature of the research. In a content analysis study, for example, human subjects are not involved.

There are many different types of descriptive studies, and classifying them is not easy. However, a logical way to initially categorize them is in terms of how data are collected, through self-report or observation. In a self-report study, information is solicited from individuals using, for example, questionnaires, interviews, or standardized attitude scales. In an observation study, individuals are not asked for information; rather, the researcher obtains the desired data through other means such as direct observation. These two categories are not, of course, mutually exclusive; a self-report study may involve observation and vice versa. A case study, for example, is primarily observational in that information is collected *about* an individual or group. However, one or more instruments may be administered in order to more fully describe the characteristics of the individual or group under study.

Self-report Research

There are several major types of self-report research studies. The most well known and most-often used is probably survey research, which generally utilizes questionnaires or interviews to collect data.

Types of Self-report Research

While survey research is the most frequently encountered type of self-report research, developmental, follow-up, and sociometric studies also rely primarily on self-reported information.

Survey Research

A survey is an attempt to collect data from members of a population in order to determine the current status of that population with respect to one or more variables. Populations may be broadly defined, such as the American voting public, or narrowly defined, such as all parents of school-age children in Teenytown, U.S.A. Determining "current status . . . with respect to some variable" may involve assessment of a variety of types of information such as attitudes, opinions, characteristics, and demographic information. Surveys are generally viewed with some disdain because many people have encountered poorly planned, poorly executed survey studies utilizing poorly developed instruments. You should not condemn survey research, however, just because it has often been misused. After all, you do not dislike telephones just because a few people use them to make obscene phone calls! Descriptive research at its best can provide very valuable data. It represents considerably more than asking questions and reporting answers; it involves careful design and execution of each of the components of the research process, including the formulation of hypotheses, and may describe variables and relationships between variables. Surveys are used in many fields, including political science, sociology, economics, and education. In education their most common use is for the collection of data by schools or about schools. Surveys conducted by schools are usually prompted by a need for certain kinds of information related to instruction, facilities, or the student population. Surveys conducted to collect data about schools are initiated by a variety of groups, including governmental agencies and researchers.

Surveys are either sample surveys or census surveys, but usually the former. In a sample survey, as the name suggests, the researcher infers information about a population of interest based on the responses of a sample drawn from that population; preferably, the sample is either a simple-random or a stratified-random sample. In a census survey, an attempt is made to acquire data from each and every member of a population; a census survey is usually conducted when a population is relatively small and readily accessible, such as when a superintendent collects data from each principal in his or her system. Sample surveys are sometimes referred to as cross-sectional since information is collected at some point in time from a sample which hopefully represents all relevant subgroups in the population. Surveys concerned with the current status of construct variables (such as achievement or attitude), as opposed to concrete variables (such as number of professional journals to which English teachers subscribe, or number of pupils per class), involve not only careful selection from, and/or definition of, a population, but also require care in selection or development of the data-gathering instrument. It is considerably easier to develop a valid, reliable instrument for determining the percentage of teachers in each school who are teaching "out-of-field" than it is to develop one for assessing teachers' attitudes toward required, in-service teacher education programs.

There are a variety of types of surveys, many of which are familiar to most people. The results of various public opinion polls, for example, are frequently reported by the media. Such polls represent an attempt to determine how *all* the members of a population (be it the American public in general or citizens of Skunk Hollow) feel about a political, social, educational, or economic issue, not just vocal special-interest groups within the population. Public opinion polls are almost always sample surveys. Samples are selected to properly represent relevant subgroups (in terms of such variables as socioeconomic status, sex, and geographic location) and results are often reported separately for each of those subgroups as well as for the total group.

One type of survey unique to education is the school survey which may involve the study of an individual school or of all the schools in a particular system. School surveys are generally conducted for the purpose of internal or external evaluation or for assessment and projection of needs and usually are conducted as a cooperative effort between local school personnel and a visiting team of experts, typically from local educational agencies and institutions. Resulting recommendations and/or projections are based upon the collection of data concerning the current status of variables such as community characteristics, institutional and administrative personnel, curriculum and instruction, finances, and physical facilities. School surveys can provide necessary and valuable information to both the schools studied and to other agencies and groups (such as boards of public instruction) whose operations are school related.

Developmental Studies

Developmental studies are concerned primarily with behavior variables that differentiate children at different levels of age, growth, or maturation. Developmental studies may investigate progression along a number of dimensions, such as intellectual, physical, emotional, or social development. The children under study may be a relatively heterogeneous group, such as fourth graders in general, or may comprise a more narrowly defined homogeneous group, such as the study of the gifted, children with high intellectual potential. Knowledge concerning developmental patterns of various student groups can be applied in order to make the curriculum and instruction for various student populations more appropriate and relevant. Knowing that 4-year-old and 5-year-old children typically enjoy skill-testing games (such as jumping rope and bouncing balls) but do not enjoy group work or activities involving competition would certainly be helpful to a preschool teacher in developing lesson plans.[1]

Developmental studies may be cross-sectional or longitudinal; both methods have their own relative advantages and disadvantages. When the cross-sectional approach is used, different children at various stages of development are simultaneously studied; when the longitudinal method is used, the same group of children is studied over a period of time as the children progress from level to level. Suppose, for example, you were interested in studying the development of abstract thinking in elementary school students. If you used a cross-sectional approach, you would study samples of children at each of the six grade levels, including first graders to sixth graders; the children studied at one level would be different children from those studied at another level. If you use a longitudinal approach, you could select a sample of first graders and study the development of their abstract thinking as they progressed from grade to grade; the group studied at the sixth-grade level would be the same group that was studied at the first-grade level. The advantage of the cross-sectional method is that larger groups can be studied. In longitudinal studies, samples tend to shrink as time goes by; keeping track of subjects over periods of time can be difficult, as can maintaining their participation in the study. A major concern in a cross-sectional study is selecting samples of children that truly represent children at their level; a further related problem is selecting samples at different levels that are comparable on relevant variables such as intelligence. An advantage of the longitudinal method is that this latter concern about comparability is not a problem in that the same group is involved at each level. A major disadvantage of the longitudinal method is that an extended commitment must be made by the researcher, the subjects, and all others involved. Although for particular problems one of the methods may be clearly more appropriate, the cross-sectional approach is generally preferable because of the typically larger samples.

Follow-Up Studies

A follow-up study is conducted to determine the status of a group of interest after some period of time. Like school surveys, follow-up studies are often conducted by educational institutions for the purpose of internal or external evaluation of

---

1. Strang, R.M. *An introduction to child study* (4th ed.). New York: Macmillan, 1959.

their instructional program, or some aspect of it. Accreditation agencies, for example, typically require systematic follow-up of teacher education program graduates. Such follow-up efforts typically seek objective information regarding the current status of the former students (Are you presently employed?) as well as attitudinal and opinion data concerning the graduates' perceptions of the adequacy of their training. If a majority of graduates should indicate, for example, that they feel the career counseling they received was poor, this finding would suggest an area in need of improvement. Similarly, if a number of graduates should indicate that they have been unable to obtain employment due to a lack of certain competencies, this information would also be valuable input for the upgrading of the program of interest. Of course the results of such a follow-up study may also be very positive, indicating a high degree of satisfaction with the program.

Follow-up studies may also be conducted solely for research purposes. A researcher may be interested, for example, in assessing the degree to which initial treatment effects have been maintained over time. A study might demonstrate that students participating in preschool training are better adjusted socially and achieve higher academically in the first grade. A follow-up study could be conducted to determine if this initial advantage is still in evidence at the end of the third grade. Many treatments which have an initial impact do not have a lasting effect; initial differences "wash out" or disappear after some period of time. A treatment may temporarily change attitudes, for example, but when the subjects are removed from the experimental setting they may gradually regress to their original point of view. Conversely, some treatments do not result in initial differences but may produce long-range effects. Delayed feedback concerning adequacy of test performance, for example, is a technique which does not necessarily improve initial achievement but does seem to facilitate long-term retention.[2] If follow-up data were not collected, it would be erroneously concluded that delayed feedback has no effect. Thus, in many areas of research, a follow-up study is essential to a more complete understanding of the effects of a given approach or technique.

Sociometric Studies

Sociometry is the assessment and analysis of the interpersonal relationships within a group of individuals. By analyzing the expressed choices or preferences of group members for other members of the group, degree of acceptance or rejection for members of the group can be determined. The basic sociometric process involves asking each member to indicate with which other members she or he would most like to engage in a particular activity. For example, you might ask subjects to list in order of preference the three individuals they would most like to work with on a cooperative project. As you well know, choices will vary depending upon the activity; the person you would most enjoy going with to a party is not necessarily the same person with whom you would like to write a joint term paper. The choices made by the group members are graphically depicted in a diagram called a sociogram. A sociogram may take many forms and use a variety of symbols,

---

2. See, for example, English, R.A., & Kinzer, J.R. The effect of immediate and delayed feedback on retention of subject matter. *Psychology in the Schools,* 1966, *3,* 143–147.

but basically it shows who chose whom. A sociogram will clearly identify "stars"—members chosen quite frequently, "isolates"—members not chosen, and "cliques"—small subgroups of individuals who mutually select each other.

Sociometric techniques are utilized by both researchers and practitioners. A number of educational research studies have been concerned with the relationship between group status and other variables such as personality characteristics. Another type of research study involves assessment of initial interpersonal relationship patterns, introduction of a treatment designed to change the existing pattern, and postassessment to determine pattern changes. A similar procedure may be utilized by teachers in an attempt, for example, to bring isolates into the group. If Clancy Clutz were identified as being an isolate, his teacher could make a concerted effort to provide opportunities for Clancy to interact with other members of the group. Thus, the sociometric process is one that is relatively simple to apply and can provide data useful for the solution of immediate social problems and for the development of theories concerning interpersonal relationships within a group.

Conducting Self-report Research

Self-report research requires the collection of standardized, quantifiable information from all members of a population or sample. In other words, in order to obtain comparable data from all subjects, the same questions must be asked. Any of the types of tests described in chapter 5 (i.e., achievement, character and personality, intelligence, aptitude) can be used in a self-report research study. Two additional commonly used procedures for collecting self-report data are the questionnaire study and the interview study.

Conducting a Questionnaire Study

Criticisms of questionnaires are related not to their use but to their misuse. Too many carelessly and incompetently constructed questionnaires have unfortunately been administered and distributed. Development of a sound questionnaire requires both skill and time. However, the use of a questionnaire has some definite advantages over other methods of collecting data that are not available through other sources. In comparison to use of an interview procedure, for example, a questionnaire is much more efficient in that it requires less time, is less expensive, and permits collection of data from a much larger sample. Questionnaires may be administered to subjects but are usually mailed. Although a personally administered questionnaire has some of the same advantages inherent in the use of an interview, such as the opportunity to establish rapport with respondents, explain the purposes of the study, and clarify individual items, it is not usually the case that the members of a sample of interest are conveniently found together in one location. Attempting to travel to each respondent in order to administer the questionnaire is generally impracticable and eliminates the advantage of being able to contact a large sample.

The steps in conducting a questionnaire study are essentially the same as for other types of research, although data collection involves some unique considerations.

Statement of the Problem   The problem under investigation, and the topic of the questionnaire, must be of sufficient significance to motivate subjects to respond; questionnaires dealing with trivial issues usually end up in the circular file of potential respondents. The problem must be defined in terms of specific objectives concerning the kind of information needed; specific hypotheses or questions must be formulated and every item on the questionnaire should directly relate to them.

Selection of Subjects   Subjects should be selected using an appropriate sampling technique (or an entire population may be used), and identified subjects must be persons who (1) have the desired information and (2) are likely to be willing to give it. Individuals who possess the desired information but are not sufficiently interested, or for whom the topic under study has little meaning, are not likely to respond. It is sometimes worth the effort to do a preliminary check of potential responders to determine their receptivity. In some cases it is more productive to send the questionnaire to a person of authority rather than directly to the person with the desired information; if a person's boss passes along a questionnaire and asks the person to complete and return it, that person is more likely to do so than if *you* ask him or her!

Construction of the Questionnaire   As a general guideline, the questionnaire should be as attractive and brief, and as easy to respond to, as possible. Sloppy looking questionnaires turn people off, lengthy questionnaires turn people off, questionnaires requiring lengthy responses to each question *really* turn people off! Turning people off is not the way to get them to respond. To meet this guideline you must carefully plan both the content and the format of the questionnaire. No item should be included that does not directly relate to the objectives of the study, and structured, or closed-form, items should be used if at all possible. A structured item consists of a question and a list of alternative responses from which the respondent selects. The list of alternatives should include all possible responses, and each possible response should be distinctly different from the rest. In some cases, a very short written response may be required, but generally a structured item is multiple-choice in nature (yes or no, A, B, C, D, or E). In addition to facilitating response, structured items also facilitate data analysis; scoring is very objective and efficient. A potential disadvantage is the possibility that a subject's true response in not listed among the alternatives. Therefore, questionnaires should include an "other" category for each item, a space for a subject to write in a response not anticipated by the researcher. An unstructured item format, in which the responder has complete freedom of response (questions are asked with no possible responses indicated), is sometimes defended on the grounds that it permits greater depth of response and may permit insight into the reasons for responses. While this may be true, and unstructured items are simpler to construct, the disadvantages of this approach generally outweigh the advantages; subjects often provide information extraneous to the objectives of the study, responses are difficult to score and analyze, and subjects are not happy with an instrument that requires written responses. For certain topics or purposes unstructured items may be necessary and some questionnaires contain both structured and unstructured items. In general, however, structured items are to be preferred.

Individual items should also be constructed according to a set of guidelines. The number one rule is that each question should deal with a single concept and be worded as clearly as possible; any term or concept that might mean different things to different people should be defined. Do not ask, for example, "Do you spend a lot of time each week preparing for your classes?"; one teacher might consider one hour per day "a lot" while another might consider one hour per week "a lot." Instead, ask "how many hours per week do you spend preparing for your classes" or "how much time do you spend per week preparing for your classes—(A) less than 30 minutes, (B) between 30 minutes and an hour, (C) between 1 and 3 hours, (D) between 3 and 5 hours, (E) more than 5 hours." Also, when necessary, questions should indicate a point of reference. Do not ask, for example, "How much time do you spend preparing for your classes?" Instead, ask, "How much time do you spend *per day* (or per whatever time period you wish) preparing for your classes?" As another example, if you were interested not only in how many hours were actually spent in preparation but also in teachers' perceptions concerning that time, you would not ask, "Do you think you spend a lot of time preparing for classes?" Instead, you would ask, "Do you think you spend a lot of time *compared to other teachers* (or compared to whatever you wished) preparing for your classes?" As several of the above examples illustrate, underlining (in a typed questionnaire) or italicizing (in a printed one) key phrases may also help to clarify questions.

There are also a number of "don'ts" to keep in mind when constructing items. First, avoid leading questions which suggest that one response may be more appropriate than another. Second, avoid touchy questions to which the respondent might not reply honestly. Asking a teacher, for example, if he or she sets high standards for achievement is like asking a mother if she loves her children; the answer in both cases is going to be "of course!" Another major "don't" is not to ask a question that assumes a fact not necessarily in evidence; such questions present alternatives that are all unacceptable. The classic question of this nature is, "Have you stopped beating your wife?" The question calls for a simple "yes" or "no" response, but how does a husband respond who has never beaten his wife?! If he answers "yes," it suggests that he *used* to beat his wife but he has stopped; if he answers "no," it suggests that he is *still* beating his wife!

As with organization of the review of related literature, and for similar reasons, each developed item should be placed on a separate index card. This facilitates arrangement of the items so that they will be presented in a logical order; it is much easier to reorder index cards than to redo a questionnaire once it is developed. After the items have been developed, and their order determined, directions to respondents must be written. Standardized directions promote standardized, comparable responses. Directions should specify how the subject is to respond and where. When determining how subjects should respond, you should consider how the results will be tabulated. If results are to be machine-scored, for example, you might have subjects use a separate answer sheet and 'a number two pencil instead of having them circle responses on the questionnaire.

Validation of the Questionnaire   A too-often-neglected procedure is validation of the questionnaire in order to determine if it measures what it was developed to measure. Validation is probably not done more often because it is not easy and requires much additional time and effort. However, anything worth doing is worth doing well. The appropriate validation procedure for a given questionnaire will depend upon the nature of the instrument. A questionnaire developed to determine the classroom behavior of teachers, for example, might be validated by observing a sample of respondents to determine the degree to which their actual behavior is consistent with their self-reported behavior.

Preparation of the Cover Letter   Every mailed questionnaire must be accompanied by a cover letter that explains what is being asked of the respondent and why, and which hopefully motivates the responder to fulfill the request. The letter should be brief, neat, and addressed specifically to the potential responder (Dear Dr. Zhivago, not Dear Sir). The letter should also explain the purpose of the study, emphasizing its importance and significance, and give the responder a good reason for cooperating; the fact that you need the data for your thesis or dissertation is not a good reason. If at all possible, it should state a commitment to share the results of the study when completed. It usually helps if you can get the endorsement of an organization, institution, group, or administrator with which the responder is associated, or which the responder views with respect (such as a professional organization). If the group is too heterogeneous, or has no identifiable affiliation in common, a general appeal to professionalism can be made. Sometimes even humor and a little psychology are used. For example, a major car manufacturer sent out a questionnaire concerning one of their models to owners of that model. A quarter was enclosed along with a note indicating that the company was aware that the recipient of the questionnaire was quite busy and that the quarter was a gesture of appreciation for the anticipated cooperation. Besides being mildly amusing, the technique had the effect of making recipients feel like they "owed" the company a response. If possible, having the letter signed by a respected, well-known person also helps.

If the questions to be asked are at all threatening (such as items dealing with sex or attitudes toward the local administration), anonymity or confidentiality of responses must be assured. Complete anonymity probably increases the truthfulness of responses as well as the precentage of returns. On the other hand, anonymity makes follow-up efforts extremely difficult since you do not know who responded and who did not. It also makes subgroup comparisons impossible (for example, secondary teachers versus elementary teachers) unless specific classification items are included in the questionnaire itself (for example, "What grade do you teach?"). If identification is deemed necessary, complete confidentiality of responses must be guaranteed.

A specific deadline date by which the completed questionnaire is to be returned should be given. This date should give subjects enough time to respond but discourage procrastination; two to three weeks will usually be sufficient. Each letter to be sent should be signed individually. When many questionnaires are to be sent, individually signing each letter will admittedly take considerably more time than making copies of one signed letter, but it adds a personal touch which might make a difference in the potential respondent's decision to comply or not comply. Finally, the act of responding should be made as painless as possible. A stamped, addressed, return envelope should be included; if not, your letter and questionnaire will very likely be placed into the circular file along with the mail

```
CHARLES E. MERRILL PUBLISHING COMPANY              SERVING AMERICA'S SCHOOLS SINCE 1842
A BELL & HOWELL COMPANY


1300 Alum Creek Drive  Columbus, Ohio 43216    (614) 258-8441

July 18, 1980




Professor Ima Teecher
College of Education - 201
University of Brillyunce
Brillyunce, California
               99999

Dear Professor Teecher:

As a publisher in speech pathology, it is our goal to publish the
most useful, professional and attractive textbooks for your courses.
The enclosed questionnaire is designed to solicit your opinions
concerning the content and format features of an anatomy and
physiology of speech text which would best meet your needs and
preferences.  Your suggestions will be reflected in a book to be
developed during the coming year.

We would greatly appreciate it if you would complete the questionnaire
and return it in the enclosed addressed, stamped envelope by August 1.
We realize that your time is valuable and to express our appreciation
for your assistance we will be pleased to send you any two of the books
listed on the attached sheet.  Just check the books of your choice and
return the sheet with your questionnaire.

We sincerely thank you for your cooperation.


Best regards,

Marianne Taflinger
Marianne Taflinger
Sponsoring Editor
```

Figure 7.1.
Sample cover letter for a questionnaire.

addressed to "occupant"! (See Figure 7.1 for an example of a properly written cover letter.)

Pretesting the Questionnaire   The questionnaire should be tried out in a field test just as a research plan should be executed first as a pilot study, and for essentially the same reasons. Pretesting the questionnaire yields data concerning instrument deficiencies as well as suggestions for improvement. Having two or three available people complete the questionnaire first will result in the identification of major problems. The subsequently revised instrument and the cover letter should then be sent to a small sample from your intended population or a highly similar population. Pretest subjects should be encouraged to make comments and suggestions concerning directions, recording procedures, and specific items. If the percentage of returns is very low, then both the letter and the instrument should be carefully reexamined. The feedback from those who do respond should be carefully studied and considered. Lastly, proposed data tabulation and analysis procedures should be applied to the pretest data. The end product of the pretest will be a revised instrument ready to be mailed to the already selected subjects.

Follow-Up Activities   Not everyone to whom you send a questionnaire is going to return it (what an understatement!). Some recipients have no intention of completing it, others mean to but put it off so long that they either forget it or lose it. It is for this latter group that follow-up activities are primarily conducted. The higher your percentage of returns, the better. Although you should not expect 100%, you should not be satisfied with whatever you get after your first mailing. If your percentage of returns is not at *least* 70%, the validity of your conclusions will be weak. Given all the work you have already done, it makes no sense to end up with shaky findings and a study of limited value when some additional effort on your part can make a big difference.

An initial follow-up strategy is to simply send out a reminder postcard. This will prompt those who meant to fill it out but put it off and have not yet lost it! If responses are not anonymous you can mail a card only to those who have not responded. If they are anonymous, and you do not know who has and who has not responded, simply send a card to everyone; include a statement like the ones used by finance companies—"If you have already responded, please disregard this reminder and thank you for your cooperation." Full-scale follow-up activities are usually begun shortly after the deadline for responding has passed. A second set of questionnaires is sent to subjects, but with a new cover letter, and of course another stamped envelope. The new letter should suggest that you know they *meant* to respond but that they may have misplaced the questionnaire or maybe they never even received it. In other words, do not scold them; provide them with an acceptable reason for their nonresponse. The significance and purpose of the study should be repeated and the importance of *their* input should be reemphasized. The letter should suggest subtly that many others are responding; this implies that their peers have found the study to be important and so should they.

If the second mailing does not result in an overall acceptable percentage of return, be creative. Magazine subscription agencies have developed follow-up procedures to a science and have become very creative. I once let a subscription to a popular weekly magazine lapse and received several gentle reminders and "sensational one-time-only offers." One afternoon I received a long-distance call from several thousand miles away and the sweet voice at the other end suggested that my mail was apparently not getting through and wouldn't I like to renew my subscription. I bit! The point is that phone calls, if feasible, may be used, or any other method of written, verbal, or personal communication which might induce additional subjects to respond. They may grow to admire your persistence!

If your questionnaire is well constructed, and your cover letter well written, you should get at least an adequate response rate. First mailings will typically produce at least a 40% return. A second mailing should bring your percentage up to at least 70%; mailings beyond a second are generally not too effective. After a second mailing, use other approaches until an acceptable percentage of returns is achieved.

Dealing with Nonresponse   Despite all your initial and follow-up efforts, you may find yourself with an unacceptably low response percentage, say 60%. The problem is one of generalizability of results since you do not know if the 60% represents the population from which the sample was originally selected as well as the total original sample. If you knew that the responding subjects were essentially a random sample of the total sample, there would be no problem; but you do not know that. The subjects who responded may be different in some systematic way from nonresponders (the old volunteer syndrome); they may be better educated, feel more strongly about the issue (positively or negatively), or be more success-ful. In follow-up studies of program graduates discussed previously, successful graduates might tend to respond more than unemployed graduates or those in low-paying jobs. Generalizations based on information provided by responders only would suggest a rosier picture than if all graduates responded.

The usual approach to dealing with excessive nonresponse is to try to deter-mine if nonresponders are different from responders in some systematic way by randomly selecting a small subsample of nonresponders and interviewing them, either in person or by phone. Through an interview, the researcher can not only obtain responses to questionnaire items but can also try to determine any distin-guishing characteristics. If responses are essentially the same for the interviewed subjects as for the original responders, it may be assumed that the response group is representative and the results generalizable. If they are significantly different, such differences as well as resulting limitations to generalizability must be discus-sed in the research report. For example, instead of concluding that program graduates express general satisfaction with their training, you might conclude that at least *successful* program graduates express satisfaction (naturally!).

Analysis of Results   When presenting the results of a questionnaire study, the response rate for each item should be given as well as the total sample size and the overall percentage of returns, since all respondents may not answer all questions. The simplest way to present the results is to indicate the percentage of responders who selected each alternative for each item. For example, "on item 4 dealing with possession of a master's degree, 50% said yes, 30% said no, and 20% said they were working on one." In addition to simply determining choices, relationships between variables can be investigated by comparing responses on one item with reponses on other items. For example, it might be determined that 80% of those reporting possession of a master's degree expressed favorable attitudes toward individualized instruction, while only 40% of those reporting lack of a master's degree expressed a favorable attitude. Thus, possible explanations for certain attitudes and behaviors can be explored by identifying factors that seem to be related to certain responses. This type of relationship analysis can also be used to test hypotheses. For example, it might be hypothesized that teachers with advanced degrees are more receptive to nontraditional methods of instruc-tion. The above finding concerning master's degrees and attitudes toward in-dividualized instruction would be data in support of the hypothesis. Establishment of a direct cause-effect relationship between training and attitudes would not, however, be warranted. Due to lack of manipulation of variables it would not be possible to determine whether increased training *results* in increased receptivity to new ideas or whether receptive teachers seek out additional education. Resolution of such issues would require conducting a study using another method of research.

Conducting an Interview Study

An interview is essentially the oral, in-person, administration of a questionnaire to each member of a sample. The interview has a number of unique advantages and disadvantages. When well conducted it can produce in-depth data not possible with a questionnaire; on the other hand, it is expensive and time consuming, and generally involves smaller samples. The interview is most appropriate for asking questions which cannot effectively be structured into a multiple-choice format, such as questions of a personal nature. In contrast to the questionnaire, the interview is flexible; the interviewer can adapt the situation to each subject. By establishing rapport and a trust relationship, the interviewer can often obtain data that subjects would not give on a questionnaire. The interview may also result in more accurate and honest responses since the interviewer can explain and clarify both the purpose of the research and individual questions. Another advantage of the interview is that the interviewer can follow up on incomplete or unclear responses by asking additional probing questions. Reasons for particular responses can also be determined.

Direct interviewer-interviewee contact also has its disadvantages. The responses given by a subject may be biased and affected by her or his reaction to the interviewer, either positive or negative. For example, a subject may become hostile or uncooperative if the interviewer reminds him of his first wife's mother! Another disadvantage is that it is very time consuming and expensive, and the number of subjects that can be handled is generally considerably less than the number which can be sent a questionnaire; interviewing 500 people would be a monumental task as compared to mailing 500 questionnaires. Also, the interview requires a level of skill usually beyond that of the beginning researcher. It requires not only research skills, such as knowledge of sampling and instrument development, but also a variety of communication and interpersonal relations skills.

The steps in conducting an interview study are basically the same as for a questionnaire study, with some unique differences. The process of selecting and defining a problem and formulating hypotheses is essentially the same. Samples of subjects who possess the desired information are selected in the usual manner except that they are typically smaller. An effort must be made to get a commitment of cooperation from selected subjects. Subjects who do not attend interviews present the same problems as subjects who do not return questionnaires. The problem is more serious for interviews, however, since the sample size is smaller to begin with. The major differences between an interview study and a questionnaire study are the nature of the instrument involved (an interview guide versus a questionnaire), the need for human relations and communication skills, methods for recording responses, and nature of pretest activities.

Construction of the Interview Guide   The interviewer must have a written guide which indicates what questions are to be asked and in what order, and what additional prompting or probing is permitted. In order to obtain standardized, comparable data from each subject, all interviews must be conducted in essentially the same manner. As with a questionnaire, each question in the interview should relate to a specific study objective. Also as with a questionnaire, questions may be structured or unstructured. Since an interview is usually used when a questionnaire is not really appropriate, it usually involves unstructured or semi-structured questions. Structured questions, which require the interviewee to select from alternatives, are of course easier to analyze but tend to defeat the purpose of an interview. Completely unstructured questions, on the other hand, which allow absolute freedom of response, can yield in-depth responses and provide otherwise unobtainable insights, but produce data that are very difficult to quantify and tabulate. Therefore most interviews use a semistructured approach involving the asking of structured questions followed by clarifying unstructured, or open-ended, questions. The unstructured questions facilitate explanation and understanding of the responses to the structured questions. Thus, a combination of objectivity and depth can be obtained, and results can be tabulated as well as explained.

Many of the guidelines for constructing questionnaires apply to the construction of interview guides. The interview should be as brief as possible, and questions should be worded as clearly as possible. Terms should be defined when necessary and a point of reference given when appropriate. Also, leading questions should be avoided, as should questions based on the assumption of a fact not in evidence ("tell me, have you stopped beating your wife?").

Communication During the Interview   Effective communication during the interview is critical, and interviewers should be well trained before the study begins. Since first impressions can make a big difference, getting the interview "off on the right foot" is important. Before the first formal question is asked, some time should be spent in establishing rapport and putting the interviewee at ease. The purpose of the study should be explained and strict confidentiality of responses assured. As the interview proceeds, the interviewer should make full use of the advantages of the interview situation. The interviewer can, for example, explain the purpose of any question whose relevance to the purpose of the study is unclear to the subject. The interviewer should also be sensitive to the reactions of the subject and proceed accordingly. If a subject appears to be threatened by a particular line of questioning, for example, the interviewer should move on to other questions and return to the threatening questions later, when perhaps the interviewee is more relaxed. Or, if the subject gets carried away with a question and gets "off the track," the interviewer can gently get him or her back on target. Above all, the interviewer should avoid words or actions that may make the subject unhappy or feel threatened. Frowns and disapproving looks have no place in an interview!

Recording Responses   Responses made during an interview can be recorded manually by the interviewer or mechanically by a recording device. If the interviewer records the responses, space is provided after each question in the interview guide, and responses are recorded either during the interview as it progresses or shortly after the interview is completed. If responses are recorded during the interview it may tend to slow things down, especially if responses are at all lengthy; it also may make some subjects nervous to have someone writing down every word they say. If responses are recorded after the interview, the interviewer is not likely to recall every response exactly as given, especially if many questions are asked. On the other hand, if a recording device such as a cassette recorder is used, the interview moves more quickly, and responses are recorded exactly as given. If responses need clarifying, several persons can listen to the recordings independently, and classifications can be compared. A recorder, of course, may also initially make subjects nervous, but usually they tend to forget its presence as the interview progresses, whereas they are constantly aware when someone is writing down their responses. In general, mechanical recording is more objective and efficient.

Pretesting the Interview Procedure   The interview guide, interview procedures, and analysis procedures should be tried out, before the main study begins, using a small sample from the same or a very similar population to the one being used in the study. Feedback from a small pilot study can be used to revise questions in the guide that are apparently unclear, do not solicit the desired information, or produce negative reactions in subjects. Insights into better ways to handle certain questions can also be acquired. Finally, the pilot study will determine whether the resulting data can be quantified and analyzed in the manner intended. As with the pretesting of a questionnaire, feedback should be sought from pilot subjects as well as from the interviewers. As always, a pretest of procedures is a good use of the researcher's time.

Observational Research

In an observational study, the current status of a phenomenon is determined not by *asking* but by *observing*. For certain research questions, observation is clearly the most appropriate approach. For example, you could ask teachers how they handle discipline in their classrooms, but more objective information would probably be obtained by actually observing several of each teacher's classes. The value of observational research is illustrated by a study conducted in the Southwest on the classroom interaction between teachers and Mexican-American students.[3] Many teachers claimed that Mexican-American children are difficult to teach due to their lack of participation in classroom activities, their failure to ask or answer questions, and the like. Systematic observation, however, revealed that the main reason they did not answer questions, for example, was that they were not asked very many! Observation revealed that teachers tended to talk less often and less favorably to Mexican-American children and to ask them fewer questions. Thus, observation not only provided more accurate information than teacher reports but also made the teachers aware that they were unintentionally part of the problem. Observational techniques may also be used to collect data in nondescriptive studies. In an experimental study designed to determine the effect of behavior modification techniques on disruptive behavior, for example, students could be observed prior to and following the introduction of behavior modification in order to determine if instances of disruptive behavior were reduced in number.

---

3. Jackson, G., & Cosca, C. The inequality of educational opportunity in the Southwest: An observational study of ethnically mixed classrooms. *American Educational Research Journal,* 1974, *11*(3), 219–229.

Observational data can be collected on inanimate objects such as books as well as human beings. In either case, an observational study must be planned and executed just as carefully as any other type of research study.

Types of Observational Research

The major types of observational research are nonparticipant observation, participant observation, and ethnography. Nonparticipant observation includes naturalistic observation, simulation observation, case studies, and content analysis. Although you may encounter other applications of the observational approach, the above mentioned are the ones most commonly used in educational research.

Nonparticipant Observation

In nonparticipant observation, the observer is not directly involved in the situation to be observed. In other words, the observer is on the outside looking in and does not intentionally interact with, or affect, the object of the observation.

Naturalistic Observation   Certain kinds of behavior can only be (or best be) observed as they occur naturally. In such situations the observer purposely controls or manipulates nothing, and in fact works very hard at not affecting the observed situation in any way.[4] The intent is to record and study behavior as it normally occurs. As an example, classroom behavior—behavior of the teacher, behavior of the student, and the interactions between teacher and student—can best be studied through naturalistic observation. Insights gained as a result of naturalistic observation often form the foundation for more controlled research in an area. The work of Piaget, for example, involved primarily naturalistic observation of children. His research, and the research which it stimulated, have provided education with many important findings regarding concept development in children.

Simulation Observation   In simulation observation the researcher creates the situation to be observed and tells subjects what activities they are to engage in. This technique allows the researcher to observe behavior that occurs infrequently in natural situations or not at all (for example, having a teacher trainee role play a teacher-parent conference). The major disadvantage of this type of observation is of course that it is not natural, and the behavior exhibited by subjects may not be the behavior that would occur in a natural setting. Subjects may behave the way they think they should behave rather than the way they really would behave. In reality, this potential problem is not as serious as it may sound. Subjects tend to get carried away with their roles and often exhibit very true-to-life emotions. Besides, even if subjects "fake it" at least they show that they are aware of the correct way to behave. A student who demonstrates the correct way to interact with an irate parent at least *knows* what should be done.

Two major types of simulation are individual role playing and team role playing. In individual role playing the researcher is interested in the behavior of

4. Agnew, N.M., & Pyke, S.W. *The science game: An introduction to research in the behavioral sciences.* Englewood Cliffs, N.J.: Prentice-Hall, 1978.

one person, although other "players" are involved. The individual is given a role, a situation, and a problem to solve. The observer then records and evaluates the subject's solution to the problem and the way in which she or he executes it. As an example, a teacher trainee might be told:

> Yesterday Billy Bungle was caught drawing pictures on his desk. You made him stay after school and wash and wax all the desks. The principal has just informed you that a very upset Mrs. Bungle is on her way to see you. What will you say to Mrs. Bungle?

In a team role-playing situation, a small group is presented with a situation and a problem and solutions are recorded and evaluated. Qualities such as leadership ability may also be studied. As an example, a group might be told:

> The faculty has appointed you a committee of six. Your charge is to come up with possible solutions to the problem of student fights in the halls, an occurrence which has been increasing.

The Case Study   A case study is the in-depth investigation of an individual, group, or institution. In education, case studies are typically conducted to determine the background, environment, and characteristics of children with problems. The primary purpose of a case study is to determine the factors, and relationships among the factors, that have resulted in the current behavior or status of the subject of the study. In other words, the purpose of a case study is to determine *why,* not just what. The major problems with case studies are possible observer bias (the observer sees what he or she wants to see) and lack of generalizability. The insights which may be acquired concerning a particular case may not apply to any other case. Therefore the major use of case studies is in individual counseling, not the solution of research problems. Case studies may, however, suggest hypotheses which can be tested using another method of research.

Content Analysis   Content analysis is the systematic, quantitative description of the composition of the object of the study. Typical subjects for content analysis include books, documents, and creative productions such as musical compositions, works of art, and photographs. Textbooks are frequently analyzed to determine such things as readability level and the existence or extent of bias in presentation of material. Content analysis, for example, can be used to determine if a particular textbook is appropriate for the intended grade level by analyzing such variables as frequency of certain vocabulary words and average sentence length. Content analysis studies may be quite simple, involving primarily frequency counts, or very sophisticated and complex, involving investigation of the existence of bias or prejudice in a textbook.

Participant Observation

In participant observation, the observer actually becomes a part of, a participant in, the situation to be observed. The rationale for participant observation is that in many cases the view from the inside is somewhat different than the view from the outside looking in. There are, of course, degrees of participation, and observation may be overt or covert. For example, if a researcher obtains permission to attend faculty meetings at a local high school in order to study principal-teacher interactions, the observation is more overt. If the researcher manages to get hired as a teacher, the intent being to study principal-teacher interactions without anyone being aware that such observation is occurring, the degree of participation is greater and the observation is covert. It is very likely that the conclusions drawn from the two approaches would differ. Although the covert observation might provide more valid findings, this type of observation has some obvious drawbacks. First and foremost is the highly questionable ethics involved in observing people without their knowledge and, more than likely, recording conversations with concealed recording devices. Another major problem is the issue of the impact of the observer's participation on the situation observed. In other words, the situation is somewhat different than it would have been if the observer did not participate. Also, there is the possibility that the greater the participation, the greater the bias. All observers strive to be totally objective. But in the above example, it is possible that the observer would tend to identify with the role of teacher, and observations and/or interpretations of principal-teacher interactions would be affected by this role identification.

Participant observation studies also vary in the degree of structure involved in the inquiry. Participant observation studies may be designed to test hypotheses, to derive hypotheses, or both. Those which are oriented toward hypothesis testing are more structured and more focused in terms of the behaviors to be observed and recorded. More typically, however, such studies are hypothesis generating. Thus, participant observation research is characterized by the collection of large amounts of data that are difficult to analyze. This problem is illustrated and described in the following statement made by a participant observer:

> . . . our files contain approximately five thousand single-spaced pages of such material. Faced with such a quantity of "rich" but varied data, the researcher faces the problem of how to analyze it systematically and then to present . . . conclusions so as to convince other scientists of their validity.[5]

Thus, the good news is that participant observation typically yields an abundance of potentially useful data. The bad news is that analyzing such data and drawing defensible conclusions in not an easy task.

Ethnography

A relatively recent trend in education is a growing interest in ethnographic methods of research. The main reason for the enthusiasm for ethnography is probably dissatisfaction with more traditional approaches for investigating certain kinds of educational problems. While application of ethnographic methodology may be new to education, it is not a new research strategy. It has been used extensively by anthropologists for years and is in fact frequently referred to as the anthropological approach.

---

5. Becker, H.S. Problems of inference and proof in participant observation. *American Sociological Review*, 1958, *23*(6).

Definition Ethnography involves intensive data collection, that is, collection of data on many variables over an extended period of time, in a naturalistic setting. The unit of observation in an ethnographic study is typically a classroom, or even a school. Rather than, for example, studying the teaching-learning process by collecting test scores before and after some treatment, the ethnographer works more inductively by observing many aspects of the learning environment and attempting to identify factors associated with effective and ineffective environments.[6] The rationale behind the use of ethnography is the research-based belief that behavior is significantly influenced by the environment in which it occurs. In other words, behavior occurs in a context, and accurate understanding of the behavior requires understanding of the context in which it occurs. Organizations such as schools, for example, definitely influence the behavior of persons within them.[7] Relatedly, ethnographers point out that if we wish to generalize our findings to real-world settings, the findings should be derived from research conducted in real-world settings.

Method Ethnographic research may involve nonparticipant observation, participant observation, or both. Typically, ethnographic studies are characterized by some type of participant observation at an overt level. Ethnography, however, represents "multi-instrument" research, and the ethnographer uses a variety of data collection strategies in conjunction with observation. Preliminary participant observation provides data that guides the researcher in selecting other appropriate approaches. Pelto and Pelto classify the possibilities as verbal and nonverbal.[8] Verbal techniques involve interactions between the researcher and persons in the research environment, and include tools such as questionnaires, interviews, attitude scales, and other psychological instruments. Nonverbal techniques are less obstrusive, that is, less likely to affect the behaviors being studied, and include such strategies as the use of recording devices and examination of written records.

The fact that ethnographic research is characterized by participant observation and a more inductive approach does not mean that it is unsystematic or haphazard. Ethnographers plan their research studies just as carefully as researchers conducting other types of research. Having refined the research problem of interest, the ethnographic researcher makes informed decisions concerning the most appropriate environment, or setting, to study, and the most effective level of participation. These decisions involve related decisions such as which persons in the environment should be interacted with, and what should be the nature of the interaction, for example, what kinds of questions should be asked. These decisions are guided by tentative, preliminary hypotheses. Recall that in chapter 2 it was stated that a tentative hypothesis guides the review of related literature which in turn guides the formulation of a specific, testable hypothesis. The same basic process is involved in ethnography. The tentative hypothesis or hypotheses guide

6. Fienberg, S.E. The collection and analysis of ethnographic data in educational research. *Anthropology & Education Quarterly,* 1979, *10*(3), 50–57.

7. Wilson, S. The use of ethnographic techniques in educational research. *Review of Educational Research,* 1977, *47*(2), 245–265.

8. Pelto, P.J., & Pelto, G.H. *Anthropological research: The structure of inquiry* (2nd ed.). New York: Cambridge University Press, 1978.

the initial data collection strategies. Initial data collection efforts suggest other appropriate strategies, and so forth. Following completion of the study, which may last for months, the researcher analyzes the mass of data collected and attempts to derive specific, testable hypotheses that explain the observed behavior. These hypotheses can then be tested in other studies.

The major difference between ethnographic and traditional approaches is that the review of related literature, the study of previous research and theory, does not result in testable hypotheses, to be supported or not supported by the results of the study. Instead, the study of previous work results in tentative, working hypotheses and strategies only. The ethnographer does not want to be overly influenced by findings produced by the application of other methods of research; such studies probably did not involve careful study of the environment in which the results were obtained or, more likely, the results were obtained in an environment different from the one to which the results were intended to be generalizable.

When ethnography was first applied to the investigation of educational problems, it was utilized by persons with training in anthropological methods. As its popularity has grown, it has increasingly been used by persons with more traditional, hypothesis-testing-oriented backgrounds. The result has been the emergence of a modified anthropological approach, an approach that could be characterized as more-structured ethnography. Rist describes this shift as follows:

> Finally, there is the matter of how to employ the method. The traditional assumption was that a single individual (sometimes a couple) would go to the field site, become enmeshed in the life of that site, and only after a long and involved period of time, begin to formulate a framework for the analysis. Theory was "grounded" in experience. Recently, there are several examples in which the number of ethnographers has not been one or two, but upwards to 60 working on a single study. The conventional single site case study has been complemented by a multisite approach frequently used in policy analysis and program evaluation. Furthermore, the idea of going into the field and allowing the issues and problems to emerge from extensive time on site has also given way to the preformulation of research problems, to the specifying of precise activities that are to be observed, and to the analytic framework within which the study is to be conducted. And all of this is prior to the *first* site visit. The end result is a structured and predetermined approach to data collection and analysis.[9]

While some view this adaptation of ethnography as a distortion of the method, most see it as an improvement.

An Example   The application of ethnography to the investigation of educational problems is illustrated in a study by Schultz and Florio. The purpose of the research was to study one aspect of the socialization process involved when children enter a school environment. Through socialization children learn which behaviors are appropriate and which are inappropriate in a variety of situations. One important aspect of socialization is recognizing when the context has changed

---

9. Rist, R.C. Blitzkrieg ethnography: On the transformation of a method into a movement. *Educational Researcher,* 1980, *9*(2), 8–10. Copyright 1980, American Educational Research Association, Washington, D.C.

sufficiently to necessitate a change in behavior. The prime agent for socialization in the school setting is, of course, the teacher. The Schultz and Florio study focused on the techniques used by one kindergarten teacher to alert students to a change in context. Specifically, the changes in context that occurred during an open activity period called "worktime" were studied.

The research took place in a kindergarten/first-grade classroom in a suburb of Boston. The study concentrated on identifying "what it is that children need to know in order to act in a manner that is considered appropriate in the classroom." Toward this end the researchers examined the various contexts as well as the related teacher-student interactions. Seventy hours of videotape were collected over a two-year period, and supplementary field notes were taken. During the second year of the study, a participant observer spent several days a week collecting information related to the videotaped behavior.

Based on their analysis of the data, the authors concluded that consistent contextual changes in behavior required a systematic set of behaviors on the part of the teacher.

Children associate certain teacher behaviors with the requirement to pay attention. If the teacher fails to exhibit these behaviors at any time, the children fail to pay attention and exhibit inappropriate behavior.[10]

Educational Ethnography: In Summary   By now you should have a reasonably good understanding of the ethnographic method. Its drawbacks are obvious, although not necessarily unique. Proper application of the approach requires the accurate recording of large amounts of data, over long periods of time, by persons thoroughly trained in observational methods. Results are difficult to analyze and, given the length of the typical study, findings are difficult to replicate. At a practical level, ethnographic research tends to be more costly than other approaches. A more serious problem is the fact that we are usually dealing with an N of one. In other words, since the unit under study is typically a classroom or a school, the number of "subjects" is one. Thus, findings may be very unique to the unit studied.[11]

A current problem with ethnography is not a fault of the method, but rather the way in which it is being used. As more and more people have gotten into the ethnography act, some with little or no related training, there has been an increase in the number of poorly conducted, allegedly ethnographic studies. As Rist puts it, ethnography "is becoming a mantle to legitimate much work that is shoddy, poorly conducted, and ill conceived."[12] Such research is characterized by the taking of shortcuts such as minimal time being spent in the setting being studied. Rist humorously refers to these abbreviated versions of ethnographic research as "blitzkrieg ethnography."

When properly used, however, ethnography has the potential for providing insights not obtainable with other methods. The hypotheses generated by ethno-

---

10. Schultz, J., & Florio, S. Stop and freeze: The negotiation of social and physical space in a kindergarten/first grade classroom. *Anthropology & Education Quarterly,* 1979, *10*(3), 166–181.
11. See footnote 6.
12. See footnote 9.

graphic studies are in many cases more valid than those based on theory alone. It is, of course, unrealistic to believe that a method that has been used successfully in another field, that is anthropology, can be adopted and used in toto in education. The approach is undergoing constant refinement and adaptation in the direction of a more-structured ethnography. This trend is viewed as a positive one with the potential result being a research method incorporating the best features of the integrated approaches.

Conducting Observational Research

The steps in conducting observational research are essentially the same as for other types of descriptive research. Selection and definition of the problem are essentially the same, as is "subject" selection. Like the interview technique, observation is time consuming and typically involves smaller samples. While nonparticipant observation, participant observation, and ethnography involve some unique procedures, all observation involves definition of the variables to be observed, recording of observations, and training and monitoring of observers.

Definition of Observational Variables

There is no way that an observer can observe and record everything that goes on during a session, especially in a natural setting such as a classroom. What will be observed is determined by the research hypothesis or question. Thus, for a former example concerning the effectiveness of behavior modification in reducing instances of disruptive behavior, attention would be focused only on "disruptive behavior." The term "disruptive behavior," however, does not have universal meaning; therefore, once the behavior to be observed is determined, the researcher must clearly define what specific behaviors do and do not match the intended behavior. In the above example, "disruptive behavior" might include talking out of turn, making extraneous noises, throwing things, and getting out of one's seat, whereas doodling would probably not be considered disruptive.

Once a behavioral unit is defined, observations must be quantified so that all observers will count the same way. If Gorgo screams *and* tips over his chair at the same time, that could be considered as one instance of disruptive behavior or as two instances. Researchers typically divide observation sessions into a number of specific observation periods, that is, they define a time unit. Thus for a one-hour session, a time unit of 30 seconds might be agreed upon resulting in a total of 120 observations per hour. The length of the time unit will usually be a function of both the behavior to be observed and the frequency with which it normally occurs. If it is simply a matter of observing and recording a high-frequency behavior, the time unit may be 10 seconds. If any judgments or inferences are required on the part of the observer, or if the behavior is a low-frequency behavior, the time unit is typically longer, perhaps 30 seconds or 1 minute. There should be correspondence between actual frequency and recorded frequency. Once the time unit has been established, the observer then records what occurred during the observation period. If during a 15-second interval a student exhibits disruptive behavior, this would be indicated, regardless of how often disruptive behavior occurred.

After the variables have been defined and the time unit established, a decision must be made as to when observations will be made. For example, if behavior varies with factors such as day of the week and time of day, it would be unwise to observe every Tuesday morning only. One solution is to randomly select observation times so that different days and different times of day are reflected in the observations. A second solution is to avoid selecting observation times and to simply observe all the possibilities (i.e., all day every day). The latter approach, of course, is only feasible for short periods of time and for a limited number of subjects. You could observe one boy or girl for a week, but observing a group of children for a month would be a little unreasonable.[13]

Recording of Observations

One point, which at first reading may seem obvious, is that observers should have to observe and record only one behavior at a time. Even if you are interested in two types of behavior, for example teacher behavior and student behavior, the observer should only have to make one decision at a time. Thus, if two types of behavior are to be observed they should probably be observed alternately. In other words, for the teacher-student observation example, teacher behavior might be observed during the first, third, fifth, seventh (and so forth) observation periods, and student behavior during the second, fourth, sixth, and eighth. Such a procedure would present a fairly accurate picture concerning what occurred in the observed classroom. It is also a good idea to alternate observation periods and recording periods, especially if any inference is required on the part of the observers. Thus we might have the observers observe for 15 seconds, record for 5 seconds, observe for 15 seconds, record for 5 seconds, and so forth. This approach controls for the fact that the observer is not paying complete attention while recording, and tends to increase the reliability of observations.

While the point is debatable, as a general rule it is probably better to record observations as the behavior occurs. Since each observation must be made within a set period of time, for example 15 seconds, the recording process should be as simplified as possible. Most observation studies facilitate recording by using an agreed-upon code, or set of symbols, and a recording instrument. Often the task is not just to determine whether a behavior occurred or not, but to record *what* occurred. The Flanders System, for example, which is widely used for classroom observation, classifies all teacher behavior and all student behavior into one of 10 categories, each of which is represented by a number.[14] Thus, if a teacher praises a student, the observer records that "2" occurred (see Figure 7.2).

Some very good coding systems have been developed by researchers working in the area of behavior modification. Such codes are typically designed for

---

13. Webb, E.J., Campbell, D.T., Schwartz, R.D., & Sechrest, L. *Unobtrusive measures: Nonreactive research in the social sciences.* Chicago: Rand McNally, 1966.

14. The Flanders System was developed at the Far West Laboratory for Educational Research and Development by the staff of the Teacher Education Division under the direction of N.A. Flanders. The interaction analysis materials are available from P.F. Amidon & Associates, 1966 Benson Avenue, St. Paul, Minn. 55116.

Teacher Talk	Response	1. *Accepts feeling.* Accepts and clarifies an attitude or the feeling tone of a student in a nonthreatening manner. Feelings may be positive or negative. Predicting and recalling feelings are included. 2. *Praises or encourages.* Praises or encourages students; says "um hum" or "go on"; makes jokes that release tension, but not at the expense of a student. 3. *Accepts or uses ideas of students.* Acknowledges student talk. Clarifies, builds on, or asks questions based on student ideas.
		4. *Asks questions.* Asks questions about content or procedure, based on teacher ideas, with the intent that a student will answer.
	Initiation	5. *Lectures.* Offers facts or opinions about content or procedures; expresses *his own* ideas, gives *his own* explanation, or cites an authority other than a student. 6. *Gives directions.* Gives directions, commands, or orders to which a student is expected to comply. 7. *Criticizes student or justifies authority.* Makes statements intended to change student behavior from nonacceptable to acceptable patterns; corrects student answers; bawls someone out. Or, states why the teacher is doing what he is doing; uses extreme self-reference.
Student Talk	Response	8. *Student talk—response.* Student talk in response to teacher contact which structures or limites the situation. Freedom to express own ideas is limited.
	Initiation	9. *Student talk—initiation.* Students initiate or express own ideas either spontaneously or in response to teacher's soliciting initiation. Freedom to develop opinions and a line of thought; going beyond existing structure.
Silence		10. *Silence or confusion.* Pauses, short periods of silence, and periods of confusion in which communication cannot be understood by the observer.

Note: There is no scale implied by these numbers. Each number is classificatory; it designates a particular kind of communication event. To write these numbers down during observation is to enumerate, not to judge a position on a scale.

Figure 7.2
Flanders' interaction analysis categories (FIAC).

recording the behavior of one individual. Bijou, Peterson, and Ault, for example, recorded occurrences of vocalizations (V), proximity (P) or physical contact (T) with another person, contact with physical objects (E) or with children and whether the interaction was parallel play (A) or shared play (C). The basic symbols were adapted as needed. For example, aggressive vocalizations were recorded as $\widehat{V}$. Other symbols were used as needed. A bracket on the top of the recording form at a particular number, indicated a change in activity on the subject's part. An "x" indicated teacher approval for appropriate (i.e., verbal or proximity) behavior.[15] As Figure 7.3 (from the Bijou, Peterson, and Ault study) indicates, during 24 observation periods, the subject changed activities 12 times. During observation periods 16, 17, and 18, she talked (V), touched (T) and physically interacted with another child, and received approval (x) for these behaviors.

15. Bijou, S.W., Peterson, R.F., & Ault, M.H. A method to integrate descriptive and experimental field studies at the level of data and empirical concepts. *Journal of Applied Behavior Analysis*, 1968, *1*(2), 175–191.

Figure 7.3.
Sample line from a data sheet of a nursery school girl who changed activities with high frequency. (Table 1 from Bijou, Peterson, and Ault, 1968. Copyright 1968 by the Society for the Experimental Analysis of Behavior, Inc. Reproduced by permission.)

There are a number of different types of forms that are used to record observations. Probably the most often used, and the most efficient, is a checklist that lists all behaviors to be observed so that the observer can simply check each behavior as it occurs. This permits the observer to spend his or her time thinking about what is occurring rather than how to record it. The Flanders System, for example, uses a recording form which is basically a checklist (see Figure 7.4). In Figure 7.4, the various codes explained in Figure 7.2 are listed on the vertical axis, and the observation periods are indicated across the top (1–30). With the exception of categories 1 and 2, which must be specified, other categories are indicated with a checkmark. The timeline shows the sequence of events that occurred over a period of time. During observation periods 1 and 2, the teacher was asking questions (4). During the next four periods students were expressing their ideas, and so forth. Thus, Figure 7.4 represents a classroom interaction in which the students are doing most of the talking and the teacher is encouraging and supporting their participation.

Rating scales are also sometimes used. These require the observer to evaluate the behavior and give it a rating from, for instance, 1 to 3. For example, an observer might rate a teacher's explanation as 1, not very clear, 2, clear, or 3, very clear. Although as many as five categories (infrequently more than five) are used, three is probably the ideal number. The more categories, the more difficult it becomes to correctly classify. An observer could probably discriminate between "not very clear" and "clear" fairly easily; deciding between "very unclear" and "not very clear" would not be as simple.

Before developing your own observation form, you should check to see if there is a standardized observation form available that is appropriate for your study.

Figure 7.4.
Recording form for Flanders' interaction analysis categories.

Using a standardized observation form has the same advantages as using a standardized test in terms of time saved, validity, and reliability. Also, as with standardized tests, the results of your study can be compared with the results of other studies that have used the same form. The Flanders System, for example, has been used in a number of studies such as the one previously described dealing with the class participation of Mexican-American children. You should also check journals such as the *Journal of Applied Behavior Analysis* for observation systems that have been used in other studies. You may find one that appears to meet your needs.

Assessing Observer Reliability

Unreliable observations are as useless as data based on an unreliable test. Determining observer reliability generally requires that at least two observers independently make observations; their recorded judgments as to what occurred can then be compared to see how well they agree. If we wanted to estimate the reliability of scoring for a short-answer test, we could correlate the scores resulting from two independent scorings of the same answers. In other words, all of the tests would be scored twice, and the correlation between the two sets of scores would be our estimate of the reliability of scoring. When we observe behavior, however, we are not typically dealing with scores, but rather with frequencies, that is, how frequently certain behaviors occurred. In these cases reliability is generally calculated based on percent agreement. For example, we might have two independent observers recording number of disruptive behaviors exhibited by a selected student during a one-hour period. If one observer recorded 20 incidents and the other recorded 25 incidents, we could compute interobserver reliability by dividing the smaller total (20) by the larger total (25) to obtain a percentage of agreement score of 80%.

As Hersen and Barlow point out, however, while 80% agreement may be considered satisfactory in most situations, if many frequencies are involved over a long period of time, the possibility exists that the two observers are not recording the same behaviors at the same time.[16] One observer, for example, may have under-recorded during the first half of a session and over-recorded during the second half; the other observer may have done just the opposite. Thus, their totals might agree quite well even though their observations did not. One reasonable solution to this potential problem, as suggested by Bijou, Peterson, Harris, Allen, and Johnston, is to use shorter observation periods and to base reliability calcualtions on both agreements and disagreements on occurrences and nonoccurrences of behavior.[17] Bijou and associates argue that with shorter observation periods it is easier to determine whether observers are recording the same events at the same time. To calculate reliability using both observer agreement and disagreement, we divide the number of agreements by the total number of agreements and disagreements. To use our disruptive behavior example, suppose

---

16. Hersen, M., & Barlow, H. *Single-case experimental designs.* New York: Pergamon Press, 1976.
17. Bijou, S.W., Peterson, R.F., Harris, F.R., Allen, K.E., & Johnston, M.S. Methodology for experimental studies of young children in natural settings. *Psychological Record,* 1969, *19,* 177–210.

that during the first 30 minutes of the observation period the two observers agreed on the occurrence of 9 instances of disruptive behavior but disagreed on the occurrence of 3 instances. To calculate interobserver reliability we would divide the number of agreements (9) by the total of the agreements and the disagreements (9 + 3 = 12), and the resulting reliability estimate would be 9/12 or 75%. There are a number of different situations for which slightly different approaches for calculating reliability are recommended. Hersen and Barlow discuss a number of these situations and refer the reader to appropriate references.

Sometimes it is not possible to have several observers observe the same situation at the same time. One solution is to record the to-be-observed situation, with a videotape or audiotape recorder, for example. This allows each observer to play back tapes at a time convenient for her or him. Another advantage to recording a situation is that you can replay it as often as you like. If behaviors to be observed are at all complex or occur at a fairly rapid rate, for example, it may be difficult to obtain reliable observations. If you record the behavior, you can play it back to your heart's content, as can other observers. This is especially useful if judgment and evaluation are required on the part of the observer. Regardless of whether observations are recorded as they occur or while viewing or listening to a tape, and assuming usage of a valid, reliable observation system, the best way to increase observer reliability is by thoroughly training and monitoring observers.

Training Observers

In order to determine agreement among observers, at least two observers are required. That means that there will be at least one other person besides yourself (or two, if you are not going to personnaly observe) who needs to be familiar with the observational procedures. Additional observers need to be trained in order to have some assurance that all observers are observing and recording the same behaviors in the same way. Thus, they must be instructed as to what behaviors to observe, how behaviors are to be coded, how behaviors are to be recorded, and how often (time unit). Observers should participate in numerous practice sessions at which they observe situations similar to those to be involved in the study and compare their recordings. Each point of disagreement should be discussed so that the observer who is incorrect understands why. Practice sessions using recordings of behavior are most effective since segments with which observers have difficulty can be replayed for discussion and feedback purposes. Estimates of observer reliability should be calculated periodically to determine the effectiveness of the training and practice; observer reliability should increase with each session. Training may be terminated when a satisfactory level of agreement is achieved (say 80%).

Monitoring Observers

Training of observers only guarantees that the initial level of reliability is satisfactory. It does not guarantee that this level will be maintained throughout the study. Also, as we have noted, observers may be exhibiting acceptable levels of reliability and yet not be observing the same behaviors in the same way at the same time.

As Hersen and Barlow point out, the major way to insure continued satisfactory levels of reliability is to monitor the recording activities of observers. The ideal would be to constantly monitor all observers. This technique is usually not feasible, however. At the very least, spot checks should be made.[18] As a general rule, the more monitoring that can reasonably be managed, the better.

Reducing Observation Bias

Observers should be made aware of two factors that may seriously affect the validity of observations—observer bias and observee bias.[19] Observer bias refers to invalid observations that result from the way in which the observer observes. Observee bias refers to invalid observations that result from the fact that observees may behave differently simply because they are being observed. Each observer brings to the observation session a unique background that may affect the way he or she perceives the situation. Having observers record independently helps to detect the presence of bias but does not eliminate it. Training and practice sessions should help to reduce it by making observers aware of its existence and by providing feedback when it appears to be occurring. Other types of observer bias are similar to those described in chapter 5 concerning rating scales and are referred to as response sets. A response set is the tendency of an observer to rate the majority of observees as above average, average, or below average regardless of the observees' actual behavior. A related problem is the "halo effect" whereby initial impressions concerning an observee (positive or negative) affect subsequent observations. A final major source of observer bias occurs when the observer's knowledge concerning observees or the purposes of the study affect observations. In the previously discussed study of the effectiveness of behavior modification in reducing disruptive behavior, the observer might tend to see what was expected, namely a decrease in disruptive behavior. In this instance, having observers view recordings rather than live behavior would help since they would not have to be told which recordings were made *before* the introduction of behavior modification and which were made *after*. The above discussion should have made obvious the problems associated with using data recorded by untrained observers such as anecdotal records on students made by teachers. Such data tend to be subjective and biased and not useful for research purposes unless, of course, the purpose of the study is to compare perceptions of different groups.

The other side of the problem, observee bias, refers to the phenomenon whereby persons being observed behave atypically simply because they are being observed. Solutions to this problem such as those depicted on television medical shows (one-way mirrors, for example) may seem intriguing but are hardly ever practicable in observational settings. Classrooms, for example, rarely are equipped with such devices. The best way to handle the problem is to make observers

---

18. Reid, J.B., & DeMaster, B. The efficacy of the spot-check procedure in maintaining the reliability of data collected by observers in quasi-natural settings: Two pilot studies. *Oregon Research Bulletin*, 1972, *12*(8).

19. Observee is a term used by the author (with apologies to Webster) meaning "a person being observed." You are the observer, the person being observed is the observee.

aware of it so that they can attempt to be as unobtrusive (inconspicuous) as possible. Observees apparently tend to ignore the presence of an observer after a few sessions. Thus, simply observing a few sessions prior to recording any data is an effective technique. Observers should also be instructed not to discuss the purpose of the observations with the observees. The fact that they may be behaving differently is bad enough; having them behave the way they think you want them to behave is worse! Another approach to the problem of observee bias is to eliminate observees. If the same information can be determined by observing inanimate objects (referred to as unobtrusive measures), use them. School suspension lists, for example, have never been known to act differently because they were being observed; such lists might be one unobtrusive measure of disruptive behavior on the part of students. The following newspaper article, although not exactly educationally relevant, does illustrate the concept of unobtrusive measures:

> Maury Graham—known in the world of freight train hoboes as "Steamtrain Maury"—reports that the current U. S. economy is in frightful shape.
> The former "King of the Hoboes" says that hoboes can gauge the seriousness of inflation by the length of the cigar and cigarette butts found along the streets.
> Says Steamtrain Maury, "The longer they are, the better times are. And right now the butts are awful short. People are smoking them right down to the end."[20]

Another amusing example is found in the statement of a police officer to the effect that one way to identify car thieves is by examining license plates. Police officers look for clean cars with dirty license plates and dirty cars with clean license plates, because thieves usually switch plates.[21]

---

20. Krebs, A. Notes on people. *New York Times,* September 11, 1974. © 1974 by the New York Times Company. Reprinted by permission.

21. Reddy, J. Heady thieves find Wheeling their Waterloo. *Chicago Sun Times,* February 28, 1965, *18,* 66.

The Correlational Method

Enablers

After reading chapter 8, you should be able to:

1. Briefly state the purpose of correlational research.
2. List and briefly describe the major steps involved in the basic correlational research process.
3. Describe the range of numerical values associated with a correlation coefficient.
4. Describe how the size of a correlation coefficient affects its interpretation with respect to (a) statistical significance, (b) its use in prediction, and (c) its use as an index of validity and reliability.
5. State two major purposes of relationship studies.
6. Identify and briefly describe the steps involved in conducting a relationship study.
7. Briefly describe two methods for computing correlation coefficients.
8. Describe the difference between a linear and a curvilinear relationship.
9. Identify and briefly describe two factors that may contribute to an inaccurate estimate of relationship.
10. Briefly define or describe "predictor variables" and "criterion variables."
11. State three major purposes of prediction studies.
12. State the major difference between data collection procedures in a prediction study and a relationship study.
13. Explain why cross-validation is an important procedure associated with multiple regression equations.

Definition and Purpose

Correlational research is sometimes treated as a type of descriptive research, primarily because it does describe an existing condition. However, the condition it describes is distinctly different from the conditions typically described in self-report or observational studies; a correlational study describes in quantitative terms the degree to which variables are related. Correlational research involves collecting data in order to determine whether, and to what degree, a relationship exists between two or more quantifiable variables. Degree of relationship is expressed as a correlation coefficient. If a relationship exists between two variables, it means that scores within a certain range on one measure are associated with scores within a certain range on another measure. For example, there is a relationship between intelligence and academic achievement; persons who score highly on intelligence tests tend to have higher grade point averages, and persons who score low on intelligence tests tend to have lower grade point averages. The purpose of a correlational study may be to determine relationships between variables, or to use relationships in making predictions.

Relationship studies typically investigate a number of variables believed to be related to a major, complex variable such as achievement. Variables found not to be highly related are eliminated from further consideration; variables that are highly related may suggest causal-comparative or experimental studies to determine if the relationships are causal. As discussed in chapter 1, the fact that there is a relationship between self-concept and achievement does not imply that self-concept "causes" achievement or that achievement "causes" self-concept. Regardless of whether a relationship is a cause-effect relationship, the existence of a high relationship permits prediction. For example, as discussed in chapter 1, high school grade point average (GPA) and college GPA are highly related; students who have high GPAs in high school tend to have high GPAs in college, and students who have low GPAs in high school tend to have low GPAs in college. Therefore, high school GPA can be, and is, used to predict college GPA. Also, as discussed in chapter 5, correlational procedures are used to establish certain types of instrument validity and reliability.

Correlational studies provide an estimate of just how related two variables are. If two variables are highly related, a correlation coefficient near $+1.00$ (or -1.00) will be obtained; if two variables are not related, a coefficient near .00 will be obtained. The more highly related two variables are, the more accurate are predictions based on their relationship. While relationships are rarely perfect, a number of variables are sufficiently related to permit useful predictions.

The Basic
Correlational Research Process

While relationship studies and prediction studies have unique features which differentiate them, their basic processes are very similar.

Problem Selection

Correlational studies may be designed either to determine which variables of a list of likely candidates are related, or to test hypotheses regarding expected relationships. Variables to be included should be selected on the basis of either a deductive or an inductive rationale. In other words, the relationships to be investigated should be suggested by theory or derived from experience. Correlational treasure hunts in which the researcher correlates all sorts of variables to see "what turns up" are to be strongly discouraged. This research strategy (appropriately referred to as the "shotgun approach") does not involve hypothesis testing and is very inefficient. While it may lead to the discovery of an important relationship, it more often produces spurious correlation coefficients, that is, coefficients that do not accurately reflect the degree of relationship between two variables and which are not found if the variables are correlated again using another sample.

Sample and Instrument Selection

The sample for a correlational study is selected using an acceptable sampling method, and 30 subjects are generally considered to be a minimally acceptable sample size. As with any study, it is important to select or develop valid, reliable measures of the variables being studied. If inadequate data are collected, the resulting correlation coefficient will represent an inaccurate estimate of the degree of relationship. Further, if the measures used do not really measure the intended variables, the resulting coefficient will not indicate the intended relationships. Suppose, for example, you wanted to determine the relationship between achievement in mathematics and physics achievement. If you selected and administered a valid, reliable test of computational skill and a valid, reliable test of physics achievement, the resulting correlation coefficient would not be an accurate estimate of the intended relationship. Computational skill is only one kind of mathematical achievement; the resulting coefficient would indicate the relationship between physics achievement and *one kind* of mathematical achievement, computational skill. Thus, care must be taken to select measures that are valid *for your purposes*.

Design and Procedure

The basic correlational design is not complicated; two (or more) scores are obtained for each member of a selected sample, one score for each variable of interest, and the paired scores are then correlated. The resulting correlation coefficient indicates the degree of relationship between the two variables. Different studies investigate different numbers of variables, and some utilize complex statistical procedures, but the basic design is similar in all correlational studies.

Data Analysis and Interpretation

When two variables are correlated the result is a correlation coefficient. A correlation coefficient is a decimal number, between .00 and +1.00, or .00 and −1.00, which indicates the degree to which two variables are related. If the coefficient is near +1.00, the variables are positively correlated. This means that a person with a high score on one variable is likely to have a high score on the other variable, and a person with a low score on one is likely to have a low score on the other; an increase on one variable is associated with an increase on the other variable. If the coefficient is near .00, the variables are not related. This means that a person's score on one variable is no indication of what the person's score is on the other variable. If the coefficient is near −1.00, the variables are inversely related. This means that a person with a high score on one variable is likely to have a low score on the other variable, and a person with a low score on one is likely to have a high score on the other; an increase in one variable is associated with a decrease on the other variable, and vice versa (see Table 8.1). Table 8.1 presents four scores for each of eight twelfth-grade students: IQ, GPA, weight, and errors on a 20-item final exam. As Table 8.1 illustrates, IQ is positively related to achievement, not related to weight, and negatively, or inversely, related to errors. The students with progressively higher IQs have progressively higher GPAs. On the other hand, students with higher IQs tend to make fewer errors (makes sense!). The relationships are not perfect, and it would be very strange if they were. One's GPA, for example, is related to other variables beside intelligence, such as motivation. The data do indicate, however, that IQ is one major variable related to both GPA and examination errors. The data also illustrate an important concept often misunderstood by beginning researchers, namely that a high negative relationship is just as strong as a high positive relationship; -1.00 and $+1.00$ indicate equally perfect relationships. A coefficient near .00 indicates no relationship; the further away from .00 the coefficient is, in *either* direction (toward -1.00 or $+1.00$), the stronger the relationship. Both high positive and high negative relationships are equally useful for making predictions; knowing that Iggie has a low IQ score would enable you to predict both a low GPA and a high number of errors.

What a correlation coefficient *means* is difficult to explain. Some beginning researchers erroneously think that a correlation coefficient of .50 means that two variables are 50% related. Not true. In research talk, a correlation coefficient squared indicates the amount of common variance shared by the variables (WHAT??!!). Now, in English. Each of two variables will result in a range of scores; there will be score variance, that is, everyone will not get the same score. In Table 8.1, for example, IQ scores vary from 85 to 140 and GPAs from 1.0 to 3.8. Common variance refers to the variation in one variable that is attributable to its tendency to vary with the other. If two variables are not related, then the variability of one set of scores has nothing to do with the variability of the other set; if two variables are perfectly related, then variability of one set of scores has everything to do with variability in the other set. Thus with no relationship the variables have no common variance, but with a perfect relationship all variance, or 100% of the variance is shared, common variance. The percent of common variance is generally less than the numerical value of the correlation coefficient. In fact, to determine

Table 8.1
Hypothetical Sets of Data Illustrating
a High Positive Relationship Between Two Variables,
No Relationship, and a High Negative Relationship

	High Positive Relationship		No Relationship		High Negative Relationship	
	IQ	GPA	IQ	Weight	IQ	Errors
1. Iggie	85	1.0	85	156	85	16
2. Hermie	90	1.2	90	140	90	10
3. Fifi	100	2.4	100	120	100	8
4. Teenie	110	2.2	110	116	110	5
5. Tiny	120	2.8	120	160	120	9
6. Tillie	130	3.4	130	110	130	3
7. Millie	135	3.2	135	140	135	2
8. Jane	140	3.8	140	166	140	1

common variance you simply square the correlation coefficient. A correlation coefficient of .80 indicates $(.80)^2$, or .64, or 64% common variance. A correlation coefficient of .00 indicates $(.00)^2$, or .00, or 00% common variance, and a coefficient of 1.00 indicates $(1.00)^2$, or 1.00, or 100% common variance. Thus, a coefficent of .50 may look pretty good at first but it actually means that the variables have 25% common variance.

Interpretation of a correlation coefficient depends upon how it is to be used. In other words, how large it needs to be in order to be useful depends upon the purpose for which it was computed. In a study designed to explore or test hypothesized relationships, a correlation coefficient is interpreted in terms of its statistical significance. In a prediction study, statistical significance is secondary to the value of the coefficient in facilitating accurate predictions. Statistical significance refers to whether the obtained coefficient is really different from zero and reflects a true relationship, not a chance relationship; the decision concerning statistical significance is made at a given level of probability.[1] In other words, based on one sample of a given size, you cannot determine positively whether there is or is not a true relationship between the variables, but you can say there probably is or probably is not such a relationship. Relatedly, a hypothesis concerning relationship or lack of it (the null hypothesis) can be supported or not supported, not proven or disproven. To determine statistical significance, you only have to consult a table that tells you how large your coefficient needs to be in order to be significant at a given probability level, and given the size of your sample (see Table A.2 in the Appendix). For the same probability level, or significance level, a larger coefficient is required when smaller samples are involved. We can generally have a lot more confidence in a coefficient based on 100 subjects than one based on 10 subjects. Thus, for example, at the 95% confidence level, with 10 cases, you would need a coefficient of at least .6319 in order to conclude the existence of a relationship; on the other hand, with 102 cases you would need a coefficient of only .1946.[2] This concept makes sense if you consider the case when you would collect data on *every* member of a population, not just a sample. In this case, no inference would be involved, and regardless of how small the actual correlation coefficient were, it would represent the true degree of relationship between the variables *for that population.* Even if the coefficient were only .11, for example, it would still indicate the existence of a relationship, a low one, but a relationship just the same. The larger the sample, the more closely it approximates the population and therefore the more probable it is that a given coefficient represents a true relationship.

You may also have noticed another related concept; for a given sample size, the value of the correlation coefficient needed for significance increases as the level of confidence increases. As the level of confidence increases, the *p* value in the table gets smaller; the 95% confidence level corresponds to $p = .05$ and the

---

1. The concepts of statistical significance, level of significance, and degrees of freedom will be discussed further in chapter 13.
2. In case you are trying to read Table A.2, a 95% level of confidence corresponds to $p = .05$, and 10 cases correspond to $df = 8$; degrees of freedom, df, are equal to N (number in the sample) $- 2$, thus $10 - 2$ or 8. For 100 cases, df equals $100 - 2$ which equals 98.

99% level to $p = .01$. Thus for 10 subjects ($df = 8$), and $p = .05$, a coefficient of .6319 is required; for 10 subjects and $p = .01$, however, a coefficient of .7646 is required. In other words, the more confident you wish to be that your decision concerning significance is the correct one, the larger the coefficient must be. Beware, however, of confusing significance with strength. No matter how significant a coefficient is, a low coefficient represents a low relationship. The level of significance only indicates the probability that a given relationship is a true one, regardless of whether it is a weak relationship or a strong relationship.

Prediction is another story. The utility of a correlation coefficient goes beyond its statistical significance in a prediction study. With a sample of 102 subjects, for example, a coefficient of .1946 is significant at $p = .05$. This relationship would be of little value for most prediction purposes. Since the relationship is so low (the common variance is only $(.1946)^2$, or .0379, or 3.8%), knowing a person's score on one variable would be of little help in predicting her or his score on the other. A correlation coefficient much below .50 is generally useless for either group prediction or individual prediction, although a combination of several variables in this range may yield a reasonably satisfactory prediction. Coefficients in the .60s and .70s are usually considered adequate for group prediction purposes, and coefficients in the .80s and above for individual prediction purposes.

When correlation coefficients are used to estimate the validity or reliability of measuring instruments, the criterion of acceptability is even higher. A correlation coefficient of .40, for example, would be considered useful in a relationship study, not useful in a prediction study, and terrible in a reliability study; a coefficient of .60 would be considered useful in a prediction study but would still probably be considered unsatisfactory as an estimate of reliability. As discussed in chapter 5, what does constitute an acceptable level of reliability is partly a function of the type of instrument. While all reliabilities in the .90s are acceptable, for certain kinds of instruments, such as personality measures, a reliability in the low .70s might be acceptable. The standards for acceptable observer reliability are similar to those for test reliability. A researcher would be very happy with observer reliabilities in the .90s, satisfied with the .80s, minimally accepting of the .70s, and would be progressively more unhappy with the .60s, .50s, and so forth.

When interpreting a correlation coefficient you must always keep in mind that you are talking about a relationship only, not a cause-effect relationship. A significant correlation coefficient may *suggest* a cause-effect relationship but does not establish one. The only way to establish a cause-effect relationship is by conducting an experiment. When one finds a high relationship between two variables it is often very tempting to conclude that one "causes" the other. In fact, it may be that neither one is the cause of the other; there may be a third variable which "causes" both of them. To use a former example, the existence of a positive relationship between self-concept and achievement could mean one of three things: a higher self-concept leads to higher achievement, higher achievement tends to increase self-concept, or there is a variable which results in both higher self-concept and higher achievement. It might be, for example, that parental behavior is a major factor in both self-concept and achievement; parents who praise their children may also encourage them to do well in school. Which of the alternatives is in fact the true explanation cannot be determined through a correlational study.

Relationship Studies

Relationship studies are conducted in an attempt to gain insight into the factors or variables that are related to complex variables such as academic achievement, motivation, and self-concept. Variables found not to be related can be eliminated from further consideration. Identification of related variables serves several major purposes. First, such studies give direction to subsequent causal-comparative and experimental studies. Experimental studies are costly in more ways than one; correlational studies are an effective way of reducing unprofitable experimental studies and suggesting potentially productive ones. Also, in both causal-comparative and experimental research studies, the researcher is concerned with controlling for variables, other than the independent variable, which might be related to performance on the dependent variable. In other words, the researcher tries to identify variables that are correlated with the dependent variable and to remove their influence so that it will not be confused with that of the independent variable. Relationship studies help the researcher to identify such variables, to control for them, and therefore to investigate the effects of the intended variable. If you were interested in comparing the effectiveness of different methods of reading instruction for first graders, for example, you would probably want to control for initial differences in reading readiness.

The relationship study strategy of attempting to understand a complex variable by identifying and analyzing variables related to it has been more productive for some complex variables than for others. For example, while a number of variables correlated with achievement have been identified, factors significantly related to success in areas such as administration and teaching have not been as easy to pin down. Either some wholes are greater than the sum of their parts, or all the relevant parts have not yet been identified. If nothing else, however, relationship studies that have not uncovered useful relationships have at least identified variables which can be excluded from future studies, a necessary step in science.

Data Collection

In a relationship study the researcher first identifies, either inductively or deductively, variables potentially related to the complex variable under study. For example, if you were interested in factors related to self-concept, you might identify variables such as intelligence, past academic achievement, and socioeconomic status. As pointed out previously, you should have some reason for including variables in the study. The shotgun approach, which involves checking all conceivable variables for possible relationships, is very inefficient and often misleading. The more correlation coefficients that are computed at one time, the more likely it is that the wrong conclusion will be reached for some of them concerning the existence of a relationship. If only one correlation coefficient is computed, and if we are working at a probability level of .05, the odds are greatly in our favor that we are making the correct decision. On the other hand, if 100 coefficients are computed, and if we are working at $p = .05$, the odds are working against us since it is likely that we will erroneously conclude relationship. A smaller number of carefully selected variables is much to be preferred to a larger number of carelessly selected variables. We may find fewer significant correlation coefficients, but we can have more confidence that the ones we do find represent true relationships, not chance ones which are not likely to be found again.

The next step in data collection is to identify an appropriate population of subjects from which to select a sample. The population must be one for which data on each of the identified variables can be collected, and one whose members are available to the researcher. Although data on some variables can be collected without direct access to subjects, variables such as past achievement which can be found in cumulative records, many relationship studies require the administration of one or more instruments and in some cases observation. Any of the types of instruments so far discussed, such as standardized tests and questionnaires, may be used in a relationship study, and each must be selected with care. One advantage of a relationship study is that all the data may be collected within a relatively short period of time. Instruments may be administered at one session or several sessions in close succession. If school children are the subjects, as is often the case, time demands on students and teachers are relatively small compared to those required for experimental studies, and it is usually easier to obtain administrative approval.

Data Analysis and Interpretation

In a relationship study, the scores for each variable are in turn correlated with the scores for the complex variable of interest. Thus, there results one correlation coefficient for each variable; each coefficient represents the relationship between a particular variable and the complex variable under study. In a study investigating factors related to self-concept, a measure of self-concept might be correlated with a measure of intelligence, a measure of past achievement, a measure of socio-economic status, and with each of any other identified variables. Since the end result in each case is a correlation coefficient, a number between -1.00 and $+1.00$, clearly each variable must be expressible in numerical form, that is, must be quantifiable. For the variable "past achievement," for example, simply classifying students as good students, average students, or poor students would not do. Past achievement would have to be expressed numerically, in terms of GPA, for example.

There are a number of different methods of computing a correlation coefficient; which one is appropriate depends upon the type of data represented by each variable.[3] The most commonly used technique is the product moment correlation coefficient, usually referred to as the Pearson r, which is appropriate when both variables to be correlated are expressed as ratio data or interval data. Since most instruments used in education, such as achievement measures and personality measures, are expressed in the form of interval data, the Pearson r is usually the appropriate coefficient for determining relationship. Further, since the Pearson r results in the most reliable estimate of correlation, its use is preferred even when other methods may be applied.

If the data for one of the variables are expressed as ranks, the appropriate correlation coefficient is the rank difference correlation coefficient, usually referred

---

3. Actual computation of a correlation coefficient, as well as the various types of data, will be described and discussed in chapters 11 and 12.

to as the Spearman rho.[4] Rank data are involved when, instead of using a score for each subject, subjects are arranged in order of score and each subject is assigned a rank from one to however many subjects there are. For a group of 30 subjects, for example, the subject with the highest score would be assigned a rank of 1, the subject with the second highest score 2, and the subject with the lowest score 30. If two subjects have the same score, their ranks are averaged; if two subjects, for example, have the same, highest score they are each assigned the average of rank 1 and rank 2, namely 1.5. If only one of the variables to be correlated is in rank order, say class standing at the time of graduation, then the other variables to be correlated with it must also be expressed in terms of ranks in order to use the Spearman rho technique. Thus, if intelligence were to be correlated with class standing, students would have to be ranked in terms of intelligence, and IQ scores per se would not be involved in actual computation of the correlation coefficient. Although the Pearson r is more precise, with a small number of subjects (less than 30) the Spearman rho is much easier to compute and results in a coefficient very close to the one which would have been obtained had a Pearson r been computed. When the number of subjects is large, however, the process of ranking becomes more time consuming and the Spearman rho loses its only advantage over the Pearson r.

There are also a number of other correlational techniques which are encountered less often but which should be used when appropriate. Some variables, for example, can only be expressed in terms of a dichotomy. Since an individual is usually either male or female, the variable of sex cannot be expressed on a scale from 1 to 30. Thus sex is typically expressed as a 1 or 0 (female versus male) or as a 1 or 2 (female versus male). A 2, however, does not mean more of something than a 1, and 1 does not mean more than 0; these numbers indicate difference only, not difference in amount. Other variables which may be expressed as a dichotomy include political affiliation (Democrat versus Republican), smoking status (smoker versus nonsmoker), and educational status (high school graduate versus high school dropout). The above examples illustrate "true" dichotomies in that a person is or is not a female, a democrat, a smoker, or a high school graduate. Artificial dichotomies may also be created by operationally defining a midpoint and categorizing subjects as falling above it or below it. Subjects with IQ scores of 100 or above might be classified as "high IQ subjects," for example, and subjects with IQ scores of 99 or below might be classified as "low IQ students." Such classifications are also typically translated into a "score" of 1 or 0.[5]

Most correlational techniques are based on the assumption that the relationship being investigated is a linear one. If a relationship is linear, then plotting the scores on the two variables will result in something resembling a straight line. If a relationship is perfect, (+1.00 or −1.00), the line will be perfectly straight; if there is no relationship, the points will form no pattern but will instead be scattered in a

---

4. Pearson and Spearman are the men credited with the development of their respective techniques for computing correlation coefficients.

5. For additional discussion concerning alternative techniques for calculating correlation coefficients see Glass, G.V., & Stanley, J.C. *Statistical methods in education and psychology.* Englewood Cliffs, N.J.: Prentice-Hall, 1970.

random fashion. Figure 8.1, which plots the data presented in Table 8.1, illustrates the concept of a linear relationship. Not all relationships, however, are linear; some are curvilinear. If a relationship is curvilinear, an increase in one variable is associated with a corresponding increase in another variable *to a point,* at which point further increase in the first variable results in a corresponding decrease in the other variable (or vice versa). The relationship between age and agility, for example, is a curvilinear one (see Figure 8.2). As Figure 8.2 illustrates, agility increasingly improves with age, peaks or reaches its maximum somewhere in the twenties, and then progressively decreases as age increases. If a relationship is suspected of being curvilinear, then a correlational technique which results in an eta ratio is required. If you try to use a correlational technique which assumes a linear relationship when the relationship is in fact curvilinear, your estimate of the degree of relationship will be way off base. Since it will in no way resemble a straight line, the coefficient will generally indicate little or no relationship; the

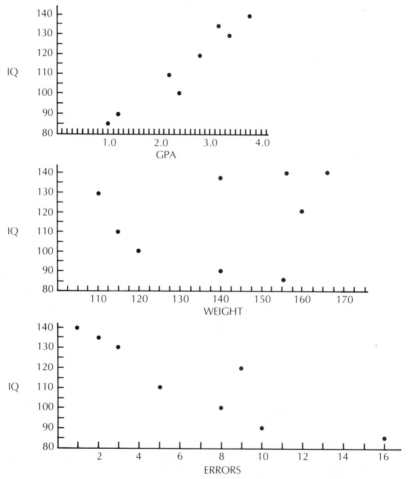

Figure 8.1.
Data points for scores presented in Table 8.1 illustrating a high positive relationship (IQ and GPA), no relationship (IQ and weight), and a high negative relationship (IQ and errors).

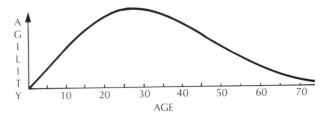

Figure 8.2.
The curvilinear relationship between age and agility.

positive relationship and negative relationship which combine to form a high curvilinear relationship will in a sense cancel each other out if a technique that assumes linearity (totally positive or totally negative) is applied.[6]

In addition to computing correlation coefficients for a total sample group, it is sometimes profitable to examine relationships separately for certain defined subgroups. The relationship between two variables may be different, for example, for females and males, college graduates and noncollege graduates, or high-ability students and low-ability students. When the subgroups are lumped together, such differential relationships may be obscured. There are also other factors that may contribute to an inaccurate estimate of relationship. Attenuation, for example, refers to the principle that correlation coefficients tend to be lowered due to the fact that less-than-perfectly-reliable measures are utilized. In relationship studies a correction for attenuation can be applied that provides an estimate of what the coefficient would be if both measures were perfectly reliable. If such a correction is used, it must be kept in mind that the resulting coefficient does not represent what was actually found. Such a correction is not used in prediction studies since predictions must be made based on existing measures, not hypothetical, perfectly reliable, instruments. Another factor that may lead to a coefficient representing an underestimate of the true relationship between two variables is a restricted range of scores. The more variability there is in each set of scores, the higher the coefficient is likely to be. The correlation coefficient for IQ and grades, for example, tends to decrease as these variables are measured at higher educational levels. Thus, the relationship will not be found to be as high for college seniors as for high school seniors. The reason is that not many low IQ individuals are college seniors; low IQ individuals either do not enter college or drop out long before their senior year. In other words, the range of IQ scores is much smaller, or more restricted, for college seniors, and a correlation coefficient based on such scores will tend to be reduced. There is also a correction for restriction in range that may be applied to obtain an estimate of what the coefficient would be if the range of scores were not restricted. It should be interpreted with the same caution as the correction for attenuation since it does not represent what was acutally found.

Prediction Studies

If two variables are highly related, scores on one variable can be used to predict scores on the other variable. High school grades, for example, can be used to

---

6. For further discussion concerning eta, as well as other advanced correlational procedures such as factor analysis and partial correlation, see Nunnally, J.C. *Psychmetric theory.* New York: McGraw-Hill, 1967.

predict college grades. The variable upon which the prediction is made is referred to as the predictor, and the variable predicted is referred to as the criterion. Prediction studies are often conducted to facilitate decision making concerning individuals or to aid in the selection of individuals. Prediction studies are also conducted to test theoretical hypotheses concerning variables believed to be predictors of a criterion, and to determine the predictive validity of individual measuring instruments. The results of prediction studies are used, for example, to predict an individual's likely level of success in a specific course, such as first-year algebra, to predict which of a number of individuals are likely to succeed in college or in a vocational training program, and to predict in which area of study an individual is most likely to be successful. Thus, the results of prediction studies are used by a number of groups besides researchers, such as counselors and admissions personnel. If several predictor variables each correlate well with a criterion, then a prediction based on a combination of those variables will be more accurate than a prediction based on any one of them. For example, a prediction of probable level of success (GPA) in college is usually based on a combination of factors such as high school GPA, rank in graduating class, and scores on college entrance exams. Although there are several major differences between prediction studies and relationship studies, both involve determining the relationship between a number of identified variables and a complex variable.

Data Collection

As with a relationship study, subjects must be selected from whom the desired data can be collected and who are available to the researcher. Instruments selected must also be valid measures of the variables of interest. It is especially important that the measure of the criterion variable be a valid one. If the criterion were "success on the job," success would have to be carefully defined in quantifiable terms. Size of desk would probably not be a valid measure of success (although you never know!), whereas number of promotions or salary increases probably would be. The major difference in data collection procedures for a relationship study and a prediction study is that in a relationship study data on all variables are collected within a relatively short period of time, whereas in a prediction study predictor variables are measured some period of time before the criterion variable is measured. In determining the predictive validity of a physics aptitude test, for example, success in physics would probably be measured at the end of a course of study whereas the aptitude test would be administered some time prior to the beginning of the course.

Data Analysis and Interpretation

As with a relationship study, each predictor variable is correlated with the criterion variable. Since a combination of variables usually results in a more accurate prediction than any one variable, prediction studies often result in a prediction equation referred to as a multiple regression equation. A multiple regression equation uses all variables that individually predict the criterion to make a more accurate prediction. College admissions personnel, for example, use prediction equations that include a number of variables in order to predict college GPA.

Since relationships are rarely perfect, predictions made by a multiple regression equation are not perfect. Thus, predicted scores are generally placed in a confidence interval. For example, a predicted college GPA of 1.20 might be placed in an interval of .80 to 1.60. In other words, students with a predicted GPA of 1.20 would be predicted to earn a GPA somewhere in the range between .80 and 1.60. A college that does not accept all applicants will probably as a general rule fail to accept any applicants with such a projected GPA range even though it is very likely that some of those students would be successful if admitted. Although the predictions for any given individual might be way off (either too high or too low), for the total group of applicants predictions are quite accurate on the whole; most applicants predicted to succeed, do so. As with relationship studies, and for similar reasons, prediction equations may be formulated for each of a number of subgroups as well as for a total group.

An interesting phenomenon characteristic of multiple regression equations is referred to as shrinkage; shrinkage is the tendency of a prediction equation to become less accurate when used with a different group, a group other than the one on which the equation was originally formulated. The reason for shrinkage is that an initial equation may be the result of chance relationships that will not be found again with another group of subjects. Thus, any prediction equation should be validated with at least one other group, and variables that are no longer found to be related to the criterion measure should be taken out of the equation; this procedure is referred to as cross-validation.

The Causal-Comparative Method

Definition and Purpose

Like correlational research, causal-comparative research is sometimes treated as a type of descriptive research since it too describes conditions that already exist. Causal-comparative research, however, also attempts to determine reasons, or causes, for the current status of the phenomena under study. The causal-comparative method entails procedures distinctly different from those involved in self-report or observational research, and qualifies as a separate method of reaearch. Causal-comparative, or ex post facto, research is that research in which the researcher attempts to determine the cause, or reason, for existing differences in the behavior or status of groups of individuals. In other words, it is observed that groups are different on some variable and the researcher attempts to identify the major factor that has led to this difference. Such research is reffered to as "ex post facto" (Latin—"after the fact") since both the effect and the alleged cause have already occurred and are studied by the researcher in retrospect. For example, as a possible explanation of apparent differences in social adjustment among first graders, a researcher might hypothesize that participation in preschool education was the major contributing factor. The researcher would then select a group of first graders who had participated in preschool education and a group who had not and would then compare the social adjustment of the two groups. If

197

the group that did participate in preschool education exhibited a higher level of social adjustment, the researcher's hypothesis would be supported.

The basic causal-comparative approach, therefore, involves starting with an effect and seeking possible causes. A variation of the basic approach involves starting with a cause and investigating its effect on some variable. Such research is concerned with "what is the effect of 'X'" questions. For example, a researcher might wish to investigate what long-range effect failure to be promoted to the seventh grade has on the self-concept of children not promoted. The researcher might hypothesize that children who are "socially promoted" have higher self-concepts at the end of the seventh grade than children who are "held back" and made to repeat the sixth grade. At the end of a school year, the researcher would identify a group of seventh graders who had been socially promoted to the seventh grade the year before, and a group of sixth graders who had been held back the year before and made to repeat the sixth grade. The self-concepts of the two groups would be compared. If the socially-promoted group exhibited a higher level of self-concept, the researcher's hypothesis would be supported.

Beginning researchers often confuse causal-comparative research with both correlational research and experimental research. Correlational and causal-comparative research are probably confused because of the lack of manipulation common to both and the similar cautions regarding interpretation of results. There are definite differences, however. Causal-comparative studies *attempt* to identify cause-effect relationships, correlational studies do not. Causal-comparative studies typically involve two (or more) groups and one independent variable, whereas correlational studies typically involve two (or more) variables and one group. Also, causal-comparative studies involve comparison, whereas correlational studies involve correlation.

It is understandable that causal-comparative and experimental research are at first difficult to distinguish; both attempt to establish cause-effect relationships and both involve group comparisons. In an experimental study, however, the researcher creates the "cause," deliberately makes the groups different, and then observes what effect that difference has on some dependent variable. In contrast, in a causal-comparative study the researcher first observes an effect and then tries to determine the cause; in other words, the researcher attempts to determine what difference between the groups has led to the observed difference on some dependent variable. To put it as simply as possible, the major difference between them is that in experimental research the independent varable, the alleged cause, is manipulated; in causal-comparative research it is not, it has already occurred. In experimental research, the researcher can randomly form groups and manipulate a variable—can determine "who" is *going to get* "what," "what" being the independent variable. In causal-comparative research, the groups are already formed and *already different* on the independent variable. Causal-comparative groups are already different in that one group may have had an experience which the other did not have, or one group may possess a characteristic which the other group does not. In any event, the difference between the groups (the independent variable) was not brought about by the researcher.

Independent variables in causal-comparative studies are variables that cannot be manipulated (such as socioeconomic status), should not be manipulated (such as number of cigarettes smoked per day), or simply are not manipulated but could be (such as method of reading instruction). There are a number of important educational problems for which it is impossible or not feasible to manipulate the independent variable. Ethical considerations often prevent manipuation of a variable that *could* be manipulated but *should not* be, such as number of cigarettes smoked. If the nature of the independent variable is such that it may cause physical or mental harm to subjects, it should not be manipulated. For example, if a researcher were interested in determining the effect of prenatal care for the mother on the developmental status of a child at age one, it would not be ethical to deprive a group of mothers-to-be of prenatal care for the sake of science when such care is considered to be extremely important to both the mother's and the child's welfare. Thus, causal-comparative research permits investigation of a number of variables that cannot be studied experimentally.

Causal-comparative studies also identify relationships that may lead to experimental studies. As mentioned previously, experimental studies are costly in more ways than one and should be conducted only when there is good reason to believe the effort will be fruitful. Like correlational studies, causal-comparative studies help to identify variables worthy of experimental investigation. In fact, causal-comparative studies are sometimes conducted solely for the purpose of determining the probable outcome of an experimental study. Suppose, for example, a superintendent was considering the adoption of systems reading in her or his school system. The superintendent might consider trying it out on an experimental basis for a year in a number of schools or classrooms before initiating total implementation. However, even such limited adoption would be costly in terms of materials and teacher training. Thus, as a preliminary measure, to facilitate her or his decision, the superintendent might conduct a causal-comparative study and compare the reading achievement of students in school districts currently using systems reading with students in school districts not currently using systems reading. Since most districts have yearly testing programs assessing the status of students in areas such as reading, acquisition of the necessary data would not be difficult. If the results indicated that the students learning through systems reading were achieving higher, the superintendent would probably decide to go ahead with an experimental tryout of systems reading in her or his own districts. If no differences were found, the superintendent would probably not go ahead with the experimental tryout and would thus not unnecessarily waste time, money, and effort.

Despite its many advantages, the causal-comparative method does have some serious limitations which should also be kept in mind. Since the independent variable has already occurred, the same kinds of controls cannot be exercised as in an experimental study. Extreme caution must be applied in interpreting results. An apparent cause-effect relationship may not be as it appears. As with a correlational study, only a relationship is established, not necessarily a causal one. The alleged cause of an observed effect may in fact be the effect, or there may be a third variable that has "caused" both the identified cause and effect. For example, suppose a researcher hypothesized that self-concept is a determinant of achievement. The researcher would identify two groups, one group with high self-concepts and one group with low self-concepts, and would then compare their achievement. If the high self-concept group did indeed show higher achievement, the temptation would be to conclude that self-concept affects achievement. This conclusion would not be warranted since it would not be possible to establish that self-concept *comes before,* or precedes, achievement. The exact opposite might be true; it might be that achievement affects self-concept. Since both the independent and dependent variables would have already occurred, it would not be possible to determine which came first, which affected the other. If the study was reversed, and a group of high achievers was compared with a group of low achievers, it might well be that they would be different on self-concept, thus suggesting that achievement causes self-concept. Even worse, it would even be possible (in fact, very plausible) that some third variable, such as parental attitude, might be the "cause" of both self-concept and achievement; parents who praise their children might also encourage high academic achievement. Thus, cause-effect relationships established through causal-comparative research are at best tenuous and tentative. Only experimental research, which guarantees that the alleged cause, or independent variable, *does come before* the observed effect, or dependent variable, can truly establish cause-effect relationships. As discussed previously, however, causal-comparative studies do have their place; they permit investigation of variables that cannot or should not be investigated experimentally, facilitate decision making, provide guidance for experimental studies, and are less costly on all dimensions.

Conducting a
Causal-Comparative Study

The basic causal-comparative design is quite simple, and although the independent variable is not manipulated, there are control procedures that can be exercised. Causal-comparative studies also involve a wider variety of statistical techniques than the other methods of research thus far discussed.

Design and Procedure

The basic causal-comparative design involves selecting two groups differing on some independent variable and comparing them on some dependent variable (see Figure 9.1). As Figure 9.1 indicates, the researcher selects two groups of subjects, loosely referred to as experimental and control groups, although it is probably more accurate to refer to them as comparison groups. The groups may differ in that one group possesses a characteristic that the other does not or has had an experience which the other has not (Case A), *or,* the groups may differ in degree; one group may possess more of a characteristic than the other or the two groups may have had different kinds of experiences (Case B). An example of Case A would be two groups, one of which was composed of hyperactive children, or two groups, one of which had received preschool training. An example of Case B would be two groups, one group composed of high self-concept individuals, and one group composed of low self-concept individuals, or two groups, one which had learned algebra via programmed instruction and one which had learned algebra via computer-assisted instruction. In both cases, the groups are compared on some dependent variable. The researcher may administer a test of the dependent variable (any of the types of instruments thus far

	Group	Independent Variable	Dependent Variable
Case A	(E)	(X)	O
	(C)		O

OR

	Group	Independent Variable	Dependent Variable
Case B	(E)	(X_1)	O
	(C)	(X_2)	O

Symbols:

(E) = experimental group; ( ) indicates no manipulation
(C) = control group
(X) = independent variable
O = dependent variable

Figure 9.1.
The basic causal-comparative design.

discussed) or collect already available data, such as the results of standardized testing conducted by a school.

Definition and selection of the comparison groups is a very important part of the causal-comparative procedure. The characteristic or experience differentiating the groups must be clearly and operationally defined, as each group will represent a different population. The way in which the groups are defined will affect the generalizability of the results. If a researcher was to compare a group of students with an "unstable" home life with a group of students with a "stable" home life, the terms unstable and stable would have to be operationally defined. An unstable home life could refer to any number of things such as a home with a drinking mother, a brutal father, or a combination of factors. If samples are to be selected from the defined population, random selection is generally the preferred method of selection. The important consideration is to select samples that are representative of their respective populations and similar with respect to critical variables other than the independent variable. As with experimental studies, the goal is to have groups that are as similar as possible on all relevant variables except the independent variable. In order to determine the equality of groups, information on a number of background and current status variables may be collected. In order to promote equality, or to correct for identified inequalities, there are a number of control procedures available to the researcher.

Control Procedures

Lack of randomization, manipulation, and control which characterize experimental studies are all sources of weakness in a causal-comparative design. Randomization of subjects to groups, for example, is probably the best single way to try to insure equality of groups. This is not possible in causal-comparative studies since the groups already exist, and furthermore, have already received the "treatment," or independent variable. A problem already discussed is the possibility that the groups are different on some other major variable besides the identified independent variable, and it is this other variable which is the real cause of the observed difference between the groups. For example, if a researcher simply compared a group of students who had received preschool education with a group who had not, the conclusion might be drawn that preschool education results in better reading achievement in first grade. What if, however, in the region in which the study was conducted, all preschool programs were private and required high tuitions. In this case, the researcher would really be investigating the effects not just of preschool education, but also of membership in a well-to-do family. It might very well be that mothers in such families provide early informal reading instruction for their children. It would be very difficult to evaluate only the effect of preschool education. If, however, the researcher was aware of the situation, he or she could *control* for this variable by only studying children of well-to-do parents. Thus, the two groups to be compared, one of which had attended a preschool program, would be equated with respect to income level of their parents, an extraneous variable. The above example is but one illustration of a number of statistical and nonstatistical methods that can be applied in an attempt to control for extraneous variables.[1]

Matching

Matching is a control technique that is also sometimes used in experimental studies. If a researcher has identified a variable believed to be related to performance on the dependent variable, she or he may control for that variable by pair-wise matching of subjects. In other words, for each subject in one group, the researcher finds a subject in the second group with the same or a similar score on the control variable. If a subject in either group does not have a suitable match, the subject is eliminated from the study. Thus, the resulting matched groups are identical or very similar with respect to the identified extraneous variable. For example, if a researcher matched on IQ, then a subject in one group with an IQ of 140 would have a match in the other group, a subject with an IQ at or near 140. As you may have deduced (if you have an IQ of 140!), a major problem with pair-wise matching is that there are invariably subjects who have no match and must therefore be eliminated from the study. The problem becomes even more serious when the researcher attempts to simultaneously match on two or more variables.

Comparing Homogeneous Groups or Subgroups

Another way of controlling an extraneous variable, which is also used in experimental research, is to compare groups which are homogeneous with respect to that variable. For example, if IQ were an identified extraneous variable, the researcher might limit groups to contain only subjects with IQs between 85 and

---

1. Several of these methods will be discussed further, and in more detail, in regard to their use in experimental research.

The resulting matched groups are identical or very similar with respect to the identified extraneous variable.

115 (average IQ). Of course this procedure also lowers the numbers of subjects in the study and additionally restricts the generalizability of the findings.

A similar but more satisfactory approach is to form subgroups within each group that represent all levels of the control variable. For example, each group might be divided into high (116 and above), average (85 to 115), and low (84 and below) IQ subgroups. The comparable subgroups in each group can be compared, for example, high IQ with high IQ. In addition to controlling for the variable, this technique has the added advantage of permitting the researcher to see if the independent variable affects the dependent variable differently at different levels of the control variable. If this question is of interest, the best approach is not to do several separate analyses but to build the control variable right into the design and analyze the results with a statistical technique called factorial analysis of variance. Factorial analysis of variance allows the researcher to determine the effect of the independent variable and the control variable, both separately and in combination. In other words, it permits the researcher to determine if there is an interaction between the independent variable and the control variable such that the independent variable operates differently at different levels of the control variable. For example, IQ might be a control variable in a causal-comparative study of the effects of two different methods of learning fractions. It might be found that a method involving manipulation of blocks is more effective for low IQ students who may have difficulty thinking abstractly.

Analysis of Covariance

The analysis of covariance, which is also used in experimental studies, is a statistical method that can be used to equate groups on one or more variables. In essence, analysis of covariance adjusts scores on a dependent variable for initial differences on some other variable (assuming that performance on the "other variable" is related to performance on the dependent variable, which is what control is all about anyway). For example, in the study comparing the effectiveness of two methods of learning fractions, one could covary on IQ, thus equating scores on a measure of achievement in fractions.[2] Analysis of covariance entails application of a nasty little formula but fortunately there are computer programs readily available that can do the calculations for you if you know how to use them (or know sombody who knows!).

Data Analysis and Interpretation

Analysis of data in causal-comparative studies involves a variety of descriptive and inferential statistics. All of the statistics that may be used in a causal-comparative study may also be used in an experimental study, and a number of them will be described in Part Seven. Briefly, however, the most commonly used descriptive statistics are the mean, which indicates the average performance of a group on a measure of some variable, and the standard deviation, which indicates how spread out a set of scores is, that is, whether the scores are relatively close together and clustered around the mean or spread out covering a wide range of scores. The most commonly used inferential statistics are the t test, which is used to see if there is a significant difference between the means of two groups, analysis of variance, which is used to see if there is a significant difference among the means of three or more groups, and the chi square test, which is used to compare group frequencies, that is, to see if an event occurs more frequently in one group than another.

As repeatedly pointed out, interpretation of the findings in a causal-comparative study requires considerable caution. Due to lack of randomization, manipulation, and other types of control characteristic of experimental studies, it is difficult to establish cause-effect relationships with any great degree of confidence. The cause-effect relationship may in fact be the reverse of the one hypothesized (the alleged cause may be the effect and vice versa), or there may be a third factor which is the "real" cause of both the alleged cause (independent variable) and effect (dependent bariable). In some cases, reversed causality is not a reasonable alternative and need not be considered. For example, preschool training may "cause" increased reading achievement in first grade but reading achievement in first grade cannot "cause" preschool training. Similarly, one's sex may affect one's achievement in mathematics, but one's achievement in mathematics cer-

---

2. Analysis of variance, factorial analysis of variance, and analysis of covariance will be discussed further in chapter 13.

tainly does not affect one's sex! In other cases, however, reversed causality is more plausible and should be investigated. For example, it is equally plausible that achievement affects self-concept and that self-concept affects achievement. It is also equally plausible that excessive absenteeism causes, or leads to, involvement in criminal activities as well as that involvement in criminal activities causes, or leads to, excessive absenteeism. The way to determine the correct order of causality, which variable caused which, is to determine which one occurred *first*. If, in the above example, it could be demonstrated that a period of excessive absenteeism was frequently followed by a student getting in trouble with the law, then it could more reasonably be concluded that excessive absenteeism leads to involvement in criminal activities. On the other hand, if it were determined that prior to a student's first involvement in criminal activities his or her attendance was good, but following it, poor, then the hypothesis that involvement in criminal activities leads to excessive absenteeism would be more reasonable.

The possibility of a third, common cause is plausible in many situations. Recall the example that parental attitude may affect both self-concept and achievement. One way to control for a potential common cause is to equate groups on the suspected variable. In the above example, students in both the high self-concept group and low self-concept group could be selected from among subjects whose parents had similar attitudes. It is clear that in order to investigate or control for alternative hypotheses, the researcher must be aware of them when they are plausible and must present evidence that they are not in fact the true explanation for the behavioral differences being investigated.

The Experimental Method

Enablers

After reading chapter 10, you should be able to:

1. Briefly state the purpose of experimental research.
2. List the basic steps involved in conducting an experiment.
3. Describe three ways in which a variable can be manipulated.
4. Explain the purpose of control.
5. Briefly define or describe "internal validity" and "external validity."
6. Identify and briefly describe eight major threats to the internal validity of an experiment.
7. Identify and briefly describe five major threats to the external validity of an experiment.
8. Briefly define or describe the concept of experimenter bias.
9. Briefly discuss the purpose of experimental design.
10. Identify and briefly describe five ways to control extraneous variables (and you better not leave out randomization!).
11. For each of the pre-experimental, true experimental, and quasi-experimental group designs discussed in this chapter, (a) draw a diagram, (b) list the steps involved in its application, and (c) identify major problems (e.g., sources of invalidity) with which it is associated.
12. Briefly describe the definition and purpose of a factorial design.
13. Briefly explain what is meant by the term interaction.
14. For each of the A-B-A single-subject designs discussed in this chapter, (a) draw a diagram, (b) list the steps involved in its application, and (c) identify major problems with which it is associated.
15. Briefly describe the procedures involved in using a multiple-baseline design.

Definition and Purpose

The experimental method is the only method of research that can truly test hypotheses concerning cause-and-effect relationships. It represents the most valid approach to the solution of educational problems, both practical and theoretical, and to the advancement of education as a science. In an experimental study, the researcher manipulates at least one independent variable, controls other relevant variables, and observes the effect on one or more dependent variables. The researcher determines "who gets what," which group of subjects gets which treatment. This manipulation of the independent variable is the one characteristic that differentiates all experimental research from the other methods of research. The independent variable, also referred to as the experimental variable, the cause, or the treatment, is that activity or characteristic believed to make a difference. In educational research independent variables typically manipulated include method of instruction, type of reinforcement, frequency of reinforcement, arrangement of learning environment, type of learning materials, and size of learning group. The above list is of course by no means exhaustive. The dependent variable, also referred to as the criterion variable, effect, or posttest, is the outcome of the study, the change or difference in groups that occurs as a result of manipulation of the independent variable. It is referred to as the dependent variable since it is "dependent" on the independent variable. The dependent variable may be measured by a test, but not necessarily. Since the independent variable is a variable which the researcher believes will make things "better," increase good things or decrease bad things, the dependent variable may also be such variables as attendance, number of suspensions, attention span, or even number of books checked out of the library. The only restriction on the dependent variable is that it represents an outcome that is measurable.

The experimental method is both the most demanding and the most productive method of research. When well conducted, experimental studies produce the soundest evidence concerning hypothesized cause-effect relationships. The results of experimental research permit prediction, but not the kind characteristic of correlational research. A correlational prediction is specific and predicts a particular score for a particular individual. Predictions based on experimental findings are more global and take the form, "if you use approach X you will probably get better results than if you use approach Y." Experimental research has repeatedly confirmed, for example, that systematically applied positive reinforcement leads to improved behavior. Although there are a number of alternative designs from which a researcher can select, the basic experimental process is the same in all studies.

The Experimental Process

The steps in an experimental study are basically the same as for other types of research: selection and definition of a problem, selection of subjects and measuring instruments, selection of a design, execution of procedures, analysis of data, and formulation of conclusions. An experimental study is guided by at least one hypothesis that states an expected causal relationship between two variables. The actual experiment is conducted in order to confirm (support) or disconfirm the experimental hypothesis. In an experimental study, the researcher is in on the action from the very beginning; the researcher forms or selects the groups, decides what is going to happen to each group, tries to control all relevant factors besides the change that she or he has introduced, and observes or measures the effect on the groups at the end of the study.

An experiment typically involves two groups, an experimental group and a control group (although as you will see later, there may be only one group, or there may be three or more groups). The experimental group typically receives a new, or novel treatment, a treatment under investigation, while the control group usually either receives a different treatment or is treated as usual. The control group is needed for comparison purposes to see if the new treatment is more effective than the usual or traditional approach, or to see if one approach is more effective than another. A common misconception among beginning researchers is that a control group always receives nothing. This would hardly be fair. If in a study, for example, the independent variable was the type of reading instruction, the experimental group might be instructed with a new method, while the control group was instructed with a traditional method. The control group would still receive reading instruction; it would not sit in a closet while the study was being conducted. Otherwise you would not be evaluating the effectiveness of a new method as compared to a traditional method, but rather the effectiveness of a new method as compared to no reading instruction at all! Any method of instruction is bound to be more effective than no instruction at all. Thus, the control group also receives a form of the independent variable. The two groups that are to receive different treatments are equated on all other variables that might be related to performance on the dependent variable, for example, reading readiness. In other words, the researcher makes every effort to ensure that the two groups are as equivalent as possible on all variables *except* the independent variable.

After the groups have been exposed to the treatment for some period of time, the researcher administers a test of the dependent variable (or otherwise measures it) and then determines whether there is a significant difference between the groups. In other words, the researcher determines whether the treatment *made a difference*. One problem associated with experimental studies in education is that subjects are often not exposed to the experimental treatment for a sufficient period of time. No matter how effective peer counseling is, for example, it is not likely to reduce suspensions if students are exposed to it for only one hour. Thus, to adequately test a hypothesis concerning the effectiveness of peer counseling, the experimental group would need to be exposed to it over a period of time. The experimental treatment should be given a "chance to work."

Another problem associated with experimental research is that the treatments received by the groups are not sufficiently different to make a difference. For example, if your study were comparing team teaching with traditional teaching it would be vital that team teaching be operationalized according to its generally accepted meaning. If in your study team teaching meant nothing more than two teachers taking turns lecturing, it would not be very different from traditional teaching. Thus, you would be very unlikely to find a major difference between your experimental and control groups at the end of the study, even though you might have if team teaching had been correctly operationalized to include such things as large-group and small-group instruction.

Manipulation and Control

Direct manipulation by the researcher of at least one independent variable is the one single characteristic that differentiates all experimental research from other methods of research. Manipulation of an independent variable seems to be a difficult concept for some beginning researchers to grasp. Quite simply it means that the researcher decides what forms or values the independent variable (or cause) will take and which group will get which form. For example, if the independent variable was number of reviews, the researcher might decide that there should be three groups, one group receiving no review, a second group receiving one review, and a third group receiving two reviews. There are many independent variables in education that can be manipulated (active variables), and many which cannot (assigned variables). You can manipulate such variables as method of instruction and size of group; you cannot manipulate such variables as sex or socioeconomic status. In other words, you can require students to receive one method of instruction or another, but you cannot require students to be male or female; they *already are* male or female. In order to manipulate a variable, *you* have to decide who is going to be what or who is going to get what. Although the design of an experimental study may include assigned variables, at least one variable must be manipulated.

The different values or forms that the independent variable may take are basically presence versus absence (*A* versus no *A*), presence in varying degrees (a lot of *A* versus a little *A*), or presence of one kind versus presence of another kind (*A* versus *B*). An example of *A* versus no *A* would be a study comparing the effectivenss of review versus no review in teaching history. An example of "a lot of *A* versus a little *A*" would be a study comparing the effectiveness of different numbers of examples in teaching algebra; one group might receive two examples per concept, and another group might receive five examples per concept. An example of *A* versus *B* would be a study to compare the effectiveness of peer counseling versus individual counseling in reducing referrals for discipline. Experimental designs may get quite complex and involve simultaneous manipulation of several independent variables. At this stage of the game, however, you had better stick to just one!

Control refers to efforts on the part of the researcher to remove the influence of any variable (other than the independent variable) that might affect performance on the dependent variable. In other words, the researcher wants the groups to be as similar as possible, so that the only major difference between them is the independent variable, the difference caused by the researcher. To illustrate the importance of control, suppose you conducted a study to compare the effectiveness of student tutors versus parent tutors in teaching first graders to read. Student tutors might be older children from higher grade levels, and parent tutors might be members of the P.T.A. Now suppose student tutors helped each member of one group for 1 hour per day for a month, while the parent tutors helped each member of a second group for 2 hours per week for a month. Would the comparison be fair? Certainly not. Subjects with the student tutors would have received two-and-one-half times as much help (5 hours per week versus 2 hours per week). Thus, one variable which would need to be *controlled* would be *time*. In order for the comparison to be fair, members of both groups would have to be helped in reading for the same amount of time. Then the researcher could truly compare the effectiveness of different *kinds* of help, not different *amounts*. The above is just one example of the kinds of factors which must be considered in planning an experiment. Some variables which need controlling may be relatively obvious; in the above example, variables such as reading readiness and intelligence would need to be considered. Other variables in need of control may not be as obvious; in the above study, for example, the researcher would need to ensure that both groups used the same reading texts and materials. Thus, we see that there are really two different kinds of variables that need to be controlled, subject variables (such as reading readiness), variables on which subjects in the different groups might differ, and environmental variables (such as learning materials), variables that might cause unwanted differences between groups. The researcher strives to ensure that the characteristics and experiences of the groups are as equal as possible on all important variables except, of course, the independent variable. If at the end of some period of time groups differ in performance on the dependent variable, the difference can be attributed to the independent variable, or treatment. Control is not easy in an experiment, especially in educational research where real live subjects are involved; it is a lot easier to control solids, liquids, and gases! The task is not an impossible one, however, since the researcher can concentrate on identifying and controlling only those variables that might really affect the dependent variable. If two groups differed significantly with respect to shoe size, for example, the results of the study would probably not be affected. Also, there are a number of techniques at the researcher's disposal that can be used to control for extraneous variables.[1]

You should keep in mind that, even though experimental research is the only type of research which can truly establish cause-effect relationships, it is only useful when it is appropriate. There are many problems in education for which the experimental method is inappropriate. For example, if a researcher wanted to determine at what ages children are capable of different levels of abstract thinking, a descriptive study would probably be the appropriate research method.

Threats to Experimental Validity

Any uncontrolled extraneous variables affecting performance on the dependent variable are threats to the validity of an experiment. An experiment is valid if results obtained are due only to the manipulated independent variable, and if they are generalizable to situations outside of the experimental setting. The two conditions which must be met are referred to as internal validity and external validity. *Internal validity* refers to the condition that observed differences on the dependent variable are a direct result of manipulation of the independent variable, not some other variable. In other words, the outcome of the study is the result of what the researcher did, not something else. If someone can come up with an alternative explanation (a rival hypothesis) for your results, your study was not internally valid. To use a former example, if the student tutors had worked with subjects for five hours per week, and the parent tutors only two, and if the student-tutored group out-performed the parent-tutored group, then time, or amount of tutoring, would be a plausible alternative explanation for the results. The degree to which results are attributable to manipulation of the independent variable is the degree to which an experimental study is internally valid. *External validity* refers to the condition that results are generalizable, or applicable, to groups and environments outside of the experimental setting. In other words, the results of the study, the confirmed cause-effect relationship, can be expected to be reconfirmed with other

---

1. These will be discussed later in the chapter.

groups, in other settings, at other times, as long as the conditions are similar to those of the study. If a study was conducted using groups of gifted ninth graders, for example, the results should be applicable to other groups of gifted ninth graders. As mentioned previously, if research results were not generalizable to any other situation outside of the experimental setting, then no one could profit from anyone else's research, and each and every effect would have to be reestablished over and over and over. An experimental study can only contribute to educational theory or practice if there is some assurance that confirmed relationships and observed effects are replicable and likely to occur at other times and places with other groups. The term *ecological validity* is sometimes used to refer to the degree to which results can be generalized to other environments. If results cannot be replicated in other environments by other researchers, the study has low ecological validity.

So all one has to do in order to conduct a valid experiment is to maximize internal validity and maximize external validity, right? Wrong. Unfortunately, there is a "catch-22" complicating the researcher's experimental life. Maximization of internal validity requires exercise of very rigid control over subjects and conditions in a laboratory-like environment. The more a situation is controlled, however, the less realistic it becomes, and the less generalizable to nonlaboratory settings the results become. In other words, lab findings are generalizable to other labs. A study can contribute little to educational practice, for example, if there is no assurance that a technique found to be effective in a controlled laboratory setting will also be effective in a natural classroom setting. On the other hand, the more natural the experimental setting becomes, the more difficult it becomes to control extraneous variables. It is very difficult, for example, to conduct a well-controlled study in an actual classroom. Thus the researcher must strive for a balance between control and realism. If a choice is involved, the researcher should err on the side of too much control rather than too little. A study that is not internally valid is worthless. In fact, one research strategy is first to demonstrate an effect in a highly controlled environment (for the sake of internal validity) and then to redo the study in a more natural setting (for the sake of external validity).

Although lab-like settings are generally preferred for the investigation of theoretical problems, experimentation in natural, or field, settings has its advantages, especially for certain practical problems. In the final analysis, however, the researcher usually strives for a compromise, or an environment somewhere between a lab setting and a natural educational setting. Many studies, for example, are conducted in simulated-classroom settings that the researcher makes as much like a natural classroom as possible. This permits the researcher to exercise sufficient control to ensure adequate internal validity, while at the same time maintaining a degree of realism necessary for generalizability.

In the pages to come many threats to internal and external validity will be discussed. Some extraneous variables are definite threats to internal validity, some are definite threats to external validity, and some may be threats to both. How potential threats are classified, or labeled, is not the important thing; what is important is that you, as a researcher, be aware of their existence and make efforts to control for them. As you read, you may begin to feel that there are just too many of them for one little researcher to control all at the same time. The task is not as formidable as it may at first appear, however. As you will see later, there are a number of experimental designs that control many threats for you; all you have to do is to select a "good" design and go from there. Also, each of the threats to be discussed is only a potential threat that may not be a problem in a particular study.

Threats to Internal Validity

Probably the most authoritative source regarding experimental design and threats to experimental validity is the work of Donald Campbell and Julian Stanley.[2] Campbell and Stanley have identified eight major threats to internal validity, or to put it another way, sources of internal invalidity.

History

History refers to the occurrence of any event which is not part of the experimental treatment but which may affect performance on the dependent variable. The longer a study lasts, the more likely it is that history may be a problem. Happenings such as a bomb scare, an epidemic of influenza, or even current events are examples of history. For example, suppose you showed a series of films designed to increase tolerance toward noncapitalistic countries such as the Soviet Union. Suppose that between the time you showed the films and the time you administered some posttest measure of tolerance, the news media announced that the Soviet Union was reported to be responsible for the death of an American pilot shot down in Turkey, near the border of the Soviet Union. Such an event could easily wipe out any effect the films might have had; posttest scores might show considerable intolerance when they might otherwise have shown increased tolerance. Thus, while the researcher has no control over the occurrence of such events, he or she can select a design which controls *for* their occurrence.

Maturation

Maturation refers to physical or mental changes that may occur within the subjects over a period of time. These changes may affect the subjects' performance on the measure of the dependent variable. Especially in studies which last for any length of time, subjects may become, for example, older, more coordinated, unmotivated, anxious, or just plain bored. Maturation is more of a threat in some studies than in others. It would be much more likely to be a problem, for example, in a study designed to test the effectiveness of a psychomotor training program than in a study designed to compare two methods of teaching algebra, especially if preadolescent students were involved; such students are typically undergoing rapid biological changes. As with history, the researcher cannot control the occurrence of maturation but can control *for* its occurrence.

Testing

Testing refers to improved scores on a posttest resulting from subjects having taken a pretest. In other words, taking a pretest may improve performance on a

---

2. Campbell, D.T., & Stanley, J.C.: *Experimental and quasi-experimental designs for research.* Chicago: Rand McNally, 1971.

posttest, regardless of whether there is any treatment or instruction in between. Testing is more likely to be a threat when the time between testings is short; a pretest taken in September is not likely to affect performance on a posttest taken in June. This phenomenon is also more likely to occur in some studies than in others, for example, when the tests measure factual information that can be recalled; taking a pretest on algebraic equations, on the other hand, is much less likely to improve performance on a similar posttest. One obvious way to control for testing is to use a design that does not involve a pretest. Another way to attempt to control for testing is to use alternate forms, one form for the pretest and another for the posttest. It is a factor which should at least be considered when selecting both the measuring instrument and the experimental design.

Instrumentation

Instrumentation refers to unreliability, or lack of consistency, in measuring instruments which may result in an invalid assessment of performance. Instrumentation may occur in several different ways. If two different tests are used for pretesting and posttesting, and the tests are not of equal difficulty, instrumentation may occur; if the posttest is more difficult, it may fail to show improvement which is actually present, whereas if the posttest is less difficult, it may indicate an improvement that is not present. If data are collected through observation, observers may not be observing or evaluating behavior the same way at the end of the study as at the beginning. In fact, if they are aware of the nature of the study, they may unconsciously tend to see and record what they know the researcher is hypothesizing. If data are collected through the use of a mechanical device, such as an ergometer, it may be suffering from some malfunction resulting in inaccurate measurement. Thus, the researcher must take care in selecting tests, caution observers, and check mechanical devices. In addition, the researcher can select an experimental design that controls for this factor.

Statistical Regression

Statistical regression usually occurs when subjects are selected on the basis of their extreme scores and refers to the tendency of subjects who score highest on a pretest to score lower on a posttest, and of subjects who score lowest on a pretest to score higher on a posttest. The tendency is for scores to regress, or move toward, the mean (average) or expected score. For example, suppose a researcher wished to determine the effectivenss of a new method of spelling instruction in improving the spelling ability of poor spellers. The researcher might administer a 100-item, 4-alternative, multiple-choice spelling pretest. Each question might read, "Which of the following four words is spelled incorrectly?" The researcher might then select for the study the 30 students who scored lowest. Now suppose none of the pretested students knew *any* of the words and guessed on *every* single question. With 100 items, and 4 choices for each item, a student would be expected to receive a score of 25 just by guessing. Some students, however, just due to rotten guessing, would receive scores much lower than 25, and other students, just by chance, would receive much higher scores than 25. If they were administered the test a second time, *without* any instruction intervening, their expected score would still be 25. Thus students who scored very low the first time would be expected to have a second score closer to 25, and students who scored very high the first time would also be expected to score closer to 25 the second time. In the above study, if students were selected because of their very low pretest scores, they would be expected to do better on the posttest, regardless of the treatment. The researcher might erroneously attribute their improved spelling ability to the new method of spelling instruction. The researcher must therefore be aware of statistical regression and if at all possible select a design that controls for this phenomenon.

Differential Selection of Subjects

Differential selection of subjects usually occurs when already formed groups are used and refers to the fact that the groups may be different before the study even begins, and this initial difference may at least partially account for posttest differences. Suppose, for example, you received permission to use two of Ms. Hynee's English classes in your study; there would be no guarantee that the two classes were at all equivalent. If your luck was really bad, one class might be the honors English class and one class might be the remedial English class. It would not be too surprising if the first class did much better on the posttest! Thus, using already formed groups should be avoided if possible. If they must be used, groups should be selected which are as similar as possible, and a pretest should be administered to check for initial equivalence.

Mortality

First, let me make it perfectly clear that mortality *does not* mean that subjects die! Mortality, or attrition, is more likely to occur in longer studies and refers to the fact that subjects who drop out of a group may share a characteristic such that their absence has a significant effect on the results of the study. Subjects who drop out of a study may be less motivated, for example; this is especially a problem when volunteers are used. Volunteers rarely drop out of control groups because few or no demands are made on them. Volunteers may, however, drop out of an experimental group if too much effort is required for participation. The experimental group that remains at the end of the study may as a whole represent a more-motivated group than the control group. As another example of the problem of mortality, suppose Suzy Shiningstar (high IQ and all that) got the measles and dropped out of one's control group. Now, suppose that before Suzy dropped out she managed to give the measles to her friends in the control group. Since birds of a feather flock together, Suzy's control group friends would probably also be "high IQ and all that." The experimental group might end up looking pretty good when compared to the control group simply because many of the good students dropped out of the control group. Thus, the researcher cannot assume that subjects drop out of a study in a random fashion and should if possible select a design that controls for mortality.

Selection-Maturation Interaction, Etc.

The "etc." means that selection may also interact with factors such as history and testing, although selection-maturation interaction is more common. What this means is that if already formed groups are used, one group may profit more (or less) from a treatment, or have an initial advantage, because of maturation, history, or testing factors. Suppose, for example, that you received permission to use two of Ms. Hynee's English classes, and both classes were average English classes and apparently equivalent on all relevant variables. Suppose, however, that for some reason one day Ms. Hynee had to miss one of her classes but not the other (maybe she had a toothache), and Ms. Alma Mater took over Ms. Hynee's class. Suppose further that as luck would have it Ms. Mater covered much of the material now included in your posttest (remember history?). Unbeknownst to you, your experimental group would have a definite advantage to begin with, and it might be this initial advantage which caused posttest differences, rather than your independent variable. Thus, the researcher must select a design that controls for this potential problem or make every effort to determine if it is operating in the study.

Threats to External Validity

There are also several major threats to external validity that limit, or make questionable, generalization to nonexperimental populations.

Pretest-Treatment Interaction

Pretest-treatment interaction occurs when subjects respond or react differently to a treatment because they have been pretested. A pretest may sensitize or alert subjects to the nature of the treatment. The treatment effect may be different than it would have been had subjects not been pretested. Thus results are only generalizable to other pretested groups. The results are not even generalizable to the unpretested population from which the sample was selected. This potential problem is more or less serious depending upon the subjects, the nature of the tests, the nature of the treatment, and the duration of the study. Studies involving attitude change, for example, are especially susceptible to this problem. Campbell and Stanley illustrate the effect by pointing out the probable lack of comparability of one group viewing the antiprejudice film Gentlemen's Agreement right after taking a lengthy pretest dealing with anti-Semitism, and another group viewing the movie without a pretest. Individuals in the unpretested group could quite conceivably enjoy the movie as a good love story and be unaware that it deals with a social issue; pretested individuals would have to be pretty dense not to see a connection between the pretest and the message of the film. On the other hand, taking a pretest on algebraic algorithms would probably affect very little (if at all) a group's responsiveness to a new method of teaching algebra. The pretest-treatment interaction would also be expected to be minimized in studies involving very young children, who would probably not even see a connection between a pretest and a subsequent treatment, and in studies conducted over a relatively long period of time; any effects of a pretest taken in September would probably have worn off or greatly diminished by the time a posttest was given in June. For some studies, however, the potential interactive effect of a pretest is a more serious consideration. In such cases the researcher should select a design which either controls for the effect or allows the researcher to determine the magnitude of the effect.

Selection-Treatment Interaction

Selection-treatment interaction is similar to the "differential selection of subjects" problem associated with internal invalidity and also occurs when subjects are not randomly selected for treatments. Interaction effects aside, the very fact that subjects are not randomly selected from a population severely limits the researcher's ability to generalize since representativeness of the sample is in question. Even if intact groups are randomly selected, the possibility exists that the experimental group is in some important way different from the control group, and/or from the larger population. This nonrepresentativeness of groups may also result in a selection-treatment interaction such that the results of a study hold only for the groups involved and are not representative of the treatment effect in the intended population. While the selection-treatment interaction is a definite weakness associated with several of the poorer experimental designs, it is also an uncontrolled variable associated with the designs involving randomization. One's accessible population is often a far cry from one's target population; the way in which a given population becomes available to a researcher may make generalizability of findings questionable, no matter how internally valid an experiment may be. As Campbell and Stanley point out, if a researcher is turned down by nine school systems and accepted by a tenth, the accepting system is bound to be different from the other nine, and from the population of schools to which the researcher would like to generalize. Administrative and instructional personnel, in all probability, have "higher morale, less fear of being inspected, and more zeal for improvement" than personnel in an average school. It is therefore recommended that the researcher report problems involved in acquiring subjects, including the number of times he or she was turned down, so that the reader can judge the seriousness of a possible selection-treatment interaction.

Specificity of Variables

Like selection-treatment interaction, specificity is a threat to generalizability regardless of the experimental design used. Specificity of variables refers to the fact that a given study is conducted with a specific kind of subject, using specific measuring instruments, at a specific time, under a specific set of circumstances. For example, team teaching might be found to be effective *with* upper-middle-class second graders, and *when* achievement is measured using the Baloney Achievement Test. To deal with this issue, the researcher must (1) operationally define variables in a way that has meaning outside of the experimental setting, and (2) be careful in stating conclusions and generalizations. Defining achievement in geometry, for example, solely in terms of memorization of definitions would certainly not help the generalizability of the study since most geometry teachers measure achievement primarily in terms of problem solving. Also, a researcher would most definitely be overgeneralizing if based on a study involving fourth graders, the researcher concluded that a treatment was effective for elementary-age students.

Reactive Arrangements

Reactive arrangements refer to a number of factors associated with the way in which the study is conducted and the feelings and attitudes of the subjects involved. In an effort to maintain a high degree of control, the researcher may create an experimental environment that is highly artificial and hinders generalizability of findings to nonexperimental settings. Another type of reactive arrangement results from the subjects' knowledge that they are involved in an experiment or their feeling that they are in some way receiving "special" attention. The effect that such knowledge or feelings can have on the behavior of subjects was dramatically demonstrated at the Hawthorne Plant of the Western Electric Company in Chicago years ago. As part of their research on working conditions, researchers investigated the relationship between light intensity and worker output. The researchers increased light intensity and production went up. They increased it some more and production went up some more. The brighter the place became, the more production rose. As a check, the researchers decreased illumination, and guess what—production went up! The darker it got, the more the workers produced. The researchers soon realized that it was the attention the workers were receiving, and not the illumination, that was affecting production. To this day, the term Hawthorne effect is used to describe any situation in which subjects' behavior is affected not by the treatment per se, but by their knowledge of participation in a study.

A similar phenomenon in medical research resulted in the placebo effect, which is sort of the antidote for the Hawthorne effect. In medical research it was discovered that any "medication" could make subjects feel better, even sugar and water. To counteract this effect, the placebo approach was developed in which half of the subjects receive the true medication and half receive a placebo (sugar and water, for example); this fact is of course not known to the subjects. The application of the placebo effect in educational research is that all groups in an experiment should *appear* to be treated the same. Subjects should not feel special if they are in the experimental group, nor should they feel shortchanged if they are in the control group. Suppose, for example, you have four groups of ninth graders, two experimental and two control, and the treatment is a film designed to promote a positive attitude toward a vocational career. If the experimental subjects are to be excused from several of their classes in order to view the film, then the control subjects too should be excused and shown another film whose content is unrelated to the purpose of the study (*Donald in Mathmajic Land* would do!). As an added control you might have all the subjects told that there are two movies and that eventually all of them will see both movies. In other words, it should appear as if *all* the students are doing the same thing.

Another related effect is the novelty effect. The novelty effect refers to increased interest, motivation, or participation on the part of subjects simply because they are doing something different. In other words, a treatment may be effective because it is different, not better per se. To counteract the novelty effect, the study should be conducted over a period of time sufficient to allow the "newness" to wear off. This is especially true if the treatment involves activities very different from the subjects' usual routine.

Multiple-Treatment Interference

Multiple-treatment interference can occur when the same subjects receive more than one treatment in succession; it refers to the carry-over effects from an earlier treatment which make it difficult to assess the effectiveness of a later treatment. Suppose you were interested in comparing two different approaches to improving classroom behavior—behavior modification and corporal punishment (admittedly an extreme example used to make a point!). Let us say that for two months behavior modification techniques were systematically applied to the subjects, and at the end of this period behavior was found to be significantly better than before the study began. Now suppose that for the next 2 months the same subjects were physically punished whenever they misbehaved (hand slappings, spankings, and the like), and at the end of the 2 months behavior was equally as good as after the 2 months of behavior modification. Could you than conclude that behavior modification and corporal punishment are equally effective methods of behavior control? Cer-tain-ly not. In fact, the goal of behavior modification is to produce behavior which is self-maintaining, that is, continues after direct intervention is stopped. Thus, the good behavior exhibited by the subjects at the end of the study could well be because of the effectiveness of the previous behavior modification and exist in spite of the corporal punishment. If it is not possible to select a design in which each group receives but one treatment, the researcher should try to minimize potential muliple-treatment interference by allowing sufficient time to elapse between treatments and by investigating distinctly different types of independent variables.

Contamination and Experimenter Bias

Contamination occurs when the researcher's familiarity with the subjects affects the outcome of the study; the researcher may unintentionally influence their behavior or be subjective in evaluating their behavior. The contamination is similar to that associated with the halo effect in that knowledge of a subject's behavior in one situation may color judgment concerning his or her behavior in another. If you know Suzy Shiningstar is a good student, you may tend to rate her group leadership ability a little higher than it actually is. Further, the researcher's expectations concerning study outcomes may actually contribute to producing those outcomes. Knowing which subjects are in which group may cause the researcher to be unintentionally biased in evaluating their performance. Rosenthal has demonstrated the experimenter bias effect in a number of interesting studies. In one study, two groups of graduate students were each given rats and instructions to train the rats to perform a discrimination-learning task.[3] One group of graduate students was told that due to selective breeding their rats were "maze-bright" and would learn quickly and well; the other graduate students were told that their rats were "maze-dull." In reality both sets of rats were just average, run-of-the-mill rats which had been randomly assigned to the two groups of graduate students. Lo and behold, however, the "smart" rats significantly outperformed the "dumb" rats!

It should be noted that the studies of Rosenthal and his associates have been accused of being affected by experimenter bias! But seriously, folks, some researchers have pointed out some methodological flaws in the studies and others have

---

3. Rosenthal, R., & Fode, K.L. The effect of experimenter bias on the performance of the albino rat. *Behavioral Science*, 1963, *8*, 183–189.

suggested that the results would not have been obtained had properly trained observers been used. It is true that many of their findings have not been replicated.[4] In any event, the message to the researcher is to be on the safe side and to not be directly involved in conducting her or his own study, if at all possible. Further, the researcher should avoid communicating outcome expectations to any personnel connected with the study.

Group Experimental Designs

The validity of an experiment is a direct function of the degree to which extraneous variables are controlled. If such variables are not controlled, it is difficult to evaluate the effects of an independent variable and the generalizability of effects. The term "confounding" is sometimes used to refer to the fact that the effects of the independent variable may be confounded by extraneous variables such that it is difficult to determine the effects of each. This is what experimental design is all about—control of extraneous variables; good designs control many sources of invalidity, poor designs control few. If you recall, two types of extraneous variables in need of control were previously identified, subject variables and environmental variables. Subject variables include organismic variables and intervening variables. Organismic variables, as the term implies, are characteristics of the subject, or organism (such as sex), which cannot be directly controlled, but which can be controlled *for*. Intervening variables, as the term implies, are variables that intervene between the independent variable and the dependent variable (such as anxiety or boredom), which cannot be directly observed or controlled, but which also can be controlled *for*.

Control of Extraneous Variables

Randomization is the best single way to attempt to control for many extraneous variables all at the same time. The logical implication of the above statement is that randomization should be used whenever possible; subjects should be randomly selected from a population whenever possible, subjects should be randomly assigned to groups whenever possible, treatments should be randomly assigned to groups whenever possible, and anything else you can think of should be randomly assigned, if possible! Recall that random selection means selection by pure chance and is usually accomplished using a table of random numbers. Random assignment means assignment by pure chance and is usually accomplished by flipping a coin if two groups are involved, or by rolling a die if more than two groups are involved (heads you are in the experimental group, tails you are in the control group). Randomization is effective in creating equivalent, representative groups that are essentially the same on all relevant variables thought of by the researcher, and probably even a few not thought of. A randomly formed group is a characteristic unique to experimental research; it is a control factor not possible with causal-comparative research. The rationale is that if subjects are assigned at random to groups, there is no reason to believe that the groups are greatly different in any systematic way. Thus, the groups would be

---

4. Barber, T.X., & Silver, M.J. Fact, fiction, and the experimental bias effect. *Psychological Bulletin Monograph*, 1968, 70(6), Part II, 1–29.

expected to perform essentially the same on the dependent variable *if* the independent variable makes no difference; therefore, if the groups perform differently at the end of the study, the difference can be attributed to the treatment, or independent variable. The larger the groups, the more confidence the researcher can have in the effectiveness of randomization; recall that 15 subjects per group is an accepted minimum. In addition to equating groups on subject variables such as intelligence, randomization also equalizes groups on environmental variables. Teachers, for example, can be randomly assigned to groups so that the experimental groups will not have all the "Carmel Kandee" teachers or all the "Hester Hartless" teachers (and likewise the control groups). Clearly, the researcher should use as much randomization as possible. If subjects cannot be randomly selected, those available should at least be randomly assigned. If subjects cannot be randomly assigned to groups, then at least treatment condition should be randomly assigned to the existing groups.

In addition to randomization, there are other ways to control for extraneous variables. Certain environmental variables, for example, can be controlled by holding them constant for all groups. Recall the student tutor versus parent tutor study; help time was an important variable that had to be held constant, that is, be the same, for the two groups. Other such variables which might need to be held constant include: learning materials, meeting place and time (students might be more alert in the morning than in the afternoon), and years of experience of participating teachers. Controlling subject variables is critical. If the groups are not the same to start with, you have not even given yourself a fighting chance. Regardless of whether groups can be randomly formed, there are a number of techniques at your disposal that can be used to try to equate groups.

Matching

Matching is a technique for equating groups on one or more variables the researcher has identified as being highly related to performance on the dependent variable. The most commonly used approach to matching involves random assignment of pair members, one member to each group. In other words, for each of the available subjects, the researcher attempts to find another subject with the same or a similar score on the control variable (the variable on which subjects are being matched). If the researcher is matching on sex, obviously the "match" must be of the same sex, not a similar sex. If the researcher is matching on variables such as pretest scores, GRE scores, or IQ, however, the "similar score" concept makes sense. Unless the available number of subjects is very large, it is unreasonable to try to make exact matches. Thus, the researcher might decide that two GRE scores within 50 points of each other constitute an acceptable match. As the researcher identifies each matched pair, one member of the pair is randomly assigned to one group and the other member to the other group. If a subject does not have a suitable match, the subject is excluded from the study. The resulting matched groups are identical or very similar with respect to the identified extraneous variable.

A major problem with such matching is that there are invariably subjects who do not have a match and must be eliminated from the study. This factor may cost the researcher many subjects, especially if matching is attempted on two or more variables (imagine trying to find a match for a male with an IQ near 140 and a GPA between 1.00 and 1.50!). One way to combat loss of subjects is to match less closely. The researcher might decide that two IQ scores within 20 points constitute an acceptable match. This procedure may increase subjects but it tends to defeat the purpose of matching. A related procedure is to rank all of the subjects, from highest to lowest, based on their scores on the control variable. The first two subjects (the subjects with the highest and next highest scores) are the first pair, no matter how far apart their scores are; one member is randomly assigned to one group and one member to the other. The next two subejcts (the subjects with the third and fourth highest scores) are the next pair, and so on. The major advantage of this approach is that no subjects are lost; the major disadvantage is that it is a lot less precise than pair-wise matching. Advanced statistical procedures, such as analysis of covariance, and the availability of computer programs to compute such statistics have greatly reduced the research use of matching.

Comparing Homogeneous Groups or Subgroups

Another way of controlling an extraneous variable, which was discussed previously with respect to causal-comparative research, is to compare groups that are homogeneous with respect to that variable. For example, if IQ were an identified extraneous variable, the researcher might select a group of subjects with IQs between 85 and 115 (average IQ). The researcher would then randomly assign half of the selected subjects to the experimental group and half to the control group. Of course this procedure also lowers the number of subjects in the study and additionally restricts the generalizability of the findings. Further, if random assignment is possible, using only a homogeneous subgroup really only makes sense if one wants to have an additional guarantee concerning group equality on the control variable.

As with causal-comparative research, a similar, but more satisfactory approach is to form subgroups representing all levels of the control variable. For example, the available subjects might be divided into high (116 or above), average (85 to 115), and low (84 and below) IQ subgroups. Half of the selected subjects from each of the subgroups could then be randomly assigned to the experimental group and half to the control group. The procedure just described should sound familiar since it describes stratified sampling. If the researcher is interested not just in controlling the variable but also in seeing if the independent variable affects the dependent variable differently at different levels of the control variable, the best approach is to build the control variable right into the design and to analyze the results with a statistical technique called factorial analysis of variance.[5]

Using Subjects as Their Own Controls

Using subjects as their own controls involves exposing the same group to the different treatments, one treatment at a time. This helps to control for subject differences since the same subjects get both treatments. Of course this approach is

---

5. Analysis of variance and factorial analysis of variance will be discussed further in chapter 13.

not always feasible; you cannot teach the same algebraic concepts twice to the same group using two different methods of instruction (well, you *could* but it would not make such sense). A problem with this approach in some studies is carry-over effects of one treatment to the next. To use a previous example, it would be very difficult to evaluate the effectiveness of corporal punishment in improving behavior if the group receiving corporal punishment was the same group that had previously been exposed to behavior modification. If only one group is available, a better approach, if feasible, is to randomly divide the group into two smaller groups, each of which receives both treatments but in a different order. In the above example, the researcher could at least get some idea of the effectiveness of corporal punishment because there would be a group which received it *before* behavior modification.

Analysis of Covariance

The analysis of covariance is a statistical method for equating randomly formed groups on one or more variables. In essence, analysis of covariance adjusts scores on a dependent variable for initial differences on some other variable, such as pretest scores, IQ, reading readiness, or musical aptitude (assuming that performance on the "other variable" is related to performance on the dependent variable). In the example previously given, for a study comparing the effectiveness of two methods of learning fractions, the researcher could covary on IQ thus equating scores on a measure of achievement in fractions. Although analysis of covariance can be used in studies when groups cannot be randomly formed, its use is most appropriate when randomization is used. Despite randomization, for example, it might be found that two groups differ significantly in terms of pretest scores. Analysis of covariance can be used in such cases to "correct" or adjust posttest scores for initial pretest differences.[6] Calculation of an analysis of covariance is quite a complex, lengthy procedure and you would not want to do many by hand. Fortunately, there are computer programs readily available that can do the work for you if you know how to use them.

Types of Group Designs

A selected experimental design dictates to a great extent the specific procedures of a study. Selection of a given design dictates such factors as whether there will be a control group, whether subjects will be randomly assigned to groups, whether each group will be pretested, and how resulting data will be analyzed. Depending upon the particular combination of such factors represented, different designs are appropriate for testing different types of hypotheses, and designs vary widely in the degree to which they control the various threats to internal and external validity. In selecting a design, you must first determine which designs are appropriate for your study, for testing your hypothesis. You then determine which of those that are appropriate are also feasible given any constraints under which you may be operating. If, for example, you must use existing groups, a number of

---

6. Another important function of analysis of covariance, its ability to increase the power of a statistical test, will be discussed in chapter 13.

designs will automatically be eliminated. From the designs that are appropriate and feasible, you select the one that controls the most sources of internal and external invalidity. In other words, you select the best design you possibly can that will yield the data you need to test your hypothesis or hypotheses.

There are two major classes of experimental designs, single-variable designs, which involve one independent variable (which is manipulated), and factorial designs, which involve two or more independent variables (at least one of which is manipulated). Single-variable designs are classified as pre-experimental, true experimental, or quasi-experimental, depending upon the control they provide for sources of internal and external invalidity. Pre-experimental designs do not do a very good job of controlling threats to validity and should be avoided. In fact the results of a study based on such a design are so questionable, they are essentially worthless for all purposes except, *perhaps,* a preliminary investigation of a problem. The true experimental designs represent a very high degree of control and are always to be preferred. Quasi-experimental designs do not control as well as true experimental designs but do a much better job than the pre-experimental designs. Thus, if you have a choice between a true experimental design and a quasi-experimental design, select the true experimental design. If your choice is between a quasi-experimental design and a pre-experimental design, select the quasi-experimental design. If your choice is between a pre-experimental design or not doing the study at all, do not do the study at all. The poor designs will be discussed only so that (1) you will know what *not* to do, and (2) so that you will recognize their use in published research reports (heaven forbid) and be appropriately critical of findings.

Factorial designs are basically elaborations of true experimental designs and permit investigation of two or more variables, individually and in interaction with each other. In education, variables do not operate in isolation. After an independent variable has been investigated using a single-variable design, it is often useful then to study the variable in combination with one or more other variables; some variables work differently at different levels of another variable. Since a factorial design involves two or *more* variables, there is an almost infinite number of possibilites for such designs.

Pre-experimental Designs

Here is a research riddle for you: Can you do an experiment with only one group? The answer is . . . yes, but not a really good one. Two of the pre-experimental designs involve only one group. As Figure 10.1 illustrates, none of the pre-experimental designs does a very good job of controlling extraneous variables that jeopardize validity.

The One-Shot Case Study   The one-shot case study involves one group which is exposed to a treatment (*X*) and then posttested (*O*). All of the sources of invalidity are not relevant; testing, for example, is not a concern since there is no pretest. As Figure 10.1 indicates, however, *none* of the threats to validity that are relevant is controlled. Even if the subjects score high on the posttest, you cannot attribute their performance to the treatment since you do not even know what they knew before you administered the treatment. So, if you have a choice between using this design and not doing a study—do not do the study.

Designs	Sources of Invalidity									
	Internal								External	
	History	Maturation	Testing	Instrumentation	Regression	Selection	Mortality	Selection Interactions	Pretest-X Interaction	Multiple-X Interference
One-shot case study X O	−	−	(+)	(+)	(+)	(+)	−	(+)	(+)	(+)
One-group pretest-pottest design O X O	−	−	−	−	−	(+)	+	(+)	−	(+)
Static group comparison X O / O	+	−	(+)	(+)	(+)	−	−	−	(+)	(+)

Symbols:
X   = unusual treatment
O   = test, pretest or posttest
- - - - = groups are not randomly
           formed
Each line represents a group

+   = factor controlled for
(+) = factor controlled for
       because not revelant
−   = factor not controlled
       for

Note: Figures 10.1 and 10.2 basically follow the format used by Campbell and Stanley and are presented with a similar note of caution: The figures are intended to be supplements to, not substitutes for, textual discussions. You *should not* totally accept or reject designs because of their +'s and −'s; you *should* also be aware that which design is most appropriate for a given study is determined not only by the controls provided by the various designs but also by the nature of the study and the setting in which it is to be conducted.

While the symbols used in these figures, and their placement, vary somewhat from Campbell and Stanley's format, the intent, interpretations, and textual discussions of the two presentations are in agreement (Personal communication with Donald T. Campbell, April 22, 1975).

Figure 10.1
Sources of invalidity for pre-experimental designs.

The One-Group Pretest-Posttest Design   This design involves one group which is pretested (O), exposed to a treatment (X), and posttested (O). The success of the treatment is determined by comparing pretest and posttest scores. However, although it controls invalidity not controlled by the one-shot case study, a number of additional factors are relevant to this design that are not controlled. If subjects do significantly better on the posttest, it cannot be assumed that the improvement is due to the treatment. History and maturation are not controlled; something may happen *to* the subjects or *inside* of the subjects to make them perform better the second time. The longer the study is, the more likely this becomes. Testing and instrumentation are not controlled; the subjects may learn something on the first test that helps them on the second test, or unreliability of the measures may be responsible for the apparent improvement. Statistical regression is also not controlled for. Even if subjects are not selected on the basis of extreme scores (high or low), it is possible that a group may do very poorly, just by poor luck, on the pretest; subjects may guess badly just by chance on a multiple-choice pretest, for example, and improve on a posttest simply because their score based on guessing is more in line with an expected score. The external validity factor pretest-treatment interaction is also not controlled. Pretest-treatment interaction may cause subjects to react differently to the treatment than they would have if they have not been pretested.

To illustrate the problems associated with this design, let us examine a hypothetical study. Suppose a professor teaches a very "heavy" statistics course and is concerned that the high anxiety level of students interferes with their learning. The kindly professor therefore prepares a 100-page booklet which explains the course and tries to convince students that they will have no problems and will receive all the help they need to successfully complete the course, even if they do have a poor math background and cannot "add 2 and 2." The professor wants to see if the booklet works; at the beginning of the term he administers an anxiety scale and then gives each student a copy of the booklet with instructions to read it as soon as possible. Two weeks later he administers the anxiety scale again and sure enough the students indicate much less anxiety than at the beginning of the term. The professor is well satisfied with his booklet and its effectiveness in reducing anxiety. However, his self-satisfaction is not warranted. If you think about it, you will see that there are a number of alternative factors that could explain the decreased anxiety. Students, for example, are typically more anxious at the beginning of a course because they do not know what is coming (fear of the unknown!). After being in a course for a couple of weeks students usually find that it is not as bad as they imagined (right?). Besides, the professor would not even know if the students read his masterpiece! Unlike this example, the only situations for which the one-group pretest-posttest design is even re-motely appropriate is when the behavior to be measured is not likely to change all by itself. Certain prejudices, for example, are not likely to change unless a concerted effort is made.

The Static-Group Comparison   The static-group comparison involves at least two groups; one receives a new, or unusual, treatment and both groups are post-tested. The posttest scores of the two groups are then compared. Of course, the other group may well receive *another*, or usual treatment. Thus, the design could be written as follows:

$$X_1 O$$
$$----$$
$$X_2 O$$

In fact writing the design this way often makes beginning researchers feel more comfortable, since the other way it looks as if the control group is doing nothing. This design can be expanded to deal with any number of groups. For three groups, for example, the design would take one of the following forms:

$$
\begin{array}{ccc}
X_1 O & & X_1 O \\
---- & & ---- \\
X_2 O & \text{or} & X_2 O \\
---- & & ---- \\
O & & X_3 O
\end{array}
$$

The broken line separating the groups indicates that the groups are *not* randomly formed. The degree to which the groups are equivalent is the degree to which their comparison is reasonable. Since subjects are not randomly assigned to groups, and since there are no pretest data, however, it is difficult to determine just how equivalent they are. It is always possible that posttest differences are due to group differences, not just treatment effects (maturation, selection and selection interactions). Mortality is also a problem since if you lose subjects from the study you have no information concerning what you have lost (no pretest data). On the positive side, the presence of a control group controls for history since it is assumed that events occuring outside of the experimental setting will equally affect both groups. Of course the existence of a control group (in this and other designs) permits the occurrence of events that are group-specific, events such as a power failure or a violent storm. These events, referred to as within-group, or intrasession, history, are more likely to occur when groups are "treated" at different times. If not controlled for in some way, their occurrence should be described fully in the research report.

True Experimental Designs

The true experimental designs control for nearly all sources of internal and external invalidity. As Figure 10.2 indicates, all of the true experimental designs have one characteristic in common that none of the other designs has—random assignment of subjects to groups. Ideally subjects should be randomly selected and randomly assigned; however, to qualify as a true design, at least random assignment must be involved. Note too that all the true designs involve a control group. Also, while the posttest-only control group design may *look* like the static-group comparison design, random assignment makes them very different in terms of control.

The Pretest-Posttest Control Group Design   This design involves at least two groups, both of which are formed by random assignment; both groups are administered a pretest of the dependent variable, one group receives a new, or unusual, treatment, and both groups are posttested.[7] Posttest scores are compared to determine the effectiveness of the treatment. This design may also be represented as follows:

$$R \quad O \quad X_1 \quad O$$
$$R \quad O \quad X_2 \quad O$$

This representation indicates that both groups are being exposed to the independent variable; one group is receiving the new, or unusual treatment, and one group is receiving the usual treatment. The pretest-posttest control group design may also be expanded to include any number of treatment groups. For three groups, for example, this design would take one of the following forms:

---

7. Although a number of measures may be administered before a study begins (for stratified sampling purposes, for example) the term *pretest* usually refers to a test of the dependent variable.

Designs	Sources of Invalidity										
	Internal									External	
	History	Maturation	Testing	Instrumentation	Regression	Selection	Mortality	Selection Interactions		Pretest-X Interactions	Multiple-X Interference
TRUE EXPERIMENTAL DESIGNS											
1. Pretest-Posttest Control Group Design $R\ O\ X\ O$ $R\ O\ \ \ O$	+	+	+	+	+	+	+	+		−	(+)
2. Posttest-Only Control Group Design $R\ \ \ X\ O$ $R\ \ \ \ \ O$	+	+	(+)	(+)	(+)	+	−	+		(+)	(+)
3. Solomon Four-Group Design $R\ O\ X\ O$ $R\ O\ \ \ O$ $R\ \ \ X\ O$ $R\ \ \ \ \ O$	+	+	+	+	+	+	+	+		+	(+)
QUASI—EXPERIMENTAL DESIGNS											
4. Nonequivalent Control Group Design $O\ X\ O$ $O\ \ \ O$	+	+	+	+	−	+	+	−		−	(+)
5. Time Series Design $O\ O\ O\ O\ X\ O\ O\ O\ O$	−	+	+	−	+	(+)	+	(+)		−	(+)
6. Counterbalanced Designs $X_1O\ X_2O\ X_3O$ $X_3O\ X_1O\ X_2O$ $X_2O\ X_3O\ X_1O$	+	+	+	+	+	+	+	−		−	−

New Symbol:
R = random assignment of subjects to groups

Figure 10.2.
Sources of invalidity for true
experimental designs and quasi-experimental designs.

$$
\begin{array}{ccccccc}
R & O & X_1 & O & & R & O & X_1 & O \\
R & O & X_2 & O & \text{or} & R & O & X_2 & O \\
R & O & & O & & R & O & X_3 & O
\end{array}
$$

The combination of random assignment and the presence of a pretest and a control group serve to control for all sources of internal invalidity. Random assignment controls for regression and selection factors; the pretest controls for mortality; randomization and the control group control for maturation; and the control group controls for history, testing, and instrumentation. Testing, for example, is controlled because if pretesting leads to higher posttest scores, the advantage should be equal for both the experimental and control groups. The only definite weakness with this design is a possible interaction between the pretest and the treatment which may make the results generalizable only to other pretested groups. As discussed before, the seriousness of this potential weakness depends upon such factors as the nature of the pretest, the nature of the treatment, and the length of the study. It is more likely to occur with reactive measures such as attitude scales and in short studies. When this design is used, the researcher should assess and report the probability of its occurrence. A researcher might indicate, for example, that possible pretest interaction was believed to be minimized by the nonreactive nature of the pretest (chemical equations), and by the length of the study (9 months).

There are three basic ways in which the data can be analyzed in order to determine the effectiveness of the treatment and to test the research hypothesis; one of them is clearly inappropriate, one is not very appropriate, and one is clearly the most appropriate. One approach is to compare the pretest and posttest scores of each group; if the experimental group improves significantly but not the control group, it is concluded that the treatment is effective. This approach is inappropriate because the real question is whether the experimental group is better than the control group; thus the appropriate comparison is of the posttest scores of each group. If the researcher finds that both groups have improved significantly (e.g., each group's average posttest reading scores is significantly higher than its pretest reading score after 9 months of different instruction) this still does not indicate whether one group is significantly better than the other; we would expect both groups to improve their reading in 9 months, so the question involves which treatment has done a better job. A second approach is to compute gain, or difference, scores for each subject (posttest score minus pretest score) and then to compare the average gain of the experimental group with the average gain of the control group. Gain scores entail problems, however. For one thing, all students do not have the same "room" to gain. On a 100-item test, who is better, a student who goes from a pretest score of 80 to a posttest score of 99 (a gain of 19), or a student who goes from a pretest score of 20 to a posttest score of 70 (a gain of 50)? The third approach, and the one usually recommended, is to simply compare the posttest scores of the two groups. The pretest is used to see if the groups are essentially the same on the dependent variable. If they are, posttest scores can be directly compared using a t test, if they are not (random assignment does not *guarantee* equality), posttest scores can be analyzed using analysis of covariance.[8] Recall that covariance adjusts posttest scores for initial differences on any variable, including pretest scores.

A variation of the pretest-posttest control group design involves random assignment of members of matched pairs to the groups, one member to each group in order to more closely control for one or more extraneous variables. There is really no advantage to this technique, however, since any variable that can be controlled through matching can be better controlled using other procedures such as analysis of covariance.

---

8. Even if groups are not significantly different initially, covariance may be used to increase the power of the statistical test. This concept will be discussed further in chapter 13.

The Posttest-Only Control Group Design This design is exactly the same as the pretest-posttest control group design *except* there is no pretest; subjects are randomly assigned to groups, exposed to the independent variable, and post-tested. Posttest scores are then compared to determine the effectiveness of the treatment. This design may also be represented as follows:

$$R \qquad X_1 \quad O$$
$$R \qquad X_2 \quad O$$

This representation indicates that both groups are being exposed to the independent variable; one group is receiving the new, or unusual, treatment and one group is receiving the usual treatment. As with the pretest-posttest control group design, the posttest-only control group design can be expanded to include more than two groups.

The combination of random assignment and the presence of a control group serve to control for all sources of internal invalidity except mortality. Mortality is not controlled for because of the absence of pretest data on subjects. However, mortality may or may not be a problem depending upon the study. If the study is relatively short in duration, for example, no subjects may be lost. In this case the researcher may report that while mortality is a potential threat to validity with this design, it did not prove to be a threat in his or her particular study since the group sizes remained constant throughout the duration of the study. Thus, if the probability of differential mortality is low, the posttest-only design can be a very effective design. Of course if there is any chance that the groups may be different with respect to initial knowledge related to the dependent variable (despite random assignment), the pretest-posttest control group design should be used. Which design is "best" depends upon the study. If the study is to be short, and if it can be assumed that neither group has any knowledge related to the dependent variable, then the posttest-only design may be the "best." If the study is to be lengthly (good chance of mortality), or if there is a chance that the two groups differ on initial knowledge related to the dependent variable, then the pretest-posttest control group design may be the best. What if, however, you face the following dilemma:

1. The study is going to last 2 months.

2. Assessment of initial knowledge is essential.

3. The pretest is an attitude scale and the treatment is designed to change attitudes.

Here we have a classic case where pretest-treatment interaction is probable. Do we throw our hands up in despair? Of course not. One solution is to select the lesser of the two evils, perhaps take our chances with mortality. Another solution, if sufficient subjects are available, is to use the Solomon four-group design, to be discussed next. If you look at Figure 10.2 you will see that the Solomon four-group design is simply a combination of the pretest-posttest control group design (the top two lines) and the posttest-only control group design (the third and fourth lines).

A variation of the posttest-only control group design involves random assignment of members of matched pairs to the groups, one member to each group, in order to more closely control for one or more extraneous variables. As with the pretest-posttest control group design, however, there is really no advantage to this technique; any variable that can be controlled through matching can better be controlled using other procedures.

The Solomon Four-Group Design   The Solomon four-group design involves random assignment of subjects to one of four groups. Two of the groups are pretested and two are not; one of the pretested groups and one of the unpretested groups receive the experimental treatment. All four groups are posttested. As Figure 10.2 indicates, this design is a combination of the pretest-posttest control group design and the posttest-only control group design, each of which has its own major source of invalidity (pretest-treatment interaction and mortality, respectively). The combination of these two designs results in a design which controls for pretest-treatment interaction *and* for mortality. The correct way to analyze data resulting from application of this design is to use a 2 × 2 factorial analysis of variance. The two independent variables are the treatment variable and the pretest variable; in other words, whether a group is pretested or not is an independent variable, just as the experimental variable is. The factorial analysis tells the researcher whether the treatment is effective *and* whether there is an interaction between the treatment and the pretest. To put it as simply as possible, if the pretested experimental group performs differently on the posttest than the unpretested experimental group, there is probably a pretest-treatment interaction. If no interaction is found, then the researcher can have more confidence in the generalizability of treatment differences.

A common misconception among beginning researchers is that since the Solomon four-group design controls for so many sources of invalidity, it is the "best" design. This is not true. For one thing, this design requires twice as many subjects as either of the other true experimental designs, and subjects are often hard to come by. Further, if mortality is not likely to be a problem, and pretest data are not needed, then the posttest-only design may be the best; if pretest-treatment interaction is unlikely, and testing is a normal part of the subjects' environment (such as when classrooms are used), then the pretest-posttest control group design may be the "best." Which design is the "best" depends upon the nature of the study and the conditions under which it is to be conducted.

Quasi-Experimental Designs

Sometimes it is just not possible to randomly assign subjects to groups. In order to receive permission to use school children in a study, for example, a researcher often has to agree to use existing classrooms. When this occurs, however, there are still a number of designs available to the researcher that provide adequate control of sources of invalidity; these designs are referred to as quasi-experimental designs. Although Campbell and Stanley discuss a number of such designs, only three of the major ones will be discussed here. Keep in mind that designs such as these are *only* to be used when it is not feasible to use a true experimental design.

The Nonequivalent Control Group Design   This design should be familiar to you since it looks very much like the pretest-posttest control group design; the only difference is that the nonequivalent control group design does not involve random assignment of subjects to groups (although treatment should be randomly assigned to groups, if possible). Two existing groups are pretested, administered a treatment, and posttested. The lack of random assignment adds sources of invalidity not associated with the pretest-posttest control group design—possible regression and interaction between selection and variables such as maturation, history, and testing. The more similar the groups are, the better; the researcher should make every effort to use groups that are as equivalent as possible. Comparing an advanced algebra class with a remedial algebra class, for example, would not do. If differences between the groups on any major extraneous variable are identified, analysis of covariance can be used to statistically equate the groups. An advantage of this design is that since classes are used "as is," possible effects from reactive arrangements are minimized. Subjects may not even be aware that they are involved in a study. As with the pretest-posttest control group design, the nonequivalent control group design may be represented as X_1 and X_2 rather than X versus no X and may also be extended to include more than two groups.

The Time-Series Design   The time-series design is actually an elaboration of the one-group pretest-posttest design. One group is repeatedly pretested, exposed to a treatment, and then repeatedly posttested. If a group scores essentially the same on a number of pretests and then significantly improves following a treatment, the researcher has more confidence in the effectiveness of the treatment than if just one pretest and one posttest are administered. To use a former example, if our statistics professor measured anxiety several times before giving the students his booklet, he would be able to see if anxiety was declining naturally. History is still a problem with this design, however, since something might happen between the last pretest and the first posttest, the effect of which might be confused with the treatment. Instrumentation may also be a problem but not an expected problem unless for some reason the researcher changes measuring instruments during the study. Pretest-treatment interaction is also a validity problem. It should be clear that if one pretest can interact with a treatment, more than one pretest can only make matters worse!

   While statistical analyses appropriate for this design are rather advanced, determining the effectiveness of the treatment basically involves analysis of the pattern of the test scores. Figure 10.3 illustrates several possible patterns which might be found; Campbell and Stanley discuss a number of other possibilities. In Figure 10.3 the vertical line between O_4 and O_5 indicates the point at which the treatment was introduced. Pattern A does not indicate a treatment effect; performance was increasing before the treatment was introduced, and continued to increase at the same rate following introduction of the treatment. In fact pattern A represents the reverse situation to that encountered by our statistics professor and his anxiety-reducing booklet. Patterns B and C do indicate a treatment effect; the effect appears to be more permanent in pattern C than in pattern B. Pattern D does not indicate a treatment effect even though student scores are higher on O_5 than O_4. The pattern is too erratic. Scores appear to be fluctuating up and down: the O_4 to O_5 fluctuation cannot be attributed to the treatment. The four patterns

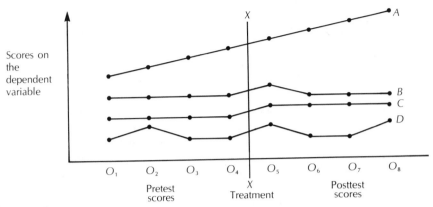

Figure 10.3.
Possible patterns for the results of a study based on a time-series design.

shown illustrate that just comparing O_4 and O_5 is not sufficient; in all four cases O_5 indicates a higher score than O_4, but only in two of the patterns does it appear that the difference is due to a treatment effect.

A variation of the time-series design, which is referred to as the multiple time-series design, involves the addition of a control group to the basic design as follows:

$$O \quad O \quad O \quad O \quad X \quad O \quad O \quad O \quad O$$
$$O \quad O \quad O \quad O \qquad \quad O \quad O \quad O \quad O$$

This variation eliminates history and instrumentation as threats to validity and thus represents a design with no probable sources of internal invalidity. This design can be more effectively used in situations where testing is a naturally occurring event not likely to be noticed, such as research involving school classrooms.

Counterbalanced Designs   In a counterbalanced design, all groups receive all treatments but in a different order. Although Figure 10.2 represents the design for three groups and three treatments, any number of groups may be involved (two or more); the only restriction is that the number of groups equals the number of treatments. The order in which the groups receive the treatments is randomly determined. While subjects may be pretested, this design is usually employed when intact groups must be used and when administration of a pretest is not possible or feasible. The static group comparison also can be used in such situations, but the counterbalanced design controls several additional sources of invalidity. In the situation shown in Figure 10.2, there are three groups and three treatments (or two treatments and a control group). The first horizontal line indicates that group 1 receives treatment 1 and is posttested, then receives treatment 2 and is posttested, and then treatment 3 and is posttested. The second line indicates that group 2 receives treatment 3, then treatment 1, and then treatment 2, and is posttested after each treatment. The third line indicates that group 3 receives threatment 2, then treatment 3, then treatment 1, and is pottested after each treatment. To put it another way, the first column indicates that at time 1, while group 1 is receiving treatment 1, group 2 is receiving treatment 3 and group 3 is receiving treatment 2. All three groups are posttested and the treatments are shifted to produce the second column. The second column indicates that at time 2, while group 1 is receiving treatment 2, group 2 is receiving treatment 1, and group 3 is receiving treatment 3. The groups are then posttested again and the treatments are again shifted to produce the third column. The third column indicates that now, at time 3, group 1 is receiving treatment 3, group 2 is receiving treatment 2, and group 3 is receiving treatment 1. All groups are posttested again. Thus, each row represents a replication of the study. In order to determine the effectiveness of the treatments, the average performance of the groups for each treatment can be compared. In other words, the posttest scores for all the groups for the first treatment can be compared to the posttest scores of all the groups for the second treatment, and so forth, depending upon the number of groups and treatments.

A unique weakness of this design is potential multiple-treatment interference that can result when the same group receives more than one treatment. Thus, a counterbalanced design should really only be used when the treatments are such that exposure to one will not affect evaluation of the effectiveness of another. Of course, there are not too many situations in education where this condition can be met. You cannot, for example, teach the same geometric concepts to the same group using several different methods of instruction. There are, however, sophisticated analysis procedures which can be applied to determine both the effects of treatments and the effects of the order of those treatments.

Factorial Designs

Factorial designs involve two or more independent variables, at least one of which is manipulated by the researcher. They are basically elaborations of true experimental designs and permit investigation of two or more variables, individually and in interaction with each other. In education, variables do not operate in isolation. After an independent variable has been investigated using a single-variable design, it is often useful then to study the variable in combination with one or more other variables. Some variables work differently at different levels of another variable; one method of math instruction may be more effective for high-aptitude students while another method may be more effective for low-aptitude students. The term "factorial" refers to the fact that the design involves several factors; in the above example, method of instruction is a factor and aptitude is a factor. Each factor has two or more levels; in the above example, the factor "method of instruction" has two levels since there are two types of instruction, and the factor of aptitude has two levels, high aptitude and low aptitude. Thus, a 2 × 2 factorial design has two factors and each factor has two levels. The 2 × 2 is the simplest factorial design. As another example, a 2 × 3 factorial design has two factors, one factor has two levels and the second factor has three levels (such as high, average, and low aptitude).

The simplest factorial design, the 2 × 2, requires four groups as Figure 10.4 illustrates. In Figure 10.4 there are two factors; one factor, type of instruction, has two levels, programmed and traditional, and the other factor, IQ, has two levels, high and low. Each of the groups represents a combination of one level of one factor and one level of the other factor. Thus, group 1 is composed of high

Type of Instruction

		Programmed	Traditional
IQ	High	Group 1	Group 2
	Low	Group 3	Group 4

Figure 10.4
An example of the basic 2 × 2 factorial design.

IQ students receiving programmed instruction (PI), group 2 is composed of high IQ students receiving traditional instruction (TI), group 3 is composed of low IQ students receiving PI, and group 4 is composed of low IQ students receiving TI. If this design were used, a number of high IQ students would be randomly assigned to either group 1 or group 2, and an equal number of low IQ students would be randomly assigned to either group 3 or group 4. In such a design both variables may be manipulated, but the 2 × 2 design usually involves one manipulated, or experimental, variable and one nonmanipulated variable; the nonmanipulated variable is often referred to as a control variable. In the above example, IQ is a control variable. Control variables are usually physical or mental characteristics of the subjects such as sex, IQ, or math aptitude.

The purpose of a factorial design is to determine whether the effects of an experimental variable are generalizable across all levels of a control variable or whether the effects are specific to specific levels of the control variable. Also, a factorial design can demonstrate relationships that a single-variable experiment cannot. For example, a variable found not to be effective in a single-variable experiment may be found to interact significantly with another variable. The second example in Figure 10.5 illustrates this possibility.

Figure 10.5 represents two possible outcomes for an experiment involving a 2 × 2 factorial design. The number in each box, or cell, represents the average posttest score of that group. Thus, in the top example, the high IQ students under method A had an average posttest score of 80. The marginal row and column numbers outside of the boxes represent average scores across boxes, or cells. Thus, in the top example, the average score for high IQ subjects was 60 (found by averaging the scores for all high IQ subjects regardless of treatment), and for low IQ students the average score was 40. The average score for students under method A was 70 (found by averaging the scores of all the subjects under method A regardless of IQ level), and for students under method B, 30. By examining the cell averages, we see that method A was better than method B for high IQ students (80 versus 40), and method A was also better for low IQ students (60 versus 20). Thus, method A was better, regardless of IQ level; there was *no interaction* between method and IQ. The high IQ students in each method outperformed the low IQ students in each method (no big surprise), and the subjects in method A outperformed the subjects in method B at each IQ level. The graph to the right of the results illustrates the lack of interaction.

In the bottom example, which method was better, A or B? The answer is, it depends! Depends on what? Depends on which IQ level we are talking about. For high IQ students, method A was better (80 versus 60); for low IQ students, method B was better (20 versus 40). Even though high IQ students did better than low IQ students regardless of method, how well they did depended upon

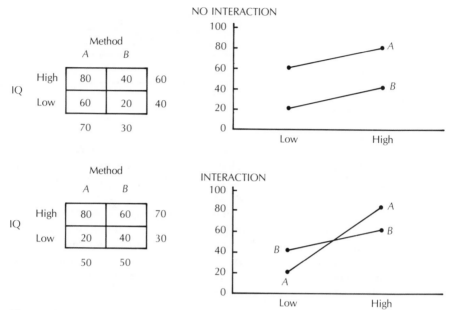

Figure 10.5
Illustration of interaction and no
interaction in a 2 × 2 factorial experiment.

which method they were under. It cannot be said that either method was better in general; which method was better *depended* upon the IQ level. Now suppose the study had not used a factorial design but had simply compared two groups of subjects, one group receiving method A and one group receiving method B; each group would have been composed of both high and low IQ students. The researcher would have concluded that method A and method B were equally effective, since the overall average score for method A was 50 and the overall average score for method B was 50! By using a factorial design it was determined that an *interaction* appears to exist between the variables such that each of the methods is differentially effective depending upon the IQ level of the subjects. The graph to the right of the results illustrates the interaction.

There are a lot of possible factorial designs depending upon the nature and the number of independent variables. Theoretically, a researcher could simultaneously investigate 10 factors in a 2 × 2 × 2 × 2 × 2 × 3 × 3 × 3 × 4 × 4 design, for example. In reality, however, more than 3 factors are rarely used. For one thing, each additional factor increases the number of subjects that are required. For another thing, when too many factors are involved, resulting interactions become difficult, if not impossible, to interpret. Interpretation of a two-way interaction, such as the one illustrated in Figure 10.5, is relatively straightforward. But how, for example, would you interpret a five-way interaction between teaching method, IQ, sex, aptitude, and anxiety! Such interactions tend to have no meaning. Besides, it is not easy to graph a five-way interaction! When used correctly and reasonably, however, factorial designs are very effective for testing certain research hypotheses that cannot be tested with a single-variable design.

Single-Subject Experimental Designs

As you would probably guess, single-subject experimental designs are designs that can be applied when the sample size is one. They can also be applied when a number of individuals are considered as one group. They are typically used to study the behavior change an individual exhibits as a result of some intervention, or treatment. In single-subject designs each subject serves as his or her own control in variations on a time-series design. Basically, the subject is alternately exposed to a nontreatment and a treatment condition, or phase, and performance is repeatedly measured during each phase. The nontreatment condition is symbolized as A and the treatment condition is symbolized as B. For example, we might (1) observe and record out-of-seat behavior on five occasions, (2) apply a behavior modification procedure and observe behavior on five more occasions, and (3) stop the behavior modification procedure and observe five more times. Our design would be symbolized as A-B-A. While single-subject designs have their roots in clinical psychology and psychiatry, they are useful in many educational settings. As an example, federally funded programs for handicapped students typically have a requirement that the effectiveness of the program be demonstrated for *each* participant.

The use of single-subject designs has increased steadily since about the mid sixties, paralleling the increased application of behavior modification techniques. Publication of the first issue of the *Journal of Applied Behavior Analysis* in 1968 by The Society for the Experimental Analysis of Behavior, signaled a new acceptance for single-subject research, an acceptance based on an improved methodology. Whereas previously single-subject research was generally equated with a descriptive, case-study approach, it now became associated with a more controlled, experimental approach.

Single-Subject Versus Group Designs

As single-subject designs have become progressively more refined and capable of dealing with threats to experimental validity, they have come to be viewed as acceptable substitutes for traditional group designs in a number of situations. At the very least they are considered to be valuable complements to such designs.

Most experimental research problems require traditional group designs for their investigation. This is mainly because the results are intended to be applied *to groups*, for example, classrooms. As an example, if we were investigating the comparative effectiveness of two approaches to teaching reading, we would be interested in which approach *in general* produces better results. The schools cannot provide individual tutors or programs for each student and therefore seek strategies that are relatively more beneficial to groups of children. Our research study would, therefore, require the application of a group comparison design such as the pretest-posttest control group design. In addition to being inappropriate, a single-subject design would also be very impractical for such a research problem. Single-subject designs require multiple measurements during each phase (i.e., no treatment, treatment, no treatment) of the study. Recall that in a previous example 15 separate observation periods were involved. It would be highly impractical to administer a reading achievement test 15 times to the same students.

There are, however, a number of research questions for which traditional group designs are not appropriate for two major reasons. First, group comparison designs are frequently opposed on ethical or philosophical grounds. By definition such designs involve a control group that does not receive the experimental treatment. Withholding students with a demonstrated need from a potentially beneficial program, or intervention, may be opposed or actually prohibited, as in the case of certain federally funded programs. The fact that the effectiveness of the treatment has not yet been demonstrated, and in fact the purpose of the research is to assess its effectiveness, is irrelevant. That the treatment is *potentially* effective is sufficient to raise objections if an attempt is made to prevent any eligible subjects from receiving it. Second, application of a group comparison design is not possible in many cases because of the size of the population of interest. There may simply not be enough subjects of a given kind to permit the formulation of two equivalent groups. If the treatment, for example, is aimed at improving the social skills of profoundly retarded children, the number of such children available in any one locale may be quite small. If there are say 10 such children, application of a single-subject design is clearly preferable to the formulation of two more-or-less equivalent groups of 5 children each.

External Validity

A major criticism frequently leveled at single-subject research studies is that they suffer from low external validity, that is, results cannot be generalized to the population of interest as they can with group designs. While this allegation is basically true, it is also true that the results of a study using a group design cannot be directly generalized to any individual within the group. If we randomly select subjects and randomly assign them to groups, the result is two relatively heterogeneous groups. The average posttest performance of the treatment *group* may not adequately reflect the performance of any individual within the group. Thus, group designs and single-subject designs each have their own generalizability problems. If your concern is with improving the functioning of an individual, a group design is not going to be appropriate.

Usually, however, we are interested in generalizing the results of our research to persons other than those directly involved in the study. For single-subject designs, the key to generalizability is replication. If a researcher applies the same treatment using the same single-subject design to a number of subjects, and gets essentially the same results in every case (or even in most cases), our confidence in the findings is increased; there is evidence for the generalizability of the results for other subjects. If other researchers in other settings apply the same treatment to other subjects and get essentially the same results, the case for the efficacy of the treatment becomes stronger. The more diverse the replications are (i.e., different kinds of subjects, different settings), the more generalizable the results are.

One generalizability problem associated with many single-subject designs is the possible effect of the baseline condition on the subsequent effects of the treatment condition. We can never be sure that the treatment effects are the same as they would have been if the treatment phase had been the *first* phase. This problem of course parallels the pretest-treatment interaction problem associated with a number of the group designs.

Internal Validity

If proper controls are exercised in connection with the application of a single-subject design, the internal validity of the resulting study may be quite good.[9]

Repeated and Reliable Measurement

As with a time-series design, pretest performance is measured a number of times prior to implementation of the treatment or intervention. In single-subject designs these sequential measures of pretest performance are referred to as baseline measures. As a result of these measures taken over some period of time, sources of invalidity such as maturation are controlled for in the same way as for the time-series design. Unlike the time-series design, however, performance is also measured at various points in time while the treatment is being applied. This added dimension greatly reduces the potential threat to validity from history, a threat to internal validity associated with the time-series design.

One very real threat to the internal validity of most single-subject designs is instrumentation. Recall that instrumentation refers to unreliability, or inconsistency, in measuring instruments that may result in an invalid assessment of performance. Since repeated measurement is a characteristic of all single-subject designs, it is especially important that measurement of the target behavior, or performance, be done in exactly the same way every time, or as nearly the same as is humanly possible. Typically, studies using single-subject designs are concerned with some type of behavior requiring observation as the major data collection strategy. In such studies it is critical that the observation conditions (e.g., location, time of day) be standardized. If one observer makes all the observations, then intraobserver reliability should be estimated. If more than one observer is involved, then interobserver reliability should be estimated. Consistency of measurement is especially crucial as we move from phase to phase. For example, if a change in measurement procedures occurs at the same time we move from a baseline to a treatment phase, the result will be an invalid assessment of the effect of the treatment.

Relatedly, the nature and conditions of the treatment should be specified in sufficient detail to permit replication. Some single-subject designs involve reinstatement of the treatment phase following measurement of posttest performance. For example, with an A-B-A-B design, we have a baseline phase, a treatment phase, a return to baseline conditions (withdrawal of the treatment), and a second treatment phase. If its effects are to be validly assessed, the treatment must involve precisely the same procedures every time it is introduced. Also, since the key to generalizability for single-subject designs is replication, it is

---

9. Most of the discussion to follow is based on discussion presented in Hersen, M., & Barlow, H. *Single-case experimental designs.* New York: Pergamon Press, 1976. The student should consult this source for in-depth discussion of all topics in this section.

clearly a necessity for the treatment to be sufficiently standardized to permit other researchers to apply it as it was originally applied and as it was intended to be applied.

Baseline Stability

Another factor related to the internal validity of single-subject designs is the length of the baseline and treatment phases. A major question is, "How many measurements of behavior should be taken before treatment is introduced?" There is no easy answer to this question. The purpose of the baseline measurements is to provide a description of the target behavior as it naturally occurs *without* the treatment. Thus, the baseline serves as the basis of comparison for assessing the effectiveness of the treatment.

If most behaviors were very stable, there would be no problem. But human behavior is variable. For example, if the performance being measured were disruptive behavior, we would not expect a child to exhibit exactly the same number of disruptive acts during each observation period. There would be fluctuations and the child would be more disruptive at some times than at others. Such fluctuations, however, usually fall within some consistent range. Therefore, a sufficient number of baseline measurements are usually taken to establish a pattern. The establishment of a pattern is referred to as baseline stability. We might observe, for example, that the child normally exhibits between 5 and 10 disruptive behaviors during a 30-minute period. These figures then become our basis of comparison for assessing the effectiveness of the treatment. If during the treatment phase the number of disruptive behaviors ranges from say 0 to 3, or steadily decreases until it reaches 0, and if the number of disruptive behaviors increases when treatment is withdrawn, the effectiveness of the treatment is demonstrated. If the target behavior is found to be getting progressively worse, there are progressively more incidents of disruptive behavior for example, fewer measurements are required to establish the baseline pattern. If, on the other hand, the behavior is naturally getting progressively better, there is no point in introducing the treatment until, or unless, the behavior stabilizes and ceases to improve naturally.

Normally, the length of the treatment phase, and the number of measurements taken during the treatment phase, parallel the length and measurements of the baseline phase. If, for example, baseline stability is established after 10 observation periods, then the treatment phase will include 10 observation periods. There are reasons for varying phase length, however. For example, for ethical reasons we might continue a treatment condition indefinitely if a previously self-destructive child stopped engaging in self-destructive behaviors while under treatment.

The Single Variable Rule

An important principle of single-subject research is that only one variable should be manipulated throughout the experiment. In other words, as we move from phase to phase, only one variable should be changed. Sometimes an attempt is made to simultaneously manipulate two variables in order to assess their interactive effects. This practice is not sound and prevents us from assessing adequately the effects of either variable.

Types of Single-Subject Designs

Single-subject designs can be classified into two major categories, A-B-A designs and multiple-baseline designs. A-B-A designs basically involve alternate phases of baseline (A) and treatment (B). In some cases treatment cannot or should not be withdrawn once it is applied. In such cases a multiple-baseline design is often appropriate.

A-B-A Designs

There are a number of variations of the basic A-B-A design, the least complex of which is the A-B design. Variations not discussed in this section are used very infrequently in educational research studies.

The A-B Design   Although this design is an improvement over the simple case-study approach, its internal validity is suspect. When this design is used baseline measurements are repeatedly made until stability is presumably established, treatment is then introduced and an appropriate number of measurements are made during treatment. If behavior improves during the treatment phase, the effectiveness of the treatment is allegedly demonstrated. We could symbolize this design as follows:

Of course the specific number of measurements (O) involved in each phase will vary from experiment to experiment. The problem is that we don't know if behavior improved *because of* the treatment or for some other reason. It is always possible that the observed behavior change occurred as a result of the influence of some other, unknown variable, or that the behavior would have improved naturally, without the treatment.

The A-B-A Design   By simply adding a second baseline phase to the A-B design we get a much improved design, the A-B-A design. If the behavior is better during the treatment phase than during either baseline phase, the effectiveness of the treatment has presumably been demonstrated. Using familiar symbolism, we could represent this design in the following way:

As an example, during an initial baseline phase we might observe on-task behaviors during five observation sessions. We might then introduce tangible reinforcement in the form of small toys for on-task behaviors and observe on-task behaviors during five observation periods in the treatment phase. Lastly, we might stop the tangible reinforcement and observe on-task behaviors during an additional five sessions. If on-task behavior was greater during the treatment phase, we would conclude that the tangible reinforcement was the probable cause. This example represents a withdrawal design, that is, a design in which the treatment is actually stopped prior to the second baseline phase.

In some cases, when it is feasible and ethical to do so, the treatment may actually be reversed during the second baseline phase. If such is the case, we refer to the design as a reversal design. In a reversal design the treatment phase is not followed by a control, baseline phase but rather by a treatment reversal phase. In other words, a condition that is essentially the opposite of the treatment condition is implemented. In the above example, if a reversal design were used, the tangible reinforcement for on-task behavior phase would be followed by a tangible reinforcement for off-task behavior phase. On-task behaviors would probably be drastically reduced during this phase. When applicable, a reversal design typically produces more dramatic results than a withdrawal design. The major problem with this design is that its application is not very often feasible or desirable. If we were trying to reduce violent outbursts of behavior, for example, encouraging them for the sake of treatment reversal would not be advisable for obvious reasons.

The internal validity of the A-B-A design is superior to that of the A-B design. With the A-B design it is possible that behaviors would have improved without treatment intervention. It is very unlikely, however, that behavior would coincidentally improve during the treatment phase *and* coincidentally deteriorate during the subsequent baseline phase (assuming a withdrawal design). The major problem with this design is an ethical one since the experiment ends with the subject *not* receiving the treatment. Of course if the treatment has not been shown to be effective, there is no problem. But if it has been found to be beneficial, the desirability of removing it is questionable. This problem is taken care of by the A-B-A-B design.

The A-B-A-B Design   The A-B-A-B design is basically the A-B-A design with the addition of a second treatment phase. Not only does this design overcome the ethical objection to the A-B-A design, but by ending the experiment during a treatment phase, it also greatly strengthens the conclusions of the study by demonstrating the effects of the treatment *twice*. The second treatment phase can of course be extended beyond the termination of the actual study, indefinitely if desired. The A-B-A-B design can be symbolized in the following manner:

O O O O X O X O X O X O	O O O O X O X O X O X O
baseline phase A	treatment phase B
baseline phase A	treatment phase B

When application of this design is feasible, it provides the most convincing evidence of treatment effectiveness.

The A-B-A-B design was utilized in a classic study conducted by Hall, Fox, Willard, Goldsmith, Emerson, Owen, Davis, and Porcia.[10] In a series of experi-

---

10. Hall, R.V., Fox, R., Willard, D., Goldsmith, L., Emerson, M., Owen, M., Davis, F., and Porcia, E. The teacher as observer and experimenter in the modification of disputing and talking-out behaviors. *Journal of Applied Behavior Analysis*, 1971, 4, 141–149.

ments, the disputing and "talking-out" behaviors of a number of students in special education classes and regular classes, from middle class and poverty areas, ranging from first grade to junior high school, were studied. As an example, in one experiment the talking-out behavior of a 10-year-old boy in a class for educable mentally retarded children was studied. His teacher indicated that his behavior greatly influenced the behavior of the other children. His talking-out behavior (instances when he spoke without the teacher's permission) was recorded during 15-minute periods. Behavior was observed by the teacher and also tape recorded. Another teacher made an independent tally of talking-out behavior, using the tape, as a reliability check. The correspondence between the two tallies was 100% for all phases of the experiment. The four phases of the experiment were as follows:

Baseline (A): The teacher responded as usual to talking-out behavior. Talking-out behavior was recorded during a 15-minute period for 5 consecutive days (see Figure 10.6).

Treatment (B): For the next 5 days the teacher ignored the subject when he exhibited talking-out behavior and paid him special attention when he was quiet and productive. As Figure 10.6 indicates, talking-out behavior had decreased to zero by the fourth day of the treatment phase (session 9).

Baseline 2(A): The teacher again responded to talking-out behavior and ceased paying special attention to quiet, productive behavior. Talking-out behavior increased to its original level.

Treatment 2(B): Treatment conditions were reinstated and talking-out behavior again decreased to zero by the fourth session of this phase (session 19).

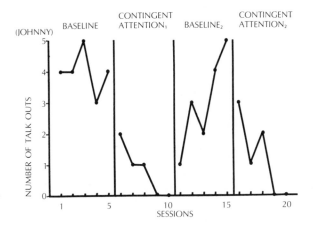

Figure 10.6.
A record of talking-out behavior of an educable mentally retarded student. Baseline—before experimental conditions. Contingent Teacher Attention₁—systematic ignoring of talking-out and increased teacher attention to appropriate behavior. Baseline₂—reinstatement of teacher attention to talking-out behavior. Contingent Teacher Attention₂—return to systematic ignoring of talking-out and increased attention to appropriate behavior. (Figure 2 from Hall, Fox, Willard, Goldsmith, Emerson, Owen, Davis, and Porcia, 1971. Copyright 1971 by the Society for the Experimental Analysis of Behavior, Inc. Reproduced by permission.)

Thus the effectiveness of paying attention only to appropriate behaviors was demonstrated twice. Note that if the experiment had ended after the second baseline phase (baseline$_2$), the design would have been on A-B-A design.

Multiple-Baseline Designs

Multiple-baseline designs are used when the only alternative would be an A-B design. This is the case when the treatment is such that it is not possible to withdraw it and return to baseline or when it would not be ethical to withdraw it or reverse it. In the most extreme case, the treatment might be some kind of surgical procedure. Multiple-baseline designs are also used when treatment can be withdrawn but the effects of the treatment "carry over" into the second baseline phase and a return to baseline conditions is difficult or impossible. The effects of many treatments do not disappear when treatment is removed (see Figure 10.3, pattern C). Actually, in many cases it is highly desirable if they do not. Reinforce-ment techniques, for example, are designed to produce improved behavior that will be maintained when external reinforcements are withdrawn.

With a multiple-baseline design, instead of collecting baseline data for one subject and one target behavior, we collect baseline data on several behaviors for one subject or one behavior for several subjects. We then systematically, over a period of time, apply the treatment to each behavior (or each subject) one at a time until all behaviors (or subjects) are under treatment. If measured perform-ance improves in each case only after treatment is introduced, then the treatment is judged to be effective. Application of this design might be symbolized as follows:

	Case 1			Case 2	
behavior 1	A-B-B-B-B		subject 1	A-B-B-B-B
behavior 2	A-A-B-B-B	OR	subject 2	A-A-B-B-B
behavior 3	A-A-A-B-B		subject 3	A-A-A-B-B

The above would represent the situation in which the treatment, once applied, would not be withdrawn. We could also symbolize case 1 as follows:

behavior 1	O	O	O X O X O X O X O X O X O X O X O X O X O X O X O
behavior 2	O	O	O O O O X O X O X O X O X O X O X O X O X O
behavior 3	O	O	O O O O O O O X O X O X O X O X O X O

In this example, treatment was applied to behavior 1 first and then behavior 2 and then behavior 3 until all 3 behaviors were under treatment. If measured perform-ance improved in each case only after treatment was introduced, then the treat-ment would be judged to be effective. We could symbolize case 2 in the same manner. In either case, the more behaviors or subjects are treated, the more convincing the evidence is for the effectiveness of the treatment. Note that this design requires that the behaviors be able to be treated independently. If we apply treatment to behavior 1, for example, the other target behaviors should remain at baseline levels. If other behaviors change when behavior 1 is treated, the design is not valid for assessing treatment effectiveness.

While multiple-baseline designs are generally used when there is a problem with returning to basline conditions, that is, baseline levels are not recoverable, they can be used very effectively for situations in which baseline is recoverable. We could, for example, target talking-out behavior, out-of-seat behavior and aggressive behavior. It would be possible to return to baseline conditions with these behaviors. If we applied an A-B-A design within a multiple-baseline framework, the result could be symbolized as follows:

taking-out behavior	A-B-A-A-A
out-of-seat behavior	A-A-B-A-A
aggressive behavior	A-A-A-B-A

OR

talking-out behavior	O	O	O X O X O X O	O	O	O	O	O	O	O	O	O
out-of-seat behavior	O	O	O	O	O	O X O X O X O	O	O	O	O	O	O
aggressive behavior	O	O	O	O	O	O	O	O	O X O X O X O	O	O	O

Such a design would combine the best features of an A-B-A design and a multiple-baseline design and would provide very convincing evidence regarding treatment effects. In essence it would represent three replications of an A-B-A experiment. Whenever baseline is recoverable and there are no carry-over effects, any of the A-B-A designs can be applied within a multiple-baseline framework.

Summary

Chapter 6/The Historical Method

Definition and Purpose

1. Historical research is the systematic collection and objective evaluation of data related to past occurrences, in order to test hypotheses concerning causes, effects, or trends of these events that may help to explain present events and anticipate future events.

The Historical Research Process

2. The steps involved in conducting a historical research study are essentially the same as for other types of research; definition of a problem, formulation of hypotheses (or questions to be answered), systematic collection of data, objective evaluation of data, and confirmation or disconfirmation of hypotheses.

Definition of a Problem

3. The purpose of a historical research study should be to explain or predict, not to rehash.

4. The historical researcher is basically limited to whatever data are already available.

5. It is much better to study in depth a well-defined problem with one or more specific, well-stated hypotheses, than to investigate either a too-broadly stated problem with a fuzzy hypothesis, or a problem for which insufficient data are available.

Data Collection

6. In a historical research study, the review of related literature and study procedures are part of the same process.

7. The term "literature" takes on a much broader meaning in a historical study and refers to all sorts of written communication; in addition, identification, acquisition, and review of such "literature" is considerably more complex.

8. The written communication may be in the form of legal documents, records, minutes of meetings, letters, and other documents which will not normally be indexed alphabetically by subject, author, and title in a library.

9. A historical research study in education may also involve interviews with persons who participated in the event or process under investigation, if it occurred in the recent past.

10. Primary sources constitute firsthand information, such as original documents and reports by actual participants or direct observers; secondary sources constitute secondhand information, such as reference books (encyclopedias, for example) or reports by relatives of actual participants or observers.

11. A common criticism of historical research is excessive reliance on secondary sources.

Data Analysis: External and Internal Criticism

12. All sources of historical data must be subjected to rigorous scientific analysis to determine both their authenticity (external criticism) and their accuracy (internal criticism).

13. In determining the accuracy of documents, there are at least four factors that must be considered: knowledge and competence of the author, the time delay between the occurrence and recording of events, biased motives of the author, and consistency of the data.

Data Synthesis

14. As with a review of related literature, historical data should be organized and synthesized, and conclusions and generalizations formulated.

15. Since summarization of historical research data involves logical analysis rather than statistical analysis, the researcher must take care to be as objective as possible.

Chapter 7/The Descriptive Method

Definition, Purpose, and Process

16. Descriptive research involves collecting data in order to test hypotheses or to answer questions concerning the current status of the subject of the study.

17. The researcher must give careful thought to sample selection and data collection; which population has the desired information is not always readily apparent.

18. Frequently, since one is generally asking questions that have not been asked before, or seeking information that is not already available, a descriptive study requires the development of an instrument appropriate for obtaining the desired information.

19. A logical way to initially categorize descriptive studies is in terms of how data are collected, through self-report or observation. In a self-report study, information is

solicited from individuals using, for example, questionnaires, interviews, or standard-ized attitude scales. In an observation study, individuals are not asked for informa-tion; rather, the researcher obtains the desired data through other means such as direct observation.

Self-report Research

Types of Self-report Research

Survey Research

20. A survey is an attempt to collect data from members of a population in order to determine the current status of that population with respect to one or more variables.

21. In a sample survey, the researcher infers information about a population of interest based on the responses of a selected sample drawn from that population; preferably, the sample is either a simple-random or stratified-random sample.

22. In a census survey, an attempt is made to acquire data from each and every member of a population; a census survey is usually conducted when a population is relatively small and readily accessible.

23. Sample surveys are sometimes referred to as cross-sectional since information is collected at some point in time from a sample which hopefully represents all relevant subgroups in the population.

24. One type of survey unique to education is the school survey which may involve the study of an individual school or of all the schools in a particular system.

25. School surveys are generally conducted for the purpose of internal or external evaluation or for assessment and projection of needs and usually are conducted as a cooperative effort between local school personnel and a visiting team of experts, typically from local educational agencies and institutions.

Developmental Studies

26. Developmental studies are concerned primarily with behavior variables that dif-ferentiate children at different levels of age, growth, or maturation.

27. When the cross-sectional approach is used, different children at various stages of development are simultaneously studied; when the longitudinal method is used, the same group of children is studied over a period of time as the children progress from level to level.

Follow-Up Studies

28. A follow-up study is conducted to determine the status of a group of interest after some period of time.

29. Like school surveys, follow-up studies are often conducted by educational institutions for the purpose of internal or external evaluation of their instructional programs.

30. Follow-up studies may also be conducted solely for research purposes.

Sociometric Studies

31. Sociometry is the assessment and analysis of the interpersonal relationships within a group of individuals.

32. The basic sociometric process involves asking each member to indicate with which other members she or he would most like to engage in a particular activity.

33. The choices made by the group members are graphically depicted in a diagram called a sociogram.

Conducting Self-Report Research

34. Self-report research requires the collection of standardized, quantifiable information from all members of a population or sample.

Conducting a Questionnaire Study

35. In comparison to use of an interview procedure, a questionnaire is much more efficient in that it requires less time, is less expensive, and permits collection of data from a much larger sample.

36. Questionnaires may be administered to subjects but are usually mailed.

Statement of the Problem

37. The problem under investigation, and the topic of the questionnaire, must be of sufficient significance to motivate subjects to respond.

38. The problem must be defined in terms of specific objectives concerning the kind of information needed; specific hypotheses or questions must be formulated and every item on the questionnaire should directly relate to them.

Selection of Subjects

39. Subjects should be selected using an appropriate sampling technique (or an entire population may be used), and identified subjects must be persons who (1) have the desired information and (2) are likely to be willing to give it.

Construction of the Questionnaire

40. As a general guideline, the questionnaire should be as attractive and brief, and as easy to respond to, as possible.

41. No item should be included that does not directly relate to the objectives of the study, and structured, or closed-form, items should be used if at all possible.

42. A structured item consists of a question and a list of alternative responses from which the respondent selects.

43. In addition to facilitating response, structured items also facilitate data analysis; scoring is very objective and efficient.

44. An unstructured item format, in which the responder has complete freedom of response (questions are asked with no possible reponses indicated), is sometimes defended on the grounds that it permits greater depth of response and may permit insight into the reasons for responses.

45. With respect to item construction, the number one rule is that each question should deal with a single concept and be worded as clearly as possible; any term or concept that might mean different things to different people should be defined.

46. When necessary, questions should indicate a point of reference.

47. Avoid leading questions which suggest that one response may be more appropriate than another.

48. Do not ask a question that assumes a fact not necessarily in evidence.

Validation of the Questionnaire

49. A too-often-neglected procedure is validation of the questionnaire in order to determine if it measures what it was developed to measure.

Preparation of the Cover Letter

50. Every mailed questionnaire must be accompanied by a cover letter that explains what is being asked of the respondent, and why, and which hopefully motivates the responder to fulfill the request.

51. The cover letter should be brief, neat, and addressed specifically to the potential responder.
52. The letter should explain the purpose of the study, emphasizing its importance and significance, and give the responder a good reason for cooperating.
53. It usually helps if you can get the endorsement of an organization, institution, group, or administrator with which the responder is associated or which the responder views with respect (such as a professional organization).
54. If the questions to be asked are at all threatening (such as items dealing with sex or attitudes toward the local administration), anonymity or confidentiality of responses must be assured.
55. A specific deadline date by which the completed questionnaire is to be returned should be given.
56. The act of responding should be made as painless as possible. A stamped, addressed, return envelope should be included.

Pretesting the Questionnaire

57. The questionnaire should be tried out in a field test just as a research plan should be executed first as a pilot study, and for essentially the same reasons.
58. Pretesting the questionnaire yields data concerning instrument deficiencies as well as suggestions for improvement.

Follow-Up Activities

59. If your percentage of returns is not at *least* 70%, the validity of your conclusions will be weak.
60. An initial follow-up strategy is to simply send out a reminder postcard.
61. Full-scale follow-up activities are usually begun shortly after the deadline for responding has passed.

Dealing with Nonresponse

62. If your response rate is below 70%, you have a problem with generalizability of results since you do not know if the persons who did respond represent the population from which the sample was originally selected as well as the original sample.
63. The usual approach to dealing with excessive nonresponse is to try to determine if nonresponders are different from responders in some systematic manner by randomly selecting a small subsample of nonresponders and interviewing them, either in person or by phone.

Analysis of Results

64. The simplest way to present the results is to indicate the percentage of responders who selected each alternative for each item.
65. Relationships between variables can be investigated by comparing responses on one item with responses on other items.

Conducting an Interview Study

66. An interview is essentially the oral, in-person administration of a questionnaire to each member of a sample.
67. When well conducted it can produce in-depth data not possible with a questionnaire; on the other hand, it is expensive and time consuming, and generally involves smaller samples.
68. The steps in conducting an interview study are basically the same as for a questionnaire study, with some unique differences.

Construction of the Interview Guide

69. The interviewer must have a written guide which indicates what questions are to be asked and in what order, and what additional prompting or probing is permitted.

70. In order to obtain standardized, comparable data from each subject, all interviews must be conducted in essentially the same manner.

71. As with a questionnaire, each question in the interview should relate to a specific study objective.

72. Most interviews use a semistructured approach involving the asking of structured questions followed by clarifying unstructured, or open-ended, questions.

73. Many of the guidelines for constructing a questionnaire apply to the construction of interview guides.

Communication During the Interview

74. Before the first formal question is asked, some time should be spent in establishing rapport and putting the interviewee at ease.

75. The interviewer should also be sensitive to the reactions of the subject and proceed accordingly.

Recording Responses

76. Responses made during an interview can be recorded manually by the interviewer or mechanically by a recording device.

77. In general, mechanical recording is more objective and efficient.

Pretesting the Interview Procedure

78. Feedback from a small pilot study can be used to revise questions in the guide that are apparently unclear, do not solicit the desired information, or produce negative reactions in subjects. Insights into better ways to handle certain questions can also be acquired.

79. The pilot study will determine whether the resulting data can be quantified and analyzed in the manner intended.

Observational Research

Types of Observational Research

Nonparticipant Observation

80. In nonparticipant observation, the observer is not directly involved in the situation to be observed.

Naturalistic Observation

81. In naturalistic observation the observer purposely controls or manipulates nothing, and in fact works very hard at not affecting the observed situation in any way.

Simulation Observation

82. In simulation observation the researcher creates the situation to be observed and tells subjects what activities they are to engage in.

83. This technique allows the researcher to observe behavior that occurs infrequently in natural situations or not at all.

84. Two major types of simulation are individual role playing and team role playing.

The Case Study

85. A case study is the in-depth investigation of an individual, group, or institution.

86. The primary purpose of a case study is to determine the factors, and relationships among the factors, that have resulted in the current behavior or status of the subject of the study.

Content Analysis

87. Content analysis is the systematic, quantitative description of the composition of the object of the study.

88. Typical subjects for content analysis include books, documents, and creative productions such as musical compositions, works of art, and photographs.

Participant Observation

89. In participant observation, the observer actually becomes a part of, a participant in, the situation to be observed.

90. There are degrees of participation, and observation may be overt or covert.

91. Participant observation studies vary in the degree of structure involved in the inquiry. Such studies may be designed to test hypotheses, to derive hypotheses, or both.

92. More typically, participant observation studies are hypothesis generating. Thus, participant observation research is characterized by the collection of large amounts of data that are difficult to analyze.

Ethnography

Definition

93. Ethnography involves intensive data collection, that is, collection of data on many variables over an extended period of time, in a naturalistic setting.

94. The unit of observation in an ethnographic study is typically a classroom, or even a school.

Method

95. Ethnographic research may involve nonparticipant observation, participant observation, or both.

96. Typically, ethnographic studies are characterized by some type of participant observation at an overt level.

97. Ethnography represents "multi-instrument" research, and the ethnographer uses a variety of data collection strategies in conjunction with observation.

98. Having refined the research problem of interest, the ethnographic researcher makes informed decisions concerning the most appropriate environment to study and the most effective level of participation.

99. In ethnography, a tentative hypothesis or hypotheses guide the initial data collection strategies. Initial data collection efforts suggest other appropriate strategies, and so forth.

100. The major difference between ethnographic and traditional approaches is that the review of related literature, the study of previous research and theory, does not result in testable hypotheses, to be supported or not supported by the results of the study. Instead, the study of previous work results in tentative, working hypotheses and strategies only. The researcher analyzes the mass of data collected and attempts to derive specific, testable hypotheses that explain the observed behavior.

Educational Ethnography: In Summary

101. In an ethnographic study, results are difficult to analyze, findings are difficult to replicate, the process is costly, and we are usually dealing with an N of one.

102. When properly used, ethnography has the potential for providing insights not obtainable with other methods.

103. The approach is undergoing constant refinement in the direction of a more-structured ethnography.

Conducting Observational Research

104. The steps in conducting observational research are essentially the same as for other types of descriptive research.

Definition of Observational Variables

105. Once the behavior to be observed is determined, the researcher must clearly define what specific behaviors do and do not match the intended behavior.

106. Once a behavioral unit is defined, observations must be quantified so that all observers will count the same way.

107. Researchers typically divide observation sessions into a number of specific observation periods, that is, define a time unit. There should be correspondence between actual behavior frequency and recorded frequency.

108. Observation times may be randomly selected, so that different days and times of day are reflected in the observations, or all possibilities may be observed. The latter approach is only feasible for short periods of time and for a limited number of subjects.

Recording of Observations

109. Observers should have to observe and record only one behavior at a time.

110. It is also a good idea to alternate observation periods and recording periods, especially if any inference is required on the part of the observers.

111. As a general rule, it is probably better to record observations as the behavior occurs.

112. Most observation studies facilitate recording by using an agreed-upon code, or set of symbols, and a recording instrument.

113. Probably the most often used type of recording form, and the most efficient, is a checklist that lists all behaviors to be observed so that the observer can simply check each behavior as it occurs. Rating scales are also sometimes used.

Assessing Observer Reliability

114. Determining observer reliability generally requires that at least two observers independently make observations; their recorded judgments as to what occurred can then be compared to see how well they agree.

115. One approach to increasing reliability is to use shorter observation periods and to base reliability calculations on both agreements and disagreements on occurrences and nonoccurrences of behavior. With this approach it is easier to determine whether observers are recording the same events at the same time.

116. Recording situations to be observed allows each observer to play back tapes at a time convenient for him or her, and to play them back as often as needed.

Training Observers

117. Observers need to be trained in order to have some assurance that all observers are observing and recording the same behaviors in the same way.

118. Observers must be instructed as to what behaviors to observe, how behaviors are to be coded, how behaviors are to be recorded, and how often.

119. Practice sessions using recordings of behaviors are most effective since segments with which observers have difficulty can be replayed for discussion and feedback purposes.

120. Training may be terminated when a satisfactory level of reliability is achieved (say 80%).

Monitoring Observers

121. The major way to ensure continued satisfactory levels of reliability is to monitor the recording activities of observers.

122. As a general rule, the more monitoring that can reasonably be managed, the better.

Reducing Observation Bias

123. Observer bias refers to invalid observations that result from the way in which the observer observes.

124. A response set is the tendency of an observer to rate the majority of observees as above average, average, or below average, regardless of the observees' actual behavior.

125. The "halo effect" refers to the phenomenon whereby initial impressions concerning an observee (positive or negative) affect subsequent observations.

126. Data recorded by untrained observers, such as anecdotal records on students made by teachers, tend to be subjective and biased and usually not useful for research purposes.

127. Observee bias refers to the phenomenon whereby persons being observed behave atypically simply because they are being observed.

128. The best way to handle the problem of observee bias is to make observers aware of it so that they can attempt to be as unobtrusive as possible.

129. Another approach to the problem of observee bias is to eliminate observees. If the same information can be determined by observing inanimate objects (referred to as unobtrusive measures), use them.

Chapter 8/The Correlational Method

Definition and Purpose

130. Correlational research involves collecting data in order to determine whether, and to what degree, a relationship exists between two or more quantifiable variables.

131. Degree of relationship is expressed as a correlation coefficient.

132. If a relationship exists between two variables, it means that scores within a certain range on one measure are associated with scores within a certain range on another measure.

133. The fact that there is a relationship between variables does not imply that one is the cause of the other.

134. Correlational studies provide an estimate of just how related two variables are. If two variables are highly related, a correlation coefficient near 1.00 (or −1.00) will be obtained; if two variables are not related, a coefficient near .00 will be obtained.

135. The more highly related two variables are, the more accurate are predictions based on their relationship.

The Basic Correlational Research Process

Problem Selection

136. Correlational studies may be designed either to determine which variables of a list of likely candidates are related or to test hypotheses regarding expected relationships.

Sample and Instrument Selection

137. The sample for a correlational study is selected using an acceptable sampling method, and 30 subjects are generally considered to be a minimally acceptable sample size.

138. It is important to select or develop valid, reliable measures of the variables being studied.

Design and Procedure

139. The basic correlational design is not complicated; two (or more) scores are obtained for all members of a selected sample, one score for each variable of interest, and the paired scores are then correlated.

Data Analysis and Interpretation

140. A correlation coefficient is a decimal number between .00 and +1.00, or .00 and −1.00, which indicates the degree to which the two variables are related.

141. If the coefficient is near +1.00, the variables are positively related. This means that a person with a high score on one variable is likely to have a high score on the other variable, and a person with a low score on one is likely to have a low score on the other; an increase on one variable is associated with an increase on the other.

142. If the coefficient is near .00, the variables are not related.

143. If the coefficient is near −1.00, the variables are inversely related. This means that a person with a high score on one variable is likely to have a low score on the other variable, and a person with a low score on one is likely to have a high score on the other; an increase on one variable is associated with a decrease on the other variable, and vice versa.

144. A correlation coefficient squared indicates the amount of common variance shared by the variables.

145. How large a correlation coefficient needs to be in order to be useful depends upon the purpose for which it was computed.

146. In a study designed to explore or test hypothesized relationships, a correlation coefficient is interpreted in terms of its statistical significance.

147. In a prediction study, statistical significance is secondary to the value of the coefficient in facilitating accurate predictions.

148. Statistical significance refers to whether the obtained coefficient is really different from zero and reflects a true relationship, not a chance relationship.

149. To determine statistical significance you only have to consult a table that tells you how large your coefficient needs to be in order to be significant at a given level of confidence, and given the size of your sample.

150. For the same level of confidence, or significance level, a larger coefficient is required when smaller samples are involved.

151. For a given sample size, the value of the correlation coefficient needed for significance increases as the level of confidence increases.

152. No matter how significant a coefficient is, a low coefficient represents a low relationship.

153. A correlation coefficient much below .50 is generally useless for either group prediction or individual prediction, although a combination of several variables in this area may yield a reasonably satisfactory prediction.

154. Coefficients in the .60s and .70s are usually considered adequate for group prediction purposes, and coefficients in the .80s and above for individual prediction purposes.

155. While all reliabilities in the .90s are acceptable, for certain kinds of instruments, such as personality measures, a reliability in the low .70s might be acceptable.

156. When interpreting a correlation coefficient you must always keep in mind that you are talking about a relationship only, not a cause-effect relationship.

Relationship Studies

157. Relationship studies are conducted in an attempt to gain insight into the factors, or variables, that are related to complex variables such as academic achievement, motivation, and self-concept.

158. Such studies give direction to subsequent causal-comparative and experimental studies. Also, in both causal-comparative and experimental research studies, the researcher is concerned with controlling for variables, other than the independent variable, which might be related to performance on the dependent variable. Relationship studies help the researcher to identify such variables.

Data Collection

159. In a relationship study the researcher first identifies, either inductively or deductively, variables potentially related to the complex variable under study.

160. The shotgun approach, which involves checking all conceivable variables for possible relationships, is very inefficient and often misleading.

161. A smaller number of carefully selected variables is much to be preferred to a large number of carelessly selected variables.

162. The population must be one for which data on each of the identified variables can be collected, and one whose members are available to the researcher.

163. One advantage of a relationship study is that all the data may be collected within a relatively short period of time.

Data Analysis and Interpretation

164. In a relationship study, the scores for each variable are in turn correlated with the scores for the complex variable of interest.

165. Each variable must be expressable in numerical form, that is, must be quantifiable.

166. The most commonly used technique is the product moment correlation coefficient, usually referred to as the Pearson r, which is appropriate when both variables to be correlated are expressed as ratio data or interval data.

167. If data for one of the variables are expressed as ranks, the appropriate correlation coefficient is the rank difference correlation coefficient, usually referred to as the Spearman rho.

168. There are also a number of other correlational techniques which are encountered less often but which should be used when appropriate.

169. Most correlational techniques are based on the assumption that the relationship being investigated is a linear one.

170. If a relationship is curvilinear, an increase in one variable is associated with a corresponding increase in another variable *to a point,* at which point further increase in the first variable results in a corresponding decrease in the other variable (or vice versa).

171. In addition to computing correlation coefficients for a total sample group, it is sometimes profitable to examine relationships separately for certain defined sub-groups.

172. Attenuation refers to the principle that correlation coefficients tend to be lowered due to the fact that less-than-perfectly-reliable measures are utilized.

173. In relationship studies, a correction for attenuation can be applied that provides an estimate of what the coefficient would be if both measures were perfectly reliable.

174. Another factor that may lead to a coefficient representing an underestimate of the true relationship between two variables is a restricted range of scores.

175. There is a correction for restriction in range that may be applied to obtain an estimate of what the coefficient would be if the range of scores were not restricted.

Prediction Studies

176. If two variables are highly related, scores on one variable can be used to predict scores on the other variable.

177. The variable upon which the prediction is made is referred to as the predictor, and the variable predicted is referred to as the criterion.

178. Prediction studies are often conducted to facilitate decision making concerning individuals or to aid in the selection of individuals.

179. Prediction studies are also conducted to test theoretical hypotheses concerning variables believed to be predictors of the criterion, and to determine the predictive validity of individual measuring instruments.

180. If several predictor variables each correlate well with a criterion, then a prediction based on a combination of those variables will be more accurate than a prediction based on any one of them.

Data Collection

181. As with a relationship study, subjects must be selected from whom the desired data can be collected and who are available to the researcher.

182. The major difference in data collection precedures for a relationship study and a prediction study is that in a relationship study data on all variables are collected within a relatively short period of time, whereas in a prediction study predictor variables are measured some period of time before the criterion variable is measured.

Data Analysis and Interpretation

183. As with a relationship study, each predictor variable is correlated with the criterion variable.

184. Since a combination of variables usually results in a more accurate prediction than any one variable, prediction studies often result in a prediction equation referred to as a multiple regression equation.

185. A multiple regression equation uses all variables that individually predict the criterion to make a more accurate prediction.

186. Since relationships are not perfect, predictions made by a multiple regression equation are not perfect.

187. Predicted scores are generally placed in a confidence interval.

188. As with relationship studies, and for similar reasons, prediction equations may be formulated for each of a number of subgroups as well as for the total group.

189. Shrinkage is the tendency of a prediction equation to become less accurate when used with a different group, a group other than the one on which the equation was originally formulated.

190. Any prediction equation should be validated with at least one other group, and variables that are no longer found to be related to the criterion measure should be taken out of the equation; this procedure is referred to as cross-validation.

Chapter 9/The Causal-Comparative Method

Definition and Purpose

191. Causal-comparative, or ex post facto, research is that research in which the researcher attempts to determine the cause, or reason, for existing differences in the behavior or status of groups of individuals.

192. The basic causal-comparative approach involves starting with an effect and seeking possible causes.

193. A variation of the basic approach involves starting with a cause and investigating its effect on some variable.

194. Causal-comparative studies *attempt* to identify cause-effect relationships, correlational studies do not.

195. The major difference between experimental research and causal-comparative research is that in experimental research the independent variable, the alleged cause, is manipulated, and in causal-comparative research it is not, it has already occurred.

196. In experimental research the researcher can randomly form groups and manipulate a variable—can determine "who" is *going to get* "what," "what" being the independent variable; in causal-comparative research the groups are already formed and *already different* on the independent variable.

197. Causal-comparative groups are already different in that one group may have had an experience which the other did not have, or one group may possess a characteristic which the other group does not; in any event, the difference between the groups (the independent variable) was not determined by the researcher.

198. Independent variables in causal-comparative studies are variables that cannot be manipulated (such as socioeconomic status), should not be manipulated (such as number of cigarettes smoked per day), or simply are not manipulated, but could be (such as method of reading instruction).

199. Causal-comparative studies identify relationships that may lead to experimental studies.

200. As with a correlational study, only a relationship is established, not necessarily a causal one.

201. The alleged cause of an observed effect may in fact be the effect, or there may be a third variable that has "caused" both the identified cause and effect.

202. Cause-effect relationships established through causal-comparative research are at best tenuous and tentative.

203. Only experimental research, which guarantees that the alleged cause, or independent variable, does *come before* the observed effect, or dependent variable, can truly establish cause-effect relationships.

Conducting a Causal-Comparative Study

Design and Procedure

204. The basic causal-comparative design involves selecting two groups differing on some independent variable and comparing them on some dependent variable.

205. The groups may differ in that one group possesses a characteristic that the other does not, *or* the groups may differ in degree; one group may possess more of a characteristic than the other or the two groups may have had different kinds of experiences.

206. The important consideration is to select samples that are representative of their respective populations and similar with respect to critical variables other than the independent variable.

207. In order to determine the equality of groups, information on a number of background and current status variables may be collected.

Control Procedures

208. Lack of the randomization, manipulation, and control which characterize experimental studies are all sources of weakness in a causal-comparative design.

209. A problem is the possibility that the groups are different on some other major variable besides the identified independent variable, and it is this other variable which is the real cause of the observed difference between the groups.

Matching

210. For each subject in one group the researcher finds a subject in the second group with the same or a similar score on the control variable.

211. A major problem with pair-wise matching is that there are invariably subjects who have no match and must therefore be eliminated from the study.

Comparing Homogeneous Groups or Subgroups

212. Another way of controlling an extraneous variable, which is also used in experimental research, is to compare groups which are as homogeneous as possible.

213. A similar but more satisfactory approach is to form subgroups within each group that represent all levels of the control variable. In addition to controlling for the variable, this technique has the added advantage of permitting the researcher to see if the independent variable affects the dependent variable differently at different levels of the control variable. If this question is of interest, the best approach is not to do several separate analyses but to build the control variable right into the design and analyze the results with a statistical technique called factorial analysis of variance.

Analysis of Covariance

214. The analysis of covariance, which is also used in experimental studies, is a statistical method that can be used to equate groups on one or more variables.

215. In essence, analysis of covariance adjusts scores on a dependent variable for initial differences on some other variable (assuming that performance on the "other variable" is related to performance on the dependent variable, which is what control is all about anyway).

Data Analysis and Interpretation

216. Analysis of data in causal-comparative studies involves a variety of descriptive and inferential statistics.

217. The most commonly used descriptive statistics are the mean, which indicates the average performance of a group on a measure of some variable, and the standard deviation, which indicates how spread out a set of scores is, that is, whether the scores are relatively close together and clustered around the mean or spread out covering a wide range of scores.

218. The most commonly used inferential statistics are the *t* test, which is used to see if there is a significant difference between the means of two groups, analysis of variance, which is used to see if there is a significant difference among the means of three or more groups, and the chi square test, which is used to compare group frequencies, that is, to see if an event occurs more frequently in one group than another.

219. As repeatedly pointed out, interpretation of the findings in a causal-comparative study requires considerable caution.

220. The alleged cause-effect relationship may in fact be the reverse of the one hypothesized (the alleged cause may be the effect and vice versa).

221. There may be a third factor which is the real "cause" of both the alleged cause (independent variable) and effect (dependent variable).

222. The way to determine the correct order of causality, which variable caused which, is to determine which one occurred *first*.

223. One way to control for a potential common cause is to equate groups on the suspected variable.

Chapter 10/The Experimental Method

Definition and Purpose

224. In an experimental study, the researcher manipulates at least one independent variable, controls other relevant variables, and observes the effect on one or more dependent variables.

225. The independent variable, also referred to as the experimental variable, the cause, or the treatment, is that activity or characteristic believed to make a difference.

226. The dependent variable, also referred to as the criterion variable, effect, or posttest, is the outcome of the study, the change or difference in groups that occurs as a result of manipulation of the independent variable.

227. When well conducted, experimental studies produce the soundest evidence concerning hypothesized cause-effect relationships.

228. Predictions based on experimental findings (in contrast to those based on correlational studies) are more global and take the form "if you use approach X you will probably get better results than if you use approach Y."

The Experimental Process

229. The steps in an experimental study are basically the same as for other types of research: selection and definition of a problem, selection of subjects and measuring instruments, selection of a design, execution of procedures, analysis of data, and formulation of conclusions.

230. An experimental study is guided by at least one hypothesis that states an expected causal relationship between two variables.

231. In an experimental study, the researcher is in on the action from the very beginning; the researcher forms or selects the groups, decides what is going to happen to each group, tries to control all other relevant factors besides the changes that she or he has introduced, and observes or measures the effect on the groups at the end of the study.

232. An experiment typically involves two groups, an experimental group and a control group (although there may be only one group, or there may be three or more groups).

233. The experimental group typically receives a new, or novel, treatment, a treatment under investigation, while the control group either receives a different treatment, or is treated as usual.

234. The two groups that are to receive different treatments are equated on all other variables that might be related to performance on the dependent variable.

235. After the groups have been exposed to the treatment for some period of time, the researcher administers a test of the dependent variable (or otherwise measures it) and then determines whether there is a significant difference between the groups.

Manipulation and Control

236. Direct manipulation by the researcher of at least one independent variable is the one single characteristic that differentiates all experimental research from other methods of research.

237. The different values or forms that the independent variable may take are basically presence versus absence (A versus no A), presence in varying degrees (a lot of A versus a little A), or presence of one kind versus presence of another kind (A versus B).

238. Control refers to efforts on the part of the researcher to remove the influence of any variable (other than the independent variable) that might affect performance on the dependent variable.

239. There are really two different kinds of variables that need to be controlled, subject variables, such as reading readiness, variables on which subjects in the different groups might differ, and environmental variables, variables such as learning materials, variables which might cause unwanted differences between groups.

Threats to Experimental Validity

240. Any uncontrolled extraneous variables affecting performance on the dependent variable are threats to the validity of an experiment.

241. An experiment is valid if results obtained are due only to the manipulated independent variable, and if they are generalizable to situations outside of the experimental setting.

242. *Internal validity* refers to the condition that observed differences on the dependent variable are a direct result of manipulation of the independent variable, not some other variable.

243. *External validity* refers to the condition that results are generalizable, or applicable, to groups and environments outside of the experimental setting.

244. The term *ecological validity* is sometimes used to refer to the degree to which results can be generalized to other environments.

245. The researcher must strive for a balance between control and realism. If a choice is involved, the researcher should err on the side of too much control rather than too little.

246. Although lab-type settings are generally preferred for the investigation of theoretical problems, experimentation in natural, or field, settings has its advantages, especially for certain practical problems.

Threats to Internal Validity

History

247. History refers to the occurrence of any event that is not part of the experimental treatment but which may affect performance on the dependent variable.

Maturation

248. Maturation refers to physical or mental changes that may occur within the subjects over a period of time. These changes may affect the subjects' performance on the measure of the dependent variable.

Testing

249. Testing refers to improved scores on a posttest resulting from subjects having taken a pretest.

Instrumentation

250. Instrumentation refers to unreliability, or lack of consistency, in measuring instruments which may result in invalid assessment of performance.

Statistical Regression

251. Statistical regression usually occurs when subjects are selected on the basis of their extreme scores and refers to the tendency of subjects who score highest on a pretest to score lower on a posttest, and of subjects who score lowest on a pretest to score higher on a posttest.

Differential Selection of Subjects

252. Differential selection of subjects usually occurs when already-formed groups are used and refers to the fact that the groups may be different before the study even begins, and this initial difference may at least partially account for posttest differences.

Mortality

253. Mortality, or attrition, is more likely to occur in longer studies and refers to the fact that subjects who drop out of a study may share a characteristic such that their absence has a significant effect on the results of the study.

Selection-Maturation Interaction, Etc.

254. The "etc." means that selection may also interact with factors such as history and testing, although selection-maturation interaction is more common. What this means is that if already formed groups are used, one group may profit more (or less) from a treatment or have an initial advantage (or disadvantage) because of maturation, history, or testing factors.

Threats to External Validity

Pretest-Treatment Interaction

255. Pretest-treatment interaction occurs when subjects respond or react differently to a treatment because they have been pretested. The treatment effect is different than it would have been had subjects not been pretested.

Selection-Treatment Interaction

256. Selection-treatment interaction is similar to the "differential selection of subjects" problem associated with internal invalidity and also occurs when subjects are not randomly selected for treatments.

257. Interaction effects aside, the very fact that subjects are not randomly selected from a population severely limits the researcher's ability to generalize since representativeness of the sample is in question.

258. This nonrepresentativeness of groups may also result in a selection-treatment interaction such that the results of a study hold only for the groups involved and are not representative of the treatment effect in the intended population.

Specificity of Variables

259. Specificity is a threat to generalizability regardless of the experimental design.

260. Specificity of variables refers to the fact that a given study is conducted with a specific kind of subject, using specific measuring instruments, at a specific time, under a specific set of circumstances.

261. To deal with this issue the researcher must (1) operationally define variables in a way that has meaning outside of the experimental setting and (2) be careful in stating conclusions and generalizations.

Reactive Arrangements

262. Reactive arrangements refer to a number of factors associated with the way in which the study is conducted and the feelings and attitudes of the subjects involved.

263. In an effort to maintain a high degree of control, the researcher may create an experimental environment that is highly artificial and which hinders generalizability of findings to nonexperimental settings.

264. Another type of reactive arrangement results from the subjects' knowledge that they are involved in an experiment or their feeling that they are in some way receiving "special" attention (the Hawthorne effect).

265. The placebo effect is sort of the antidote for the Hawthorne effect. Its application in educational research is that all groups in an experiment should *appear* to be treated the same.

266. The novelty effect refers to increased interest, motivation, or participation on the part of the subjects simply because they are doing something different.

Multiple-Treatment Interference

267. Multiple-treatment interference can occur when the same subjects receive more than one treatment in succession; it refers to the carry-over effects from an earlier treatment which make it difficult to assess the effectiveness of a later treatment.

Contamination and Experimenter Bias

268. Contamination occurs when the researcher's familiarity with the subjects affects the outcome of the study; the researcher may unintentionally influence their behavior or be subjective in evaluating their behavior.

269. Further, the researcher's expectations concerning study outcomes may actually contribute to producing those outcomes (experimenter bias).

Group Experimental Designs

270. The validity of an experiment is a direct function of the degree to which extraneous variables are controlled.

271. This is what experimental design is all about—control of extraneous variables; good designs control many sources of invalidity, poor designs control few.

272. Subject variables include organismic variables and intervening variables.

273. Organismic variables are characteristics of the subject, or organism (such as sex), which cannot be directly controlled, but which can be controlled *for*.

274. Intervening variables are variables that intervene between the independent variable and the dependent variable (such as anxiety or boredom), which cannot be directly observed or controlled, but which can be controlled *for*.

Control of Extraneous Variables

275. Randomization is the best single way to attempt to control for many extraneous variables at the same time.

276. Randomization should be used whenever possible; subjects should be randomly selected from a population whenever possible, subjects should be randomly assigned to groups whenever possible, treatments should be randomly assigned to groups whenever possible, and anything else you can think of should be randomly assigned if possible!

277. Randomization is effective in creating equivalent, representative groups that are essentially the same on all relevant variables thought of by the researcher, and probably even a few not thought of.

278. A randomly formed group is a characteristic unique to experimental research; it is a control factor not possible with causal-comparative research.

279. Certain environmental variables can be controlled by holding them constant for all groups.

280. Controlling subject variables is critical.

Matching

281. Matching is a technique for equating groups on one or more variables the researcher has identified as being highly related to performance on the dependent variable.

282. The most commonly used approach to matching involves random assignment of pair members, one member to each group.

283. A major problem with such matching is that there are invariably subjects who do not have a match and must be eliminated from the study.

284. One way to combat loss of subjects is to match less closely.

285. A related procedure is to rank all of the subjects, from highest to lowest, based on their scores on the control variable; each two adjacent scores constitute a pair.

Comparing Homogeneous Groups or Subgroups

286. Another way of controlling an extraneous variable is to compare groups that are homogeneous with respect to that variable.

287. As with causal-comparative research, a similar, but more satisfactory approach is to form subgroups representing all levels of the control variable.

288. If the researcher is interested not just in controlling the variable but also in seeing if the independent variable affects the dependent variable differently at different levels of the control variable, the best approach is to build the control variable right into the design and to analyze the results with a statistical technique called factorial analysis of variance.

Using Subjects as Their Own Controls

289. Using subjects as their own controls involves exposing the same group to the different treatments, one treatment at a time.

Analysis of Covariance

290. The analysis of covariance is a statistical method for equating randomly formed groups on one or more variables.

291. In essence, analysis of covariance adjusts scores on a dependent variable for initial differences on some other variable, such as pretest scores, IQ, reading readiness, or musical aptitude (assuming that performance on the "other variable" is related to performance on the dependent variable).

Types of Group Designs

292. A selected experimental design dictates to a great extent the specific procedures of a study.

293. Selection of a given design dictates such factors as whether there will be a control group, whether subjects will be randomly assigned to groups, whether each group will be pretested, and how resulting data will be analyzed.

294. Depending upon the particular combination of such factors represented, different designs are appropriate for testing different types of hypotheses and designs vary widely in the degree to which they control the various threats to internal and external validity.

295. From the designs that are appropriate and feasible, you select the one that controls the most sources of internal and external invalidity.

296. There are two major classes of experimental designs, single-variable designs, which involve one independent variable (which is manipulated), and factorial designs, which involve two or more independent variables (at least one of which is manipulated).

297. Single-variable designs are classified as pre-experimental, true experimental, or quasi-experimental, depending upon the control they provide for sources of internal and external invalidity.

298. Pre-experimental designs do not do a very good job of controlling threats to validity and should be avoided.

299. The true experimental designs represent a very high degree of control and are always to be preferred.

300. Quasi-experimental designs do not control as well as true experimental designs but do a much better job than the pre-experimental designs.

301. Factorial designs are basically elaborations of true experimental designs and permit investigation of two or more variables, individually and in interaction with each other.

Pre-Experimental Designs

The One-Shot Case Study

302. The one-shot case study involves one group which is exposed to a treatment (X) and then posttested (O).

303. None of the threats to validity that are relevant is controlled.

The One-Group Pretest-Posttest Design

304. This design involves one group which is pretested (O), exposed to a treatment (X), and posttested (O).

305. Although it controls several sources of invalidity not controlled by the one-shot case study, a number of additional factors are relevant to this design that are not controlled.

The Static-Group Comparison

306. The static-group comparison involves at least two groups; one receives a new, or unusual, treatment and both groups are posttested.

307. Since subjects are not randomly assigned to groups, and since there is no pretest data, it is difficult to determine just how equivalent they are.

True Experimental Designs

308. The true experimental designs control for nearly all sources of internal and external invalidity.

309. All of the true experimental designs have one characteristic in common that none of the other designs has—random assignment of subjects to groups.

310. Ideally, subjects should be randomly selected and randomly assigned; however, to qualify as a true design, at least random assignment must be involved.

311. Note too that all the true designs involve a control group.

The Pretest-Posttest Control Group Design

312. This design involves at least two groups, both of which are formed by random assignment; both groups are administered a pretest of the dependent variable, one group receives a new, or unusual, treatment, and both groups are posttested.

313. The combination of random assignment and the presence of a pretest and a control group serve to control for all sources of internal invalidity.

314. The only definite weakness with this design is a possible interaction between the pretest and the treatment which may make the results generalizable only to other pretested groups.

315. The best approach to data analysis is to simply compare the posttest scores of the two groups. The pretest is used to see if the groups are essentially the same on the dependent variable. If they are, posttest scores can be directly compared using a *t* test; if they are not (random assignment does not *guarantee* equality), posttest scores can be analyzed using analysis of covariance.

316. A variation of the pretest-posttest control group design involves random assignment of members of matched pairs to the groups, one member to each group, in order to more closely control for one or more extraneous variables.

The Posttest-Only Control Group Design

317. This design is exactly the same as the pretest-posttest control group design *except* there is no pretest; subjects are randomly assigned to groups, exposed to the independent variable, and posttested. Posttest scores are then compared to determine the effectiveness of the treatment.

318. The combination of random assignment and the presence of a control group serve to control for all sources of invalidity except mortality. Mortality is not controlled for because of the absence of pretest data on the subjects.

319. A variation of the posttest-only control group design involves random assignment of members of matched pairs to the groups, one member to each group, in order to more closely control for one or more extraneous variables.

The Solomon Four-Group Deisgn

320. The Solomon four-group design involves random assignment of subjects to one of four groups. Two of the groups are pretested and two are not; one of the pretested groups and one of the unpretested groups receive the experimental treatment. All four groups are posttested.

321. This design is a combination of the pretest-posttest control group design and the posttest-only control group design, each of which has its own source of invalidity (pretest-treatment interaction and mortality, respectively). The combination of these two designs results in a design which controls for pretest-treatment interaction *and* for mortality.

322. The correct way to analyze data resulting from application of this design is to use a 2×2 factorial analysis of variance. The factorial analysis tells the researcher whether there is an interaction between the treatment and the pretest.

323. Which design is the "best" depends upon the nature of the study.

Quasi-Experimental Designs

324. Sometimes it is just not possible to randomly assign subjects to groups. When this occurs, however, quasi-experimental designs are available to the researcher. They provide adequate control of sources of invalidity.

The Nonequivalent Control Group Design

325. This design looks very much like the pretest-posttest control group design; the only difference is that the nonequivalent control group design does not involve random assignment.

326. The lack of random assignment adds a source of invalidity not associated with the pretest-posttest control group design—possible interactions between selection and variables such as maturation, history, and testing.

327. The researcher should make every effort to use groups that are as equivalent as possible.

328. If differences between the groups on any major extraneous variable are identified, analysis of covariance can be used to statistically equate the groups.

329. An advantage of this design is that since classes are used "as is," possible effects from reactive arrangements are minimized.

The Time-Series Design

330. The time-series design is actually an elaboration of the one-group pretest-posttest design. One group is repeatedly pretested, exposed to a treatment, and then repeatedly posttested.

331. If a group scores essentially the same on a number of pretests and then significantly improves following a treatment, the researcher has more confidence in the effectiveness of the treatment than if just one pretest and one posttest are administered.

332. History is still a problem, however, since something might happen between the last pretest and the first posttest, the effect of which might be confused with the treatment. Pretest-treatment interaction is also a validity problem.

333. While statistical analyses appropriate for this design are rather advanced, determining the effectiveness of the treatment basically involves analysis of the pattern of the test scores.

334. A variation of the time series design, which is referred to as the multiple time-series design, involves the addition of a control group to the basic design. This variation eliminates history and instrumentation as threats to validity, and thus represents a design with no probable sources of internal invalidity.

Counterbalanced Designs

335. In a counterbalanced design, all groups receive all treatments but in a different order.

336. The only restriction is that the number of groups equals the number of treatments.

337. While subjects may be pretested, this design is usually employed when intact groups must be used and when administration of a pretest is not possible or feasible.

338. In order to determine the effectiveness of the treatments, the average performance of the groups for each treatment can be compared.

339. A unique weakness of this design is potential multiple-treatment interference that can result when the same group receives more than one treatment.

340. A counterbalanced design should really only be used when the treatments are such that exposure to one will not affect evaluation of the effectiveness of another.

Factorial Designs

341. Factorial designs involve two or more independent variables, at least one of which is manipulated by the researcher.

342. They are basically elaborations of true experimental designs and permit investigation of two or more variables, individually and in interaction with each other.

343. In education, variables do not operate in isolation.

344. The term "factorial" refers to the fact that the design involves several factors. Each factor has two or more levels.

345. The 2×2 is the simplest factorial design.

346. Both variables may be manipulated, but the 2×2 design usually involves one manipulated, or experimental, variable and one nonmanipulated variable; the non-manipulated variable is often referred to as a control variable.

347. Control variables are usually physical or mental characteristics of the subjects such as sex, IQ, or math aptitude.

348. The purpose of a factorial design is to determine whether the effects of an experimental variable are generalizable across all levels of a control variable or whether the effects are specific to specific levels of the control variable. Also, a factorial design can demonstrate relationships that a single-variable experiment cannot.

349. If one value of the independent variable is more effective regardless of level of the control variable, there is no interaction.

350. If an interaction exists between the variables, different values of the independent variable are differentially effective depending upon the level of the control variable.

351. Theoretically, a researcher can simultaneously investigate any number of factors.

352. In reality, however, more than three factors are rarely used.

Single-Subject Experimental Designs

353. Single-subject experimental designs are designs that can be applied when the sample size is one.

354. Single-subject designs are typically used to study the behavior change an individual exhibits as a result of some intervention, or treatment.

355. Basically, the subject is alternately exposed to a nontreatment and a treatment condition, or phase, and performance is repeatedly measured during each phase.

356. The nontreatment condition is symbolized as A and the treatment condition is symbolized as B.

Single-Subject Versus Group Designs

357. At the very least, single-subject designs are considered to be valuable complements to group designs.

358. Most experimental research problems require traditional group designs for their investigation. This is mainly because the results are intended to be applied to *groups,* e.g., classrooms.

359. There are a number of research questions for which traditional group designs are not appropriate for two major reasons. First, group comparison designs are frequently opposed on ethical or philosophical grounds since by definition such designs involve a control group that does not receive the experimental treatment. Second, application of a group comparison design is not possible in many cases because of the small size of the population of interest.

External Validity

360. Results of single-subject research cannot be generalized to the population of interest as they can with group design research.

361. It is also true that the results of a study using a group design cannot be directly generalized to any individual within the group.

362. For single-subject designs, the key to generalizability is replication.

363. One generalizability problem associated with many single-subject designs is the possible effect of the baseline condition on the subsequent effects of the treatment condition.

Internal Validity

Repeated and Reliable Measurement

364. As with a time-series design, pretest performance is measured a number of times prior to implementation of the treatment or intervention. In single-subject designs these sequential measures of pretest performance are referred to as baseline measures.

365. As a result of these measures taken over some period of time, sources of invalidity such as maturation are controlled for in the same way as for the time-series design.

366. Unlike the time-series design, however, performance is also measured at various points in time while the treatment is being applied. This added dimension greatly reduces the potential threat to validity from history.

367. One very real threat to the internal validity of most single-subject designs is instrumentation. Since repeated measurement is a characteristic of all single-subject designs, it is especially important that measurement of the target behavior, or performance, be done in exactly the same way every time, or as nearly the same as is humanly possible.

368. In single-subject studies it is critical that the observation conditions (e.g., location, time of day) be standardized.

369. If one observer makes all the observations, then intraobserver reliability should be estimated. If more than one observer is involved, then interobserver reliability should be estimated.

370. The nature and conditions of the treatment should be specified in sufficient detail to permit replication. If its effects are to be validly assessed, the treatment must involve precisely the same procedures every time it is introduced, either in the same study or in another study by another researcher.

Baseline Stability

371. The purpose of the baseline measurements is to provide a description of the target behavior as it naturally occurs *without* the treatment. The baseline serves as the basis of comparison for assessing the effectiveness of the treatment.

372. A sufficient number of baseline measurements are usually taken to establish a pattern. The establishment of a pattern is referred to as baseline stability.

373. Normally, the length of the treatment phase, and the number of measurements taken during the treatment phase, parallel the length and measurements of the baseline phase.

The Single Variable Rule

374. An important principle of single-subject research is that only one variable should be manipulated throughout the experiment.

Types of Single-Subject Designs

A-B-A Designs

The A-B Design

375. When this design is used baseline measurements are repeatedly made until stability is

presumably established, treatment is then introduced and an appropriate number of measurements are made during treatment. If behavior improves during the treatment phase, the effectiveness of the treatment is allegedly demonstrated.

376. The problem is that we don't know if behavior improved *because of* the treatment or for some other reason.

The A-B-A Design

377. By simply adding a second baseline phase to the A-B design we get a much improved design, the A-B-A design.

378. In some cases, when it is feasible and ethical to do so, the treatment may actually be reversed during the second baseline phase. If such is the case, we refer to the design as a reversal design, and a condition that is essentially the opposite of the treatment condition is implemented.

379. The internal validity of the A-B-A design is superior to that of the A-B design. With the A-B design it is possible that behaviors would have improved without treatment intervention. It is very unlikely, however, that behavior would coincidentally improve during the treatment phase *and* coincidentially deteriorate during the subsequent baseline phase.

380. The major problem with this design is an ethical one since the experiment ends with the subject *not* receiving the treatment.

The A-B-A-B Design

381. The A-B-A-B design is basically the A-B-A design with the addition of a second treatment phase.

382. Not only does this design overcome the ethical objection to the A-B-A design, by ending the experiment during a treatment phase, it also greatly strengthens the conclusions of the study by demonstrating the effects of the treatment *twice*.

383. The second treatment phase can be extended beyond the termination of the actual study, indefinitely if desired.

384. When application of the A-B-A-B design is feasible, it provides the most convincing evidence of treatment effectiveness.

Multiple-Baseline Designs

385. Multiple-baseline designs are used when the only alternative would be an A-B design. This is the case when the treatment is such that it is not possible to withdraw it and return to baseline or when it would not be ethical to withdraw it or reverse it.

386. Multiple-baseline designs are also used when treatment can be withdrawn but the effects of the treatment "carry over" into the second baseline phase and a return to baseline conditions is difficult or impossible.

387. With a multiple-baseline design, instead of collecting baseline data for one subject and one target behavior, we collect baseline data on several behaviors for one subject or one behavior for *several* subjects. We then systematically, over a period of time, apply the treatment to each behavior (or each subject) one at a time until all behaviors (or subjects) are under treatment. If measured performance improves in each case only after treatment is introduced, then the treatment is judged to be effective.

388. The more behaviors or subjects are treated, the more convincing the evidence is for the effectiveness of the treatment.

389. This design requires that the behaviors be able to be treated independently.

390. Whenever baseline is recoverable and there are no carry-over effects, any of the A-B-A designs can be applied within a multiple-baseline framework.

Task 6 Performance Criteria

The description of subjects should describe the population from which the sample was selected (allegedly of course!) including its size and major characteristics.

The description of the instrument(s) should describe the purpose of the instrument (what it is intended to measure), and available validity and reliability coefficients.

The description of the design should indicate why it was selected, potential threats to validity associated with the design, and aspects of the study that are believed to have minimized their potential effects. A figure should be included illustrating how the selected design was applied in the study. For example, you might say:

Since random assignment of subjects to groups was possible, and since administration of a pretest was not advisable due to the reactive nature of the dependent variable (attitudes toward school), the posttest-only control group design was selected for this study (see Figure 1).

Group	Assignment	N	Treatment	Posttest
I	Random	25	Daily Homework	So-so Attitude Scale
II	Random	25	No Homework	So-so Attitude Scale

Figure 1.
Experimental design.

The description of procedures should describe in detail all steps which were executed in conducting the study. The description should include: (1) the manner in which the sample was selected and the groups formed; (2) how and when pretest data were collected; (3) the ways in which the groups were different (the independent variable, or treatment); (4) aspects of the study that were the same or similar for all groups; and (5) how and when posttest data were collected.

Note: If the dependent variable was measured with a test (collection of pretest and posttest data), the specific test or tests administered should be named. If a test was administered strictly for selection-of-subjects purposes, that is, not as pretest of the dependent variable, it too should be described.

See the *Student Guide* for practice problems and for examples of Task 6.

Part Seven

Data Analysis and Interpretation
Or . . .
The Word is "Statistics," not "Sadistics"

Does it look bad? Is it? What will it turn into?

Statistics is a set of procedures for describing, synthesizing, analyzing, and interpreting quantitative data. One thousand scores, for example, can be represented with a single number. As another example, you would not expect two groups to perform *exactly* the same on a posttest, even if they were essentially equal. Application of the appropriate statistic helps you to decide if the difference between groups is big enough to represent a true difference, not a chance difference.

Choice of appropriate statistical techniques is determined to a great extent by the design of the study and by the kind of data to be collected. The posttest-only control group design and the Solomon four-group design, for example, suggest different statistical analyses for investigating group differences. As with the design, statistical procedures and techniques are identified and described in detail in the research plan. Analysis of the data is as important as any other component of the research process. Regardless of how well the study is conducted, inappropriate analyses can lead to inappropriate conclusions. The complexity of the analysis is not an indication of its "goodness"; a simple statistic is often more appropriate than a more complicated one. The choice of statistical techniques is largely determined by the research hypothesis to be tested.

There are a wide variety of statistics available to the researcher. This part will describe and explain only those most commonly used in educational research. The intent is that you be able to apply and interpret these statistics, *not* that you necessarily understand their theoretical rationale and mathematical derivation. Despite what you have heard, statistics is easy. In order to calculate the statistics to be described you only need to know how to add, subtract, multiply, and divide. That is all there is. All formulas, no matter how gross they may look, turn into arithmetic problems when applied to your data. The arithmetic problems involve only the operations of addition, subtraction, multiplication, and division; the formulas tell you how often, and in what order, to perform those operations. Now, if you are a smarty, you are probably thinking, "What about square roots?" While it is true that many of the formulas involve square roots, you do not have to know how to find the square root of anything. All the "square rootin'" has been done for you and the square root of any reasonable number (six trillion is not a reasonable number) can be located in a table (see Table A.3 in the Appendix).

Even if you have a hangup about math and have not had a math course since junior high school, you will be able to calculate statistics; no calculus is required. The very hardest formula still requires arithmetic, maybe sixth grade arithmetic if you have to divide by a big number, but arithmetic just the same. In fact, you do not even have to divide big numbers if you do not want to. You are allowed to use a calculator! All you have to do is follow the steps as presented, and you cannot go wrong. You are going to be pleasantly surprised to see just how easy statistics is. Trust me.

The goal of Part Seven is for you to be able to select, apply, and correctly interpret analyses appropriate for a given study. After you have read Part Seven, you should be able to perform the following task.

Task 7

Based on Tasks 2–6 which you have already completed, write the results section of a research report. Generate data for each of the subjects in your study, summarize and describe the data using descriptive statistics, statistically analyze the data using inferential statistics, and interpret the results in terms of your original research hypothesis. Present the results of your data analyses in a summary table.

(See Performance Criteria, p. 369)

11

Preanalysis Procedures

Enablers

After reading chapter 11, you should be able to:

1. List the steps involved in scoring
   (a) standardized tests, and
   (b) self-developed tests.
2. Identify and describe the four scales of measurement.
3. List three examples of each of the four scales of measurement.

Preparing Data for Analysis

Execution of a research study usually produces a mass of raw data resulting from the administration of one or more standardized or self-developed instruments or from the collection of naturally available data (such as grade point averages). Collected data must be accurately scored, if appropriate, and systematically organized in a manner that facilitates analysis.

Scoring Procedures

All instruments administered should be scored accurately and consistently; each subject's test should be scored using the same procedures and criteria. When a standardized instrument is used, the scoring process is greatly facilitated. The test manual usually spells out the steps to be followed in scoring each test (or answer sheet), and a scoring key is often provided. If the manual is followed conscientiously and each test is scored carefully, scoring errors are minimized. As an extra check it is usually a good idea to recheck all tests, or at least some percentage of them, say 25% (every fourth test).

Scoring self-developed instruments is more complex, especially if open-ended items are involved.[1] There is no manual to follow, and the researcher has to develop and refine a scoring procedure. Steps for scoring each item and for arriving at a total score must be delineated and carefully followed. If other than

---

1. Projective tests also involve complex scoring procedures. The skills and experience required for valid scoring and interpretation of such tests are generally beyond the capabilities of beginning researchers.

objective-type items (such as multiple-choice questions) are to be scored it is advisable also to have at least one other person score the tests as a reliability check. Tentative scoring procedures should always be tried out beforehand by administering the instrument to a group of subjects from the same or a similar population as the one from which subjects will be selected for the actual study. Problems with the instrument or with scoring procedures can be identified and corrected before it is too late to do anything about them. The procedure ultimately used to score study data should be described in detail in the final research report.

If a test scoring service is available on your campus, and if your test questions can be responded to on a standard, machine-scorable answer sheet, you can save yourself a lot of time and increase the accuracy of the scoring process if you take advantage of the service. If tests are to be machine scored, answer sheets should be checked carefully for stray pencil marks and a percentage of them should be scored by hand just to make sure that the key is correct and that the machine is scoring properly. The fact that your tests are being scored by a machine does not relieve you of the responsibility of carefully checking your data before and after processing.

Tabulation Procedures

After instruments have been scored, the results are transferred to summary data sheets and/or data cards. Recording of the scores in a systematic manner facilitates examination of the data as well as data analysis. If analysis is to consist of a simple comparison of the posttest scores of two or more groups, data are generally placed in columns, one for each group, in ascending or descending order. If pretest scores are involved, similar, additional columns are formed. If planned analyses involve subgroup comparisons, scores should be tabulated separately for each subgroup. For example, in a study investigating the interaction between two types of mathematics instruction and two levels of aptitude (a 2 × 2 factorial design), four subgroups are involved, as shown in Table 11.1. The same is true for questionnaires. If the research hypotheses or questions are concerned with subgroup comparisons, responses to each should be tallied by subgroup. To use a former example, a superintendent might be interested in comparing the attitude toward unions of elementary-level teachers with those of secondary teachers. Thus, for a question such as, "Would you join a union if given the opportunity?" the superintendent would tally the number of "yes," "no," and "undecided" responses separately for elementary- and secondary-level teachers.

When a number of different kinds of data are collected for each subject, such as several test scores and biographical information, data are frequently recorded on data cards, one card for each subject. The card for each subject follows the same format, and both the variable names and the actual data are frequently coded. The variable "pretest reading comprehension scores," for example, may be coded as PRC, and sex of subject may be recorded as "1" or "2" (male versus female). When a number of different analyses are to be performed, data cards facilitate analysis since they can be easily sorted and resorted to form the piles, or subgroups, required for each analysis.

If complex or multiple analyses are to be performed, or if a large number of

Table 11.1
Hypothetical Summary Data Sheet for the
Results of a Study Based on a 2 × 2 Factorial Design

	Method A	Method B
	68	55
	72	60
	76	65
	78	70
	80	72
	84	74
	84	74
	85	75
High Aptitude	86	75
	86	76
	88	76
	90	76
	91	78
	92	82
	96	87
	50	60
	58	66
	60	67
	62	68
	64	69
	64	69
	65	70
	65	70
Low Aptitude	66	71
	67	71
	70	72
	72	75
	72	76
	75	77
	78	79

subjects are involved, researchers frequently let computers do the calculations. If a computer is to be used, data must be presented in a machine-readable form, usually on punched cards. Using a procedure called keypunching, which is similar to typing, data can be transferred from data sheets or data cards onto special cards which are "fed into" the computer. In essence, a keypunch machine translates numbers into a series of punched holes in a card the computer can read and "understand." Since keypunching represents an extra step and therefore one more place where mistakes can be made, it is imperative that data be recorded systematically and consistently on data sheets or cards so that keypunch errors are minimized. Of course keypunched data cards should always be checked against original data sheets or cards before analysis.[2]

Once the data have been prepared for analysis, the choice of statistical procedures to be applied is determined not only by the research hypothesis and design but also by the type of measurement scale represented by the data.

---

2. More will be said concerning the use of the computer in data analysis in Chapter 14.

Types of Measurement Scales

Data for analysis result from the measurement of one or more variables. Depending upon the variables, and the way in which they are measured, different kinds of data result, representing different scales of measurement. There are four types of measurement scales: nominal, ordinal, interval, and ratio. It is important to know which type of scale is represented by your data since different statistics are appropriate for different scales of measurement.

Nominal Scales

A nominal scale represents the lowest level of measurement. Such a scale classifies persons or objects into two or more categories. Whatever the basis for classification, a person can only be in one category, and members of a given category have a common set of characteristics. Classifying subjects as tall versus short, male versus female, or introverted versus extroverted, are all examples of nominal scales. When a nominal scale is used, the data simply indicate how many subjects are in each category. For 100 first graders, for example, it might be determined that 40 attended kindergarten and 60 did not.

For identification purposes, categories are sometimes numbered from 1 to however many categories there are, say 4. It is important to realize, however, that the category labeled 4 is only different from the category labeled 3; 4 is not more, or higher, than 3, only different from 3. To avoid confusion, it is sometimes a good idea to label categories with letters instead of numbers, in other words, A, B, C, D instead of 1, 2, 3, 4. While nominal scales are not very precise, occasionally their use is necessary.

Ordinal Scales

An ordinal scale not only classifies subjects but also ranks them in terms of the degree to which they possess a characteristic of interest. In other words, an ordinal scale puts the subjects in order from highest to lowest, from most to least. With respect to height, for example, 50 subjects might be ranked from 1 to 50; the subject with rank 1 would be the tallest and the subject with rank 50 would be the shortest. It would be possible to say that one subject was taller or shorter than another subject. Indicating one's rank in a graduating class, or expressing one's score as a percentile rank, are measures of relative standing that represent ordinal scales.

Although ordinal scales do indicate that some subjects are higher, or better, than others, they do not indicate how much higher or how much better. In other words, intervals between ranks are not equal; the difference between rank 1 and rank 2 is not necessarily the same as the difference between rank 2 and rank 3, as the example below illustrates:

Rank	Height
1	6' 2"
2	6' 1"
3	5' 11"
4	5' 7"
5	5' 6"

Rank	Height
6	5′ 5″
7	5′ 4″
8	5′ 3″
9	5′ 2″
10	5′ 0″

The difference in height between the subject with rank 1 and the subject with rank 2 is 1 inch; the difference between rank 2 and rank 3 is 2 inches. In the example given, differences in height represented by differences in rank range from 1 inch to 4 inches. Thus, while an ordinal scale results in more precise measurement than a nominal scale, it still does not allow the level of precision usually desired in a research study.

Interval Scales

An interval scale has all the characteristics of a nominal scale and an ordinal scale, but in addition it is based upon predetermined equal intervals. Most of the tests used in educational research, such as achievement tests, aptitude tests, and intelligence tests, represent interval scales. Therefore, you will most often be working with statistics appropriate for interval data. When we talk about "scores," we are usually referring to interval data. When scores have equal intervals it is assumed, for example, that the difference between a score of 30 and a score of 40 is essentially the same as the difference between a score of 50 and a score of 60. Similarly, the difference between 81 and 82 is approximately the same as the difference between 82 and 83. If height is considered as an interval scale, then clearly the difference between a height of 5′ 6″ and 5′ 5″ (1 inch) is the same as the difference between 5′ 4″ and 5′ 3″. Thus, with an interval scale we can say not just that Egor is taller than Ziggie, but also that Egor is 7 feet tall and Ziggie is 5 feet tall. Interval scales, however, do not have a true zero point. Such scales typically have an arbitrary maximum score and an arbitrary minimum score, or zero point. If an IQ test produces scores ranging from 0 to 200, a score of 0 does not indicate the absence of intelligence nor does a score of 200 indicate possession of the ultimate intelligence. A score of 0 only indicates the lowest level of performance possible on that particular test and a score of 200 represents the highest level. Thus, scores resulting from administration of an interval scale can be added and subtracted, but not multiplied or divided. We can say that an achievement test score of 90 is 45 points higher than a score of 45 but we cannot say that a person scoring 90 knows twice as much as a person scoring 45. Similarly, a person with a measured IQ of 140 is not necessarily twice as smart, or twice as intelligent, as a person with a measured IQ of 70. For most educational measurement, however, such generalizations are not needed.

Ratio Scales

A ratio scale represents the highest, most precise, level of measurement. A ratio scale has all the advantages of the other types of scales and in addition it has a meaningful, true zero point. Height, weight, and time are examples of ratio scales.

The concept of "no time," for example, is a meaningful one. Because of the true zero point, not only can we say that the difference between a height of 3' 2" and a height of 4' 2" is the same as the difference between 5' 4" and 6' 4", but also that a man 6' 4" is twice as tall as a child 3' 2". Similarly, 60 minutes is 3 times as long as 20 minutes, and 40 pounds is 4 times as heavy as 10 pounds. Thus, with a ratio scale we can say that Egor is tall and Ziggie is short (nominal scale), Egor is taller than Ziggie (ordinal scale), Egor is 7 feet tall and Ziggie is 5 feet tall (interval scale), *and* that Egor is seven-fifths as tall as Ziggie. Since most physical measures represent ratio scales, but not psychological measures, ratio scales are not used very often in educational research.

A statistic appropriate for a lower level of measurement may be applied to data representing a higher level of measurement. A statistic appropriate for ordinal data, for example, may be used with interval data, since interval data possess all the characteristics of ordinal data and more. The reverse, however, is not true. A statistic appropriate for interval data cannot be applied to ordinal data since such a statistic requires equal intervals.

12

Descriptive Statistics

Enablers

After reading chapter 12 you should be able to:

1. List the steps involved in constructing a frequency polygon.
2. .Define or describe three measures of central tendency.
3. Define or describe three measures of variability.
4. List four characteristics of normal distributions.
5. List two characteristics of
   (a) positively skewed distributions, and
   (b) negatively skewed distributions.
6. Define or describe two measures of relationship.
7. Define or describe four measures of relative position.
8. Generate a column of 10 numbers each between 1 and 10 (in other words, make them up). You may use any number more than once. Assume those numbers represent scores on a posttest. Using these "scores" give the formula and compute the following (show your work):
   (a) mean,
   (b) standard deviation,
   (c) Pearson r (divide the column in half and make two columns of five scores each), and
   (d) z scores.

Types of Descriptive Statistics

The first step in data analysis is to describe, or summarize, the data using descriptive statistics. In some studies, such as certain questionnaire surveys, the entire analysis procedure may consist solely of calculating and interpreting descriptive statistics. Descriptive statistics permit the researcher to meaningfully describe many, many scores with a small number of indices. If such indices are calculated for a sample drawn from a population, the resulting values are referred to as statistics; if they are calculated for an entire population, they are referred to as parameters.

The major types of descriptive statistics are measures of central tendency, measures of variability, measures of relationship, and measures of relative position. Measures of central tendency are used to determine the typical or average score of a group of scores; measures of variability indicate how spread out a group of scores are; measures of relationship indicate to what degree two sets of scores are related; and measures of relative position describe a subject's performance compared to the performance of all other subjects. Before actually calculating any of these measures, it is often useful to present the data in graphic form.

Graphing Data

As discussed previously, data are often recorded on summary sheets, in columns, and placed in ascending order. Data in this form are easily graphed. Graphing data permits the researcher to see what the distribution of scores looks like. The shape of the distribution may not be self-evident, especially if a large number of scores are involved, and, as we shall see later, the shape of the distribution may influence our choice of certain descriptive statistics.

The most common method of graphing research data is to construct a frequency polygon. The first step in constructing a frequency polygon is to list all scores and to tabulate how many subjects received each score. If 85 tenth-grade students were administered an achievement test, the results might be as shown in Table 12.1.

Table 12.1
Frequency Distribution Based
on 85 Hypothetical Achievement Test Scores

Score	Frequency of Score
78	1
79	4
80	5
81	7
82	7
83	9
84	9
85	12
86	10
87	7
88	6
89	3
90	4
91	1
Total:	85 Students

Once the scores are tallied, the steps are as follows:

1. Place all the scores on a horizontal axis, at equal intervals, from lowest score to highest.

2. Place the frequencies of scores at equal intervals on the vertical axis, starting with zero.

3. For each score, find the point where the score intersects with its frequency of occurrence and make a dot.

4. Connect all the dots with straight lines (see Figure 12.1).

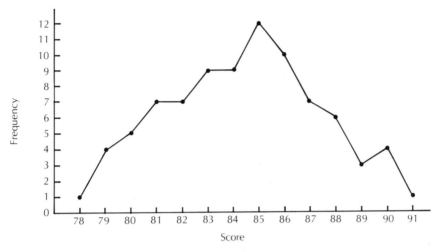

Figure 12.1.
Frequency polygon based on 85 hypothetical achievement test scores.

From Figure 12.1 we can see that most of the tenth graders scored at or near 85, with progressively fewer students achieving higher or lower scores. In other words, the scores appear to form a relatively normal distribution, a concept to be discussed a little later. This knowledge would be helpful in selecting an appropriate measure of central tendency.

Measures of Central Tendency

Measures of central tendency give the researcher a convenient way of describing a set of data with a single number. The number resulting from computation of a measure of central tendency represents the average or typical score attained by a group of subjects. The three most frequently encountered indices of central tendency are the mode, the median, and the mean. Each of these indices is appropriate for a different scale of measurement; the mode is appropriate for nominal data, the median for ordinal data, and the mean for interval or ratio data. Since most measurement in educational research represents an interval scale, the mean is the most frequently used measure of central tendency.

The Mode

The mode is the score that is attained by more subjects than any other score. For the data presented in Figure 12.1, for example, the mode is 85 since 12 subjects achieved that score. The mode is not established through calculation; it is determined by looking at a set of scores or at a graph of scores and seeing which score occurs most frequently. There are several problems associated with the mode, and it is therefore of limited value and seldom used. For one thing, a set of scores may have two (or more) modes, in which case it is referred to as bimodal. Another problem with the mode is that it is an unstable measure of central tendency; equal-sized samples randomly selected from the same accessible population are likely to have different modes. When nominal data are involved, however, the mode is the only appropriate measure of central tendency.

The Median

The median is that point in a distribution above and below which are 50% of the scores; in other words, the median is the midpoint. If there are an odd number of scores, the median is the middle score (assuming the scores are arranged in order). For example, for the scores 75, 80, 82, 83, 87, the median is 82, the middle score. If there are an even number of scores, the median is the point halfway between the two middle scores. For example, for the scores 21, 23, 24, 25, 26, 30, the median is 24.5; for the scores 50, 52, 55, 57, 59, 61, the median is 56. Thus, the median is not necessarily the same as one of the scores.

The median is only the midpoint of the scores and does not take into account each and every score; it ignores, for example, extremely high scores and extremely low scores. Two quite different sets of scores may have the same median. For example, for the scores 60, 62, 65, 67, 72, the median is 65; for the scores 60, 62, 65, 67, 89, the median is also 65. As we shall see shortly, this apparent lack of precision may be advantageous at times.

The median is the appropriate measure of central tendency when the data represent an ordinal scale. For certain distributions, the median may be selected as the most appropriate measure of central tendency even though the data represent an interval or ratio scale. While the median appears to be a rather simple index to determine, it cannot always be arrived at by simply looking at the scores; it does not always nearly fall between two different scores. For example, determining the median for the scores 80, 82, 84, 84, 84, 88 would require application of a relatively complex formula.[3]

The Mean

The mean is the arithmetic average of the scores and is the most frequently used measure of central tendency. It is calculated by adding up all of the scores and dividing that total by the number of scores. By the very nature of the way in which it is computed, the mean takes into account, or is based on, each and every score. Unlike the median, the mean is definitely affected by extreme scores. Thus, in certain cases, the median may actually give a more accurate estimate of the typical score.

In general, however, the mean is the preferred measure of central tendency. It is appropriate when the data represent either an interval or a ratio scale and is a more precise, stable index than both the median and the mode. If equal-sized samples are randomly selected from the same population, the means of those samples will be more similar to each other than either the medians or the modes. While the mode is almost never the most appropriate measure of central tendency when the data represent an interval or ratio scale, the median may be. In the situation described previously, in which there are one or more extreme scores, the median will not be the most accurate representation of the performance of the total group but it will be the best index of typical performance. As an example of this concept, suppose you had the following IQ scores: 96, 96, 97, 99, 100, 101, 102, 104, 155. For these scores, the measures of central tendency are:

---

3. For an explanation of the procedure used to determine the median, see Downie, N.M., & Heath, R.W. *Basic statistical methods* (4th ed.) New York: Harper & Row, 1974.

mode = 96 (most frequent score)
median = 100 (middle score)
mean = 105.6 (arithmetic average)

In this case, the median clearly best represents the typical score. The mode is too low, and the mean is higher than all of the scores except one. The mean is "pulled up" in the direction of the 155 score whereas the median essentially ignores it. The different pictures presented by the different measures are part of the reason for the phrase "lying with statistics." And in fact, by selecting one index of central tendency over another one may present a particular point of view in a stronger light. In a labor-versus-management union dispute over salary, for example, very different estimates of typical employee salaries will be obtained depending upon which index of central tendency is used. Let us say that the following are typical of employee salaries in a union company: $6,000, $7,000, $7,000, $8,000, $9,000, $10,000, $25,000. For these salaries, the measures of central tendency are:

mode = $7,000 (most frequent salary)
median = $8,000 (middle salary)
mean = $10,286 (arithmetic average)

Both labor and management could overstate their case, labor by using the mode and management by using the mean. The mean is higher than every salary except one, $25,000, which in all likelihood would be the salary of a company manager. Thus, in this case, the most appropriate, and most accurate, index of typical salary would be the median.

In research, we are not interested in "making cases" but rather in describing the data in the most accurate way. For the majority of sets of data the mean is the appropriate measure of central tendency.

Measures of Variability

Although measures of central tendency are very useful statistics for describing a set of data, they are not sufficient. Two sets of data that are very different can have identical means or medians. As an example, consider the following sets of data:

set A: 79   79   79   80   81   81   81
set B: 50   60   70   80   90   100   110

The mean of both sets of scores is 80 and the median of both is 80, but set A is very different from set B. In set A the scores are all very close together and clustered around the mean. In set B the scores are much more spread out; in other words, there is much more variation, or variability, in set B. Thus, there is a need for a measure that indicates how spread out the scores are, how much variability there is. There are a number of descriptive statistics that serve this purpose, and they are referred to as measures of variability. The three most frequently encountered are the range, the quartile deviation, and the standard deviation. While the standard deviation is by far the most often used, the range is the only appropriate measure of variability for nominal data, and the quartile deviation is the appropriate index of variability for ordinal data. As with measures of central tendency, measures of variability appropriate for nominal and ordinal data may be used with interval or ratio data even though the standard deviation is generally the preferred index for such data.

The Range

The range is simply the difference between the highest score and the lowest score in a distribution and is determined by subtraction. As an example, the range for the scores 79, 79, 79, 80, 81, 81, 81 is 2, while the range for the scores 50, 60, 70, 80, 90, 100, 110 is 60. Thus, if the range is small the scores are close together, whereas if the range is large the scores are more spread out. Like the mode, the range is not a very stable measure of variability, and its chief advantage is that it gives a quick, rough estimate of variability.

The Quartile Deviation

In "research talk" the quartile deviation is one-half of the difference between the upper quartile and the lower quartile in a distribution. In English, the upper quartile is the 75th percentile, that point below which are 75% of the scores; the lower quartile, correspondingly, is the 25th percentile, that point below which are 25% of the scores. By subtracting the lower quartile from the upper quartile and then dividing the result by two, we get a measure of variability. If the quartile deviation is small the scores are close together, whereas if the quartile deviation is large the scores are more spread out. The quartile deviation is a more stable measure of variability than the range and is appropriate whenever the median is appropriate. Calculation of the quartile deviation involves a process very similar to that used to calculate the median, which just happens to be the second quartile.[4]

The Standard Deviation

The standard deviation is appropriate when the data represent an interval or ratio scale and is by far the most frequently used index of variability. Like the mean, its counterpart measure of central tendency, the standard deviation is the most stable measure of variability and takes into account each and every score. In fact, the first step in calculating the standard deviation involves finding out how far each score is from the mean, that is, subtracting the mean from each score. Now, (concentrate!), if we square each difference, add up all the squares, and divide by the number of scores, we have a measure of variability called variance. If the variance is small, the scores are close together; if the variance is large, the scores are more spread out. The square root of the variance is called the standard deviation and, like variance, a small standard deviation indicates that scores are

---

4. For an explanation of the procedure used to determine the quartile deviation, see Downie & Heath.

close together and a large standard deviation indicates that the scores are more spread out.

If you know the mean and the standard deviation of a set of scores you have a pretty good picture of what the distribution looks like. An interesting phenomenon associated with the standard deviation is the fact that if the distribution is relatively normal (about which we will have more to say shortly), then the mean plus 3 standard deviations and the mean minus 3 standard deviations encompasses just about all the scores, over 99% of them. In other words, each distribution has its own mean and its own standard deviation that are calculated based on the scores. Once they are computed, three times the standard deviation added to the mean, and three times the standard deviation subtracted from the mean, includes just about all the scores.[5] The symbol for the mean is $\bar{X}$ and the standard deviation is usually abbreviated as SD. Thus, the above described concept can be expressed as follows:

$$\bar{X} \pm 3 \, SD = 99 + \% \text{ of the scores}$$

As an example, suppose that for a set of scores the mean $(\bar{X})$ is calculated to be 80 and the standard deviation (SD) to be 1. In this case the mean plus three standard deviations, $\bar{X} + 3 \, SD$, is equal to $80 + 3(1) = 80 + 3 = 83$. The mean minus three standard deviations, $\bar{X} - 3 \, SD$, is equal to $80 - 3(1) = 80 - 3 = 77$. Thus, almost all the scores fall between 77 and 83. This makes sense since, as we mentioned before, a small standard deviation (in this case $SD = 1$) indicates that the scores are close together, not very spread out.

As another example, suppose that for another set of scores the mean $(\bar{X})$ is again calculated to be 80, but this time the standard deviation (SD) is calculated to be 4. In this case the mean plus three standard deviations, $\bar{X} + 3 \, SD$, is equal to $80 + 3(4) = 80 + 12 = 92$. In case you still do not see,

$$80 \text{ plus } 1 \, SD = 80 + 4 = 84$$
$$80 \text{ plus } 2 \, SD = 80 + 4 + 4 = 88$$
$$80 \text{ plus } 3 \, SD = 80 + 4 + 4 + 4 = 92.$$

Or, to explain it another way, 80 plus 1 $SD = 80 + 4 = 84$, plus another $SD = 84 + 4 = 88$, plus one more (the third) $SD = 88 + 4 = 92$. Now, the mean minus three standard deviations, $\bar{X} - 3 \, SD$, is equal to $80 - 3(4) = 80 - 12 = 68$. In other words,

$$80 \text{ minus } 1 \, SD = 80 - 4 = 76$$
$$80 \text{ minus } 2 \, SD = 80 - 4 - 4 = 72$$
$$80 \text{ minus } 3 \, SD = 80 - 4 - 4 - 4 = 68.$$

Or, to explain it another way, 80 minus 1 $SD = 80 - 4 = 76$, minus another $SD = 76 - 4 = 72$, minus one more (the third) $SD = 72 - 4 = 68$. Thus, almost

---

5. The number 3 is a constant. In other words, for any normal distribution of scores, the standard deviation multiplied by 3 and then added to the mean and subtracted from the mean will include almost all the scores in the distribution.

all the scores fall between 68 and 92. This makes sense since a larger standard deviation (in this case $SD = 4$) indicates that the scores are more spread out. Clearly, if you know the mean and standard deviation of a set of scores you have a pretty good idea of what the scores look like. You know the average score and you know how spread out, or how variable, the scores are. Thus, together they describe a set of data quite well.

The Normal Curve

The ±3 concept is valid only when the scores are normally distributed, that is, form a normal, or bell-shaped, curve. Most of you are probably familiar with the concept of grading "on the normal curve." When this is done, a certain percentage of students receive a grade of C, a smaller percentage receive Bs and Ds and an even smaller percentage receive As and Es, or Fs. Such grading is based on the assumption (which may or may not be true in a given case) that the students' scores do indeed form a normal curve. Many, many variables, such as height, weight, IQ scores, and achievement scores, do yield a normal curve if a sufficient number of subjects are measured.

Normal Distributions

If a variable is normally distributed, that is, does form a normal curve, then several things are true. First, 50% of the scores are above the mean and 50% of the scores are below the mean. Second, the mean, the median, and the mode are the same. Third, most scores are near the mean and the farther from the mean a score is, the fewer the number of subjects who attained that score. Fourth, the same number, or percentage, of scores is between the mean and plus one standard deviation ($\bar{X} + 1\,SD$) as is between the mean and minus one standard deviation ($\bar{X} - 1\,SD$), and similarly for $\bar{X} \pm 2\,SD$ and $\bar{X} \pm 3\,SD$ (see Figure 12.2). In Figure 12.2, the symbol σ (the Greek letter sigma) is used to represent the standard deviation, that is, $1\sigma = 1\,SD$, and the mean ($\bar{X}$) is designated as 0. The vertical lines at each of the SD (σ) points delineate a certain percentage of the total area under the curve. As Figure 12.2 indicates, if a set of scores forms a normal distribution, the $\bar{X} + 1\,SD$ includes 34.13% of the scores and the $\bar{X} - 1\,SD$ includes 34.13% of the scores. Each succeeding standard deviation encompasses a constant percentage of the cases. Since the $\bar{X} \pm 2.58\,SD$ (approximately 2½ SDs) includes 99% of the cases, we see that $\bar{X} \pm 3\,SD$ includes almost all the scores, as pointed out previously.

Below the row of SDs is a row of percentages. As you move from left to right, from point to point, the cumulative percentage of scores which fall below each point is indicated. Thus, at the point which corresponds to $-3\,SD$, we see that only .1% of the scores fall below this point. The numerical value corresponding to $+1\,SD$, on the other hand, is a figure higher than 84.1% (rounded to 84% on the next row) of the scores. Relatedly, the next row, percentile equivalents, also involves cumulative percentages. The figure 20 in this row, for example, indicates that 20% of the scores fall below this point. While we will discuss percentiles and the remaining rows further as we proceed through this chapter, we will look at one more row at this time. Near the bottom of Figure 12.2, under Wechsler Scales, is a row labeled Deviation IQs. This row indicates that the mean IQ

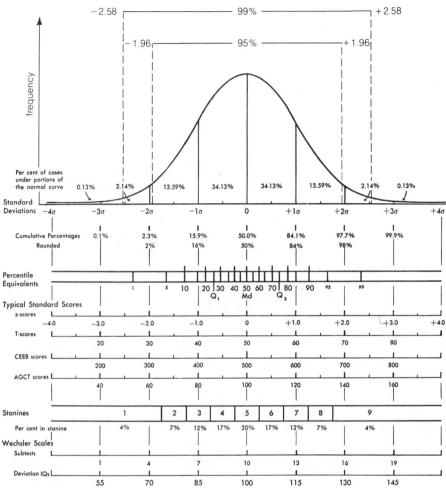

Figure 12.2.
Characteristics of the normal curve.
Note: Based on a figure appearing in *Test Service Bulletin* No. 48,
January, 1955 of The Psychological Corporation.

for the Wechsler Scale is 100 and the standard deviation is 15 (115 is in the column corresponding to +1 *SD* (+1σ) and since the mean is 100, 115 represents $\bar{X}$ + 1 *SD* = 100 + 15 = 115. An IQ of 145 represents a score 3 *SD*s above the mean (average) IQ. If your IQ is in this neighborhood you are certainly a candidate for MENSA! An IQ of 145 corresponds to a percentile of 99.9. On the other side of the curve we see that an IQ of 85 corresponds to a score one standard deviation below the mean ($\bar{X}$ − 1 *SD* = 100 − 15 = 85) and to the 16th percentile. Note that the mean always corresponds to the 50th percentile. In other words, the average score is always that point above which are 50% of the cases and below which are 50% of the cases. Thus, if scores are normally distributed the following statements are true:

$\overline{X} \pm 1.0\,SD$ = approximately 68% of the scores
$\overline{X} \pm 2.0\,SD$ = approximately 95% of the scores
                (1.96 SD is exactly 95%)
$\overline{X} \pm 2.5\,SD$ = approximately 99% of the scores
                (2.58 SD is exactly 99%)
$\overline{X} \pm 3.0\,SD$ = approximately 99+% of the scores

And similarly, the following are always true:

$\overline{X} - 3.0\,SD$ = approximately the .1 percentile
$\overline{X} - 2.0\,SD$ = approximately the 2nd percentile
$\overline{X} - 1.0\,SD$ = approximately the 16th percentile
$\overline{X}$ = the 50th percentile
$\overline{X} + 1.0\,SD$ = approximately the 84th percentile
$\overline{X} + 2.0\,SD$ = approximately the 98th percentile
$\overline{X} + 3.0\,SD$ = approximately the 99+ percentile

You may have noticed that the ends of the curve never touch the baseline and that there is no definite number of standard deviations which corresponds to 100%. This is because the curve allows for the existence of unexpected extremes at either end and because each additional standard deviation includes only a tiny fraction of a percent of the scores. As an example, for the IQ test the mean plus 5 standard deviations would be $100 + 5(15) = 100 + 75 = 175$. Surely 5 SDs would include everyone. Wrong! There has been a very small number of persons who have scored near 200, which corresponds to +6.67 SDs. Thus, while ±3 SDs includes just about everyone, the exact number of standard deviations required to include every score varies from variable to variable.

As mentioned earlier, many variables form a normal distribution, including physical measures, such as height and weight, and psychological measures, such as intelligence and aptitude. In fact, most variables measured in education form normal distributions *if* enough subjects are tested. In other words, a variable that is normally distributed in a population may not be in a small sample. In Figure 12.2, the standard deviation is symbolized as σ, instead of SD, to indicate that the curve represents the scores of a population, not a sample. Depending upon the size and nature of a particular sample, the assumption of a normal curve may or may not be a valid one. Since research studies deal with a finite number of subjects, and often a not very large number, research data only more or less approximate a normal curve; correspondingly all of the equivalencies (standard deviation, percentage of cases, and percentile) are also only approximations.[6] This is an important point since most statistics used in educational research are based on the assumption that the variable is normally distributed. If this assumption is badly violated in a given sample then certain statistics should not be used.

In general, however, the fact that most variables are normally distributed allows us quickly to determine many useful pieces of information concerning a set of data.

---

6. Thus, we see the fallacy of some normal-curve grading which assumes that each class forms a normal distribution of ability and effort, a highly improbable event.

Skewed Distributions

When a distribution is not normal, it is said to be skewed. A normal distribution is symmetrical and the values of the mean, the median, and the mode are the same. A distribution which is skewed is not symmetrical, and the values of the mean, the median, and the mode are different. In a symmetrical distribution, there are approximately the same number of extreme scores (very high and very low) at each end of the distribution. In a skewed distribution there are more extreme scores at one end than the other. If the extreme scores are at the lower end of the distribution, the distribution is said to be negatively skewed; if the extreme scores are at the upper, or higher, end of the distribution, the distribution is said to be positively skewed (see Figure 12.3).

As we can see by looking at the negatively skewed distribution, most of the subjects did well but a few did very poorly. Conversely, for the positively skewed distribution, most of the subjects did poorly but a few did very well. In both cases, the mean is "pulled" in the direction of the extreme scores. Since the mean is affected by extreme scores and the median is not, the mean is always closer to the extreme scores than the median. Thus, for a negatively skewed distribution the mean ($\overline{X}$) is always lower, or smaller, than the median (md); for a positively skewed distribution the mean is always higher, or greater, than the median. Since the mode is not affected by extreme scores, no "always" statements can be made concerning its relationship to the mean and the median in a skewed distribution. Usually, however, as Figure 12.3 indicates, in a negatively skewed distribution the mean and median are lower, or smaller, than the mode, whereas in a positively skewed distribution the mean and the median are higher, or greater, than the mode. To summarize:

negatively skewed: mean < median < mode

positively skewed: mean > median > mode

Since the relationship between the mean and the median is a constant, the skewness of a distribution can be determined without constructing a frequency polygon. If the mean is less than the median, the distribution is negatively skewed; if the mean and the median are the same, or very close, the distribution is symmetrical; if the mean is greater than the median, the distribution is positively skewed. The farther apart the mean and the median are, the more skewed is the

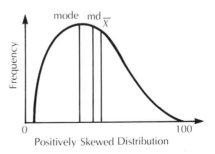

Negatively Skewed Distribution   Positively Skewed Distribution

Figure 12.3.
A positively skewed distribution and a negatively skewed distribution, each resulting from the administration of a 100-item test.

distribution. If the distribution is very skewed, then the assumption of normality required for many statistics is violated.

Measures of Relationship

Correlational research was discussed in detail in chapter 8. You will recall that correlational research involves collecting data in order to determine whether and to what degree, a relationship exists between two or more quantifiable variables—not a causal relationship, just a relationship. Degree of relationship is expressed as a correlation coefficient which is computed based on the two sets of scores. The correlation coefficient provides an estimate of just how related two variables are. If two variables are highly related, a correlation coefficient near +1.00 (or −1.00) will be obtained; if two variables are not related, a coefficient near .00 will be obtained. There are a number of different methods of computing a correlation coefficient; which one is appropriate depends upon the scale of measurement represented by the data. The two most frequently used correlational analyses are the rank difference correlation coefficient, usually referred to as the Spearman rho, and the product moment correlation coefficient, usually referred to as the Pearson r.

The Spearman Rho

If the data for one of the variables are expressed as ranks instead of scores, the Spearman rho is the appropriate measure of correlation.[7] The Spearman rho is thus appropriate when the data represent an ordinal scale (although it may be used with interval data) and is used when the median and quartile deviation are used.[8] If only one of the variables to be correlated is in rank order, for example class standing at time of graduation; then the other variable to be correlated with it must also be expressed in terms of ranks in order to use the Spearman rho technique. Thus, if intelligence were to be correlated with class standing, students would have to be ranked in terms of intelligence, and IQ scores per se would not be involved in actual computation of the correlation coefficient.

Although the Spearman rho is interpreted in the same way as the Pearson r and produces a coefficient somewhere between −1.00 and +1.00 (if a group of subjects achieve identical ranks on two variables the coefficient will be +1.00), there is one difference between the techniques which should be mentioned. The Pearson r permits several subjects to have the same score on a given variable but the Spearman rho does not permit several subjects to have the same rank. If more than one subject receives the same score then their ranks are averaged. In other words, if two subjects have the same, highest score they are each assigned the average of rank 1 and rank 2, namely rank 1.5. Similarly, the 24th and 25th highest scores, if identical, would each be assigned the rank 24.5.[9]

---

7. Rho is a Greek letter and is pronounced like row, row, row your boat.
8. Statistics appropriate for ordinal data are referred to as nonparametric. This concept will be discussed in chapter 13.
9. For a description of the procedures involved in calculating the Spearman rho, see Downie & Heath.

The Pearson r

The Pearson r is the most appropriate measure of correlation when the sets of data to be correlated represent either interval or ratio scales. Like the mean and the standard deviation, the Pearson r takes into account each and every score in both distributions; it is also the most stable measure of correlation. Since most educational measures represent interval scales, the Pearson r is usually the appropriate coefficient for determing relationship. An assumption associated with the application of the Pearson r is that the relationship between the variables being correlated is a linear one. If this is not the case, the Pearson r will not yield a valid indication of relationship. If there is any question concerning the linearity of the relationship, the two sets of data should be plotted as previously shown in Figure 8.1.

Measures of Relative Position

Measures of relative position indicate where a score is in relation to all other scores in the distribution. In other words, measures of relative position permit you to express how well an individual has performed as compared to all other individuals in the sample who have been measured on the same variable. A major advantage of such measures is that they make it possible to compare the performance of an individual on two or more different tests. For example, if Ziggy's score in reading is 40 and his score in math is 35 it does not follow that he did better in reading; 40 may have been the lowest score on the reading test and 35 the highest score on the math test! Measures of relative position express different scores on a common scale, a common frame of reference. The two most frequently used measures of relative position are percentile ranks and standard scores.

Percentile Ranks

A percentile rank indicates the percentage of scores that fall below a given score. If a score of 65 corresponds to a percentile rank of 80, the 80th percentile, this means that 80% of the scores in the distribution are lower than 65. Or, to put it another way, if Suzy Smart scored at the 95th percentile, this would mean that she did better than 95% of the other students who took the same test. Conversely, if Dudley Veridull scored at the 2nd percentile this would mean that Dudley only did better than, or received a higher score than, 2% of the students.

Percentiles are appropriate for data representing an ordinal scale, although they are frequently computed for interval data. The median of a set of scores corresponds to the 50th percentile which makes sense since the median is the middle point and therefore the point below which are 50% of the scores. While percentile ranks are not used very often in research studies, they are frequently used in the public schools to report test results of students in a form which is understandable by most audiences.

Standard Scores

Figure 12.2 depicts a number of standard scores. Basically, a standard score is a derived score that expresses how far a given raw score is from some reference point, typically the mean, in terms of standard deviation units. A standard score is a measure of relative position which is appropriate when the test data represent an interval or ratio scale of measurement. The most commonly reported and used standard scores are z scores, T scores (or Z scores), and stanines. Standard scores allow scores from different tests to be compared on a common scale and, unlike percentiles, we can validly perform mathematical operations on them in order to average them, for example. Averaging scores on a series of classroom tests in order to arrive at a final grade is like averaging apples and oranges and getting an "orapple." Such tests are likely to vary in level of difficulty and variability of scores. By converting test scores to standard scores, however, we can average them and arrive at a valid final grade.

The normal curve equivalencies indicated in Figure 12.2 for the various standard scores are accurate only to the degree to which the distribution is normal. Further, standard score equivalencies hold only if all the derived scores are based on the raw scores of the same group. A CEEB (College Entrance Examination Board) score of 700, for example, is not equivalent to a Wechsler IQ of 130 because the tests were normed on different groups. If a set of raw scores is normally distributed then so are the standard score equivalents. But all distributions are not normal, even if the variable being measured is. Height, for example, is normally distributed, but the measured heights of the girls in a seventh-grade gym class may not be for a variety of reasons. There is a procedure for transforming a set of raw scores which insures that the distribution of standard scores will be normal. Raw scores thus transformed are referred to as normalized scores. All resulting standard scores are normally distributed and the normal curve equivalencies are accurate.

z Scores   A z score is the most basic standard score. It expresses how far a score is from the mean in terms of standard deviation units. A score which is exactly "on" the mean corresponds to a z of 0; a score which is exactly 1 standard deviation above the mean (such as an IQ of 115) corresponds to a z of +1.00; a z score which is exactly 2 standard deviations below the mean (such as an IQ of 70) corresponds to a z of −2.00. Get it? As Figure 12.2 indicates, if a set of scores is transformed into a set of z scores (each score is expressed as a z score), the new distribution has a mean of 0 and a standard deviation of 1.

The major advantage of z scores is that they allow scores from different tests or subtests to be compared. As an example, suppose Bobby Bonker's mother, a woman who is really on top of things, comes in and asks his teacher, "How is Bobby doing in the basic skills area?" If the teacher tells her that Bobby's reading score was 50 and his math score was 40, she still does not know how well Bobby is doing. In fact, she might get the false impression that he is better in reading when in fact 50 might be a very low score on the reading test and 40 may be a very good score on the math test. Now suppose Bobby's teacher also tells his mother that the average score (the mean, $\bar{X}$) on the reading test was 60, and the average score on the math test was 30. Aha! Now it looks as if Bobby is better in math than in reading. Further, if the standard deviation (*SD*) on both tests was 10, Bobby's true status becomes even more evident. Since his score in reading is exactly 1 *SD* below the mean (60 − 10 = 50), his z score is −1.00. On the other hand, his score in math is 1 *SD* above the mean (30 + 10 = 40) and his z score is

+1.00. Converting z scores to percentiles shows that Bobby is clearly better in math than in reading:

	Raw Score	X̄	SD	z	Percentile
Reading	50	60	10	−1.00	16th
Math	40	30	10	+1.00	84th

Of course, scores do not always happen to be exactly 1 *SD* (or 2 *SD*, 3 *SD*) above or below the mean. Usually we have to apply the following formula to convert a raw score to a z score:

$$z = \frac{X - \bar{X}}{SD}, \qquad \text{where } X = \text{the raw score}$$

The only problem with z scores is that they involve negative numbers and decimals. It would be pretty hard to explain to Mrs. Bonker that her son was a −1.00. How do you tell a mother her son is a negative?! A simple solution is to transform z scores into *T* (or *Z*) scores. As Figure 12.2 indicates, z scores are actually the building blocks for a number of standard scores. Other standard scores represent transformations of z scores that communicate the same information in a more generally understandable form by eliminating negatives and/or decimals.

T Scores   A *T* score is nothing more than a z score expressed in a different form. To transform a z score to a *T* score, you simply multiply the z score by 10 and add 50. In other words, $T = 10z + 50$. Thus a z score of 0 (the mean score) becomes a *T* score of 50 [$T = 10(0) + 50 = 0 + 50 = 50$]. A z score of +1.00 becomes a *T* score of 60 [$T = 10(1.00) + 50 = 10 + 50 = 60$], and a z score of −1.00 becomes a *T* score of 40 [$T = 10(−1.00) + 50 = −10 + 50 = 40$]. Thus, when scores are transformed to *T* scores, the new distribution has a mean of 50 and a standard deviation of 10 (see Figure 12.2). It would clearly be much easier to communicate to Mrs. Bonker that Bobby is a 40 in reading and a 60 in math and that the average score is 50 than to tell her that he is a +1.00 and a −1.00 and the average score is .00.

If the raw score distribution is normal, then so is the z score distribution. If this is the case, then the transformation $10z + 50$ produces a *T* distribution. If, on the other hand, the original distribution is not normal (such as when a small sample group is involved), then neither is the z score distribution. In such cases the distribution resulting from the $10z + 50$ transformation is more accurately referred to as a *Z* distribution. Of course even with a set of raw scores that are not normally distributed, we can produce a set of normalized *Z* scores. In either case, we can use the normal curve equivalencies to convert such scores into corresponding percentiles, or vice versa. As Figure 12.2 indicates, for example, at *T* of $50 = P_{50}$. Similarly, the second percentile corresponds to a *T* of 30 and a *T* of 60 corresponds to the 84th percentile. The same is true for the other standard score transformations illustrated in Figure 12.2. The CEEB distribution is formed by multiplying *T* scores by 10 in order to eliminate decimals; it is calculated directly using CEEB $= 100z + 500$. The AGCT (Army General Classification Test) distribution is formed by multiplying T scores by 2, and is formed directly using AGCT = $200z$ + 100. In both cases, given values can be converted to percentiles (and vice versa) using normal curve equivalencies. Thus, a CEEB score of 400 corresponds to the 16th percentile and the 98th percentile corresponds to an AGCT score of 140.

Stanines Stanines are standard scores that divide a distribution into nine parts. Stanine (short for "standard nine") equivalencies are derived using the formula $2z$ + 5 and rounding resulting values to the nearest whole number. Stanines 2 through 8 each represent ½SD of the distribution; stanines 1 and 9 include the remainder. In other words, stanine 5 includes ½SD around the mean ($\overline{X}$); that is, it equals $\overline{X} \pm$ ¼SD. Stanine 6 goes from +¼SD to +¾SD (¼SD + ½SD = ¾SD), and so forth. Stanine 1 includes any score that is less than −1¾ SD (−1.75 SD) below the mean, and stanine 9 includes any score that is greater than +1¾ SD (+1.75 SD) above the mean. As figure 12.2 indicates (see the row of figures directly beneath the stanines), stanine 5 includes 20% of the scores, stanines 4 and 6 each contain 17%, stanines 3 and 7 each contain 12%, 2 and 8 each contain 7%, and 1 and 9 each contain 4% of the scores (percentages approximate).

Like percentiles, stanines are very frequently reported in norms tables for standardized tests. They are very popular with school systems because they are so easy to understand and to explain to others. While they are not as exact as other standard scores, they are useful for a variety of purposes. They are frequently used as a basis for grouping, and are also used as a criterion for selecting students for special programs. A remediation program, of example, may select students who scored in the first and second (and perhaps the third) stanine on a standardized reading test.

Calculation for Interval Data

Since most data in educational research studies represent interval scales, we will calculate the measure of central tendency, variability, relationship, and relative position appropriate for interval data. There are several alternate formulas available for computing each of these measures; in each case, however, we will use the easiest formula, the raw score formula. At first glance some of the formulas may look scary but they are really easy. The only reason they look hard is because they involve symbols with which you are unfamiliar. As promised, however, each formula transforms "magically" into an arithmetic problem in one easy step; all you have to do is substitute the correct numbers for the correct symbols.

Symbols

Before we start calculating you should get acquainted with a few basic symbols. First, "X" is usually used to symbolize a raw score, any score. If you see a column of numbers, and at the top of that column is an X, you know that the column represents a set of scores. If there are two sets of scores they may be labeled X_1 and X_2 or X and Y, it does not matter which.

Another symbol used frequently is the Greek letter Σ, which is used to indicate addition: Σ means "the sum of," or "add them up." Thus ΣX means "add up all the Xs," and ΣY means "add up all the Ys." Isn't this easy?

Now, if any symbol has a bar over it, such as $\overline{X}$, that indicates the mean, or arithmetic average, of the scores. Thus $\overline{X}$ refers to the mean of the X scores and $\overline{Y}$ refers to the mean of the Y scores.

A capital N refers to the number of subjects; $N = 20$ means that there are 20 subjects (N for number makes sense, doesn't it?). If one analysis involves several groups, the number of subjects in each group is indicated with a lowercase letter n and a subscript indicating the group. If there are three groups, and the first group has 15 subjects, the second group has 18 subjects, and the third group has 20 subjects, this is symbolized as $n_1 = 15$, $n_2 = 18$, and $n_3 = 20$. The total number of subjects is represented as $N = 53$ $(15 + 18 + 20 = 53)$.

Finally, you must get straight the difference between ΣX^2 and $(\Sigma X)^2$; they do not mean the same thing. Different formulas may include one or the other or both and it is very important to interpret each correctly; a formula tells you what to do and you must do exactly what it tells you. Now let us look at ΣX^2. What does it tell you? The Σ tells you that you are supposed to add something up. What you are supposed to add up are X^2 s. What do you suppose X^2 means? Right. It means the square of the score; if $X = 4$, then $X^2 = 4^2 = 4 \times 4 = 16$. Thus, ΣX^2 says to square each score and *then* add up all the squares. Now let us look at $(\Sigma X)^2$. Since whatever is in the parentheses is always done first, the first thing we do is ΣX. You already know what that means, it means "add up all the scores." And then what? Right. You add up all the scores and *then* you square the total. Do you see the difference between ΣX^2 (square each number and then add up all the squares) and $(\Sigma X)^2$ (add up all the scores and then square the total)? Good.

To summarize, symbols commonly used in statistical formulas are as follows:

$$X = \text{any score}$$
$$\Sigma = \text{the sum of; add them up}$$
$$\Sigma X = \text{the sum of all the scores}$$
$$\overline{X} = \text{the mean, or arithmetic average, of the scores}$$
$$N = \text{total number of subjects}$$
$$n = \text{number of subjects in a particular group}$$
$$\Sigma X^2 = \text{the sum of all the squares; square each score}$$
$$\text{and add up all the squares}$$
$$(\Sigma X)^2 = \text{the square of the sum; add up all the scores}$$
$$\text{and square the sum, or total}$$

The Mean

Although a sample size of 5 is hardly ever considered to be acceptable, we will work with this number for the sake of illustration. In other words, all of our calculations will be based on the test scores for five subjects so that you can concentrate on how the calculation is being done and will not get lost in the numbers. For the same reason we will also use very small numbers. Now let us assume we have the following scores for some old friends of ours and we want to compute the mean, or arithmetic average.

	X
Iggie	1
Hermie	2
Fifi	3
Teenie	4
Tiny	5

Remember that a column labeled X means "here come the scores!"

The formula for the mean is $\overline{X} = \dfrac{\Sigma X}{N}$

You are now looking at a statistic. Looks bad, right? Now let us first see what it really *says*. It reads "the mean ($\overline{X}$) is equal to the sum of the scores (ΣX) divided by the number of subjects (N)." So, in order to find $\overline{X}$ we need ΣX and N.

$$\begin{array}{c} X \\ 1 \\ 2 \\ 3 \\ 4 \\ \underline{5} \\ \Sigma X = 15 \end{array}$$

Clearly, $\Sigma X = 1 + 2 + 3 + 4 + 5 = 15$
$N = 5$ (there are 5 subjects right?)

Now we have everything we need to find the mean and all we have to do is substitute the correct number for each symbol.

$$\overline{X} = \frac{\Sigma X}{N} = \frac{15}{5}$$

Now what do we have? Right! An arithmetic problem. A hard arithmetic problem? No! An elementary school arithmetic problem? Yes! And all we did was to substitute each symbol with the appropriate number. Thus,

$$\overline{X} = \frac{\Sigma X}{N} = \frac{15}{5} = 3$$

and the mean is equal to 3. If you look at the scores you can see that 3 is clearly the average score. Was that hard? Cer-tain-ly not! And guess what—you just learned how to do a statistic! Are they all going to be that easy? Of course!

The Standard Deviation

Earlier we discussed the fact that the standard deviation is the square root of the variance which is based on the distance of each score from the mean. To calculate the standard deviation (SD), however, we do not have to calculate deviation scores; we can use a raw score formula which gives us the same answer with less grief. Now, before you look at the formula remember that no matter how bad it looks it is going to turn into an easy arithmetic problem. Ready?

$$SD = \sqrt{\frac{SS}{N}}, \text{ where } SS = \Sigma X^2 - \frac{(\Sigma X)^2}{N}$$

In other words, the *SD* is equal to the square root of the sum of squares (SS) divided by *N*. Now just relax and look at each piece of the formula; you already know what each piece means. Starting with the easy one, *N* refers to what? Right—the number of subjects. How about (ΣX)? Right—the sum of the scores. And $(\Sigma X)^2$? Right—the square of the sum of the scores. That leaves ΣX^2 which means the sum of what? . . . . Fantastic. The sum of the squares. Okay, let us use the same scores we used to calculate the mean. The first thing we need to do is to square each score and then add those squares up—while we are at it we can also go ahead and add up all the scores.

	X	X²	
Iggie	1	1	
Hermie	2	4	$\Sigma X = 15$
Fifi	3	9	$\Sigma X^2 = 55$
Teenie	4	16	$N = 5$
Tiny	5	25	
	$\Sigma X = 15$	$\Sigma X^2 = 55$	

Do we have everything we need? Does the formula ask for anything else? We are in business. Substituting each symbol with its numerical equivalent we get:

$$SS = \Sigma X^2 - \frac{(\Sigma X)^2}{N} = 55 - \frac{(15)^2}{5}$$

Now what do we have? A statistic? No! An arithmetic problem? Yes! A hard arithmetic problem? No! It is harder than 15/5 but it is not *hard*. If we just do what the formula tells us to do we will have no problem at all. The first thing it tells us to do is to square 15:

$$SS = \Sigma X^2 - \frac{(\Sigma X)^2}{N} = 55 - \frac{(15)^2}{5} = 55 - \frac{225}{5}$$

So far so good? Now, just in case you are not too good at squaring ($15 \times 15 = 225$), many numbers have been squared for you in Table A.3 in the Appendix. The next thing the formula tells you to do is to divide 225 by 5:

$$= 55 - 45$$

It is looking a lot better; now it is *really* an easy arithmetic problem. Okay the next step is to subtract 45 from 55:

$$SS = 10$$

Mere child's play. Think you can figure out the next step? Terrific! Now that we have SS, we simply substitute it into the *SD* formula as follows:

$$SD = \sqrt{\frac{SS}{N}} = \sqrt{\frac{10}{5}} = \sqrt{2}$$

H-m-m-m, you say you are not good at square rootin'. As luck would have it, and as you may have already discovered, Table A.3 includes square roots for many numbers, including 2. Thus,

$$SD = \sqrt{2} = 1.4$$

and the standard deviation is 1.4. If we had calculated the standard deviation for the IQ distribution shown in Figure 12.2 what would we have gotten? Right—15. Now you know how to do *two* statistics. Were they hard? No! Just keep remembering that when you look at the next formula; no matter how bad it looks, it is really just an arithmetic problem.[10]

The Pearson r

The formula for the Pearson r *looks* very, very complicated, but it is not (have I lied to you so far?). It looks bad because it has a lot of pieces but each piece is quite simple to calculate. Now, to calculate a Pearson r we need two sets of scores. Let us assume we have the following sets of scores for two variables for our old friends:

	X	Y
Iggie	1	2
Hermie	2	3
Fifi	3	4
Teenie	4	3
Tiny	5	5

The question is, "Are these two variables related?" Positively? Negatively? Not at all?

In order to answer those questions we apply the formula for the Pearson r to the data. Here goes!

$$r = \frac{\Sigma XY - \frac{(\Sigma X)(\Sigma Y)}{N}}{\sqrt{\left[\Sigma X^2 - \frac{(\Sigma X)^2}{N}\right]\left[\Sigma Y^2 - \frac{(\Sigma Y)^2}{N}\right]}}$$

Now, if you look at each piece you will see that you already know how to calculate all of them except one. You should have no problem with ΣX, ΣY, ΣX^2, or ΣY^2. And even though there are 10 scores there are only 5 subjects so $N = 5$. What is left? The only new symbol in the formula is ΣXY. What could that mean? Well, you know that it is the sum of something, namely the XYs, whatever they are. An XY is just what you would guess it is—the product of an X score and its corresponding Y score. Thus, Iggie's XY score is $1 \times 2 = 2$, and Teenie's XY score is $4 \times 3 = 12$. Okay, let us get all the pieces we need:

---

10. Remember, it is perfectly all right to use a calculator. In fact, it is a good idea! Some calculators will compute square roots for you.

	X	Y	X²	Y²	XY
Iggie	1	2	1	4	2
Hermie	2	3	4	9	6
Fifi	3	4	9	16	12
Teenie	4	3	16	9	12
Tiny	5	5	25	25	25
	15	17	55	63	57
	ΣX	ΣY	ΣX²	ΣY²	ΣXY

Now guess what we are going to do. Right! We are going to turn that horrible-looking statistic into a horrible-looking arithmetic problem! Of course it will really be an easy arithmetic problem if we do it one step at a time.

$$r = \frac{\Sigma XY - \frac{(\Sigma X)(\Sigma Y)}{N}}{\sqrt{\left[\Sigma X^2 - \frac{(\Sigma X)^2}{N}\right]\left[\Sigma Y^2 - \frac{(\Sigma Y)^2}{N}\right]}} = \frac{57 - \frac{(15)(17)}{5}}{\sqrt{\left[55 - \frac{(15)^2}{5}\right]\left[63 - \frac{(17)^2}{5}\right]}}$$

It still does not look good but you have to admit it looks better! Let us start with the numerator (for you nonmathematical types, the top part). The first thing the formula tells you to do is to multiply 15 by 17:

$$= \frac{57 - \frac{225}{5}}{\sqrt{\left[55 - \frac{(15)^2}{5}\right]\left[63 - \frac{(17)^2}{5}\right]}}$$

The next step is to divide 255 by 5:

$$= \frac{57 - 51}{\sqrt{\left[55 - \frac{(15)^2}{5}\right]\left[63 - \frac{(17)^2}{5}\right]}}$$

The next step is a real snap. All you have to do is subtract 51 from 57:

$$= \frac{6}{\sqrt{\left[55 - \frac{(15)^2}{5}\right]\left[63 - \frac{(17)^2}{5}\right]}}$$

So much for the numerator. Was that hard? NO! Au contraire, it was very easy. Right? Right. Now for the denominator (the bottom part). If you think hard you will realize that you have seen part of the denominator before. Hint: It was not in connection with the mean. Let us go through it step by step anyway just in case you did not really understand what we were doing the last time we did it. The first thing the formula says to do is square 15:

$$= \frac{6}{\sqrt{\left[55 - \frac{225}{5}\right]\left[63 - \frac{(17)^2}{5}\right]}}$$

Now we divide 225 by 5:

$$= \frac{6}{\sqrt{\left[55 - 45\right]\left[63 - \frac{(17)^2}{5}\right]}}$$

Did you get that? All we did was divide 225 by 5 and we got 45. Can you figure out the next step? Good. We subtract 45 from 55:

$$= \frac{6}{\sqrt{\left[10\right]\left[63 - \frac{(17)^2}{5}\right]}}$$

It is looking a lot better, isn't it? Okay, now we need to square 17 (do not forget Table A.3):

$$= \frac{6}{\sqrt{\left[10\right]\left[6) - \frac{289}{5}\right]}}$$

Next, we divide 289 by 5:

$$= \frac{6}{\sqrt{[10]\ [63 - 57.8]}}$$

We are getting there. Now we subtract 57.8 from 63. Do not let the decimals scare you:

$$\frac{6}{\sqrt{[10][63 - 57.8]}} = \frac{6}{\sqrt{[10][5.2]}} \qquad \text{Note:} \quad \begin{array}{r} 63.0 \\ -57.8 \\ \hline 5.2 \end{array}$$

Can you figure out what to do next? If you can, you are smarter than you thought. Next, we multiply 10 by 5.2:

$$\frac{6}{\sqrt{[10]\ [5.2]}} = \frac{6}{\sqrt{52}} \qquad \text{Note:} \quad \begin{array}{r} 10 \\ 5.2 \\ \hline 20 \\ 50 \\ \hline 52.0 \end{array}$$

Now it is time for Table A.3 again because we need the square root of 52:

$$\frac{6}{\sqrt{52}} = \frac{6}{7.2}$$

Almost done. All we have to do is divide 6 by 7.2:

$$\frac{6}{7.2} = .83 \quad \text{Note: } 7.2\,\overline{)6}$$

$$= 72\,\overline{)60.000}^{\,.833}$$

$$\underline{576}$$

$$240$$

$$\underline{216}$$

$$240$$

$$\underline{216} \text{ etc.}$$

Fanfare! Ta-ta-ta-ta! We are through. In case you got lost in the action, .83 is the correlation coefficient, the Pearson r. In other words, $r = +.83$.

Is .83 good? Does it represent a true relationship? Is .83 significantly different from .00? If you recall the related discussion in chapter 8, you know that to determine whether .83 represents a true relationship we need a table. We need a table which indicates how large our r needs to be in order to be significant, given the number of subjects we have and the level of significance at which we are working (see Table A.2 in the Appendix). The number of subjects affects the degrees of freedom which for the Pearson r are always computed by the formula $N - 2$. Thus, for our example, degrees of freedom $(df) = N - 2 = 5 - 2 = 3$. If we select $p = .05$ as our level of significance, we are now ready to use Table A.2.[11] Look at Table A.2 and find the column labeled df and run your left index finger down the column until you hit 3, the df associated with our r; keep your left finger right there for the time being. Now run your right index finger across the top of the table until you come to .05, the significance level we have selected. Now, run your left finger straight across the table and your right finger straight down the table until they meet. If you follow directions well, you should have ended up at .8783, which rounds off to .88. Now we compare our coefficient to the table value. Is .83 $\geq$ .88? No, .83 is not greater than or equal to .88. Therefore, our coefficient does not indicate a true relationship between X and Y. Even though it *looks* big, it is not big enough given that we only have five subjects. We are not positive that there is no relationship, but the odds are against it. Note that if we had had just one more subject ($N = 6$) our df would have been 4 ($N - 2 = 6 - 2 = 4$) and our coefficient would have indicated a significant relationship (.83 *is* $\geq$ .81). Note too, that the same table would have been used if r had been a negative number, $-.83$. The table does not know or care whether the r is positive or negative. It only tells you how large r must be in order to indicate a relationship significantly different from .00, a true relationship.

Do not forget, however, that even if a correlation coefficient is statistically significant it does not necessarily mean that the coefficient has any practical significance. Whether the coefficient is useful depends upon the use to which it will be put; a coefficient to be used in a prediction study needs to be much higher than a coefficient to be used in a relationship study.

---

11. Degrees of freedom and level of significance will be explained further in chapter 13.

Standard Scores

Your brain has definitely earned a rest. Therefore, we will conclude this section with a "cinchy" statistic, z. Thus, the formula for a z score is:

$$z = \frac{X - \bar{X}}{SD}$$

Compared to some of the winners we have been working with, the z score formula should be a snap! To convert scores to z scores we simply apply that formula to each score. Therefore, the first thing we need to do is to subtract the mean from each score:

	X	$\bar{X}$	$X - \bar{X}$	
Iggie	1	3	-2	We previously
Hermie	2	3	-1	computed the
Fifi	3	3	0	mean and it
Teenie	4	3	1	was 3.
Tiny	5	3	2	

Now all we have to do is to divide each score by the standard deviation which we have also already calculated; it is 1.4. Let us see how Iggie works out:

$$\text{Iggie } z = \frac{X - \bar{X}}{SD} = \frac{-2}{1.4} = -1.43$$

In case you have forgotten, if the signs are the same (two positives or two negatives), the answer in a multiplcation or division problem is a positive number; if the signs are different, the answer is a negative number, as in Iggie's case. For the rest of our friends, the results are:

$$\text{Hermie } z = \frac{X - \bar{X}}{SD} = \frac{-1}{1.4} = -.71$$

$$\text{Fifi } \quad z = \frac{X - \bar{X}}{SD} = \frac{0}{1.4} = .00$$

$$\text{Teenie } z = \frac{X - \bar{X}}{SD} = \frac{1}{1.4} = +.71$$

$$\text{Tiny } \quad z = \frac{X - \bar{X}}{SD} = \frac{2}{1.4} = +1.43$$

Notice that since Fifi's score was the same as the mean score, her z score is .00; her score is *no* distance from the mean.

If we want to eliminate the negatives, we can convert each z score to a Z score. Remember those? To do that we multiply each z score by 10 and add 50:

$$Z = 10z + 50$$

If we apply this formula to our z scores we get the following results:

$$
\begin{aligned}
\text{Iggie} \quad Z = 10z + 50 &= 10(-1.43) + 50 \\
&= -14.3 + 50 \\
&= 50 - 14.3 \\
&= 35.7 \\
\text{Hermie} \quad Z = 10z + 50 &= 10(-.71) + 50 \\
&= -7.1 + 50 \\
&= 50 - 7.1 \\
&= 42.9 \\
\text{Fifi} \quad Z = 10z + 50 &= 10(.00) + 50 \\
&= .00 + 50 \\
&= 50.0 \\
\text{Teenie} \quad Z = 10z + 50 &= 10(+.71) + 50 \\
&= 7.1 + 50 \\
&= 50 + 7.1 \\
&= 57.1 \\
\text{Tiny} \quad Z = 10z + 50 &= 10(+1.43) + 50 \\
&= 14.3 + 50 \\
&= 50 + 14.3 \\
&= 64.3
\end{aligned}
$$

I told you it would be easy!

Almost always in a research study, descriptive statistics such as the mean and standard deviation are computed separately for each group in the study. A correlation coefficient is usually only computed in a correlational study (unless it is used to compute the reliability of an instrument used in a causal-comparative or experimental study). Standard scores are rarely used in research studies. In order to test our hypothesis, however, we almost always need more than descriptive statistics; application of one or more inferential statistics is usually required.

13

Inferential Statistics

Enablers

After reading chapter 13, you should be able to:

1. Explain the concept of standard error.
2. Describe how sample size affects standard error.
3. Define or describe the null hypothesis.
4. State the purpose of a test of significance.
5. Define or describe Type I and Type II errors.
6. Define or describe the concept of significance level (probability level).
7. Describe one-tailed and two-tailed tests.
8. Explain the difference between parametric tests and nonparametric tests.
9. State the purpose, and explain the strategy, of the t test.
10. Define or describe independent and nonindependent samples.
11. State the purpose of the t test for independent samples (when is it used).
12. State the purpose of the t test for nonindependent samples.
13. Describe one major problem associated with analyzing gain scores (difference scores).
14. State the purpose of the simple analysis of variance.
15. State the purpose of multiple comparison procedures.
16. State the purpose of a factorial analysis of variance.
17. State a major purpose of analysis of covariance.
18. State the purpose of chi square.
19. Generate three columns of five one-digit numbers ("scores"), compute each of the following statistics (give the formula and show your work), state whether each result is statistically significant at $p = .05$, and interpret each result:
    (a) t test for independent samples (use columns 1 and 2),
    (b) t test for nonindependent samples (use columns 2 and 3),
    (c) simple analysis of variance for 3 groups (use all 3 columns),
    (d) the Scheffe' test (based on (c) above), and
    (e) chi square (sum the numbers in each column and treat them as if they were the total number of people responding "yes," "no," and "undecided," respectively, in a survey).

Concepts Underlying Application

Inferential statistics deal with, of all things, inferences. Inferences about what? Inferences about populations based on the behavior of samples. Most educational research studies deal with samples. Recall that "goodness" of the various sampling techniques is a function of their effectiveness in producing representative samples; the more representative a sample is, the more generalizable the results will be to the population from which the sample was selected. Results which only hold for the sample upon which they are based are of very limited value. Consequently, random samples are preferred since they seem to do the job best. Inferential statistics are concerned with determining how likely it is that results based on a sample or samples are the same results that would have been obtained for the entire population.

Sample values, such as the mean, are referred to as statistics. The corresponding values in the population are referred to as parameters. Thus, if a mean is based on a sample, it is a statistic; if it is based on an entire population, it is a parameter. Inferential statistics are used to make inferences concerning parameters, based on sample statistics. If a difference between means is found for two groups at the end of a study, the question of interest is whether a similar difference exists in the population from which the samples were selected. It could be that no real difference exists in the population and that the difference found for the samples was a chance one; if two different samples had been used it is likely that no difference would have been found. And now we get to the heart of inferential statistics, the concept of "how likely is it"; if I find a difference between two sample means and conclude that the difference is large enough to infer that a true difference exists in the population, how likely is it that I am wrong? In other words, inferences concerning populations are only probability statements; the researcher is only probably correct when he or she makes an inference and concludes that there is a true difference, or true relationship, in the population.

There are a number of concepts underlying the application of inferential statistics with which you should be familiar. Before the various types of inferential statistics are described, and several major ones calculated, these concepts will be discussed.

Standard Error

Inferences concerning populations are based on the behavior of samples. The chances of the composition of a sample being identical to that of its parent population, however, are virtually nil. If we randomly select a number of samples from the same population and compute the mean for each, it is very likely that each mean will be somewhat different from each other mean, and that none of the means will be identical to the population mean. This expected, chance variation among the means is referred to as sampling error. Recall that in chapter 4 we discussed the fact that unlike sampling bias, sampling error is not the researcher's fault. Sampling error just happens and is as inevitable as taxes! Thus, if a difference is found between sample means, the question of interest is whether the difference is a result of sampling error or a reflection of a true difference.

An interesting characteristic of sampling errors is that they are normally distributed. Errors vary in size (small errors versus large errors) and these errors form a normal curve. Although sampling errors are random fluctuations, they actually behave in a very orderly manner. Thus, if a sufficiently large number of equal-sized large samples are randomly selected from a population, all samples will not have the same mean on the variable measured, *but* the means of those samples will be normally distributed around the population mean. The mean of all the sample means will yield a good estimate of the population mean.[1] Most of the sample means will be very close to the population mean; the number of means which are considerably different from the population mean (as estimated by the mean of the sample means) will decrease as the size of the difference increases. In other words, very few means will be much higher or much lower than the population mean. An example may help to clarify this concept. Let us suppose that we do not know what the population mean IQ is on the Stanford-Binet, Form LM. Further suppose we randomly select 100 samples of $N = 50$ and calculate the mean IQ of each. We might get the following results:

64	82	87	94	98	100	104	108	114	121
67	83	88	95	98	101	104	109	115	122
68	83	88	96	98	101	105	109	116	123
70	84	89	96	98	101	105	110	116	124
71	84	90	96	98	102	105	110	117	125
72	84	90	97	99	102	106	111	117	127
74	84	91	97	99	102	106	111	118	130
75	85	92	97	99	103	107	112	119	131
75	86	93	97	100	103	107	112	119	136
78	86	94	97	100	103	108	113	120	142

If we compute the mean of all these means we get $10038/100 = 100.38$, which is a darn good estimate of the population mean, which we know is 100. Further, if you check the scores, you will discover that 71% of the scores fall between 84 and 116, and 96% fall between 68 and 132. Since we know that the standard deviation is 16, our distribution approximates a normal curve quite well; the percentage of cases falling within each successive standard deviation is very close to the percentage characteristic of a normal curve (71% as compared to 68%, and 96% as compared to 95%). The concept illustrated by the above example is a comforting one. It tells us, in essence, that most of the sample means we obtain will be close to the population mean and only a few will be very far away. In other words, once in a while, just by chance, we will get a sample which is quite different from the population, but not very often.

As with any normally distributed set of scores, a distribution of sample means has not only its own mean but also its own standard deviation. The standard deviation of the sample means (the standard deviation of sampling errors) is usually referred to as the standard error of the mean. The standard error of the mean ($SE_{\bar{x}}$) tells us by how much we would expect our sample means to differ if

---

1. To find the mean of the sample means you simply add up all the sample means and divide by the number of means, assuming that the size of each sample is the same as the size of every other sample.

we used other samples from the same population. According to normal curve percentages, we can say that approximately 68% of the sample means will fall between plus and minus one standard error of the mean (remember the standard error of the mean is a standard deviation), 95% will fall between plus and minus two standard errors, and 99+% will fall between plus and minus three standard errors. In other words, if the mean is 60, and the standard error of the mean is 10, we can expect 95% of the sample means to fall between 40 and 80 [60 ± 2(10)]. Thus a sample mean might very well be 65, but a sample mean of 95 is highly unlikely. Thus, given a number of large, randomly selected samples we can estimate quite well population parameters by computing the mean and standard deviation of the sample means.

It is not necessary, however, to select a large number of samples in order to estimate standard error. If we know the standard deviation of the population, we can estimate the standard error of the mean by dividing the standard deviation by the square root of our sample size ($\sqrt{N}$). In most cases, however, we do not know the mean or standard deviation of the population. In these cases, we estimate the standard error by dividing the standard deviation of the sample by the square root of the sample size minus one:

$$SE_{\bar{x}} = \frac{SD}{\sqrt{N-1}}$$

Using this estimate of the $SE_{\bar{x}}$, the sample mean, $\bar{X}$, and characteristics of the normal curve, we can estimate probable limits within which the population mean falls. These limits are referred to as confidence limits. Thus, if a sample $\bar{X}$ is 80, and $SE_{\bar{x}}$ is 1.00, if we say that the population mean falls between 79 and 81 ($\bar{X} \pm 1\ SE_{\bar{x}}$), we have approximately a 68% chance of being correct; if we say that the population mean falls between 78 and 82 ($\bar{X} \pm 2\ SE_{\bar{x}}$), we have approximately a 95% chance of being correct; if we say that the population mean falls between 77 and 83 ($\bar{X} \pm 3\ SE_{\bar{x}}$), we have approximately a 99+% chance of being correct. In other words, the probability of the population mean being less than 78 or greater than 82 is only 5/100, or 5%. Note that as our degree of confidence increases, the limits get farther apart. This makes sense since we are 100% confident that the population mean is somewhere between our sample mean plus infinity and minus infinity!

You have probably come to the realization by now that the smaller the standard error of the mean is, the better; a smaller standard error indicates less sampling error. The major factor affecting the standard error of the mean is sample size. As the size of the sample increases, the standard error of the mean decreases. This makes sense since if we used the whole population there would be no sampling error at all. A large sample is more likely to represent a population than a small sample. This discussion should help you to understand why samples should be as large as possible; smaller samples entail more error than larger samples. Another factor affecting the standard error of the mean is the size of the population standard deviation. If it is large, members of the population are very spread out on the variable of interest, and sample means will also be very spread out. Of course the researcher has no control over the size of the population standard deviation but the researcher can control sample size to some extent.

Thus, the researcher should make every effort to acquire as many subjects as possible so that inferences about the population of interest will be as correct as possible.

All of the above discussion has been in reference to the standard error of a mean. An estimate of standard error, however, can also be computed for other measures of central tendency as well as measures of variability, relationship, and relative position. Further, an estimate of standard error can also be determined for the difference between means. In other words, at the conclusion of an experimental study we may have two sample means, one mean for the experimental group, and one for the control group. In order to determine whether or not the difference between those means probably represents a true population difference, we need an estimate of the standard error of the difference between two means. Differences between two sample means are normally distributed around the mean difference in the population. Most differences will be close to the true difference and a few will be way off. In order to determine whether a difference found between sample means probably represents a true difference or a chance difference, tests of significance are applied to the data; tests of significance allow us to determine whether or not there is a significant difference between the means. Many tests of significance are based upon an estimate of standard error and they typically test a null hypothesis.

The Null Hypothesis

When we talk about the difference between two sample means being a true difference we mean that the difference was caused by the treatment (the independent variable), and not by chance. In other words, the difference is either caused by the treatment, as stated in the research hypothesis, or is the result of chance, random sampling error. The chance explanation for the difference is called the null hypothesis. The null hypothesis says in essence that there is no true difference or relationship between parameters in the populations and that any difference or relationship found for the samples is the result of sampling error. A null hypothesis might state:

> There is no significant difference between the mean reading comprehension of first-grade students who receive individualized reading instruction and first-grade students who receive group reading instruction.

This hypothesis says that there really is not any difference between the two methods and if you find one in your study, it is not a true difference, but a chance difference resulting from sampling error.

The null hypothesis for a study is usually (although not necessarily) different from the research hypothesis.[2] The research hypothesis usually states that one method is expected to be more effective than another. Why have both? It is difficult to explain simply, but essentially the reason is that rejection of a null

---

2. Sometimes our research hypothesis states the expectation that two approaches are equally effective. Recall a previous example concerning the comparative effectiveness of parent volunteers versus paid paraprofessionals.

hypothesis is more conclusive support for a positive research hypothesis. In other words, if the results of your study support your research hypothesis, you only have one piece of evidence based upon one situation. If you reject a null hypothesis, your case is stronger. As an analogy, suppose you hypothesize that all research textbooks contain a chapter on sampling. If you examine a research textbook and it does contain such a chapter, you have not *proven* your hypothesis, you have just found one little piece of evidence to support your hypothesis. If, on the other hand, the textbook you examine does not contain a chapter on sampling, your hypothesis is *disproven*. In other words, 1 book is enough to disprove your hypothesis, but 1,000 books are not enough to prove it; there may always be a book somewhere that does not contain a chapter on sampling. In a research study, the test of significance selected to determine whether a difference between means is a true difference provides a test of the null hypothesis. As a result, the null hypothesis is either rejected, as being probably false, or not rejected, being probably true. Notice the word "probably." We never know for sure whether we are making the correct decision; what we can do is to estimate the probability of our being wrong. After we make the decision to reject or not reject the null hypothesis, we make an inference back to our research hypothesis. If, for example, our research hypothesis states that A is better than B, and if we reject the null hypothesis that $A = B$, and if the mean for A is greater than the mean for B (and not vice versa), then we conclude that our research hypothesis was supported. If we do not reject the null hypothesis $A = B$, then we conclude that our research hypothesis was not supported.

In order to test a null hypothesis we need a test of significance and we need to select a probability level which indicates how much risk we are willing to take that the decision we make is wrong.

Tests of Significance

At the end of an experimental research study the researcher typically has two or more group means. These means are very likely to be at least a little different. The researcher must then decide whether the means are significantly different, different enough to conclude that they represent a true difference. In other words, the researcher must make the decision whether or not to reject the null hypothesis. The researcher does not make this decision based on her or his own best guess. Instead, the researcher selects and applies an appropriate test of significance. The test of significance helps us to decide whether we can reject the null hypothesis and infer that the difference is significantly greater than a chance difference. If the difference is too large to attribute to chance, we reject the null hypothesis, if not, we do not reject it.

The test of significance is made at a preselected probability level and allows us to state that we have rejected the null hypothesis because we would expect to find a difference as large as we have found by chance only 5 times out of every 100 studies, or only 1 time in every 100 studies, or whatever; therefore, we conclude that the null hypothesis is *probably* false and reject it. Obviously, if we can say we would expect such a difference by chance only 1 time in 100 studies we are more confident in our decision than if we say we would expect such a chance difference 5 times in 100. How confident we are depends upon the level of significance, or probability level, at which we perform our test of significance.

There are a number of different tests of significance which can be applied in research studies, one of which is more appropriate in a given situation. Factors such as the scale of measurement represented by the data, method of subject selection, the number of groups, and the number of independent variables determine which test of significance should be selected for a given experiment. Shortly, we will discuss and calculate several frequently used tests of significance—the t test, analysis of variance, and chi square.

Decision Making: Levels of Significance and Type I and Type II Errors

Based on a test of significance the researcher will either reject or not reject the null hypothesis as a probable explanation for results. In other words, the researcher will make the decision that the difference between the means is, or is not, too large to attribute to chance. The researcher never knows for sure whether he or she is right or wrong, only whether he or she is probably correct. Actually, there are four possibilities. If the null hypothesis is really true, and the researcher agrees that it is true (does not reject it), the researcher makes the correct decision. Similarly, if the null hypothesis is false, and the researcher rejects it (says there is a difference), the researcher also makes the correct decision. But what if the null hypothesis is true, there really is no difference, and the researcher rejects it and says there is a difference? The researcher makes an incorrect decision. Similarly, if the null hypothesis is false, there really is a significant difference between the means, but the researcher concludes that the null hypothesis is true and does not reject it, the researcher also makes an incorrect decision. These wrong decisions that can be made by researchers have names. If the researcher rejects a null hypothesis that is really true, the researcher makes a Type I error; if the researcher fails to reject a null hypothesis that is really false, the researcher makes a Type II error. Figure 13.1 illustrates the four possible outcomes of decision making.

When the researcher makes the decision to reject or not reject the null hypothesis, she or he does so with a given probability of being correct. This probability of being correct is referred to as the significance level, or probability level, of the test of significance. If the decision is made to reject the null hypothesis, the means are concluded to be significantly different—too different to be the result of chance error. If the null hypothesis is not rejected, the means are

		The true status of the null hypothesis. It is really	
		True (should not be rejected)	False (should be rejected)
The researcher's decision. The researcher concludes that the null hypothesis is	True (does not reject)	Correct Decision	Type II Error
	False (rejects)	Type I Error	Correct Decision

Figure 13.1.
The four possible outcomes of decision making concerning rejection of the null hypothesis.

determined to be not significantly different. The level of significance, or probability level, selected determines how large the difference between the means must be in order to be declared significantly different. The most commonly used probability level (symbolized as p) is the .05 level. Some studies use $p = .01$ and occasionally an exploratory study will use $p = .10$.

The probability level selected determines the probability of committing a Type I error, that is, of rejecting a null hypothesis that is really true. Thus, if you select $p = .05$ you have a 5% probability of making a Type I error whereas if you select $p = .01$ you have only a 1% probability of committing a Type I error. The less chance of being wrong you are willing to take, the greater the difference between the means must be. As an example, examine the six possible outcomes presented below and decide whether you think the means are significantly different. Assume that the means indicate the mean final performance on a 100-item test for two groups of 20 subjects each:

	Group A	Group B
1.	70.0	70.4
2.	70.0	71.0
3.	70.0	72.0
4.	70.0	75.0
5.	70.0	80.0
6.	70.0	90.0

How about outcome one? Is 70.0 significantly different from 70.4 (a difference of .4)? Probably not. How about outcome two, 70.0 versus 71.0 (a difference of 1.0)? Probably not significantly different. How about outcome six, 70.0 versus 90.0 (a difference of 20.0)? That difference probably is significant. How about five, 70.0 versus 80.0? Probably a significant difference. How about four, 70.0 versus 75.0? H-m-m-m. Is a 5-point difference a big enough difference? Up to a certain point the difference is probably too small to represent a true difference. Beyond a certain point the difference becomes large enough to be probably a true difference. Where is that magic point? At what point does a difference stop being too small and become "big enough?" The answer to these questions depends upon the probability level at which we perform our selected test of significance. The smaller our probability level is, the larger the difference must be. In the above example, if we were working at $p = .05$, then a difference of 5 (say 70.0 versus 75.0) might be big enough. If, on the other hand, we were working at $p = .01$ (a smaller chance of being wrong), a difference of at least 10 might be required (say 70.0 versus 80.0). Got the idea?

Thus, if you are working at $p = .05$, and as a result of your test of significance you reject the null hypothesis, you are saying in essence that you do not believe the null hypothesis is true because the chances are only 5 out of 100 (.05) that a difference as large (or larger) as the one you have found would occur just by chance as a result of sampling error. In other words, there is a 95% chance that the difference resulted from manipulation of the independent variable, not chance. Similarly, if you are working at $p = .01$ and reject the null hypothesis, you are saying that a difference as large as the one you have found would be expected to occur by chance only once for every 100 studies (1 out of 100, or .01). So why not set p at .000000001 and hardly ever be wrong? Good question; I am glad you asked it. If you select p to be very, very small, you definitely decrease your chances of committing a Type I error; you will hardly ever reject a true null hypothesis. *But,* guess what happens to your chances of committing a Type II error? Right. As you decrease the probability of committing a Type I error, you increase the probability of committing a Type II error, that is, of not rejecting a null hypothesis when you should (catch-22 again!) For example, you might conduct a study for which a mean difference of 9.5 represents a true difference. If you set p at .0001, however, you might require a mean difference of 20.0. If the difference actually found was 11.0, you would not reject the null hypothesis (11.0 is less than 20.0) although there really is a difference (11.0 is greater than 9.5). How do you decide which p level to work at, and when do you decide?

The choice of a probability level, p, is made prior to execution of the study. The researcher considers the relative-seriousness of committing a Type I versus a Type II error and selects p accordingly. In other words, the researcher compares the consequences of making the two possible wrong decisions. As an example, suppose you are a teacher and one day your principal comes up to you and says: "I understand you have research training and I want you to do a study for me. I'm considering implementing the Whoopee Reading System in the school next year. This System is very costly, however; if implemented, we will have to spend a great deal of money on materials and inservice training. I don't want to do that unless it *really* works. I want you to conduct a pilot study this year with several groups and then tell me if the Whoopee System really results in better reading achievement. You know what you're doing so you'll have my complete support in setting up the groups the way you want to and in implementing the study." In this case, which would be more serious, a Type I error or a Type II error? Suppose you conclude that the groups are significantly different, that the Whoopee System really works. Suppose it really does not. Supoose you make a Type I error. In this case, the principal is going to be *very* upset if he makes a big investment based on your decision and at the end of a year's period there is no difference in achievement. On the other hand, suppose you conclude that the groups are not significantly different, that the Whoopee System does not really make a difference. Suppose it really does. Suppose you make a Type II error. In this case, what will happen? Nothing. You will tell the principal the System does not work, he will thank you for the input, the System will not be implemented, and life will go on as usual. No one will ever know you made the wrong decision. Therefore, for this situation, which would *you* rather commit, a Type I error or a Type II error? Obviously, a Type II error. You want to be very sure you do not commit a Type I error. Therefore you would select a very small p, perhaps $p = .01$ or even $p = .001$. You want to be pretty darn sure there is a difference before you say there is.

As another example, suppose you are going to conduct an exploratory study to investigate the effectiveness of a new counseling technique. If you conclude that it is more effective, does make a difference, further research will be conducted. If you conclude that it does not make a difference, the new technique will be labeled as being not very promising. Now, which would be more serious, a Type I error or a Type II error? If you conclude there is a difference, and there really is not (Type I error), no real harm will be done and the only real consequence will be that further research will probably disconfirm your finding. If, on the other hand, you conclude that the technique makes no difference, and it really does (Type II error), a technique may be prematurely abandoned; with a little refinement, this new technique might make a real difference. In this case, you would probably rather commit a Type I error than a Type II error. Therefore, you might select a p level as low as .10.

For most studies, $p = .05$ is a reasonable probability level. The consequences of committing a Type I error are usually not too serious. A no-no in selecting a probability level is to compute a test of significance, such as a t test, and then see "how significant it is." If the results just happen to be significant at $p = .01$ you do not say "oh goodie" and report that the t was significant at the .01 level. You put your cards on the table before you play the game.

A common misconception among beginning researchers is the notion that if you reject a null hypothesis you have "proven" your research hypothesis. Rejection of a null hypothesis, or lack of rejection, only supports or does not support a research hypothesis. If you reject a null hypothesis and conclude that the groups are really different, it does not mean that they are different for the reason you hypothesized. They may be different for some other reason. On the other hand, if you fail to reject the null hypothesis it does not necessarily mean that your research hypothesis is wrong. The study, for example, may not have represented a fair test of your hypothesis. To use a former example, if you were investigating peer counseling versus individualized counseling and each group received its respective treatment for one day, you probably would not find any differences between the groups. This would not mean that peer counseling does not work; if your study were conducted over a 6-month period it might very well make a difference.

Two-Tailed and One-Tailed Tests

Tests of significance are almost always two-tailed. The null hypothesis states that there is no difference between the groups ($A = B$), and a two-tailed test allows for the possibility that a difference may occur in either direction; either group mean may be higher than the other ($A > B$ or $B > A$). A one-tailed test assumes that a difference can only occur in one direction; the null hypothesis states that one group is not better than another ($A \not> B$), and the one-tailed test assumes that if a difference occurs it will be in favor of that particular group ($A > B$). As an example, suppose a research hypothesis was:

Kindergarten children who receive a mid-morning snack exhibit better behavior during the hour before lunch than kindergarten students who do not receive a mid-morning snack.

For this research hypothesis the null hypothesis would state:

There is no difference between the behavior during the hour before lunch of kindergarten students who receive a mid-morning snack and kindergarten students who do not receive a mid-morning snack.

A two-tailed test of significance would allow for the possibility that either the group that received a snack or the group that did not might exhibit better behavior. For a one-tailed test, the hypothesis might state:

Kindergarten children who receive a mid-morning snack do not exhibit better behavior during the hour before lunch than kindergarten children who do not receive a mid-morning snack.

In this case, the assumption would be that if a difference were found between the groups it would be in favor of the group that received the snack. In other words, the researcher would consider it highly unlikely that not receiving a snack could result in better behavior than receiving one.

As mentioned before, tests of significance are almost always two-tailed. To select a one-tailed test of significance the researcher has to be pret-ty darn sure that a difference can only occur in one direction; this is not very often the case. When appropriate, a one-tailed test has one major advantage. The value resulting from application of the test of significance required for significance is smaller. In other words, it is "easier" to find a significant difference. It is difficult to explain simply why this is so, but it has to do with p. Suppose you are computing a t test of significance at $p = .05$. If your test is two-tailed you are allowing for the possibility of a positive t or a negative t; in other words, you are allowing that the mean of the first group may be higher than the mean of the second group ($\bar{X}_1 - \bar{X}_2 = $ a positive number), or that the mean of the second group may be higher than the mean of the first group ($\bar{X}_1 - \bar{X}_2 = $ a negative number). Thus, our p value, say .05, has to be divided in half, half for each possibility, .025 and .025 ($.025 + .025 = .05$). For a one-tailed test, the entire p value, say .05, is concentrated on one possible outcome, a positive t. Since .025 is a smaller probability of committing a Type I error than .05, for example, a larger t value is required. The above explanation applies to any p value and to other tests of significance besides the t test. While the above is definitely not the most scientific explanation of two-tailed and one-tailed tests, it should give you some conceptual understanding.

Degrees of Freedom

After you have determined whether the test will be two-tailed or one-tailed, selected a probability level, and computed a test of significance, you are ready to consult the appropriate table in order to determine the significance of your results. As you may recall from our discussion of the significance of r in chapter 8, the appropriate table is usually entered at the intersection of your probability level and your degrees of freedom, df. Degrees of freedom are a function of such factors as the number of subjects and the number of groups. Recall that for the correlation coefficient, r, the appropriate degrees of freedom were determined by the formula $N - 2$, number of subjects minus 2. It is difficult to explain in plain English what the concept of degrees of freedom *means* but an illustration may help. Suppose I ask you to name any five numbers. You agree and say "25, 44, 62, 84, 2". In this case N is equal to 5 and you had 5 choices, or 5 degrees of freedom. Now suppose I tell you to name 5 more and you say "1, 2, 3, 4, . . .," and I say "Wait! The mean of the five numbers must be 4." Now you have no choice—the last number *must* be 10 because $1 + 2 + 3 + 4 + 10 = 20$ and 20 divided by $5 = 4$. You lost one degree of freedom because of that one restriction, the restriction that the mean must be 4. In other words, instead of having $N = 5$ degrees of freedom, you only had $N = 1$ or $4(5 - 1)$ degrees of freedom. Got the idea?

Each test of significance has its own formula for determining degrees of freedom. For the correlation coefficient, r, for example, the formula is $N - 2$. The number 2 is a constant. In other words, degrees of freedom are always determined for r by subtracting 2 from N, the number of subjects. Each of the inferential statistics we are about to discuss also has its own formula for degrees of freedom.

Tests of Significance: Types

Different tests of significance are appropriate for different sets of data. It is important that the researcher select an appropriate test; an incorrect test can lead to incorrect conclusions. The first decision in selecting an appropriate test of significance is whether a parametric test may be used or whether a nonparametric test must be selected. Parametric tests are usually more powerful and generally to be preferred. By "more powerful" is meant more likely to reject a null hypothesis that is false; in other words, the researcher is less likely to commit a Type II error, less likely to not reject a null hypothesis that should be rejected.

Parametric tests, however, require that certain assumptions be met in order for them to be valid. One of the major assumptions underlying use of parametric tests is that the variable measured is normally distributed in the population (or at least that the form of the distribution is known). Since most variables studied in education are normally distributed, this assumption is usually met. A second major assumption is that the data represent an interval or a ratio scale of measurement. Again, since most measures used in education represent interval data, this assumption is usually met. In fact, this is one major advantage of using an interval scale—it permits application of a parametric test to the data. A third assumption is that subjects are selected independently for the study; in other words, that selection of one subject in no way affects selection of any other subject. Recall that the definition of random sampling is sampling in which *every* member of the population has an equal and *independent* chance of being selected for the sample. Thus, if randomization is involved in subject selection, the assumption of independence is met. Another assumption is that the variances of the population comparison groups are equal (or at least that the ratio of the variances is known). Recall that the variance of a group of scores is nothing more than the standard deviation squared.

With the exception of independence, some violation of one or more of these assumptions usually does not make too much difference, in other words, the same decision is made concerning the statistical significance of the results. However, if one or more assumptions are greatly violated, such as if the distribution is extremely skewed, parametric statistics should not be used. In such cases, a nonparametric test should be used. Nonparametric tests make no assumptions about the shape of the distribution. They are usually used when the data represent an ordinal or nominal scale, when a parametric assumption has been greatly violated, or when the nature of the distribution is not known.

If the data represent an interval or ratio scale, a parametric test should be used unless another of the assumptions is greatly violated. As mentioned before, parametric tests are more powerful. It is more difficult with a nonparametric test to reject a null hypothesis at a given level of significance; it usually takes a larger sample size to reach the same level of significance. Another advantage of parametric statistics is that they permit tests of a number of hypotheses that cannot be tested with a nonparametric test; there are a number of parametric statistics that have no counterpart among nonparametric statistics. Since parametric statistics seem to be relatively hearty, that is, do their job even with moderate assumption violation, they will usually be selected for analysis of research data.

With one exception, all of the statistics to be discussed are parametric statistics. Of course, we are not going to discuss each and every statistical test available to the researcher. A number of useful, commonly used statistics will be described, and a smaller number of the most frequently used statistics will be calculated. Whether any of these statistics are appropriate for data resulting from application of single-subject designs is debatable. Typically, the results of single-subject research are presented graphically and summarized using simple descriptive statistics. The need for inferential statistics depends somewhat on the nature of the results. For example, in many studies the differences between baseline and treatment scores are of such a magnitude as to make application of inferential statistics unnecessary. In other studies, treatment effects are not so clear-cut and the case for using inferential statistics is stronger. In these instances, if a sufficient number of measurements are made during each phase, baseline measures, or scores, can be compared to treatment measures. In some studies, a *t* test is an appropriate statistic for determining whether the differences between baseline and treatment means are statistically significant.

The t Test

The *t* test is used to determine whether two means are significantly different at a selected probability level. In other words, for a given sample size the *t* indicates how often a difference $(\bar{X}_1 - \bar{X}_2)$ as large or larger would be found when there is no true population difference. The *t* test makes adjustments for the fact that the distribution of scores for small samples becomes increasingly different from a normal distribution as sample sizes become increasingly smaller. Distributions for smaller samples, for example, tend to be higher at both the mean and the ends. For a given *p* level, the values of *t* required to reject a null hypothesis are progressively higher for progressively smaller samples; as the size of the samples becomes larger (approaches infinity) the score distribution approaches normality.

The strategy of the *t* test is to compare the *actual* mean difference observed $(\bar{X}_1 - \bar{X}_2)$ with the difference *expected* by chance. The *t* test involves forming the ratio of these two values. In other words, the numerator for a *t* test is the difference between the sample means $\bar{X}_1$ and $\bar{X}_2$, and the denominator is the chance difference which would be expected if the null hypothesis were true—the standard error of the difference between the means. The denominator, or error term, is a function of both sample size and group variance. Smaller sample sizes and greater variation within groups are associated with an expectation of greater random differences between groups. To explain it one more way, even if the null hypothesis is true you do not expect two sample means to be identical; there is going to be some chance variation. The t ratio determines whether the observed difference is sufficiently larger than a difference which would be expected by chance. After the numerator is divided by the denominator, the resulting t value is compared to the appropriate t table value (depending upon the probability level and the degrees of freedom); if the calculated t value is equal to or greater than the table value then the null hypothesis is rejected.

There are two different types of t tests, the t test for independent samples and the t test for nonindependent samples.

The t Test for Independent Samples

Independent samples are samples that are randomly formed, that is, formed without any type of matching. The members of one group are not related to members of the other group in any systematic way other than that they are selected from the same population. If two groups are randomly formed, the expectation is that they are essentially the same at the beginning of a study with respect to performance on the dependent variable. Therefore, if they are essentially the same at the end of the study, the null hypothesis is probably true; if they are different at the end of the study, the null hypothesis is probably false, that is, the treatment does make a difference. The key word is *essentially*. We do not expect them to be identical at the end, they are bound to be somewhat different; the question is whether they are significantly different. Thus, the t test for independent samples is used to determine whether there is probably a significant difference between the means of two independent samples.

The t Test for Nonindependent Samples

Nonindependent samples are samples formed by some type of matching. The ultimate matching, of course, is when the two samples are really the same sample group at two different times, such as one group which receives two different treatments at two different times or which is pretested before a treatment and then posttested. When samples are not independent, the members of one group are systematically related to the members of a second group (especially if it is the same group at two different times). If samples are nonindependent, scores on the dependent variable are expected to be correlated and a special t test for correlated, or nonindependent, means must be used. When samples are nonindependent, the error term of the t test tends to be smaller and therefore there is a higher probability that the null hypothesis will be rejected. Thus, the t test for nonindependent samples is used to determine whether there is probably a significant difference between the means of two matched, or nonindependent, samples or between the means for one sample at two different times.

Analysis of Gain Scores (Difference Scores)

When two groups are pretested, administered a treatment, and then posttested, the t test may or may not be the appropriate analysis technique. Many beginning researchers (and some not-so-beginning researchers) assume that the logical procedure is to (1) subtract each subject's pretest score from his or her posttest score (resulting in a gain, or difference, score), (2) compute the mean gain, or difference, score for each group, and (3) calculate a t value for the difference between the two average mean differences. There are a number of problems associated with this approach, however, the major one being lack of equal opportunity to grow. Every subject does not have the same room to gain. A subject who scores very low on a pretest has a lot of room, and a subject who scores very high only has a little room (referred to as the ceiling effect). Who has improved, or gained, more—a subject who goes from 20 to 70 (a gain of 50) or a subject who goes from 85 to 100 (a gain of only 15 but perhaps a perfect score)?

The correct analysis of posttest scores for two groups depends upon the performance of the two groups on the pretest. If both groups are essentially the same on the pretest, for example, neither group knows anything, then posttest scores can be directly compared using a t test. If, on the other hand, there is a difference between the groups on the pretest, the preferred posttest analysis is analysis of covariance. Recall that analysis of covariances adjusts posttest scores for initial differences on some variable (in this case the pretest) related to performance on the dependent variable. Thus, in order to determine whether analysis of covariance is necessary, a Pearson r can be calculated to determine if there is a significant relationship between pretest scores and posttest scores. If not, a simple t test can be computed on posttest scores (or as we shall see shortly, analysis of covariance may be computed anyway, but for a different reason).

Simple Analysis of Variance

Simple, or one-way, analysis of variance (ANOVA) is used to determine whether there is a significant difference between two or more means at a selected probability level. In a study involving three groups, for example, the ANOVA is the appropriate analysis technique. Three (or more) posttest means are bound to be different; the question is whether the differences represent true differences or chance differences resulting from sampling error. To answer this question at a given probability level the ANOVA is applied to the data and an F ratio is computed. You may be wondering why you cannot just compute a lot of t tests, one for each pair of means. Aside from some statistical problems concerning resulting distortion of your probability level, it is more convenient to perform one ANOVA than several t's. For four means, for example, six separate t tests would be required ($\bar{X}_1 - \bar{X}_2$, $\bar{X}_1 - \bar{X}_3$, $\bar{X}_1 - \bar{X}_4$, $\bar{X}_2 - \bar{X}_3$, $\bar{X}_2 - \bar{X}_4$, $\bar{X}_3 - \bar{X}_4$).

The concept underlying ANOVA is that the total variation, or variance, of scores can be attributed to two sources—variance between groups (variance caused by the treatment), and variance within groups (error variance). As with the t test, a ratio is formed (the F ratio) with group differences as the numerator (variance between groups) and an error term as the denominator (variance within groups). Randomly formed groups are assumed to be essentially the same at the beginning of a study on a measure of the dependent variable. At the end of the study, after administration of the independent variable (treatment), we determine whether the between groups (treatment) variance differs from the within groups (error) variance by more than what would be expected by chance. In other words, if the treatment variance is enough larger than the error variance, a significant F

ratio results, the null hypothesis is rejected, and it is concluded that the treatment had a significant effect on the dependent variable. If, on the other hand, the treatment variance and error variance are essentially the same (do not differ by more than what would be expected by chance), the resulting F ratio is not significant and the null hypothesis is not rejected. The greater the difference, the larger the F ratio. To determine whether or not the F ratio is significant an F table is entered at the place corresponding to the selected probability level and the appropriate degrees of freedom. The degrees of freedom for the F ratio are a function of the number of groups and the number of subjects.

Multiple Comparisons

If the F ratio is determined to be nonsignificant, the party is over. But what if it is significant? What do you know? All you know is that there is at least one significant difference somewhere, you do not know where that difference is; you do not know which means are significantly different from which other means. It might be, for example, that three means are equal but all greater than a fourth mean, that is, $\bar{X}_1 = \bar{X}_2 = \bar{X}_3$ and each mean is $> \bar{X}_4$ ($\bar{X}_1$, $\bar{X}_2$, and $\bar{X}_3$ might represent three treatments and $\bar{X}_4$ might represent a control group). Or it might be that $\bar{X}_1 = \bar{X}_2$, and $\bar{X}_3 = \bar{X}_4$, but $\bar{X}_1$ and $\bar{X}_2$ are each greater than $\bar{X}_3$ and $\bar{X}_4$. When the F ratio is significant, and more than two means are involved, multiple comparison procedures are used to determine which means are significantly different from which other means. There are a number of different multiple comparison techniques available to the researcher. In essence, they involve calculation of a special form of the t test, a form for which the error term is based on the combined variance of all the groups, not just the groups being compared. This special t adjusts for the fact that many tests are being executed. What happens is that when many tests are performed, the probability level, p, tends to increase; if p is supposed to be .05, it will actually end up being greater, maybe .90, if many tests are performed. Thus, the chance of finding a significant difference is increased but so is the chance of committing a Type I error. Which mean comparisons are to be made should generally be decided upon *before* the study is conducted, not after, and should be based upon research hypotheses. In other words, application of a multiple comparison technique should not be essentially a "fishing expedition" in which the researcher looks for any difference she or he can find.[3]

Of the many multiple comparison techniques available probably the most often used is the Scheffe' test. The Scheffe' test is appropriate for making any and all possible comparisons involving a set of means. The calculations for this approach are quite simple and sample sizes do not have to be equal, as is the case with some multiple comparison techniques. The Scheffe' test is very conservative, which is good news and bad news. The good news is that the probability of

---

3. It is possible to obtain a nonsignificant F ratio and yet to find a significant difference between two or more means. Some statisticians believe that it is legitimate to investigate this possibility if the F ratio is nonsignificant (most do not). All statisticians and researchers, however, agree that multiple comparison techniques should not be applied with abandon in the hopes that "something will turn up."

committing a Type I error for any comparison of means is never greater than the p level selected for the original analysis of variance. The bad news is that it is entirely possible, given the comparisons selected for investigation, to find no significant differences even though the F for the analysis of variance was significant. In general, however, the flexibility of the Scheffe' test and its ease of application make it useful for a wide variety of situations.

Factorial Analysis of Variance

If a research study is based upon a factorial design and investigates two or more independent variables and the interactions between them, the appropriate statistical analysis is a factorial, or multifactor, analysis of variance. Such an analysis yields a separate F ratio for each independent variable and one for each interaction. Analysis of the data presented in Figure 10.5, for example, would yield three Fs—one for the manipulated, independent variable, Method, one for the control independent variable, IQ, and one for the interaction between Method and IQ. For the No Interaction example, the F for Method would probably be significant since method A appears to be significantly more effective than method B (70 versus 30); the F for IQ would also probably be significant since high IQ subjects appear to have performed significantly better than low IQ subjects (60 versus 40); the F for the interaction between Method and IQ would not be significant since method A is more effective than method B for both IQ groups, not differentially effective for one level of IQ or another (80 > 40, 60 > 20). On the other hand, for the Interaction example, the F for Method would not be significant since method A is equally as effective as method B overall (50 = 50); the F for IQ would probably be significant since high IQ subjects still appear to have performed significantly better than low IQ subjects (70 versus 30); the F for the interaction between Method and IQ, however, would probably be significant since the methods appear to be differentially effective depending upon the IQ level; method A is better for high IQ subjects (80 versus 60) and method B is better for low IQ subjects (20 versus 40). Another way of looking at it is to see that for the No Interaction example (80 + 20) = (60 + 40); for the Interaction example (80 + 40) = (20 + 60).

A factorial analysis of variance is not as difficult to calculate as you may think. If no more than two variables are involved, and if you have access to a calculator, one can be performed without too much difficulty. Most statistics texts outline the procedure to be followed. If more than two variables are involved, it is usually better to use a computer if possible. Use of the computer in data analysis will be discussed in chapter 14.

Analysis of Covariance

Analysis of covariance (ANCOVA) is used in two major ways, as a technique for controlling extraneous variables and as a means of increasing power. Covariance is a form of ANOVA and is a statistical, rather than an experimental, method that can be used to equate groups on one or more variables. Use of covariance is essentially equivalent to matching groups on the variable or variables to be controlled.[4] In a number of situations, covariance is the preferred approach to control. As pointed out previously, for example, analysis of pretest-posttest gain scores has several disadvantages. Thus, for a study based on a pretest-posttest control group design, covariance is a superior method for controlling for pretest differences.

Essentially, ANCOVA adjusts posttest scores for initial differences on some variable and compares adjusted scores. In other words, the groups are equalized with respect to the control variable and then compared. Any variable that is correlated with the dependent variable can be controlled for using covariance. Pretest performance, IQ, readiness, and specific aptitude are frequently controlled for in educational research studies through the use of analysis of covariance. If the variable to be controlled is a variable such as IQ which is very unlikely to be affected by manipulation of the independent variable under study, then it does not really matter when such data are collected—prior to, during, or following the experiment. Otherwise, as in the case of a pretest of the dependent variable, the covariate data must be collected prior to the initiation of treatments. By using covariance we are attempting to reduce variation in posttest scores which is attributable to another variable. Ideally, we would like all posttest variance to be attributable to the treatment conditions.

Analysis of covariance is a control technique used in both causal-comparative studies in which already-formed, not necessarily equal, groups are involved and in experimental studies in which either existing groups or randomly formed groups are involved; randomization does not guarantee that groups will be equated on all variables. Unfortunately, the situation for which ANCOVA is least appropriate is the situation for which it is most often used. Covariance is based on the assumption that subjects have been randomly assigned to treatment groups. It is therefore best used in conjunction with true experimental designs. If existing, or intact, groups are involved but treatments are assigned to groups randomly, covariance may still be used but results must be interpreted with due caution. If covariance is used with existing groups and nonmanipulated independent variables, as in causal-comparative studies, the results are likely to be misleading at best. There is evidence, for example, that improper use of covariance tends to give an artificial advantage to whichever group scores higher initially on the variable to be controlled. Thus, for example, if an experimental group has a higher pretest score than a control group, it is difficult to interpret results if the experimental group scores significantly higher than the control group on the posttest.[5] There are other assumptions associated with the use of analysis of covariance. Violation of these assumptions is not as serious, however, if subjects have been randomly assigned to treatment groups.[6]

---

4. Roscoe, J.T. *Fundamental research statistics for the behavioral sciences.* New York: Holt, Rinehart and Winston, 1975.

5. Campbell, D.T., & Boruch, R.F. Making the case for randomized assignment to treatments by considering the alternatives: Six ways in which quasi-experimental evaluations in compensatory education tend to underestimate effects. In C.A. Bennett and A.A. Lumsdaine (Eds.), *Evaluation and experiment: Some critical issues in assessing social programs.* Seattle: Academic Press, 1975.

6. For further discussion of these concepts see: Elashoff, J.D. Analysis of covariance: A delicate instrument. *American Educational Research Journal,* 1969, *6*(3), 383–401; Evans, S.H., & Anastasio, E.J. Misuse of analysis of covariance when treatment effect and covariate are confounded. *Psychological Bulletin,* 1968, *69*(4), 225–234; and Winer, B.J. *Statistical principles in experimental design* (2nd ed.). New York: McGraw-Hill, 1971.

A second, not previously discussed, function of ANCOVA is that it increases the power of a statistical test by reducing within-group (error) variance. Although increasing sample size also increases power, the researcher is often limited to samples of a given size because of financial and practical reasons. The power-increasing function of ANCOVA is directly related to the degree of randomization involved in formation of the groups; the results of ANCOVA are least likely to be valid when already formed groups to which treatments have not been randomly assigned are used. Further, since randomization increases the validity of ANCOVA, and since randomization can generally be counted on to equate groups on relevant variables, Huck and others urge that researchers should consider the primary value of analysis of covariance to be its ability to increase power rather than its ability to equate groups on extraneous variables.[7]

As pointed out before, application of the analysis of covariance technique is quite a complex, lengthy procedure which is hardly ever hand calculated. Almost all researchers use computer programs for reasons of accuracy and sanity!

Chi Square

Chi square, symbolized as χ^2, is a nonparametric test of significance appropriate when the data are in the form of frequency counts occurring in two or more mutually exclusive categories.[8] Chi square is not appropriate when the data are in the form of test scores. A chi square test compares proportions actually observed in a study with proportions expected, to see if they are significantly different. Expected proportions are usually the frequencies which would be expected if the groups were equal, although they may be based on past data. The chi square value increases as the difference between observed and expected frequencies increases. Whether the chi square value is significant is determined by consulting a chi square table.

The chi square can be used to compare frequencies occurring in different categories or the categories may be groups, so that the chi square is comparing groups with respect to the frequency of occurrence of different events. As an example, suppose you stopped 90 shoppers in a supermarket and asked them to taste three different brands of peanut butter (unidentified to the shoppers, of course) and to tell you which one tasted better. Suppose that 40 shoppers chose brand X, 30 chose brand Y, and 20 chose brand Z. If the null hypothesis were true, if the three brands tasted essentially the same, you would expect an equal number of shoppers to select each brand—30, 30, and 30. To determine whether the observed frequencies (40, 30, 20) were significantly different from the ex-pected frequencies (30, 30, 30) a chi square test could be applied. If the chi square were significant, the null hypothesis would be rejected, and it would be concluded that the brands do taste different.

As another example, you might wish to compare the effectiveness of two different types of reinforcement, social and token, to see which is more effective in reducing instances of classroom misbehavior. At the end of a 6-month study you might have observers observe each group for a week. Tabulation might reveal

7. Huck, S.W. The analysis of covariance: Increased power through reduced variability. *The Journal of Experimental Education*, 1972, *41*(1), 42–46.

8. Chi is pronounced KEYE, like those things you see with, not CHI as in child.

that the social reinforcement group exhibited a total of 100 instances of misbehavior and the token reinforcement group 80 instances. Would this represent a true difference or a chance difference? In this case, the total number of instances of misbehavior was 180 (100 + 80); if the groups were essentially the same you would expect each group to exhibit the same number of instances of misbehavior, namely, 180 ÷ 2 = 90. In order to determine whether the groups were significantly different, you would compare the observed frequencies (100, 80) with the expected frequencies (90, 90) using a chi square test of significance.

The chi square may also be used when frequencies are categorized along more than one dimension, sort of a factorial chi square. In the above study, for example, instances of behavior could be classified by type of reinforcement and by sex, a two-way classification, in order to determine if effectiveness of type of reinforcement is independent of the sex of the subject. When a two-way classification is used, determination of expected frequencies is a little more complex, but still not difficult.

Figure 13.2 summarizes the conditions for which each of the statistics discussed in this section are appropriate.

Statistic	Number of Groups	Number of Variables	Type of Data	Related Designs[a]
t test for independent samples	2	1	interval or ratio	1 (if groups are = on pretest), 2,4
t test for nonindependent samples	2	1	interval or ratio	4 (if groups are matched)
simple ANOVA	≥2	1	interval or ratio	1,2,4
Scheffe' test	≥2	1	interval or ratio	1,2,4
factorial ANOVA	≥2	≥2	interval or ratio	3
analysis of covariance	≥2	≥2	interval or ratio	1,2,3,4
chi square	≥2	≥1	nominal	1,2,3,4

[a] See Figure 10.2.

Figure 13.2
Summary of conditions for which selected statistics are appropriate.

Calculation and Interpretation of Selected Tests of Significance

There are many tests of significance available to the researcher, some of which are used much more frequently than others. We will calculate and interpret those which are both frequently appropriate and not beyond your current level of

research competence: the *t* test for independent samples, the *t* test for nonindependent samples, simple (or one-way) analysis of variance, the Scheffe' test, and
chi square. In each case the easiest formula will be used. At first glance some of
the formulas may look horrible but they are really easy. Just like the descriptive
statistics, they only *look* hard. You are already familiar with most of the symbols
involved so they may not look so scary after all. Regardless of how it looks,
however, each formula will transform "magically" into an arithmetic problem in
one easy step. Although a sample size of five is hardly ever considered to be
acceptable, we will again work with this number for the sake of illustration. In
other words, all of our calculations (except for the chi square) will be based on the
scores for groups each containing five subjects so that you can concentrate on
how the calculation is being done and will not get lost in the numbers. For the
same reason, we will also use very small numbers.

The t Test for Independent Samples

Suppose we have the following sets of posttest scores for two randomly formed
groups:

Group 1	Group 2
3	2
4	3
5	3
6	3
7	4

Are these two sets of scores significantly different? They are different, but are they
significantly different? The appropriate test of significance to use in order to
answer this question is the *t* test for independent samples. The formula is:

$$t = \frac{\bar{X}_1 - \bar{X}_2}{\sqrt{\left(\dfrac{SS_1 + SS_2}{n_1 + n_2 - 2}\right)\left(\dfrac{1}{n_1} + \dfrac{1}{n_2}\right)}}$$

Does it look bad? Is it? What will it turn into?[9] If you look at the formula you will
see that you are already familiar with each of the pieces. The numerator is simply
the difference between the two means $\bar{X}_1$ and $\bar{X}_2$. Each of the *ns* refers to the
number of subjects in each group; thus, $n_1 = 5$ and $n_2 = 5$. What about the SSs?
How do we find them? Right! We calculate each SS in the same way as we did for
the standard deviation. Thus:

$$SS_1 = \Sigma X_1^2 - \frac{(\Sigma X_1)^2}{n_1} \quad \text{and} \quad SS_2 = \Sigma X_2^2 - \frac{(\Sigma X_2)^2}{n_2}$$

Remember? Okay, now let's find each piece.

---

9. The answers are: Yes! No! An arithmetic problem.

First, let's calculate means, sums, and sums of squares, and let's label the scores for group 1 as X_1 and the scores for group 2 as X_2:

X_1	X_1^2	X_2	X_2^2
3	9	2	4
4	16	3	9
5	25	3	9
6	36	3	9
7	49	4	16
$\Sigma X_1 = 25$	$\Sigma X_1^2 = 135$	$\Sigma X_2 = 15$	$\Sigma X_2^2 = 47$

$$\bar{X}_1 = \frac{25}{5} = 5 \qquad\qquad \bar{X}_2 = \frac{15}{5} = 3$$

Next, we need the SSs:

$$SS_1 = \Sigma X_1^2 - \frac{(\Sigma X_1)^2}{n_1} \qquad SS_2 = \Sigma X_2^2 - \frac{(\Sigma X_2)^2}{n_2}$$

$$= 135 - \frac{(25)^2}{5} \qquad\qquad = 47 - \frac{(15)^2}{5}$$

$$= 135 - 125 \qquad\qquad = 47 - 45$$

$$= 10 \qquad\qquad\qquad = 2$$

Now we have everything we need and all we have to do is substitute the correct number for each symbol in the formula:

$$t = \frac{\bar{X}_1 - \bar{X}_2}{\sqrt{\left(\frac{SS_1 + SS_2}{n_1 + n_2 - 2}\right)\left(\frac{1}{n_1} + \frac{1}{n_2}\right)}} = \frac{5 - 3}{\sqrt{\left(\frac{10 + 2}{5 + 5 - 2}\right)\left(\frac{1}{5} + \frac{1}{5}\right)}}$$

Now what do we have? A statistic? No! An arithmetic problem? Yes! A hard arithmetic problem? No! Now, if we just do what the formula tells us to do we will have no problem at all. The first thing it says to do is to subtract 3 from 5:

$$= \frac{2}{\sqrt{\left(\frac{10 + 2}{5 + 5 - 2}\right)\left(\frac{1}{5} + \frac{1}{5}\right)}}$$

So far so good? Terrific. Now, the next thing it says is to add 10 and 2. That does not sound too tough:

$$= \frac{2}{\sqrt{\left(\frac{12}{5 + 5 - 2}\right)\left(\frac{1}{5} + \frac{1}{5}\right)}}$$

Okay, the next step is to add 5 and 5 and subtract 2:

$$= \frac{2}{\sqrt{\left(\frac{12}{8}\right)\left(\frac{1}{5}+\frac{1}{5}\right)}}$$

Did you follow that? $5 + 5 - 2 = 10 - 2 = 8$. Next, we add 1/5 to 1/5 and get guess what:

$$= \frac{2}{\sqrt{\left(\frac{12}{8}\right)\left(\frac{2}{5}\right)}}$$

Right! $1/5 + 1/5 = 2/5$. Before we go any further, this would be a good time to convert those fractions to decimals. To convert a fraction to a decimal you simply divide the numerator by the denominator:

$$\begin{array}{r} 1.5 \\ 8\overline{)12.0} \\ 8 \\ \hline 40 \\ 40 \\ \hline \end{array} \qquad \begin{array}{r} .4 \\ 5\overline{)2.0} \\ 20 \\ \hline \end{array}$$

Thus, $12/8 = 1.5$ and $2/5 = .4$
Substituting the decimals for the fractions we have:

$$t = \frac{2}{\sqrt{\left(\frac{12}{8}\right)\left(\frac{2}{5}\right)}} = \frac{2}{\sqrt{(1.5)\,(.4)}}$$

Since the parentheses indicate multiplication, we next multiply 1.5 by .4. In case you have forgotten how to do that:

$$\begin{array}{r} 1.5 \\ .4 \\ \hline .60 \end{array} \qquad \text{(there are \textit{two} decimal places)}$$

Now we have:

$$t = \frac{2}{\sqrt{(1.5)(.4)}} = \frac{2}{\sqrt{.60}}$$

We are almost through, but now we have to find the square root of .60. H-m-m-m. I promised you that you would not have to do any square rootin' and a promise is a promise. The square root table, however, only contains whole numbers. What shall we do? Fortunately, there is a neat little procedure which you can follow to find the square root of a decimal using a table. The procedure is as follows:

1. Multiply the decimal by 100 (move the decimal point two places to the right).

2. Look the new number up in a square root table.

3. Divide the identified square root by 10 (move the decimal point one place to the left).

Applying.this procedure[10] to .60 and using table A.3, we get:

1. .60 $\times$ 100 = 60.

2. the square root of 60 = 7.75

3. 7.75 $\div$ 10 = .775 or .78

Substituting in our square root we have:

$$t = \frac{2}{\sqrt{.60}} = \frac{2}{.78}$$

One more step! Once we divide 2 by .78 we will be through. Just in case you are not sure about how to divide a whole number by a decimal:

$$.78\overline{)2} = 78\overline{)200.00} \quad \begin{array}{r} 2.56 \\ \hline \end{array}$$

$$\begin{array}{r} 2.56 \\ 78\overline{)200.00} \\ \underline{156} \\ 440 \\ \underline{390} \\ 500 \\ \underline{468} \\ 32 \end{array}$$

Therefore, $t = \dfrac{2}{.78} = 2.56$

Assuming we selected p = .05, the only thing we need before we go the the t table is the appropriate degrees of freedom. For the t test for independent samples, the formula for degrees of freedom is $n_1 + n_2 - 2$. For our example, df = $n_1 + n_2 - 2 = 5 + 5 - 2 = 8$. Therefore, t = 2.56, p = .05, df = 8. Now go to Table A.4 in the Appendix. Run the index finger of your right hand across the probability row at the top of the table until you get to .05. Now run the index finger of your left hand down the degrees of freedom column until you get to 8. Now move your right index finger down the column and your left index finger across; they will intersect at 2.306. The value 2.306 is the t value required for rejection of the null hypothesis with p = .05 and df = 8. Is our value 2.56 >

---

10. This procedure is not really magic, it just looks like it! If you apply the procedure to .49 you will find that the square root is .7 which makes sense since you know that the square root of 49 is 7.

2.306? Yes, and therefore we reject the null hypothesis. Are the means different? Yes. Are they significantly different? Yes. Was that hard? Of course not. Are all the tests of significance going to be that easy? Of course!

Suppose our t value has been 2.29. What would we have concluded? We would have concluded that there is no significant difference between the groups. How about if we concluded that our t was *almost* significant? Boooo! A t is not *almost* significant or *really* significant; it is or it is not significant. You will never see a research report that says "aw shucks, almost made it" or "pret-ty close!"

The t Test for Nonindependent Samples

Let us assume that we have the following sets of scores for two matched groups:

X_1	X_2
2	4
3	5
4	4
5	7
6	10

Are these two sets of scores significantly different? They are different, but are they significantly different? The appropriate test of significance to use in order to answer this question is the t test for nonindependent samples. The formula is:

$$t = \frac{\bar{D}}{\sqrt{\dfrac{\Sigma D^2 - \dfrac{(\Sigma D)^2}{N}}{N(N-1)}}}$$

Except for the Ds the formula should look very familiar. If the Ds were Xs you would know exactly what to do. Whatever Ds are, we are going to find their mean, $\bar{D}$, add up their squares, ΣD^2, and square their sum $(\Sigma D)^2$. What do you suppose D could possibly stand for? Right! D stands for difference. The difference between what? Right, D is the difference between the matched pairs. Thus, each D equals $X_2 - X_1$. For our data, the first pair of scores is 2 and 4 and $D = +2$. Got it? Okay, let us find the Ds for each pair of scores. While we are at it we might as well get the squares, the sums, and the mean. The mean of the Ds is found the same way as any other mean, by adding up the Ds and dividing by the number of Ds:

X_1	X_2	D	D^2
2	4	+2	4
3	5	+2	4
4	4	0	0
5	7	+2	4
6	10	+4	16
		$\Sigma D = 10$	$\Sigma D^2 = 28$

$$\bar{D} = \frac{\Sigma D}{N} = \frac{10}{5} = 2$$

Now we have everything we need, and all we have to do is substitute the correct number for the correct symbol in the formula:

$$t = \frac{\bar{D}}{\sqrt{\dfrac{\Sigma D^2 - \dfrac{(\Sigma D)^2}{N}}{N(N-1)}}} = \frac{2}{\sqrt{\dfrac{28 - \dfrac{(10)^2}{5}}{5(5-1)}}}$$

Now what do we have? Right! An easy arithmetic problem. Now that you are an old pro, we can solve this arithmetic problem rather quickly. Below, the steps are executed one at a time with an explanation for each step to the right of the step:

$$t = \frac{2}{\sqrt{\dfrac{28 - \dfrac{(10)^2}{5}}{5(5-1)}}}$$

$$= \frac{2}{\sqrt{\dfrac{28 - \dfrac{100}{5}}{5(5-1)}}} \qquad 10^2 = 100$$

$$= \frac{2}{\sqrt{\dfrac{28 - 20}{5(5-1)}}} \qquad \frac{100}{5} = 20$$

$$= \frac{2}{\sqrt{\dfrac{8}{5(5-1)}}} \qquad 28 - 20 = 8$$

$$= \frac{2}{\sqrt{\dfrac{8}{5(4)}}} \qquad (5-1) = 4$$

$$= \frac{2}{\sqrt{\dfrac{8}{20}}} \qquad 5(4) = 20$$

$$= \frac{2}{\sqrt{.4}} \qquad \frac{8}{20} = \frac{4}{10} = .4$$

$$= \frac{2}{.63} \qquad \sqrt{.4} = .63$$

$$= 3.17$$

Thus, $t = 3.17$. Assuming $p = .05$, the only thing we need before we go to the t table is the appropriate degrees of freedom. For the t test for nonindependent samples, the formula for degrees of freedom is $N - 1$, the number of pairs minus 1. For our example, $N - 1 = 5 - 1 = 4$. Therefore, $t = 3.17$, $p = .05$, $df = 4$. Now go to Table A.4 again (the t table does not know whether our t is for independent or nonindependent samples). For $p = .05$ and $df = 4$, the table value for t required for rejection of the null hypothesis is 2.776. Is our value 3.17 > 2.776? Yes, and therefore we reject the null hypothesis. Are the groups different? Yes. Are they significantly different? Yes. We are really rolling now, aren't we?

Simple Analysis of Variance (ANOVA)

Suppose we have the following sets of posttest scores for three randomly formed groups:

X_1	X_2	X_3
1	2	4
2	3	4
2	4	4
2	5	5
3	6	7

These sets of data are different, but are they significantly different? The appropriate test of significance to use in order to answer this question is the simple, or one-way, analysis of variance. Recall that the total variation, or variance, is a combination of between (treatment) variance and within (error) variance. In other words:

total sum of squares = between sum of squares + within
sum of squares or,

$$SS_{total} = SS_{between} + SS_{within}$$

In order to compute an ANOVA we need each term, *but*, since $C = A + B$, or $C(SS_{total}) = A(SS_{between}) + B(SS_{within})$, we only have to compute any two terms and we can easily get the third. Since we only have to calculate two we might as well do the two easiest, SS_{total} and $SS_{between}$. Once we have these we can get SS_{within} by subtraction; SS_{within} will equal $SS_{total} - SS_{between}$ ($B = C - A$). The formula for $SS_{between}$ is as follows:

$$SS_{between} = \frac{(\Sigma X_1)^2}{n_1} + \frac{(\Sigma X_2)^2}{n_2} + \frac{(\Sigma X_3)^2}{n_3} - \frac{(\Sigma X)^2}{N}$$

How easy can you get? For the first three terms all we have to do is add the scores in each group, square the total, and divide by the number of scores in the group. For the fourth term all we have to do is add up *all* the scores $(X_1 + X_2 + X_3)$, square the total and divide by the total $N(n_1 + n_2 + n_3)$. Before we do this let us look at the formula for SS_{total}:

$$SS_{total} = \Sigma X^2 - \frac{(\Sigma X)^2}{N}$$

That is even easier yet. We will already know what $(\Sigma X)^2/N$ is equal to after we calculate $SS_{between}$. The only new thing we will need is ΣX^2. You know how to do that; all we have to do is square *every* score in all three groups and add up the squares. Note that if an X or N refers to a particular group it is subscripted $(X_1, X_2, X_3$ and $n_1, n_2, n_3)$. If an X or N is not subscripted it refers to the total for all the groups. So, what do we need? We need the sum of scores for each group and the total of all the scores, and the sum of all the squares. That should be easy, let's do it:

X_1	X_1^2	X_2	X_2^2	X_3	X_3^2
1	1	2	4	4	16
2	4	3	9	4	16
2	4	4	16	4	16
2	4	5	25	5	25
3	9	6	36	7	49
10	22	20	90	24	122
ΣX_1	ΣX_1^2	ΣX_2	ΣX_2^2	ΣX_3	ΣX_3^2

$$\Sigma X = \Sigma X_1 + \Sigma X_2 + \Sigma X_3 = 10 + 20 + 24 = 54$$
$$\Sigma X^2 = \Sigma X_1^2 + \Sigma X_2^2 + \Sigma X_3^2 = 22 + 90 + 122 = 234$$
$$N = n_1 + n_2 + n_3 = 5 + 5 + 5 = 15$$

Now we are ready. First let us do SS_{total}:

$$SS_{total} = \Sigma X^2 - \frac{(\Sigma X)^2}{N}$$

$$= 234 - \frac{(54)^2}{15}$$

$$= 234 - \frac{2916}{15} \qquad (54^2 = 2916)$$

$$= 234 - 194.4 \qquad (2916 \div 15 = 194.4)$$

$$= 39.6$$

That was easy, easy, easy. Now let us do $SS_{between}$:

$$SS_{between} = \frac{(\Sigma X_1)^2}{n_1} + \frac{(\Sigma X_2)^2}{n_2} + \frac{(\Sigma X_3)^2}{n_3} - \frac{(\Sigma X)^2}{N} \text{ [11]}$$

$$= \frac{(10)^2}{5} + \frac{(20)^2}{5} + \frac{(24)^2}{5} - 194.4$$

$$= \frac{100}{5} + \frac{400}{5} + \frac{576}{5} - 194.4$$

$$= 20 + 80 + 115.2 - 194.4$$

$$= 215.2 - 194.4$$

$$= 20.8$$

(We already computed the last term, remember?)

$10^2 = 100$

$20^2 = 400$

$24^2 = 576$

$\dfrac{100}{5} = 20$

$\dfrac{400}{5} = 80$

$\dfrac{576}{5} = 115.2$

$20 + 80 + 115.2 = 215.2$

Now how are we going to get SS_{within}? Right. We subtract $SS_{between}$ from SS_{total}:

$$SS_{within} = SS_{total} - SS_{between}$$
$$= 39.6 - 20.8$$
$$= 18.8$$

Now we have everything we need to begin! Seriously, we have all the pieces but we are not quite there yet. Let us fill in a summary table with what we have and you will see what is missing:

Source of Variation	Sum of Squares		df	Mean Square	F
Between	20.8	$(K - 1)$			
Within	18.8	$(N - K)$			
Total	39.6	$(N - 1)$			

The first thing you probably noticed is that each term has its own formula for degrees of freedom. The formula for the between term is $K - 1$, where K is the number of treatment groups; thus, the degrees of freedom are $K - 1 = 3 - 1 = 2$. The formula for the within term is $N - K$, where N is the total sample size and K is still the number of treatment groups; thus, degrees of freedom for the within term $N - K = 15 - 3 = 12$. We do not need them, but for the total term $df =$

---

11. For more than three groups, the ANOVA procedure is exactly the same except that $SS_{between}$ has one extra term for each additional group. For four groups, for example,

$$SS_{between} = \frac{(\Sigma X_1)^2}{n_1} + \frac{(\Sigma X_2)^2}{n_2} + \frac{(\Sigma X_3)^2}{n_3} + \frac{(\Sigma X_4)^2}{n_4} - \frac{(\Sigma X)^2}{N}$$

$N - 1 = 15 - 1 = 14$. Now what about mean squares? Mean squares are found by dividing each sum of squares by its appropriate degrees of freedom. In other words,

$$\text{Mean Square} = \frac{\text{sum of squares}}{\text{degrees of freedom}}$$

or,

$$\text{MS} = \frac{\text{SS}}{df}$$

For between, MS_B, we get:

$$\text{MS}_B = \frac{\text{SS}_B}{df}$$
$$= \frac{20.8}{2}$$
$$= 10.40$$

For within, MS_W, we get:

$$\text{MS}_W = \frac{\text{SS}_W}{df}$$
$$= \frac{18.8}{12}$$
$$= 1.57$$

Now all we need is our F ratio. The F ratio is a ratio of MS_B and MS_W:

$$F = \frac{\text{MS}_B}{\text{MS}_W}$$

Therefore for our example:

$$F = \frac{\text{MS}_B}{\text{MS}_W}$$
$$= \frac{10.40}{1.57}$$
$$= 6.62$$

Filling in the rest of our summary table we have:

Source of Variation	Sum of Squares	df		Mean Square	F
Between	20.8	$(K - 1)$	2	10.40	6.62
Within	18.8	$(N - K)$	12	1.57	
Total	39.6	$(N - 1)$	14		

Thus, $F = 6.62$ with 2 and 12 degrees of freedom. Assuming $p = .05$, we are now ready to go to our F table, Table A.5 in the Appendix. Across the top of Table A.5, the row labeled n_1 refers to the degrees of freedom for the between term, in our case 2. Find it? Down the extreme left-hand side of the table, in the column labeled n_2, are the degrees of freedom for the within term, in our case 12. Find it? Good. Now, where these two values intersect (go down the 2 column and across the 12 row) we find 3.88, the value of F required for significance (required in order to reject the null hypothesis) if $p = .05$. The question is whether our F value 6.62 is greater than 3.88. It is. Therefore we reject the null hypothesis and conclude that there is a significant difference among the group means.

 WHEW!! That was long, *but* it was not hard, was it?

The Scheffe' Test

In the above example the only thing the F ratio told us was that there was at least one significant difference *somewhere*. In order to find out *where* we will apply the Scheffe' test. The Scheffe' test involves calculation of an F ratio for each mean comparison of interest. As you study the following formula, you will notice that we already have almost all of the information we need to apply the Scheffe' test:

$$F = \frac{(\bar{X}_1 - \bar{X}_2)^2}{MS_W\left(\dfrac{1}{n_1} + \dfrac{1}{n_2}\right)(K - 1)} \quad \text{with } df = (K - 1)(N - K)$$

Where in the world do we get MS_W? Correct! MS_W is the MS_W from the analysis of variance which is 1.57. The degrees of freedom are also from the ANOVA, 2 and 12. Of course the above formula is for the comparison of $\bar{X}_1$ and $\bar{X}_2$. To compare any other two means we simply change the $\bar{X}$s and the ns. So before we can apply the Scheffe' test, the only thing we have to calculate is the mean for each group. Looking back at our ANOVA example, the sums for each group were 10, 20, and 24, respectively. Thus, the three means are:

$$\bar{X}_1 = \frac{\Sigma X_1}{n_1} = \frac{10}{5} = 2.00$$

$$\bar{X}_2 = \frac{\Sigma X_2}{n_2} = \frac{20}{5} = 4.00$$

$$\bar{X}_3 = \frac{\Sigma X_3}{n_3} = \frac{24}{5} = 4.80$$

Applying the Scheffe' test to $\bar{X}_1$ and $\bar{X}_2$ we get:

$$F = \frac{(\bar{X}_1 - \bar{X}_2)^2}{MS_W\left(\dfrac{1}{n_1} + \dfrac{1}{n_2}\right)(K - 1)} = \frac{(2.00 - 4.00)^2}{1.57\left(\dfrac{1}{5} + \dfrac{1}{5}\right)2}$$

$$= \frac{(-2.00)^2}{1.57 \left(\frac{2}{5}\right) 2}$$

$$= \frac{4}{1.57(.4)2}$$

$$= \frac{4}{1.57(.8)}$$

$$= \frac{4}{1.256}$$

$$= 3.18$$

Since the value of F required for significance is 3.88 if $p = .05$ and $df = 2$ and 12, and since $3.18 < 3.88$, we conclude that there is no significant difference between $\bar{X}_1$ and $\bar{X}_2$.

Applying the Scheffe' test to $\bar{X}_1$ and $\bar{X}_3$ we get:

$$F = \frac{(\bar{X}_1 - \bar{X}_3)^2}{MS_W \left(\frac{1}{n_1} + \frac{1}{n_3}\right)(K-1)} \qquad = \frac{(2.00 - 4.80)^2}{1.57 \left(\frac{1}{5} + \frac{1}{5}\right) 2}$$

$$= \frac{(-2.80)^2}{1.256}$$

$$= \frac{7.84}{1.256}$$

$$= 6.24$$

Since $6.24 > 3.88$, we conclude that there is a significant difference between $\bar{X}_1$ and $\bar{X}_3$. Note that since the ns are equal in our example, that is, $n_1 = n_2 = n_3$, the denominator is the same as for the $\bar{X}_1$ and $\bar{X}_2$ comparison. And similarly for $\bar{X}_2$ and $\bar{X}_3$ we get:

$$F = \frac{(\bar{X}_2 - \bar{X}_3)^2}{MS_W \left(\frac{1}{n_2} + \frac{1}{n_3}\right)(K-1)} \qquad = \frac{(4.00 - 4.80)^2}{1.57 \left(\frac{1}{5} + \frac{1}{5}\right) 2}$$

$$= \frac{(-.80)^2}{1.256}$$

$$= \frac{.64}{1.256}$$

$$= .51$$

Since $.51 < 3.88$, we conclude that there is no significant difference between $\bar{X}_2$ and $\bar{X}_3$. In other words, group 3 performed significantly better than group 1 and that is the only significant difference. Even though group 2 performed better than group 1 ($\bar{X}_1 = 2.00$, $\bar{X}_2 = 4.00$), the difference, 2.00, is not a significant difference.

The Scheffe' test can also be used to compare combinations of means. Suppose, for example, that group 1 was a control group and we wanted to compare the mean of group 1 to the mean of groups 2 and 3 combined. First we would have to combine the means for groups 2 and 3 as follows:

$$\bar{X}_{2+3} = \frac{n_2\bar{X}_2 + n_3\bar{X}_3}{n_2 + n_3} = \frac{5(4.00) + 5(4.80)}{5 + 5}$$

$$= \frac{20.00 + 24.00}{10}$$

$$= \frac{44.00}{10}$$

$$= 4.40$$

Of course, since $n_2 = n_3$, we could have simply averaged the means as follows:

$$\bar{X}_{2+3} = \frac{\bar{X}_2 + \bar{X}_3}{2} = \frac{4.00 + 4.80}{2} = \frac{8.80}{2} = 4.40$$

Next, we simply calculate the F ratio using $\bar{X}_1 = 2.00$ and the combined mean $\bar{X}_{2+3} = 4.40$:

$$F = \frac{(\bar{X}_1 - \bar{X}_{2+3})^2}{MS_W \left(\frac{1}{n_1} + \frac{1}{n_2 + n_3}\right)(K-1)} = \frac{(2.00 - 4.40)^2}{1.57 \left(\frac{1}{5} + \frac{1}{10}\right)2}$$

$$= \frac{(-.40)^2}{1.57(.2 + .1)2}$$

$$= \frac{5.76}{1.57(.3)2}$$

$$= \frac{5.76}{.94}$$

$$= 6.13$$

Since $6.13 > 3.88$, we would conclude that there is a significant difference between $\bar{X}_1$ and $\bar{X}_{2+3}$. In other words, the experimental groups performed significantly better than the control group.

Chi Square

A one-dimensional chi square (x^2) is the easiest statistic of all. To use our peanut butter example, we asked 90 people to indicate which brand they thought tasted better; 40 picked brand X, 30 picked brand Y, and 20 picked brand Z. If there were no difference between the brands we would expect the same number of people to choose each brand, 30 (90 ÷ 3 = 30). Therefore, we have the following table:

Brand

	X	Y	Z	
observed	40	30	20	total: 90
expected	30	30	30	

In order to determine whether the observed frequencies are significantly different from the expected frequencies we apply the following formula:

$$x^2 = \sum \left[\frac{(fo - fe)^2}{fe} \right]$$

All this formula says is that for each category (X, Y, and Z) we subtract the expected frequency (fe) from the observed frequency (fo), square the difference, $(fo - fe)^2$, and then divide by the expected frequency, fe. The big Σ says that after we do the above for each term we add up the resulting values. Thus, substituting our table values into the formula we get:

$$
\begin{array}{ccccc}
& X & & Y & & Z \\
& fo \quad fe & & fo \quad fe & & fo \quad fe \\
x^2 = & \dfrac{(40 - 30)^2}{30} & + & \dfrac{(30 - 30)^2}{30} & + & \dfrac{(20 - 30)^2}{30} \\
& fe & & fe & & fe \\
= & \dfrac{(10)^2}{30} & + & \dfrac{(0)^2}{30} & + & \dfrac{(-10)^2}{30} \\
= & \dfrac{100}{30} & + & 0 & + & \dfrac{100}{30} \\
= & 3.33 & + & 0 & + & 3.33 \\
= & 6.66 & & & &
\end{array}
$$

Thus $x^2 = 6.66$. The degrees of freedom for a one-dimensional chi square are determined by the formula $(K - 1)$ where K equals the number of categories, in our case 3. Thus $df = K - 1 = 3 - 1 = 2$. Therefore, we have $x^2 = 6.66$, $p = .05$, $df = 2$. To determine whether the differences between observed and expected frequencies are significant, we compare our chi square value to the appropriate value in Table A.6 in the Appendix. Run the index finger of your right hand across the top until you find $p = .05$. Now run the index finger of your left hand down the extreme left-hand column and find $df = 2$. Run your left hand across and your right hand down and they will intersect at 5.991. Is our value of 6.66 > 5.991? Yes. Therefore, we reject the null hypothesis. There is a significant difference between observed and expected proportions; the brands of peanut butter compared do taste different! Suppose we had selected $p = .01$. The chi square value required for significance would be 9.210. Is our value of 6.66 > 9.210? No. Therefore, we would not reject the null hypothesis and we would conclude that there is no significant difference between observed and expected frequencies; the three brands of peanut butter taste the same. Thus, you can see that selection of a p level is important; different conclusions may very well be drawn with different p levels.

14

Using the Computer for
Data Analysis

Enablers

After reading chapter 14, you should be able to:

1. Describe the three major costs associated with using the computer for data analysis.

2. List the major steps involved in using the computer for data analysis.

When to Use the Computer

The computer can save the researcher many hours of computation time and rechecking time. The computer, however, is not magic, nor is it a gigantic toy. Some beginning researchers think that all they have to do is turn over their data to the computer and "poof!" out will come the analyses. Beginning researchers also have a tendency to want to analyze everything is sight; after all they do not have to do the work, the computer will. The decision to use the computer, however, is not an automatic one. Preparing data for computer analysis takes time and actual processing costs money. For many studies the researcher may actually save time and money by *not* using the computer. If sample sizes are not large, if a limited number of variables are involved, and if relatively simple statistical analyses are to be performed, use of a calculator may be the most efficient approach to data analysis. Of course if the opposite is true, the computer is a logical choice of an analysis tool. Some statistical analyses, such as analysis of covariance and factorial analysis of variance, are rarely done by hand by experienced researchers.

A good guideline for beginning researchers, however, is that you should not use the computer to perform an analysis that you have never done yourself by hand. After you have performed several analyses of variance on various sets of data, for example, you will have the knowledge and comprehension necessary to effectively use the computer for subsequent analyses. Instructions for preparing data for computer processing will make sense to you and you will know what the resulting output sheets should look like. After you have acquired first-hand experience with a variety of statistics you will be in a position to judge whether the data for a given study can more efficiently be handled by computer analysis.

Most universities have computer facilities. If you ever plan to use the computer you should become familiar with the facilities, services, and equipment available and should sign up for the related instruction which is usually available. To use an analogy, you do not just hand your money to a bank officer, tell him or her to take care of it, and hope everything turns out all right. Before you put your money in a bank you try to find out as much about it as possible. Before you open an account you want to know the bank's hours, services available, and charges associated with each service. When you receive your monthly statement you check it very carefully for errors and you make sure you understand every number on the printout. The same care should be taken in using a computer center. Before you start processing data you should learn as much as you can, and when you get your output sheet it should be as understandable to you as a bank statement; you should know where all the numbers come from and what they mean.

Costs Associated with Computer Use

In many cases, computer services are free to graduate students; when they are not, they are usually within the beginning researcher's budget. The major costs associated with computer analysis are for programming, keypunching, and computer time. Programming costs for statistical analyses are usually nil or very minimal. This is because programs for many standard analyses have already been written and are available for use by the researcher. Typically, a number of such programs are available in a collection referred to as a statistical package. All of the programs in a given package have a set of instructions in common and specific instructions for each program. These instructions are typically described in manuals that are usually available in college and university bookstores. The statistical package that is probably available at more computer centers than any other is SPSS, *Statistical Package for the Social Sciences*. SPSS includes programs for many statistics frequently used in research studies. For most analyses, the information you need for using SPSS will be included in the *SPSS Primer*.[1] More detailed information on features and statistical procedures is contained in the complete manual upon which the primer is based.[2] Another frequently used statistical package is the BMD package.[3] The BMD package also provides for application of a wide variety of statistics frequently used in educational research.

Occasionally an existing program may require some modification but usually you will be able to locate one that does exactly what you need done. Keypunching costs usually involve paying a keypuncher so much an hour to transform your data from data sheets to the punched cards that are fed into the computer. Keypunching is a relatively simple process, however, which is worth your while to learn. Doing your own keypunching not only saves you money but also may reduce keypunching errors since you can read your data sheets better than anyone else. The third major cost, charges for computer time, is usually very

1. Klecka, W.R., Nie, N.H., & Hull, C.H. *SPSS Primer: Statistical package for the social sciences primer.* New York: McGraw-Hill, 1975.

2. Nie, N.H., Hull, C.H., Jenkins, J.G., Steinbrenner, K., & Bent, D.H. *SPSS: Statistical package for the social sciences* (2nd ed.). New York: McGraw-Hill, 1975.

3. Dixon, W.J. (Ed.). *BMD: Biomedical computer programs.* Berkeley: University of California Press, 1973.

reasonable (if not free for students). While the costs per hour for computer processing time are high, the analyses typically required for a research project usually use no more than a few minutes. Thus, if you use an existing program, keypunch your own data, and are given free processing time, the entire operation may cost you nothing but time.

Steps in Using the Computer

The first step in using the computer is to select an appropriate program. The program selected will indicate how the data may be keypunched and what instruction cards need to be punched. Instruction cards tell the computer all about your data, including such information as sample sizes, number of variables, and how the data are arranged on the data cards. Then the data and the instructions are keypunched onto 80-column cards. All resulting cards must be checked for accuracy. In fact, many computer centers have a machine which will print out on a sheet the information punched on your cards. When you are through, you are ready to turn in your program deck for processing. It is always a good idea to make a second set of cards just in case something happens to the first deck. Most computer centers also have a machine that will make a duplicate deck for you. Turnaround time, or how long it takes to get your output after you have submitted your cards, depends usually on how busy the center is at the time. You may have to wait only a few minutes or you may be advised to come back after some specified period of time. When you pick up your output the first things you look for are error messages. They tell you that the analyses were not performed because you did something wrong, anything from not following program instructions to putting a card in the wrong place. If your program has run successfully you then examine the output figures to see if they make sense. If you read your data in wrong, the program may be executed correctly but you may have "wrong answers." For example, if your data are IQ scores, and the output tells you that the mean IQ was 10.4, you probably misplaced a decimal point somewhere!

Postanalysis Procedures

Enablers

After reading chapter 15, you should be able to:

1. List at least six guidelines to be followed in verifying and storing data.
2. Explain how a rejected null hypothesis relates to a research hypothesis.
3. Explain how a null hypothesis which is not rejected relates to a research hypothesis.
4. Identify the major use of significant unhypothesized relationships.
5. Explain the difference between statistical and practical significance.
6. Define or describe replication.

Verification and Storage of Data

After you have completed all the statistical analyses necessary to describe your data and test your hypothesis, you do not say, "thank goodness, I'm done!" and happily throw away all your data and your work sheets. The data must be thoroughly checked and stored in an organized manner.

Verification

The very first thing you should do when you think you are done is to recheck all your work. You should have double-checked test scores before you started data analysis; make sure all scores were correctly recorded onto data sheets or cards, if you have not already done so. Then carefully check all your calculations. You may have noticed that we applied each statistic step by step, leaving no steps to the imagination. This was probably helpful to some and annoying to others. Math superstar types seem to derive great satisfaction from doing several steps in a row "in their heads" and writing down the results instead of separately recording the result of each step. This may save time in the short run but not necessarily in the long run. If you end up with a result that just does not look right it is a lot easier to spot an error if every step is in front of you.

Also, do not just check the steps you followed after you had an arithmetic problem; check every value that you substituted into the formula in order to make it an arithmetic problem. A very frustrated student once came to me with the very sad tale that he had been up all night, had rechecked his work over and over and over, and still kept getting a negative sum of squares in his ANOVA. He was at the point where he could easily have been convinced that squares can be negative! An inspection of his work revealed very quickly that the problem was not in his execution of ANOVA but in the numbers he was trying to do ANOVA with. Early in the game he had added ΣX_1^2, ΣX_2^2, and ΣX_3^2 and obtained a number much, much larger than their actual sum. From that point on, he was doomed. The moral of the story is that if you have checked a set of figures several times and they are still correct, do not check them 50 more times, look elsewhere. Make sure you are using the correct formula and make sure you have substituted the correct numbers. The anecdote also illustrates that the results should make sense. If your scores range from 20 to 94 and you get a standard deviation of 1.2 you have probably made a mistake somewhere because 1.2 does not look reasonable. Similarly, if your means are 24.2 and 26.1 and you get a t ratio of 44.82 you had better recheck everything ve-ry carefully.

The above discussion applies equally well regardless of whether you do your analyses by hand, with the aid of a calculator, or with the aid of a computer. There is really no need for anyone to do any analysis by hand when calculators are so readily available. In fact, purchase of an inexpensive one (they sell for under $10.00) which performs only addition, subtraction, multiplication, and division is an excellent investment for a beginning researcher. Besides making life easier for you, it also reduces the likelihood of computational errors. If you punch the correct numbers in, they almost always give you the correct answer. Some of the more sophisticated desk models also provide a record of your work on a tape. Most campuses have at least one such machine somewhere.

If you use the computer you should double-check your input. Make sure you are giving the computer the correct data and the correct directions concerning what to do with the data. Also, although you can usually be pretty safe in assuming that the computer will accurately execute each analysis, it is a good idea to spot check. The computer only does what it has been programmed to do and programming errors do occur. Thus, if the computer gives you six F ratios, calculate at least one yourself; if it agrees with the one the computer gave you, the rest are most probably correct.

Storage

When you are convinced that your work is accurate, all data sheets or cards, work sheets, and records of calculations should be labeled, organized, and filed in a safe place. You never know when you might need your data again. Sometimes an additional analysis is desired either by the original researcher or by another researcher who wishes to analyze the data using a different statistical technique. Also, it is not highly unusual to use data from one study in a later study. Therefore, all of the data should be carefully labeled with as many identification labels as possible, labels such as the dates of the study, the nature of each treatment group, and whether data are pretest data, posttest data, or data for a control variable (such as IQ). All work sheets should also be clearly labeled to indicate the identity of the group(s), the analysis, and the scores, for example, "social reinforcement group/standard deviation/posttest." If the same analysis covers more than one page, fully label each page and indicate "page 1 of 4, page 2 of 4, . . ." A convenient, practical way to store data is in loose-leaf ring binders, or notebooks. Notebooks can be labeled on the binding, for example, "Reinforcement Study, Spring, 1976," and pages are not likely to slip out and become lost as when manila folders are used. Lastly, find a safe place for all and guard it very carefully. A few years ago the author learned a lesson the hard way. In the process of moving from one location to another, the box containing all the data for a major study got lost in the action, never to be seen again. Naturally, since that time several requests for the data have been received. Also, since that tragic event, all subsequent records have been given a royal escort whenever similiar journeys have been called for.

Interpretation of Results

The result of the application of a test of significance is a number and only a number, a value which is statistically significant or not statistically significant. What it actually *means* requires interpretation by the researcher. The results of statistical analyses need to be interpreted in terms of the purpose of the study, the original research hypothesis, and with respect to other studies that have been conducted in the same area of research.

Hypothesized Results

The researcher must discuss whether the results support the research hypothesis and why or why not, and whether the results are in agreement with other findings and why or why not. If your results are not in agreement with other research, reasons for the discrepancy must be discussed. There may have been validity problems in your study or you may have discovered a relationship previously not uncovered. The work of Yvonne Brackbill is a good example of the latter. The results of her studies suggested that contrary to previous evidence derived from animal studies, immediate feedback is not necessarily superior to delayed feedback when human beings are involved, especially with respect to delayed retention.[1] Subsequent studies have confirmed her findings. On the other hand, if you reject a null hypothesis, your research hypothesis may be supported but it is not proven. One study does not prove anything; it only shows that in one instance the hypothesis was supported. Also, a supported research hypothesis does not necessarily mean that your treatment would "work" with different populations, different materials, and different dependent variables. As an example, if token reinforcement is found to be effective in improving the behavior of first graders this does not mean that token reinforcement will necessarily be effective in reducing referrals to the principal at the high school level. In other words, do not overgeneralize.

If you do not reject the null hypothesis, and your research hypothesis is not supported, you do not apologize. The natural reaction is this situation for beginning researchers is to be very disappointed. In the first place, failure to reject a null hypothesis does not necessarily mean that your research hypothesis is false, but even if it is, it is just as important to know what does not work as what does, which variables are not related as which are. Of course if there were some serious validity problems with your study you should describe them in detail. Also, if for

---

1. See, for example, Brackbill, Y., & Kappy, M.S. Delay of reinforcement and retention. *Journal of Comparative and Physiological Psychology.* 1962, 55(1), 14–18.

some reason you lost a lot of subjects you should discuss why, and how the study may have been affected.[2] But do not rationalize. If your study was well planned and well conducted, and no unforeseen mishaps occurred, do not try to come up with *some* reason why your study did not "come out right." It may very well have "come out right"; the null hypothesis might be true. But you do not know that. All you know is that it was not rejected in your study. In other words, there is no evidence either way concerning the truth or falsity of the hypothesized relationship.

Unhypothesized Results

Unhypothesized results should be interpreted with great care. Often during a study an apparent relationship will be noticed which was not hypothesized. You might notice, for example, that experimental subjects appear to require fewer examples to learn new math concepts, an unhypothesized relationship. You do not go and change your original hypothesis, nor do you slip in a new one; hypotheses must be formulated a priori based on deductions from theory and/or experience. A true test of a hypothesis comes from its ability to explain and predict what *will* happen, not what *is* happening. You can, however, collect and analyze data on these unforeseen relationships and present your results as such. These findings may then form the basis for a later study, conducted by yourself or another investigator, specifically designed to test a hypothesis related to your findings. Do not fall into the trap, however, of searching frantically for *something* that might be significant if your study does not appear to be going as hypothesized. Fishing expeditions in experimental studies are just as bad as fishing expeditions in correlational studies.

Statistical Versus Practical Significance

The fact that results are statistically significant does not automatically mean that they are of any educational value. Statistical significance only means that your results would be likely to occur by chance a certain percentage of the time, say 5%. This only means that the observed relationship or difference is probably a real one, not necessarily an important one. With very large samples, for example, a very small correlation coefficient may be statistically significant but of no real practical use to anybody. Similarly, the error term of the t test is affected by the sample size; as the sample size increases, the error term (denominator) tends to decrease, and thus the t ratio increases. Thus, with very large samples a very small mean difference may yield a significant t. A mean difference of two points might be statistically significant but probably not worth the effort of revising a curriculum.

Thus, in a way, the smaller sample sizes typically used in educational research studies actually have a redeeming feature. Given that smaller sample sizes mean

---

2. Recall that an insufficient number of subjects affects the power of a study and that power refers to statistical ability to reject a false null hypothesis. In other words, if your sample size is too small you may lack the power to reject the null hypothesis even if it is false. Power is also affected by the type of statistic used (parametric tests are more powerful than nonparametric tests) and by group variance on the dependent variable.

less power, and given that a greater mean difference is probably required for rejection of the null hypothesis, more observed relationships are probably practically significant than if larger samples were involved. Of course, by the same token, our lack of power may keep us from finding some important relationships. In any event, you should always take care in interpreting results. The fact that method A is significantly more effective than method B *statistically* does not mean that the whole world should immediately adopt method A!

Replication of Results

Perhaps the strongest support for a research hypothesis comes from replication of results. Replication means that the study is done again. The second (third, etc.) study may be a repetition of the original study, using the same or different subjects, or it may represent an alternative approach to testing the same hypothesis. Although repeating the study with the same subjects (which is feasible only in certain types of research, such as those involving single-subject designs) supports the reliability of results, repeating the study with different subjects in the same or different settings, increases the generalizability of the findings.[3] Brackbill's hypothesis concerning the effectiveness of delayed feedback, for example, was increasingly supported as other researchers repeatedly demonstrated the effect with other types of subjects and other learning tasks. The need for replication is especially great when an unusual or new relationship is found in a study, or when the results have practical significance and the treatment investigated might really make a difference. Interpretation and discussion of a replicated finding will invariably be less "hedgey" than a first-time-ever finding, and rightly so.

The significance of a relationship may also be enhanced if it is replicated in a more natural setting. A highly controlled study, for example, might find that method A is more effective than method B *in a laboratory-like environment.* Interpretation and discussion of the results in terms of practical significance and implications for classroom practice would have to be stated with due caution. If the same results could then be obtained in a classroom situation, however, the researcher could be less tentative concerning their generalizability.

Summary

Chapter 11/Preanalysis Procedures

Preparing Data for Analysis

Scoring Procedures

1. All instruments administered should be scored accurately and consistently; each subject's test should be scored using the same procedures and criteria.

---

3. Sidman, M. *Tactics of scientific research: Evaluating experimental data in psychology.* New York: Basic Books, 1960.

2. When a standardized instrument is used, the scoring process is greatly facilitated; the test manual usually spells out the steps to be followed in scoring each test (or answer sheet), and a scoring key is often provided.

3. Scoring self-developed instruments is more complex, especially if open-ended items are involved. Steps for scoring each item and for arriving at a total score must be delineated and carefully followed. If other than objective-type items are to be scored it is advisable to also have at least one other person score the tests as a reliability check. Tentative scoring procedures should always be tried out beforehand by administering the instrument to a group of subjects from the same or a similar population as the one from which subjects will be selected for the actual study.

4. If a test scoring service is available on your campus, and if your questions can be responded to on a standard, machine-scorable answer sheet, you can save yourself a lot of time and increase the accuracy of the scoring process if you take advantage of the service.

Tabulation Procedures

5. After instruments have been scored, the results are transferred to summary data sheets and/or data cards.

6. If planned analyses involve subgroup comparisons, scores should be tabulated for each subgroup.

7. When a number of different kinds of data are collected for each subject, such as several test scores and biographical information, data are frequently recorded on data cards, one card for each subject.

8. The card for each subject follows the same format, and both the variable names and the actual data are frequently coded.

9. If a computer is to be used, data must be presented in a machine-readable form, usually on punched cards.

Types of Measurement Scales

10. Depending upon the variables, and the way in which they are measured, different kinds of data result, representing different scales of measurement.

11. It is important to know which type of scale is represented by your data since different statistics are appropriate for different scales of measurement.

Nominal Scales

12. A nominal scale represents the lowest level of measurement.

13. Such a scale classifies persons or objects into two or more categories.

14. Whatever the basis for classification, a person can only be in one category, and members of a given category have a common set of characteristics.

Ordinal Scales

15. An ordinal scale not only classifies subjects but also ranks them in terms of the degree to which they possess a characteristic of interest.

16. Intervals between ranks are not equal.

Interval Scales

17. An interval scale has all the characteristics of a nominal scale and an ordinal scale, but in addition it is based upon predetermined equal intervals.

18. Most of the tests used in educational research, such as achievement tests, aptitude tests, and intelligence tests, represent interval scales.

19. Interval scales do not have a true zero point.

Ratio Scales

20. A ratio scale represents the highest, most precise, level of measurement.

21. A ratio scale has all the advantages of the other types of scales and in addition it has a meaningful, true zero point.

22. Because of the true zero point, not only can we say that the difference between a height of 3′ 2″ and a height of 4′ 2″ is the same as the difference between 5′ 4″ and 6′ 4″, but also that a man 6′ 4″ is twice as tall as a child 3′ 2″.

23. Since most physical measures represent ratio scales, but not psychological measures, ratio scales are not used very often in educational research.

24. A statistic appropriate for a lower level of measurement may be applied to data representing a higher level of measurement; the reverse is not true.

Chapter 12/Descriptive Statistics

Types of Descriptive Statistics

25. The first step in data analysis is to describe, or summarize, the data using descriptive statistics.

26. Descriptive statistics permit the researcher to meaningfully describe many, many scores with a small number of indices.

27. If such indices are calculated for a sample drawn from a population, the resulting values are referred to as statistics; if they are calculated for an entire population, they are referred to as parameters.

Graphing Data

28. The shape of the distribution may not be self-evident, especially if a large number of scores are involved.

29. The most common method of graphing research data is to construct a frequency polygon.

30. The first step in constructing a frequency polygon is to list all the scores and to tabulate how many subjects received each score. Once the scores are tallied, the steps are as follows: place all the scores on a horizontal axis, at equal intervals, from lowest score to highest; place the frequencies of scores at equal intervals on the vertical axis, starting with zero; for each score, find the point where the score intersects with its frequency of occurrence and make a dot; connect all the dots with straight lines.

Measures of Central Tendency

31. Measures of central tendency give the researcher a convenient way of describing a set of data with a single number.

32. The number resulting from computation of a measure of central tendency represents the average or typical score attained by a group of subjects.

33. Each index of central tendency is appropriate for a different scale of measurement; the mode is appropriate for nominal data, the median for ordinal data, and the mean for interval or ratio data.

The Mode

35. The mode is the score that is attained by more subjects than any other score.

36. The mode is not established through calculation; it is determined by looking at a set of scores or at a graph of scores and seeing which score occurs most frequently.

37. There are several problems associated with the mode, and it is therefore of limited value and seldom used. For one thing, a set of scores may have two (or more) modes, in which case it is referred to as bimodal. Another problem with the mode is that it is an unstable measure of central tendency; equal-sized samples randomly selected from the same accessible population are likely to have different modes.

38. When nominal data are involved, however, the mode is the only appropriate measure of central tendency.

The Median

39. The median is that point in a distribution above and below which are 50% of the scores; in other words, the median is the midpoint.

40. The median does not take into account each and every score; it ignores, for example, extremely high scores and extremely low scores.

The Mean

41. The mean is the arithmetic average of the scores and is the most frequently used measure of central tendency.

42. By the very nature of the way in which it is computed, the mean takes into account, or is based on, each and every score.

43. It is appropriate when the data represent either an interval or a ratio scale and is a more precise, stable index than both the median and the mode.

44. In situations in which there are one or more extreme scores, the median will be the best index of typical performance.

Measures of Variability

45. Two sets of data that are very different can have identical means or medians.

46. Thus, there is a need for a measure that indicates how spread out the scores are, how much variability there is.

47. While the standard deviation is by far the most often used, the range is the only appropriate measure of variability for nominal data, and the quartile deviation is the appropriate index of variability for ordinal data.

48. As with measures of central tendency, measures of variability appropriate for nominal and ordinal data may be used with interval or ratio data even though the standard deviation is generally the preferred index of variability.

The Range

49. The range is simply the difference between the highest and lowest score in a distribution and is determined by subtraction.

50. Like the mode, the range is not a very stable measure of variability, and its chief advantage is that it gives a quick, rough estimate of variability.

The Quartile Deviation

51. The quartile deviation is one-half of the difference between the upper quartile (the 75th percentile) and lower quartile (the 25th percentile) in a distribution.

52. The quartile deviation is a more stable measure of variability than the range and is appropriate whenever the median is appropriate.

The Standard Deviation

53. Like the mean, its counterpart measure of central tendency, the standard deviation is the most stable measure of variability and takes into account each and every score.

54. If you know the mean and the standard deviation of a set of scores, you have a pretty good picture of what the distribution looks like.

55. If the distribution is relatively normal, then the mean plus 3 standard deviations and the mean minus 3 standard deviations encompasses just about all the scores, over 99% of them.

The Normal Curve

56. Many, many variables do yield a normal curve if a sufficient number of subjects are measured.

Normal Distributions

57. If a variable is normally distributed, that is, does form a normal curve, then several things are true. First, 50% of the scores are above the mean and 50% of the scores are below the mean. Second, the mean, the median, and the mode are the same. Third, most scores are near the mean and the farther from the mean a score is, the fewer the number of subjects who attained that score. Fourth, the same number, or percentage, of scores is between the mean and plus one standard deviation ($\bar{X} + 1$ SD) as is between the mean and minus one standard deviation ($\bar{X} - 1$ SD), and similarly for $\bar{X} \pm 2$ SD and $\bar{X} \pm 3$ SD.

58. If scores are normally distributed, the following are true statements:

$\bar{X} \pm 1.0$ SD = Approximately 68% of the scores
$\bar{X} \pm 2.0$ SD = Approximately 95% of the scores
          (1.96 SD is exactly 95%)
$\bar{X} \pm 2.5$ SD = Approximately 99% of the scores
          (2.58 SD is exactly 99%)
$\bar{X} \pm 3.0$ SD = Approximately 99+% of the scores

And similarly, the following are always true:

$\bar{X} - 3.0$ SD = Approximately the .1 percentile
$\bar{X} - 2.0$ SD = Approximately the 2nd percentile
$\bar{X} - 1.0$ SD = Approximately the 16th percentile
$\bar{X}$ = The 50th percentile
$\bar{X} + 1.0$ SD = Approximately the 84th percentile
$\bar{X} + 2.0$ SD = Approximately the 98th percentile
$\bar{X} + 3.0$ SD = Approximately the 99+ percentile

59. Many variables form a normal distribution, including physical measures, such as height and weight, and psychological measures, such as intelligence and aptitude.

60. Since research studies deal with a finite number of subjects, and often a not very large number, research data only more or less approximate a normal curve.

Skewed Distributions

61. When a distribution is not normal, it is said to be skewed.

62. A distribution which is skewed is not symmetrical, and the values of the mean, the median, and the mode are different.

63. In a skewed distribution, there are more extreme scores at one end than the other. If the extreme scores are at the lower end of the distribution, the distribution is said to be negatively skewed; if the extreme scores are at the upper, or higher, end of the distribution, the distribution is said to be positively skewed.

64. In both cases, the mean is "pulled" in the direction of the extreme scores.

65. For a negatively skewed distribution the mean ($\overline{X}$) is always lower, or smaller, than the median (md); for a positively skewed distribution the mean is always higher, or greater, than the median. Usually, in a negatively skewed distribution the mean and the median are lower, or smaller, than the mode, whereas in a positively skewed distribution the mean and the median are higher, or greater, than the mode.

Measures of Relationship

66. Degree of relationship is expressed as a correlation coefficient which is computed based on the two sets of scores.

67. If two variables are highly related, a correlation coefficient near +1.00 (or −1.00) will be obtained; if two variables are not related, a coefficient near .00 will be obtained.

The Spearman Rho

68. If the data for one of the variables are expressed as ranks instead of scores, the Spearman rho is the appropriate measure of correlation.

69. The Spearman rho is thus appropriate when the data represent an ordinal scale (although it may be used with interval data) and is used when the median and quartile deviation are used.

70. If only one of the variables to be correlated is in rank order, for example, class standing at time of graduation, then the other variable to be correlated with it must also be expressed in terms of ranks.

71. The Spearman rho is interpreted in the same way as the Pearson r and produces a coefficient somewhere between −1.00 and +1.00.

72. If more than one subject receives the same score then their ranks are averaged.

The Pearson r

73. The Pearson r is the most appropriate measure of correlation when the sets of data to be correlated represent either interval or ratio scales.

74. Like the mean and the standard deviation, the Pearson r takes into account each and every score in both distributions; it is also the most stable measure of correlation.

75. Since most educational measures represent interval scales, the Pearson r is usually the appropriate coefficient for determining relationship.

76. An assumption associated with the application of the Pearson r is that the relationship between the variables being correlated is a linear one.

Measures of Relative Position

77. Measures of relative position indicate where a score is in relation to all other scores in the distribution.

78. A major advantage of such measures is that they make it possible to compare the performance of an individual on two or more different tests.

Percentile Ranks

79. A percentile rank indicates the percentage of scores that fall below a given score.

80. Percentiles are appropriate for data representing an ordinal scale, although they are frequently computed for interval data.

81. The median of a set of scores corresponds to the 50th percentile.

Standard Scores

82. A standard score is a measure of relative position which is appropriate when the data represent an interval or ratio scale.

83. A z score expresses how far a score is from the mean in terms of standard deviation units.

84. If a set of scores is transformed into a set of z scores, the new distribution has a mean of 0 and a standard deviation of 1.

85. The major advantage of the z score is that it allows scores from different tests to be compared.

86. The only problem with z scores is that they involve negative numbers and decimals. A simple solution is to transform z scores into Z scores. To do this you simply multiply the z score by 10 and add 50.

87. Stanines are standard scores that divide a distribution into nine parts.

Calculation for Interval Data

Symbols

88. Symbols commonly used in statistical formulas are as follows:

$$X = \text{any score}$$
$$\Sigma = \text{the sum of; add them up}$$
$$\Sigma X = \text{the sum of all the scores}$$
$$\bar{X} = \text{the mean, or arithmetic average, of}$$
$$\text{the scores}$$
$$N = \text{total number of subjects}$$
$$n = \text{number of subjects in a particular}$$
$$\text{group}$$
$$\Sigma X^2 = \text{the sum of all the squares; square each}$$
$$\text{score and add up all the squares}$$
$$(\Sigma X)^2 = \text{the square of the sum; add up all the scores}$$
$$\text{and square the sum, or total.}$$

The Mean

89. The formula for the mean is $\bar{X} = \dfrac{\Sigma X}{N}$

The Standard Deviation

90. The formula for the standard deviation is

$$SD = \sqrt{\frac{SS}{N}}, \text{ where } SS = \Sigma X^2 - \frac{(\Sigma X)^2}{N}$$

The Pearson r

91. The formula for the Pearson r is

$$r = \frac{\Sigma XY - \frac{(\Sigma X)(\Sigma Y)}{N}}{\sqrt{\left[\Sigma X^2 - \frac{(\Sigma X)^2}{N}\right]\left[\Sigma Y^2 - \frac{(\Sigma Y)^2}{N}\right]}}$$

92. The formula for degrees of freedom for the Pearson r is $N - 2$.

Standard Scores

93. The formula for a z score is $z = \frac{X - \bar{X}}{SD}$.

94. The formula for a Z score is $Z = 10z + 50$.

Summary/Chapter 13

Concepts Underlying Application

95. Inferential statistics deal with inferences about populations based on the behavior of samples.

96. Inferential statistics are concerned with determining how likely it is that results based on a sample or samples are the same results that would have been obtained for the entire population.

97. Sample values, such as the mean, are referred to as statistics. The corresponding values in the population are referred to as parameters.

98. Inferential statistics are used to make inferences concerning parameters, based on sample statistics.

99. If a difference between means is found for two groups at the end of a study, the question of interest is whether a similar difference exists in the population from which the samples were selected.

100. Inferences concerning populations are only probability statements; the researcher is only probably correct when he or she makes an inference and concludes that there is true difference, or true relationship, in the population.

Standard Error

101. Expected, chance variation among the means is referred to as sampling error.

102. If a difference is found between sample means, the question of interest is whether the difference is a result of sampling error or a reflection of a true difference.

103. An interesting characteristic of sampling errors is that they are normally distributed.

104. If a sufficiently large number of equal-sized large samples are randomly selected from a population, all samples will not have the same mean on the variable measured, *but* the means of those samples will be normally distributed around the population mean. The mean of all the sample means will yield a good estimate of the population mean.

105. As with any normally distributed set of scores, a distribution of sample means has not only its own mean but also its own standard deviation. The standard deviation of the sample means (the standard deviation of sampling errors) is usually referred to as the standard error of the mean.

106. The standard error of the mean ($SE_{\bar{x}}$) tells us by how much we would expect our sample means to differ if we used other samples from the same population.

107. According to normal curve percentages, we can say that approximately 68% of the sample means will fall between plus and minus one standard error of the mean (remember the standard error of the mean is a standard deviation), 95% will fall between plus and minus two standard errors, and 99+% will fall between plus and minus three standard errors.

108. If we know the standard deviation of the population, we can estimate the standard error of the mean by dividing the standard deviation by the square root of our sample size ($\sqrt{N}$).

109. In most cases, however, we do not know the mean or standard deviation of the population. In these cases, we estimate the standard error by dividing the standard deviation of the sample by the square root of the sample minus one:

$$SE_{\bar{x}} = \frac{SD}{\sqrt{N-1}}$$

110. The smaller the standard error of the mean is, the better; a smaller standard error indicates less sampling error.

111. The major factor affecting the standard error of the mean is sample size. As the size of the sample increases, the standard error of the mean decreases.

112. The researcher should make every effort to acquire as many subjects as possible so that inferences about the population of interest will be as correct as possible.

113. An estimate of standard error can also be computed for other measures of central tendency as well as measures of variability, relationship, and relative position. Further, an estimate of standard error can also be determined for the difference between means.

114. Differences between two sample means are normally distributed around the mean difference in the population.

The Null Hypothesis

115. When we talk about the difference between two sample means being a true difference we mean that the difference was caused by the treatment (the independent variable), and not by chance.

116. The null hypothesis says in essence that there is no true difference or relationship between parameters in the populations and that any differences or relationship found for the samples is the result of sampling error.

117. The null hypothesis for a study is usually (although not necessarily) different from the research hypothesis.

118. Rejection of a null hypothesis is more conclusive support for a positive research hypothesis.

119. In a research study, the test of significance selected to determine whether a difference between means is a true difference provides a test of the null hypothesis. As a result, the null hypothesis is either rejected, as being probably false, or not rejected, being probably true.

120. After we make the decision to reject or not reject the null hypothesis, we make an inference back to our research hypothesis.

121. In order to test a null hypothesis we need a test of significance, and we need to select a probability level which indicates how much risk we are willing to take that the decision we make is wrong.

Tests of Significance

122. The test of significance helps us to decide whether we can reject the null hypothesis and infer that the difference is a true one, a population difference, not a chance one resulting from sampling error.

123. The test of significance is made at a preselected probability level and allows us to state that we have rejected the null hypothesis because we would expect to find a difference as large as we have found by chance only 5 times out of every 100 studies, or only 1 time in every 100 studies, or whatever; therefore we conclude that the null hypothesis is *probably* false and reject it.

124. There are a number of different tests of significance which can be applied in research studies, one of which is more appropriate in a given situation.

125. Factors such as the scale of measurement represented by the data, method of subject selection, the number of groups, and the number of independent variables determine which test of significance should be selected for a given experiment.

Decision Making: Levels of Significance and Type I and Type II Errors

126. The researcher makes a decision that the difference between the means is, or is not, too large to attribute to chance. The researcher never knows for sure whether he or she is right or wrong, only whether he or she is probably correct.

127. There are four possibilities. If the null hypothesis is really true, and the researcher agrees that it is true (does not reject it), the researcher makes the correct decision. Similarly, if the null hypothesis is false, and the researcher rejects it (says there *is* a difference), the researcher also makes the correct decision. But if the null hypothesis is true, there really is no difference, and the researcher rejects it and says there is a difference, the researcher makes an incorrect decision referred to as a Type I error. Similarly, if the null hypothesis is false, there really is a significant difference between the means, but the researcher concludes that the null hypothesis is true and does not reject it, the researcher also makes an incorrect decision referred to as a Type II error.

128. When the researcher makes the decision to reject or not reject the null hypothesis, she or he does so with a given probability of being correct. This probability of being correct is referred to as the significance level, or probability level, of the test of significance.

129. If the decision is made to reject the null hypothesis, the means are concluded to be significantly different—too different to be the result of chance error. If the null hypothesis is not rejected, the means are determined to be not significantly different.

130. The level of significance, or probability level, selected determines how large the difference between the means must be in order to be declared significantly different.

131. The most commonly used probability level (symbolized as p) is the .05 level. Some studies use $p = .01$ and occasionally an exploratory study will use $p = .10$.

132. The probability level selected determines the probability of committing a Type I error, that is, of rejecting a null hypothesis that is really true.

133. The smaller our probability level is, the larger the mean difference must be in order to be a significant difference.

134. As you decrease the probability of committing a Type I error, you increase the probability of committing a Type II error, that is, of not rejecting a null hypothesis when you should.

135. The choice of a probability level, p, is made prior to execution of the study. The researcher considers the relative seriousness of committing a Type I versus a Type II error and selects p accordingly.

136. Rejection of a null hypothesis, or lack of rejection, only supports or does not support a research hypothesis; it does not "prove" anything.

Two-Tailed and One-Tailed Tests

137. Tests of significance are almost always two-tailed.

138. The null hypothesis states that there is no difference between the groups ($A = B$) and a two-tailed test allows for the possibility that a difference may occur in either direction, either group mean may be higher than the other ($A > B$ or $B > A$).

139. A one-tailed test assumes that a difference can only occur in one direction; the null hypothesis states that one group is not better than another ($A \not> B$), and the one-tailed test assumes that if a difference occurs it will be in favor of that particular group ($A > B$).

140. To select a one-tailed test of significance the researcher has to be pret-ty sure that a difference can only occur in one direction; this is not very often the case.

141. When appropriate, a one-tailed test has one major advantage. The value resulting from application of the test of significance required for significance is smaller. In other words, it is "easier" to find a significant difference.

Degrees of Freedom

142. After you have determined whether the test will be two-tailed or one-tailed, selected a probability level, and computed a test of significance, you are ready to consult the appropriate table in order to determine the significance of your results.

143. The appropriate table is usually entered at the intersection of your probability level and your degrees of freedom, df.

144. Degrees of freedom are a function of such factors as the number of subjects and the number of groups.

145. Each test of significance has its own formula for determining degrees of freedom.

Tests of Significance: Types

146. Different tests of significance are appropriate for different sets of data.

147. It is important that the researcher select an appropriate test; an incorrect test can lead to incorrect conclusions.

148. The first decision in selecting an appropriate test of significance is whether a parametric test may be used or whether a nonparametric test must be selected.

149. Parametric tests are more powerful and are generally to be preferred. By "more powerful" is meant more likely to reject a null hypothesis that is false; in other words, the researcher is less likely to commit a Type II error, less likely to not reject a null hypothesis that should be rejected.

150. Parametric tests require that certain assumptions be met in order for them to be valid.

151. One of the major assumptions underlying use of parametric tests is that the variable measured is normally distributed in the population (or at least that the form of the distribution is known).

152. A second major assumption is that the data represent an interval or ratio scale of measurement.

153. A third assumption is that subjects are selected independently for the study; in other words, that selection of one subject in no way affects selection of any other subject. Recall that the definition of random sampling is sampling in which every member of the population has an equal and independent chance of being selected for the sample.

154. Another assumption is that the variances of the population comparison groups are equal (or at least that the ratio of the variances is known).

155. With the exception of independence, some violation of one or more of these assumptions usually does not make too much difference, in other words, the same decision is made concerning the statistical significance of the results.

156. If one or more of the parametric assumptions are greatly violated, a nonparametric test should be used. Nonparametric tests make no assumptions about the shape of the distribution.

157. Nonparametric tests are used when the data represent an ordinal or nominal scale, when a parametric assumption has been greatly violated, or when the nature of the distribution is not known.

158. If the data represent an interval or ratio scale, a parametric test should be used unless another of the assumptions is greatly violated.

159. Besides being more powerful, parametric tests also have the advantage that they permit tests of a number of hypotheses that cannot be tested with a nonparametric test; there are a number of parametric statistics that have no counterpart among nonparametric statistics.

160. Typically, the results of single-subject research are presented graphically and summarized using simple descriptive statistics. The need for inferential statistics depends somewhat on the nature of the results.

The t Test

161. The t test is used to determine whether two means are significantly different at a selected probability level.

162. For a given sample size, the t indicates how often a difference as large or larger $(\bar{X}_1 - \bar{X}_2)$ would be found when there is no true population difference.

163. The t test makes adjustments for the fact that the distribution of scores for small samples becomes increasingly different from a normal distribution as sample sizes become increasingly smaller.

164. Distributions for smaller samples, for example, tend to be higher at both the mean and the ends.

165. For a given p level, the values of t required to reject a null hypothesis are progres-

sively higher for progressively smaller samples; as the size of the samples becomes larger (approaches infinity) the score distribution approaches normality.

166. The strategy of the t test is to compare the *actual* mean difference observed $(\bar{X}_1 - \bar{X}_2)$ with the difference *expected* by chance. The t test involves forming the ratio of these two values. In other words, the numerator for a t test is the difference between the sample means $\bar{X}_1$ and $\bar{X}_2$, and the denominator is the chance difference which would be expected if the null hypothesis were true—the standard error of the difference between the means.

167. The denominator is a function of both sample size and group variance.

168. Smaller sample sizes and greater variation within groups are associated with an expectation of greater random differences between groups.

169. The t ratio determines whether the observed difference is sufficiently larger than a difference which would be expected by chance.

170. After the numerator is divided by the denominator, the resulting t value is compared to the appropriate t table value (depending upon the probability level and the degrees of freedom); if the calculated t value is equal to or greater than the table value then the null hypothesis is rejected.

171. There are two different types of t tests, the t test for independent samples and the t test for nonindependent samples.

The t Test for Independent Samples

172. Independent samples are samples that are randomly formed, that is, formed without any type of matching.

173. If two groups are randomly formed, the expectation is that they are essentially the same at the beginning of a study with respect to performance on the dependent variable. Therefore, if they are essentially the same at the end of the study, the null hypothesis is probably true; if they are different at the end of the study, the null hypothesis is probably false, that is, the treatment probably makes a difference.

174. The t test for independent samples is used to determine whether there is a significant difference between the means of two independent samples.

The t Test for Nonindependent Samples

175. Nonindependent samples are samples formed by some type of matching. The ultimate matching, of course, is when the two samples are really the same sample group at two different times, such as one group which receives two different treatments at two different times or which is pretested before a treatment and then posttested.

176. When samples are not independent, the members of one group are systematically related to the members of a second group (especially if it is the same group at two different times).

177. If samples are nonindependent, scores on the dependent variable are expected to be correlated and a special t for correlated, or nonindependent, means must be used.

178. The t test for nonindependent samples is used to determine whether there is probably a significant difference between the means of two matched, or nonindependent, samples or between the means for one sample at two different times.

Analysis of Gain Scores (Difference Scores)

179. There are a number of problems associated with this approach, the major one being lack of equal opportunity to grow. Every subject does not have the same room to gain.

180. If two groups are essentially the same on a pretest, their posttest scores can be directly compared using a *t* test.

181. If there is a difference between the groups on the pretest, the preferred posttest analysis is analysis of covariance.

Simple Analysis of Variance

182. Simple, or one-way, analysis of variance (ANOVA) is used to determine whether there is a significant difference between two *or more* means at a selected probability level.

183. The concept underlying ANOVA is that the total variation, or variance, of scores can be attributed to two sources—variance between groups (variance caused by the treatment) and variance within groups (error variance).

184. As with the *t* test, a ratio is formed (the *F* ratio) with group differences as the numerator (variance between groups) and an error term as the denominator (variance within groups).

185. At the end of the study, after administration of the independent variable (treatment), we determine whether the between groups (treatment) variance differs from the within groups (error) variance by more than what would be expected by chance.

186. The degrees of freedom for the *F* ratio are a function of the number of groups and the number of subjects.

Multiple Comparisons

187. Multiple comparison procedures are used following ANOVA to determine which means are significantly different from which other means.

188. In essence, they involve calculation of a special form of the *t* test, a form for which the error term is based on the combined variance of all the groups, not just the groups being compared. This special *t* adjusts for the fact that many tests are being executed. When many tests are performed, the probability level, *p*, tends to increase; if *p* is supposed to be .05, it will actually end up being greater, maybe .90, if many tests are performed.

189. Which mean comparisons are to be made should generally be decided upon *before* the study is conducted, not after, and should be based upon the research hypotheses.

190. Of the many multiple comparison techniques available probably the most often used is the Scheffe' test, which is a very conservative test.

191. The Scheffe' test is appropriate for making any and all possible comparisons involving a set of means.

192. The calculations for the Scheffe' test are quite simple and sample sizes do not have to be equal.

Factorial Analysis of Variance

193. If a research study is based upon a factorial design and investigates two or more independent variables and the interactions between them, the appropriate statistical analysis is a factorial, or multifactor, analysis of variance.

194. Such an analysis yields a separate *F* ratio for each independent variable and one for each interaction.

Analysis of Covariance

195. Analysis of covariance (ANCOVA) is used in two major ways, as a technique for controlling extraneous variables and as a means of increasing power.

196. Covariance is a form of ANOVA and is a statistical, rather than experimental, method that can be used to equate groups on one or more variables.

197. Essentially, ANCOVA adjusts posttest scores for initial differences on some variable (such as pretest performance or IQ) and compares adjusted scores.

198. Covariance is based on the assumption that subjects have been randomly assigned to treatment groups. It is therefore best used in conjunction with true experimental designs. If existing, or intact, groups are involved but treatments are assigned to groups randomly, covariance may still be used but results must be interpreted with due caution.

199. Covariance increases the power of a statistical test by reducing within-group (error) variance.

Chi Square

200. Chi square, symbolized as X^2, is a nonparametric test of significance appropriate when the data are in the form of frequency counts occurring in two or more mutually exclusive categories.

201. A chi square compares proportions actually observed in a study with proportions expected to see if they are significantly different.

202. Expected frequencies are usually the frequencies which would be expected if the groups were equal, although they may be based on past data.

203. The chi square can be used to compare frequencies occurring in different categories or the categories may be groups, so that the chi square is comparing groups with respect to the frequency of occurrence of different events.

204. The chi square may also be used when frequencies are categorized along more than one dimension, sort of a factorial chi square.

Calculation and Interpretation of Selected Tests of Significance

The t Test for Independent Samples

205. The formula is:

$$t = \frac{\bar{X}_1 - \bar{X}_2}{\sqrt{\left(\dfrac{SS_1 + SS_2}{n_1 + n_2 - 2}\right)\left(\dfrac{1}{n_1} + \dfrac{1}{n_2}\right)}}$$

206. The formula for the degrees of freedom is

$$n_1 + n_2 - 2$$

207. If your t value is equal to or greater than the t table value, you reject the null hypothesis; the means are significantly different at a selected p level.

The *t* Test for Nonindependent Samples

208. The formula is:

$$t = \frac{\bar{D}}{\sqrt{\dfrac{\Sigma D^2 - \dfrac{(\Sigma D)^2}{N}}{N(N-1)}}}$$

209. The formula for degrees of freedom is $N - 1$, the number of pairs minus 1.

210. If your *t* value is equal to or greater than the *t* table value, you reject the null hypothesis; the means are significantly different at a selected *p* level.

Simple Analysis of Variance (ANOVA)

211. $SS_{total} = SS_{between} + SS_{within}$

212. $SS_{between} = \dfrac{(\Sigma X_1)^2}{n_1} + \dfrac{(\Sigma X_2)^2}{n_2} + \dfrac{(\Sigma X_3)^2}{n_3} + \ldots + \ldots - \dfrac{(\Sigma X)^2}{N}$

213. $SS_{total} = \Sigma X^2 - \dfrac{(\Sigma X)^2}{N}$

214. The formula for degrees of freedom for the between term is $K - 1$, where K is the number of groups.

215. The formula for the degrees of freedom for the within term is $N - K$, where N is the total sample size and K is still the number of treatment groups.

216. Mean square $= \dfrac{\text{sum of squares}}{\text{degrees of freedom}}$

217. $F = \dfrac{MS_B}{MS_W}$

218. If your F value is greater than the F table value, you reject the null hypothesis; there is a significant difference among the means.

The Scheffe' Test

219. The Scheffe' test involves calculation of an F ratio for each mean comparison.

220. For example, to compare $\bar{X}_1$ with $\bar{X}_2$, the formula is:

$$F = \frac{(\bar{X}_1 - \bar{X}_2)^2}{MS_W \left(\dfrac{1}{n_1} + \dfrac{1}{n_2}\right)(K-1)} \quad \text{with } df = (K-1)(N-K)$$

221. The MS_W in the formula is the MS_W from the analysis of variance.

222. The significance of each F is determined using the degrees of freedom from the analysis of variance.

Chi Square

223. $\chi^2 = \sum \left[\dfrac{(fo - fe)^2}{fe} \right]$

224. The formula for degrees of freedom for a one-dimensional chi square is $K - 1$, where K equals the number of categories.

225. If your chi square value is equal to or greater than the chi square table value, you reject the null hypothesis; there is a significant difference between observed and expected proportions.

Chapter 14/Using the Computer for Data Analysis

When to Use the Computer

226. If sample sizes are not large, if a limited number of variables are involved, and if relatively simple statistical analyses are to be performed, use of a calculator may be the most efficient approach to data analysis.

227. Some statistical analyses, such as analysis of covariance and factorial analysis of variance, are rarely done by hand by experienced researchers.

228. A good guideline for beginning researchers is that you should not use the computer to perform an analysis that you have never done yourself by hand.

229. Most universities have computer facilities. If you ever plan to use the computer you should become familiar with the facilities, services, and equipment available and should sign up for the related instruction which is usually available.

Costs Associated with Computer Use

230. The major costs associated with computer analysis are for programming, keypunching, and computer time.

231. Programs for many standard analyses have already been written and are available for use by the researcher.

232. Doing your own keypunching not only saves you money but may reduce keypunching errors since you can read your data sheets better than anyone else.

233. While the costs per hour for computer processing time are high, the analyses typically required for a research project generally use no more than a few minutes.

234. If you use an existing program, keypunch your own data, and are given free processing time, the entire operation may cost you nothing but time.

Steps in Using the Computer

235. The first step in using the computer is to select an appropriate program.

236. The program selected will indicate how the data may be keypunched and what instruction cards need to be punched.

237. Instruction cards tell the computer all about your data, including such information as sample sizes, number of variables, and how the data are arranged on the data cards.

238. Data and instructions are keypunched onto 80-column cards.

239. When you pick up your output the first things you look for are error messages.

240. If your program has run successfully you then examine the output figures to see if they make sense.

Chapter 15/Postanalysis Procedures

Verification and Storage of Data

Verification

241. The very first thing you should do when you think you are done is to recheck all your work.

242. It is easier to check calculations if analyses have been performed and recorded step by step, leaving no steps to the imagination.

243. Do not just check the steps you followed after you had an arithmetic problem; check every value that you substituted into the formula.

244. If you have checked a set of figures several times and they are still correct, do not check them 50 more times, look elsewhere for errors.

245. Results should make logical sense.

246. There is really no need for anyone to do any analysis by hand when calculators are so readily available. Besides making life easier for you, they also reduce the likelihood of computational errors.

247. If you use the computer you should double-check your input.

Storage

248. When you are convinced that your work is accurate, all data sheets or cards, work sheets, and records of calculations should be labeled, organized, and filed in a safe place.

249. All of the data should be carefully labeled with as many identification labels as possible, labels such as the dates of the study, the nature of each treatment group, and whether data are pretest data, posttest data, or data for a control variable (such as IQ).

250. A convenient, practical way to store data is in loose-leaf ring binders or notebooks.

251. Find a nice safe place for it all and guard it very carefully.

Interpretation of Results

252. The results of statistical analyses need to be interpreted in terms of the purpose of the study, the original research hypothesis, and with respect to other studies that have been conducted in the same area of research.

Hypothesized Results

253. The researcher must discuss whether the results support the research hypothesis and why or why not, and whether the results are in agreement with other findings and why or why not.

254. If you reject a null hypothesis, your research hypothesis may be supported but it is not proven.

255. A supported research hypothesis does not necessarily mean that your treatment would "work" with different populations, different materials, and different dependent variables.

256. Failure to reject a null hypothesis does not necessarily mean that your research hypothesis is false, but even if it is, it is just as important to know what does not work as what does, what variables are not related as which are.

257. If you do not reject the null hypothesis, there is no evidence either way concerning the truth or falsity of the hypothesized relationship.

Unhypothesized Results

258. Unhypothesized results should be interpreted with great care.

259. Often during a study an apparent relationship will be noticed which was not hypothesized.

260. A true test of a hypothesis comes from its ability to explain and predict what *will* happen, not what *is* happening.

261. You can, however, collect and analyze data on these unforeseen relationships and present your results as such.

262. These findings may then form the basis for a later study, conducted by yourself or another investigator, specifically designed to test a hypothesis related to your findings.

Statistical Versus Practical Significance

263. The fact that results are statistically significant does not automatically mean that they are of any educational value.

264. With very large samples a very small mean difference may yield a significant *t*. A mean difference of two points might be statistically significant but probably not worth the effort of revising a curriculum.

Replication of Results

265. Perhaps the strongest support for a research hypothesis comes from replication of results.

266. Replication means that the study is done again. The second study may be a repetition of the original study, using different subjects, or it may represent an alternative approach to testing the same hypothesis.

267. The need for replication is especially great when an unusual or new relationship is found in a study, or when the results have practical significance and the treatment investigated might really make a difference.

268. The significance of a relationship may also be enhanced if it is replicated in a more natural setting.

Task 7 Performance Criteria

The data which you generate (scores you make up for each subject) should make sense. If your dependent variable is IQ, for example, do not generate scores for your subjects like 2, 11, and 15; generate scores like 84, 110, and 120. Got it? Unlike a real study, you can make your study turn out any way you want!

Depending upon the scale of measurement represented by your data, select and compute the appropriate descriptive statistics.

Depending upon the scale of measurement represented by your data, your research hypothesis, and your research design, select and compute the appropriate test of significance. Determine the statistical significance of your results for a selected probability level. Present your results in a summary statement and in a summary table, and relate how the significance or nonsignificance of your results supports or does not support your original research hypothesis. For example, you might say:

> Computation of a t test for independent samples indicated that the group which received weekly reviews retained significantly more than the group which received daily reviews (see Table 1). Therefore, the original hypothesis that "ninth-grade algebra students who receive a weekly review will retain significantly more algebraic concepts than ninth-grade algebra students who receive a daily review" was supported.

Table 1
Means, Standard Deviations, and t for the Daily-Review
and Weekly-Review Groups on the Delayed Retention Test

Review Group	Mean	SD	t
Daily	44.82	5.12	2.56*
Weekly	52.68	6.00	

Note: Maximum score = 75.
* $df = 38$, $p < .05$.

Note: Task 7 should look like the results sections of a research report. Although your actual calculations should not be part of Task 7, they should be attached to it.

See the *Student Guide* for practice problems and examples of Task 7.

Part Eight

Research Reports

The research report should . . . reflect scholarship. . . .

There are a variety of reasons for which people conduct research. The motivation for doing a research project may be no more than that such a project is a degree requirement, or it may come from a strong desire to contribute to educational theory or practice. Whatever the reason for their execution, most research studies culminate with the production of a research report.

A number of manuals are available which describe various formats and styles for writing research reports although there are a number of elements which are common to most reports regardless of the format followed. Virtually all research reports, for example, contain a statement of the problem, a description of procedures, and a presentation of results. Further, all research reports have a common purpose, namely, to communicate as clearly as possible the purpose, procedures, and findings of the study. A well-written report describes a study in sufficient detail to permit replication by another researcher.

You have already written many of the components of a research report through your work in Parts 2 through 7. In Part 8 you will integrate all your previous efforts to produce a complete report.

The goal of Part 8 is for you, having conducted a study, to be able to produce a complete report. After you have read Part Eight, you should be able to perform the following task.

Task 8

Based on Tasks 2, 6, and 7, prepare a research report which follows the general format for a thesis or dissertation.

(See Performance Criteria, p. 394.)

16

Preparation of a Research Report

Enablers

After reading chapter 16, you should be able to:

1. List 10 general rules for writing and preparing a research report.
2. Identify and briefly describe the major sections and subsections of a research report.
3. List four major differences between a research report prepared as a thesis or dissertation and a research report prepared as a manuscript for publication.
4. List two guidelines for presenting a paper at a professional meeting.

General Guidelines

If you carefully prepare a research plan before you conduct your study, you have a good head start on writing your research report, especially the introduction section. While you are conducting your study, you can profitably utilize any free time you have by revising and refining the introduction and method sections of the report. The study may not be executed exactly as planned, but the procedures should not diverge drastically from the original plan. When the study is completed, the final draft of the method section can incorporate any final changes in procedures. After all the data are analyzed you are ready to write the final sections of the report. The major guideline previously described for analyzing, organizing, and reporting related literature is applicable to this task—make an outline. The chances of your results and conclusions being presented in an organized, logical manner are greatly increased if the sequence is thought through before anything is actually written. Formulation of an outline greatly facilitates the "thinking through" process. To review briefly, development of an outline involves identification and ordering of major topics followed by differentiation of each major heading into logical subheadings. The time spent in working on an outline is well worth it since it is much easier to reorganize an outline that is not quite right than to reorganize a document written in prargraph form. Of course this does not mean that your first report draft will be your last. Two or three revisions of each section are to be expected. Each time you read a section you will see ways to improve its organization or clarity. Also, other persons who review your report for you will see areas in need of rethinking or rewording that you have not noticed.

While the research plan may have been written in the future tense ("subjects *will be* randomly selected . . .") by the time you get to the research report the party is over and each section is written in the past tense ("subjects *were* randomly selected"). Further, in addition to conscientiously following a selected style and format, there are several general rules of good report writing which the researcher should be aware of and follow.

General Rules for Writing and Typing

Probably the foremost rule of research report writing is that the writer must be as objective as possible in reporting the study. A research report is a scientific document, not a novel or treatise. In other words, the report should not contain subjective statements ("*clearly* group instruction is no good"), overstatements ("wow, what fantastic results!"), or emotional statements ("every year thousands of school children are the poor, innocent victims of an ineffective reading program"). Further, the report should not be written as if it were a legal brief intended to present arguments in favor of a position ("the purpose of this study was to prove . . ."). The research report should contain an objective, factual description of past research and the study upon which the report is based.[1] Consistent with the goal of objective reporting, personal pronouns such as *I, my, we,* and *our* should be avoided like the plague. Instead, impersonal pronouns and the passive voice should be used. Phrases such as "*it* was determined" and "subjects *were* randomly *selected*" should be used instead of "*I* determined" and "*I* randomly *selected* subjects."

The research report should be written in a clear, simple, straightforward style; you do not have to be boring, just concise. In other words, say what you have to say in the fewest number of words and using the simplest language. For example, instead of saying "the population comprised all students who matriculated for the fall quarter at Egghead University," it would be better to say "the population was all students enrolled for the fall quarter at Egghead University." The research report should also reflect scholarship; correct spelling, grammatical construction, and punctuation are not too much to expect of a scientific report. And do not say that you are the world's worst speller; everyone has access to a dictionary. If there is any doubt in your mind concerning the correct spelling of a word, correct construction of a sentence, or correct punctuation, consult the appropriate reference book. It is also a good idea to have someone you know, someone who is perhaps stronger in these areas, review your manuscript for you and indicate errors.

While different style manuals suggest different rules of writing, there are several which are common to most manuals. Use of abbreviations and contractions, for instance, is generally discouraged. Do not say, for example, "the American Psychological Assn.," say "the American Psychological Association." Also words like *shouldn't, isn't,* and *won't* should be avoided. Exceptions to the abbreviation rule include commonly used and understood abbreviations (such as IQ and GPA)

---

1. A little more latitude is permitted the researcher in discussing implications of the study and in making recommendations for future research or action.

and abbreviations defined by the researcher to promote clarity, simplify presentation, or reduce repetition. If the same sequence of words is going to be used repeatedly, the researcher will often define an abbreviation in parentheses the first time the sequence is used and thereafter use only the abbreviation. In a study by Doughtie, Wakefield, Sampson, and Alston (1974), for example, the Illinois Test of Psycholinguistic Ability was referred to throughout the research report as the ITPA.[2] Also, as the above sentence illustrates, authors of cited references are usually referred to by last name only in the main body of the report; first names, initials, and titles are not given. Instead of saying "Professor Dudley Q. McStrudle (1976) concluded . . ." you normally would say "McStrudle (1976) concluded. . . ." The above described guidelines, of course, hold only for the main body of the report. Tables, figures, footnotes, and references may include abbreviations; footnotes and references usually give at least the author's initials. Another convention followed by most style manuals is with respect to numbers. If the first word of a sentence is a number ("Six schools were contacted . . ."), or if the number is nine or less ("a total of five lists . . ."), numbers are usually expressed as words. Otherwise, numbers are generally expressed as arabic numerals ("a total of 500 questionnaires was sent to the various groups of interest").

The same standards of scholarship should be applied to the typing of the report as to the writing of the report. When you read a report full of typos you cannot help but wonder if the study was conducted in the same careless manner as the report was proofread. If you are not highly proficient in typing, find yourself a typist who is. Present the typist with a manuscript which is in final, correct form; the typist's job is to type, not to polish your report. I once gave a paper to my secretary that I was going to read at a meeting. In the middle of page 7 I wrote a note which said "see attached document"; the attached document had a paragraph marked that I wanted included in the paper. While proofreading the typed paper, much to my chagrin, I discovered that she had typed "see attached document" right in the middle of a page. When I asked her about it she told me sweetly "I type what I see, not what you mean!" The point is that you should not expect your typist to "know" what you want. If you have any special instructions (such as not to split words at the end of a line), share them with your typist and be sure they are understood. It is also a good idea to give your typist a copy of the style manual you are following to ensure that required guidelines (such as size of margins) are followed. Finally, no matter how good your typist is, nobody is perfect. The final typed report should be proofread carefully at least twice. Reading the report silently to yourself will usually be sufficient to identify major typing errors. If you have a willing listener, however, reading the manuscript out loud often helps you to identify grammatical or constructional errors. Sometimes sentences do not make nearly as much sense when you hear them as when you write them; also, your listener will frequently be helpful in bringing to your attention sections that are unclear. Reading the report backwards, last sentence first, will also help you to identify poorly constructed or unclear sentences.

---

2. Doughtie, E.B., Wakefield, J.A. Jr., Sampson, R.N., & Alston, H.L. A statistical test of the theoretical model for the representational level of the Illinois Test of Psycholinguistic Ability. *Journal of Educational Psychology,* 1974, *66*(3), 410–415.

Format and Style

Most research reports consistently follow a selected system for format and style. While many such systems are available, a given report usually strictly follows one of them. Format refers to the general pattern of organization and arrangement of the report. The number and types of headings and subheadings to be included in the report are determined by the format used. Style refers to the rules of spelling, capitalization, punctuation, and typing followed in preparing the report. While specific formats may vary in terms of specific headings included, all research reports follow a very similar format that parallels the steps involved in conducting a study. One format may call for a Discussion section, for example, while another may require a Summary, Conclusions, and Recommendations section (or both), but all formats for a research report entail a section in which the results of the study are discussed and interpreted. All research reports also include a condensed description of the study, whether it be a summary of a dissertation or an abstract of a journal article.

Most colleges, universities, and professional journals either have developed their own, required style manual or have selected one that must be followed. One such manual, which is increasingly being adopted as the required guide for theses and dissertations, is the *Publication Manual of the American Psychological Association*.[3] This format is becoming increasingly popular, primarily because it eliminates the need for formal footnotes. If you are not bound by any particular format and style system, the APA manual is recommended. In addition to acquiring and studying a copy of the selected manual, it is also very helpful to study several reports that have been written following the same manual. Such reports serve as useful models and help the writer translate abstract guidelines into practice.

Types of Research Reports

Research reports usually take the form of a thesis, dissertation, journal article, or paper to be read at a professional meeting. In fact, the same report may take several forms; dissertation studies are frequently described at professional meetings and prepared for publication. As mentioned previously, and as you probably noticed when you reviewed the literature related to your problem, the components of all research reports are very similar. Depending upon its form, the report may be divided into sections or chapters but these divisions are similar in content.

Theses and Dissertations

While specifics will vary considerably, most research reports prepared for a degree requirement follow the same general format. Figure 16.1 presents an outline of the typical contents of such a report. As Figure 16.1 indicates, theses and dissertations include a set of fairly standard preliminary pages, components which directly parallel the research process, and supplementary information, which is included in appendices.

---

3. *Publication Manual of the American Psychological Association (Second edition)*. Washington, D.C.: American Psychological Association, 1974.

PRELIMINARY PAGES
  Title page
  Acknowledgment page
  Table of Contents
  List of Tables
  List of Figures
MAIN BODY OF THE REPORT
  Introduction
    Statement of the Problem
    Review of Related Literature
    Statement of the Hypothesis
  Method
    Subjects
    Instruments
    Design
    Procedure
  Results
  Conclusions and Recommendations (Discussion)
  Summary
  References (Bibliography)
APPENDICES

Figure 16.1
Common components of
a research report submitted for a degree requirement.

Preliminary Pages

The preliminary pages set the stage for the report to follow and indicate where in the report each component, table, and figure can be found.

The Title Page   The title page usually includes the title of the report, the author's name, the degree requirement being fulfilled, the name and location of the college or university awarding the degree, the date of submission of the report, and signatures of approving committee members. The title should be brief (15 words or less, as a rule of thumb), and at the same time it should describe the purpose of the study as clearly as possible. One way to reduce the size of the title is to omit unnecessary words such as "a study of. . . ," "an investigation of. . . ," and "an experimental study to determine. . . ." The title should, however, at least indicate the major independent and dependent variables, and sometimes it names the population studied. Volume 72, issue 1, of the *Journal of Educational Psychology,* for example, includes the following titles:

Test Anxiety and Academic Performance: The Effects of Study-Related Behaviors.[4]

Maternal Teaching Strategies and Cognitive Styles in Chicano Families.[5]

---

4. Culler, R.E., & Holahan, C.J. Test anxiety and academic performance: The effects of study-related behaviors, *Journal of Educational Psychology,* 1980, 72(1), 16–20.

5. Laosa, L.M. Maternal teaching strategies and cognitive styles in Chicano families. *Journal of Educational Psychology,* 1980, 72(1), 45–54.

Classroom Learning Style and Cooperative Behavior of Elementary School Children.[6]

Do Teacher Standards for Assigning Grades Affect Student Evaluations of Instruction?[7]

Each one of these titles specifies the cause-effect relationship that was investigated. A good title should clearly communicate what the study was about. Recall that when you reviewed the literature and looked under key words in the various indexes, you made decisions based on titles listed concerning whether the articles were probably related or not related to your problem. When the titles were well constructed it was fairly easy to determine probable relationship or lack of relationship to your problem; when they were vaguely worded it was often difficult to determine without examining the report of the study. Thus, after you write your title apply the communication test; would *you* know what the study was about if you read the title in an index?

The Acknowledgment Page   Most theses and dissertations include an acknowledgment page. This page permits the writer to express appreciation to persons who have contributed significantly to the completion of the report. Notice the word significant. Everyone who had anything to do with the study or the report cannot (and should not!) be mentioned. It is acceptable to thank your major professor for his or her guidance and assistance; it is not acceptable to thank your third-grade teacher for giving you confidence in your ability.

The Table of Contents, List of Tables, and List of Figures   The table of contents is basically an outline of your report which indicates on which page each major section (or chapter) and subsection begins. The list of tables, which is presented on a separate page, gives the number and title of each table and the page on which it can be found. As an example:

LIST OF TABLES

TABLE   Page

1. Means and standard deviations for all tests by group and experiment 22
2. Analysis of variance of delayed retention scores for review and non-review subjects for experiment II 25

The list of figures, which is also presented on a new page, gives the number and title of each figure and the page on which it can be found:

---

6. Hertz-Lazarowitz, R., Sharan, S., & Steinberg, R. Classroom learning style and cooperative behavior of elementary school children. *Journal of Educational Psychology,* 1980, 72(1), 99–106.

7. Abrami, P.C., Dickens, W.J., Perry, R.P., & Leventhal, L. Do teacher standards for assigning grades affect student evaluations of instruction? *Journal of Educational Psychology,* 1980, 72(1), 107–117.

LIST OF FIGURES

FIGURE   Page

1. Experimental designs for experiment I and experiment II 14
2. Plot of test scores for all groups before and after each learning and
   review session 23

Entries listed in the table of contents should be identical to headings and sub-headings in the report, and table titles and figure titles should be the same titles that are given for the actual tables and figures in the main body of the report.

The Main Body of the Report

With the exception of the section for Conclusions and Recommendations, you are already quite familiar with the components of a research report. Therefore, we will review each of these components briefly and will discuss the section Conclusions and Recommendations in more depth.

Introduction   As mentioned previously, the introduction to a research report is already written and in pretty good shape if the researcher carefully developed a research plan prior to conducting the study. The introduction section includes a description of the problem, a review of related literature, a statement of hypotheses, and definition of terms. A well-written statement of a problem generally indicates the variables, and the specific relationship between those variables, investigated in the study. The statement of the problem should be accompanied by a presentation of the background of the problem, including a justification for the study in terms of the significance of the problem.

The review of related literature describes and analyzes what has already been done related to your problem. The review of related literature is not a series of abstracts or annotations but rather an analysis of the relationships and differences among related studies and reports. The review should flow in such a way that the least-related references are discussed first and the most-related references are discussed last, just prior to the statement of the hypothesis. The review should conclude with a brief summary of the literature and its implications.

A good hypothesis states as clearly and concisely as possible the expected relationship (or difference) between two variables and defines those variables in operational, measurable terms. The hypothesis (or hypotheses) logically follows the review of related literature and it is based upon the implications of previous research. A well-developed hypothesis is testable, that is, can be confirmed or disconfirmed.

The introduction also includes operational definition of terms used in the study which do not have a commonly known meaning. Some institutions require that one section of the introduction be devoted to defining all the terms in one place. Usually, however, it is better to define each term the first time it appears in the report.

Method   As with the introduction, the method section of the report is already written and included in the research plan. The procedure section may require some revision, but it should be in reasonably good shape. The method section includes a description of subjects, instruments, design, procedure, assumptions, and limitations. The description of subjects includes a definition and description of the population from which the sample was selected and may describe the method used in selecting the sample or samples (or the method of selection may be described in the procedure section). The description of the population should indicate its size and major characteristics such as age, grade level, ability level, and socioeconomic status. Information should be provided on any variables which might be related to performance on the dependent variable. A good description of the population enables the reader of the report to determine how similar study subjects were to the population with which she or he is involved, and thus, how applicable results might be. If method of sample selection is presented here it should be very specific.

The description of instruments should identify and describe all instruments used to collect data pertinent to the study, be they tests, questionnaires, interview forms, or observation forms. The description of each instrument should relate the function of the instrument in the study (for example, selection of subjects or a measure of the dependent variable), what the instrument is intended to measure, and data related to validity and reliabiltiy. If an instrument has been developed by the researcher, the description needs to be more detailed and should also relate the manner in which it was developed, a description of pretesting efforts and subsequent instrument revisions, steps involved in scoring, and guidelines for interpretation. A copy of the instrument itself, accompanying scoring keys, and other pertinent data related to a newly developed test are generally placed in the appendix of the thesis or dissertation.

The description of the design is especially important in an experimental study. In other types of research the description of the design may be combined with procedure. In an experimental study, the description of the basic design (or variation of a basic design) applied in the study should include a rationale for selection and a discussion of sources of invalidity associated with the design, and why they may have been minimized in the study being reported.

The procedure section should describe each step followed in conducting the study, in chronological order, in sufficient detail to permit the study to be replicated by another researcher. If not done so earlier, the method of subject selection should be described in detail. It should be clear exactly how subjects were assigned to groups and how treatments were assigned to groups. Time and conditions of pretest administration (if appropriate) should be described, followed by a detailed explanation of the study itself. The ways in which groups were different (treatment) should be clearly delineated as well as ways in which they were similar (control procedures). Any unforeseen events which occurred which might have affected the results should be discussed in terms of their seriousness and probable consequences. Also, any insights regarding ways to improve procedures should be shared so that other researchers may profit from the investigator's experiences.

Results   The results section describes the statistical techniques that were applied to the data and the results of each analysis. For each hypothesis, the statistical test of significance selected and applied to the data is described followed by a statement indicating whether the hypothesis was supported or not supported. Tables and figures are used to present findings in summary or graph form and add clarity to the presentation. Tables present numerical data in rows and columns and usually include descriptive statistics, such as means and standard deviations, and the results of tests of significance, such as t and F ratios. While a figure may be any nontabular presentation of information (such as a diagram or chart), figures in the results sections are usually graphical presentations of data. Figures can often be used to show relationships not evident in tabular presentations of data. Interactions, for example, are clearer when illustrated in a figure. If figures are based on numerical data, that data should be presented in a table or in the figure itself. Good tables and figures are uncluttered and self-explanatory; it is better to use two tables (or figures) than one that is crowded. They should stand alone, that is, be interpretable without the aid of related textual material. Tables and figures follow their related textual discussion and are referred to by number, not name or location. In other words, the text should say "see Table 1" not "see the table with the means" or "see the table on the next page."

Figure 16.2 illustrates appropriate use and format of tables and figures. It presents Table 3 and Figure 2 from a study by Winne and Marx which appeared in a 1980 issue of the *Journal of Educational Psychology*.[8] Table 3 includes descriptive statistics for the results (the means, *M*, and the standard deviations, *SD*). Figure 2 graphically presents the means from Table 3 and clearly depicts an interaction which is not evident from an examination of Table 3. If you consult a copy of the 1974 edition of the *Publication Manual of the American Psychological Association*, you will notice that the formats of Table 3 and Figure 2 do not match the formats prescribed by the manual. This is because the manual is undergoing revision and the third edition may or may not be available by the time you read this. In the meantime, submitted manuscripts with tables and figures that adhere to the specifications of the second edition are being revised as shown in Figure 16.2, prior to publication.

Conclusions and Recommendations   Every research report has a section that discusses and interprets the results, draws conclusions and implications, and makes recommendations. Interpretation of results may be presented in a separate section titled "Discussion" or it may be included in the same section as the other analysis of results items. If only one hypothesis was tested, and (or) if the discussion is brief, it may be included in the results section. What this section (or sections) is called is unimportant; what is important is how well it is done. Each result is discussed in terms of the original hypothesis to which it relates, and in terms of its agreement or disagreement with previous results obtained by other researchers in other studies. For example, in a study investigating the effectiveness of reviews in increasing retention of mathematical rules (Gay, 1973), it was hypothesized that ". . . for the mathematical task involved in this study . . . one review will significantly enhance retention . . ." and "temporal position of one review will not be a significant effect. . . ."[9] The results section of the research

8. Winne, P.H., & Marx, R.W. Matching students' cognitive responses to teaching skills. *Journal of Educational Psychology*, 1980, 72(2), 257–264.

9. Gay, L.R. Temporal position of reviews and its effect on the retention of mathematical rules. *Journal of Educational Psychology*. 1973, 64(2), 171–182. Temporal position refers to when the

Table 3

*Means and Standard Deviations for Groups on
Mean of Posttraining Quizzes in Experiment 2*

Group	Structural	Functional
Prose		
M	4.82	5.27
SD	1.19	.95
Prose plus video		
M	6.07	5.39
SD	.76	1.07
Placebo		
M	5.19	
SD	1.36	

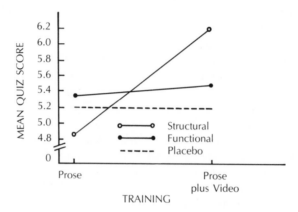

Figure 2. Mean achievement for trained and placebo
groups in Experiment 2.

Figure 16.2
Example of a table and a figure illustrating appropriate use
and format. (From Winne and Marx, 1980. Copyright 1980 by the
American Psychological Association. Reprinted by permission.)

report stated that: "It was found that while review groups retained significantly
more than the no-review group ($F = 6.96$, $df = 1/48$, $p < .05$) the effect of
temporal position of the reviews was not significant." And the Discussion section
stated that "The results of experiment I indicate that the temporal position of one
review is not an important factor in retention of mathematical rules. These findings
are consistent with those of Peterson et al. (1935), Sones and Stroud (1940), and
Ausubel (1966) involving meaningful verbal learning."[10]

---

review was received. In this study subjects received a review 1 day, 1 week, or 2 weeks following
the day of original learning.

10. Peterson, H.A., Ellis, M., Toohill, N., & Kloess, P. Some measurements of the effects of
reviews. *Journal of Educational Psychology*, 1935, *26*, 65–72; Sones, A.M., & Stroud, J.B.
Review, with special reference to temporal position. *Journal of Educational Psychology*, 1940, *31*,
665–676; and Ausubel, D.P. Early versus delayed review in meaningful learning. *Psychology in the
Schools*, 1966, *3*, 195–198.

Two common errors committed by beginning researchers are to confuse results and conclusions, and to overgeneralize results. A result is the outcome of a test of significance, for example, the mean of group 1 is found to be significantly larger than the mean of group 2. The corresponding conclusion is that the original hypothesis was supported and that method A was more effective than method B. Overgeneralization refers to the statement of conclusions that are not warranted by the results. For example, if a group of first graders receiving individualized instruction were found to achieve significantly higher on a test of reading comprehension than a group receiving traditional instruction, it would be an overgeneralization to conclude that individualized instruction is a superior method of instruction for elementary students.

The researcher should also discuss the theoretical and practical implications of the findings and make recommendations for future research or future action. In this portion of the report the researcher is permitted more freedom in expressing opinions that are not necessarily direct outcomes of data analysis. The researcher is free to discuss any possible revisions or additions to existing theory and to encourage studies designed to test hypotheses suggested by the results. The researcher may also discuss implications of the findings for educational practice and suggest studies designed to replicate the study in other settings, with other subjects, and in other curricular areas, in order to increase the generalizability of the findings. The researcher may also suggest next-step studies designed to investigate another dimension of the problem investigated. For example, a study finding type of feedback to be a factor in retention might suggest that amount of feedback may also be a factor and recommend further research in that area.

Summary The size of the summary will determine the amount of detail permitted and its emphasis. Summaries are often required to be no more than a given maximum number of words, usually between 100 and 500. Shorter summaries usually concentrate more on the problem and the results than on the method. Since the summary of a report is often the only part read (remember when you did your review of related literature?) it should describe the most important aspects of the study, including the problem investigated, the type of subjects and instruments involved, the design, the procedures, and the major results and the major conclusions. A reader should be able to tell from a summary exactly what a study was about and what it found. For example, a 100-word summary for a study investigating the comparative effectiveness of individualized versus traditional instruction for eighth grade low-ability students might read as follows:

The purpose of this study was to investigate the comparative effectiveness of individualized versus traditional methods of mathematics instruction for low-ability eighth graders. Using a posttest-only control group design and applying a *t*-test for independent samples, it was found that the group taught using the individualized method of instruction achieved significantly higher posttest scores on the Stanford Achievement Test: Arithmetic Test (level 7.0–9.9) than the control group. It was concluded that the individualized method was more effective in teaching basic math concepts to low-ability eighth-grade mathematics students than traditional methods.[11]

---

11. Based on a paper by G.E. Colton, Florida International University, Miami, 1974. Used by permission.

References The references, or bibliography, section of the report lists all the sources, alphabetically by authors' last names, that were directly used in writing the report. Most of the references will, of course, appear in the introduction section of the report. Every source cited in the paper must be included in the references, and every entry listed in the references must appear in the paper; in other words, the sources in the paper and the sources in the references must correspond exactly. If sources were consulted that were not directly cited in the main body of the report, these may be listed separately as Additional References. Any secondary sources should be described separately as Secondary References. For example, if you described the results of a dissertation study based on a reading of an abstract, and you could not or did not acquire the entire dissertation, the reference to the dissertation study would be a secondary reference. In thesis and dissertation studies, since the list of references is likely to be lengthy, references are often subdivided into sections such as Books, Articles, and Unpublished.

The style manual being followed will determine the form which each reference must take. This form is usually different for journal articles and books. It is important that whatever form is used it is followed consistently. If the style manual to be used is known while the review of related literature is being conducted, the researcher can save time by writing each reference in the proper form initially.

Appendices

Appendices are usually necessary in thesis and dissertation reports. Appendices include information and data pertinent to the study which either are not important enough to be included in the main body of the report or are too lengthy. Appendices contain such entries as materials especially developed for the study (for example, tests, questionnaires, and cover letters), raw data, and data analysis sheets. Infrequently, an index may be required. An index alphabetically lists all items of importance or interest in the report and the page on which each can be found. The longer the document, the more useful an index will be. Also, a number of universities ask that a vita be included. A vita is a short autobiography describing professionally related activities and experiences of the author. Information typically included in a vita describes educational training and degrees earned, professional work experience, memberships in professional organizations, and publications, if any.

Journal Articles

Preparation of a research report for publication in a professional journal serves the interests of the professional community as well as those of the researcher. Progress in educational research requires that researchers share their efforts so that others may profit from and build upon them. Dissertations and theses are not read nearly as often as professionals journals; thus, publication in a frequently read journal permits the largest possible audience to read about and use the findings of a research study. From a personal point of view, it is definitely to the researcher's advantage, especially the new graduate, to have a publication. When applying for a position, for example, most of what a perspective employer knows about you is what he or she reads about you in your vita. Since a newly graduated individual is likely to be short on professional experience, having a publication definitely gives her or him an edge. Having a publication in a respected journal indicates not only that you conducted a worthwhile study but also that you had the ability *and* the energy to prepare, submit, and publish a scholarly report.

Selection and Analysis of a Journal

Based on your review of related literature and your references, you should be able to identify two or three journals which publish studies in the area of research represented by your study. If you do not know, you should check with someone who does in order to determine which journal of those identified is the most respected in your field. Examination of a recent issue should give you some guidance concerning the format, style, and length acceptable to the selected journal. There is usually a section in the front or back of the journal that gives instructions for submitting manuscripts. The *Journal of Educational Psychology,* for example, strongly advises authors to use the *Publication Manual of the American Psychological Association* in preparing the manuscript and requires an abstract of 100 to 120 words. Authors are instructed to submit manuscripts in triplicate to the editor. Although the journal may not specify a definite maximum manuscript length, shorter manuscripts, all things being equal, have a higher probability of being published. Space in a journal is at a premium and most editors try to publish as many articles per issue as possible. If too long, an otherwise acceptable manuscript may be returned for revision and shortening.

Preparation of the Manuscript

The contents and format of a journal article are very similar to those of a thesis or dissertation except that, as just pointed out, the journal article is much shorter. In fact, some complex or lengthy theses or dissertations may best be submitted as two shorter articles; this is especially true in studies with two or more substudies. None of the preliminary pages of a thesis or dissertation become part of a journal article; only the title remains. The introduction section is usually considerably shorter, describing primarily those studies directly related to the hypothesis of the study. The method section is also much shorter, describing the subjects, instruments, design, and procedure in much less detail. The author must exercise judgment in determining which are the critical aspects of the study and which components require more in-depth description. The results section is usually of greater interest to the reader and thus typically gets reduced less than preceding sections of the paper. Correspondingly, the discussion section will probably not require too much revision. Instead of a summary, many journals require an abstract of a given length. The abstract serves the same purpose as a summary but is not included as part of the manuscript; it is submitted on a separate sheet. When published, the abstract generally precedes the complete description of the study.[12] Limits are not usually put on the number of references permitted, and all pertinent sources are included. As with the preliminary pages, the supplementary

---

12. Theses and dissertations are also frequently required to be accompanied by an abstract.

pages of the thesis or dissertation are not part of the manuscript. Usually a footnote in the manuscript is used to indicate how and where interested readers may obtain copies of tests and other materials usually included in appendices.

Submission and Evaluation of Manuscripts

Before submitting a manuscript to a journal editor, you should have at least one other person read it. If you are in a university setting, you will probably know several persons who have publications who can read your manuscript with the critical eye of a journal review editor. The required number of copies of the manuscript and a brief cover letter indicating the title of the article and your mailing address should be mailed first class to the journal. The editorial board members who review your manuscript will independently determine whether your research, in their opinion, represents a significant contribution, was well conducted, and is well reported. If your manuscript is not accepted for publication, you will usually be given copies of the reviewers' comments or be informed in a summary statement as to the reasons for its rejection. Often you can use this input to revise your manuscript before submitting it to another journal. While it is not ethical to send your article to several journals simultaneously, it is perfectly all right to send it to a second journal after you have been rejected by another.

Papers Read at Professional Meetings

There are a number of professional organizations that hold annual national meetings and in some cases more frequent regional meetings. Some of these organizations include members from a wide variety of professional areas; this is the case with the American Educational Research Association and the American Psychological Association. Others, such as the National Association of Social Studies Teachers, are more specialized and members represent either one specific professional area or a small number of related areas. Whatever their scope, the major focus of their meetings is typically to have members share new knowledge and research findings. While a great deal of informal exchange occurs, the structured, scheduled portion of meetings usually takes the form of paper presentations. A new Ph.D., for example, may describe his or her dissertation study. Papers with a common theme (such as retention of verbal learning, programs for the culturally disadvantaged, or computer-assisted instruction) are presented together at one (or several) sessions. Thus, while at any given time a number of different paper sessions may be going on simultaneously in different locations, a person is free to select and attend those sessions that appear to be most closely related to her or his personal interests or needs.

Usually at least 6 months prior to the date of the meeting, the sponsoring association publishes a "call for papers" in one of its journals or newsletters. The call for papers indicates guidelines and deadlines for submitting papers. An understood restriction is that the information to be presented has not already been published and truly represents "new" knowledge. Typically a full report is not required but rather an abstract of a specified length (1,000 words, for example). Submitted abstracts are sent out for review and a certain number selected for presentation. If you receive notification that your paper has been accepted, you are committed to being present at the meeting to give your paper and to having copies of a complete report available.

Research reports presented at meetings follow the same general format as all research reports and, in fact, the paper you prepare for presentation may resemble very closely a manuscript you are submitting to a journal.[13] It is not unethical to present the results of a study which is to be published as long as the publication date follows the paper presentation date. In fact, a major purpose of professional meetings is to share knowledge more quickly than can be done through the reading of journals. The length of time that typically elapses between the date on which a manuscript is submitted and the date on which it first appears in print in a journal is considerably longer than the 6 to 9 months that typically elapse between a call for papers and a professional meeting.

Since the time allotted for presenting a given paper is generally in the neighborhood of 10 minutes (the range is normally from 5 to 20 minutes), it is usually not possible to read the entire research report. In fact, reading a report verbatim is not a good idea anyway, especially since copies of a complete report should be available to interested persons.[14] It is a much more efficient use of limited time to give a brief informal summary of the study, emphasizing results, conclusions, and any other important aspects of the study. An audience appreciates a presenter who *talks* to them rather than *reads* to them. It is usually helpful to either prepare an outline of what you want to say (and to which you can refer), prepare a much-shortened version of the paper ("10-minutes-worth" of the paper, for example), or underline key points in the full report. It is also a good idea to practice your presentation by making it to anyone who will listen.

Summary/Chapter 16

General Guidelines

1. If you carefully prepare a research plan before you conduct your study, you have a good head start on writing your research report.

2. The major guideline previously described for analyzing, organizing, and reporting related literature is applicable to this task—make an outline.

3. Development of an outline involves identification and ordering of major topics followed by differentiation of each major heading into logical subheadings.

4. A research report is written in the past tense.

---

13. If a journal article represents a version of a paper previously presented at a professional meeting, this fact should be discussed in a footnote at the beginning of the manuscript. This footnote should indicate the name, location, and date of the meeting at which it was presented.

14. Most presenters bring a limited number of copies of the complete report to the meeting itself and honor additional requests by mailing copies. Sometimes a request for a paper will be received months after a presentation is made; these requests must also be honored, just as promptly as initial requests.

General Rules for Writing and Typing

5. Probably the foremost rule of research report writing is that the writer must be as objective as possible in reporting the study.

6. Consistent with the goal of objective reporting, personal pronouns such as *I, my, we,* and *our* should be avoided; instead impersonal pronouns and the passive voice should be used.

7. The research report should be written in a clear, simple, straightforward style; you do not have to be boring, just concise.

8. Correct spelling, grammatical construction, and punctuation are not too much to expect of a scientific report.

9. Use of abbreviations and contractions is generally discouraged.

10. Authors of cited references are usually referred to by last name only in the main body of the report; first names, initials, and title are not given. Tables, footnotes, and references may include abbreviations; footnotes and references usually give at least the author's initials.

11. If the first word of a sentence is a number, or if the number is nine or less, numbers are usually expressed as words. Otherwise, numbers are generally expressed as arabic numerals.

12. The same standards of scholarship should be applied to the typing of the report as to the writing of the report.

13. Present the typist with a manuscript which is in final correct form; the typist's job is to type, not to polish your report.

14. If you have any special instructions, share them with the typist and be sure they are understood.

15. It is also a good idea to give your typist a copy of the style manual you are following to insure that required guidelines (such as size of margins) are followed.

16. The final typed report should be proofread carefully.

Format and Style

17. Most research reports consistently follow a selected system for format and style.

18. Format refers to the general pattern of organization and arrangement of the report.

19. Style refers to the rules of spelling, capitalization, punctuation, and typing followed in preparing the report.

20. While specific formats may vary in terms of specific headings included, all research reports follow a very similar format that parallels the steps involved in conducting a study.

21. Most colleges, universities, and professional journals either have developed their own, required style manual or have selected one that must be followed.

22. In addition to acquiring and studying a copy of the selected manual, it is also very helpful to study several reports that have been written following the same manual.

Types of Research Reports

23. Research reports usually take the form of a thesis, dissertation, journal article, or paper to be read at a professional meeting.

24. Depending upon its form, the report may be divided into sections or chapters but these divisions are similar in content.

Theses and Dissertations

Preliminary Pages

The Title Page

25. The title page usually includes the title of the report, the author's name, the degree requirement being fulfilled, the name and location of the college or university awarding the degree, the date of submission of the report, and signatures of approving committee members.

26. The title should be brief (15 words or less, as a rule of thumb), and at the same time it should describe the purpose of the study as clearly as possible.

27. The title should, however, at least indicate the major independent and dependent variables, and sometimes it names the population studied.

The Acknowledgment Page

28. This page permits the writer to express appreciation to persons who have contributed significantly to the completion of the report.

The Table of Contents, List of Tables, and List of Figures

29. The table of contents is basically an outline of your report which indicates on which page each major section (or chapter) and subsection begins.

30. The list of tables, which is presented on a separate page, gives the number and title of each table and the page on which it can be found.

31. The list of figures, which is also presented on a new page, gives the number and title of each figure and the page on which it can be found.

The Main Body of the Report

Introduction

32. The introduction section includes a description of the problem, a review of related literature, a statement of the hypothesis, and definition of terms.

33. A well-written statement of a problem generally indicates the variables, and the specific relationship between those variables, investigated in the study.

34. The review of related literature describes and analyzes what has already been done related to your problem.

35. A good hypothesis states as clearly and concisely as possible the expected relationship (or difference) between two variables, and defines those variables in operational, measurable terms.

36. The introduction also includes operational definition of terms used in the study which do not have a commonly known meaning.

Method

37. The method section includes a description of subjects, instruments, design, procedure, assumptions, and limitations.

38. The description of subjects includes a definition and description of the population from which the sample was selected and may describe the method used in selecting the sample or samples (or the method of selection may be described in the procedure section).

39. The description of each instrument should relate the function of the instrument in the study (for example, selection of subjects or a measure of the dependent variable), what the instrument is intended to measure, and data related to validity and reliability.

40. In an experimental study, the description of the basic design (or variation of a basic design) applied in the study should include a rationale for selection and a discussion of sources of invalidity associated with the design, and why they may have been minimized in the study being reported.

41. The procedure section should describe each step followed in conducting the study, in chronological order, in sufficient detail to permit the study to be replicated by another researcher.

Results

42. The results section describes the statistical techniques that were applied to the data and the results of each analysis.

43. For each hypothesis, the statistical test of significance selected and applied to the data is described followed by a statement indicating whether the hypothesis was supported or not.

44. Tables and figures are used to present findings in summary or graph form and add clarity to the presentation.

45. Tables present numerical data in rows and columns and usually include descriptive statistics, such as means and standard deviations, and the results of tests of significance such as t and F ratios.

46. Good tables and figures are uncluttered and self-explanatory; it is better to use two tables (or figures) than one that is crowded.

47. Tables and figures follow their related textual discussion and are referred to by number, not name or location.

Conclusions and Recommendations

48. Every research report has a section that discusses and interprets the results, draws conclusions and implications, and makes recommendations.

49. Each result is discussed in terms of the original hypothesis to which it relates, and in terms of its agreement or disagreement with previous results obtained by other researchers in other studies.

50. A result is the outcome of a test of significance; the corresponding conclusion is whether or not an original hypothesis was supported.

51. Overgeneralization refers to the statement of conclusions that are not warranted by the results.

52. The researcher should discuss the theoretical and practical implications of the findings and make recommendations for future research or future action.

Summary

53. Summaries are often required to be no more than a given maximum number of words, usually between 100 and 500.

54. Since the summary of a report is often the only part read, it should describe the most important aspects of the study, including the problem investigated, the type of subjects

and instruments, the design, the procedures, and the major results and the major conclusions.

References

55. The references, or bibliography, section of the report lists all the sources, alphabetically by authors' last names, that were directly used in writing the report.

56. Every source cited in the paper must be included in the references, and every entry listed in the references must appear in the paper; in other words, the sources in the paper and the sources in the references must correspond exactly.

57. If sources were consulted that were not directly cited in the main body of the report, these may be listed separately as Additional References.

58. Any secondary sources should also be described separately as Secondary References.

59. In thesis and dissertation studies, since the list of references is likely to be lengthy, references are often subdivided into sections such as Books, Articles, and Unpublished.

Appendices

60. Appendices include information and data pertinent to the study which either are not important enough to be included in the main body of the report or are too lengthy.

61. Appendices contain such entries as materials especially developed for the study (for example, tests, questionnaires, and cover letters), raw data, and data analysis sheets.

62. An index alphabetically lists all items of importance or interest in the report and the page on which each can be found.

63. A vita is a short autobiography describing professionally related activities and experiences of the author.

Journal Articles

Selection and Analysis of a Journal

64. Based on your review of related literature and your references, you should be able to identify two or three journals which publish studies in the area of research represented by your study.

65. Examination of a recent issue should give you some guidance concerning the format, style, and length acceptable to the selected journal.

66. All things being equal, shorter manuscripts have a higher probability of being published.

Preparation of the Manuscript

67. The contents and format of a journal article are very similar to those of a thesis or dissertation except that the journal article is much shorter.

68. None of the preliminary pages of a thesis or dissertation become part of a journal article; only the title remains.

69. The results section is usually of greater interest to the reader and thus typically gets reduced less than preceding sections of the paper. Correspondingly, the discussion section will probably not require too much revision.

70. Instead of a summary, many journals require an abstract of a given length.

71. Limits are not usually put on the number of references permitted, and all pertinent sources are included.

72. Supplementary pages of the thesis or dissertation are not part of the manuscript.

Submission and Evaluation of Manuscripts

73. Before submitting a manuscript to a journal editor, you should have at least one other person read it.

74. The required number of copies of the manuscript and a brief cover letter indicating the title of the article and your mailing address should be mailed first class to the journal.

Papers Read at Professional Meetings

75. The major focus of professional meetings is typically to have members share new knowledge and research findings.

76. While a great deal of informal exchange occurs, the structured, scheduled portion of meetings usually takes the form of paper presentations.

77. If you receive notification that your paper has been accepted, you are committed to being present at the meeting to give your paper and to having copies of a complete report available.

78. Research reports presented at meetings follow the same general format as all other reports and, in fact, the paper you prepare for presentation may resemble very closely a manuscript you are submitting to a journal.

79. A major purpose of professional meetings is to share knowledge more quickly than can be done through the reading of journals.

80. Reading a report verbatim is not a good idea, especially since copies of a complete report should be available to interested persons.

81. It is usually helpful either to prepare an outline of what you want to say, prepare a much-shortened version of the paper, or underline key points in the full report.

82. It is also a good idea to practice your presentation by making it to anyone who will listen.

Task 8 Performance Criteria

Your research report should include all the components presented in Figure 16.1 with the possible exceptions of an acknowledgment page and appendices.

Development of Task 8 basically involves combining Tasks 2, 6, and 7, writing Conclusions and Recommendations, writing a Summary, and preparing the appropriate preliminary pages and References. In other words, you have already written most of Task 8.

See the *Student Guide* for examples of Task 8.

Part Nine
Research Critiques

Anyone who reads a newspaper, listens to the radio, or watches television is a consumer of research. We are constantly bombarded with the latest research findings concerning the relationship between smoking and cancer, the positive effects of vitamin E, and the cavity-reducing powers of toothpaste, to name a few. Many people tend to uncritically accept and act on such findings if they are labeled the results of "scientific research" or if they are transmitted by anyone in a white lab coat. Very few people question the control procedures utilized or the generalizability of findings based on rats to human beings. You, as a professional, are required to possess critical evaluation skills. In addition to being critical of data transmitted by the media, you have a responsibility to be informed concerning the latest findings in your professional area and to be able to differentiate "good" research from "poor" research. Decisions made based on invalid research are likely to be bad ones and may result in the adoption of ineffective procedures.

Just because a study is reported in a journal does not necessarily mean that it was a good study; results are frequently published which are based on research involving one or more serious flaws. When you reviewed the literature related to your problem, you did not critically evaluate references; you simply determined whether or not each was related to your problem and if so in what way. Normally a researcher critically evaluates each reference and does not consider the results of poorly executed research. When you reviewed the literature you did not yet possess the competencies required to make quality discriminations. Competent evaluation of a research study requires knowledge of each of the components of the research process. Your work in previous chapters has given you that knowledge.

The goal of Part Nine is for you to be able to critically analyze and evaluate research reports. After you have read Part Nine, you should be able to perform the following task.

Task 9

Given a reprint of a research report and an evaluation form, evaluate the components of the report.

(See Performance Criteria, p. 406)

17

Evaluation of a Research Report

Enablers

After reading chapter 17, you should be able to:

1. For *each* of the major sections and subsections of a research report, list at least three questions which should be asked in determining its adequacy.

2. For each of the following types of research, list at least three questions which should be asked in determining the adequacy of a study representing that type:

> Historical Research
> Descriptive Research
>   Questionnaire Studies
>   Interview Studies
>   Observation Studies
> Correlational Research
>   Relationship Studies
>   Prediction Studies
> Causal-Comparative Research
> Experimental Research

General Evaluation Criteria

At your current level of expertise you will not be able to evaluate every component of every study. You would not be able to determine, for example, whether the appropriate degrees of freedom were used in the calculation of an analysis of covariance. There are, however, a number of basic errors or weaknesses which you should be able to detect in a research study. You should, for example, be able to identify the sources of invalidity associated with a study based on a one-group pretest-posttest design. You should also be able to detect obvious indications of experimenter bias which may have affected the results. A statement in a research report that "the purpose of this study was to prove . . ." should alert you to a probable bias effect.

As you read a research report, either as a consumer of research keeping up with the latest findings in your professional area or as a producer of research reviewing literature related to a defined problem, there are a number of questions you should ask yourself concerning the adequacy of execution of the various components. The answers to some of these questions are more critical than the answers to others. An inadequate title is not a critical flaw; an inadequate design is. Some questions are difficult to answer if the study is not directly in your area of expertise. If your area of specialization is reading, for example, you are probably not in a position to judge the adequacy of a review of literature related to anxiety effects on learning. And, admittedly, the answers to some questions are more subjective than objective. Whether or not a good design was used is pretty objective; most everyone would agree that the randomized posttest only control group design is a good design. Whether or not the most appropriate design was used, given the problem under study, involves a degree of subjective judgment; the need for inclusion of a pretest, for example, might be a debatable point. Despite the lack of complete precision, however, evaluation of a research report is a worthwhile process. Major problems and shortcomings are usually readily identifiable, and by mentally responding to a number of questions one formulates an overall impression concerning the validity of the study. For each component of a research report a number of evaluative questions are listed for your consideration. This forthcoming list is by no means exhaustive and, as you read it, you may very well think of additional questions which might be asked.

Introduction

Problem

Is there a statement of the problem?

Is the problem "researchable," that is, can it be investigated through the collection and analysis of data?

Is background information on the problem presented?

Is the educational significance of the problem discussed?

Does the problem statement indicate the variables of interest and the specific relationship between those variables which were investigated?

When necessary, are variables directly or operationally defined?

Review of Related Literature

Is the review comprehensive?

Are all references cited relevant to the problem under investigation?

Are the sources mostly primary or were a number of secondary sources cited?

Have references been critically analyzed and the results of various studies compared and contrasted or is the review basically a series of abstracts or annotations?

Is the review well organized, does it logically flow in such a way that the least-related references to the problem are discussed first and the most-related references are discussed last?

Does the review conclude with a brief summary of the literature and its implications for the problem investigated?

Do the implications discussed form an empirical or theoretical rationale for the hypotheses which follow?

Hypotheses

Are specific questions to be answered listed or specific hypotheses to be tested stated?

Does each hypothesis state an expected relationship or difference between two variables?

If necessary, are variables directly or operationally defined?

Is each hypothesis testable?

Method

Subjects

Are the size and major characteristics of the population studied described?

Was the entire population studied?

Was a sample selected?

Is the method of selecting a sample clearly described?

Is the method of sample selection described one that is likely to result in a representative, unbiased sample?

Were volunteers used?

Are the size and major characteristics of the sample described?

Does the sample size meet the suggested guideline for minimum sample size appropriate for the method of research represented?

Instruments

Is a rationale given for selection of the instruments used?

Is each instrument described in terms of purpose and content?

Are the instruments appropriate for measuring the intended variables?

If an instrument was developed specifically for the study, are the procedures involved in its development and validation described?

Is evidence presented that indicates that each instrument is appropriate for the sample under study?

Is instrument validity discussed and coefficients given if appropriate?

Is reliability discussed in terms of type and size of reliability coefficients?

If appropriate, are subtest reliabilities given?

If an instrument was specifically developed for the study, are administration, scoring, and interpretation procedures fully described?

Design and Procedure

Is the design appropriate for testing the hypotheses of the study?

Are procedures described in sufficient detail to permit them to be replicated by another researcher?

Was a pilot study conducted?

If a pilot study was conducted are its execution and results described as well as its impact on the subsequent study?

Are control procedures described?

Are there any potentially confounding variables which were not controlled?

Results

Are appropriate descriptive statistics presented?

Was the probability level, p, at which the results of the tests of significance were evaluated, specified in advance of data analysis?

If parametric tests were used is there any evidence that one or more of the required assumptions were greatly violated?

Are the tests of significance described appropriate, given the hypotheses and design of the study?

Was every hypothesis tested?

Are the tests of significance interpreted using the appropriate degrees of freedom?

Are the results clearly presented?

Are the table and figures (if any) well organized and easy to understand?

Are the data in each table and figure described in the text?

Conclusions and Recommendations

Is each result discussed in terms of the original hypothesis to which it relates?

Is each result discussed in terms of its agreement or disagreement with previous results obtained by other researchers in other studies?

Are generalizations made that are not warranted by the results?

Are the possible effects of uncontrolled variables on the results discussed?

Are theoretical and practical implications of the findings discussed?

Are recommendations for future action made?

Based only on statistical significance, are suggestions for educational action made that are not justified by the data; in other words, has the author confused statistical significance and practical significance?

Are recommendations for future research made?

Summary (or Abstract)

Is the problem restated?

Are the number and type of subjects and instruments described?

Is the design used identified?

Are procedures described?

Are the major results and conclusions restated?

Method-Specific Evaluation Criteria

In addition to general criteria that can be applied to almost any study, there are additional questions that should be asked depending upon the method of research represented by the study. In other words, there are concerns that are specific to historical studies, and likewise to descriptive, correlational, causal-comparative, and experimental studies.

Historical Research

Were the sources of data related to the problem mostly primary or mostly secondary?

Was each piece of data subjected to external criticism?

Was each piece of data subjected to internal criticism?

Descriptive Research

Questionnaire Studies

Are questionnaire validation procedures described?

Was the questionnaire pretested?
Are pilot study procedures and results described?
Are directions to questionnaire respondents clear?
Does each item in the questionnaire relate to one of the objectives of the study?
Does each questonnaire item deal with a single concept?
When necessary, is a point of reference given for questionnaire items?
Are leading questions avoided in the questionnaire?
Are there sufficient alternatives for each questionnaire item?
Does the cover letter explain the purpose and importance of the study and give
   the potential respondent a good reason for cooperating?
If appropriate, is confidentiality of responses assured in the cover letter?
Was the percentage of returns at least 70%?
Are follow-up activities described?
If the response rate was low, was any attempt made to determine any major
   differences between responders and nonresponders?

Interview Studies

Were the interview procedures pretested?
Are pilot study procedures and results described?
Does each item in the interview guide relate to a specific objective of the study?
When necessary, is a point of reference given in the guide for interview items?
Are leading questions avoided in the interview guide?
Does the interview guide indicate the type and amount of prompting and probing
   that was permitted?
Are the qualifications and special training of the interviewers described?
Is the method that was used to record responses described?
Is there a more reliable, unbiased method of recording responses that could have
   been used?
How were responses to semistructured and unstructured items quantified and
   analyzed?

Observation Studies

Are observational variables defined?
Were observers required to observe more than one behavior at a time?
Was a coded recording instrument used?
Are the qualifications and special training of the observers described?
Is the level of observer reliability reported?
Is the level of observer reliability sufficiently high?
Were possible observer and observee biases discussed?
Could an unobtrusive measure have been used instead to collect the data?

Correlational Research

Relationship Studies

Were variables carefully selected or was a shotgun approach used?
Is the rationale for variable selection described?
Are conclusions and recommendations based on values of correlation coefficients
   corrected for attenuation or restriction in range?

Do the conclusions indicate causal relationships between the variables investigated?

Prediction Studies

Is a rationale given for selection of predictor variables?
Is the criterion variable well defined?
Was the resulting prediction equation validated with at least one other group?

Causal-Comparative Research

Are the characteristics or experiences that differentiate the groups (the independent variable) clearly defined or described?
Are critical extraneous variables identified?
Were any control procedures applied to equate the groups on extraneous variables?
Are causal relationships found discussed with due caution?
Are plausible alternative hypotheses discussed?

Experimental Research

Was an appropriate experimental design selected?
Is a rationale for design selection given?
Are sources of invalidity associated with the design identified and discussed?
Is the method of group formation described?
Was the experimental group formed in the same way as the control group?
Were existing groups used or were groups randomly formed?
Were treatments randomly assigned to groups?
Were critical extraneous variables identified?
Were any control procedures applied to equate groups on extraneous variables?
Is there any evidence to suggest reactive arrangements (for example, the Hawthorne effect)?

Summary/Chapter 17

General Evaluation Criteria

1. There are a number of basic errors or weaknesses which even a beginning researcher should be able to detect in a research study.
2. You should be able to detect obvious indications of experimenter bias which may have affected the results.
3. As you read a research report, either as a consumer of research keeping up with the latest findings in your professional area or as a producer of research reviewing

literature related to a defined problem, there are a number of questions you should ask yourself concerning the adequacy of execution of the various components.

4. The answers to some of these questions are more critical than the answers to others.
5. Major problems and shortcomings are usually readily identifiable, and by mentally responding to a number of questions one formulates an overall impression concerning the validity of the study.

Introduction

6. Problem .... See page 400
7. Review of Related Literature .... See page 400
8. Hypotheses .... See page 400

Method

9. Subjects .... See page 401
10. Instruments .... See page 401
11. Design and Procedure .... See page 401

Results
12. .... See page 401

Conclusions and Recommendations
13. .... See page 402

Summary
14. .... See page 402

Method-Specific Evaluation Criteria

15. In addition to general criteria which can be applied to almost any study, there are additional questions which should be asked depending upon the method of research represented by the study.

Historical Research
16. .... See page 402

Descriptive Research
17. Questionnaire Studies .... See page 402
18. Interview Studies .... See page 403
19. Observation Studies .... See page 403

Correlational Research
20. Relationship Studies .... See page 403
21. Prediction Studies .... See page 404

Causal-Comparative Research
22.

See page 404

Experimental Research
23.

See page 404

Task 9 Performance Criteria

The evaluation form will list a series of questions about an article to which you must indicate a yes or no response. For example, you might be asked if there is a statement of hypotheses. If the answer is yes, you must indicate where the asked-for component is located in the study. For example, you might indicate a statement of a hypothesis on page 4, paragraph 3, lines 2–6.

In addition, if the study is experimental you will be asked to identify and diagram the experimental design which was applied.

See the *Student Guide* for a practice example for Task 9.

Appendix A

Reference Tables

Table A.1.
Ten Thousand Random Numbers

	00— 04	05— 09	10— 14	15— 19	20— 24	25— 29	30— 34	35— 39	40— 44	45— 49
00	54463	22662	65905	70639	79365	67382	29085	69831	47058	08186
01	15389	85205	18850	39226	42249	90669	96325	23248	60933	26927
02	85941	40756	82414	02015	13858	78030	16269	65978	01385	15345
03	61149	69440	11268	88218	58925	03638	52862	62733	33451	77455
04	05219	81619	81619	10651	67079	92511	59888	72095	83463	75577
05	41417	98326	87719	92294	46614	50948	64886	20002	97365	30976
06	28357	94070	20652	35774	16249	75019	21145	15217	47286	76305
07	17783	00015	10806	83091	91530	36466	39981	62481	49177	75779
08	40950	84820	29881	85966	62800	70326	84740	62660	77379	90279
09	82995	64157	66164	41180	10089	41757	78258	96488	88629	37231
10	96754	17676	55659	44105	47361	34833	86679	23930	53249	27083
11	34357	88040	53364	71726	45690	66334	60332	22554	90600	71113
12	06318	37403	49927	57715	50423	67372	63116	48888	21505	80182
13	62111	52820	07243	79931	89292	84767	85693	73947	22278	11551
14	47534	09243	67879	00544	23410	12740	02540	54440	32949	13491
15	98614	75993	84460	62846	59844	14922	49730	73443	48167	34770
16	24856	03648	44898	09351	98795	18644	39765	71058	90368	44104
17	96887	12479	80621	66223	86085	78285	02432	53342	42846	94771
18	90801	21472	42815	77408	37390	76766	52615	32141	30268	18106
19	55165	77312	83666	36028	28420	70219	81369	41943	47366	41067
20	75884	12952	84318	95108	72305	64620	91318	89872	45375	85436
21	16777	37116	58550	42958	21460	43910	01175	87894	81378	10620
22	46230	43877	80207	88877	89380	32992	91380	03164	98656	59337
23	42902	66892	46134	01432	94710	23474	20523	60137	60609	13119
24	81007	00333	39693	28039	10154	95425	39220	19774	31782	49037
25	68089	01122	51111	72373	06902	74373	96199	97017	41273	21546
26	20411	67081	89950	16944	93054	87687	96693	87236	77054	33848
27	58212	13160	06468	15718	82627	76999	05999	58680	96739	63700
28	70577	42866	24969	61210	76046	67699	42054	12696	93758	03283
29	94522	74358	71659	62038	79643	79169	44741	05437	39038	13163
30	42626	86819	85651	88678	17401	03252	99547	32404	17918	62880
31	16051	33763	57194	16752	54450	19031	58580	47629	54132	60631
32	08244	27647	33851	44705	94211	46716	11738	55784	95374	72655
33	59497	04392	09419	89964	51211	04894	72882	17805	21896	83864
34	97155	13428	40293	09985	58434	01412	69124	82171	59058	82859
35	98409	66162	95763	47420	20792	61527	20441	39435	11859	41567
36	45476	84882	65109	96597	25930	66790	65706	61203	53634	22557
37	89300	69700	50741	30329	11658	23166	05400	66669	48708	03887
38	50051	95137	91631	66315	91428	12275	24816	68091	71710	33258
39	31753	85178	31310	89642	98364	02306	24617	09609	83942	22716
40	79152	53829	77250	20190	56535	18760	69942	77448	33278	48805
41	44560	38750	83635	56540	64900	42912	13953	79149	18710	68618
42	68328	83378	63369	71381	39564	05615	42451	64559	97501	65747
43	46939	38689	58625	08342	30459	85863	20781	09284	26333	91777
44	83544	86141	15707	96256	23068	13782	08467	89469	93842	55349
45	91621	00881	04900	54224	46177	55309	17852	27491	89415	23466
46	91896	67126	04151	03795	59077	11848	12630	98375	53068	60142
47	55751	62515	22108	80830	02263	29303	37204	96926	30506	09808
48	85156	87689	95493	88842	00664	55017	55539	17771	69448	87530
49	07521	56898	12236	60277	39102	62315	12239	07105	11844	01117

Reprinted by permission from *Statistical Methods* by George W. Snedecor and William G. Cochran, sixth edition © 1967 by Iowa State University Press, pp. 543–46.

Table A.1 (continued).

	50— 54	55— 59	60— 64	65— 69	70— 74	75— 79	80— 84	85— 89	90— 94	95— 99
00	59391	58030	52098	82718	87024	82848	04190	96574	90464	29065
01	99567	76364	77204	04615	27062	96621	43918	01896	83991	51141
02	10363	97518	51400	25670	98342	61891	27101	37855	06235	33316
03	96859	19558	64432	16706	99612	59798	32803	67708	15297	28612
04	11258	24591	36863	55368	31721	94335	34936	02566	80972	08188
05	95068	88628	35911	14530	33020	80428	33936	31855	34334	64865
06	54463	47237	73800	91017	36239	71824	83671	39892	60518	37092
07	16874	62677	57412	13215	31389	62233	80827	73917	82802	84420
08	92494	63157	76593	91316	03505	72389	96363	52887	01087	66091
09	15669	56689	35682	40844	53256	81872	35213	09840	34471	74441
10	99116	75486	84989	23476	52967	67104	39495	39100	17217	74073
11	15696	10703	65178	90637	63110	17622	53988	71087	84148	11670
12	97720	15369	51269	69620	03388	13699	33423	67453	43269	56720
13	11666	13841	71681	98000	35979	39719	81899	07449	47985	46967
14	71628	73130	78783	75691	41632	09847	61547	18707	85489	69944
15	40501	51089	99943	91843	41995	88931	73631	69361	05375	15417
16	22518	55576	98215	82068	10798	86211	36584	67466	69373	40054
17	75112	30485	62173	02132	14878	92879	22281	16783	86352	00077
18	80327	02671	98191	84342	90813	49268	94551	15496	20168	09271
19	60251	45548	02146	05597	48228	81366	34598	72856	66762	17002
20	57430	82270	10421	00540	43648	75888	66049	21511	47676	33444
21	73528	39559	34434	88586	54086	71693	43132	14414	79949	85193
22	25991	65959	70769	64721	86413	33475	42740	06175	82758	66248
23	78388	16638	09134	59980	63806	48472	39318	35434	24057	74739
24	12477	09965	96657	57994	59439	76330	24596	77515	09577	91871
25	83266	32883	42451	15579	38155	29793	40914	65990	16255	17777
26	76970	80876	10237	39515	79152	74798	39357	09054	73579	92359
27	37074	65198	44785	68624	98336	84481	97610	78735	46703	98265
28	83712	06514	30101	78295	54656	85417	43189	60048	72781	72606
29	20287	56862	69727	94443	64936	08366	27227	05158	50326	59566
30	74261	32592	86538	27041	65172	85532	07571	80609	39285	65340
31	64081	49863	08478	96001	18888	14810	70545	89755	59064	07210
32	05617	75818	47750	67814	29575	10526	66192	44464	27058	40467
33	26793	74951	95466	74307	13330	42664	85515	20632	05497	33625
34	65988	72850	48737	54719	52056	01596	03845	35067	03134	70322
35	27366	42271	44300	73399	21105	03280	73457	43093	05192	48657
36	56760	10909	98147	34736	33863	95256	12731	66598	50771	83665
37	72880	43338	93643	58904	59543	23943	11231	83268	65938	81581
38	77888	38100	03062	58103	47961	83841	25878	23746	55903	44115
39	28440	07819	21580	51459	47971	29882	13990	29226	23608	15873
40	63525	94441	77033	12147	51054	49955	58312	76923	96071	05813
41	47606	93410	16359	89033	89696	47231	64498	31776	05383	39902
42	52669	45030	96279	14709	52372	87832	02735	50803	72744	88208
43	16738	60159	07425	62369	07515	82721	37875	71153	21315	00132
44	59348	11695	45751	15865	74739	05572	32688	20271	65128	14551
45	12900	71775	29845	60774	94924	21810	38636	33717	67598	82521
46	75086	23537	49939	33595	13484	97588	28617	17979	70749	35234
47	99495	51534	29181	09993	38190	42553	68922	52125	91077	40197
48	26075	31671	45386	36583	93459	48599	52022	41330	60651	91321
49	13636	93596	23377	51133	95126	61496	42474	45141	46660	42338

Table A.1 (continued).

	00—04	05—09	10—14	15—19	20—24	25—29	30—34	35—39	40—44	44—49
50	64249	63664	39652	40646	97306	31741	07294	84149	46797	82487
51	26538	44249	04050	48174	65570	44072	40192	51153	11397	58212
52	05845	00512	78630	55328	18116	69296	91705	86224	29503	57071
53	74897	68373	67359	51014	33510	83048	17056	72506	82949	54600
54	20872	54570	35017	88132	25730	22626	86723	91691	13191	77212
55	31432	96156	89177	75541	81355	24480	77243	76690	42507	84362
56	66890	61505	01240	00660	05873	13568	76082	79172	57913	93448
57	41894	57790	79970	33106	86904	48119	52503	24130	72824	21627
58	11303	87118	81471	52936	08555	28420	49416	44448	04269	27029
59	54374	57325	16947	45356	78371	10563	97191	53798	12693	27928
60	64852	34421	61046	90849	13966	39810	42699	21753	76192	10508
61	16309	20384	09491	91588	97720	89846	30376	76970	23063	35894
62	42587	37065	24526	72602	57589	98131	37292	05967	26002	51945
63	40177	98590	97161	41682	84533	67588	62036	49967	01990	72308
64	82309	76128	93965	26743	24141	04838	40254	26065	07938	76236
65	79788	68243	59732	04257	27084	14743	17520	94501	55811	76099
66	40538	79000	89559	25026	42274	23489	34502	75508	06059	86682
67	64016	73598	18609	73150	62463	33102	45205	87440	96767	67042
68	49767	12691	17903	93871	99721	79109	09425	26904	07419	76013
69	76974	55108	29795	08404	82684	00497	51126	79935	57450	55671
70	23854	08480	85983	96025	50117	64610	99425	62291	86943	21541
71	68973	70551	25098	78033	98573	79848	31778	29555	61446	23037
72	36444	93600	65350	14971	25325	00427	52073	64280	18847	24768
73	03003	87800	07391	11594	21196	00781	32550	57158	58887	73041
74	17540	26188	36647	78386	04558	61463	57842	90382	77019	24210
75	38916	55809	47982	41968	69760	79422	80154	91486	19180	15100
76	64288	19843	69122	42502	48508	28820	59933	72998	99942	10515
77	86809	51564	38040	39418	49915	19000	58050	16899	79952	57849
78	99800	99566	14742	05028	30033	94889	55381	23656	75787	59223
79	92345	31890	95712	08279	91794	94068	49337	88674	35355	12267
80	90363	65162	32245	82279	79256	80834	06088	99462	56705	06118
81	64437	32242	48431	04835	39070	59702	31508	60935	22390	52246
82	91714	53662	28373	34333	55791	74758	51144	18827	10704	76803
83	20902	17646	31391	31459	33315	03444	55743	74701	58851	27427
84	12217	86007	70371	52281	14510	76094	96579	54853	78339	20839
85	45177	02863	42307	53571	22532	74921	17735	42201	80540	54721
86	28325	90814	08804	52746	47913	54577	47525	77705	95330	21866
87	29019	28776	56116	54791	64604	08815	46049	71186	34650	14994
88	84979	81353	56219	67062	26146	82567	33122	14124	46240	92973
89	50371	26347	48513	63915	11158	25563	91915	18431	92978	11591
90	53422	06825	69711	67950	64716	18003	49581	45378	99878	61130
91	67453	35651	89316	41620	32048	70225	47597	33137	31443	51445
92	07294	85353	74819	23445	68237	07202	99515	62282	53809	26685
93	79544	00302	45338	16015	66613	88968	14595	63836	77716	79596
94	64144	85442	82060	46471	24162	39500	87351	36637	42833	71875
95	90919	11883	58318	00042	52402	28210	34075	33272	00840	73268
96	06670	57353	86275	92276	77591	46924	60839	55437	03183	13191
97	36634	93976	52062	83678	41256	60948	18685	48992	19462	96062
98	75101	72891	85745	67106	26010	62107	60885	37503	55461	71213
99	05112	71222	72654	51583	05228	62056	57390	42746	39272	96659

Table A.1 (continued).

	50— 54	55— 59	60— 64	65— 69	70— 74	75— 79	80— 84	85— 89	90— 94	95— 99
50	32847	31282	03345	89593	69214	70381	78285	20054	91018	16742
51	16916	00041	30236	55023	14253	76582	12092	86533	92426	37655
52	66176	34037	21005	27137	03193	48970	64625	22394	39622	79085
53	46299	13335	12180	16861	38043	59292	62675	63631	37020	78195
54	22847	47839	45385	23289	47526	54098	45683	55849	51575	64689
55	41851	54160	92320	69936	34803	92479	33399	71160	64777	83378
56	28444	59497	91586	95917	68553	28639	06455	34174	11130	91994
57	47520	62378	98855	83174	13088	16561	68559	26679	06238	51254
58	34978	63271	13142	82681	05271	08822	06490	44984	49307	61617
59	37404	80416	69035	92980	49486	74378	75610	74976	70056	15478
60	32400	65482	52099	53676	74648	94148	65095	69597	52771	71551
61	89262	86332	51718	70663	11623	29834	79820	73002	84886	03591
62	86866	09127	98021	03871	27789	58444	44832	36505	40672	30180
63	90814	14833	08759	74645	05046	94056	99094	65091	32663	73040
64	19192	82756	20553	58446	55376	88914	75096	26119	83898	43816
65	77585	52593	56612	95766	10019	29531	73064	20953	53523	58136
66	23757	16364	05096	03192	62386	45389	85332	18877	55710	96459
67	45989	96257	23850	26216	23309	21526	07425	50254	19455	29315
68	92970	94243	07316	41467	64837	52406	25225	51553	31220	14032
69	74346	59596	40088	98176	17896	86900	20249	77753	19099	48885
70	87646	41309	27636	45153	29988	94770	07255	70908	05340	99751
71	50099	71038	45146	06146	55211	99429	43169	66259	99786	59180
72	10127	46900	64984	75348	04115	33624	68774	60013	35515	62556
73	67995	81977	18984	64091	02785	27762	42529	97144	80407	64524
74	26304	80217	84934	82657	69291	35397	98714	35104	08187	48109
75	81994	41070	56642	64091	31229	02595	13513	45148	78722	30144
76	59337	34662	79631	89403	65212	09975	06118	86197	58208	16162
77	51228	10937	62396	81460	47331	91403	95007	06047	16846	64809
78	31089	37995	29577	07828	42272	54016	21950	86192	99046	84864
79	38207	97938	93459	75174	79460	55436	57206	87644	21296	43393
80	88666	31142	09474	89712	63153	62333	42212	06140	42594	43671
81	53365	56134	67582	92557	89520	33452	05134	70628	27612	33738
82	89807	74530	38004	90102	11693	90257	05500	79920	62700	43325
83	18682	81038	85662	90915	91631	22223	91588	80774	07716	12548
84	63571	32579	63942	25371	09234	94592	98475	76884	37635	33608
85	68927	56492	67799	95398	77642	54913	91583	08421	81450	76229
86	56401	63186	39389	88798	31356	89235	97036	32341	33292	73757
87	24333	95603	02359	72942	46287	95382	08452	62862	97869	71775
88	17025	84202	95199	62272	06366	16175	97577	99304	41587	03686
89	02804	08253	52133	20224	68034	50865	57868	22343	55111	03607
90	08298	03879	20995	19850	73090	13191	18963	82244	78479	99121
91	59883	01785	82403	96062	03785	03488	12970	64896	38336	30030
92	46982	06682	62864	91837	74021	89094	39952	64158	79614	78235
93	31121	47266	07661	02051	67599	24471	69843	83696	71402	76287
94	97867	56641	63416	17577	30161	87320	37752	73276	48969	41915
95	57364	86746	08415	14621	49430	22311	15836	72492	49372	44103
96	09559	26263	69511	28064	75999	44540	13337	10918	79846	54809
97	53873	55571	00608	42661	91332	63956	74087	59008	47493	99581
98	35531	19162	86406	05299	77511	24311	57257	22826	77555	05941
99	28229	88629	25695	94932	30721	16197	78742	34974	97528	45447

Table A.2.
Values of the Correlation Coefficient
for Different Levels of Significance (p)

df	.10	.05	.01	.001
1	.98769	.99692	.99988	
2	.90000	.95000	.99000	.99999
3	.8054	.8783	.95873	.99900
4	.7293	.8114	.91720	.99116
5	.6694	.7545	.8745	.97406
6	.6215	.7067	.8343	.95074
7	.5822	.6664	.7977	.92493
8	.5494	.6319	.7646	.8982
9	.5214	.6021	.7348	.8721
10	.4973	.5760	.7079	.8471
11	.4762	.5529	.6835	.8233
12	.4575	.5324	.6614	.8010
13	.4409	.5139	.6411	.7800
14	.4259	.4973	.6226	.7603
15	.4124	.4821	.6055	.7420
16	.4000	.4683	.5897	.7246
17	.3887	.4555	.5751	.7084
18	.3783	.4438	.5614	.6932
19	.3687	.4329	.5487	.6787
20	.3598	.4227	.5368	.6652
25	.3233	.3809	.4869	.6524
30	.2960	.3494	.4487	.5974
35	.2746	.3246	.4182	.5541
40	.2573	.3044	.3932	.5189
45	.2428	.2875	.3721	.4896
50	.2306	.2732	.3541	.4648
60	.2108	.2500	.3248	.4433
70	.1954	.2319	.3017	.4078
80	.1829	.2172	.2830	.3799
90	.1726	.2050	.2673	.3568
100	.1638	.1946	.2540	.3375
				.3211

Table A.2 is taken from Table VII of Fisher and Yates: *Statistical Tables for Biological, Agricultural and Medical Research,* published by Longman Group Ltd., London (previously published by Oliver and Boyd, Edinburgh), and by permission of the authors and publishers.

Table A.3.
Squares and Square Roots

Number	Square	Square Root	Number	Square	Square Root
1	1	1.000	51	26 01	7.141
2	4	1.414	52	27 04	7.211
3	9	1.732	53	28 09	7.280
4	16	2.000	54	29 16	7.348
5	25	2.236	55	30 25	7.416
6	36	2.449	56	31 36	7.483
7	49	2.646	57	32 49	7.550
8	64	2.828	58	33 64	7.616
9	81	3.000	59	34 81	7.681
10	1 00	3.162	60	36 00	7.746
11	1 21	3.317	61	37 21	7.810
12	1 44	3.464	62	38 44	7.874
13	1 69	3.606	63	39 69	7.937
14	1 96	3.742	64	40 96	8.000
15	2 25	3.873	65	42 25	8.062
16	2 56	4.000	66	43 56	8.124
17	2 89	4.123	67	44 89	8.185
18	3 24	4.243	68	46 24	8.246
19	3 61	4.359	69	47 61	8.307
20	4 00	4.472	70	49 00	8.367
21	4 41	4.583	71	50 41	8.426
22	4 84	4.690	72	51 84	8.485
23	5 29	4.796	73	53 29	8.544
24	5 76	4.899	74	54 76	8.602
25	6 25	5.000	75	56 25	8.660
26	6 76	5.099	76	57 76	8.718
27	7 29	5.196	77	59 29	8.775
28	7 84	5.292	78	60 84	8.832
29	8 41	5.385	79	62 41	8.888
30	9 00	5.477	80	64 00	8.944
31	9 61	5.568	81	65 61	9.000
32	10 24	5.657	82	67 24	9.055
33	10 89	5.745	83	68 89	9.110
34	11 56	5.831	84	70 56	9.165
35	12 25	5.916	85	72 25	9.220
36	12 96	6.000	86	73 96	9.274
37	13 69	6.083	87	75 69	9.327
38	14 44	6.164	88	77 44	9.381
39	15 21	6.245	89	79 21	9.434
40	16 00	6.325	90	81 00	9.487
41	16 81	6.403	91	82 81	9.539
42	17 64	6.481	92	84 64	9.592
43	18 49	6.557	93	86 49	9.644
44	19 36	6.633	94	88 36	9.695
45	20 25	6.708	95	90 25	9.747
46	21 16	6.782	96	92 16	9.798
47	22 09	6.856	97	94 09	9.849
48	23 04	6.928	98	96 04	9.899
49	24 01	7.000	99	98 01	9.950
50	25 00	7.071	100	1 00 00	10.000

Table A.3 (continued).

Number	Square	Square Root	Number	Square	Square Root
101	1 02 01	10.050	151	2 28 01	12.288
102	1 04 04	10.100	152	2 31 04	12.329
103	1 06 09	10.149	153	2 34 09	12.369
104	1 08 16	10.198	154	2 37 16	12.410
105	1 10 25	10.247	155	2 40 25	12.450
106	1 12 36	10.296	156	2 43 36	12.490
107	1 14 49	10.344	157	2 46 49	12.530
108	1 16 64	10.392	158	2 49 64	12.570
109	1 18 81	10.440	159	2 52 81	12.610
110	1 21 00	10.488	160	2 56 00	12.649
111	1 23 21	10.536	161	2 59 21	12.689
112	1 25 44	10.583	162	2 62 44	12.728
113	1 27 69	10.630	163	2 65 69	12.767
114	1 29 96	10.677	164	2 68 96	12.806
115	1 32 25	10.724	165	2 72 25	12.845
116	1 34 56	10.770	166	2 75 56	12.884
117	1 36 89	10.817	167	2 78 89	12.923
118	1 39 24	10.863	168	2 82 24	12.961
119	1 41 61	10.909	169	2 85 61	13.000
120	1 44 00	10.954	170	2 89 00	13.038
121	1 46 41	11.000	171	2 92 41	13.077
122	1 48 84	11.045	172	2 95 84	13.115
123	1 51 29	11.091	173	2 99 29	13.153
124	1 53 76	11.136	174	3 02 76	13.191
125	1 56 25	11.180	175	3 06 25	13.229
126	1 58 76	11.225	176	3 09 76	13.266
127	1 61 29	11.269	177	3 13 29	13.304
128	1 63 84	11.314	178	3 16 84	13.342
129	1 66 41	11.358	179	3 20 41	13.379
130	1 69 00	11.402	180	3 24 00	13.416
131	1 71 61	11.446	181	3 27 61	13.454
132	1 74 24	11.489	182	3 31 24	13.491
133	1 76 89	11.533	183	3 34 89	13.528
134	1 79 56	11.576	184	3 38 56	13.565
135	1 82 25	11.619	185	3 42 25	13.601
136	1 84 96	11.662	186	3 45 96	13.638
137	1 87 69	11.705	187	3 49 69	13.675
138	1 90 44	11.747	188	3 53 44	13.711
139	1 93 21	11.790	189	3 57 21	13.748
140	1 96 00	11.832	190	3 61 00	13.784
141	1 98 81	11.874	191	3 64 81	13.820
142	2 01 64	11.916	192	3 68 64	13.856
143	2 04 49	11.958	193	3 72 49	13.892
144	2 07 36	12.000	194	3 76 36	13.928
145	2 10 25	12.042	195	3 80 25	13.964
146	2 13 16	12.083	196	3 84 16	14.000
147	2 16 09	12.124	197	3 88 09	14.036
148	2 19 04	12.166	198	3 92 04	14.071
149	2 22 01	12.207	199	3 96 01	14.107
150	2 25 00	12.247	200	4 00 00	14.142

Table A.3 (continued).

Number	Square	Square Root	Number	Square	Square Root
201	4 04 01	14.177	251	6 30 01	15.843
202	4 08 04	14.213	252	6 35 04	15.875
203	4 12 09	14.248	253	6 40 09	15.906
204	4 16 16	14.283	554	6 45 16	15.937
205	4 20 25	14.318	255	6 50 25	15.969
206	4 24 36	14.353	256	6 55 36	16.000
207	4 28 49	14.387	257	6 60 49	16.031
208	4 32 64	14.422	258	6 65 64	16.062
209	4 36 81	14.457	259	6 70 81	16.093
210	4 41 00	14.491	260	6 76 00	16.125
211	4 45 21	14.526	261	6 81 21	16.155
212	4 49 44	14.560	262	6 86 44	16.186
213	4 53 69	14.595	263	6 91 69	16.217
214	4 57 96	14.629	264	6 96 96	16.248
215	4 62 25	14.663	265	7 02 25	16.279
216	4 66 56	14.697	266	7 07 56	16.310
217	4 70 89	14.731	267	7 12 89	16.340
218	4 75 24	14.765	268	7 18 24	16.371
219	4 79 61	14.799	269	7 23 61	16.401
220	4 84 00	14.832	270	7 29 00	16.432
221	4 88 41	14.866	271	7 34 41	16.462
222	4 92 84	14.900	272	7 39 84	16.492
223	4 97 29	14.933	273	7 45 29	16.523
224	5 01 76	14.967	274	7 50 76	16.553
225	5 06 25	15.000	275	7 56 25	16.583
226	5 10 76	15.033	276	7 61 76	16.613
227	5 15 29	15.067	277	7 67 29	16.643
228	5 19 84	15.100	278	7 72 84	16.673
229	5 24 41	15.133	279	7 78 41	16.703
230	5 29 00	15.166	280	7 84 00	16.733
231	5 33 61	15.199	281	7 89 61	16.763
232	5 38 24	15.232	282	7 95 24	16.793
233	5 42 89	15.264	283	8 00 89	16.823
234	5 47 56	15.297	284	8 06 56	16.852
235	5 52 25	15.330	285	8 12 25	16.882
236	5 56 96	15.362	286	8 17 96	16.912
237	5 61 69	15.395	287	8 23 69	16.941
238	5 66 44	15.427	288	8 29 44	16.971
239	5 71 21	15.460	289	8 35 21	17.000
240	5 76 00	15.492	290	8 41 00	17.029
241	5 80 81	15.524	291	8 46 81	17.059
242	5 85 64	15.556	292	8 52 64	17.088
243	5 90 49	15.588	293	8 58 49	17.117
244	5 95 36	15.620	294	8 64 36	17.146
245	6 00 25	15.652	295	8 70 25	17.176
246	6 05 16	15.684	296	8 76 16	17.205
247	6 10 09	15.716	297	8 82 09	17.234
248	6 15 04	15.748	298	8 88 04	17.263
249	6 20 01	15.780	299	8 94 01	17.292
250	6 25 00	15.811	300	9 00 00	17.321

Table A.3 (continued).

Number	Square	Square Root	Number	Square	Square Root
301	9 06 01	17.349	351	12 32 01	18.735
302	9 12 04	17.378	352	12 39 04	18.762
303	9 18 09	17.407	353	12 46 09	18.788
304	9 24 16	17.436	354	12 53 16	18.815
305	9 30 25	17.464	355	12 60 25	18.841
306	9 36 36	17.493	356	12 67 36	18.868
307	9 42 49	17.521	357	12 74 49	18.894
308	9 48 64	17.550	358	12 81 64	18.921
309	9 54 81	17.578	359	12 88 81	18.947
310	9 61 00	17.607	360	12 96 00	18.974
311	9 67 21	17.635	361	13 03 21	19.000
312	9 73 44	17.664	362	13 10 44	19.026
313	9 79 69	17.692	363	13 17 69	19.053
314	9 85 96	17.720	364	13 24 96	19.079
315	9 92 25	17.748	365	13 32 25	19.105
316	9 98 56	17.776	366	13 39 56	19.131
317	10 04 89	17.804	367	13 46 89	19.157
318	10 11 24	17.833	368	13 54 24	19.183
319	10 17 61	17.861	369	13 61 61	19.209
320	10 24 00	17.889	370	13 69 00	19.235
321	10 30 41	17.916	371	13 76 41	19.261
322	10 36 84	17.944	372	13 83 84	19.287
323	10 43 29	17.972	373	13 91 29	19.313
324	10 49 76	18.000	374	13 98 76	19.339
325	10 56 25	18.028	375	14 06 25	19.365
326	10 62 76	18.055	376	14 13 76	19.391
327	10 69 29	18.083	377	14 21 29	19.416
328	10 75 84	18.111	378	14 28 84	19.442
329	10 82 41	18.138	379	14 36 41	19.468
330	10 89 00	18.166	380	14 44 00	19.494
331	10 95 61	18.193	381	14 51 61	19.519
332	11 02 24	18.221	382	14 59 24	19.545
333	11 08 89	18.248	383	14 66 89	19.570
334	11 15 56	18.276	384	14 74 56	19.596
335	11 22 25	18.303	385	14 82 25	19.621
336	11 28 96	18.330	386	14 89 96	19.647
337	11 35 69	18.358	387	14 97 69	19.672
338	11 42 44	18.385	388	15 05 44	19.698
339	11 49 21	18.412	389	15 13 21	19.723
340	11 56 00	18.439	390	15 21 00	19.748
341	11 62 81	18.466	391	15 28 81	19.774
342	11 69 64	18.493	392	15 36 64	19.799
343	11 76 49	18.520	393	15 44 49	19.824
344	11 83 36	18.547	394	15 52 36	19.849
345	11 90 25	18.574	395	15 60 25	19.875
346	11 97 16	18.601	396	15 68 16	19.900
347	12 04 09	18.628	397	15 76 09	19.925
348	12 11 04	18.655	398	15 84 04	19.950
349	12 18 01	18.682	399	15 92 01	19.975
350	12 25 00	18.708	400	16 00 00	20.000

Table A.3 (continued).

Number	Square	Square Root	Number	Square	Square Root
401	16 08 01	20.025	451	20 34 01	21.237
402	16 16 04	20.050	452	20 43 04	21.260
403	16 24 09	20.075	453	20 52 09	21.284
404	16 32 16	20.100	454	20 61 16	21.307
405	16 40 25	20.125	455	20 70 25	21.331
406	16 48 36	20.149	456	20 79 36	21.354
407	16 56 49	20.174	457	20 88 49	21.378
408	16 64 64	20.199	458	20 97 64	21.401
409	16 72 81	20.224	459	21 06 81	21.424
410	16 81 00	20.248	460	21 16 00	21.448
411	16 89 21	20.273	461	21 25 21	21.471
412	16 97 44	20.298	462	21 34 44	21.494
413	17 05 69	20.322	463	21 43 69	21.517
414	17 13 96	20.347	464	21 52 96	21.541
415	17 22 25	20.372	465	21 62 25	21.564
416	17 30 56	20.396	466	21 71 56	21.587
417	17 38 89	20.421	467	21 80 89	21.610
418	17 47 24	20.445	468	21 90 24	21.633
419	17 55 61	20.469	469	21 99 61	21.656
420	17 64 00	20.494	470	22 09 00	21.679
421	17 72 41	20.518	471	22 18 41	21.703
422	17 80 84	20.543	472	22 27 84	21.726
423	17 89 29	20.567	473	22 37 29	21.749
424	17 97 76	20.591	474	22 46 76	21.772
425	18 06 25	20.616	475	22 56 25	21.794
426	18 14 76	20.640	476	22 65 76	21.817
427	18 23 29	20.664	477	22 75 29	21.840
428	18 31 84	20.688	478	22 84 84	21.863
429	18 40 41	20.712	479	22 94 41	21.886
430	18 49 00	20.736	480	23 04 00	21.909
431	18 57 61	20.761	481	23 13 61	21.932
432	18 66 24	20.785	482	23 23 24	21.954
433	18 74 89	20.809	483	23 32 89	21.977
434	18 83 56	20.833	484	23 42 56	22.000
435	18 92 25	20.857	485	23 52 25	22.023
436	19 00 96	20.881	486	23 61 96	22.045
437	19 09 69	20.905	487	23 71 69	22.068
438	19 18 44	20.928	488	23 81 44	22.091
439	19 27 21	20.952	489	23 91 21	22.113
440	19 36 00	20.976	490	24 01 00	22.136
441	19 44 81	21.000	491	24 10 81	22.159
442	19 53 64	21.024	492	24 20 64	22.181
443	19 62 49	21.048	493	24 30 49	22.204
444	19 71 36	21.071	494	24 40 36	22.226
445	19 80 25	21.095	495	24 50 25	22.249
446	19 89 16	21.119	496	24 60 16	22.271
447	19 98 09	21.142	497	24 70 09	22.293
448	20 07 04	21.166	498	24 80 04	22.316
449	20 16 01	21.190	499	24 90 01	22.338
450	20 25 00	21.213	500	25 00 00	22.361

Table A.3 (continued).

NUMBER	SQUARE	SQUARE ROOT	NUMBER	SQUARE	SQUARE ROOT
501	25 10 01	22.383	551	30 36 01	23.473
502	25 20 04	22.405	552	30 47 04	23.495
503	25 30 09	22.428	553	30 58 09	23.516
504	25 40 16	22.450	554	30 69 16	23.537
505	25 50 25	22.472	555	30 80 25	23.558
506	25 60 36	22.494	556	30 91 36	23.580
507	25 70 49	22.517	557	31 02 49	23.601
508	25 80 64	22.539	558	31 13 64	23.622
509	25 90 81	22.561	559	31 24 81	23.643
510	26 01 00	22.583	560	31 36 00	23.664
511	26 11 21	22.605	561	31 47 21	23.685
512	26 21 44	22.627	562	31 58 44	23.707
513	26 31 69	22.650	563	31 69 69	23.728
514	26 41 96	22.672	564	31 80 96	23.749
515	26 52 25	22.694	565	31 92 25	23.770
516	26 62 56	22.716	566	32 03 56	23.791
517	26 72 89	22.738	567	32 14 89	23.812
518	26 83 24	22.760	568	32 26 24	23.833
519	26 93 61	22.782	569	32 37 61	23.854
520	27 04 00	22.804	570	32 49 00	23.875
521	27 14 41	22.825	571	32 60 41	23.896
522	27 24 84	22.847	572	32 71 84	23.917
523	27 35 29	22.869	573	32 83 29	23.937
524	27 45 76	22.891	574	32 94 76	23.958
525	27 56 25	22.913	575	33 06 25	23.979
526	27 66 76	22.935	576	33 17 76	24.000
527	27 77 29	22.956	577	33 29 29	24.021
528	27 87 84	22.978	578	33 40 84	24.042
529	27 98 41	23.000	579	33 52 41	24.062
530	28 09 00	23.022	580	33 64 00	24.083
531	28 19 61	23.043	581	33 75 61	24.104
532	28 30 24	23.065	582	33 87 24	24.125
533	28 40 89	23.087	583	33 98 89	24.145
534	28 51 56	23.108	584	34 10 56	24.166
535	28 62 25	23.130	585	34 22 25	24.187
536	28 72 96	23.152	586	34 33 96	24.207
537	28 83 69	23.173	587	34 45 69	24.228
538	28 94 44	23.195	588	34 57 44	24.249
539	29 05 21	23.216	589	34 69 21	24.269
540	29 16 00	23.238	590	34 81 00	24.290
541	29 26 81	23.259	591	34 92 81	24.310
542	29 37 64	23.281	592	35 04 64	24.331
543	29 48 49	23.302	593	35 16 49	24.352
544	29 59 36	23.324	594	35 28 36	24.372
545	29 70 25	23.345	595	35 40 25	24.393
546	29 81 16	23.367	596	35 52 16	24.413
547	29 92 09	23.388	597	35 64 09	24.434
548	30 03 04	23.409	598	35 76 04	24.454
549	30 14 01	23.431	599	35 88 01	24.474
550	30 25 00	23.452	600	36 00 00	24.495

Table A.3 (continued).

Number	Square	Square Root	Number	Square	Square Root
601	36 12 01	24.515	651	42 38 01	25.515
602	36 24 04	24.536	652	42 51 04	25.534
603	36 36 09	24.556	653	42 64 09	25.554
604	36 48 16	24.576	654	42 77 16	25.573
605	36 60 25	24.597	655	42 90 25	25.593
606	36 72 36	24.617	656	43 03 36	25.612
607	36 84 49	24.637	657	43 16 49	25.632
608	36 96 64	24.658	658	43 29 64	25.652
609	37 08 81	24.678	659	43 42 81	25.671
610	37 21 00	24.698	660	43 56 00	25.690
611	37 33 21	24.718	661	43 69 21	25.710
612	37 45 44	24.739	662	43 82 44	25.729
613	37 57 69	24.759	663	43 95 69	25.749
614	37 69 96	24.779	664	44 08 96	25.768
615	37 82 25	24.799	665	44 22 25	25.788
616	37 94 56	24.819	666	44 35 56	25.807
617	38 06 89	24.839	667	44 48 89	25.826
618	38 19 24	24.860	668	44 62 24	25.846
619	38 31 61	24.880	669	44 75 61	25.865
620	38 44 00	24.900	670	44 89 00	25.884
621	38 56 41	24.920	671	45 02 41	25.904
622	38 68 84	24.940	672	45 15 84	25.923
623	38 81 29	24.960	673	45 29 29	25.942
624	38 93 76	24.980	674	45 42 76	25.962
625	39 06 25	25.000	675	45 56 25	25.981
626	39 18 76	25.020	676	45 69 76	26.000
627	39 31 29	25.040	677	45 83 29	26.019
628	39 43 84	25.060	678	45 96 84	26.038
629	39 56 41	25.080	679	46 10 41	26.058
630	39 69 00	25.100	680	46 24 00	26.077
631	39 81 61	25.120	681	46 37 61	26.096
632	39 94 24	25.140	682	46 51 24	26.115
633	40 06 89	25.159	683	46 64 89	26.134
634	40 19 56	25.179	684	46 78 56	26.153
635	40 32 25	25.199	685	46 92 25	26.173
636	40 44 96	25.219	686	47 05 96	26.192
637	40 57 69	25.239	687	47 19 69	26.211
638	40 70 44	25.259	688	47 33 44	26.230
639	40 83 21	25.278	689	47 47 21	26.249
640	40 96 00	25.298	690	47 61 00	26.268
641	41 08 81	25.318	691	47 74 81	26.287
642	41 21 64	25.338	692	47 88 64	26.306
643	41 34 49	25.357	693	48 02 49	26.325
644	41 47 36	25.377	694	48 16 36	26.344
645	41 60 25	25.397	695	48 30 25	26.363
646	41 73 16	25.417	696	48 44 16	26.382
647	41 86 09	25.436	697	48 58 09	26.401
648	41 99 04	25.456	698	48 72 04	26.420
649	42 12 01	25.475	699	48 86 01	26.439
650	42 25 00	25.495	700	49 00 00	26.458

Table A.3 (continued).

Number	Square	Square Root	Number	Square	Square Root
701	49 14 01	26.476	751	56 40 01	27.404
702	49 28 04	26.495	752	56 55 04	27.423
703	49 42 09	26.514	753	56 70 09	27.441
704	49 56 16	26.533	754	56 85 16	27.459
705	49 70 25	26.552	755	57 00 25	27.477
706	49 84 36	26.571	756	57 15 36	27.495
707	49 98 49	26.589	757	57 30 49	27.514
708	50 12 64	26.608	758	57 45 64	27.532
709	50 26 81	26.627	759	57 60 81	27.550
710	50 41 00	26.646	760	57 76 00	27.568
711	50 55 21	26.665	761	57 91 21	27.586
712	50 69 44	26.683	762	58 06 44	27.604
713	50 83 69	26.702	763	58 21 69	27.622
714	50 97 96	26.721	764	58 36 96	27.641
715	51 12 25	26.739	765	58 52 25	27.659
716	51 26 56	26.758	766	58 67 56	27.677
717	51 40 89	26.777	767	58 82 89	27.695
718	51 55 24	26.796	768	58 98 24	27.713
719	51 69 61	26.814	769	59 13 61	27.731
720	51 84 00	26.833	770	59 29 00	27.749
721	51 98 41	26.851	771	59 44 41	27.767
722	52 12 84	26.870	772	59 59 84	27.785
723	52 27 29	26.889	773	59 75 29	27.803
724	52 41 76	26.907	774	59 90 76	27.821
725	52 56 25	26.926	775	60 06 25	27.839
726	52 70 76	26.944	776	60 21 76	27.857
727	52 85 29	26.963	777	60 37 29	27.875
728	52 99 84	26.981	778	60 52 84	27.893
729	53 14 41	27.000	779	60 68 41	27.911
730	53 29 00	27.019	780	60 84 00	27.928
731	53 43 61	27.037	781	60 99 61	27.946
732	53 58 24	27.055	782	61 15 24	27.964
733	53 72 89	27.074	783	61 30 89	27.982
734	53 87 56	27.092	784	61 46 56	28.000
735	54 02 25	27.111	785	61 62 25	28.018
736	54 16 96	27.129	786	61 77 96	28.036
737	54 31 69	27.148	787	61 93 69	28.054
738	54 46 44	27.166	788	62 09 44	28.071
739	54 61 21	27.185	789	62 25 21	28.089
740	54 76 00	27.203	790	62 41 00	28.107
741	54 90 81	27.221	791	62 56 81	28.125
742	55 05 64	27.240	792	62 72 64	28.142
743	55 20 49	27.258	793	62 88 49	28.160
744	55 35 36	27.276	794	63 04 36	28.178
745	55 50 25	27.295	795	63 20 25	28.196
746	55 65 16	27.313	796	63 36 16	28.213
747	55 80 09	27.331	797	63 52 09	28.231
748	55 95 04	27.350	798	63 68 04	28.249
749	56 10 01	27.368	799	73 84 01	28.267
750	56 25 00	27.386	800	64 00 00	28.284

Table A.3 (continued).

NUMBER	SQUARE	SQUARE ROOT	NUMBER	SQUARE	SQUARE ROOT
801	64 16 01	28.302	851	72 42 01	29.172
802	64 32 04	28.320	852	72 59 04	29.189
803	64 48 09	28.337	853	72 76 09	29.206
804	64 64 16	28.355	854	72 93 16	29.223
805	64 80 25	28.373	855	73 10 25	29.240
806	64 96 36	28.390	856	73 27 36	29.257
807	65 12 49	28.408	857	73 44 49	29.275
808	65 28 64	28.425	858	73 61 64	29.292
809	65 44 81	28.443	859	73 78 81	29.309
810	65 61 00	28.460	860	73 96 00	29.326
811	65 77 21	28.478	861	74 13 21	29.343
812	65 93 44	28.496	862	74 30 44	29.360
813	66 09 69	28.513	863	74 47 69	29.377
814	66 25 96	28.531	864	74 64 96	29.394
815	66 42 25	28.548	865	74 82 25	29.411
816	66 58 56	28.566	866	74 99 56	29.428
817	66 74 89	28.583	867	75 16 89	29.445
818	66 91 24	28.601	868	75 34 24	29.462
819	67 07 61	28.618	869	75 51 61	29.479
820	67 24 00	28.636	870	75 69 00	29.496
821	67 40 41	28.653	871	75 86 41	29.513
822	67 56 84	28.671	872	76 03 84	29.530
823	67 73 29	28.688	873	76 21 29	29.547
824	67 89 76	28.705	874	76 38 76	29.563
825	68 06 25	28.723	875	76 56 25	29.580
826	68 22 76	28.740	876	76 73 76	29.597
827	68 39 29	28.758	877	76 91 29	29.614
828	68 55 84	28.775	878	77 08 84	29.631
829	68 72 41	28.792	879	77 26 41	29.648
830	68 89 00	28.810	880	77 44 00	29.665
831	69 05 61	28.827	881	77 61 61	29.682
832	69 22 24	28.844	882	77 79 24	29.698
833	69 38 89	28.862	883	77 96 89	29.715
834	69 55 56	28.879	884	78 14 56	29.732
835	69 72 25	28.896	885	78 32 25	29.749
836	69 88 96	28.914	886	78 49 96	29.766
837	70 05 69	28.931	887	78 67 69	29.783
838	70 22 44	28.948	888	78 85 44	29.799
839	70 39 21	28.965	889	79 03 21	29.816
840	70 56 00	28.983	890	79 21 00	29.833
841	70 72 81	29.000	891	79 38 81	29.850
842	70 89 64	29.017	892	79 56 64	29.866
843	71 06 49	29.034	893	79 74 49	29.883
844	71 23 36	29.052	894	79 92 36	29.900
845	71 40 25	29.069	895	80 10 25	29.917
846	71 57 16	29.086	896	80 28 16	29.933
847	71 74 09	29.103	897	80 46 09	29.950
848	71 91 04	29.120	898	80 64 04	29.967
849	72 08 01	29.138	899	80 82 01	29.983
850	72 25 00	29.155	900	81 00 00	30.000

Table A.3 (continued).

Number	Square	Square Root	Number	Square	Square Root
901	81 18 01	30.017	951	90 44 01	30.838
902	81 36 04	30.033	952	90 63 04	30.854
903	81 54 09	30.050	953	90 82 09	30.871
904	81 72 16	30.067	954	91 01 16	30.887
905	81 90 25	30.083	955	91 20 25	30.903
906	82 08 36	30.100	956	91 39 36	30.919
907	82 26 49	30.116	957	91 58 49	30.935
908	82 44 64	30.133	958	91 77 64	30.952
909	82 62 81	30.150	959	91 96 81	30.968
910	82 81 00	30.166	960	92 16 00	30.984
911	82 99 21	30.183	961	92 35 21	31.000
912	83 17 44	30.199	962	92 54 44	31.016
913	83 35 69	30.216	963	92 73 69	31.032
914	83 53 96	30.232	964	92 92 96	31.048
915	83 72 25	30.249	965	93 12 25	31.064
916	83 90 56	30.265	966	93 31 56	31.081
917	84 08 89	30.282	967	93 50 89	31.097
918	84 27 24	30.299	968	93 70 24	31.113
919	84 45 61	30.315	969	93 89 61	31.129
920	84 64 00	30.332	970	94 09 00	31.145
921	84 82 41	30.348	971	94 28 41	31.161
922	85 00 84	30.364	972	94 47 84	31.177
923	85 19 29	30.381	973	94 67 29	31.193
924	85 37 76	30.397	974	94 86 76	31.209
925	85 56 25	30.414	975	95 06 25	31.225
926	85 74 76	30.430	976	95 25 76	31.241
927	85 93 29	30.447	977	95 45 29	31.257
928	86 11 84	30.463	978	95 64 84	31.273
929	86 30 41	30.480	979	95 84 41	31.289
930	86 49 00	30.496	980	96 04 00	31.305
931	86 67 61	30.512	981	96 23 61	31.321
932	86 86 24	30.529	982	96 43 24	31.337
933	87 04 89	30.545	983	96 62 89	31.353
934	87 23 56	30.561	984	96 82 56	31.369
935	87 42 25	30.578	985	97 02 25	31.385
936	87 60 96	30.594	986	97 21 96	31.401
937	87 79 69	30.610	987	97 41 69	31.417
938	87 98 44	30.627	988	97 61 44	31.432
939	88 17 21	30.643	989	97 81 21	31.448
940	88 36 00	30.659	990	98 01 00	31.464
941	88 54 81	30.676	991	98 20 81	31.480
942	88 73 64	30.692	992	98 40 64	31.496
943	88 92 49	30.708	993	98 60 49	31.512
944	89 11 36	30.725	994	98 80 36	31.528
945	89 30 25	30.741	995	99 00 25	31.544
946	89 49 16	30.757	996	99 20 16	31.559
947	89 68 09	30.773	997	99 40 09	31.575
948	89 87 04	30.790	998	99 60 04	31.591
949	90 06 01	30.806	999	99 80 01	31.607
950	90 25 00	30.822	1000	100 00 00	31.623

Table A.4.
Distribution of t

df				
			p	
	.10	.05	.01	.001
1	6.314	12.706	63.657	636.619
2	2.920	4.303	9.925	31.598
3	2.353	3.182	5.841	12.924
4	2.132	2.776	4.604	8.610
5	2.015	2.571	4.032	6.869
6	1.943	2.447	3.707	5.959
7	1.895	2.365	3.499	5.408
8	1.860	2.306	3.355	5.041
9	1.833	2.262	3.250	4.781
10	1.812	2.228	3.169	4.587
11	1.796	2.201	3.106	4.437
12	1.782	2.179	3.055	4.318
13	1.771	2.160	3.012	4.221
14	1.761	2.145	2.977	4.140
15	1.753	2.131	2.947	4.073
16	1.746	2.120	2.921	4.015
17	1.740	2.110	2.898	3.965
18	1.734	2.101	2.878	3.922
19	1.729	2.093	2.861	3.883
20	1.725	2.086	2.845	3.850
21	1.721	2.080	2.831	3.819
22	1.717	2.074	2.819	3.792
23	1.714	2.069	2.807	3.767
24	1.711	2.064	2.797	3.745
25	1.708	2.060	2.787	3.725
26	1.706	2.056	2.779	3.707
27	1.703	2.052	2.771	3.690
28	1.701	2.048	2.763	3.674
29	1.699	2.045	2.756	3.659
30	1.697	2.042	2.750	3.646
40	1.684	2.021	2.704	3.551
60	1.671	2.000	2.660	3.460
120	1.658	1.980	2.617	3.373
∞	1.645	1.960	2.576	3.291

Table A.4 is taken from Table III of Fisher and Yates: *Statistical Tables for Biological, Agricultural and Medical Research*, published by Longman Group Ltd., London (previously published by Oliver and Boyd, Edinburgh), and by permission of the authors and publishers.

Table A.5.
Distribution of F

	$p = .10$					
	n_1*					
n_2**	1	2	3	4	5	6
4	4.54	4.32	4.19	4.11	4.05	4.01
5	4.06	3.78	3.62	3.52	3.45	3.40
6	3.78	3.46	3.29	3.18	3.11	3.05
7	3.59	3.26	3.07	2.96	2.88	2.83
8	3.46	3.11	2.92	2.81	2.73	2.67
9	3.36	3.01	2.81	2.69	2.61	2.55
10	3.28	2.92	2.73	2.61	2.52	2.46
11	3.23	2.86	2.66	2.54	2.45	2.39
12	3.18	2.81	2.61	2.48	2.39	2.33
13	3.14	2.76	2.56	2.43	2.35	2.28
14	3.10	2.73	2.52	2.39	2.31	2.24
15	3.07	2.70	2.49	2.36	2.27	2.21
16	3.05	2.67	2.46	2.33	2.24	2.18
17	3.03	2.64	2.44	2.31	2.22	2.15
18	3.01	2.62	2.42	2.29	2.20	2.13
19	2.99	2.61	2.40	2.27	2.18	2.11
20	2.97	2.59	2.38	2.25	2.16	2.09
21	2.96	2.57	2.36	2.23	2.14	2.08
22	2.95	2.56	2.35	2.22	2.13	2.06
23	2.94	2.55	2.34	2.21	2.11	2.05
24	2.93	2.54	2.33	2.19	2.10	2.04
25	2.92	2.53	2.32	2.18	2.09	2.02
26	2.91	2.52	2.31	2.17	2.08	2.01
27	2.90	2.51	2.30	2.17	2.07	2.00
28	2.89	2.50	2.29	2.16	2.06	2.00
29	2.89	2.50	2.28	2.15	2.06	1.99
30	2.88	2.49	2.28	2.14	2.05	1.98
40	2.84	2.44	2.23	2.09	2.00	1.93
60	2.79	2.39	2.18	2.04	1.95	1.87
120	2.75	2.35	2.13	1.99	1.90	1.82
∞	2.71	2.30	2.08	1.94	1.85	1.77

*n_1 = degrees of freedom for the mean square between
**n_2 = degrees of freedom for the mean square within

Table A.5 is taken from Table V of Fisher and Yates: *Statistical Tables for Biological, Agricultural and Medical Research,* published by Longman Group Ltd., London (previously published by Oliver and Boyd, Edinburgh), and by permission of the authors and publishers.

Table A.5 (continued).

			$p = .05$			
			n_1*			
n_2**	1	2	3	4	5	6
4	7.71	6.94	6.59	6.39	6.26	6.16
5	6.61	5.79	5.41	5.19	5.05	4.95
6	5.99	5.14	4.76	4.53	4.39	4.28
7	5.59	4.74	4.35	4.12	3.97	3.87
8	5.32	4.46	4.07	3.84	3.69	3.58
9	5.12	4.26	3.86	3.63	3.48	3.37
10	4.96	4.10	3.71	3.48	3.33	3.22
11	4.84	3.98	3.59	3.36	3.20	3.09
12	4.75	3.88	3.49	3.26	3.11	3.00
13	4.67	3.80	3.41	3.18	3.02	2.92
14	4.60	3.74	3.34	3.11	2.96	2.85
15	4.54	3.68	3.29	3.06	2.90	2.79
16	4.49	3.63	3.24	3.01	2.85	2.74
17	4.45	3.59	3.20	2.96	2.81	2.70
18	4.41	3.55	3.16	2.93	2.77	2.66
19	4.38	3.52	3.13	2.90	2.74	2.63
20	4.35	3.49	3.10	2.87	2.71	2.60
21	4.32	3.47	3.07	2.84	2.68	2.57
22	4.30	3.44	3.05	2.82	2.66	2.55
23	4.28	3.42	3.03	2.80	2.64	2.53
24	4.26	3.40	3.01	2.78	2.62	2.51
25	4.24	3.38	2.99	2.76	2.60	2.49
26	4.22	3.37	2.98	2.74	2.59	2.47
27	4.21	3.35	2.96	2.73	2.57	2.46
28	4.20	3.34	2.95	2.71	2.56	2.44
29	4.18	3.33	2.93	2.70	2.54	2.43
30	4.17	3.32	2.92	2.69	2.53	2.42
40	4.08	3.23	2.84	2.61	2.45	2.34
60	4.00	3.15	2.76	2.52	2.37	2.25
120	3.92	3.07	2.68	2.45	2.29	2.17
∞	3.84	2.99	2.60	2.37	2.21	2.10

*n_1 = degrees of freedom for the mean square between
**n_2 = degrees of freedom for the mean square within

Table A.5 (continued).

			$p = .01$			
			$n_1{}^*$			
$n_2{}^{**}$	1	2	3	4	5	6
4	21.20	18.00	16.69	15.98	15.52	15.21
5	16.26	13.27	12.06	11.39	10.97	10.67
6	13.74	10.92	9.78	9.15	8.75	8.47
7	12.25	9.55	8.45	7.85	7.46	7.19
8	11.26	8.65	7.59	7.01	6.63	6.37
9	10.56	8.02	6.99	6.42	6.06	5.80
10	10.04	7.56	6.55	5.99	5.64	5.39
11	9.65	7.20	6.22	5.67	5.32	5.07
12	9.33	6.93	5.95	5.41	5.06	4.82
13	9.07	6.70	5.74	5.20	4.86	4.62
14	8.86	6.51	5.56	5.03	4.69	4.46
15	8.68	6.36	5.42	4.89	4.56	4.32
16	8.53	6.23	5.29	4.77	4.44	4.20
17	8.40	6.11	5.18	4.67	4.34	4.10
18	8.28	6.01	5.09	4.58	4.25	4.01
19	8.18	5.93	5.01	4.50	4.17	3.94
20	8.10	5.85	4.94	4.43	4.10	3.87
21	8.02	5.78	4.87	4.37	4.04	3.81
22	7.94	5.72	4.82	4.31	3.99	3.76
23	7.88	5.66	4.76	4.26	3.94	3.71
24	7.82	5.61	4.72	4.22	3.90	3.67
25	7.77	5.57	4.68	4.18	3.86	3.63
26	7.72	5.53	4.64	4.14	3.82	3.59
27	7.68	5.49	4.60	4.11	3.78	3.56
28	7.64	5.45	4.57	4.07	3.75	3.53
29	7.60	5.42	4.54	4.04	3.73	3.50
30	7.56	5.39	4.51	4.02	3.70	3.47
40	7.31	5.18	4.31	3.83	3.51	3.29
60	7.08	4.98	4.13	3.65	3.34	3.12
120	6.85	4.79	3.95	3.48	3.17	2.96
∞	6.64	4.60	3.78	3.32	3.02	2.80

$*n_1$ = degrees of freedom for the mean square between
$**n_2$ = degrees of freedom for the mean square within

Table A.5 (continued).

	$p = .001$					
	$n_1{}^*$					
$n_2{}^{**}$	1	2	3	4	5	6
4	74.14	61.25	56.18	53.44	51.71	50.53
5	47.18	37.12	33.20	31.09	29.75	28.84
6	35.51	27.00	23.70	21.92	20.81	20.03
7	29.25	21.69	18.77	17.19	16.21	15.52
8	25.42	18.49	15.83	14.39	13.49	12.86
9	22.86	16.39	13.90	12.56	11.71	11.13
10	21.04	14.91	12.55	11.28	10.48	9.92
11	19.69	13.81	11.56	10.35	9.58	9.05
12	18.64	12.97	10.80	9.63	8.89	8.38
13	17.81	12.31	10.21	9.07	8.35	7.86
14	17.14	11.78	9.73	8.62	7.92	7.43
15	16.59	11.34	9.34	8.25	7.57	7.09
16	16.12	10.97	9.00	7.94	7.27	6.81
17	15.72	10.66	8.73	7.68	7.02	6.56
18	15.38	10.39	8.49	7.46	6.81	6.35
19	15.08	10.16	8.28	7.26	6.62	6.18
20	14.82	9.95	8.10	7.10	6.46	6.02
21	14.59	9.77	7.94	6.95	6.32	5.88
22	14.38	9.61	7.80	6.81	6.19	5.76
23	14.19	9.47	7.67	6.69	6.08	5.65
24	14.03	9.34	7.55	6.59	5.98	5.55
25	13.88	9.22	7.45	6.49	5.88	5.46
26	13.74	9.12	7.36	6.41	5.80	5.38
27	13.61	9.02	7.27	6.33	5.73	5.31
28	13.50	8.93	7.19	6.25	5.66	5.24
29	13.39	8.85	7.12	6.19	5.59	5.18
30	13.29	8.77	7.05	6.12	5.53	5.12
40	12.61	8.25	6.60	5.70	5.13	4.73
60	11.97	7.76	6.17	5.31	4.76	4.37
120	11.38	7.32	5.79	4.95	4.42	4.04
∞	10.83	6.91	5.42	4.62	4.10	3.74

$*n_1$ = degrees of freedom for the mean square between
$**n_2$ = degrees of freedom for the mean square within

Table A.6.
Distribution of χ^2

df	.10	.05	.01	.001
			p	
1	2.706	3.841	6.635	10.827
2	4.605	5.991	9.210	13.815
3	6.251	7.815	11.345	16.266
4	7.779	9.488	13.277	18.467
5	9.236	11.070	15.086	20.515
6	10.645	12.592	16.812	22.457
7	12.017	14.067	18.475	24.322
8	13.362	15.507	20.090	26.125
9	14.684	16.919	21.666	27.877
10	15.987	18.307	23.209	29.588
11	17.275	19.675	24.725	31.264
12	18.549	21.026	26.217	32.909
13	19.812	22.362	27.688	34.528
14	21.064	23.685	29.141	36.123
15	22.307	24.996	30.578	37.697
16	23.542	26.296	32.000	39.252
17	24.769	27.587	33.409	40.790
18	25.989	28.869	34.805	42.312
19	27.204	30.144	36.191	43.820
20	28.412	31.410	37.566	45.315
21	29.615	32.671	38.932	46.797
22	30.813	33.924	40.289	48.268
23	32.007	35.172	41.638	49.728
24	33.196	36.415	42.980	51.179
25	34.382	37.652	44.314	52.620
26	35.563	38.885	45.642	54.052
27	36.741	40.113	46.963	55.476
28	37.916	41.337	48.278	56.893
29	39.087	42.557	49.588	58.302
30	40.256	43.773	50.892	59.703
32	42.585	46.194	53.486	62.487
34	44.903	48.602	56.061	65.247
36	47.212	50.999	58.619	67.985
38	49.513	53.384	61.162	70.703
40	51.805	55.759	63.691	73.402
42	54.090	58.124	66.206	76.084
44	56.369	60.481	68.710	78.750
46	58.641	62.830	71.201	81.400
48	60.907	65.171	73.683	84.037
50	63.167	67.505	76.154	86.661

Table A.6 is taken from Table IV of Fisher and Yates: *Statistical Tables for Biological, Agricultural and Medical Research,* published by Longman Group Ltd., London (previously published by Oliver and Boyd, Edinburgh), and by permission of the authors and publishers.

Appendix B

Glossary

A-B design A single-subject design in which baseline measurements are repeatedly made until stability is presumably established, treatment is introduced, and an appropriate number of measurements are made during treatment.

A-B-A design A single-subject design in which baseline measurements are repeatedly made until stability is presumably established, treatment is introduced, and an appropriate number of measurements are made, and the treatment phase is followed by a second baseline phase.

A-B-A-B design A single-subject design in which baseline measurements are repeatedly made until stability is presumably established, treatment is introduced, and an appropriate number of measurements are made, and the treatment phase is followed by a second baseline phase which is followed by a second treatment phase.

achievement test An instrument that measures the current status of individuals with respect to proficiency in given areas of knowledge or skill.

analysis of covariance A statistical method for equating groups on one or more variables and for increasing the power of a statistical test; adjusts scores on a dependent variable for initial differences on some variable such as pretest performance or IQ.

applied research Research conducted for the purpose of applying, or testing, theory and evaluating its usefulness in solving problems.

aptitude test A measure of potential used to predict how well someone is likely to perform in a future situation.

assumption Any important "fact" presumed to be true but not actually verified; assumptions should be described in the procedures section of a research plan or report.

attenuation Refers to the principle that correlation coefficients tend to be lowered because less-than-perfectly reliable measures are used.

basic research Research conducted for the purpose of theory development or refinement.

case study An in-depth investigation of an individual, group, or institution to determine the factors, and relationship among the factors, which have resulted in the current behavior or status of the subject of the study.

causal-comparative research Research that attempts to determine the cause, or reason, for existing differences in the behavior or status of groups of individuals; also referred to as ex post facto research.

census survey Descriptive research that attempts to acquire data from each and every member of a population.

chi square   A nonparametric test of significance appropriate when the data are in the form of frequency counts; it compares proportions actually observed in a study with proportions expected to see if they are significantly different.

cluster sampling   Sampling in which intact groups, not individuals, are randomly selected.

common variance   The variation in one variable that is attributable to its tendency to vary with another variable.

concurrent validity   The degree to which the scores on a test are related to the scores on another, already established test administered at the same time, or to some other valid criterion available at the same time.

construct validity   The degree to which a test measures an intended hypothetical construct, or nonobservable trait, which explains behavior.

contamination   The researcher's familiarity with the subjects affects the outcome of the study.

content analysis   The systematic, quantitative description of the composition of the object of the study.

content validity   The degree to which a test measures an intended content area; it is determined by expert judgment and requires both item validity and sampling validity.

control   Efforts on the part of the researcher to remove the influence of any variable other than the independent variable that might affect performance on a dependent variable.

control group   The group in a research study that either receives a different treatment than the experimental group or is treated as usual.

control variable   A nonmanipulated variable, usually a physical or mental characteristic of the subjects (such as IQ).

correlational research   Research that involves collecting data in order to determine whether, and to what degree, a relationship exists between two or more quantifiable variables.

correlation coefficient   A decimal number between .00 and ±1.00 that indicates the degree to which two variables are related.

counterbalanced design   A quasi-experimental design in which all groups receive all treatments, each group receives the treatments in a different order, the number of groups equals the number of treatments, and all groups are posttested after each treatment.

criterion   In a prediction study, the variable that is predicted.

cross-validation   Validation of a prediction equation with at least one group other than the group on which it was based; variables that are no longer found to be related to the criterion measure are removed from the equation.

curvilinear relationship   An increase in one variable is associated with a corresponding increase in another variable to a point, at which point further increase in the first variable is associated with a corresponding decrease in the other variable (or vice versa).

deductive hypothesis   A hypothesis derived from theory which provides evidence which supports, expands, or contradicts the theory.

dependent variable   The change or difference in behavior that occurs as a result of the independent variable; also referred to as the criterion variable, the effect, the outcome, or the posttest.

descriptive statistics   Data analysis techniques enabling the researcher to meaningfully describe many scores with a small number of numerical indices.

developmental studies   Studies concerned with behavior variables that differentiate children at different levels of age, growth, or maturation.

diagnostic test   A type of achievement test yielding multiple scores for each area of achievement measured that facilitate identification of specific areas of deficiency.

differential selection of subjects   Groups may be different before a study even begins, and this initial difference may at least partially account for posttest differences.

ecological validity   The degree to which results can be generalized to environments outside of the experimental setting.

educational research   The formal, systematic application of the scientific method to the study of educational problems.

environmental variable   A variable in the setting in which a study is conducted that might cause unwanted differences between groups (e.g., learning materials).

equivalent forms   Two tests identical in every way except for the actual items included.

equivalent-forms reliability   Indicates score variation that occurs from form to form of a test; also referred to as alternate-forms reliability.

ethnography   The collection of data on many variables over an extended period of time in a naturalistic setting.

evaluation   The systematic process of collecting and analyzing data in order to make decisions.

experimental group   The group in a research study that typically receives a new, or novel, treatment, a treatment under investigation.

experimental research   Research in which at least one independent variable is manipulated, other relevant variables are controlled, and the effect on one or more dependent variables is observed.

experimenter bias   The researcher's expectations concerning the outcomes of the study actually contribute to producing various outcomes.

ex post facto research   See causal-comparative research.

external criticism   The scientific analysis of data to determine their authenticity.

external validity   The degree to which results are generalizable, or applicable, to groups and environments outside of the experimental setting.

factorial analysis of variance   The appropriate statistical analysis if a study is based on a factorial design and investigates two or more independent variables and the interactions between them; yields a separate F ratio for each independent variable and one for each interaction.

factorial design   An experimental design that involves two or more independent variables (at least one of which is manipulated) in order to study the effects of the variables individually and in interaction with each other.

follow-up study   A study conducted to determine the status of a group of interest after some period of time.

generosity error   The tendency to give an individual the benefit of the doubt whenever there is insufficient knowledge to make an objective judgment.

halo effect   The phenomenon whereby initial impressions concerning an individual (positive or negative) affect subsequent measurements.

Hawthorne effect   A type of reactive arrangement resulting from the subjects' knowledge that they are involved in an experiment or their feeling that they are in some way receiving "special" attention.

historical research   The systematic collection and objective evaluation of data related to past occurrences in order to test hypotheses concerning causes, effects, or trends of those events which may help to explain present events and anticipate future events.

history   Any event which is not part of the experimental treatment but which may affect performance on the dependent variable.

hypothesis   A tentative, reasonable, testable explanation for the occurrence of certain behaviors, phenomena, or events.

independent variable   An activity or characteristic believed to make a difference with respect to some behavior; also referred to as the experimental variable, the cause, and the treatment.

inductive hypothesis   A generalization based on observation.

inferential statistics   Data analysis techniques for determining how likely it is that results based on a sample or samples are the same results that would have been obtained for an entire population.

instrumentation   Unreliability in measuring instruments that may result in invalid assessment of subjects' performance.

interaction   Refers to the situation in which different values of the independent variable are differentially effective depending upon the level of the control variable.

interjudge reliability   The consistency of two (or more) independent scorers, raters, or observers.

internal criticism   The scientific analysis of data to determine their accuracy which takes into consideration the knowledge and competence of the author, the time delay between the occurrence and recording of events, biased motives of the author, and consistency of the data.

internal validity   The degree to which observed differences on the dependent variable are a direct result of manipulation of the independent variable, not some other variable.

interval scale   A measurement scale that classifies and ranks subjects, is based upon predetermined equal intervals, but does not have a true zero point.

intervening variable   A variable which intervenes between, or alters the relationship between, an independent variable and a dependent variable, which cannot be directly observed or controlled (e.g., anxiety) but which can be controlled for.

intrajudge reliability   The consistency of the scoring, rating, or observing of an individual.

item validity   The degree to which test items represent measurement in the intended content area.

John Henry effect   The phenomenon whereby if for any reason members of a control group feel threatened or challenged by being in competition with an experimental group, they may outdo themselves and perform way beyond what would normally be expected.

Likert scale   An instrument that asks an individual to respond to a series of statements by indicating whether she or he strongly agrees (SA), agrees (A), is undecided (U), disagrees (D), or strongly disagrees (SD) with each statement.

limitation   An aspect of a study which the researcher knows may negatively affect the results or generalizability of the results, but over which he or she has no control.

linear relationship The situation in which an increase (or decrease) in one variable is associated with a corresponding increase (or decrease) in another variable.

matching A technique for equating groups on one or more variables, resulting in each member of one group having a direct counterpart in another group.

maturation Physical or mental changes which occur within subjects over a period of time and which may affect their performance on a measure of the dependent variable.

mean The arithmetic average of a set of scores.

measures of central tendency Indices representing the average or typical score attained by a group of subjects.

measures of variability Indices indicating how spread out the scores are in a distribution.

median That point in a distribution above and below which are 50% of the scores.

mode The score that is attained by more subjects in a group than any other score.

mortality Refers to the fact that subjects who drop out of a study may share a characteristic such that their absence has a significant effect on the results of the study.

multiple-baseline design A single-subject design in which baseline data are collected on several behaviors for one subject or one behavior for several subjects, treatment is applied systematically over a period of time to each behavior (or each subject) one at a time until all behaviors (or subjects) are under treatment.

multiple comparisons Procedures used following application of analysis of variance to determine which means are significantly different from which other means.

multiple regression equation A prediction equation using two or more variables that individually predict a criterion to make a more accurate prediction.

multiple time-series design A variation of the time-series design that involves the addition of a control group to the basic design.

multiple-treatment interference Refers to the carry-over effects from an earlier treatment that make it difficult to assess the effectiveness of a later treatment.

naturalistic observation Observation in which the observer purposely controls or manipulates nothing, and in fact works very hard at not affecting the observed situation in any way.

negatively skewed distribution A distribution in which there are more extreme scores at the lower end than at the upper, or higher, end.

nominal scale The lowest level of measurement which classifies persons or objects into two or more categories; a person can only be in one category, and members of a category have a common set of characteristics.

nonequivalent control group design A quasi-experimental design involving at least two groups, both of which are pretested; one group receives the experimental treatment, and both groups are posttested.

nonparametric test A test of significance appropriate when the data represent an ordinal or nominal scale, when a parametric assumption has been greatly violated, or when the nature of the distribution is not known.

nonparticipant observation Observation in which the observer is not directly involved in the situation to be observed, i.e., the observer does not intentionally interact with or affect the object of the observation.

novelty effect A type of reactive arrangement resulting from increased interest, motivation, or participation on the part of subjects simply because they are doing something different.

null hypothesis States that there is no relationship (or difference) between variables and that any relationship found will be a chance relationship, the result of sampling error, not a true one.

observation research Descriptive research in which the desired data is obtained not by asking individuals for it but through such means as direct observation.

observee bias The phenomenon whereby persons being observed behave atypically simply because they are being observed, thus producing invalid observations.

observer bias The phenomenon whereby an observer does not observe objectively and accurately, thus producing invalid observations.

one-group pretest-posttest design A pre-experimental design involving one group which is pretested, exposed to a treatment, and posttested.

one-shot case study A pre-experimental design involving one group which is exposed to a treatment and then posttested.

operational definition One which defines concepts in terms of processes, or operations.

ordinal scale A measurement scale that classifies subjects and ranks them in terms of the degree to which they possess a characteristic of interest.

organismic variable A characteristic of a subject, or organism (e.g., sex), which cannot be directly controlled but which can be controlled for.

parameter A numerical index describing the behavior of a population.

parametric test A test of significance appropriate when the data represent an interval or ratio scale of measurement and other assumptions have been met.

participant observation Observation in which the observer actually becomes a part of, a participant in, the situation to be observed.

Pearson r A measure of correlation appropriate when the data represent either interval or ratio scales; it takes into account each and every score and produces a coefficient between .00 and ±1.00.

percentile rank A measure of relative position indicating the percentage of scores that fall at or below a given score.

pilot study A small-scale study conducted prior to the conducting of the actual study; the entire study is conducted, every procedure is followed, and the resulting data are analyzed—all according to the research plan.

population The group to which the researcher would like the results of a study to be generalizable.

positively skewed distribution A distribution in which there are more extreme scores at the upper, or higher, end than at the lower end.

posttest-only control group design A true experimental design involving at least two randomly formed groups; one group receives a new, or unusual, treatment and both groups are posttested.

prediction study An attempt to determine which of a number of variables are most highly related to a criterion variable, a complex variable to be predicted.

predictive validity The degree to which a test is able to predict how well an individual will do in a future situation.

predictor In a prediction study, the variable upon which the prediction is based.

pretest-posttest control group design A true experimental design which involves at least two randomly formed groups; both groups are pretested, one group receives a new, or unusual treatment, and both groups are posttested.

pretest-treatment interaction   Refers to the fact that subjects may respond or react differently to a treatment because they have been pretested.

primary source   Firsthand information such as the testimony of an eyewitness, an original document, a relic, or a description of a study written by the person who conducted it.

problem statement   A statement which indicates the variables of interest to the researcher and the specific relationship between those variables which is to be, or was, investigated.

quartile deviation   One-half of the difference between the upper quartile (the 75th percentile) and the lower quartile (the 25th percentile) in a distribution.

random sampling   The process of selecting a sample in such a way that all individuals in the defined population have an equal and independent chance of being selected for the sample.

range   The difference between the highest and lowest score in a distribution.

rationale equivalence reliability   An estimate of internal consistency based on a determination of how all items on a test relate to all other items and to the total test.

ratio scale   The highest level of measurement that classifies subjects, ranks subjects, is based upon predetermined equal intervals, and has a true zero point.

reactive arrangements   Threats to the external validity of a study associated with the way in which a study is conducted and the feelings and attitudes of the subjects involved.

readiness test   A test administered prior to instruction or training in a specific area in order to determine whether and to what degree a student is ready for, or will profit from, instruction.

relationship study   An attempt to gain insight into the variables, or factors, that are related to a complex variable such as academic achievement, motivation, and self-concept.

reliability   The degree to which a test consistently measures whatever it measures.

replication   Refers to when a study is done again; the second study may be a repetition of the original study, using different subjects, or it may represent an alternative approach to testing the same hypothesis.

research   The formal, systematic application of the scientific method to the study of problems.

research hypothesis   A statement of the expected relationship (or difference) between two variables.

research plan   A detailed description of a proposed study designed to investigate a given problem.

response set   The tendency of an observer to rate the majority of observees the same regardless of the observees' actual behavior.

review of literature   The systematic identification, location, and analysis of documents containing information related to a research problem.

sample   A number of individuals selected from a population for a study, preferably in such a way that they represent the larger group from which they were selected.

sample survey   Research in which information about a population is inferred based on the responses of a sample selected from that population.

sampling   The process of selecting a number of individuals (a sample) from a population, preferably in such a way that the individuals selected represent the larger group from which they were selected.

sampling bias Systematic sampling error; two major sources of sampling bias are the use of volunteers and the use of available groups.

sampling error Expected, chance variation in variables that occurs when a sample is selected from a population.

sampling validity The degree to which a test samples the total intended content area.

Scheffe' test A conservative multiple comparison technique appropriate for making any and all possible comparisons involving a set of means.

secondary source Secondhand information, such as a brief description of a study written by someone other than the person who conducted it.

selection-maturation interaction Refers to the fact that if already formed groups are used in a study, one group may profit more (or less) from treatment or have an initial advantage (or disadvantage) because of maturation factors; selection may also interact with factors such as history and testing.

selection-treatment interaction Refers to the fact that if nonrepresentative groups are used in a study the results of the study may hold only for the groups involved and may not be representative of the treatment effect in the population.

self-report research Descriptive research in which information is solicited from individuals using, for example, questionnaires or interviews.

semantic differential scale An instrument that asks an individual to give a quantitative rating to the subject of the attitude scale on a number of bipolar adjectives such as good-bad, friendly-unfriendly, positive-negative.

shrinkage Refers to the tendency of a prediction equation to become less accurate when used with a different group, a group other than the one on which the equation was originally formulated.

simple analysis of variance (ANOVA) A parametric test of significance used to determine whether there is a significant difference between or among two or more means at a selected probability level.

simulation observation Observation in which the researcher creates the situation to be observed and tells the subjects what activities they are to engage in.

single-subject experimental designs Designs applied when the sample size is one; used to study the behavior change which an individual exhibits as a result of some intervention, or treatment.

single-variable designs A class of experimental designs involving only one independent variable (which is manipulated).

skewed distribution A nonsymetrical distribution in which there are more extreme scores at one end of the distribution than the other.

sociometric study A study that assesses and analyzes the interpersonal relationships within a group of individuals.

Solomon four-group design A true experimental design that involves random assignment of subjects to one of four groups; two groups are pretested, two are not; one of the pretested groups and one of the unpretested groups receive the experimental treatment, and all four groups are posttested.

Spearman rho A measure of correlation appropriate when the data for at least one of the variables are expressed as ranks; it produces a coefficient between .00 and ± 1.00.

specificity of variables Refers to the fact that a given study is conducted with a specific kind of subject, using specific measuring instruments, at a specific time, under a specific set of circumstances, factors that affect the generalizability of the results.

split-half reliability A type of reliability that is based on the internal consistency of a test and is estimated by dividing a test into two equivalent halves and correlating the scores on the two halves.

standard deviation The most stable measure of variability which takes into account each and every score in a distribution.

standard error of the mean The standard deviation of sample means which indicates by how much the sample means can be expected to differ if other samples from the same population are used.

standard error of measurement An estimate of how often one can expect errors of a given size in an individual's test score.

standard score A derived score that expresses how far a given raw score is from some reference point, typically the mean, in terms of standard deviation units.

stanines Standard scores that divide a distribution into nine parts.

static group comparison A pre-experimental design that involves at least two nonrandomly formed groups; one receives a new, or unusual, treatment and both are posttested.

statistic A numerical index describing the behavior of a sample or samples.

statistical regression The tendency of subjects who score highest on a pretest to score lower on a posttest, and of subjects who score lowest on a pretest to score higher on a posttest.

statistical significance The conclusion that results are unlikely to have occurred by chance; the observed relationship or difference is probably a real one.

stratified sampling The process of selecting a sample in such a way that identified subgroups in the population are represented in the sample in the same proportion that they exist in the population or in equal proportion.

structured item A question and a list of alternative responses from which the responder selects; also referred to as a closed-form item.

subject variable A variable on which subjects in different groups in a study might differ, e.g., intelligence.

survey An attempt to collect data from members of a population in order to determine the current status of that population with respect to one or more variables.

systematic sampling Sampling in which individuals are selected from a list by taking every Kth name, where K equals the number of individuals on the list divided by the number of subjects desired for the sample.

T score A standard score derived from a z score by multiplying the z score by 10 and adding 50.

t test for independent samples A parametric test of significance used to determine whether there is a significant difference between the means of two independent samples at a selected probability level.

t test for nonindependent samples A parametric test of significance used to determine whether there is a significant difference between the means of two matched, or nonindependent, samples at a selected probability level.

test A means of measuring the knowledge, skill, feelings, intelligence, or aptitude of an individual or group.

testing A threat to experimental validity which refers to improved scores on a posttest which are a result of subjects having taken a pretest.

test objectivity Refers to a situation in which an individual's score is the same, or essentially the same, regardless of who is doing the scoring.

test-retest reliability The degree to which scores on a test are consistent, or stable, over time.

test of significance A statistical test used to determine whether or not there is a significant difference between or among two or more means at a selected probability level.

time-series design A quasi-experimental design involving one group which is repeatedly pretested, exposed to an experimental treatment, and repeatedly posttested.

Type I error The rejection by the researcher of a null hypothesis which is actually true.

Type II error The failure of a researcher to reject a null hypothesis which is really false.

unobtrusive measures Inanimate objects (such as school suspension lists) which can be observed in order to obtain desired information.

unstructured item A question giving the responder complete freedom of response.

validity The degree to which a test measures what it is intended to measure; a test is valid for a particular purpose and for a particular group.

variable A concept that can assume any one of a range of values, e.g., intelligence, height, aptitude.

z score The most basic standard score that expresses how far a score is from a mean in terms of standard deviation units.

Z score See *T* score.

Author Index

Abrami, P. C., 380
Agnew, N. M., 169
Allen, K. E., 179
Alston, H. L. A., 377
Anastasio, E. J., 324
Archibald, R. D., 73
Ault, M. H., 177
Ausubel, D. P., 47, 384

Barber, T. X., 220
Barlow, H., 179, 239
Becker, H. S., 171
Bennett, C. A., 324
Bent, D. H., 344
Bijou, S. W., 177, 179
Boruch, R. F., 324
Brackbill, Y., 349
Brandhorst, W. T., 39
Buros, O. K., 124, 133

Campbell, D. T., 176, 213, 216, 231, 324
Chave, E. J., 127
Colton, G. E., 385
Cosca, C., 168
Culler, R. E., 379

Davis, F., 242, 243
De Master, B., 181
Dickens, W. J., 380
Dixon, W. J., 344
Doughtie, E. B., 377
Downie, N. M., 284, 286, 292

Ebel, R., 26, 38
Elashoff, J. D., 324
Ellis, M., 69, 384
Emerson, M., 242, 243
English, R. A., 158
Evans, S. H., 324

Fienberg, S. E., 172, 174
Flanders, N. A., 176
Florescu, R., 152
Florio, S., 174
Fode, K. L., 219

Ford, J. D., 38
Fox, L., 242, 243

Gay, L. R., 48, 69, 382
Glass, G. V., 191
Goldsmith, L., 242, 243
Good, C. V., 28
Gorsuch, R. L., 47
Guilford, J. P., 128
Guttman, L., 127

Hall, R. V., 242, 243
Harris, F. R., 179
Heath, R. W., 284, 286, 292
Hersen, M., 179, 239
Hertz-Lazarowitz, R., 380
Holahan, C. J., 379
Howder, M. L., 39
Huck, S. W., 325
Hull, C. H., 344

Jackson, G., 168
Jenkins, J. G., 344
Johnston, M. S., 179

Kappy, M. S., 349
Katz, M. B., 147
Kinzer, J. R., 158
Klecka, W. R., 344
Kloess, P., 69, 384
Krebs, A., 182

Laosa, L. M., 379
Lehmann, I. J., 132
Leventhal, L., 380
Li, J. C. R., 98
Likert, R. A., 126
Lumsdaine, A. A., 324
Lushene, R. E., 48

McNally, R. T., 152
Marx, R. W., 380
Meder, Z., 151
Mehrens, W. A., 132
Michael, J. A., 64

439

Miel, A., 146

Nie, N. H., 344
Nunnally, J. C., 117, 193

Osgood, C. E., 126, 127
Owen, M., 242, 243

Pelto, G. H., 172
Pelto, P. J., 172
Perry, R. P., 380
Peterson, H. A., 69, 384
Peterson, R. F., 177, 179
Porcia, E., 242, 243
Pugh, E., 39
Pyke, S. W., 169

Reddy, J., 182
Reid, J. B., 181
Rist, R. C., 173, 174
Roscoe, J. T., 98, 324
Rosenthal, R., 219

Sampson, R. N., 377
Schultz, J., 174
Schwartz, R. D., 176
Sechrest, L., 176
Sharan, S., 380
Sidman, M., 351
Silver, M. J., 220

Smith, H. A., 38
Snider, J. G., 127
Sones, A. M., 69, 384
Spielberger, C. D., 47
Stanley, J. C., 191, 213, 216, 231
Steinberg, R., 380
Steinbrenner, K., 344
Strang, R. M., 157
Stroud, J. B., 69, 384
Suci, G. J., 126

Tannenbaum, P. H., 126
Thurstone, L. L., 127
Toohill, N., 69, 384
Torrance, E. N., 129
Travers, R. M. W., 38
Tyack, D. B., 147

Villoria, R. L., 73
Von Däniken, E., 12

Wakefield, J. A., 377
Webb, E. J., 176
Weber, E., 39
Weinberger, J. A., 64
Weinstein, C. S., 38
Willard, D., 242, 243
Wilson, S., 172
Winer, B. J., 324
Winne, P. H., 380

Subject Index

α. *See p*
A-B-A designs, 241–44
Achievement tests, 124–25
Action research, 10
Active variables, 210
Adjective check list, 125
AERA. *See* American Educational Research
    Association
Alternate-forms reliability, 118–19
American Educational Research Association
    (AERA), 388
American Psychological Association (APA):
    bibliographic reference form, 42; and ethical
    standards for conducting research, 64;
    Publication Manual, 42, 378
Analysis of covariance, 204, 223, 229, 321, 343
Analysis of variance, 203, 321, 323, 333–37,
    343
Annual Review of Psychology, 35
APA. *See* American Psychological Association
Applied research, 8–9
Aptitude tests, 130–32
Assigned variables, 210
Assumptions, 71–72
Attenuation, correction for, 193

Baseline stability, 240
Base rate, 115
Basic research, 8–9
Between group variance, 321
Buckley Amendment, 64

California Achievement Test Battery, 124
California Psychological Inventory, 125
California Test of Mental Maturity, 130–31
Case studies, 170
Causal-comparative research: comparison with
    correlational research, 197, 198; comparison
    with experimental research, 14, 198; control
    procedures in, 201–4; analysis of covariance,
    204, comparing homogenous groups or
    subgroups, 202–4; matching, 202; data
    analysis in, 204; definition and purpose,
    14–16, 197–200; design and procedure in,

200–201; examples of, 16, 197, 199–205;
    interpretation of results in, 204–5
Cause-effect relationships: causal-comparative
    research, 14–15, 199–200, 204–5;
    correlational research, 13–14, 184, 188;
    experimental research, 14–15, 209, 211;
    reversed causality, 204
Census surveys, 156
Change scores. *See* Gain scores
Character and personality tests, 125–30
Chi square, 204, 325–26, 339–41
Child Development Abstracts and Bibliography,
    35
CIJE. *See Current Index to Journals in
    Education*
Cluster sampling: definition and purpose, 93;
    disadvantages of, 95; example of, 94–95;
    steps in, 93–94
Coefficient of equivalence, 119
Coefficient of internal consistency, 119–21
Coefficient of stability, 118; and equivalence,
    119
Computer, use of in literature searches: costs,
    40; initiation of, 39, 40; data sources for,
    39–40, 41; search strategy, specification of,
    41; use of in data analysis, 277, 343–45, 348
Concurrent validity, 113–14
Construct validity, 112–13
Constructs 112–13
Contamination, 219
Content analysis, 170
Content validity, 111–12
Control group, 71, 201, 209
Control variables, 235
Correlation coefficients: and common variance,
    186, and corrections: for attenuation, 193; for
    restriction in range, 193; and curvilinear
    relationships, 192; definition, 14;
    interpretation of, 14, 117, 122–23, 190–93,
    292, 303, 350; in a prediction study, 188; in
    a relationship study, 187; statistical
    significance, 187–88, 292; as a validity or
    reliability estimate, 117, 122–23; and linear
    relationships, 191; types of: Pearson *r*, 190,

Correlation coefficients: *(cont.)*
293, 300–303; Spearman rho, 190, 292
Correlational research: data analysis in, 185–88
(*see also* Correlation coefficients); definition
and purpose, 13, 183; examples of, 14; steps
in, 184–88; types of, 189–95 (*see also*
Prediction studies; Relationship studies)
Criterion variables, 113–16
Cross-sectional surveys, 156
Cross-validation, 116, 195
Culture-Fair Intelligence Test, 131
Current Index to Journals in Education (CIJE),
33, 36–37
Curvilinear relationships, 192

Data analysis: scoring procedures, 110, 135,
275–76; storage of data, 348; tabulation
procedures, 276–77; use of computer in, 277,
343–45; verification of data, 347 (*see also*
Descriptive statistics; Inferential statistics;
Scales, types of)
Degrees of freedom, 317; for analysis of
variance; 322, 335; for chi square, 340; for
the Pearson r, 187, 303; for Scheffe' test, for t
test for independent samples, 330; for t test
for nonindependent samples, 333
Dependent variables, 14–15, 209
Descriptive research: definition and purpose, 12,
153; examples of, 13, 154, 156–58; steps in,
154, types of: observational research, 168–82
(*see also* Observational research), self-report
research, 155–68 (*see also* Self-report
research)
Descriptive statistics: central tendency, measures
of: mean, 204, 184–85, 291, 297–98;
median, 284, 291; mode, 283, 291; graphing
data, 282–83; normal curve: normal
distributions, 288–90, 308, 318; skewed
distributions, 291; purpose of, 281;
relationship, measures of: Pearson r, 293,
300–303, 321; Spearman rho, 292; relative
position, measures of: percentile ranks, 293,
standard scores; 293, 304, symbols in, 296;
variability, measures of: range, 286; quartile
deviation, 286; standard deviation, 204,
286–88, 298–300, 309–10
Design, 69–70, *See also* Experimental designs;
Factorial designs; Pre-experimental designs;
Quasi-experimental designs; Single-subject
experimental designs
Developmental studies, 157
Diagnostic tests, 125
Dictionary of Education, 28
Difference scores. *See* Gain scores
Differential Aptitude Tests, 132
Dissertation Abstracts International, 34
Dissertation reports. *See* Thesis report,
components of
Divergent thinking, measures of, 128

Ecological validity, 212
Education Index, 32–33, 34, 35
Educational research: classification by method,
11–17; classification by purpose, 8–11;
definition, 6; purpose, 6; steps in, 7; types of,

see Action research; Applied research; Basic
research; Causal-comparative research;
Correlational research; Descriptive research;
Evaluation research; Experimental research;
Historical research; Research and
development
Educational Resources Information Center. *See*
ERIC
Edwards Personal Preference Schedule, 125
Empirical validity, 111
Encyclopedia of Educational Research, 26, 38
Equivalent-forms reliability, 118–19
ERIC (Educational Resources Information
Center), 31, 35–37; clearinghouses, 37;
Current Index to Journals in Education,
36–37; Document Reproduction Service, 37;
Research in Education, 36; *Thesaurus of
ERIC Descriptors,* 36
Error variance, 321, 325, 333–36
Errors of measurement, 117
Eta ratio, 192
Ethics of research, 63
Ethnography: definition of, 172; methods,
172–73; an example of, 173–74
Evaluation of a research report. *See* Research
report, evaluation of
Evaluation research, 9–10
Experimental designs, 208–9, 223–24; types of:
factorial, 234–36; pre-experimental, 224–27;
quasi-experimental, 231–34; true
experimental, 227–31; single-subject, 237–45
Experimental research: comparison with
causal-comparative research, 14, 204;
contamination, 219; control in, 209–11;
220–23; analysis of covariance, 223;
comparing homogeneous groups or
subgroups, 222; matching, 221;
randomization, 220; using subjects as their
own controls, 222; definition and purpose,
15, 207; designs in, 69–70, 223–45 (*see also*
Experimental designs; Factorial designs;
Pre-experimental designs; Quasi-experimental
designs; Single-subject designs); examples of,
15, 210, 218–20; 325; experimenter bias,
219; external validity: and multiple-treatment
interference, 218; and pretest-treatment
interaction, 69, 216; and reactive
arrangements, 217; and selection-treatment
interaction, 217; and specificity of variables,
217; internal validity: and differential selection
of subjects, 215; and history, 213; and
instrumentation, 214; and maturation, 213;
and mortality, 215; and selection-maturation
interaction, etc., 215; and statistical regression,
214; and testing, 213; manipulation in,
209–10; steps in conducting, 208–9
Experimenter bias, 219
Ex post facto research. *See* Causal-comparative
research
External criticism of data, 12, 149–50
External validity. *See* Experimental research
Extraneous variables, 220–23

F ratio, 321, 322, 323, 335–36
Face validity, 111

Factorial analysis of variance, 203, 223, 231, 343
Factorial designs, 224, 234–36, 276
Family Educational Rights and Privacy Act of 1974, 64
Figures, 380–81, 383
Follow-up studies, 157–58
Frequency: expected, 325, 340; observed, 325, 340; polygon, 282–83

Gain scores, 229, 253
Gantt chart, 73–74
Generosity error, 128
Guttman scales, 127

Halo effect 128, 181
Hawthorne effect, 218
Historical research: definition and purpose, 11, 145–46; examples of, 12, 146, 149, 151–52; evaluation of data: external criticism, 12, 149; internal criticism, 12, 149; sources of data: primary, 11, 148; secondary, 11, 148; steps in, 146–51
History of Education Quarterly, 147
Hypotheses: characteristics of, 46; definition and purpose, 45; statement of, 49, 67; testing, 50, 349–50; types: declarative, 48, 49; deductive, 48–49; inductive, 47; null, 47, 48–50, 311–17, 320, 349; research 48, 311, 316, 349; statistical, 48
Hypothetical constructs, 112–13

Independence, 88, 96, 318, 319, 320
Independent variables, 14–16, 207; manipulation of, 209–10
Inferential statistics, concepts underlying application of: degrees of freedom, 317; level of significance *(p)*, 187, 303, 313–17, 319, 322, 330; null hypothesis, 47, 48–50, 311–317, 320, 325, 349; standard error, 308–11, 319; tests of significance, 311, 312, 316, 317; two-tailed and one-tailed tests, 316–17; Type I and Type II errors, 313–16; gain scores, 320; interpretation of results: hypothesized results, 349–50; replicated results, 351; statistical versus practical significance, 350–51; unhypothesized results, 350; parametric versus nonparametric, 318–19, 325; purpose of, 308; tests of significance, types: analysis of variance, 204, 321–22, 333–37; analysis of covariance, 204, 223, 229, 321, 323–24; chi square, 204, 325–26, 339; factorial analysis of variance, 203, 222, 231, 323; multiple comparisons, 322–23, 337–39; *t* test for independent samples, 320, 327–31; *t* test for nonindependent samples, 320, 331–33
Informed consent, 64
Intelligence tests, 130–31
Interaction, 224, 234, 323
Interaction analysis system, Flanders', 176–78
Interjudge reliability, 122
Internal consistency reliability, 119–21
Internal criticism of data, 12, 149–50
Internal validity. *See* Experimental research

International Index, 34
Interpretation of results. *See* Inferential statistics
Interrater reliability, 122
Interscorer reliability, 122
Interval scales, 279, 284, 293, 296, 318–19
Interview studies (*see also* Self-report research): advantages and disadvantages of, 166; communication during, 167; interview guide construction, 166; pretesting of procedures, 168; recording responses, 168; steps in conducting, 166
Intrajudge reliability, 122
Intrarater reliability, 122
Intrascorer reliability, 122
Item validity, 111

Journal articles, preparation and submission of, 386–88
Journal of Educational Measurement, 134
Journal of Educational Psychology, 387

KR–20, KR–21, 121
Kuder-Richardson formulas, 121
Kuder Interest Inventory-Vocational, 129

Legal restrictions on research, 63–64
Level of significance, 197, 303, 313–17, 319, 322, 330
Likert scales, 126
Limitations, 72
Linear relationships, 191–92
Literature, review of. *See* Related literature, review of
Logical validity, 111

Matching, 202, 221, 320
Mean, 204, 285, 291, 304; calculation of, 297–98
Mean square: between, 335–36; within, 335–36, 337
Measurement scales. *See* Scales, types of
Measures of central tendency, 283–85, 291, 297–98, 304
Measures of variability, 285–88, 298–300, 305
Median, 284, 291
Mental Measurement Yearbooks, 124, 133–34
Minnesota Multiphasic Personality Inventory, 125
Mode, 283, 291
Mooney Problem Check List, 125
Multi-aptitude batteries, 132
Multifactor analysis of variance. *See* Factorial analysis of variance
Multiple-baseline designs, 244–45
Multiple comparisons, 322–23, 337–39
Multiple regression equations, 194–95

National Association of Social Studies Teachers, 388
National Research Act of 1974, 64
Naturalistic observation, 169
New York Times Index, The, 34
Nominal scales, 278, 283, 319
Nonparametric statistics, 318–19; chi square, 325, 339–41

Nonparticipant observation; definition of, 169; types of: naturalistic, 169; simulation, 169; case study, 170; content analysis, 170

Nonprojective tests: definition and purpose, 125; types: attitude, 126; creativity, 128; interest, 129; personality, 125–26

Normal curve: normal distributions, 288–91, 308, 318, 319, skewed distributions, 291

Novelty effect, 218

Null hypothesis, 47, 48–50, 311–17, 320, 325, 349

Observational research, conducting: observer reliability, 179; definition of variables, 175; recording of observations, 176; training observers, 180; definition and purpose, 168; examples of, 13, 168, 169; observee bias, 181; observer bias, 181; types of: case studies, 170; content analysis, 170; ethnography, 171–75; naturalistic observation, 169; nonparticipant, 169–70; participant, 170–71; simulation observation, 169; unobtrusive measures, 182

Operational definitions, 28, 209

Ordinal scales, 278–79, 284, 292, 293, 318

p, 187, 303, 313–19, 319, 322, 330

Papers read at professional meetings, 388–89

Parameter, 308

Parametric statistics, 291, 318–19, See also Inferential statistics

Participant observation, 171

Pearson r, 190, 293, 321; calculation of, 300–303

Percentiles, 289, 293

Personality tests, 125–30

Pilot study, 74–75

Placebo effect, 218

Plan, research. See Research plan

Population, 86–87

Power, of test of significance, 318–19, 323–25, 350

Prediction studies: data analysis in, 194; data collection in, 194; definition and purpose, 14, 184; examples of, 14, 193

Predictive validity, 114–16

Predictor variables, 115

Pre-experimental designs, 224–27; the one-group pretest-posttest design, 225–26; the one-shot case study, 224; the static-group comparison, 226–27

Primary sources of data, 11, 32, 148–49

Problem: characteristics of, 27–28; selection of, 25–27; statement of, 28–29, 67; sources of, 27

Product moment correlation coefficient, 190, 293; calculation of, 300–303

Projective tests, 129, 275

Proportional stratified sampling, 90–91

Proposal, research. See Research plan

Psychological Abstracts, 34–35, 134

Publication Manual of the American Psychological Association, 42, 378

Quartile deviation, 286

Quasi-experimental designs, 224, 231–34; counterbalanced designs, 233; multiple time-series design, 232–33; nonequivalent control group design, 232; time-series design, 233–34

Questionnaire studies (*see also* Self-report research): analysis of results, 165, 276; anonymity of response, 162; construction of a questionnaire, 160–61; cover letter preparation, 162; follow-up activities, 164; nonresponse, dealing with, 165; pretesting a questionnaire, 163; problem statement, 160; subject selection, 160; validation of questionnaire, 161

Random assignment, 70, 220, 324–25

Random numbers, table of, 88

Random sampling, 318, 324; advantages of, 88; definition of 88, 318; example of, 89–90; random numbers, table of, 88; steps in, 88–89

Range, 286

Rank difference correlation coefficient, 190, 292

Rating scales, 127–28

Ratio scales, 279–80, 284, 293, 294, 318, 319

Rationale equivalence reliability, 121

Readers' Guide to Periodical Literature, 33–34

Readiness tests, 132

Related literature, review of: coding references, 42; procedure for, 41–43; analyzing, organizing, and reporting, procedures for, 43–45, 67; definition and purpose, 29–31; preparation for: key word identification, 31; library services, 31; scope, 30; sources, 32–38; primary, 32; secondary, 32 (*see also* Computer searches)

Relationship studies: data analysis in, 190–92 (*see also* Correlation coefficients); data collection in, 189; definition and purpose, 13–14, 184, 189; examples of, 14, 190

Reliability: definition of, 92; long form versus short form, 135; and scoring, 122; and standard error of measurement, 123; of subtests, 123; types of: alternate forms, 118; coefficient of equivalence, 119; coefficient of stability, 118; coefficient of stability and equivalence, 119; equivalent-forms, 118–19; rationale equivalence, 121; split-half, 119; test-retest, 118

Replication, 72, 351

Report, research. See Research report

Research assistants, training of, 66

Research, definiton of, 6. See also Educational research

Research and development, 10

Research in Education (RIE), 36

Research hypothesis, 48, 311, 316, 349

Research plan, components of: budget, 74; data analysis, 72–73; introduction, 67; method, 67–72; time schedule, 73; definition and purpose, 61–62; evaluation of, 74–75

Research problem. See Problem

Research proposal. See Research plan

Research report, evaluation of: general criteria, 399–402; method-specific criteria, 402–4;

Research report, evaluation of: *(cont.)*
preparation of: format and style, 378; writing and typing of, 375; types: dissertations, 378–86; journal articles, 386–88; papers read at professional meetings, 388–89; theses, 378–86 (*see also* Thesis report, components of)
Response set, 126, 181
Restriction in range, correction for, 193
Review of Educational Research, 26, 32, 38
Review of related literature. *See* Related literature, review of
Role playing, 169–70
Rorschach Ink Blot Test, 129

Sample size. *See* Sampling
Sample surveys, 156
Sampling, bias: reporting, 100; sources of, 99–100; definition and purpose, 85–86; methods of (*see* Cluster sampling; Random sampling; Stratified sampling; Systematic sampling); population, definition of, 86; sample size, 97–98, 319, 325, 350; sampling error, 98–99, 308–15; steps in, 87
Sampling error. *See.* Sampling
Sampling validity, 111
Scales, types of: interval, 279, 284, 286, 293, 295, 319; nominal, 278, 283, 319; ordinal, 278–79, 284, 292, 319; ratio, 279–80, 284, 286, 293, 319
Scheffé's test for multiple comparisons, 322–23, 337–39
Scholastic aptitude tests, 130–31
School surveys, 156
Scientific method: application in education, 6–7; steps in, 7
Second Handbook of Research on Teaching, 38
Secondary sources of data, 11, 32, 148
Selection of a sample. *See* Sampling
Self-concept, measures of, 127
Self-report research: conducting, 159–69 (*see also* Interview studies; Questionnaire studies); examples of, 13, 157; instruments used in, 125; types of: development studies, 157; follow-up studies, 157; sociometric studies, 158; survey research, 155–56
Semantic differential scales, 126
Sequential Tests of Educational Progress (STEP), 132
Shot-gun approach, 184, 189
Shrinkage, 195
Significance level. *See* Level of significance
Simple analysis of variance, 204, 321–22, 333–37
Simulation observation, 169
Single-subject experimental designs, 237–45; external validity and, 238–39; internal validity and, 239–40; types of: A-B-A, 241–44, multiple-baseline, 244–45; versus group designs, 237–38; statistical analysis of, 319
Single-variable rule, 240
Sixteen Personality Factor Questionnaire, 125
Smithsonian Science Information Exchange (SSIE), 37–38
Sociometric studies, 158

Spearman-Brown prophecy formula, 120–21
Spearman rho, 190, 292
Split-half reliability, 119–20
Standard deviation, 204, 286, 305, 309–10; calculation of, 298–300
Standard error: of difference between means, 311, 319; of mean, 308–11; of measurment, 123
Standard scores, 293; calculation of, 304
Standardized tests. *See* Tests, standardized
Stanford-Binet Intelligence Scale, 131
Stanines, 296
Statistic, definition of, 308
Statistical significance. *See* Inferential statistics
Statistics. *See* Descriptive statistics; Inferential statistics; Scales, types of
Stratified sampling: definition and purpose, 90; example of, 92; proportional, 90; steps in, 91
Strong Vocational Interest Blank, 129
Subtest reliability, 123
Sum of squares: between, 333–36; total, 333–36; within, 333–36
Systematic sampling: comparison with random sampling, 96; definition of, 96; example of, 96–97; steps in, 96

t test, 204, 229, 319–22; for independent samples, 320; for nonindependent samples, 320
T scores, 295, 304–5
Table of random numbers, 88
Tables, 380–81, 383
Tests in Print, 133
Test of significance, 311, 312, 316, 318–26 *See also* Inferential statistics
Tests, standardized: administration of, 109–10; 135; advantages of using, 108; characteristics of, 109; (*see also* Reliability; Validity); definition of, 109; individually versus group administered, 108; long versus short forms of, 108; scoring of, 108, 110: 276–78; selection of, 134–36; sources of information on, 133–34; types: achievement, 124–25; character and personality, 125–30 (*see also* Nonprojective tests; Projective tests), diagnostic, 125; intelligence, 130–31: multiple-aptitude batteries, 132; use of in schools, 135–36
Test-retest reliability, 118
Thematic Apperception Test, 129
Thesaurus of ERIC Descriptors, 36
Thesis report, components of: appendices, 386; main body: conclusions and recommendations, 383–85; introduction, 381; method, 381; references, 386; results, 382; summary, 389; preliminary pages: acknowledgment page, 380; list of figures, 380; list of tables, 380; table of contents, 380; title page, 379
Thurstone scales, 126
Treatment variables. *See* Independent variables
Treatment variance, 321–22
True experimental designs. *See* Experimental designs
True score, 117, 123–24

Two-tailed and one-tailed tests, 316–17
Type I and Type II errors, 313–16
Types of data. *See* Scales, types of

Unobtrusive measures, 182

Validity (*see also* Experimental research):
    definition of, 110; types: concurrent, 113–14;
    construct, 112–13; content, 111–12;
    predictive, 114–16
Variables: definition, 13; importance of defining,
    28; types of: active, 210; assigned, 210;
    control, 235; criterion, 113–16; dependent,
    14–16, 207; independent, 14–16, 207,
    210–11; predictor, 115; extraneous, 212,
    220–23
Variance, 286, 298, 318; between groups, 321,
    333–37; within groups, 321, 325, 333–37.
    See also Inferential statistics
Volunteers as subjects, 99–100, 165, 217

Wechsler Adult Intelligence Scale, 131
Wechsler Intelligence Scale for Children, 131
Wechsler Preschool and Primary Scale of
    Intelligence, 131
Within group variance, 321, 325

z score, 293, 304
Z score, 295, 304–5